Catalunya
& the Costa Brava

Damien Simonis

D0307860

LONELY PLANET PUBLICATIONS
Melbourne • Oakland • London • Paris

CATALUNYA

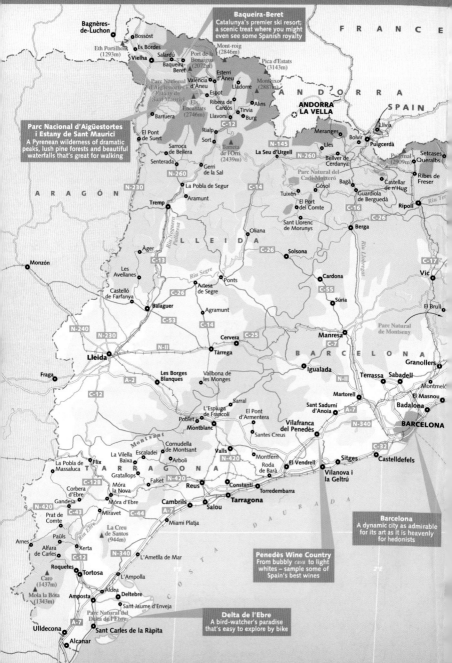

Baqueira-Beret
Catalunya's premier ski resort;
a scenic treat where you might
even see some Spanish royalty

**Parc Nacional d'Aigüestortes
i Estany de Sant Maurici**
A Pyrenean wilderness of dramatic
peaks, lush pine forests and beautiful
waterfalls that's great for walking

Barcelona
A dynamic city as admirable
for its art as it is heavenly
for hedonists

Penedès Wine Country
From bubbly cava to light
whites – sample some of
Spain's best wines

Delta de l'Ebre
A bird-watcher's paradise
that's easy to explore by bike

FRANCE

ANDORRA

SPAIN

Bagnères-
de-Luchon
Bossòst
Es Bòrdes
Eth Portilhon
(1293m)
Vielha
Salardú
Baqueira-
Beret
Port de la
Bonaigua
(2072m)
Mont-roig
(2846m)
Pica d'Estats
(3143m)
València
d'Àneu
Esterri
d'Àneu
Lladorre
Montcaubo
(2887m)
Espot
Ribera de
Cardós
Tírvia
Alins
ANDORRA
LA VELLA
Parc Nacional
d'Aigüestortes i
Estany de
Sant Maurici
Els
Encantats
(2746m)
Barruera
Llavorsí
Burg
C-12
Llívia
El Pont
de Suert
Rialp
Sort
Torreta
de l'Orri
(2439m)
N-145
La Seu d'Urgell
N-260
Meranges
Lles
Bolvir
Puigcerdà
Setcases
Queralbs
Puigmal
(2909m)
Sarroca
de Bellera
Gerri
de la Sal
Bellver de
Cerdanya
Ribes de
Freser
Senterada
N-260
La Pobla de Segur
Parc Natural del
Cadí-Moixeró
Gósol
Bagà
Castellar
de n'Hug
Tremp
Aramunt
C-14
Tuixén
El Pont
del Comte
Guardiola
de Berguedà
Ripoll
Riu Ter
C-16
ARAGÓN
N-230
Àger
Riu Noguera Pallaresa
LLEIDA
Oliana
Sant Llorenç
de Morunys
Berga
C-17
Les
Avellanes
C-13
Riu Segre
Solsona
C-26
Vic
Monzón
Castelló
de Farfanya
Artesa
de Segre
Ponts
C-26
Cardona
C-55
Súria
El Brull
Balaguer
Agramunt
C-53
C-14
Cervera
C-25
Manresa
Parc Natural
de Montseny
N-240
N-230
N-II
Tàrrega
C-7
BARCELONA
Granollers
Lleida
Les Borges
Blanques
A-2
Vallbona de
les Monges
Sarral
Igualada
N-II
Terrassa
Sabadell
Montmeló
Fraga
C-12
L'Espluga
de Francolí
El Pont
d'Armentera
Sant Sadurní
d'Anoia
Martorell
A-7
El Masnou
Badalona
Poblet
Montblanc
Santes Creus
Vilafranca
del Penedès
N-340
BARCELONA
Montsant
Cornudella
de Montsant
Escaladei
Arbolí
La Vilella
Baixa
Valls
Montferri
C-32
La Pobla de
Massaluca
Flix
TARRAGONA
Gratallops
Faket
N-420
Roda de Barà
El Vendrell
Vilanova i
la Geltrú
Sitges
Castelldefels
Móra
la Nova
Reus
Constantí
Corbera
d'Ebre
Gandesa
C-12B
Móra d'Ebre
C-44
Cambrils
Salou
Torredembarra
Tarragona
C-43
Miravet
A-7
Prat de
Comte
Arnes
Paüls
La Creu
de Santos
(944m)
Miami Platja
N-420
Alfara
de Carles
Xerta
C-12
N-340
L'Ametlla de Mar
COSTA DAURADA
Roquetes
Caro
(1437m)
Tortosa
L'Ampolla
Mola la Bóta
(1343m)
Amposta
Aldea
Deltebre
Sant Jaume d'Enveja
Parc Natural del
Delta de l'Ebre
Riu Ebre
Ulldecona
Alcanar
Sant Carles de la Ràpita

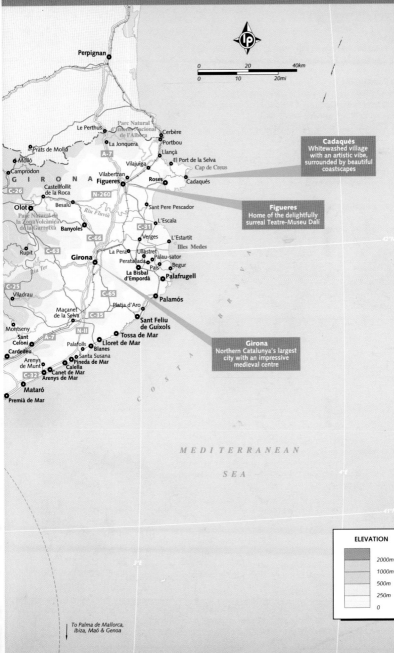

Perpignan

Le Perthus
Prats de Molló
Molló
Camprodon
Parc Natural
d'Interès Nacional
de l'Albera
Cerbère
Portbou
La Jonquera
Llançà
Vilajuïga
El Port de la Selva
Cap de Creus
Vilabertran
Figueres
Roses
Cadaqués

G I R O N A
C-26
Castellfollit
de la Roca
Besalú
Riu Fluvià
N-260
Olot
Parc Natural de
la Zona Volcànica
de la Garrotxa
Banyoles
Sant Pere Pescador
L'Escala
C-31
Verges
L'Estartit
Illes Medes
Rupit
C-63
Riu Ter
La Pera
Ullastret
Palau-sator
Girona
Peratallada
Begur
Pals
La Bisbal
d'Empordà
Palafrugell
C-25
Viladrau
C-65
Palamós
Platja d'Aro
Maçanet
de la Selva
C-35
Montseny
Sant Feliu
de Guíxols
Sant
Celoni
A-7
N-II
Tossa de Mar
Palafolls
Lloret de Mar
Cardedeu
Blanes
Santa Susana
Arenys
de Munt
Pineda de Mar
Calella
C-32
Canet de Mar
Arenys de Mar
Mataró
Premià de Mar

C O S T A

B R A V A

Cadaqués
Whitewashed village
with an artistic vibe,
surrounded by beautiful
coastscapes

Figueres
Home of the delightfully
surreal Teatre-Museu Dalí

Girona
Northern Catalunya's largest
city with an impressive
medieval centre

42°N

4°E

41°N

3°E

M E D I T E R R A N E A N

S E A

0   20   40km
0   10   20mi

To Palma de Mallorca,
Ibiza, Maó & Genoa

ELEVATION

2000m
1000m
500m
250m
0

Catalunya & the Costa Brava
1st edition – November 2001

Published by
Lonely Planet Publications Pty Ltd ABN 36 005 607 983
90 Maribyrnong St, Footscray, Victoria 3011, Australia

Lonely Planet Offices
Australia Locked Bag 1, Footscray, Victoria 3011
USA 150 Linden St, Oakland, CA 94607
UK 10a Spring Place, London NW5 3BH
France 1 rue du Dahomey, 75011 Paris

Photographs
Many of the images in this guide are available for licensing from
Lonely Planet Images.
Web site: www.lonelyplanetimages.com

Front cover photograph
Castellers (human-castle builders) wow the crowds at Vilafranca del
Penedès (Guy Moberly).

ISBN 1 86450 315 7

text & maps © Lonely Planet Publications Pty Ltd 2001
photos © photographers as indicated 2001

GR and PR are trademarks of the FFRP (Fédération Française de la
Randonnée Pédestre).

Printed through Colorcraft Ltd, Hong Kong
Printed in China

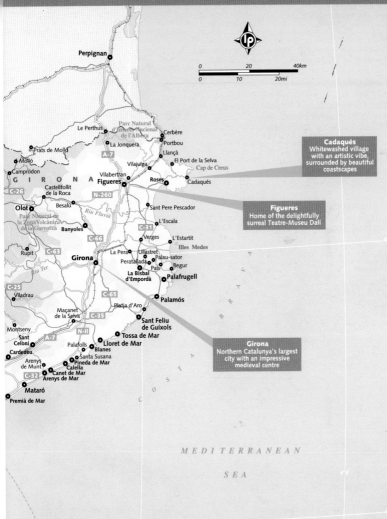

Cadaqués
Whitewashed village with an artistic vibe, surrounded by beautiful coastscapes

Figueres
Home of the delightfully surreal Teatre-Museu Dalí

Girona
Northern Catalunya's largest city with an impressive medieval centre

Perpignan

Le Perthus
Parc Natural d'Interès Nacional de l'Albera
Cerbère
La Jonquera
Portbou
Prats de Molló
Llançà
Molló
Vilajuïga
El Port de la Selva
Cap de Creus
Camprodon
Vilabertran
G I R O N A
Figueres
Roses
Cadaqués
Castellfollit de la Roca
Olot
Besalú
Riu Fluvià
Sant Pere Pescador
Parc Natural de la Zona Volcànica de la Garrotxa
Banyoles
L'Escala
Verges
L'Estartit
Rupit
Girona
La Pera
Ullastret
Illes Medes
Riu Ter
Peratallada
Palau-sator
Pals
Begur
La Bisbal d'Empordà
Palafrugell
Viladrau
Palamós
Maçanet de la Selva
Platja d'Aro
Montseny
Sant Feliu de Guíxols
Sant Celoni
Tossa de Mar
Cardedeu
Palafolls
Lloret de Mar
Blanes
Arenys de Munt
Santa Susana
Pineda de Mar
Calella
Canet de Mar
Arenys de Mar
Mataró
Premià de Mar

C O S T A   B R A V A

M E D I T E R R A N E A N

S E A

42°N

4°E

41°N

3°E

ELEVATION

2000m
1000m
500m
250m
0

To Palma de Mallorca, Ibiza, Maó & Genoa

0   20   40km
0   10   20mi

Catalunya & the Costa Brava
1st edition – November 2001

Published by
Lonely Planet Publications Pty Ltd ABN 36 005 607 983
90 Maribyrnong St, Footscray, Victoria 3011, Australia

Lonely Planet Offices
Australia Locked Bag 1, Footscray, Victoria 3011
USA 150 Linden St, Oakland, CA 94607
UK 10a Spring Place, London NW5 3BH
France 1 rue du Dahomey, 75011 Paris

Photographs
Many of the images in this guide are available for licensing from
Lonely Planet Images.
Web site: www.lonelyplanetimages.com

Front cover photograph
Castellers (human-castle builders) wow the crowds at Vilafranca del
Penedès (Guy Moberly).

ISBN 1 86450 315 7

Printed through Colorcraft Ltd, Hong Kong
Printed in China

Although the authors and Lonely Planet try to make the information as accurate as possible, we accept no responsibility for any loss, injury or inconvenience sustained by anyone using this book.

Contents – Text

Contents – Maps

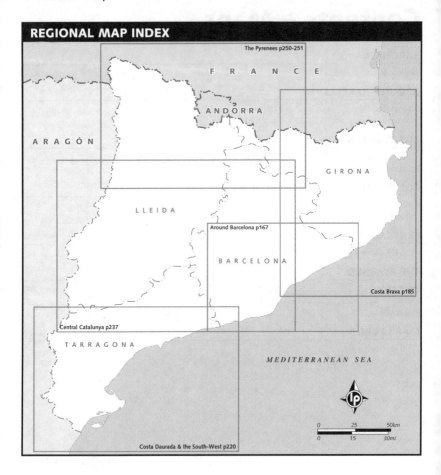

The Author

Damien Simonis

With a degree in languages and several years' reporting and sub-editing on Australian newspapers (including *The Australian* and *The Age*), Sydney-born Damien left the country in 1989. He has since lived, worked and travelled extensively throughout Europe, the Middle East and North Africa. Since 1992, writing for Lonely Planet has kept him busy, most recently on *Italy*, *Spain*, *The Canary Islands*, *Barcelona*, *Madrid*, *Venice*, *Florence* and *Tuscany*. He has also written and snapped photos for other publications in Australia, the UK and North America. When not on the road, Damien resides in Stoke Newington, north London.

FROM THE AUTHOR

Various people helped me with this book and/or simply made my time in Catalunya more than just an assignment. Special thanks, as always, go to Michael van Laake, Susan Kempster, Susana Pellicer and Rocio Vázquez (get well!). Edith López Garciá accompanied me on some great trips in the Catalan countryside and had plenty of suggestions. There's still plenty to do! Armin Teichmann and Anna Torrisi also teamed up for some fun excursions.

Thanks also to other friends – Teresa Quintana-Montero, Loreta Jaumandreu, Geoffrey Leaver-Heaton and Lola Nieto de Haro, Nick Reddel (and the band!) and Paloma and co from Carrer de Sant Pere més alt – for the good times had over these past crazy months.

Thanks also for a warm welcome from the merry journos of Spanish SCIJ, including Elisabeth Esporrin Pons, Ita Fabregas, Antonio and Cuca Campañá, Antonio Marin (thanks for the housing tips) et al. I will always regret not having taken up Ernest Udina's kind offer of lunch and help at the International Press Centre. A quiet man, a lover of the mountains and a leading journalist in Catalunya, he died while returning from an ascent of Mont Blanc in July 2001. May he rest in peace.

A particular note of thanks to Mike 'Butterfly' Lockwood out on the Solsona estate for invaluable wildlife tips. Another bottle of gin then I expect. Oh, and the pork scratchings.

Joan Ignasi Moreu, at the regional tourist board, was most helpful with contacts and ideas, some of which I could not follow up this time around. Next time!

I also owe a debt of thanks to colleague John Noble, who wrote the original text on Catalunya for LP's *Spain*, which served in turn as the launch pad for the present book. Thanks to my editor, Sally Schafer, and the rest of the crew on this book, who kept the production process nice and smooth for this old hack.

Above all, this book is dedicated to Ottobrina Voccoli, with whom I shared some of the most splendid moments of discovery of this remarkable region.

This Book

This first edition of Lonely Planet's *Catalunya & the Costa Brava* was researched and written by Damien Simonis.

From the Publisher
This book was produced in Lonely Planet's London office. Sally Schafer coordinated the editing and proofing with invaluable assistance from Jenny Lansbury, Michala Green and Heather Dickson. Ian Stokes coordinated the mapping, design and layout. James Timmins produced the climate charts and David Wenk created the map legend. Andrew Weatherill designed the front cover, Lonely Planet Images provided the photographs and Asa Andersson, Martin Harris, Jane Smith and Mick Weldon drew the illustrations. Thanks are due to Emma Koch for her patience and help with the Language chapter and to Tim Ryder and Amanda Canning for their expert answers to a barrage of questions.

Foreword

ABOUT LONELY PLANET GUIDEBOOKS

The story begins with a classic travel adventure: Tony and Maureen Wheeler's 1972 journey across Europe and Asia to Australia. Useful information about the overland trail did not exist at that time, so Tony and Maureen published the first Lonely Planet guidebook to meet a growing need.

From a kitchen table, then from a tiny office in Melbourne (Australia), Lonely Planet has become the largest independent travel publisher in the world, an international company with offices in Melbourne, Oakland (USA), London (UK) and Paris (France).

Today Lonely Planet guidebooks cover the globe. There is an ever-growing list of books and there's information in a variety of forms and media. Some things haven't changed. The main aim is still to help make it possible for adventurous travellers to get out there – to explore and better understand the world.

At Lonely Planet we believe travellers can make a positive contribution to the countries they visit – if they respect their host communities and spend their money wisely. Since 1986 a percentage of the income from each book has been donated to aid projects and human rights campaigns.

Updates Lonely Planet thoroughly updates each guidebook as often as possible. This usually means there are around two years between editions, although for more unusual or more stable destinations the gap can be longer. Check the imprint page (following the colour map at the beginning of the book) for publication dates.

Between editions up-to-date information is available in two free newsletters – the paper *Planet Talk* and email *Comet* (to subscribe, contact any Lonely Planet office) – and on our Web site at www.lonelyplanet.com. The *Upgrades* section of the Web site covers a number of important and volatile destinations and is regularly updated by Lonely Planet authors. *Scoop* covers news and current affairs relevant to travellers. And, lastly, the *Thorn Tree* bulletin board and *Postcards* section of the site carry unverified, but fascinating, reports from travellers.

Correspondence The process of creating new editions begins with the letters, postcards and emails received from travellers. This correspondence often includes suggestions, criticisms and comments about the current editions. Interesting excerpts are immediately passed on via newsletters and the Web site, and everything goes to our authors to be verified when they're researching on the road. We're keen to get more feedback from organisations or individuals who represent communities visited by travellers.

Lonely Planet gathers information for everyone who's curious about the planet – and especially for those who explore it first-hand. Through guidebooks, phrasebooks, activity guides, maps, literature, newsletters, image library, TV series and Web site we act as an information exchange for a worldwide community of travellers.

7

Research Authors aim to gather sufficient practical information to enable travellers to make informed choices and to make the mechanics of a journey run smoothly. They also research historical and cultural background to help enrich the travel experience and allow travellers to understand and respond appropriately to cultural and environmental issues.

Authors don't stay in every hotel because that would mean spending a couple of months in each medium-sized city and, no, they don't eat at every restaurant because that would mean stretching belts beyond capacity. They do visit hotels and restaurants to check standards and prices, but feedback based on readers' direct experiences can be very helpful.

Many of our authors work undercover, others aren't so secretive. None of them accept freebies in exchange for positive write-ups. And none of our guidebooks contain any advertising.

Production Authors submit their raw manuscripts and maps to offices in Australia, USA, UK or France. Editors and cartographers – all experienced travellers themselves – then begin the process of assembling the pieces. When the book finally hits the shops, some things are already out of date, we start getting feedback from readers and the process begins again …

WARNING & REQUEST

Things change – prices go up, schedules change, good places go bad and bad places go bankrupt – nothing stays the same. So, if you find things better or worse, recently opened or long since closed, please tell us and help make the next edition even more accurate and useful. We genuinely value all the feedback we receive. A well-travelled team reads and acknowledges every letter, postcard and email and ensures that every morsel of information finds its way to the appropriate authors, editors and cartographers for verification.

Everyone who writes to us will find their name in the next edition of the appropriate guidebook. They will also receive the latest issue of *Planet Talk*, our quarterly printed newsletter, or *Comet*, our monthly email newsletter. Subscriptions to both newsletters are free. The very best contributions will be rewarded with a free guidebook.

Excerpts from your correspondence may appear in new editions of Lonely Planet guidebooks, the Lonely Planet Web site, *Planet Talk* or *Comet*, so please let us know if you *don't* want your letter published or your name acknowledged.

Send all correspondence to the Lonely Planet office closest to you:

Australia: Locked Bag 1, Footscray, Victoria 3011
USA: 150 Linden St, Oakland, CA 94607
UK: 10A Spring Place, London NW5 3BH
France: 1 rue du Dahomey, 75011 Paris

Or email us at: talk2us@lonelyplanet.com.au

For news, views and updates see our Web site: www.lonelyplanet.com

HOW TO USE A LONELY PLANET GUIDEBOOK

The best way to use a Lonely Planet guidebook is any way you choose. At Lonely Planet we believe the most memorable travel experiences are often those that are unexpected, and the finest discoveries are those you make yourself. Guidebooks are not intended to be used as if they provide a detailed set of infallible instructions!

Contents All Lonely Planet guidebooks follow roughly the same format. The Facts about the Destination chapters or sections give background information ranging from history to weather. Facts for the Visitor gives practical information on issues like visas and health. Getting There & Away gives a brief starting point for researching travel to and from the destination. Getting Around gives an overview of the transport options when you arrive.

The peculiar demands of each destination determine how subsequent chapters are broken up, but some things remain constant. We always start with background, then proceed to sights, places to stay, places to eat, entertainment, getting there and away, and getting around information – in that order.

Heading Hierarchy Lonely Planet headings are used in a strict hierarchical structure that can be visualised as a set of Russian dolls. Each heading (and its following text) is encompassed by any preceding heading that is higher on the hierarchical ladder.

Entry Points We do not assume guidebooks will be read from beginning to end, but that people will dip into them. The traditional entry points are the list of contents and the index. In addition, however, some books have a complete list of maps and an index map illustrating map coverage.

There may also be a colour map that shows highlights. These highlights are dealt with in greater detail in the Facts for the Visitor chapter, along with planning questions and suggested itineraries. Each chapter covering a geographical region usually begins with a locator map and another list of highlights. Once you find something of interest in a list of highlights, turn to the index.

Maps Maps play a crucial role in Lonely Planet guidebooks and include a huge amount of information. A legend is printed on the back page. We seek to have complete consistency between maps and text, and to have every important place in the text captured on a map. Map key numbers usually start in the top left corner.

Although inclusion in a guidebook usually implies a recommendation we cannot list every good place. Exclusion does not necessarily imply criticism. In fact there are a number of reasons why we might exclude a place – sometimes it is simply inappropriate to encourage an influx of travellers.

Introduction

There probably isn't anyone who hasn't heard of Barcelona, the bustling northeastern Spanish metropolis, home to Gothic and Gaudí, economic engine for the nation and a party town for revellers of all sorts. But Catalunya, the region of which it is capital? You would hear a pin drop in the room for the embarrassed silence.

Perhaps it is a good thing that the regional government has not really devoted sufficient resources to promoting one of Spain's most fascinating and diverse regions at an international level. For everything Catalunya has to offer the visitor, it could easily rival, and on several important points beat, the likes of the much more fashionable Tuscany in Italy.

In an area where you can get pretty much anywhere within six hours' travel, you can pass from broad sandy beaches in the south to coves hidden away among the bluffs of the rugged Costa Brava. Or from the package holiday party atmosphere of coastal resorts to the remote and majestic peaks of the Catalan Pyrenees. You can hike and ski, go rafting or canyoning, dive or windsurf.

Vultures in search of more aesthetic and cerebral activity are spoiled for choice. You can explore hundreds of charming Romanesque churches around the northern half of the region; discover medieval hamlets and villages; marvel at great Gothic cathedrals in the cities of Barcelona, Tarragona, Girona and others; seek out the imposing monasteries of the interior; and poke about the sites of ancient Greek and Roman settlements (especially at Empúries and Tarragona). After these excursions, a stream of museums can fill you in with more explanation of the region's rich history and artistic legacy. Three of the giants of 20th-century painting, Picasso, Miró and Dalí, began their extraordinary careers here. And who could forget the wild architectural fantasies of Gaudí and co in Barcelona?

Even then one has barely scratched the surface, but everyone needs time off. Catalan food is among Spain's best and you'll

have plenty of opportunity to indulge the palate with an array of mouthwatering seafood delights on the coast and hearty meat and game dishes farther inland. The range is surprising, from elegant *haute cuisine* to Basque tapas in Barcelona, and from *fideuà* (a sort of noodle paella) on the coast to steaming hot *olla aranesa* (a filling stew) on winter nights in the north-western Pyrenees. And what is a satisfying meal without fine wine? Catalunya is pretty much self-sufficient there too, producing much of the nation's bubbly *(cava)* and a broad range of robust reds and strong whites.

For a long time absorbed into the centralised Spanish state, Catalunya, with its own language and customs, has always maintained a quite separate cultural identity. Since the restoration of democracy in the late 1970s, the region has acquired considerable autonomy in the running of its own affairs. Polemicists indulge ad nauseam in debates over whether or not Catalunya does, or has ever, constituted a nation. Whatever the answer to such thorny questions, it is a fascinating region with a resilient and unique identity, as the following pages will show.

Facts about Catalunya

HISTORY
From the Caves to the Plains

Evidence indicates Palaeolithic (Old Stone Age) people wandered around what is now Catalan territory as long as 70,000 years ago. Other archaeological findings in several locations show that these primitive peoples' Neolithic descendants found themselves equally at home in Catalan caves. Outdoors they not only hunted but, from about 7000 BC onwards, were engaged in rudimentary agriculture. The few but precious archaeological sites that have been explored up and down the region reveal developments in line with those elsewhere in Spain and other parts of Europe: the use of bronze and other metals from about 1800 BC, increasingly complex burial rituals and the first simple examples of housing.

These Iberian tribes rubbed along pretty much undisturbed until the 7th century BC, when the first Indo-European invasions took place. Waves of these more advanced tribes, particularly Celts, poured into Spain from northern Italy, Switzerland and beyond. Catalan historians point out the lack of place names of Celtic origin in Catalunya to suggest 'Catalan' Indo-Europeans were of a different stock. In any case they brought with them more sophisticated methods of cultivating land, rearing livestock (cattle and pigs) and building. It was during this period that the tribes began to move out of the caves and into settlements in the plains.

Phoenicians & Greeks

These early tribes were not long established when a quite different set of customers made an appearance.

The Phoenicians, a Semitic trading people from the eastern Mediterranean (particularly present-day Lebanon) who had gradually ventured west across the sea, set up small trading bases in the area, from present-day Amposta, by the Delta de l'Ebre (Ebro in Spanish), to Flix. More interested in trade than conquest, the Phoenician presence had

little impact on the peoples they encountered. In any case, they had more important bases (such as the ancient precursor of Cádiz) in the south of the peninsula. Things would be different with the arrival of the first Greeks.

As far as historians can work out, two Greek settlements were established in the 6th century BC. Of Rodes, founded by Greeks from Rhodes and possibly where modern Roses now stands, nothing remains. You can, however, still visit the site of Emporion (modern Empúries) today. Founded in about 580 BC by Greeks from Focea, in Asia Minor, the town would become, along with their bigger base at Masilia (Marseilles, France), a key link in the chain of Greek trading posts around the Mediterranean.

In the port of Emporion (meaning 'market') ships from the eastern Mediterranean unloaded wine, ceramics, olive oil, perfumes, textiles and arms. The Greeks exchanged these for local products such as cereals, honey, metals, skins and probably slaves. Before long the Greeks began minting coins in Emporion too.

The Greeks brought their powerful cultural advances to the attention of the locals, Iberians and Indo-Europeans alike, who proved amenable students. More sophisticated art (especially in ceramics), writing, and the cultivation of wine grapes and the olive all served to foment the rise of what has become known as the Iberian, or Celt-Iberian, culture.

The Iberians

There is much discussion as to who exactly the Iberians were. The name 'Iber' appears to come from the name of the Riu Ebre, and the tribes included in the definition stretched from the south of Spain to southern France. There was no Iberian people as such, more a succession of tribes with a common language, and more or less influenced by Phoenician and Greek culture.

Among the tribes in Catalunya (some of whom were already well mixed with Indo-Europeans) were the Laietani, thought by some to have been the original settlers of what would subsequently be Barcelona. Others included the Sordons, Indigets, Cossetans, Andossins (whence came the principality of Andorra), Ceretans (in what is now Cerdanya), Ausetans, Bargusins, Lacentans and Ilergets (around Lleida).

As many as a thousand Iberian settlements have been identified in Catalunya and about 100 have been excavated (Ullastret, in the Costa Brava area, is a good example). The Iberians tended to build on hill-tops and the discovery in several cases of town walls suggests that the new iron weapons they had learned to make from the Greeks were being put to use.

The Road from Rome

By the 3rd century BC, two superpowers emerged in the Mediterranean: Rome and Carthage. The inevitable conflict between them utterly changed the history of the Spanish peninsula. By the time the Carthaginian general, Hannibal, marched his huge army north through Catalunya, crushing whatever opposition the Iberians could muster, most of the coastal Phoenician and Greek settlements had already been brought under Carthaginian control (modern Cartagena in Murcia was the new Carthaginian capital in the peninsula).

Without getting bogged down in the history of the Punic wars between Rome and Carthage (suffice it to say that Rome won), it is worth noting that the wars brought Rome to Catalunya. In 218 BC, Scipio landed at Emporion to cut off Hannibal's forces (who were heading overland for Italy) from behind.

By 197 BC, all the peninsula, which the Romans called Hispania, was under Roman control. Their campaign had not been made any easier by the tendency of Iberian tribes to switch sides with disconcerting frequency. When the Carthaginians had already been beaten several Iberian tribes rose unsuccessfully against the Romans.

Rome divided Hispania in two. Hispania Citerior (including what is now Catalunya, Aragón, Valencia and Murcia) had its capital in the Roman city of Tarraco (Tarragona). The rest of the peninsula was dubbed Hispania Ulterior. By the time Emperor Augustus came to Tarraco in 26 BC, the Pax Romana had taken hold and the whole peninsula was enjoying a long period of peace. Augustus altered the administration of the territory, creating three provinces: the Betica, Lusitania and Tarraconensis. The latter's jurisdiction stretched from Catalunya to Cantabria in the west and to Almería (in Andalucía) in the south. The Val d'Aran came under the jurisdiction of Aquitania (in France), which helps explain its separate development.

Whatever you might say of the Romans, the moral force of their system of government must have been persuasive. In all Hispania they left behind only one serious army detachment in León (in the north-west) and little more than symbolic units based in Tarraco, Emporion and Denia (Valencia). No more was required to keep the peace.

In the next few hundred years, the Roman way of life was implanted. Some new towns were founded (Barcino, the Roman precursor of Barcelona, may have been one, though theories regarding its earlier settlement abound). More commonly, Iberian cities were Romanised, including Gerunda (Girona), Ilerda (Lleida), Ausa (Vic) and Baetulo (Badalona). The most important reminders of Rome's presence to survive are in Tarragona, Barcelona and Empúries.

The Roman road system revolutionised communications. The Via Augusta ran from Rome to Cádiz and branch roads led from Tarraco to Ilerda and from there north to what later became La Seu d'Urgell. Others connected Emporion with Olot and Barcino with Ausa.

The towns were organised along imperial lines, with a senate or decurion (formed of 100 well-off citizens) serving as a parliament from whose ranks two duumviri were elected annually to run town affairs. In AD 74 all free men and women in Hispania, regardless of race, were declared Roman citizens, with all the privileges and rights this implied. Children went to school, the use of Latin spread and the tenor of daily life for most people rose on the back of a prosperous imperial economy. Far-off imperial wars in the Middle East and Central Europe had little direct impact on Hispania.

Christianity had also arrived by the 3rd century AD, as documentary evidence of the existence of a bishop at Tarragona and various martyrs shows. By the end of the 4th century other major towns such as Barcelona, Girona and Lleida also had bishops, while Tarragona had confirmed its primacy with the presence of an archbishop.

Barbarian Invasions

As the Roman empire wobbled, Hispania felt the effects. It is no coincidence that the bulk of the Roman walls in Barcelona and some other Roman towns, vestiges of which remain today, went up in the 4th century AD. Marauding Franks were among the first to visit a little death and destruction on Catalunya in a prelude to what was to come – several waves of invaders flooding across the country like great Atlantic rollers. By AD 415, the comparatively Romanised Visigoths had arrived and under their leader Athaulf made a temporary capital in Barcelona. The Visigoths didn't arrive in force until the next century, when the Franks edged them out of France.

Barcelona was made capital on several occasions, but chaos was the name of the game. Wars, coups and assassinations were part of the daily diet of the Visigoths, who eventually took control of Hispania and made their capital at Toletum (Toledo). In all Hispania there were probably never more than a few hundred thousand Visigoths, but they remained the ruling class – much aided by Hispano-Roman nobility and the emerging Christian clergy.

Islam Victorious

Visigothic rule remained unsettled to the end. What no-one in Hispania could have guessed, however, was that the next surprise would come from the south.

In 711, the Muslim general Tariq landed an expeditionary force of 7000 men at present-day Gibraltar (*jebel Tariq*; Tariq's Mountain). After the death of the prophet Mohammed in 632 in distant Arabia, Muslims had swept across Asia Minor and all of North Africa, conquering and converting as they went in an unprecedented spate of divinely inspired ad hoc empire building.

In Spain Tariq found the Visigothic 'state' so rotten and divided that he had no trouble sweeping across the peninsula all the way into France, where the Muslims were only brought to a halt in 732 by the Franks at Poitiers.

All of Catalunya found itself under Muslim domination from as early as 718 but this situation would not last long. Indeed, the mountainous north-west remained largely untouched by the 'Saracens', as the Muslim warriors were known. North-east of the Riu Llobregat they contented themselves with implanting garrisons and raising taxes. To the south and west, and especially in the valley of the Riu Ebre, they settled in for the long term.

The Franks and local counts mounted counterattacks. In 785 they retook Girona and in 801 Barcelona fell after a long siege. A rough triangle of Catalunya, whose dividing line from the rest of (Muslim-controlled) Catalunya ran roughly north-west from Barcelona, was now in Christian hands. It was in 800 that Europeans started to talk of Christendom, united under the religious staff of the pope and his secular aide, the newly crowned Holy Roman Emperor, Charlemagne. It was Charlemagne's Frankish troops, under the command of Louis the Pious, who had made all the difference in the siege of Barcelona. In Catalunya (a term yet to be used) the reconquest had begun – it would be another 350 years before the last Muslims were expelled from Catalan territory.

The Spanish March or 'Catalunya Vella'

The *comtes* (counts) installed in Barcelona as Louis' lieutenants hailed from territory within and south of the Catalan Pyrenees. From the Frankish point of view the area was on the periphery and so became known as the Frankish or Spanish March – a buffer zone designed to keep the Muslims at arm's length, and to be used as a springboard for later

offensives. The area also became known as Catalunya Vella (Old Catalunya), as opposed to Catalunya Nova, the territories that would later be wrested from Muslim control.

The March was under nominal Frankish control but the real power lay with local potentates (themselves often of Frankish origin). One of these was Guifré el Pelós, or Wilfred the Hairy. According to legend, old Guifré had hair in parts most people do not (exactly which parts was never specified!). Son of Sunifred d'Urgell, he and his brothers managed to gain, through Holy Roman imperial decree and a dash of intrigue, control of most of the Catalan counties. These included Barcelona, at the time something of a glorified country town.

By 878 they had completed their task and Guifré el Pelós entered the folk mythology of Catalunya. A great funder of religious

Born in Blood

Guifré el Pelós founded the Casal de Barcelona (House of Barcelona) more or less with the consent of his Frankish overlords. But what's a new political entity without a flag of some sort? Scribblers of history and other tall tales soon hit upon a particularly gratifying account for the existence of Catalunya's national colours (the following story and several different versions began to circulate some time around the 16th century).

Called upon to join the holy fight against the wicked Muslims with an army of Frankish good guys, the gutsy Guifré fell wounded in hair-raising style on the field of battle. The Frankish emperor, Charles the Bald (this is not a joke), was so touched by his vassal's loyalty that he wanted to reward him in some way. No, not with an all-expenses-paid holiday to Rome or a gold-plated scimitar. Upon seeing Guifré's bright, golden shield embarrassingly bereft of a coat of arms, old Charles dipped his fingers in a pool of Guifré's fresh, warm blood and drew four finger stripes, *les quatre barres*, down the shield.

So much for the story-telling. From this tale came the Catalan coat of arms, concrete evidence of which first appears in 1150 in a seal of Count Ramon Berenguer IV. The same heraldic sign (said to be the fourth oldest in all Europe) can also be made out on the coffin of Ramon Berenguer II (in the cathedral in Girona), who died in 1082. Its origins remain a mystery. The coat of arms went on to become that of the so-called Crown of Aragón (Corona de Aragón), a coalition formed in 1137.

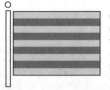

The Catalan flag (in which the stripes become horizontal) is first documented in the 13th century and became the official symbol of the modern, autonomous region of Catalunya in 1979. A symbol similar to the coat of arms, but oval in shape, was concocted in 1932 and now represents the Generalitat de Catalunya (the regional government of Catalunya). The same colour combination also appears in the heraldry of the other former members of the Crown of Aragón.

foundations in Barcelona (none of which survive) and across Catalunya (some of which do), he astutely won for himself the benevolence of the only people who could write in those days – the clergy. They began a tradition of eulogy that has never really died since. If Catalunya can be called a nation, then its 'father' was the hirsute Guifré.

Guifré and his immediate successors continued, at least in name, to be vassals of the Franks. In reality, his position as *comte de Barcelona* (count of Barcelona; even today many refer to Barcelona as the *ciutat comtal*, or city of counts) was assured in its own right.

The Comtes de Barcelona
By the late 10th century the Casal de Barcelona (House of Barcelona) was the senior of several counties (whose leaders were all related by family ties) that would soon be a single, independent principality covering most of modern Catalunya except the south, plus Roussillon (which today lies across the border in France).

One last Muslim assault came when Al-Mansur raided Barcelona in 985. Calls for Frankish aid to repulse Al-Mansur had gone unheeded, so from 988 onwards the counts refused to acknowledge Frankish suzerainty. The Franks never contested this new status quo and so Catalunya acquired tacit recognition across Europe.

Throughout Spain, a confusion of counties, principalities and kingdoms vied for local or peninsular domination. It was as common for Muslim warlords to team up with Christian rulers in local spats as for Christians and Muslims to challenge one another. These were, to say the least, interesting times. Particularly so for the counts of Barcelona, who managed to pick up a lot of booty by judicious meddling in Muslim squabbles to the south.

This booty was put to good use. The count of Barcelona, Count Ramon Berenguer I, was able to buy the counties of Carcassonne (a nice irony, since the ancestors of the counts of Barcelona had been the rulers of Carcassonne) and Béziers, north of Roussillon, with Muslim bullion.

More than any of his predecessors, it was he who established the Casal de Barcelona as overall head of all the Catalan counties. The precedent was rarely seriously put to the test thereafter. Below the count of Barcelona were other counts and below them a growing feudal aristocracy.

The counts of Barcelona would maintain ambitions in France for the following two centuries – at one point they held territory as far east as Provence. But they were constantly on the lookout for ways of recovering Catalan territory to the south.

Under Ramon Berenguer III (1097–1131) Tarragona was retaken, Catalunya launched its own fleet and sea trade developed. This was the era of great Catalan Romanesque art with its masterly church frescoes, concentrated especially in Catalunya Vella, the northern half of the region.

Marriage of Convenience?
In 1137 Ramon Berenguer IV clinched what must have seemed an unbeatable deal. He was betrothed to Petronilla, heiress to the throne of Catalunya's western neighbour Aragón, thus creating a joint state that set the scene for Catalunya's golden age. This state, the Crown of Aragón (Corona de Aragón) was ruled by *comtes-reis* (in Catalan parlance) or count-kings. Their title enshrined the continued separateness of the two original states, both of which retained many of their own laws. (Eventually the coalition included the principality of Catalunya, Aragón, Valencia, the Balearic Islands and Roussillon, in present-day France.)

Oddly, the counts of Barcelona never considered the possibility of elevating their title to 'king of Catalunya'. Thus, although in the coming centuries Catalunya (and not Aragón) would be at the forefront of the new realm's conquests and advances, to all of Europe the state would be known as Aragón. In the long term the arrangement was to have unexpected consequences as it tied Catalunya to the destiny of the rest of the peninsula in a way that ultimately would not appeal to many Catalans.

Don Ramon wasn't content to lie about with Petronilla. In the course of the 1140s he wrested control of southern Catalunya from the Muslims. This southwards expansion heralded a major shift in policy, which until then had been concerned with the north.

Don Ramon's son Alfons II styled himself as king of Aragón (on the insistence of the Aragonese nobility) but already trouble had begun to brew as Catalan rulers tended to clash with Aragonese nobles. The latter felt considerable sympathy for the Castilian rulers and the Reconquista (Reconquest), their campaign to wrest back the Iberian Peninsula from the Muslims. The Catalans viewed this enthusiasm with suspicion but Alfons was compelled to sign an agreement effectively leaving the job to the Castilians and locking the Catalans out of much of the potential territorial gains.

More pressing problems lay around the corner, however. Pere I (Alfons' successor) died in the Battle of Muret in 1213 and France pounced on virtually all Catalan possessions north of the Pyrenees.

Mediterranean Empire

The French blow induced some serious thinking in Barcelona on how to proceed. Not content to leave all the glory of the Reconquista to the Castilians, Jaume I (1213–76) embarked on some spectacular missions of his own.

He set his sights on seizing the Balearic Islands, which were in Muslim hands and frequently used as pirate bases to strangle Catalan sea trade. He eventually convinced the Aragonese nobility that by doing so they would open the doors to expanded commerce.

In 1229 Jaume, with a kind of divine fervour, set off on an expedition that involved fleets from Tarragona, Barcelona, Marseilles and other ports. His object was Mallorca, which he won. Six years later he had Ibiza and Formentera in hand. Things were going so well that, prodded by the more land-oriented Aragonese, for good measure he took control of Valencia too. This was no easy task and was completed only in 1248 after 16 years of grinding conquest.

The empire-building program shifted into top gear in the 1280s. Jaume I's son Pere II (1276–85) took Sicily in 1282. Pere

was married to the daughter of the last of the island's Hohenstaufen rulers, who opposed the claims of Charles d'Anjou (which had papal backing) to mastery of the island. Charles was dislodged on the night of the Sicilian Vespers and Pere moved in with his troops in a largely bloodless conquest.

The easternmost part of the Balearics, Menorca, was not so lucky, falling to Alfons III in 1287 in a blood bath. Most of its people were killed or enslaved and the island remained largely deserted throughout its occupation. Malta, Gozo and Athens were also taken but not held for long. A half-hearted attempt was made on Corsica but the most determined and ultimately fruitless assault began on Sardinia in 1324. The island became the Crown of Aragón's Vietnam. As late as 1423 Naples also came under the influence of the Catalo-Aragonese.

In spite of the carnage and expense of war, the western Mediterranean had been turned into a Catalan (or, if you will, Aragonese) lake. Trade proceeded apace, not only among the occupied territories but also with North Africa (through which Barcelona dominated the African gold trade) and to a lesser extent in the Levant.

The Rise of Parliament

The Crown may have been 'of Aragón' and many of its rulers may from now on have adopted the habit of using more Castilian names (no more Borrells, Berenguers etc), but the effective capital was still Barcelona. Jaume I, credited with notable legal reforms, authorised the election of a committee of top citizens to advise his officials in 1249. The idea developed and by 1274 the Consell dels Cent Jurats (Council of the Hundred Sworn-In) formed a kind of electoral college from which an executive body of five *consellers* was nominated to run city affairs. At the same time, municipal government was established in other Catalan cities.

In 1283, the Corts Catalanes met for the first time. This legislative council for all of the territory of the Crown of Aragón was made up of representatives of the nobility, clergy and high-class merchants to form a counterweight to regal power. The Corts

Catalanes met at first annually, then every three years, but had a permanent secretariat known as the Diputació del General, or Generalitat de Catalunya, based in Barcelona.

Decline & Castilian Domination

Empire began to exhaust Catalunya. Sea wars with Genoa, resistance in Sardinia, the rise of the Ottoman empire and the loss of the gold trade all drained the coffers. Commerce collapsed. The Black Death and famines killed about half of Catalunya's population in the 14th century.

At home, Pere III (1336–87) in particular seemed to be doomed to fighting one pointless war after another. Years of civil war in Aragón and Valencia achieved nothing, the natives were restless in Sardinia and Sicily, and then Pere found himself at war with Castile's Pedro I the Cruel. Aided by the house of Trastámara (which was angling for and eventually grabbed the Castilian crown), Pere was caught up in 13 years of conflict that brought him and his people nothing.

After Martí I, the last of Guifré el Pelós' dynasty, died heirless in 1410, a council elected Fernando (Ferran to the Catalans) de Antequera, a Castilian prince of the Trastámara house, to the Aragonese throne. This, the so-called Compromiso de Caspe (Casp Agreement; 1412), was engineered by the Aragonese nobility. Fernando and his successors were soon at daggers drawn with their Catalan subjects. A rebellion that began in 1462 against King Joan II ended in a devastating siege of Barcelona in 1473.

Joan II's son, Fernando, succeeded to the Aragonese throne in 1479 and his marriage to Isabel, queen of Castile, united Spain's two most powerful monarchies. Just as Catalunya had been hitched to Aragón, now the combine was hitched to Castile and Ramon Berenguer IV's clever marriage in 1137 in retrospect must have seemed like a nasty trap.

Catalunya effectively became part of the Castilian state, governed by a viceroy, although it jealously guarded its own institutions and system of law. The Reyes Católicos (Catholic Monarchs; Fernando and Isabel) introduced the Inquisition (the rooting out of those who did not practise Christianity as the Catholic church wished them to) in Catalunya against its people's wishes. The region was increasingly sidelined as Castile marched from victory to splendid victory. In 1492 the last of the Muslims were ejected from Granada. In the same year Columbus discovered the Americas – an event that in little time would bring enormous wealth to the now united Spain, but from which the Catalans would benefit little.

Castile's star shone bright all too briefly. Under Carlos I, Spain was united with the Habsburg empire and its fate was determined by Carlos' endless imperial wars and those of his successor Felipe II. By the 17th century the crown was in poor shape and the coffers empty. Increasingly Madrid sought to squeeze more taxes from the still comparatively autonomous Catalans.

Reapers War

Events precipitated themselves as King Felipe IV's advisor and effective ruler, Count-Duke Olivares, provoked a French attack on Catalan territory in the early 17th century. Olivares hoped to create a crisis that would allow him to roll back Catalunya's autonomy statutes and so impose hefty taxes and increase direct military control of the prickly region. What he provoked was the Guerra dels Segadors (Reapers War; 1640–52). It was a war on at least three levels – Spain versus France, Catalunya versus the Spanish monarchy, and the peasants against those who they saw as making their already miserable lives still less bearable.

Catalunya declared itself a 'republic' under French protection, but Cardinal Richelieu (the ruthless chief minister to Louis XIII) quickly persuaded the Catalans to swear loyalty to the French crown instead. Countryside and towns were trampled upon and Barcelona was finally besieged into submission. The French protection was less than convincing (and in the end largely resented), and seven years later, when France and Spain concluded hostilities, Louis XIV and Felipe IV signed a peace treaty that achieved little more than the loss to France of Catalan territory – in particular Roussillon and parts of Cerdanya.

War of the Spanish Succession

Catalunya seemed destined to stumble from one losing cause to another. The last of the Habsburgs, Carlos II, died in 1700 without leaving an heir and France imposed the investiture of a Bourbon, Felipe V. Schooled in French-style absolutism and centralism, Felipe soon proved vexatious to the Catalans. So Catalunya joined England, the Netherlands, some German states, Portugal and the House of Savoy in their decision to bat for an Austrian candidate. In 1702 the War of the Spanish Succession, a contest for the balance of power in Europe, broke out and 11 years later the allies signed the Treaty of Utrecht with France, which left Felipe V in charge in Madrid – and the Catalans well out on a limb. Felipe took Barcelona after a long siege on 11 September 1714 – for Catalans the blackest day in history. The fighting went on a few more days around the bastion of Cardona but the result was never in doubt.

Felipe V abolished the Generalitat, built a huge fort (the Ciutadella) to watch over

The iron-fisted Felipe V proved both a hindrance and a help to Catalunya.

Barcelona, and banned writing and teaching in Catalan. What remained of Catalunya's possessions was farmed out to the great powers: Menorca had gone to the British in 1713, Naples and Sardinia went to Austria, and Sicily to the House of Savoy. In Catalunya the so-called Nova Planta (New Plan), a policy levelling all differences between the constituent parts of the Spanish nation, was put into place.

Economic Recovery... & Collapse

Felipe V's iron fist was matched by some common sense. Politically and culturally crushed, the Catalans nevertheless found themselves with considerable room for manoeuvre economically.

The new tax system was progressive and more equitable than anything that had gone before. By the late 1720s the wheels of Catalan industry (cotton, ship-building and agriculture) were turning so well that Madrid decided to drop conscription in Catalunya, so as not to rob the region of labour.

When trade with the Americas was opened up to Catalunya in 1778, things only improved. The textiles industry – its factories concentrated in and around Barcelona – boomed. Other growing sectors included paper, cork, leather and liquor (local brandy became a successful export).

By wider European standards Catalunya's industry was still in its infancy, but it was way ahead of anything that much of the rest of the country was up to. Catalan exports to the rest of the realm rocketed.

The French Revolution of 1789 brought little but bad news for Catalunya. The Guerra Gran (1793–95; the first war with republican France), ended in a dubious peace treaty that led to the loss of commercial links with Britain. In Madrid the wheeler-dealer Manuel Godoy, the ill-suited adviser to the monarchy, managed to manoeuvre Spain into a pointless war against England in which Spain lost the bulk of its fleet at the Battle of Trafalgar (1805). Subsequently Godoy allowed Napoleon to occupy the country, ostensibly in a joint mission to conquer Portugal.

It took six years (1808–13) for a combined force of British troops under Wellington, along with Portuguese, ragtag Spaniards and some Catalans, to turf the French out. To the Catalans the conflict is known simply as the Guerra del Francès (War of the French), while to the rest of Spain it has gone down as the Guerra de Independencia (War of Independence). The net balance for Catalunya of all this fun and games was impoverishment.

The first half of the 19th century was marked by seesaw politics between absolutists, conservatives and liberals. Coups and counter-coups took place and street violence became increasingly common – a popular revolt in Barcelona in 1842 led to a bombardment of the city.

Renaixença

Even by the 1830s there were signs that industry was again picking up in and around Barcelona. The relative calm and growing wealth that came with commercial success in the second half of the century helped revive interest in all things Catalan.

The so-called Renaixença (Renaissance) was both backward- and forward-looking. Politicians and academics increasingly studied and demanded the return of former Catalan institutions and legal systems. The Catalan language was readopted by the middle and upper classes and a new Catalan literature emerged.

In 1892, the newly formed Unió Catalanista (Catalanist Union) demanded the re-establishment of the Corts Catalanes in a document known as the *Bases de Manresa*. In 1906 the suppression of Catalan newssheets was greeted by the formation of Solidaritat Catalana (Catalan Solidarity), a nationalist movement. Led by Enric Prat de la Riba, it attracted a broad band of Catalans, not all of them nationalists.

Perhaps the most dynamic expression of this Catalan renaissance occurred in the arts. Barcelona was the epicentre of Modernisme, the Catalan version of Art Nouveau.

In 1898 disaster struck again. Spain blundered into a hopeless colonial war with the USA in which it managed to lose its navy and remaining colonies – Cuba, Puerto Rico and the Philippines. The blow to the Catalan economy was immense. Many a local fortune had been made in the colonies by *'indios'*, Spaniards who had made their piles in the 'Indies'.

Years of Chaos

Catalanism was not the only source of political ferment. The rapid growth of the industrial proletariat, especially in Barcelona, led to heightened tension on the streets and radical changes in politics. From the late 1890s, bomb attacks and street violence increased as anarchists, gangsters, police, hired-guns in the pay of the big industrialists and others confronted one another.

Madrid's decision in 1909 to order a call-up of new recruits to fight Spain's nasty and largely incompetent colonial war in northern Morocco unleashed a general strike in Catalunya that quickly got out of hand. In what came to be known as the Setmana Tràgica (Tragic Week), mobs wrecked 70 religious buildings and workers were shot on the streets in reprisal. Madrid at first accused separatists of the violence, although the blame was ultimately left at the door of the anarchists. By now Barcelona had become known as the 'city of bombs'.

In 1914, Solidaritat Catalana launched the Mancomunitat de Catalunya, a kind of regional parliament that demanded a Catalan state within a Spanish federation. Made up of elected provincial politicians from around the region, it took on many administrative functions but was strangled in 1923 with the arrival of General Miguel Primo de Rivera as dictator in Madrid.

Rivera's repression of anything that smacked of separatism only succeeded in uniting, after his fall in 1930, the pent-up fervour of Catalunya's radical elements. Within days of the formation of Spain's Second Republic in 1931, leftist Catalan nationalists, Esquerra Republicana de Catalunya (ERC; Republican Left of Catalunya), led by Francesc Macià and Lluís Companys proclaimed Catalunya a republic within an imaginary 'Iberian Federation'. Madrid quickly pressured them into accepting unitary Spanish statehood, but in 1932 Catalunya got a new regional government, with the old title of Generalitat.

Francesc Macià, its first president, died in 1933 and was succeeded by Lluís Companys who, in 1934, tried again to achieve near-independence, proclaiming the 'Catalan State of the Spanish Federal Republic'. The Madrid government responded with an army bombardment of the Generalitat offices and Barcelona's city hall. The Generalitat was closed and its members given 35-year jail terms. They were released, and the Generalitat restored, when the leftist Popular Front won the February 1936 Spanish general elections. Now, briefly, Catalunya gained genuine autonomy.

But events of greater import than Catalan separatism were dragging all of Spain down the miserable path of civil war. For years the left and right had become increasingly radical. Street violence was the norm and a clash appeared inevitable. It came when General Francisco Franco led the army in his Nationalist uprising on 17 July 1936.

Civil War

By the end of 1936, Franco controlled much of southern and western Spain. Galicia and Navarra in the north were also his. Most of the east and industrialised north stood with Madrid and the Republic. Initial rapid advances on Madrid were stifled and the two sides settled in for almost three years of attrition.

While Nazi Germany and Fascist Italy aided Franco, the democratic West remained aloof. What little help trickled through to the Republic came from the USSR. The Republicans' biggest problem, however, was disunity. While radical anarchists, who in the first year of the war were the dominant force in Catalunya, wanted to pursue social revolution at all costs, the communists aimed to win the war first. That said, they devoted considerable energy to suppressing anarchists and even moderate socialists – their own allies!

The red and black colours of the anarchists fluttered over Barcelona but in May 1937 Companys ordered police to take over the anarchist-held telephone exchange on Plaça de Catalunya. After three days of street fighting, chiefly between anarchists

and the Partit Socialista Unificat de Catalunya (PSUC; Catalan communist party) the anarchists asked for a cease-fire. They were soon disarmed.

In the autumn of that year the Republican government moved to Barcelona. The last major engagement of the war took place on the Riu Ebre near Tortosa in summer 1938. It ended in defeat for the Republicans and by January of the following year Barcelona was in Nationalist hands. In March Madrid also finally fell and the war was over.

The Franco Era

Even before the war had ended Franco made the symbolic act of abolishing the Generalitat (in 1938). Up to 35,000 people were shot in his post-war purge, and the executions continued into the 1950s. Lluís Companys, who with hundreds of thousands of other refugees had fled to France, was arrested by the Gestapo in August 1940, handed over to Franco, and shot in secret on 15 October on Montjuïc hill. He is reputed to have died with the words 'Visca Catalunya!' ('Long live Catalunya!') on his lips.

Although the war ended in 1939, sporadic armed resistance continued in various parts of Spain, including Catalunya, until well into the 1940s. The most spectacular operation was a guerrilla invasion from France across the Pyrenees into the Val d'Aran in 1944. They got as far as La Pobla de Segur.

Meanwhile, Companys was succeeded as the head of the Catalan government-in-exile by Josep Irla, a former ERC MP who remained in charge until May 1954. Irla was followed by the charismatic Josep Tarradellas after the parliament-in-exile met in Mexico. Tarradellas remained at the head of the government-in-exile until after the death of Franco.

Franco embarked on a program of Castilianisation in Catalunya. He banned the public use of Catalan and had all town, village and street names rendered in Spanish. Book publishing in Catalan was allowed from the mid-1940s, but education, radio, TV and the daily press remained in Spanish.

By the 1950s opposition had turned to

JANE SMITH

General Franco did his best to Castilianise Catalunya during his dictatorship.

peaceful mass protests and strikes. In 1960 an audience at Barcelona's Palau de la Música Catalana concert hall sang a banned Catalan anthem in front of Franco. The ringleaders included a young Catholic banker, Jordi Pujol, who spent two years in jail as a result. Pujol was to become Catalunya's president in the post-Franco era.

The biggest social change in Franco's day was caused by the flood of 1.5 million immigrants during the 1950s and 1960s from poorer parts of Spain, chiefly Andalucía, attracted by economic growth in Catalunya.

A New Era

Two years after Franco's death in 1975, Josep Tarradellas was invited to Madrid to hammer out the Catalan part of a regional autonomy policy. Shortly afterwards, King Juan Carlos I decreed the re-establishment of the Generalitat de Catalunya and recognised Josep Tarradellas as its president. When Tarradellas finally returned to Barcelona he announced simply: *'Ja soc aquí'* ('I am finally here').

In Catalunya, a commission of experts had already cobbled together an autonomy statute. This got the royal seal of approval in 1979. The Catalan nationalist Jordi Pujol was elected Tarradellas' successor in April 1980 and he has remained at the helm of the Generalitat ever since.

Pujol has waged a constant war of attrition with Madrid, eking out ever more power. Catalunya has made considerable advances on this front, taking control of a range of areas including local police, education, trade, tourism, agriculture, hospitals, social security and culture. In 1996 Catalunya and other regions won the right to collect a third of national income tax. The region, an economic powerhouse for all of Spain, entered the 21st century with a greater deal of autonomy and a more assertive sense of its separate identity than at any time since 1714.

GEOGRAPHY

Catalunya forms a rough triangle, bounded by the Pyrenees and the French (and Andorran) frontier to the north, the Mediterranean Sea to the east and the region of Aragón to the west, joined at its southern extremity by the region of Valencia. The total area is 31,932 sq km.

Within that compact area is a striking variety of territory, much of it mountainous or at least hilly.

The Pyrenees

To the north, the eastern Pyrenees stretch some 200km along a dividing line that subsequently continues west across Spain and separates the Iberian peninsula from the rest of Europe. The highest peak in the Catalan Pyrenees, the Pica d'Estats (3143m), rises in the west of the region. Similar in age to the Alps (up to 100 million years old), the Pyrenees were also hit by glaciation around the same time (during the Quaternary Ice Age).

Rivers

These glaciers helped sculpt a series of river valleys that slice their way southwards through this natural fortress. Among them are: Riu Noguera Ribagorçana (along the

Aragonese border), Riu Noguera Pallaresa (a popular stretch for white-water rafting), Riu Segre and Riu Ter. The first two join the Segre on its way south-west through Lleida and on (after merging with Riu Cinca) to join one of Spain's most celebrated waterways, the Riu Ebre (Ebro in Spanish). This river enters southern Catalunya from Aragón, winds southwards and then sweeps east to empty into the Mediterranean in the broad wetlands of the Delta de l'Ebre. This is now home to a nature reserve and many species of water bird, including the flamingo.

The Coast
Back in the north, the Pyrenees drop towards the Mediterranean coast but not completely. The coastal cliffs of the Cap de Creus peninsula and the inland hills, mostly bald and windswept country, have an unruly majesty.

Farther south the coast flattens out in the Golf de Roses. Halfway along the gulf the ancient Greeks founded Emporion (present-day Empúries). South from there the coast at L'Estartit is fronted by a group of seven islets, the Illes Medes – source of the best diving in mainland Spain. Farther south again at Begur, the Costa Brava (Rugged Coast) again earns its name. From here to Tossa de Mar there are some magnificent stretches of cliff, pine stands and many charming little beaches, coves and inlets. Another trio of microscopic islets, the Illes Formigues, completes the catalogue of Catalan islands. If you travel the main roads a little way inland (for instance around Palamòs and Palafrugell), all this may not seem immediately apparent!

From there on the coast largely flattens out. The Costa del Maresme stretching down to Barcelona boasts some fine long beaches but has little character. After Barcelona comes the Costa Daurada, occasionally broken up by stretches of high cliff but largely lying low for the length of the southern Catalan coast.

The Plains
South of the Pyrenees lie a couple of plains, the Pla d'Urgell and the Plana de Vic, while closer to the northern coast, parts of the Empordà area are pretty flat too. The south-west, around Lleida for instance, although not strictly flat, hardly boasts grand mountains.

The Hills
The Pyrenees aside, there is no shortage of mountain and hill country in Catalunya. The Serra del Cadí, with its magnificent Pedraforca massif, is just one of several chains south of the Pyrenees proper that complicate the countryside in the northern half of the region.

A series of hill chains chop up the territory not far inland from the coast. These include Montseny, Montnegre, Collserola (west of Barcelona), Garraf, Prades and the Altes de l'Ebre. And who can forget the unique serrated profile of Montserrat?

CLIMATE
Catalunya's climate is as varied as its layout. This is in great part due to the presence of mountains and the sea.

The latter regulates the coastal climate, which in general is sunny and pleasant. The hottest month is usually July, closely followed by August, and on parts of the coast temperatures frequently reach 35°C. The sea contributes to humidity, especially in Barcelona and to the north, but it can also bring soothing sea breezes. The Costa Daurada is drier and more reliably sunny than areas farther north. Hotels on the *costas* (coasts) start opening for beach business as early as Easter, and often it is already warm enough to enjoy some early sunbathing in April. This is more likely on the Costa Daurada than the Costa Brava.

In the depths of winter (especially during February) it gets cold enough (average lows of around 7°C) to do some serious shivering. By March, with a little luck, things begin to thaw out. Oddly enough, you can get lucky with the weather in January, which has a tendency to be sunny if not terribly warm.

The northern coast is also frequently subject to an unrelenting north-easterly wind, the *tramuntana*, which can last for days. In summer this wind is the mortal enemy of bushland in the interior, occasionally turn-

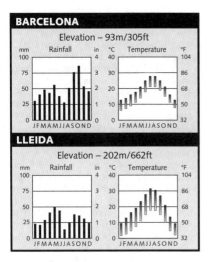

ing the frequent local outbreaks of fire into major disasters. Bush fires are an unfortunate part of the average Catalan summer.

Inland, the story can be quite different. In the flatter country to the south-west of Barcelona as far as Lleida, the summers tend to be hotter than on the coast – often 5°C or more – while in winter the temperatures drop a few degrees below those on the coast.

The various low hill and mountain ranges across the interior and leading up to the mighty Pyrenees themselves can bring changeable weather. Boiling hot days are possible but, in the Pyrenees especially, rapid changes are the norm even in summer. Frequently what starts as a bright, sparkling day can turn into a nasty storm. This unpredictability, even at fairly low altitudes in hill ranges, means you can easily be enjoying a warm sunny day on the coast while inland it's cool and wet. Barcelona and the Costa Brava are sometimes on the receiving end of summer storms that come rolling down off the mountains.

As a rule rainfall is highest in autumn and winter. In September and into October, the northern half of the region in particular gets a washdown in cracking, late summer thunderstorms that frequently lead to floods. Streams and coastal waterways known as

rieras especially have a tendency to flood seriously at this time of year, sometimes blocking major roads like the N-II.

Winter in the mountains is, unsurprisingly, more than chilly. If the average temperature in Tarragona hovers around 10°C in January, it drops as low as –5°C in the Pyrenees. Heavy snowfalls are good news for skiers but can cut off villages and close mountain passes. Typically, the best time of year for skiing is from late January to early March, although the season at the best resorts (such as Baqueira-Beret) can extend well into April. Walkers should note that snow at higher altitudes can remain an obstacle to the ill-equipped even in summer. Snowfalls in such areas are quite possible as late as June.

ECOLOGY & ENVIRONMENT

Although greener than much of the rest of Spain, Catalunya has hardly escaped the depredations on its land committed by humans. Ever since the Romans took control of the peninsula, farmers and graziers have been stripping away swathes of woodland and causing major topsoil erosion. Most of the fertile 300 sq km Delta de l'Ebre has been formed by eroded deposits in the past 600 years.

Many animal species have been depleted or destroyed by hunting. The controversial attempts to keep a handful of bears alive (and to introduce a few more) in the Pyrenees are just one example of late-20th-century reactions to earlier destruction.

Beyond Barcelona, industry is not oppressively present in Catalunya but the growth of urban sprawl, especially in the satellite towns and cities around the capital, has rendered parts of the region singularly ugly. Development along the costas, while not Spain's worst, has created eyesores and led to water pollution. Still, local councils keep beaches clean and many achieve EU (European Union) 'blue flags', indicating that they meet certain minimum standards of hygiene and facilities.

Elsewhere across the region, the general Spanish passion for constructing dams for hydroelectricity and irrigation did not leave

Catalunya untouched. Clearly these dams have caused significant change in the environment and destroyed habitats. A national plan for the massive diversion of water from the Riu Ebre to other, drier parts of Spain led to massive protests in Catalunya and neighbouring Aragón in early 2001.

The use of chemicals in agriculture is also problematic. The Delta de l'Ebre, for example, has been damaged by pesticide pollution. Air and noise pollution plague cities, especially the densely populated Barcelona.

Overall, the situation could be worse. Since the creation of the system of autonomous communities in Spain in the late 1970s, awareness of environmental issues has grown remarkably in Catalunya. Efforts have been greatly increased, especially since the late 1980s, to protect parklands and the region's flora and fauna.

FLORA & FAUNA
Flora
Trees By one estimate, 60% of Catalan territory is covered by woods of some description – more than 1.2 billion trees (how do you count something like that?). In 1987 the Generalitat classified 163 trees as 'monuments' for their uniqueness.

Among the more common species you may find in your wanderings in the remoter parts of Catalunya are: birch, silver fir, oak, cork oak, boxwood, chestnut, holm oak, ash, beech, elm, pine and European dwarf fan palm, Europe's only native palms.

The higher mountains are clothed in conifers, while cork oak and holm oak are particularly common in the lowlands.

Plants When the snows melt, the alpine and subalpine zones (below the tree line) bloom spectacularly with small rock-clinging plants and gentians, orchids, crocuses, narcissi (especially abundant in the Val d'Aran), Pyrenean lilies and sundews. About 5000 plant species have been identified in the Pyrenees.

Where there's no woodland and no agriculture, such as in parts of the Cap de Creus, the land is often covered in scrub. The short *garrigue* scrub (which prevails in the Cap de Creus) is dominated by aromatic herbs such as lavender, rosemary and thyme. Taller *maquis* scrub of gorse, juniper, heather, broom and strawberry tree also occurs. Orchids, gladioli and irises may flower beneath these shrubs, which are colourful in spring.

Fauna
Mammals Perhaps the most spectacular animal roaming the Pyrenees is the brown bear *(oso pardo)*. It is estimated that 45,000 of these bears (of various types) are left worldwide. Its Western European habitats (France, Italy, Greece and Spain) have largely been emptied. Out of these Spain is where the bear has survived best, with 80 to 90 specimens, though most of these roam the Cordillera Cantábrica range west of the Pyrenees.

It was long claimed that the bear was extinct in the Pyrenees, though some observers have always disputed that claim. Regardless, an operation to reintroduce the bear (importing specimens from Slovenia) to the French and Spanish Pyrenees around the Val d'Aran, was launched in the 1990s. The three bears (two females and one male) were tagged and have since produced four cubs. One of the adults has been killed by French farmers, displeased by the presence of animals that have a habit of eating their livestock. Heated debate continues on the presence of these bears.

The bulk of the other more interesting mammals to be found in Catalunya all stomp or skulk (depending on their habits) around the Pyrenees. They include: chamois *(isard/ rebeco)*, stoat *(ermini/armiño)*, pine marten *(marta)*, wild cat *(gat salvatge/gato salvaje)*, otter *(llúdria/nutria)*, mole *(talp/ topo)*, badger *(teixó/tejón)*, hedgehog *(eriço/ erizo)*, rabbit *(conill/conejo)*, red squirrel *(esquirol/ ardilla)*, wild boar *(porc senglar/ jabalí)*, red deer *(cérvol/ciervo)* and fallow deer *(daina/ gamo)*. The latter two have been reintroduced into several parts of the Pyrenees with varying success – it is not so uncommon to see them and also chamois and wild goats on walks high up in the mountains. Wild boar, whose numbers were once in decline, are doing well. In the extreme north-east of the region, in the Albera park, you may even come across semi-wild cows!

The *gos d'atura* is the only truly Catalan breed of dog, a hardy, hairy little specimen that is particularly smart and useful for rounding up livestock.

Birds Spring and autumn, when many migratory species can be seen, are popular times for bird-watchers.

In the Pyrenees, several kinds of raptor can be spotted, including the golden eagle *(àguila daurada/águila real)* and Bonelli's eagle *(àguila cuabarrada/águila perdicera)*.

Also flying high are limited numbers of Egyptian *(aufrany/alimoche)* and griffon vultures *(voltor comú/buitre leonado)*, as well as the majestic lammergeier *(trencalós/quebrantahuesos)*. Several other species of raptor can also occasionally be seen.

Smaller birds of the mountains and hills include goldfinches *(cadernell/jilguero)*, nightingales *(rossinyol/ruiseñor)*, black redstarts *(cuaroja/colirrojo)* and hoopoes *(puput/abubilla)*.

The wetlands reserves of the Delta de l'Ebre and the Parc Natural dels Aiguamolls de l'Empordà host a feast of water birds, the most spectacular of which are the pink flamingoes *(flamencs/flamencos)* that live and even breed in the delta. As many as 325 species of bird have been identified in the delta – some 95 of them nest there. Interestingly, the figures for the Aiguamolls park are almost identical.

Migratory birds that can be seen in these wetlands include the occasional black stork *(cigonya negra/cigüeña negra)*, heron *(ardèid/ardeido)*, tern *(xatrac/golondrina de mar)*, glossy ibis *(picaport/morito)* and spoonbill *(becplaner/espatula)*.

Among those that hang around are various types of duck *(anèc/pato)*, owl *(mussol/búho or lechuza)*, heron *(pica pedrell/garza real)*, cormorant *(cormorà/cormorán)*, harrier *(aguiló/aguilucho)* and kingfisher *(blauet/martín pescador)*.

Other Fauna There is no shortage of reptiles, insects and a varied assortment of creepy crawlies in Catalunya, though none are particularly dangerous.

National Parks & Reserves

Information on parks and reserves in Catalunya can be obtained through the region's environment *(medi ambient)* department in Barcelona (☎ 93 444 50 00, fax 93 419 75 47, Ⓦ www.gencat.es/mediamb/pn/eparcs.htm).

Of Spain's eight national parks, Catalunya counts just one, the Parc Nacional d'Aigüestortes i Estany de Sant Maurici in the north-west. It is Catalunya's most strictly protected park and covers some spectacularly beautiful territory. Everything from hunting and fishing to free camping and swimming are forbidden within the park. In the surrounding *zona perifèrica*, also considered prime parkland, some of these activities are permitted.

On the next rung down and run by various regional bodies in Catalunya are the eight *parcs naturals*, nature reserves where the controls are less stringent. In most of these there are even villages and roads within the parklands. Regulations vary from one to the next. So too do their characteristics:

Parc Natural Cadí-Moixeró
Catalunya's most extensive park, situated in the lower hills of the Pyrenees (the Pre-Pyrenees or *Prepirineus*).

Parc Natural de la Zona Volcànica de la Garrotxa
Spain's most captivating volcanic landscape, peppered with ancient volcanoes (some 40 cones) and dense with luxuriant vegetation.

Parc Natural Delta de l'Ebre
One of the most important habitats for water birds, including a blossoming population of flamingoes, in the Mediterranean. These wetlands, although inhabited and given over in part to rice production, are nevertheless a peaceful haven for birds and their observers.

Parc Natural dels Aiguamolls de l'Empordà
Another home to a varied parade of water birds are these wetlands farther north along the Catalan coast.

Parc Natural de Montserrat
The weird rock formations of Montserrat lie at the heart of this park.

Parc Natural de Montseny
This less well known park boasts a surprising

variety of landscape and flora, due in part to unexpected changes in altitude within its boundaries. Unesco declared it a biosphere reserve as far back as 1978.

Parc Natural del Cap de Creus
The stunningly bare landscape of this stretch of north Catalan coast makes for exhilarating walking in Spain's easternmost corner. The area was declared a natural park in 1998.

Parc Natural de Sant Llorenç del Munt i l'Obac
Lying between Montserrat and Montseny, this is another surprisingly attractive piece of countryside, with striking rock landscape and holm oak woods.

In addition to these are three smaller *paratges naturals*. They include the massive Pedraforca rock within the Parc Natural Cadí-Moixeró, the pretty area around Prades and the Monestir de Poblet, and the Albera park up against the French frontier in the north-east of the region.

Of the remaining principal seven designated reserves, the most important is the *reserva marina* (marine reserve) of the Illes Medes, the islet group off L'Estartit.

Four new parks are also planned. Of them, the future Parc Natural dels Ports de Tortosa-Beseit would be the second biggest in the region.

GOVERNMENT & POLITICS

The Generalitat de Catalunya, Catalunya's regional government, was resurrected by royal decree in 1977. Its power as an autonomous government is enshrined in the statutes of the national Spanish constitution of 1978, and by the Estatut d'Autonomia (devolution statute), which got the royal green light in 1979. The Govern, as the regional government is also known, is housed in the Palau de la Generalitat on Plaça de Sant Jaume in central Barcelona. The parliament sits in buildings in the Parc de la Ciutadella.

The Generalitat has wide powers over matters such as education, health, trade, industry, tourism and agriculture. Education is now nearly all in Catalan which, at the time of Franco's death, had been in some danger, not only because of the massive immigration of Castilian speakers but also because many Catalans, although they spoke Catalan, could no longer read or write it.

Since the first post-Franco regional elections in March 1980, Jordi Pujol's nationalist, right-of-centre Convergència i Unió (CiU; Convergence and Union) coalition has been at the controls. CiU does not want full independence from Spain but constantly seeks to strengthen Catalan autonomy. The pro-independence party Esquerra Republicana de Catalunya (ERC; Republican Left of Catalonia) has won only 8% to 10% of the vote in recent elections. ERC is avowedly nonviolent and there's no Catalan equivalent of the Basque Euskadi ta Askatasuna (ETA; Basque Nation & Liberty).

Generally conservative, Catalans tend to move to the left in national elections (since Spanish conservative parties are less likely to be sympathetic to regionalists than, say, the socialists). Barcelona usually votes for the left-wing Partit Socialista de Catalunya (PSC; Catalan Socialist Party) in city council elections.

The PSC, aligned with the main Spanish socialist party, the Partido Socialista Obrero Español (PSOE; Spanish Socialist Workers Party), hopes it may yet take control of the region too. It ran extremely close in the October 1999 regional polls under the leadership of the charismatic former mayor of Barcelona, Pasqual Maragall.

Elections to the Generalitat take place every four years. They are free and by direct universal suffrage. The members of each house thus elected then vote to appoint the president of the Generalitat.

The region is divided into four provinces, named after their respective capitals: Barcelona, Girona, Tarragona and Lleida. A decree of 1936 actually divided Catalunya into nine regions, although these have no administrative meaning today. The next division downwards is the *comarca*, or district, of which there are 41, each with its own administrative centre, or *consell comarcal*.

The consell comarcal of the Val d'Aran, the comarca in the extreme north-west of Catalunya, was granted more powers than the remainder of the *comarcas* under a regional law of 1990. The Val d'Aran has an identity all of its own. Its people speak a different language, Aranese *(aranés)*, which is a subdialect of the now virtually extinct Occitan. You will notice that street signs and the like here are in Aranese, not Catalan.

The final subdivision is into 76 *municipios*, or local councils, each of which is administered by an *ajuntament*.

Barcelona thus has its city government, and is the capital of the Barcelonès comarca, Barcelona province and the entire region.

ECONOMY

Since the golden empire-building days of Jaume I, Catalunya, with Barcelona as its powerhouse and window on the wider world, has always been something of an Iberian engine room. Even when marginalised by Madrid, the region managed to get along.

While rich in agricultural produce, the region is poor in raw materials needed for industry. Nevertheless, Barcelona was at the forefront of Spain's much delayed entry into the industrial age. In and around the city, small-scale textiles factories emerged in the 18th century and presaged greater things to come.

Industry properly began to take off, again mostly in and around Barcelona, in the mid-19th century. Metallurgy and engineering became sources of pride to the city. Steamships were launched here and the country's first trains were 'made in Barcelona'.

Today, Catalunya is undoubtedly the country's workhorse. Throughout the 1990s almost a quarter of all Spain's exports came from Catalunya, home to less than an eighth of the country's population. In 2000, exports from Catalunya were more than 20% up over the previous year and well ahead of the national average. The bulk of these exports go to other EU countries and total imports remain greater than total exports. Catalunya accounts for about a fifth of the national economy.

Across Catalunya about 60% of the population is employed in the services sector, 36% in industry and 4% in agriculture.

At the beginning of the 20th century half the region's population worked the land. Nowadays, machines do a lot of the work and much land has been abandoned. Still, more than 10% of the national agricultural

output is produced in Catalunya. Products include wheat, barley, olives, grapes and a range of fruit. In summer you will no doubt encounter huge sunflower plantations in coastal areas. Wood and cork are produced in mountain forest areas. Almost 20% of Spain's meat is produced in Catalunya and fishing remains an important if declining industry.

Raw materials for industry are scarce but Catalan manufacturing accounts for half the national output. Three-quarters of Spain's textiles are made in Catalunya and their production is centred above all on Barcelona's big satellite cities of Sabadell and Terrassa. Other important sectors include chemicals, metals, paper and food processing.

Tourism is big in Catalunya, which receives a little under 20% of the country's total visitors. Local authorities estimated tourism earnings at almost €7.5 million in 1999.

By European standards, Catalunya is not doing too badly in the employment stakes. According to statistics, 15% of the entire Spanish population is out of work, but in Catalunya the figure is 9.7%. Governments in Spain prefer to use a different measure – the number of people officially registered as unemployed. On that basis, 9.1% is the national rate, while in Catalunya 6.1% of the active population is out of a job. Unemployment in Catalunya is at its lowest since the 1970s. Inflation is a bigger problem in Catalunya (3.5%) than across the nation (2.9%).

POPULATION & PEOPLE

Catalunya counts some 6.1 million inhabitants, out of a total of 39.8 million for all of Spain (191 inhabitants per sq km as opposed to a national average of 77). Of these, 1.5 million live in Barcelona and a further 0.6 million in the surrounding comarca. If various satellite towns in neighbouring comarcas are included, what could be called the 'greater Barcelona area' would total about 3.8 million. Around the year 1850, all of Catalunya counted barely a million souls.

Population has not only grown constantly since the early 19th century, it has also been greatly displaced. Since the end of the Civil War especially, people have increasingly abandoned the country for the city. After Barcelona, the next five most populous centres are satellite cities and towns around the capital. Provincial capitals Tarragona and Lleida come in next and the top 10 are completed by two more towns near Barcelona. Some rural regions have remained depressingly underpopulated and many towns have been abandoned altogether. While more than 2.1 million people live in the Barcelona comarca, only 5815 live in Pallars Sobirà, a Pyrenean comarca!

The average age in Catalunya is 39½ – almost two years above that for the rest of Spain. If it weren't for a continued trickle of inward migration, population growth would stand at zero.

The *años de hambre* (years of hunger) that marked the late 1940s and 1950s sparked a process of massive internal migration. Millions of Spaniards from the poorer regions like Andalucía, Extremadura and Galicia streamed northwards and eastwards in search of a better life. Around 1.5 million people moved into Catalunya. Some statistics suggested that the newcomers actually outnumbered the locals by the end of the 1960s!

Today the influx comes from outside Spain. After an amnesty in the first half of 2000 saw about 200,000 illegal immigrants receiving residence papers, the central government in Madrid adopted a more aggressive policy on clandestine migrants. In Catalunya as elsewhere in Spain, racism has reared its ugly head. Even the wife of regional president Jordi Pujol has made public statements expressing the fear that Catalunya, along with its language, people and culture, will be flattened by the 'invasion'. Others openly worry that the newcomers will take locals' jobs, gain access to public funds denied to Spaniards and are responsible for growing crime rates.

And yet the foreign population is relatively small – legal immigrants amount to only 2.4% of the total population in the region. Counting illegals, the total is unlikely to be more than double that figure. A report in early 2000 suggested that these foreigners, mostly from North and sub-Saharan Africa, Pakistan, South America and Eastern Europe, contributed far more than they took – to the tune of a net annual addition to Catalan public coffers of almost €440 million.

EDUCATION

Education is compulsory between the ages of six and 16. Each region in Spain administers its own education system, although overall guidelines are similar throughout the country. In Catalunya about 1.3 million people are enrolled in some kind of educational institute, from pre-school to university.

Upon matriculation, students must also sit entrance exams if they want to go to university. Students tend to study for six or so years, earning qualifications such as the *diploma* after three years and the *licencia* after another two or three years' study.

The Generalitat's drive to foment the use of Catalan has meant that it is increasingly the standard language of education in schools. Some fear Spanish is being driven into the back seat.

University education is in some respects a more complex issue. Some classes are held in Castilian, but ideally the Generalitat would like to change that too. Making the speaking of Catalan a prerequisite for lecturing would exclude the rest of the country's academics from teaching in Catalunya, something that ultimately might do more harm than good.

The region boasts seven public and three private universities, as well as the Universitat Oberta de Catalunya, an Open University offering courses that don't require class attendance. Five of the universities are in Barcelona, while others are spread across the cities of Tarragona, Lleida, Girona and Vic.

Illiteracy is still an issue in Catalunya, as it is in the rest of Spain and, contrary to popular belief, in many western countries. Some 3.3% of the Catalan population is illiterate (the national average is 3.9%). Since the bulk of these people are in older age groups, it is to be supposed that the problem will gradually diminish.

ARTS

For many, Catalunya, if it is a concept at all, is thought of as a pleasant place for a beach holiday, or perhaps associated with walking and skiing in the mountains. Those who contemplate its capital, Barcelona, may think immediately of Gaudí and Modernisme, the striking Catalan version of Art Nouveau that dominated the city's architecture in the late 19th and early 20th centuries.

What is less known is that Catalunya is a remarkable repository of other artistic treasures, particularly from the Middle Ages. The region's Romanesque and, to a slightly lesser extent, Gothic heritages are as remarkable as any other comparable region's in Europe, if not more so. While in later periods Catalunya undoubtedly languished, it launched some of the greatest figures of 20th-century painting onto the world stage: Picasso, Dalí, Miró and others.

In literature and also music Catalans have had their moments, though there is no denying that in these fields they have been less prodigious than one might have expected.

Architecture
The Catalans have always been a busy lot! This can be seen especially since their golden age of empire and trade but even before that they seemed restless and active. Perhaps for that reason their most extensive artistic heritage, their most impressive portfolio if you like, lies in the bricks, stone and mortar with which they have been raising buildings great and small since the Greeks turned up on Catalan shores six centuries before Christ.

From Hill Towns to the Circus Maximus
You can get a vague idea of what Iberian hill towns were like at several locations around Catalunya, such as Ullastret (on the Costa Brava). Although not an awful lot is left of these Iron Age settlements, it is always an interesting exercise to transport yourself back three thousand years and imagine these primitive people going about their business in simple walled settlements.

A qualitative leap comes in the form of one ancient site in Catalunya, that of the Greek settlement of Emporion (now Empúries) on the Costa Brava. Again, some imagination is needed here as little rises much above knee height. Aided by the explanations scattered about the place you can see where the Greeks built their temples and laid out their *agora* (town square) at the centre. Around and about lie the remains of houses and shops and, next door, the Roman settlement that was raised after the arrival of Scipio in 218 BC.

The Romans stayed for centuries but did not populate Catalunya heavily. A fan of the empire may thus be a little disappointed by the comparative sparseness of evidence of their presence. Roman Empúries is itself engaging, and more important remains can be found in the cities. Apart from remnants of the Roman city walls and aqueduct, Barcelona offers the chance to wander around the excavated city streets below ground level in the Museu d'Història de la Ciutat. More impressive still is Tarragona, which is hardly surprising since it was the Roman provincial capital. Here you can pick your way through ruins of temples, the old Circus Maximus (in some of whose vaults now nest restaurants and bars), theatres and forum. Just outside the city are further reminders of the town's imperial past, including an impressive aqueduct.

In Martorell, not far out of Barcelona, you can contemplate the Pont del Diable (Devil's Bridge), a Gothic reconstruction of the original Roman bridge that took the Via Augusta across the river here. The foundations and grand entrance arch are Roman.

Visigothic, Pre-Romanesque & Muslim
Precious few remains of these artistic periods have survived to this day. Perhaps the best example of pre-Romanesque building, incorporating remains of earlier Visigothic constructions, is the trio of churches in Terrassa, outside Barcelona. Remains of another Visigothic church, the 4th-century Basílica de Bovalar, can be seen across the Riu Segre a little way from Seròs, a town 28km outside Lleida.

Of the hundreds of years of Muslim occupation in Catalunya, the reminders are disappointingly few. Lleida and Tortosa each retain their Islamic *suda*, or fortress, and you can visit the so-called 'Banys Àrabs' (Arab Baths) of Girona, although they are a 12th-century Christian imitation of the original idea.

Romanesque It was Lombard artisans from northern Italy who first introduced this style of monumental building to Catalunya. It is characterised by a pleasing simplicity. The exteriors of most early Romanesque edifices that have not been tampered with are virtually bereft of decoration. Churches, for instance, tend to be austere, angular constructions accompanied by tall (sometimes seven storeys), square-based bell towers. There were a few notable concessions to the curve – almost always semicircular or semi-cylindrical. These included the barrel vaulting inside the churches, the apse (or apses, for as the style was developed, up to five might be tacked on to the 'stern' of a church), and arches atop all the openings.

The main portal and windows are invariably topped with straightforward arches. When builders got a little saucy, they sometimes adorned the main entrance with several arches within one another. From the late 11th century on, stonemasons began to fill the arches with statuary, a reflection of the spread of more sophisticated European tastes in construction and decoration. The Romanesque churches of places like Lleida, Gandesa and Agramunt bear a slight Muslim influence too.

Catalunya Vella (see History earlier in this chapter) is peppered with as many as 2000 Romanesque churches in varying states of repair. Some are outstanding and provide a key to understanding the development of this form of architecture in Catalunya, as well as illuminating its medieval history.

In many respects, the most magnificent structure is the Església de Sant Vicenç in the castle complex dominating Cardona (less than an hour by car north-west of Barcelona). It is said to be the oldest basilica in Europe covered with a vaulted ceiling and dome.

As for Romanesque sculptural decoration, the main doorway to the 12th-century Monestir de Santa Maria in Ripoll, north of Barcelona in the Pyrenees, is the most extravagant display you will see in Catalunya. Another fine piece of Romanesque construction is the lovely Monestir de Sant Joan de les Abadesses, not far from Ripoll. Not far behind the Ripoll entrance is that of the 13th-century Església de la Mare de Déu dels Socors in Agramunt, while the little-visited Església de Sant Pere in Àger, north of Lleida, is also worth a look.

Perhaps one of the most spectacular settings for a massive Romanesque church and monastery complex is that of the Monestir de Sant Pere de Rodes, high up in the hills backing the northern Costa Brava. While in that area, visit Vilabertran too for its Augustinian convent.

Tarragona's magnificent cathedral also betrays some Romanesque features. Indeed quite a few churches and monasteries around Catalunya boast both Romanesque and Gothic styles, as construction tended to take long enough for one style to be superseded by another!

One of the more charming examples of simple Catalan Romanesque is the church of Sant Climent in Taüll, in north-western Catalunya, where it is by no means alone as the surrounding Vall de Boí is well worth exploring for other fine churches.

Even in Barcelona, for those who don't manage to get far out of the city, not everything was lost in the regal desire to embellish the city with Gothic jewels and so rip out all their Romanesque predecessors. The 12th-century former Benedictine monastery of Església de Sant Pau del Camp (El Raval) is a good (if rather neglected) example, especially the cloister. Just outside town you can visit the monastery complex at Sant Cugat del Vallès. Although much of it was incorporated into a later Gothic construction, it has a fine 12th-century cloister and the Lombard bell tower is Romanesque.

The list is endless and in the course of this guide only a small (if representative) sample can be offered.

The counterpoint to Romanesque architecture was the art used to decorate so many of the churches and monasteries built in the style. In this respect Barcelona is *the* place to be, as the best of Romanesque art from around Catalunya has been concentrated in the Museu Nacional d'Art de Catalunya. More can be seen in several other museums around the region. See also Painting & Sculpture later in the chapter.

Gothic This soaring form of architecture took off in France in the 13th century and spread across Europe.

In Catalunya, its emergence coincided with Jaume I's march into Valencia and annexation of Mallorca and Ibiza, accompanied by the rise and rise of a trading class and a burgeoning mercantile empire. The enormous cost of the grand new monuments could thus be covered by the steady increase in the realm's wealth.

While the many smaller towns of Catalunya Vella hung on to their Romanesque heritage, Gothic tended to be the preserve of the big cities and the grand religious orders. The best of Gothic can be seen in Barcelona, where a veritable building fever seemed to take hold of the medieval city and then leave it in a time warp. There is a reason why the heart of the old city has been dubbed the Barri Gòtic (Gothic Quarter). Barcelona is in fact one of the best places in Europe to witness both religious and civic Gothic construction.

Beyond the capital, the finest examples lie in the grand monasteries to the west and south-west, such as Poblet, Santes Creues and Sant Cugat del Vallès, as well as Pedralbes (in Barcelona itself). The cathedrals of Girona and Tarragona are also fine.

Gothic buildings did not simply pop up like mushrooms from one day to the next. The style of architecture reflected the development of building techniques. The introduction of buttresses, flying buttresses and ribbed vaulting in ceilings allowed engineers to raise edifices that were loftier and seemingly lighter than ever before. The pointed arch became a standard characteristic and the great rose windows were the principal source of light inside these enormous spaces. Think about the little hovels that most of the labourers on such enormous projects would have lived in, the precariousness of wooden scaffolding and the primitive nature of building materials available and you get some

idea of the degree of awe the great cathedrals, once completed, must have inspired.

Catalan Gothic, however, did not follow exactly the same course. Decoration tended to be more sparing than in northern Europe and the most obvious defining characteristic is the triumph of breadth over height. While some northern European cathedrals reach for the sky, Catalan Gothic has a tendency rather to push to the sides, stretching vaulting design to the limit.

In Barcelona, the Saló del Tinell (see under Museu d'Història de la Ciutat in the Barcelona chapter), with a parade of 15m arches (among the largest ever built without reinforcement) holding up the roof, is a perfect example of Catalan Gothic. Another is the enormous Reials Drassanes (Royal Shipyards) in Barcelona, which date from medieval times and are home today to the Museu Marítim.

In their churches, too, the Catalans opted for a more robust shape and lateral space – step into Barcelona's Església de Santa Maria del Mar or Església de Santa Maria del Pi (in Plaça de Sant Josep Oriol) and you'll soon get the idea. It seems that the long, narrow and high naves of many northern European Gothic churches aroused more claustrophobia than admiration in the Catalans. While on the subject of churches, a peculiarly Spanish touch that can be seen here and throughout the peninsula is the presence of a *cor*, or enclosed choir stalls, smack in the middle of the main nave – the one in Barcelona's cathedral is a good example.

Another notable departure from what you might have come to expect of Gothic beyond the Pyrenees is the lack of spires and pinnacles. Bell towers tend to terminate in a flat or nearly flat roof. Occasional exceptions prove the rule – the main facade of Barcelona's cathedral, with its three gnarled and knobbly spires, does vaguely resemble the outline that confronts you in Chartres or Cologne.

Pere III was Barcelona's big builder. In the 14th century, when he was in charge, the principality was beset by huge problems but he went ahead and built, or began to build, much of the cathedral, the Reials Drassanes,

La Llotja (in the El Born area of La Ribera; housing the stock exchange), the Saló del Tinell, the Casa de la Ciutat (which houses the Ajuntament) and numerous lesser buildings, not to mention part of the city walls. Along with the cathedral, the Església de Santa Maria del Mar and the Església de Santa Maria del Pi were completed by the end of the century.

Renaissance, Baroque & Neo-Classical

The strong Catalan affection for the Gothic style, coupled with a decline in the Crown of Aragón's fortunes, seems largely to have closed the region to the refinement that the Renaissance brought to other parts of Europe. With the exception of the occasional facade (such as on the Generalitat in Barcelona), the style did little more than graze the architectural surface of Catalunya. A particularly Spanish spin-off from the Renaissance, Plateresque, makes a rare appearance in the facade of the Església de Santa Maria la Major in Montblanc.

The extravagance of baroque was a slightly different story although even there it rarely went beyond the decoration of ex-

isting structures. The cathedrals of Girona and Tortosa got a baroque facelift, and great altarpieces were also designed in this curvaceous style.

Among the more important but restrained baroque constructions in Barcelona are the Església de la Mercè (in the Barri Gòtic), home to the medieval sculpture of Our Lady of Mercy (Barcelona's co-patron with Sant Eulàlia), the Església de Sant Felip Neri (in the Barri Gòtic) and the Jesuits' Església de Betlem, which was largely destroyed in the Civil War and since rebuilt. Also worth a look is the courtyard of the Palau de Dalmases, in Carrer de Montcada (La Ribera), reworked from the original Gothic structure.

Overall, though, baroque made less of an impact on Catalunya than on the rest of Spain, and still less than elsewhere in Europe.

Neo-classical design also had a limited impact in Catalunya. Projects of quality outside Barcelona were few and far between, although the cathedral in Vic and La Seu Nova in Lleida are two exceptions. In the capital, the facades of the Ajuntament and La Llotja are examples, as is the Plaça Reial.

Modernisme This remarkable, if brief, flurry of fantasy-filled design and architecture, which found its greatest expression in Barcelona but also made its way into other Catalan towns (and even seeped occasionally beyond Catalunya), took off in the 1880s and was already sputtering to a close by 1910.

Mention Modernisme and most people respond 'Gaudí' (often pronouncing it 'gaudy', in some cases an expression of artistic judgement).

Antoni Gaudí (1852–1926; pronounced 'gow-**di**', with the emphasis on the 'i') was born in Reus (see the Costa Daurada & the South-West chapter) and initially trained in metalwork. He obtained his architecture degree in 1878. He personifies, and in large measure transcends, a movement in architecture that brought a thunderclap of innovative greatness to Barcelona, an otherwise middle-ranking (artistically speaking) European city.

Modernisme did not appear in isolation. To the British and French the style was Art

Església de Santa Maria del Mar – Barcelona's finest example of Catalan Gothic

Nouveau; to the Italians it was *lo stile Liberty*; the Germans called it *Jugendstil* (Youth Style) and their Austrian confrères *Sezession* (Secession).

The term Modernisme is somewhat misleading. It suggests the adoption of new means of construction and/or decoration and the rejection of the old. In a sense, nothing could be further from the truth. From Gaudí down, Modernista architects looked to the past for inspiration. Gothic, Islamic and Renaissance all had something to offer. At its most playful, Modernisme was able to intelligently flout the rule books on all these styles and create new and exciting cocktails. Even many of the materials used by the Modernistas were traditional – the innovation came in their application.

The search for a source or spirit was complemented by a desire to renew and transform those sources into a new expression, or re-expression, of timeless values in a contemporary universe. Those roots and their transformation are of course more readily observed in some Modernista constructions than in others.

As many as 2000 buildings in Barcelona and throughout Catalunya display at least some Modernista traces. By far the bulk of the best work is in Barcelona, where the arrival of the style coincided with a building boom in the city.

Three Geniuses The two architects who most closely followed Gaudí in talent were Lluís Domènech i Montaner (1850–1923) and Josep Puig i Cadafalch (1867–1957), both prominent nationalists.

A quick comparison of some of the work by these three architects is enough to illustrate the difficulty in defining closely what is Modernisme. As Gaudí became more adventurous he increasingly appeared as a lone wolf. With age he became almost exclusively motivated by stark religious conviction and devoted much of the latter part of his life to what remains Barcelona's call sign – the unfinished La Sagrada Família church. His inspiration in the first instance here is clearly Gothic. But Gaudí sought the perfection of harmony and perspective he observed in nature. Straight lines were out. The curve implies movement and hence vitality and this idea informed a great deal of Art Nouveau thinking across Europe, in part inspired by long-standing tenets of Japanese art.

Others of Gaudí's key works show a similar preoccupation with the forms of nature such as the Casa Milà (La Pedrera) and Casa Batlló, both in L'Eixample district in Barcelona (see the Barcelona chapter), where not a single straight line appears anywhere.

For real contrast, just look from Casa Batlló to Puig i Cadafalch's Casa Amatller next door, where the straight line rules. This architect has also looked to the past, and to foreign influence (the gables are borrowed from the Dutch), and still managed to create a house of startling beauty and invention. Domènech i Montaner, too, clearly looks into the Gothic past, but never simply copies. Look at his Hospital de la Santa Creu i Sant Pau in L'Eixample, Barcelona. In his Palau de la Música Catalana (also in Barcelona) he comes closer to Gaudí's ideas.

Many other architects were at work raising Modernista buildings, in Barcelona and occasionally beyond. One of them was Josep Maria Jujol (1879–1949), virtually unknown outside Catalunya, who left behind some interesting examples in and around his native Tarragona.

To the Present Even before Gaudí died in 1926, Modernisme had been swept aside. In the aftermath of WWI especially, it seemed already stale, decadent and somehow unwholesome.

While other movements replaced Modernisme in the fine arts and literature, architecture took a bit of a nose dive from here on. Between the two world wars a host of neo-classical and neo-baroque edifices went up in the cities. In the aftermath of the Civil War there was little money, time or willingness for architectural fancy work. Apartment blocks and offices, designed with a realism and utilitarianism that to most mortals seem deadly dull, were now erected.

Since the death of Franco in 1975, Barcelona has been a hotbed of architectural activity – not all of it in good taste.

The Olympic Games of 1992 in particular inspired a burst of building and design activity that even today continues in massive urban renewal programs. Among leading contemporary Catalan figures are Enric Miralles (1955–2000), Josep Oriol Bohigas (born 1925) and Ricard Bofill (born 1939).

Painting & Sculpture

Ancient Art Objects from as long ago as the Early Stone Age have been unearthed in Catalunya. In the search for these objects archaeologists have also occasionally stumbled across examples of rock art showing hunting and war scenes, dance rituals and the like.

From the ancient Greeks and Iberians survive some beautiful ceramic work and bronze figurines. Mosaics (such as those at Empúries) are a potent reminder of the Roman artistic heritage, as are examples of statuary, friezes and other stonework found in Catalunya's Roman settlements.

A modest sample of all these stages in ancient art in Catalunya can be seen at the Museu d'Arqueologia in Barcelona.

Romanesque & Gothic The Roman habit of burying VIPs in impressive stone sarcophagi carried over into the early Christian period – some examples of this funerary art figure among the oldest surviving remnants of early medieval art.

Although in general medieval painters and sculptors worked in anonymity, some of their names have filtered through to us, one of which is the Mestre de Cabestany. He and his workshop were turning out marble sculpture in northern Catalunya, particularly for the Monestir de Sant Pere de Rodes in the 12th century. A few fine pieces can be observed in Barcelona's Museu de Frederic Marès.

Romanesque decorative art, which was produced from the early 11th century on into the 14th century, has come down to us in great abundance in Catalunya, generally in two forms. As a rule Romanesque churches were decorated on the inside with remarkable frescoes, while altars and other key locations were frequently adorned with wooden sculptures.

These artistic representations that to modern eyes look infantile in their slender, two-dimensional and seemingly lifeless execution served a didactic purpose. Themes were always religious and generally aimed to remind people of the other-worldliness of the Holy Trinity, the angels and saints. In more complex cases they served to communicate stories from the Bible or illustrate doctrine and matters of faith. They have to be viewed also in light of the fact that the bulk of people were illiterate, miserable and fearful.

While saints and other persons figured occasionally, by far the most common subjects of wooden carving were the Crucifixion and the Virgin Mary with the Christ child sitting in her lap. If you wander around the Museu Frederic Marès in Barcelona you will be able to confirm that the two subjects predominate.

With time the frescoes in most churches tended to degenerate. A great deal of the best examples have been preserved and transferred to the Museu Nacional d'Art de Catalunya in Barcelona. It is a truly remarkable collection. The museum at the cathedral in La Seu d'Urgell is also a rich source of Romanesque art.

In simplified terms, the move to Gothic art is defined by an increasing realism and humanity in the figures depicted, in statuary or painting. In the case of the latter, frescoes gave way to painting on wooden altarpieces, triptychs and the like.

To the untrained eye it is often not immediately apparent whether you are looking at a Romanesque or Gothic work. Dates don't always help, as the development from one style to another did not take place overnight but rather over centuries. And while in some parts of Catalunya (and the rest of Europe) artists might have been pushing back artistic boundaries, contemporaries elsewhere would have been quite happily following tried and true formulas. Add to the equation that most of the time it was the Church and its ministers who decided what or who was to be depicted and how, and you begin to understand that the artist's hands were often tied.

As already said, most artists remained anonymous. This began to change with

Gothic art. Ferrer Bassá (c.1290–1348) is considered one of Catalunya's first true masters. He was influenced by the school of Siena (Italy) and among his few surviving works are murals with a slight touch of caricature in Barcelona's Monestir de Pedralbes. The style of which he is commonly considered the originator is also known as Italo-Gothic.

The style soon displayed a more international flavour best expressed in the work of Bernat Martorell (?–1452), a master of chiaroscuro (the artistic distribution of light and dark masses in a picture) who was active in the mid-15th century. As the Flemish school gained influence, painters like Jaume Huguet (1415–92) adopted its sombre realism and lightened it with Hispanic splashes of gold, as can be seen in his *Sant Jordi* in the Museu Nacional d'Art de Catalunya. Another of his paintings hangs in the Museu Frederic Marès.

Decline & the 19th Century It is fair to say that little of greatness was achieved in the field of Catalan painting from the end of the Middle Ages on into the 19th century. Catalunya neither produced nor attracted an El Greco, a Veláquez, Zurbarán, Murillo or Goya. The Renaissance and subsequent movements in art seemed to pass the region by or were represented by occasional works of indifferent quality.

By the mid-19th century, Realisme was the modish medium on the canvas, reaching something of a zenith with the work of Marià Fortuny (1838–74). You can see some of his work, and that of his contemporaries, in the Museu Nacional d'Art Modern de Catalunya in Barcelona. The best known (and hugest) of his paintings is the 'official' version of the *Batalla de Tetuán* (1863), when Spanish arms managed a rousing victory over a ragtag Moroccan enemy in North Africa.

Modernisme As the years progressed, painters generally developed a greater eye for intimate detail and less for epic themes and this led them into Anecdotisme, out of which would emerge a fresher generation of

artists – the Modernistas of the turn of the century.

Influenced by their French counterparts (Paris was seen as Europe's artistic capital), the Modernistas allowed themselves greater freedom of interpretation, producing portraits and scenes, at times of a disturbing nature, which showed more than the 'eye' supposedly could see.

Catalunya was, however, hardly at the forefront of innovation. Ramón Casas (1866–1932) and Santiago Rusiñol (1861–1931) were easily the most important exponents of the new forms. The former was a wealthy dilettante of some talent, the latter perhaps a more earnest soul who ran a close second. Although both were the toast of the Bohemian set in turn-of-the-century Barcelona, neither was destined for greatness on the world stage.

Noucentisme From about 1910, as Modernisme fizzled, a more conservative cultural movement, Noucentisme sought, in general, to advance Catalunya. In the next 20 years, illiteracy was attacked with force, generalised education spread rapidly and telecommunications were extended across the region. Artistically speaking, Noucentisme claimed to be looking back to more classical models. A return to clarity and 'Mediterranean light' were favoured over what by some was seen as the obscure symbolism of the Modernistas.

From about 1917 a second wave of Noucentistas challenged such notions, which began to feel more like an artistic straitjacket. Some of their work was clearly influenced by the likes of Cézanne. Joaquim Sunyer (1874–1956) and Isidre Nonell (1876–1911) are among the better known of a gaggle of Noucentista painters who, just as with their Modernista predecessors, were soon largely forgotten and overshadowed by true genius.

Picasso Born in Málaga, Andalucía (in southern Spain), Pablo Ruiz Picasso (1881–1973) was already sketching by the age of nine. He and his family landed in Barcelona in 1895 and it was in Catalunya that Picasso developed.

Picasso lived and worked in the Barri Gòtic in Barcelona and got an introduction to the underside of life in the Barri Xinès. By 1900 he was a young regular of Els Quatre Gats, the Modernistas' tavern and lair of the avant-garde in Barcelona. He exhibited here and in the same year made his first trip to Paris.

By the time Picasso moved to France, definitively, in 1904, he had already explored his first personal style. In this so-called Blue Period, many of his canvases have a melancholy feel heightened by the dominance of dark blues. This was followed by the Pink Period; the subjects became merrier and the colouring leaned towards light pinks and greys.

Picasso was a turbulent character and gifted not only as a painter but as a sculptor, graphic designer and ceramicist. His work encompassed many different style changes. With *Les Demoiselles d'Avignon* (1907), Picasso broke with all forms of traditional representation, introducing a deformed perspective that would later spill over into cubism. By the mid-1920s he was dabbling with surrealism. His best-known work is *Guernica*, a complex painting portraying the horror of war inspired by the German aerial bombing of the Basque town, Gernika, in 1937.

Miró By the time the 13-year-old Picasso arrived in Barcelona, his near contemporary, Joan Miró (1893–1983), was cutting his teeth on rusk biscuits in the Barri Gòtic, where he was born and would spend all his younger years. Indeed, he passed a third of his life in his home town. Later in life he divided his time between France, the Tarragona countryside and Mallorca, where he ended his days.

His first trip to Paris came in 1920, but he was still deeply drawn to the Catalan countryside and coast. From 1919 to the early 1930s Miró wintered in Paris and spent the summers at his family's farmhouse at Montroig on the southern Catalan coast. In Paris he mixed with Picasso, Hemingway, Joyce and co and made his own mark, after several years of struggle, with an exhibition in

1925. The masterpiece from this, his so-called realist period, was *La Masia* (The Farmhouse).

During WWII, while living in seclusion in Normandy, his definitive leitmotivs finally emerged. Among Miró's most important images are women, birds (the link between earth and the heavens), stars (the unattainable heavenly world, source of imagination), and a sort of net entrapping all these levels of the cosmos. The Miró that most people are acquainted with emerged from this time – arrangements of lines and symbolic figures in primary colours, with shapes reduced to their essence.

In the 1960s and 1970s Miró devoted more time to sculpture and textiles. From 1956 he lived in Mallorca, home of his wife Pilar Juncosa.

Dalí Salvador Dalí i Domènech (1904–89) was born and died in Figueres, where he left his single greatest artistic legacy, the Teatre-Museu Dalí. Dalí created the Teatre-Museu in the former municipal theatre and it now houses a substantial portion of his life's work (see the Costa Brava chapter).

Prolific painter, showman, shameless self-promoter, or just plain weirdo, Dalí was nothing if not a character. Plunged into the world of surrealism in Paris, he was prolific – perhaps one of the best-known works of this time was *El Gran Masturbador* (1929), now in Madrid's Centro de Arte Reina Sofía. Dalí and his Russian wife Gala flitted and flirted their way from France to the USA but always returned to his home turf, mostly living at Port Lligat on the Costa Brava.

Besides painting, Dalí collaborated in the theatre and cinema, mostly working on sets, and also dabbled in writing. Everything he did seemed calculated to increase his prestige and income, and André Breton, poet and leading light of the surrealist movement, dubbed him Avida Dollars (an anagram of his name).

The 1960s saw Dalí painting pictures on a grand scale, including his 1962 reinterpretation of Marià Fortuny's *Batalla de Tetuán*. From 1979 things began to go rapidly downhill. Gala died and Dalí became a recluse.

He was buried (according to his own wish) in the Teatre-Museu Dalí.

Contemporary After such a trio, all other artists seem a little dull by comparison. But Antoni Tàpies (born 1923) is one important contemporary artist who has often been overlooked in all the commotion over the big three. Some of his work can now be seen in the Fundació Antoni Tàpies and the Museu d'Art Contemporàni de Barcelona (MACBA). Early on in his career (from the mid-1940s onwards) he seemed very keen on self-portraits, but also experimented with collage using all sorts of materials from wood to rice. This use of a broad range of material to achieve texture and depth in his works has remained a feature to this day.

To get an idea of what is happening in Catalan art today, you should make for the MACBA. There is no shortage of Catalan artists beavering away at all sorts of things. Among them are Susana Solano (born 1946), Xavier Grau (born 1951), Sergi

Aguilar (born 1946), Joan Hernàndez Pijuan (born 1931), Ignasi Aballí (born 1958), Jordi Colomer (born 1962), José Luis Pastor Calle (born 1971), Cristina Fontsaré Herraiz (born 1969), Laia Solé Coromina (born 1976) and Mercè Roura i Molas (born 1977).

Literature

Beginnings The earliest surviving documents written in Catalan date from the 12th century. Most of them are legal, economic, historical and religious texts. The oldest of them is a portion of the Visigothic law code, the *Liber Iudicorum*, rendered in the vernacular. The oldest original texts in Catalan are the *Homilies d'Organyà*, a religious work.

Catalunya's first great writer was Ramon Llull (1235–1315), who eschewed the use of either Latin or Provençal in literature. His two best-known works are perhaps *El Llibre de les Bèsties* and *El Llibre d'Amic i Amat*, the former an allegorical attack on feudal corruption and the latter a series of short pieces aimed at daily meditation – both inspired in part by Islamic works.

The count-king Jaume I (see History earlier in this chapter) was a bit of a scribbler himself and penned a rare autobiographical work, the *Llibre dels Feyts* (Book of Deeds), in the late 13th century. Ramon Muntaner (1265–1336), more of a propagandist than anything else, spent a good deal of his life eulogising various Catalan leaders and their derring-do in his *Crónica*.

Segle d'Or Everyone seems to have a 'golden century', and for Catalan writers it was the 15th. Ausiàs March (1400–59), who was actually from Valencia, announced he had abandoned the style of the troubadors and went ahead to forge a Catalan poetic tradition. His style is tormented and highly personal and continues to inspire Catalan poets to this day.

Most European peoples seem to feel it necessary to claim to have produced the first European novel. The Catalans claim it was Joanot Martorell's *Tirant lo Blanc*. Cervantes himself thought it the best book in the world. Martorell (c.1405–65) was also a busy fighting knight and his writing tells of

Salvador Dalí – surrealist, showman and shameless self-promoter

bloody battles, war, politics and sex. Some things don't change. More obscure names of the epoque include Bernat Metge (who saw out the 14th century), Roís de Corella and Jaume Roig.

Renaixença Catalan literature declined rapidly after the 15th century and suffered a seemingly mortal blow in the wake of the region's defeat by Felipe V in 1714, when use of Catalan was banned.

As Catalunya began to enjoy a burgeoning economy in the 19th century, there was sufficient leisure time for intellectuals, writers and artists to take a renewed interest in all things Catalan.

The revival of Catalan literature is commonly dated to 1833 when the rather saccharine poem *A la Pàtria* was written in Madrid by Carles Aribau (1798–1862).

From 1859, when high-minded Catalan intellectuals reintroduced the Catalan-language poetry competitions – Jocs Florals – a steady stream of material that was generally fit to be ignored started to dribble out of the tap. True quality in poetry came only with the appearance in 1877 of a country pastor, Jacint Verdaguer (1845–1902), whose *L'Atlantida* is an epic that defies easy description. To the writer's contemporaries, however, the poem confirmed Catalan's arrival as a 'great' language. Verdaguer inspired others, above all the novelist Narcís Oller (1846–1930) and playwright Àngel Guimerà (1845–1924). The former's *La Febre d'Or* (1893) describes the shaky world of speculative finance that dominated much of boom-time Barcelona.

Modernisme & Noucentisme Modernisme's main literary voice of worth was the poet Joan Maragall (1860–1911). Also noteworthy is the work of Víctor Català (1873–1966; a pseudonym of Caterina Albert). Her principal work is *Solitud*, a mysterious novel charting the awakening of a young woman whose husband has taken her to live in the Pyrenees.

Eugeni d'Ors (1881–1954), more of a journalist, critic and social commentator than writer, was one of the leading figures of Noucentisme, which aimed in part to rid

the cultural scene of Modernisme. Carles Riba (1893–1959), was the period's most outstanding poet.

To the Present Mercé Rodoreda (1909–83) was one of the major writers in Catalan of the 20th century. Her first successful novel was *Paloma* (1938), which tells the story of a young girl seduced by her brother-in-law. After the Civil War Rodoreda went into exile and in 1962 published one of her best-known works, *Plaça del Diamant*, which recounts life in Barcelona seen through the eyes of a working-class woman. The book has been translated into English and several other languages.

Josep Pla (1897–1981) was a prolific writer who, after the victory of Franco in 1939, spent many years abroad. He wrote in Catalan and Castilian and his work ranged from travel writing to histories and fiction. His complete works total 46 volumes. An important contemporary was the poet Salvador Espriu (1913–85). He started writing novels in the pre–Civil War years but during the Franco dictatorship moved to poetry, at least in part to escape censorship. Although not widely read today, his prose and verse demonstrate a meticulous attention to honing language, making his a valuable contribution to the enrichment of Catalan as a literary vehicle.

Since the demise of Franco, the amount of literature being produced in Catalan has increased greatly, but some of the region's more noteworthy scribblers write in Castilian too, and in some cases they prefer to do so.

Juan Goytisolo (born 1931) started off in the neorealist camp but his more recent works, such as *Señas de Identidad* and *Juan sin Tierra*, are decidedly more experimental. Goytisolo lives in Marrakesh. His pal, Jaime Gil de Biedma (1929–90), was one of the century's most influential poets in Catalunya and indeed across Spain.

A highly accessible writer is Barcelona-born José Luis Sampedro (born 1917). A professor of structural economics (!) and one-time senator, his novels are wide-ranging and thought-provoking. He considers *Octubre,*

Octubre his life testament. In his latest adventure, *El Amante Lesbiano*, he makes a frontal assault on what may for some be social givens.

Jorge Semprún (born 1923), who lost his home and family in the Civil War, ended up in a Nazi concentration camp for his activities with the French Resistance in WWII. He writes mostly in French. His first novel, *Le Grand Voyage*, remains one of his best.

Eduardo Mendoza (born 1943) is a Barcelona writer, whose absorbing novel *La Ciudad de los Prodigios* (published in English as *The City of Marvels*) is set in the city in the period between the Universal Exhibition of 1888 and the World Exhibition in 1929.

Terenci Moix (born 1942) is a successful columnist and writer who also tends to write in Castilian (although not exclusively). His books are fairly lightweight, but highly popular, literature exploring Spanish society and often involving a lot of gay self-discovery. A big hit was *Lleonard o el Sexo de los Ángeles*; he has also written a couple of historical novels.

Momentos Decisivos, the third novel by Félix de Azúa (born 1944), is set in the Barcelona (his home town) of the 1960s, the years before the transition from Francoist dictatorship to democracy. For Azúa, the attitudes that would awaken Spain from its torpor were formed in those 'opaque' years.

Enrique Vila-Matas (born 1948) has won fans well beyond his native Barcelona. His novels have been translated into a dozen languages. In his latest effort, *Battleby y Compañía*, a writer convinced that modern works are vapid enters a crisis, strongly attracted to nothingness.

Montserrat Roig (1946–91) crammed a lot of writing (largely in Catalan), journalistic and fiction, into her short life. Her novels include *Ramon Adéu*, *El Temps de les Cireres* and *L'Hora Violeta*.

Manuel Vázquez Montalbán (born 1939) is one of Barcelona's more prolific writers, best known for his Pepe Carvalho detective novel series.

Ana María Moix (born 1947) gained considerable acclaim in 1970 with her prize-winning *Julia*, but then fell silent until 1985, when she resurfaced with a collection of short stories, *Las Virtudes Peligrosas,* that take a caustic look at society.

Quim Monzó (born 1952) is a prolific writer of short stories, columns and essays (in Catalan). He revised the best of his stories and published them in one volume, *Vuitanta-sis Contes*, in 1999.

A promising talent is Carlos Castañer (born 1960). In his *Museo de la Soledad*, characters and stories come to melancholy life in this, the strangest of museums.

Theatre

Barcelona is possibly the most dynamic centre of theatre in Spain, although *madrileños* (citizens of Madrid) might contest this. Purely Catalan theatre was revived, amid the rhetoric of the Renaixença, in the late 19th century, with playwright and all-round Catalan nationalist Àngel Guimerà its principal driving force.

Possibly one of the wackiest theatre companies is La Fura dels Baus, which grew out of Barcelona's street-theatre culture in the late 1970s. These guys turn theatre spaces (often warehouses) into a kind of participatory apocalypse – 60 minutes of, at times, spine-chilling performance.

Tricicle is another big Barcelona name. It's a three-man mime team easily enjoyed by anyone – no need to understand Catalan. Els Comediants and La Cubana are two highly successful groups that also owe a lot to the impromptu world of street theatre.

A rising star of Barcelona theatre is director Roger Bernat (born 1968), an *enfant terrible* whose company General Elèctrica plays the main theatres but leaves the establishment perplexed with such coups as including a live sex scene in one of his works.

Music

Traditional It is hard to know into what category to put the medieval troubadors. In many respects the verses they sang (largely the plaintive cries of courtly love inspired by French traditions) represent some of the earliest medieval literature in Mediterranean Europe. Provençal and not Catalan, however, remained their universal language for a long time.

The strongest musical tradition to have survived to some degree in popular form in Catalunya is that of the *havaneres*, nostalgic songs and sea shanties brought back from Cuba by Catalans who lived, sailed and traded there. Even after Spain lost Cuba in 1898, the *havanera* tradition continued, especially in Barcelona and along the coast, as a melancholy memory of good times past (although they had not always been so great for the Cubans). Today the havaneres are enjoying something of a revival, and in some coastal towns you can turn up to listen to an evening's *cantada de havaneres*. Calella de Palafrugell on the Costa Brava is particularly well known for this, and occasionally you can hear the songs in Barcelona too.

Baroque Jordi Savall (born 1941) has assumed the task of rediscovering a Europe-wide heritage in music that predates the era of the classical greats. Born in Igualada, Savall studied at the conservatorium in Barcelona. He and his wife, the soprano Montserrat Figueras, have been largely responsible for resuscitating the beauties of medieval, Renaissance and, above all, baroque music. In 1987 Savall founded La Capella Reial de Catalunya and two years later he formed the baroque orchestra, Le Concert des Nations. He was awarded the Creu de Sant Jordi (St George Cross; a high Catalan honour) in 1990 and continues to teach, perform and record.

Anyone who has seen the film *Tous Les Matins du Monde* (1991) starring Gérard Depardieu will know his work.

Classical Spain's contribution to the world of classical music has been comparatively marginal, but Catalunya did produce a few exceptional composers.

Perhaps best known is Camprodon-born Isaac Albéniz (1860–1909), a gifted pianist who later turned his hand to composition. Among his best remembered works is the *Iberia* cycle.

Lleida's Enric Granados i Campina (1867–1916) came onto the scene early in

the 20th century. Another fine pianist, he established Barcelona's conservatorium in 1901 and composed many pieces for piano, including *Danzas Españolas*, *Cantos de la Juventud* and *Goyescas*.

Other Catalan composer/musicians of some note include Eduard Toldrà (1895–1962) and Frederic Mompou (1893–1987).

Opera Monserrat Caballé is Catalunya's most successful voice. Born in Gràcia (Barcelona) in 1933, the soprano made her debut in 1956 in Basle (Switzerland). Her home-town launch came four years later in the Gran Teatre del Liceu. In 1965 she performed at New York's Carnegie Hall to wild acclaim. She hasn't looked back and remains one of the world's top sopranos. Catalunya's other world-class opera star is the renowned tenor Josep (José) Carreras (born 1946).

Contemporary If you had to cite only one name in popular Catalan music of the past decades, it would probably be Lluís Llach (born 1948). Singer-songwriter and poet, he was born in the Alt Empordà area of north-eastern Catalunya and could be thought of as the Bob Dylan of Catalunya. A leading figure of the Nova Cançó movement that was born in the days of Franco's anti-Catalan drive, Llach was something of a musical guerrilla in the late 1960s and early 1970s. His songs of freedom sung in a language that supposedly had been censored out of existence earned Llach four years' exile in France. One of his most celebrated resistance hits was *País Petit*, which he performed and distributed on the sly. Llach is still going strong and writing songs for causes today.

A good deal of Spain's most representative modern music has grown out of the lively Barcelona *movida*, that post-Franco outburst of activity and nightlife that filled the streets of Spain in the early 1980s.

For years a big rock draw card was El Último de la Fila, a fine Barcelona duo that finally decided to quit in 1997. Milder and poppier are Los Fresones Rebeldes, a fresh-faced sextet and light-hearted departure from the trend towards indie groups and techno blare. Their first album, *Es Que No Hay*

Manera, is a bouncy punk pop offering that should ensure their continued popularity.

Mojinos Escozíos tout themselves as 'fat, ugly and heavy to the death'. Although three of the five members are from Sevilla, the other two are Catalans and all live near Barcelona. They are the latest flavour in heavy rock, a genre that gets quite a following throughout Spain.

Rock Catalá (Catalan rock) is not essentially different from rock anywhere else, except that it is sung in Catalan by local bands that appeal to local tastes. Among the most popular bands at the moment are Els Pets (one of the region's top acts), The Mad Makers, Ja T'ho Diré, Sopa de Cabra, Lax'n'Busto, Whiskyn's, Les Pellofes Radioactives, Fes-te Fotre, Glaucs, No Nem Bé, Dr Calypso, In Extremis, Obrint Pas, Baked Beans, Gore's Romance, Zea Mays and Antónia Font.

Gossos is a four-man band that specialises in folk-rock much along the lines of Crosby, Stills & Nash.

Since August 1998 the annual Senglar Rock concert has been *the* date for Catalan rock music. It was held in Montblanc at the end of June 2001, but dates and location can change, so keep your eyes peeled from early June on.

Dance

Sardana The Catalan dance, par excellence, is the *sardana*, whose roots lie in the far northern Empordà region of Catalunya. Compared with flamenco it is a sober sight indeed, but is not unlike a lot of folk dances seen in various other parts of the Mediterranean.

The dancers hold hands in a circle and wait for the 10 or so musicians to begin. The performance starts with the piping of the *flabiol*, a little wooden flute. When the other musicians join in, the dancers begin – a series of steps to the right, one back and then the same to the left. As the music 'heats up' the steps become more complex, the leaps are higher and the dancers lift their arms. Then they return to the initial steps and continue. If newcomers wish to join in, space is made for them as the dance contin-

ues and the whole thing proceeds in a more or less seamless fashion.

Cinema

In 1932, Francesc Macià, president of the Generalitat, opened Spain's first studios for making 'talkies' and a year later Metro Goldwyn Mayer had a dubbing studio in Barcelona. In the wake of Franco's victory, cinema production was concentrated in Madrid and was, in any case, a mix of propaganda and schmaltz.

In 1956, the Escola de Barcelona began to produce experimental stuff, some of which did see the light of the day. Film-makers like Vicente Aranda (born 1926) cut their teeth here. Aranda later gained fame for *Amantes* (1991), set in the Madrid of the 1950s and based on the real story of a love triangle that ends particularly badly. He followed three years later with the steamy *La Pasión Turca*.

All in all, it has been slow going in the Catalan film world. Since Franco's death any sign of restrictions on theme or use of Catalan has disappeared, but the centre of Spanish cinema remains Madrid.

Possibly the biggest name in Catalan film directing, at least for his abiding interest in the erotic, is José Juan Bigas Luna (born 1946). His *Angoixa* (Anxiety) was a worldwide success. He also directed the popular comedy *Jamón, Jamón* in 1992, his best effort in more than a decade.

Ventura Pons (born 1945) is a veteran of Catalan theatre and film-making. His *Morir (o No)*, made in 2000, follows seven stories that end in someone's death and then dovetails them into one tale in which none of the characters dies. He has churned out a feature film almost every year since he really got moving in 1989.

Daniel Calparsoro (born 1968) has tended to see the dark side in his flicks. His fourth and latest, *Asfalto* looks at some less savoury aspects of life in the mean streets of Madrid, although he insists the message is positive. His other films have been equally violent and somewhat uneven, but there is promise. Actress Laura Mañá (born 1968) turned to directing and writing with her quirky 2000 debut, *Sexo por Compasión*, in which a well-intentioned woman sets about getting her husband back by sleeping with all the neighbours.

An up-and-coming actor is Vilanova i la Geltrú's Sergi López (born 1965), whose latest success was a French movie, *Une Relation Pornographique* (2000), in which two people get together for sex and actually find lurve. He has become the screen darling of Paris with this and other Gallic hits.

SOCIETY & CULTURE

Catalans have a bit of a reputation for being reserved. That may or may not be true, but as a rule they are tolerant and courteous.

No-one really expects you to speak Catalan, but if you can stumble along good-humouredly in Castilian in shops and other situations you'll generally meet with a friendly response.

Codes of good manners differ the world over, and what can sometimes seem brusque treatment to Anglos is not intended as anything of the sort. While the latter may be obsessed with 'please' and 'thank you', you'll find your average Catalans not overly fussed. A profusion of 'por favors' is not part of the local mindset. In bars and the like you are likely to hear the most respectable people simply say 'give me...' whatever it might be. But Catalans stand on ceremony in other ways. It is common to wish all and sundry '*bon dia/buenos días*' when entering a shop or bar and to say '*adéu/adiós*' on the way out. Not mandatory, but common.

Dos & Don'ts

The standard form of greeting between men and women (even when meeting for the first time) and between women is a kiss on each cheek, right then left. Now we're not talking about big sloppy ones, a light brushing of cheeks is perfectly sufficient. Men seem to be able to take or leave handshakes on informal occasions, but they are pretty much standard in a business context.

Treatment of Animals

Although the Spanish sport of bullfighting *(la corrida)* can be witnessed in parts of Catalunya (such as Barcelona and at some rings along the coast), it is not something Catalans in general get much of a kick out of. Indeed, it has often been said that the rings (especially the one at Lloret de Mar) survive mainly because of the tourist trade.

This is not to say Catalans don't have their own ways of giving bulls a hard time. Above all in the *festes majors* (a town or village's main annual festival) of towns around the Riu Ebre, locals indulge themselves with *festes de bous* (bull festivals) much as in other parts of Spain, although with some differences. One of the most striking is the tradition of *bous embolats*, in which a bull is sent dashing around the ring with fireworks attached to its horns. One can only imagine how frightened the animal must be. In its attempts to shake loose the source of torment, the bull frequently manages only to burn its eyes and head, at which point it will be put down.

Catalunya's animal protection law allows this only in towns like Amposta (which includes such taurine torment in its August *festa major*) that can prove a historical tradition of the activity.

One local group fighting against bullfighting and the like is Anti-Bullfighting Campaign (☎ 93 278 02 94, fax 93 246 04 26) at Carrer Empordà 33, 10°, Edifici Piramidón, 08020 Barcelona.

RELIGION

Catalunya, like the rest of Spain, is largely Catholic, at least in name. But a strong anarchist and socialist tradition, which historically has almost always meant anticlericalism, has left an indelible mark here, especially in the capital Barcelona.

From the end of the 19th century through to the end of the Civil War, church-burning was a popular pastime. The two worst waves came in 1909 during the Setmana Tràgica and again at the outbreak of the Civil War in 1936. Under Franco, Catholicism was again made a state religion and the Church played a preponderant role in society.

Since Franco's demise the Church has had to content itself with a more back-seat role in Catalan society. For instance, cries that liberalising shop opening hours (extending them to Sunday) would have a negative impact on family and religious life went unheeded by the government in Madrid. Barcelona's Cardinal Ricard Maria Carles was particularly critical. 'Sunday is the day of Our Lord and of the people,' he said. 'It's loss will bring the loss of our cultural identity.'

LANGUAGE

Catalan *(català)* and Spanish (the latter is more appropriately known as *castellano*, or Castilian), have equal legal status in Catalunya. The local tongue has undergone a remarkable revival in the past 20 years, although people out in the country and smaller towns never really stopped speaking it.

Catalan should not be put on the same level as Basque, Irish, Breton or other 'marginal' languages getting intensive mouth-to-mouth treatment but still barely managing to survive. Catalan is for millions of people the main language of daily discourse. Bearing in mind that as much as half the population of Barcelona was born either elsewhere in Spain or to migrants from other parts of the country, the extent to which Catalan has become the 'norm' is remarkable.

Still, in central Barcelona and at the main tourist resorts along the coast, as well as at ski centres, you'll hear as much Spanish as Catalan. Elsewhere don't be surprised to get replies in Catalan to your questions in Spanish. Some Spaniards from other parts of the country resent this and feel the 'national' language is being marginalised; however, most Catalans will cheerfully enough speak to you in Spanish, especially once they realise you're a foreigner.

There is a third and little known linguistic anomaly. In Catalunya's extreme northwest, the people of the comarca of the Val d'Aran have their own tongue, Aranese *(aranés)*. It is a subdialect, not of Catalan but of Occitan, a tongue once spoken by much of southern medieval France.

English is not as widely spoken as you might expect, and French even less so. An effort on your part to come to grips with some of the basics of Catalan or Spanish will be a useful investment. To get you started, turn to the Language chapter.

In the course of this book priority is given to Catalan, since that is the language you will most commonly be confronted with in signs, menus and the like. Often Catalan/Spanish versions are given in that order. It's a tricky business really. From the outsider's point of view, one can only be grateful that the two languages have a fair amount in common!

Facts for the Visitor

HIGHLIGHTS

A traveller can find whatever he or she wants in Catalunya. You can belly up to the most tourist-infested bars along the party *costas* (coasts) or seek out hidden-away coves far from the madding crowd. You can explore medieval towns, join in the madness of Barcelona's September *festes* (festivals), search the region for Romanesque gems or immerse yourself in art. The mountains offer you trekking and skiing, whitewater rafting or simply village-hopping. Catalan cuisine also offers much to savour, from inland hearty meat-based meals to the seafood splendours of the coast. For a selection of more specific highlights check out the colour regional map at the beginning of the book.

SUGGESTED ITINERARIES

Even in as little as a week you could cover quite a lot of ground in Catalunya, especially with your own wheels. To really get under its skin you'd want to dedicate at least two weeks to the exercise.

Taking Barcelona as a starting point, all sorts of possibilities present themselves. Before you go screaming out of town, take the time to explore this fascinating city. It offers a wealth of architectural and artistic splendour. More appealing to some is the busy nightlife. The restaurants, bars and clubs are more than sufficient to satisfy most people's yearnings.

A southerly circuit would take you inland to the Penedès wine region and the Conca de Barberà, a pretty patch of land where you can cheerfully potter around grand monasteries and walled towns. You could close the circle by winding up in the pleasurable seaside town of Sitges, especially if you're in the mood for a bit of partying. From there the natural progression is to wind south along the coast to the one-time Roman city of Tarragona and beyond to the Delta de l'Ebre (Ebro in Spanish) parklands for some flamingo-watching.

Such a trip could be done in as little as three days.

If you have four or five days to spare, a leisurely route would take you up along the magnificent Costa Brava and its pretty little beaches. Eventually you would reach the charming town of Cadaqués and Dalí's hideaway at Port Lligat. Turning inland from the coast you won't want to miss the artist's Teatre-Museu in Figueres and the medieval towns of Girona and Besalú (all of which would also make good day trips from the coast).

Finally, the Pyrenees offer enormous scope – you could spend weeks in the mountains walking, skiing and white-water rafting. Or just pottering about hopping from one village to another.

One possible route, assuming Barcelona is your starting point, would have you heading north first to Olot. There you could indulge in some gentle walking among the volcanoes in the Parc Natural de la Zona Volcànica de la Garrotxa before embarking on a westwards haul to Ripoll (for the Romanesque architecture) and north to the Vall de Núria (for the *cremallera* train and walking). The N-152 road is the obvious route to follow west for Puigcerdà (skiing) and on to La Seu d'Urgell (more Romanesque architecture). The road west brings you to the Riu Noguera Pallaresa and white-water rafting territory. You are also on the eastern side of the Parc Nacional d'Aigüestortes i Estany de Sant Maurici, perfect for a few days' walking. The whole north-west is loaded with walking opportunities, and the region's best skiing is at Baqueira-Beret, in the remote Val d'Aran. You would want to give yourself about a week (if not more!).

PLANNING
When to Go

Visit Catalunya from April to June and in September/October. You can usually count on pleasant weather – by May (sometimes earlier) you can contemplate the beach.

Late July and August is the time to avoid: the sun positively broils, prices are inflated and you can't see the place for the swarms of holiday-makers. Only in the Pyrenees will you find any respite at this time but in August even here things can get tight. On the coast in particular, accommodation is at a premium. Inland it's not such a problem – but then it wouldn't be with such heat!

The best time for walking in the Pyrenees is from June to September. Refuges tend to open from mid-June to mid-September. It is not impossible to walk in the mountains outside this period, but the weather becomes more unpredictable and snow and ice can be a problem at higher altitudes. You should always be prepared for bad weather in the mountains.

You may prefer to organise your trip or itinerary to coincide with one or more of the festivals that dot the Catalan calendar – an obvious choice are Barcelona's Festes de la Mercè in September. To start planning around such events, turn to Public Holidays & Special Events later in the chapter.

What Kind of Trip

Many people come to Catalunya in search of sand, sea, sun and maybe some sex. That brigade tends to congregate around the rather uninspiring resorts of Lloret de Mar. But it is quite possible to build a holiday plan around the beach with a little more class. You could opt to stay a week or two at one of the more secluded beaches along the more rugged reaches of the Costa Brava and make excursions to such places as Girona, Figueres, Cadaqués and even Barcelona.

In the winter months, you could create a package for yourself taking in a week's skiing followed by a circuit of some of the region's towns and finishing in Barcelona.

Walkers have an almost infinite choice. You could base yourself for several days at a time in key spots in the mountains (such as Espot in the Parc Nacional d'Aigüestortes i Estany de Sant Maurici) and walk to your heart's content. Mixing it up with a little local exploration of villages and Romanesque churches might appeal.

In summer you could mix and match –

how about a week on the beaches followed by another exploring the mountains?

Maps

Road Atlases If you intend to drive extensively, not only in Catalunya but also in the rest of Spain, a decent road atlas is a sensible investment. Several are available, including the *Mapa Oficial de Carreteras*, put out by the Ministry of Public Works, Transport & Environment for €13.85. One of the best, and available in and outside Spain, is the *Michelin Motoring Atlas – Spain & Portugal*. In Spain it's called *Michelin Atlas de Carreteras y Turístico – España & Portugal* and costs €15.60. It is for the most part faithfully accurate.

Both atlases include maps of main towns and cities. You can find them at most decent bookshops and some petrol stations in Spain.

Regional & District Maps A good all-round map of the region, scaled at 1:250,000, is the *Mapa de Carreteres de Catalunya*, published by the Institut Cartogràfic de Catalunya. Also recommended and updated yearly is Michelin's map of Catalunya, scaled at 1:400,000. Both are fine for drivers who don't want the cost or bulk of dealing with a road atlas of all of Spain.

Lovers of more detail could start collecting the district maps *(mapes comarcales)* – all 41 of them. They are scaled at 1:50,000 and are also published by the Institut Cartogràfic de Catalunya.

City Maps Lonely Planet publishes the handy *Barcelona City Map* showing the city centre at a scale of 1:9000. It includes a metro map, walking tour and a comprehensive index of streets and sights. If you can't find a copy, another option is Michelin map No 40 (accompanied by the No 41 street directory). Various other more detailed map books are available for the long-termer. The ring-bound *Guía Urbana de Barcelona*, which is published by GeoPlaneta, is good and costs €10.25.

Suggestions for other city maps are given under the appropriate heading throughout the guide.

Walking Maps Several maps for walking are available. If possible, you will want to get hold of maps scaled at 1:25,000, as anything larger becomes less useful. The main publisher of walking maps for the Catalan Pyrenees and other hill areas in the region is Editorial Alpina. They put out a series of maps scaled at anything from 1:10,000 (Montserrat) to 1:80,000 (Costa Brava). Most of the maps you would use in the Pyrenees are at 1:25,000. The maps come packaged with a small descriptive booklet and generally cost €4.70.

Alternatively the Institut Cartogràfic de Catalunya puts out several maps, also scaled at 1:25,000. Some hikers say they are better than Editorial Alpina's maps but the trails are not always accurately marked. No 1 covers the *Parc Nacional d'Aigüestortes i Estany de Sant Maurici*. Others include *Parc Natural del Cap de Creus* (No 19), *Parc Natural dels Aiguamolls de l'Empordà* (No 4), *Alta Garrotxa – La Muga* (No 11), *Figueres* (No 2) and *Paratge Natural d'Interès Nacional de l'Albera* (No 8). They cost around €4.85.

Editorial Alpina also produces a series of maps in cooperation with the French Rando Editions, scaled at 1:40,000 and 1:50,000. They come in a predominantly yellow colour.

Maps are generally available in shops in the walking areas themselves. In Barcelona you could try the following stores:

Quera (Map 4; ☎ 93 318 07 43) Carrer de Petritxol 2. Specialist in maps and guides, including those for walking and trekking.
La Tenda (Map 2; ☎ 93 488 33 60) Carrer de Pau Claris 118–120. Camping and mountaineering equipment, as well as a broad range of walkers' maps for Catalunya and beyond.

What to Bring

Bring as little as possible. Everything you bring, you have to carry. You can buy just about anything you need in Catalunya, in any case.

Luggage If you'll be doing any walking with your luggage, even just from stations to hotels and back, a backpack is the only

sensible answer. One whose straps and openings can be zipped inside a flap is more secure. If you'll be using taxis, or your own car, you might as well take whatever luggage is easiest to open and shut, unpack and pack. Either way, a small day-pack is a useful addition.

Inscribing your name and address on the inside of your luggage, as well as labelling it on the outside, increases your chances of getting it back if it's lost or stolen. Packing things in plastic bags inside your backpack/suitcase will keep them organised and, if it rains, dry.

Clothes & Shoes In high summer you may not need more than one layer of clothing, even at 4 am. At cooler times, layers of thin clothing, which trap warm air and can be peeled off if necessary, are better than a single thick layer. See Climate in the Facts about Catalunya chapter for the kind of temperatures and rainfall you can expect. Some good (not too formal) clothes – smarter than jeans and T-shirts – for some restaurants and clubs may be handy.

A pair of strong (and if possible halfway smart) shoes is almost indispensable – they will come in handy for everything from long country walks to eating out in swankier restaurants.

Useful Items Apart from any special personal needs, or things you might require for particular kinds of trip (camping gear, walking boots, skis etc), consider the following:

- an under-the-clothes money belt or shoulder wallet, useful for protecting your money and documents in cities
- a towel and soap, often lacking in cheap accommodation
- sunscreen lotion, which can be more expensive in Spain than elsewhere
- a small Spanish dictionary and/or phrasebook (perhaps a Catalan one too, although they are harder to come by outside Catalunya and not strictly essential for survival)
- books, which can be expensive and hard to find outside main cities and tourist resorts
- photocopies of your important documents, kept separate from the originals
- a Swiss army knife

- minimal unbreakable cooking, eating and drinking gear if you plan to prepare your own food and drinks
- a medical kit (see Health later in the chapter)
- a padlock or two to secure your luggage to racks and to lock hostel lockers
- a sleeping sheet to save on sheet rental costs if you're using youth hostels (a sleeping bag is unlikely to be useful unless you're camping)
- an adapter plug for electrical appliances
- a torch (flashlight)
- an alarm clock
- sunglasses
- binoculars, if you plan to do any wildlife-spotting

RESPONSIBLE TOURISM

The first rule that anyone travelling to someone else's country should learn is 'tread softly'.

It's no doubt entirely pointless to suggest that party animals zeroing in on Barcelona or the costas might like to maintain some vague form of self-control. If lager louts could at least resist the temptation to brawl and just stick to getting wasted... The powers that be in places like Lloret de Mar, after decades of making money hand-over-fist out of cheap, mass tourism, have finally come around to thinking that maybe it's not such a good idea after all. But they are having trouble reversing the situation.

When visiting monuments, treat them with respect. At ancient sights such as the ruins at Empúries, don't go clambering over everything where you are asked not to or have no need to. By leaving things alone you do your little part to help preserve them.

Don't use the flash when photographing artworks in museums and churches. The burst of light helps damage the art.

Catalunya is a delight of nature, from its magnificent coast to its majestic mountains. Wherever you go, avoid littering. The first rule of the mountains – whatever you bring up, take it back down – should equally apply to the rest of the countryside.

In summer, be aware of the high fire hazard in the countryside. Thousands of hectares are destroyed every year as a result of negligence or, worse, because fires are deliberately lit. In the summer of 2000 and

again in 2001 thousands of hectares in the Parc Natural del Cap de Creus were lost. Park rangers say it will take 15 years to put the damage right. The north-east is particularly at risk as the vegetation is dry and burns easily, especially when a *tramuntana* (north wind) is blowing.

TOURIST OFFICES
Local Tourist Offices

In Barcelona you will find several tourist offices, one covering the region and the others specialising in the city and its surrounding province. The remaining three provincial capitals (Girona, Lleida and Tarragona) have one, three and two offices respectively, providing information on the city and/or province.

Beyond these main centres you will find that many smaller towns also have their own offices. If you ask the right questions you can find that some of these are mines of useful local information.

In addition, Catalunya's one national park, eight *parcs naturals* (nature reserves) and other protected park areas have visitor information centres.

There is a nationwide tourist information line in several languages, which might come in handy if you are calling from elsewhere in Spain. Call ☎ 901 30 06 00 any day from 9 am to 6 pm for basic information in Spanish, English and French.

Tourist Offices Abroad

There are Spanish national tourist offices in 19 countries, including:

Canada (☎ 416-961 3131, e toronto@
tourspain.es) 2 Bloor St W, 34th floor,
Toronto, Ontario M4W 3E2
France (☎ 01 45 03 82 57, e paris@tourspain
.es) 43 rue Decamps, 75784 Paris, Cedex 16
Germany (☎ 030-882 6036, e berlin@
tourspain.es) Kurfürstendamm 180, 10707
Berlin. Branches in Düsseldorf, Frankfurt-am-
Main and Munich.
Netherlands (☎ 070-346 59 00, e lahaya@
tourspain.es) Laan Van Meerdervoort 8a, 2517
The Hague
Portugal (☎ 21-357 1992, e lisboa@tourspain
.es) Avenida Sidónio Pais 28 3° Dto, 1050
Lisbon

UK (☎ 020-7486 8077, brochure request ☎ 0906 364 0630 at 60p per minute, [e] londres@tourspain.es) 22–23 Manchester Square, London W1M 5AP

USA (☎ 212-265 8822, [e] nyork@tourspain.es) 666 Fifth Ave, 35th floor, New York, NY 10103. Branches in Chicago, Los Angeles and Miami.

The Generalitat also operates a handful of tourist offices abroad, dedicated exclusively to Catalunya:

Belgium (☎ 02-732 12 60) Avenue des Cerisiers 15, 1030 Brussels

Sweden (☎ 08-411 01 06) Kungsgatan 27, 4 TR, 11156 Stockholm

UK (☎ 020-7583 8855) 3rd floor, 17 Fleet St, London EC4Y 1AA

VISAS & DOCUMENTS
Passport

Citizens of the 15 European Union (EU) member states and Switzerland can travel to Spain with their national identity card alone. If such countries do not issue ID cards – as in the UK – travellers must carry a full valid passport (UK visitor passports are not acceptable). All other nationalities must have a full valid passport.

Check that your passport's expiry date is at least some months away, otherwise you may not be granted a visa, should you need one.

By law you are supposed to have your passport or ID card with you at all times in Spain. It doesn't happen often, but it could be embarrassing if you are asked by the police to produce a document and you don't have it with you. You will usually need one of these documents for police registration when you take a hotel room.

Visas

There are no entry requirements or restrictions on EU nationals. Citizens of Australia, Canada, Israel, Japan, New Zealand and the USA do not need visas to visit Spain as tourists for up to three months. Except for people from a few other European countries (such as Switzerland), everyone else must have a Schengen Visa.

This visa is named after the Schengen Agreement, which has abolished passport controls between Austria, Belgium, Denmark, Finland, France, Germany, Greece, Iceland, Italy, Luxembourg, the Netherlands, Norway, Portugal, Spain and Sweden. A visa for any of these countries should in theory be valid throughout the area, but it pays to double-check with the embassy or consulate of each country you intend to visit. Residency status in any of the Schengen countries negates the need for a visa, whatever your nationality.

Three-month tourist (Schengen) visas are issued by Spanish embassies and consulates. You must apply for the visa in your country of residence *in person* at the consulate. Postal applications are not accepted. You'll need a valid passport and sufficient funds to finance your stay. Fees vary depending on your nationality. The visa does *not* guarantee entry.

You can apply for no more than two visas in any 12-month period and you cannot renew once inside Spain.

Visa Extensions & Residence Schengen visas cannot be extended. Nationals of EU countries, Norway and Iceland can virtually (if not technically) enter and leave Spain at will. Those wanting to stay in Spain longer than 90 days are supposed to apply during their first month for a resident's card *(tarjeta de residencia)*. This is a lengthy bureaucratic procedure: if you intend to subject yourself to it, consult a Spanish consulate before you go to Spain as you will need to take certain documents with you.

People of other nationalities who want to stay in Spain for longer than 90 days are also supposed to get a resident's card, and for them it's a truly nightmarish process, starting with a residence visa issued by a Spanish consulate in your country of residence. Start the process way in advance.

Non-EU spouses of EU citizens resident in Spain can apply for residence too. The process is lengthy and those needing to travel in and out of the country in the meantime could ask for an *exención de visado* – a visa exemption. In most cases, the spouse is obliged to make the formal application in his/her country of residence. A real pain.

Travel Insurance

A travel insurance policy to cover theft, loss of luggage or tickets, medical problems and perhaps cancellation or delays in your travel arrangements is a good idea (see Health later in the chapter for more on medical insurance).

A wide variety of policies is available and your travel agent will be able to make recommendations. The international student travel policies handled by STA Travel or other student travel organisations are usually good. Check the small print:

- Some policies exclude 'dangerous activities', which can include scuba diving, motorcycling and even trekking.
- Some policies may impose a surcharge for expensive photo equipment and the like.
- Check whether the policy covers ambulances or an emergency flight home.
- Policies often require you to pay up front for medical expenses, then to claim from the insurance company afterwards, showing receipts, but you might prefer to find a policy that involves the insurance company paying the doctor or hospital direct.

Insurance papers, and the international medical aid numbers that generally accompany them, are valuable documents, so treat them like air tickets and passports. Keep the details (photocopies or handwritten) in a separate part of your luggage.

Driving Licence & Permits

All EU member states' driving licences (pink or pink and green) are recognised (although you are supposed to get a Spanish licence if you stay for more than a year – many foreign residents ignore this requirement). The old-style UK green licence is not accepted.

Other foreign licences are supposed to be accompanied by an International Driving Permit (although in practice, for renting cars or dealing with traffic police, your national licence will suffice). The International Driving Permit is available from motoring clubs in your country and is valid for 12 months.

For information on vehicle papers and insurance see under Car & Motorcycle in the Getting There & Away chapter.

Hostel Cards

The 26 member hostels of Catalunya's official youth hostel network, the Xarxa d'Albergs de Joventut, all share a central booking service (Map 1; ☎ 93 483 83 63, fax 93 483 83 50, metro Rocafort) at Turisme Juvenil de Catalunya, Carrer de Rocafort 116–122, Barcelona.

At Xarxa hostels you need an HI card. If you don't have one, you can get one, valid until 31 December of the year you buy it, at most of the hostels in Catalunya and HI affiliates throughout Spain. You pay for the card in instalments of €1.80 for each night you spend in a hostel, up to €10.80 (people legally resident in Spain for at least a year can get a Spanish hostel card for €6). The cards are available from the Turisme Juvenil de Catalunya office.

Student, Teacher & Youth Cards

These cards can get you worthwhile discounts on travel, and reduced prices at some museums, sights and entertainments.

The International Student Identity Card (ISIC), for full-time students (€4.25 in Spain), and the International Teacher Identity Card (ITIC), for full-time teachers and professors (€6 in Spain), are issued by over 5000 organisations worldwide, most of which are student-travel related and often sell student tickets. In Catalunya, both cards are available at the Turisme Juvenil de Catalunya office (see under Hostel Cards earlier) and usit Unlimited youth travel agency (Map 1; ☎ 902 25 25 75, W www .unlimited.es, metro Rocafort), at Carrer de Rocafort 116–122 in Barcelona.

Anyone under 26 can get a GO25 card or a Euro<26 card. Both of these give similar discounts to the ISIC and are issued by most of the same organisations. The Euro<26 has a variety of names including the Under 26 Card in England and Wales and the Carnet Jove in Catalunya (Carnet Joven Europeo in the rest of Spain). For information you can contact Under 26 (☎ 020-7730 7285), 52 Grosvenor Gardens, London SW1W 0AG, UK. In Catalunya, the Euro<26 is available from the same places as the ISIC card. You don't have to be Spanish to get the card in Spain, which costs €6.

As an example of the sort of discounts you can expect, the better things on offer for Euro<26 card-holders include 20% or 25% off most 2nd-class train fares, 10% or 20% off many Trasmediterránea ferries and some bus fares, as well as discounts at some museums.

Copies

All important documents (passport data page and visa page, credit cards, travel insurance policy, air/bus/train tickets, driving licence etc) should be photocopied before you leave home. Leave one copy with someone at home and keep another with you, separate from the originals.

Another option for storing details of your vital travel documents before you leave home is Lonely Planet's on-line Travel Vault. It is safer than carrying photocopies and is the best option if you are travelling in a country with easy Internet access. Your password-protected travel vault is accessible on-line at anytime. You can create your own travel vault for free at W www .ekno.lonelyplanet.com.

EMBASSIES & CONSULATES
Your Own Embassy

It's important to realise what your own embassy can and can't do to help you if you get into trouble. Generally speaking, it won't be much help in emergencies if the trouble that you are in is remotely your own fault. Remember that you are bound by the laws of the country you are travelling in. Your embassy will not be sympathetic if you end up in jail after committing a crime locally, even if such actions are legal in your own country.

In genuine emergencies you might get some assistance, but only if other channels have been exhausted. For example, if you need to get home urgently, a free ticket

home is exceedingly unlikely – the embassy would expect you to have insurance. If you have all your money and documents stolen, it might assist with getting a new passport, but a loan for onward travel is out of the question.

Spanish Embassies & Consulates Abroad

Spanish embassies and consulates can be found in:

Andorra (☎ 82 00 13) Carrer Prat de la Creu 34, Andorra la Vella
Australia (☎ 02-6273 3555, e embespau@ mail.mae.es) 15 Arkana St, Yarralumla, Canberra, ACT 2600
  Consulates: Brisbane (☎ 07-3221 8571)
  Melbourne (☎ 03-9347 1966)
  Perth (☎ 09-9322 4522)
  Sydney (☎ 02-9261 2433)
Canada (☎ 613-747 2252, e spain@docuweb .ca) 74 Stanley Ave, Ottawa, Ontario K1M 1P4
  Consulates: Toronto (☎ 416-977 1661)
  Montreal (☎ 514-935 5235)
France (☎ 01 44 43 18 00, e ambespfr@mail .mae.es) 22 avenue Marceau, 75008 Paris, Cedex 08
Germany (☎ 030-261 60 81, e embesde@mail .mae.es) Lichtensteinallee 1, 10787 Berlin
  Consulates: Düsseldorf (☎ 0211-43 90 80)
  Frankfurt-am-Main (☎ 069-959 16 60)
  Munich (☎ 089-98 50 27)
Ireland (☎ 01-269 1640) 17A Merlyn Park, Ballsbridge, Dublin 4
Morocco (☎ 07-26 80 00, e embesjpj@mail .mae.es) 3 Zankat Madnine, Rabat
  Consulates: Rabat (☎ 07-70 41 47)
  Casablanca (☎ 02-22 07 52)
  Tangier (☎ 09-93 70 00)
Netherlands (☎ 070-364 38 14, e embespnl@ mail.mae.es) Lange Voorhout 50, 2514 EG The Hague
New Zealand See Australia
Portugal (☎ 21-347 2381, e embesppt@mail .mae.es) Rua do Salitre 1, 1250 Lisbon
UK (☎ 020-7235 5555, e espemblon@ espemblon.freeserve.co.uk) 39 Chesham Place, London SW1X 8SB
  Consulates: London (☎ 020-7589 8989), 20 Draycott Place, London SW3 2RZ
  Manchester (☎ 0161-236 1233)
  Edinburgh (☎ 0131-220 1843)
USA (☎ 202-452 0100) 2375 Pennsylvania Ave NW, Washington, DC 20037
  Consulates: Boston (☎ 617-536 2506)

Chicago (☎ 312-782 4588)
Houston (☎ 713-783 6200)
Los Angeles (☎ 213-938 0158)
Miami (☎ 305-446 5511)
New Orleans (☎ 504-525 4951)
New York (☎ 212-355 4080)
San Francisco (☎ 415-922 2995)

Embassies & Consulates in Spain

The main embassies are in Madrid. Some countries also maintain consulates in major cities. Embassies and consulates in Madrid include:

Australia (☎ 91 441 93 00) Plaza del Descubridor Diego de Ordás 3–2, Edificio Santa Engrácia 120
Canada (☎ 91 431 45 56) Calle de Núñez de Balboa 35
France (☎ 91 700 78 00) Calle del Marqués Ensenada 10
Germany (☎ 91 557 90 00) Calle de Fortuny 8
Ireland (☎ 91 436 40 95) Paseo de la Castellana 46
Netherlands (☎ 91 350 32 36) Avenida del Comandante Franco 32
New Zealand (☎ 91 523 02 26) Plaza de la Lealtad 2
Portugal (☎ 91 561 47 23) Calle de Castelló 128
  Consulate: (☎ 91 577 35 38) Calle Lagasca 88
UK (☎ 91 308 06 18) Calle de Fernando el Santo 16
  Consulate: (☎ 91 308 53 00) Calle del Marqués Ensenada 16
USA (☎ 91 577 40 00) Calle de Serrano 75

Consulates in Barcelona

Getting to Madrid may be rather a pain if you're in Catalunya, and many countries have consulates in Barcelona. They are generally open Monday to Friday from 9 or 10 am to 1 or 2 pm. You can find them listed in the phone book under Consulat/Consulado.

Australia (Map 1; ☎ 93 330 94 96) 9th floor, Gran Via de Carles III 98
Canada (Map 2; ☎ 93 215 07 04) Passeig de Gràcia 77
France (Map 3; ☎ 93 270 30 00) Ronda de l'Universitat 22B 4rt
Germany (Map 2; ☎ 93 292 10 00) Passeig de Gràcia 111
Ireland (Map 1; ☎ 93 451 90 21) Gran Via de Carles III 94
Italy (Map 2; ☎ 93 487 00 02) Carrer de Mallorca 270

Netherlands (Map 1; ☎ 93 410 62 10) Avinguda Diagonal 601
UK (Map 2; ☎ 93 419 90 44) Avinguda Diagonal 477
USA (Map 1; ☎ 93 280 02 95) Passeig de la Reina Elisenda de Montcada 23–25

CUSTOMS

People entering Spain from outside the EU are allowed to bring in, duty-free, one bottle of spirits, one bottle of wine, 50mL of perfume and 200 cigarettes.

Duty-free allowances for travel between EU countries were abolished in 1999. For *duty-paid* items bought at normal shops in one EU country and taken into another, the allowances are 90L of wine, 10L of spirits, unlimited quantities of perfume and 800 cigarettes. VAT-free shopping *is* available in the duty-free shops at airports for people travelling between EU countries.

MONEY

You can get by easily enough with a single credit or debit card enabling you to withdraw cash from automatic teller machines (ATMs) but it's sound thinking also to take some travellers cheques and a second card (if you have one). The combination gives you a fall-back if you lose a card or for some reason are unable to use it.

Currency

Spain's currency for everyday transactions until early in 2002 is the peseta (pta). This comes in coins of one, five, 10, 25, 50, 100, 200 and 500 ptas, and notes of 1000, 2000, 5000 and 10,000 ptas. A five ptas coin is known as a *duro*, and it's fairly common for small sums to be quoted in duros: *dos duros* for 10 ptas, *cinco duros* for 25 ptas, *veinte duros* for 100 ptas.

The euro (€), the new currency that Spain shares with Austria, Belgium, Finland, France, Germany, Greece, Ireland, Italy, Luxembourg, the Netherlands and Portugal, has been in use since 1999 for some noncash transactions such as bank transfers. The euro will become the currency of cash transactions too in all 12 countries early in 2002.

Euro coins and notes will appear on 1

January 2002 and then there will be a two-month transition period, in which pesetas and euros will circulate side by side and pesetas can be exchanged for euros free of charge at banks. After 28 February 2002 the euro will be the sole currency of Spain and the 11 other 'euro zone' countries.

The euro is divided into 100 cents (*céntimos* in Spain). Coin denominations will be one, two, five, 10, 20 and 50 cents, €1 and €2. The notes will be €5, €10, €20, €50, €100, €200 and €500. All euro coins of each denomination will be identical on the side showing their value, but there will be 12 different obverses, each representing one of the 12 euro zone countries. All euro notes of each denomination will be identical on both sides. *All* euro coins and notes will be legal tender throughout the euro zone.

Exchange Rates

The values of euro zone currencies against the euro (and therefore against each other) were fixed permanently in 1999. Exchange rates between euro zone and non-euro zone currencies, and between non-euro zone currencies, are variable.

country	unit		pesetas/euros
Australia	A$1	=	100 ptas/€0.60
Canada	C$1	=	129 ptas/€0.78
France	10FF	=	253 ptas/€1.52
Germany	DM1	=	85 ptas/€0.51
Japan	¥100	=	156 ptas/€0.94
New Zealand	NZ$1	=	80 ptas/€0.48
Morocco	Dr10	=	165 ptas/€0.99
Portugal	100$00	=	83 ptas/€0.50
UK	UK£1	=	277 ptas/€1.67
USA	US$1	=	197 ptas/€1.18

Exchanging Money

You can change cash or travellers cheques in currencies of the developed world without problems (except, sometimes, queues) at virtually any bank or exchange office. Many banks have ATMs.

Banks tend to offer the best exchange rates. They're common in cities, and even small villages often have one. Banks mostly open from about 8.30 am to 2 pm Monday to Friday, and 9 am to 1 pm Saturday. Some don't open on Saturday in summer. Main branches may open longer hours during the week.

Exchange offices – usually indicated by the word *canvi/cambio* (exchange) – exist mainly in tourist resorts and other places that attract high numbers of foreigners. Generally they offer longer opening hours and quicker service than banks, but worse exchange rates. In some exchange offices, the more money you change, the better the exchange rate you'll get.

Wherever you change, ask about commissions and confirm that exchange rates are as posted. Every bank seems to have a different commission structure: commissions may be different for travellers cheques and cash, and may depend on how many cheques, or how much in total, you're cashing. Typical commissions range from 1% to 3%, with a minimum of €1.80 to €3, but there are places with a minimum of €6 and sometimes €12. Places that advertise 'no commission' usually offer poor exchange rates to start with. An exception is Spain's national bank, Banco de España, which changes banknotes (only) of euro-zone currencies at the full interbank rate free of commission, up to a maximum of the equivalent of €2000 per person per day. This service is available at 23 branches in Spain including at Plaça de Catalunya 17–18, Barcelona (Map 3).

Travellers Cheques These protect your money because they can be replaced if they are lost or stolen. In Catalunya they can be cashed at many banks and exchange offices and usually attract a higher exchange rate than cash. You usually can't use them like money to actually make purchases. American Express (AmEx) and Thomas Cook are widely accepted brands with efficient replacement policies. For AmEx travellers cheque refunds you can call ☎ 900 99 44 26 from anywhere in Spain.

It doesn't really matter whether your cheques are denominated in euros or in the currency of the country you buy them in: most Spanish exchange outlets will change all developed-world currencies. Get most of your cheques in fairly large denominations (the equivalent of €100 or more) to save on per-cheque commission charges.

It's vital to keep your initial receipt, and a record of your cheque numbers and the ones you have used, separate from the cheques themselves.

Take along your passport when you go to cash travellers cheques.

ATMs & Plastic Money The exchange rate used for credit/debit card currency exchanges is usually more in your favour than for cash exchanges. Some debit cards, such as those in the Cirrus and Maestro networks, may enable you to access money in personal bank accounts from Spain without any cash-advance fee.

You can ask your card issuer before leaving home about rates and charges. It's also advisable to ask how widely usable your card will be, how to report a lost card, whether your personal identification number (PIN) will be acceptable (some European ATMs don't accept PINs of more than four digits), and to know your withdrawal/spending limits.

Payment by card is accepted by many Spanish businesses, including restaurants and places to stay (especially from the middle price range up) petrol stations, RENFE (Red Nacional de los Ferrocarriles Españoles; for long-distance rail travel) and other transport. Among the most widely accepted cards are Visa, MasterCard, EuroCard, AmEx, Cirrus, Maestro, Plus, Diners Club and JCB.

A high proportion of Spanish banks, even in small towns and some villages, have an ATM *(caixer automàtic/cajero automático)* that will dispense cash at any time if you have the right piece of plastic to slot into it. This will save you having to queue at the bank counter.

AmEx cards are among the easiest to replace if they are lost – you can call ☎ 902 37 56 37 or ☎ 91 572 03 03 (in Madrid) at any time. Always report a lost card straight away: for Visa cards call ☎ 900 97 44 45; for MasterCard/EuroCard ☎ 900 97 12 31; for Diners Club ☎ 91 547 40 00.

International Transfers You can have money transferred to you from another country, either through a bank there or using a money-transfer service such as Western Union (Ⓦ www.westernunion.com) or MoneyGram (Ⓦ www.moneygram.com). If there's money in your bank account at home, you may be able to instruct the bank yourself.

For information on Western Union services in Catalunya, call the free number ☎ 900 63 36 33; for MoneyGram call ☎ 901 20 10 10. Both have agents in cities and towns in Catalunya and around the world.

To set up a transfer through a bank, either get advice from the bank at home on a suitable pick-up bank in Catalunya, or check with a Spanish bank about how to organise it. You'll need to let the sender have the name, address and city of the Spanish bank branch, and any contact or code numbers required.

A bank-to-bank telegraphic transfer typically costs around US$20 to US$30 and can take a week. Western Union and MoneyGram are quicker (in both cases the money can supposedly be handed over to the recipient within 10 to 15 minutes of being sent), but more expensive. Their charges are on sliding scales: to transfer US$400 from the USA to Spain costs the sender around US$30 to US$40 and the recipient nothing. It's also possible to have money sent quickly by AmEx.

Security

Your money, in whatever form, is at risk unless you look after it. Carry only a limited amount of cash, and keep the bulk in more easily replaceable forms such as travellers cheques or plastic. If your accommodation has a safe, use it. If you have to leave money in your room, divide it into several stashes and hide them in different places.

For carrying money on the street the safest thing is a money belt or wallet that you can strap on under your clothes. An external money belt is only safe if it can't be sliced off by a quick knife cut. Watch out for people who touch you or seem to be getting unnecessarily close, in any situation.

Costs

If you are extremely frugal, it's just about possible to scrape by on €24 a day by staying in youth hostels, avoiding restaurants except for an inexpensive set lunch, minimising your visits to museums and bars and moving around very little. A more comfortable economy budget would be €48 a day. This could allow you up to €18 for accommodation; €2.40 for breakfast (coffee and a pastry); €6 to €9 for lunch or dinner; up to €4.80 for another light meal; €3 to €6 for admission fees to museums, sights or entertainment; and a bit over for a drink or two and intercity travel.

If you've got €120 to €150 a day you can stay in excellent accommodation, rent a car, eat some of Catalunya's finest food and perhaps indulge in a little outdoor activity (from diving to skiing).

Ways to Save Two people can travel more cheaply (per person) than one by sharing rooms. You'll also save by avoiding the peak tourist seasons, which means Christmas/New Year, winter weekends in the snow resorts, Easter and the summer (from late June to mid-September) in most places. A student or youth card, or a document such as a passport proving you're over 60, brings worthwhile savings on some travel costs and entry to some museums and sights (see Visas & Documents earlier in the chapter).

More information on accommodation, food and travel costs can be found under Accommodation later in the chapter, in the Out to Eat in Catalunya special section and in the Getting Around chapter.

Tipping & Bargaining

Tipping is a matter of personal choice – most people leave some small change if they're satisfied: 5% would normally be adequate and 10% generous. Most people leave a couple of coins at the bar or cafe tables. Porters will generally be happy with €1, and most won't turn their noses up at €0.50. Taxi drivers don't have to be tipped but a little rounding up won't go amiss.

There's not much room for bargaining, except occasionally at markets and some

cheap hotels (particularly if you're staying for a few days).

Taxes & Refunds

In Spain, value-added tax (VAT) is IVA (*ee-ba*; *impuesto sobre el valor añadido*). The 7% on accommodation and meals is usually included in quoted prices. It's 16% on retail goods and car hire. To ask 'Is IVA included?', say '*¿Está incluido el IVA?*'.

Visitors are entitled to a refund of the 16% IVA on purchases costing more than €90 from any shop if they are taking them out of the EU within three months. Ask the shop for an invoice showing the price and IVA paid for each item and identifying the vendor and purchaser. Then present the invoice to the customs booth for IVA refunds when you leave Spain. The officer will stamp the invoice and you hand it in at a bank in the airport for the reimbursement.

POST & COMMUNICATIONS
Postal Rates

A postcard or letter weighing up to 20g costs €0.42 to other European countries, €0.69 to North America, and €1.12 to Australasia or Asia. Three A4 sheets in an air-mail envelope weigh between 15g and 20g. An aerogram costs €0.51 to anywhere in the world.

Certificado (registered mail) costs an extra €1.05 for international mail. *Urgente* service, which means your letter may arrive two or three days quicker, costs an extra €1.39 for international mail. You can send mail both urgente and certificado (which costs €1.45 when added to urgente).

A day or two quicker than urgente service – but a lot more expensive – is Postal Exprés, sometimes called Express Mail Service (EMS). This uses courier companies for international deliveries. Packages weighing up to 1kg cost €24.70 to anywhere in Europe, €42.17 to North America, and €48.19 to Australia or New Zealand.

Sending Mail

Stamps are sold at most *estancos* (tobacconists' shops with 'Tabacs/Tabacos' in yellow letters on a maroon background), as well as post offices *(correus/correos)*.

Getting Addressed

Just because you have an address in your hot sweaty palm doesn't mean you will have no trouble finding what you are after. If the *pensión* you are looking for is at C/ de Montcada 23, 3°D Int, just off Av Marqués, you could be forgiven for scratching your head a little. Abbreviations contain a lot of information, and in Barcelona things are made worse by the fact that some people may give you the Catalan version of an address while others may give you the Castilian version. Here are some common abbreviations:

Av or Avda	Avinguda/Avenida
Bda	Baixada/Bajada
C/	Carrer/Calle
Cí or C°	Camí/Camino
Ctra, Ca or Cª	Carretera
Cró/Cjón	Carreró/Callejón
Gta	Glorieta (major roundabout)
Pg or P°	Passeig/Paseo
Ptge/Pje	Passatge/Pasaje
Plc/Plz	Placeta/Plazuela
Pl, Pza or Pª	Plaça/Plaza
Pt or Pte	Pont/Puente
Rbla	Rambla
Rda	Ronda
s/n	sense numeració/ sin número (without number)
Tr or Trav	Travessera
Trv	Travessia/Travesía
Urb	Urbanització/Urbanización

MICK WELDON

The following are used where there are several flats, *hostales*, offices etc in one building. They're often used in conjunction, eg, 2°C or 3°I Int:

Ent	Entresuelo (ground floor)
Pr	Principal (what Brits and co would consider the 1st floor)
1°	1st floor (2nd floor to Brits and co)
2°	2nd floor (3rd floor to Brits and co)
C	centre/centro (middle)
D	dreta/derecha (right-hand side)
Esq, I or Izq	esquerra/izquierda (left-hand side)
Int	interior (a flat or office too far inside the building to look onto any street – usually has windows onto an interior patio or shaft – the opposite is Ext, exterior)

If someone's address is Apartado de Correos 206 (which can be shortened to Apdo de Correos 206 or even Apdo 206), don't bother tramping the streets in search of it – it is a post office box.

Street names often get short shrift too. Carrer de Madrid (literally 'Street of Madrid') will often appear simply as Carrer Madrid. In spoken exchanges the word Carrer is often dropped. Thus Carrer del Comte d'Urgell will be referred to simply as Comte d'Urgell.

Cities have quite a lot of post offices and most villages have one too. Main post offices in cities and towns are usually open from about 8.30 am to 8.30 pm Monday to Friday, and from about 9 am to 1.30 pm on Saturday. Smaller offices may be open shorter hours. Estancos are usually open during normal shop hours.

It's quite safe and reliable to post your mail in the yellow street postboxes *(bústies/ buzones)* as well as at post offices.

Delivery times are erratic but ordinary mail to other Western European countries normally takes up to a week; to North America up to 10 days; and to Australia or New Zealand up to two weeks.

Receiving Mail

Delivery times are similar to those for outbound mail. All Spanish addresses have five-digit postcodes; using postcodes may help your mail arrive a bit quicker.

Poste restante mail can be addressed to you at poste restante (or better, *lista de correos*, the Spanish name for it) at any place in Catalunya that has a post office. It will be delivered to the place's main post office unless another is specified in the address. Take your passport when you pick up mail. It helps if people writing to you capitalise or underline your surname and include the postcode in the address. A typical lista de correos address looks like this:

> Jenny JONES
> Lista de Correos
> 08080 Barcelona
> Spain

For some quirks of address abbreviations, see the boxed text 'Getting Addressed'.

AmEx card or travellers cheque holders can use the free client mail-holding service at AmEx offices in Spain. You can get a list of these from AmEx offices inside or outside Spain. Take your passport when you pick up mail.

Telephone

Catalunya has many street pay phones, which are blue and easy to use for both international and domestic calls. They accept coins and phonecards *(tarjetas telefónicas)* issued by the national phone company Telefónica. Tarjetas telefónicas come in €6 and €12 denominations and, like postage stamps, are sold at post offices and estancos.

Public phones inside bars and cafes, and phones in hotel rooms, are nearly always a good deal more expensive than street pay phones.

Costs Calls from pay phones using coins or a slot-in card cost about 35% more than calls from private lines. A three-minute call from a pay phone can cost from €0.15 for a local call to €0.66 for a call to another province within Spain. Calls to Spanish mobile phones (whose numbers begin with 6) cost €1.39, as do calls to most European countries. Calls to North America cost €1.69 and to Australia €4.94. Numbers starting with 900 are free. Those beginning with 901 or 902 cost from €0.21 to €0.45 for three minutes.

All calls except those to mobile phones are cheaper between 8 pm and 8 am (6 pm to 8 am for local calls), and all day Saturday and Sunday. Calls to mobile phones are cheaper from 10 pm to 8 am Monday to Friday, 2 pm to midnight Saturday and all day Sunday. The discounts are around 50% for provincial and interprovincial calls and calls to mobile phones, and around 10% for local and international calls.

A variety of discount cards are available, which can significantly cut call costs, especially for international calls – see eKno Communication Service later in the chapter.

Domestic Dialling Spain has no telephone area codes. Phone numbers have nine digits, and you must dial all nine, wherever in the country you are calling from.

Dial ☎ 1009 to speak to a domestic operator, including for a domestic reverse-charge (collect) call *(una llamada por cobro revertido)*. For directory inquiries dial ☎ 1003; calls cost about €0.36. The Spanish Yellow Pages, Pàgines Grogues/Páginas Amarillas, are on-line at Ⓦ www.paginas amarillas.es. For emergency numbers, see the boxed text 'In Case of Emergency' later in the chapter.

International Dialling If you want to make an international call from Spain, dial the international access code (☎ 00), then the country code, area code and number you want. For international reverse-charge calls, dial ☎ 900 99 00 followed by a code for the country you're calling: ☎ 61 for Australia; ☎ 44 for the UK; ☎ 64 for New Zealand; ☎ 15 for Canada; and for the USA, ☎ 11 (AT&T) or ☎ 14 (MCI); codes for other countries – usually the normal country code – are often posted in pay phones. You'll get straight through to an operator in the country you're calling. The same numbers can be used with direct-dial calling cards.

If for some reason the above doesn't work, in most places you can get through to an English-speaking Spanish international operator on ☎ 1008.

For international directory enquiries dial ☎ 025 and be ready to pay about €0.90.

Mobile Phones Mobile phone *(teléfono móvil)* use has mushroomed in Spain. Spain uses GSM 900/1800, compatible with the rest of Europe and Australia but not with the North American GSM 1900 or the totally different system in Japan (though some North Americans have GSM 1900/900 phones that do work here). If you have a GSM phone, check with your service provider about using it in Spain, and beware of calls being routed internationally (very expensive for a 'local' call). Most Spanish towns of medium size or bigger have mobile phone shops. There are several networks with varying price plans. You can buy phones for as little as €60, generally with around €24 of calls thrown in.

Calling Spain from Abroad Spain's country code is ☎ 34. Follow this with the full nine-digit number you are calling.

Phonecards & Call Centres You'll notice a wide range of local and international discount phonecards on sale in Barcelona and occasionally elsewhere in Catalunya.

Before buying look carefully at call costs as some are really not so cheap at all. You are generally given an access number to dial and a PIN number for your card. Also springing up in Barcelona are cheap-rate call centres. Again, compare prices carefully before calling. Outside Barcelona call centres are a rarity.

eKno Communication Service Lonely Planet's eKno global communication service provides low-cost international calls – for local calls you're usually better off with a local phonecard. eKno also offers free messaging services, email, travel information and an on-line travel vault, where you can securely store all your important documents. You can join on-line at Ⓦ www .ekno.lonelyplanet.com, where you will find the local-access numbers for the 24-hour customer-service centre. Once you have joined, always check the eKno Web site for the latest access numbers for each country and updates on new features.

Fax
Most main post offices have a fax service: sending one page costs about €2.10 within Spain, €6.70 to elsewhere in Europe and €12.65 to €15 to other countries. However, you'll often find cheaper rates at shops or offices with 'Fax' signs.

Email & Internet Access
An easy way of accessing the Internet and email while you're on the road is through cybercafes and other public access points. You'll find these in Barcelona and several other centres in Catalunya. Visit Ⓦ www .netcafeguide.com for a list. Charges for an hour on-line range from €1.20 to €3.60. It's easiest to use Web-based email, which you can access anywhere in the world from any Internet-connected computer. Several such email accounts are available free, including eKno (Ⓦ www.ekno.lonelyplanet .com), Yahoo! Mail (Ⓦ www.yahoo.com) and Hotmail (Ⓦ www.hotmail.com).

If you plan to carry your notebook or palmtop computer with you, remember that the power supply voltage in Catalunya may vary from that at home, risking damage to your equipment. A universal AC adapter for your appliance will enable you to plug it in anywhere without frying the innards. Most phones in Spain use the standard US RJ-11 telephone jack. For more information on travelling with a portable computer, see **W** www.teleadapt.com or **W** www.warrior .com.

Major Internet service providers (ISPs) such as AOL (**W** www.aol.com), CompuServe (**W** www.compuserve.com) and AT&T Business Internet Services (**W** www .attbusiness.net) have dial-in nodes in Barcelona and other major Spanish cities. It's best to download a list of the dial-in numbers before you leave home, and remember that in all three cases these ISPs charge hourly surcharges on top of your regular plan rates. It generally works out cheaper to surf the net in Internet cafes.

DIGITAL RESOURCES

The World Wide Web is a rich resource for travellers. You can research your trip, hunt down bargain fares, book hotels, check weather conditions or chat with locals and other travellers about the best places to visit (or avoid!).

Start your Web explorations at the Lonely Planet Web site (**W** www.lonelyplanet.com). Here you'll find succinct summaries on travelling to Spain, postcards from other travellers and the Thorn Tree bulletin board, where you can ask questions before you go or dispense advice when you get back. You can also find travel news and updates to many of our most popular guidebooks. The subWWWay section links you to the most useful travel resources elsewhere on the Web. Lonely Planet's Spain page is at **W** www.lonelyplanet.com/destinations/ europe/spain.

The best sites dealing with Catalunya tend to concentrate on Barcelona. The following are a few of the more useful ones:

Turespaña This is the Spanish tourist office's official site, with lots of general information about the country, lists of tourist offices outside Spain and some interesting links.
W www.tourspain.es

All About Spain A varied site with information on everything from *festes* (town festivals) to hotels and a Yellow Pages guide to tour operators around the world that do trips in Spain. You can use it to search out hotels, bars and the like across Catalunya. General information is fairly superficial.
W www.red2000.com

GeoPlaneta Route and vacation planner for Spain. A search under Catalunya takes you to a list of towns and areas in the region. Clicking on these may reveal only slight information but could lead you to more detailed links.
W www.geoplaneta.com

Internet Café Guide At this site you can get a list of Internet cafes in Catalunya and beyond. It's not as up-to-date as you might expect, but it is a start (see also Email & Internet Access earlier in the chapter).
W www.netcafeguide.com

Generalitat de Catalunya The Generalitat's Web site contains some curious pages dealing with various aspects of Catalunya's history and culture. It's in Catalan, Spanish and English. There are links to government departments, universities and the like, as well as information search engines.
W www.gencat.es

Turisme Juvenil de Catalunya This site has information on Catalunya's official Xarxa d'Albergs de Joventut – which covers most of the HI youth hostels in Barcelona and the region. This is also the place to look for other information on youth and student travel and issues in Catalunya.
W www.gencat.es/tujuca/hometuju.htm

Catalunya On Line A Web portal in Catalan with links, chat forums and information on what's happening across the region.
W www.catalunyaonline.com

Ciudad Hoy This is one of the better listings sites (in Spanish) for the four provincial capitals in Catalunya (and others across Spain). Search for Girona, for example, and you are transferred to Gironahoy.com, a comprehensive site with broad listings, general news (local, national and international), links to phone directory and Yellow Pages sites and more.
W www.ciudadhoy.com

Viapolis.Com Similarly, this site has pages on Barcelona and the three other provincial capitals with copious listings and other information on each.
W www.viapolis.com

Cities.Com Search for Spain and then Cataluna (sic) on this site and it takes you to a list of about 20 other potentially interesting sites, mostly on Barcelona and some of which appear in this list.

W www.cities.com

Barcelona On Line This is the single most useful Web site on Barcelona, with numerous links to wider Catalan and Spanish topics and loads of busy pages covering restaurants, places to stay (including home stays), bars and discos, shops, tourist information, museums, weather information, Catalan and Spanish newspaper and magazine Web site links, transport information and so on. You can also plug into lots of chat forums.

W www.barcelona-on-line.es

Turisme de Barcelona Barcelona Tourism's official site, with general information on sights, eating out and other aspects of Barcelona interest, along with up-to-date details on what's on in the city. You can contact them by email on e teltur@barcelonaturisme.com. The site is in Catalan, Spanish, English and French.

W www.barcelonaturisme.com

RENFE Timetables, tickets and special offers on Spain's national rail network, including Catalunya.

W www.renfe.es

BOOKS

Most books are published in different editions by different publishers in different countries. As a result, a book might be a hard-cover rarity in one country and readily available in paperback in another. Fortunately, bookshops and libraries search by title or author, so they are best placed to advise you on the availability of the listed recommendations.

Although there is a wealth of material on Spain, comparatively little is available in English on Catalunya. There is considerably more in Spanish and Catalan, but it is mostly available in Catalunya only.

See also Literature under Arts in the Facts about Catalunya chapter.

In London there are several good bookshops devoted to the business of travel. For guidebooks and maps, Stanfords bookshop (☎ 020-7836 2121), 12–14 Long Acre, London WC2E 9LP, is acknowledged as one of the better first ports of call. A well stocked source of travel literature is Daunt Books for Travellers (☎ 020-7224 2295), 83 Marylebone High St, London W1U 4QW.

For books in Spanish, one of the best places to try is Grant & Cutler (☎ 020-7734 2012), 55–57 Great Marlborough St, London W1V 2AY.

Books on Spain (☎ 020-8898 7789, fax 8898 8812, e keithharris@books-on-spain .com, W www.books-on-spain.com), PO Box 207, Twickenham TW2 5BQ, UK, can send you mail-order catalogues of hundreds of old and new titles on Spain.

In Australia, the Travel Bookshop (☎ 02-9261 8200), 3/175 Liverpool St, Sydney, is worth a browse. In the USA, try Book Passage (☎ 415-927 0960), 51 Tamal Vista Boulevard, Corte Madera, California, and The Complete Traveler Bookstore (☎ 212-685 9007), 199 Madison Ave, New York. In France, L'Astrolabe rive gauche (☎ 01 46 33 80 06), 14 rue Serpente, Paris, is recommended.

Lonely Planet

If you plan to travel beyond Catalunya, Lonely Planet's *Spain* could be for you. On the other hand, those concentrating some effort on the regional capital should look out for *Barcelona*. Walkers with an eye on the Pyrenees will find *Walking in Spain* a very helpful guide. Lonely Planet also publishes companion guides on *Andalucía, Canary Islands* and *Madrid. World Food Spain* by Richard Sterling is a trip into Spain's culinary soul, while the *Spanish phrasebook* will enable you to fill some of the gaps between ¡hola! and ¡adiós!

Guidebooks

Apart from the book you hold in your hands, few useful guides to the region have been published in English.

If you can deal with Spanish, try the yellow and grey *Guía Total – Catalunya*, published by Anaya. In Catalan, the *Guia de Catalunya* by Josep Lluís Infiesta Pérez is a work of enormous detail covering some 1500 towns and villages in alphabetical order. It works better as a reference book than as a practical travel companion.

History, Politics & Society

Spain You may wish to acquaint yourself with the wider context of Spanish history.

For a colourful but thorough and not over-long survey of Spanish history, *The Story of Spain* by Mark Williams is hard to beat. Also concise and worthwhile is Juan Lalaguna's *A Traveller's History of Spain*.

Gerald Brenan's *The Spanish Labyrinth* (1943) is an in-depth but readable unravelling of the tangle of political and social movements in the half-century or so before the Civil War.

The Civil War is said to be the second most written-about conflict in history (after WWII) and has spawned some wonderful books. *The Spanish Civil War* by Hugh Thomas is probably the classic account of the conflict in any language. It's long and dense with detail, yet readable, even-handed and humane. Raymond Carr's more succinct *The Spanish Tragedy* is another well-written and respected account.

Paul Preston's *Franco* is the big biography of one of history's little dictators.

A highly readable overall introduction to modern Spain is *The New Spaniards* by John Hooper, a former *Guardian* Madrid correspondent, whose writings range comprehensively from the arts to politics and bullfighting to sex.

Catalunya *Homage to Catalonia* is George Orwell's story of his involvement in the Civil War, moving from the euphoria of the early days in Barcelona to disillusionment with the disastrous infighting on the Republican side.

Alastair Boyd's *The Essence of Catalonia* is an entertaining tableau of the Catalunya region.

If you feel you can deal with Catalan, *Breu Història de Catalunya* by Jesús Mestre i Godes is a delightfully readable summary of the region's ups and downs since antiquity. The book displays an irritating (but common in much contemporary Catalan history writing) tendency towards Catalanist partiality. It comes out most clearly in some of the author's elegiac exclamations. Keep an eye on this and you otherwise get a meaty account.

Homage to Barcelona (1990) by Colm Tóibín is an excellent personal introduction to the city's modern life and artistic and political history; Tóibín is an Irish journalist who lived there.

If you can, grab a copy of Eduardo Mendoza's *La Ciudad de los Prodigios* (City of Marvels), a novel set in Barcelona from the Universal Exhibition of 1888 to the World Exhibition of 1929.

An interesting look at Catalan attitudes to the changes of the past decades (notably the rise of tourism) along the Costa Brava is Norman Lewis' semi-fictional *Voices of the Old Sea*.

Art & Architecture

Barcelona (1992) by Robert Hughes is an eclectic and highly opinionated look at the city's art through its history, or perhaps the other way around. He approaches the task with mordant wit and a keen eye.

In the handy Thames & Hudson series on artistic movements, *Romanesque Art* by Meyer Schapiro covers this pre-Gothic architectural and artistic era, which probably had more impact on Catalunya than any other part of Spain.

A cross between travel guide and art history manual concentrating on the region's Romanesque treasures is the series *Viatge al Romànic Català*, published in Catalan by the RACC automobile association. At the time of writing three volumes were available and a fourth was on the way, all written by Jesús Mestre i Godes (mentioned earlier for his history of Catalunya) and Joan-Albert Adell.

Food & Wine

There are dozens of books on Spanish cookery. For more specific information on Catalan cuisine you could try *Cuina Catalana* by Pere Sans – in Catalan. Another book with the same title (and also available in Spanish) is an attractively presented recipe book by Ana Maria Calera. The single greatest tome on the subject seems to be *El Gran Llibre de la Cuina Catalana* by Josep Lladonosa i Giró. It too has been translated into Spanish.

If English is more your thing, take a look at *Catalan Cuisine* by Colman Andrews.

Flora & Fauna

Wildlife Travelling Companion: Spain by John Measures is a good traveller's guide, focusing on 150 of the best sites for viewing Spanish flora and fauna, with details of how to reach them and what you can hope to see.

The single best guide to flowers and shrubs in Spain is *Flowers of South-West Europe, A Field Guide* by Oleg Polunin & BE Smythies.

FILMS

Whit Stillman's *Barcelona* (1994) follows the loves and trials of two American cousins in post-Franco Barcelona. Interesting but hardly a hit was *Surviving Picasso* (1996), directed by James Ivory and with Anthony Hopkins as Picasso.

Believe it or not, the martial arts king has kicked and punched his way through Catalunya. Jackie Chan appeared in *Wheels on Meals*, directed by Samon Hung in 1984 and set in... Barcelona! It was a classic of kung-fu slapstick.

CD-ROMS

You'll find the odd CD-ROM with Catalan subjects, including:

Guía del Esquí A guide to the ski resorts in Spain and Andorra – check the edition year before buying (Internova; €15).

Gaudí Part of the Art Media Collection, this CD-ROM looks at the marvels of the most mesmerising of the Modernistas (€30).

Història de l'Art Catalana Prepared by teachers of the Universitat Oberta de Catalunya, this is an interesting introduction to the history of art in the region, from Romanesque to the present day (€48).

NEWSPAPERS & MAGAZINES

You can easily find a wide selection of national daily newspapers from around Europe at newsstands in central Barcelona and many of the coastal and ski resorts. Elsewhere the pickings are slimmer. The *International Herald Tribune, Time, The Economist, Le Monde, Der Spiegel* and a host of other international magazines are available.

Spanish National Press

The main Spanish dailies can be identified along roughly political lines, with the old-fashioned paper *ABC* representing the conservative right, *El País* identified with the Partido Socialista Obrero Español (PSOE; Spanish Socialist Workers Party), Spain's centre-left socialist party, and *El Mundo*, a more radical left-wing paper that prides itself on breaking political scandals. For a good spread of national and international news, *El País* is the pick. One of the best-selling dailies is *Marca*, devoted solely to sport.

Catalan Press

El País includes a daily supplement devoted to Catalunya, but the region has a lively home-grown press too. *La Vanguardia* and *El Periódico* are the main local Castilian-language dailies. The latter also publishes an award-winning Catalan version. The more Catalan-nationalist oriented daily is *Avui*. These can also be thought of as Barcelona's city papers. As you move around the region you will come across a plethora of regional and local papers in Catalan and Spanish.

RADIO

You can pick up BBC World Service broadcasts on a variety of frequencies. Broadcasts are directed at Western Europe on, among others, 648kHz, 9410kHz and 12,095kHz (short wave).

Voice of America can be found on various short-wave frequencies, including on 9700kHz, 9760kHz and 15,205kHz depending on the time of day. The BBC and VOA broadcast around the clock, but the quality of reception varies considerably.

The Spanish national network, Radio Nacional de España (RNE), has several stations (frequencies are given for Barcelona – they change as you move around the region): RNE 1 (738kHz AM; 88.3MHz FM) has general interest and current affairs programs; RNE 5 (576kHz AM) concentrates on sport and entertainment; and RNE 3 (98.7MHz FM) presents a decent range of pop and rock music. Among the most listened to rock and pop stations are 40 Principales

(93.9MHz FM), Onda Cero (89.1MHz FM) and Cadena 100 (100MHz FM).

Those wanting to get into Catalan can tune into Catalunya Ràdio (102.8MHz FM) and Ràdio Espanya Catalunya (94.9MHz FM). There is also a host of small local broadcasters.

You can hear the American InRadio program in Barcelona on 107.6MHz FM from 9 to 10 pm on Monday, Tuesday, Wednesday and Friday.

TV

TVs receive up to seven channels – two from Spain's state-run Televisión Española (TVE1 and La 2), three independent (Antena 3, Tele 5 and Canal Plus), the Catalunya regional government station, TV-3, and another Catalan station, Canal 33. Barcelona TV is the capital's local station. In some areas, especially in the Pyrenees, you will be lucky to pick up more than three of these.

News programs are generally decent and you can sometimes catch an interesting documentary or film (look out for the occasional English-language classic late at night on La 2). Otherwise, the main fare is a rather nauseating diet of soaps (many from Latin America), endless talk shows and vaudevillian variety shows (with plenty of glitz and tits). Canal Plus is a pay channel dedicated mainly to movies: you need a decoder and subscription to see the movies, but anyone can watch the other programs.

Many of the better hotels have satellite TV, serving up the usual spread of CNN, Eurosport and the like.

VIDEO SYSTEMS

Most prerecorded videos on sale in Catalunya use the PAL (phase alternation line) system common to most of Western Europe and Australia. France uses the incompatible SECAM system and North America and Japan use the incompatible NTSC system.

PHOTOGRAPHY

Most main brands of film are widely available and processing is fast and generally efficient. A roll of print film (36 exposures, ISO

100) costs around €4 and can be processed for around €7.50 (dearer for same day service), although there are often better deals if you have two or three rolls developed together. The equivalent in slide *(diapositiva)* film is around €5 plus €4.85 for processing.

TIME

Catalunya, like the rest of Spain, is on GMT/UTC plus one hour during winter and GMT/UTC plus two hours during the daylight-saving period, from the last Sunday in March to the last Sunday in October. Most other Western European countries have the same time as Spain year round, the major exceptions being Britain, Ireland and Portugal. Add one hour to these three countries' times to get Spanish time.

Spanish time is normally USA Eastern Time plus six hours and USA Pacific Time plus nine hours. But the USA tends to start daylight saving a week or two later than Spain (meaning you must add one hour to the time differences in the intervening period).

In the Australian winter (Spanish summer), subtract eight hours from Australian Eastern Standard Time to get Spanish time; in the Australian summer subtract 10 hours. The difference is nine hours for a few weeks in March.

ELECTRICITY

Electric current in Catalunya is 220V, 50Hz, as in the rest of continental Europe. Several countries outside Europe (such as the USA and Canada) use 60Hz, which means appliances from those countries with electric motors (such as some CD and tape players) may perform poorly.

Plugs have two round pins, as in the rest of continental Europe.

WEIGHTS & MEASURES

The metric system is used. Like other continental Europeans, the Spanish indicate decimals with commas and thousands with points.

LAUNDRY

Self-service laundrettes are rare. Small laundries *(lavanderías)* are fairly common; staff will usually wash, dry and fold a load for €6 to €9. Some youth hostels and a few hostales have washing machines for guests' use.

TOILETS

Public toilets are not particularly common, but it's OK to wander into most bars and cafes to use their toilet. Courtesy would suggest you buy a token drink but generally you can get away with it if you choose not to. Many toilets lack toilet paper.

HEALTH

Most travellers experience no health problems in Catalunya, which is a rather healthy corner of Europe.

Private hospitals and clinics generally provide excellent services but are expensive for those without medical insurance. That said, certain treatments in public hospitals may also have to be paid for and in such cases can be equally costly.

Your embassy or consulate in Madrid or Barcelona may be able to provide a list of recommended doctors in major towns. Tourist offices, the police and staff at your accommodation can also tell you where to find medical help or call an ambulance. If you have a specific health complaint, obtain the necessary information and referrals for treatment before leaving home.

Health Insurance

Visitors from other EU countries and Norway, Iceland and Liechtenstein are entitled to free Spanish national health emergency medical care on provision of an E111 form, which you must get in your home country before you go to Catalunya. Ask your health service how to get the form. In Britain it's issued free by post offices. If you go for treatment in Catalunya you will be asked for a photocopy of the E111.

With an E111, you will probably still have to pay at least some of the cost of medicines bought from pharmacies, even if a doctor has prescribed them (unless you are a pensioner), and perhaps for a few tests and procedures.

An E111 is no good for private consultations or treatment in Spain, which includes virtually all dentists and some of the better

Medical Kit Check List

Following is a list of items you should consider including in your medical kit – consult your pharmacist for brands available in your country.

☐ **Aspirin or paracetamol (acetaminophen in the USA)** – for pain or fever
☐ **Antihistamine** – for allergies, eg, hay fever; to ease the itch from insect bites or stings; and to prevent motion sickness
☐ **Cold and flu tablets, throat lozenges and nasal decongestant**
☐ **Multivitamins** – consider for long trips, when dietary vitamin intake may be inadequate
☐ **Antibiotics** – consider including these if you're travelling well off the beaten track; see your doctor, as they must be prescribed, and carry the prescription with you
☐ **Loperamide or diphenoxylate** –'blockers' for diarrhoea
☐ **Prochlorperazine or metaclopramide** – for nausea and vomiting
☐ **Rehydration mixture** – to prevent dehydration, which may occur, for example, during bouts of diarrhoea; particularly important when travelling with children
☐ **Insect repellent, sunscreen, lip balm and eye drops**
☐ **Calamine lotion, sting relief spray or aloe vera** – to ease irritation from sunburn and insect bites or stings
☐ **Antifungal cream or powder** – for fungal skin infections and thrush
☐ **Antiseptic (such as povidone-iodine)** – for cuts and grazes
☐ **Bandages, Band-Aids (plasters) and other wound dressings**
☐ **Water purification tablets or iodine**
☐ **Scissors, tweezers and a thermometer** – note that mercury thermometers are prohibited by airlines

clinics and surgeries, or for emergency flights home. If you want to avoid paying for these, you'll need to take out medical travel insurance. See Travel Insurance under Visas & Documents earlier in this chapter for more information.

Many US health insurance policies are valid, at least for a limited period, if you travel abroad. Most non-European national health plans aren't, so you must take out special medical insurance.

General Preparations

If you require a particular medication, take an adequate supply as well as the prescription, with the generic rather than the brand name, which will make getting replacements easier.

There are no vaccination requirements for any international travellers to Spain but it is advisable to be up to date with polio, diptheria and tetanus vaccinations.

Medical Services

If you need an ambulance anywhere in Catalunya call ☎ 061 or the general emergency number ☎ 112.

For serious medical problems, the Spanish public health service provides care to rival that of any country in the world. Seeing a doctor about something more mundane can be less than enchanting, however, because of queues and obscure appointment systems, though you should get decent attention in the end. The expense of going to a private clinic or surgery often saves time and frustration: you'll typically pay €18 to €36 for a consultation (not counting medicines). All dental practices are private.

If you want see a doctor quickly, or need emergency dental treatment, one way is to go along to the *urgències* (emergency) section of the nearest hospital. Many towns also have a *centre de salut/centro de salud* (health centre) with an emergency section.

Take along as much documentation as you can when dealing with medical services – passport, E111 with photocopies, insurance papers.

Pharmacies *(farmàcies/farmacias)* can help with many ailments. A system of duty pharmacies *(farmàcies de torn/farmacias de guardia)* ensures that each town or city district has a pharmacy open at least from around 7 am to 10 pm. When a pharmacy is closed, it posts on the door the name of the nearest open one.

Environmental Hazards

Altitude Sickness Symptoms of Acute Mountain Sickness (AMS) usually develop during the first 24 hours at altitudes of 2500m and over but may be delayed up to three weeks. Mild symptoms include headache, lethargy, dizziness, difficulty sleeping and loss of appetite. Severe symptoms include breathlessness, a dry, irritating cough, severe headache, lack of coordination and balance, confusion, irrational behaviour, vomiting, drowsiness and unconsciousness.

There is no hard-and-fast rule on what is too high: AMS has been fatal at 3000m, although 3500m to 4500m is the usual range. It is thus fairly unlikely to be a problem in the Pyrenees (the highest peak in the Catalan Pyrenees, the Pica d'Estats, is 3143m).

If difficulties occur, treat mild symptoms by resting at the same altitude until recovery, usually a day or two. You can take paracetamol or aspirin for headaches. If symptoms persist or worsen, *immediate descent is necessary*; even 500m can help.

Heat Exhaustion & Prickly Heat Dehydration and salt deficiency can cause heat exhaustion. Take time to acclimatise to high temperatures, drink sufficient liquids and be careful not to do anything too physically demanding.

Salt deficiency is characterised by fatigue, lethargy, headaches, giddiness and muscle cramps; salt tablets may help, but adding extra salt to your food is better.

Prickly heat, an itchy rash caused by excessive perspiration trapped under the skin, usually strikes people who have just arrived in a hot climate. Keeping cool, bathing often, drying the skin and using a mild talcum or prickly heat powder, or resorting to air-conditioning, may help.

Heatstroke This serious, occasionally fatal, condition can occur if the body's heat-regulating mechanism breaks down and the body temperature rises to dangerous levels. Long, continuous periods of exposure to high temperatures and insufficient fluids can leave you vulnerable to heatstroke.

The symptoms are feeling unwell, not

sweating very much (or at all) and a high body temperature (39°C to 41°C, 102°F to 106°F). Where sweating has ceased, the skin becomes flushed and red. Severe, throbbing headaches and lack of coordination will occur, and the sufferer may be confused or aggressive. Eventually the victim will become delirious or convulsive. Hospitalisation is essential, but meanwhile get victims out of the sun, remove their clothing, cover them with a wet sheet or towel and then fan continually. Give fluids if they are conscious.

Cuts, Bites & Stings
Jellyfish Jellyfish *(medusas)* generally occur either in large numbers or hardly at all. Heeding local advice is the best way to avoid them. If you are stung, dousing in vinegar will deactivate any jellyfish stingers that have not 'fired'. Calamine lotion, antihistamines and analgesics may reduce the reaction and relieve the pain.

Ticks Check for ticks all over your body if you have been walking through a potentially tick-infested area, such as long grass or woodlands in spring or summer, as ticks can cause skin infections and other more serious diseases. If a tick is found attached, press down around its head with tweezers, grab the head and gently pull upwards. Avoid pulling the rear of the body as this may squeeze the tick's gut contents through the attached mouth parts into the skin, increasing the risk of infection and disease.

Infectious Diseases
Diarrhoea Simple things like a change of water, food or climate can all cause a mild bout of diarrhoea, but a few rushed toilet trips with no other symptoms is not indicative of a major problem.

Dehydration is the main danger with any diarrhoea, particularly in children or the elderly. Under all circumstances fluid replacement (at least equal to the volume being lost) is the most important thing to remember. Weak black tea with a little sugar, soda water, or soft drinks allowed to go flat and diluted 50% with clean water are all good. With severe diarrhoea a rehydrating

solution is preferable to replace minerals and salts lost. Commercially available oral rehydration salts (ORS) are very useful. In an emergency you can make up a solution of six teaspoons of sugar and a half teaspoon of salt to a litre of clean water. Keep drinking small amounts often. Stick to a bland diet as you recover.

Gut-paralysing drugs such as loperamide or diphenoxylate can be used to bring relief from the symptoms, although they do not actually cure the problem. Only use these drugs if you do not have access to toilets (eg, if you *must* travel). Note that these drugs are not recommended for children under 12 years.

Antibiotics may be required in certain situations such as: diarrhoea with blood or mucus (dysentery), any diarrhoea with fever, profuse watery diarrhoea, persistent diarrhoea not improving after 48 hours and severe diarrhoea. These suggest a more serious cause of diarrhoea and in these situations gut-paralysing drugs should be avoided.

Hepatitis Hepatitis is a general term for inflammation of the liver. The symptoms are similar in all forms of the illness, and include fever, chills, headache, fatigue, feelings of weakness and aches and pains, followed by loss of appetite, nausea, vomiting, abdominal pain, dark urine, light-coloured faeces, jaundiced (yellow) skin and yellowing of the whites of the eyes. People who have had hepatitis should avoid alcohol for some time after the illness, as the liver needs time to recover.

Hepatitis A is transmitted by contaminated food and drinking water. You should seek medical advice, but there is not much you can do apart from resting, drinking lots of fluids, eating lightly and avoiding fatty foods.

Hepatitis B is spread through contact with infected blood, blood products or body fluids – for example through sexual contact, unsterilised needles and blood transfusions, or contact with blood via small breaks in the skin. Other risk situations include having a shave, tattoo or body piercing with contaminated equipment. The symptoms of hepatitis B may be more severe than type A and the disease can lead to long-term problems such as chronic liver damage, liver cancer or a long-term carrier state.

HIV & AIDS Infection with the human immunodeficiency virus (HIV) may lead to acquired immune deficiency syndrome (AIDS), which is a fatal disease. Any exposure to blood, blood products or body fluids may put the individual at risk. The disease is often transmitted through sexual contact or dirty needles – vaccinations, acupuncture, tattooing and body piercing can be potentially as dangerous as intravenous drug use. HIV/AIDS can also be spread through infected blood transfusions; blood used for transfusions in European hospitals is screened for HIV and should be safe.

HIV and AIDS are *VIH* and *sida*, respectively, in Spanish. The Fundación Anti-Sida España has a free information line on ☎ 900 11 10 00 and a Web site at Ⓦ www.fase.es. You can call Stop Sida on ☎ 900 60 16 01.

Sexually Transmitted Diseases Hepatitis B and HIV/AIDS can be transmitted through sexual contact – see the relevant sections earlier for more details. Other STDs include gonorrhoea, herpes and syphilis; sores, blisters or rashes around the genitals and discharges or pain when urinating are common symptoms. In some STDs, such as wart virus or chlamydia, symptoms may be less marked or not observed at all, especially in women. Chlamydia infection can cause infertility in men and women before any symptoms have been noticed. Syphilis symptoms eventually disappear completely but the disease continues and can cause severe problems in later years. While abstinence from sexual contact is the only 100% effective prevention, using condoms is also effective. The treatment of gonorrhoea and syphilis is with antibiotics. The different sexually transmitted diseases each require specific antibiotics.

Women's Health
Gynaecological Problems Antibiotic use, synthetic underwear, sweating and contraceptive pills can lead to fungal vaginal infections, especially when travelling in hot climates. Fungal infections are characterised by a rash, itch and discharge and can be treated with a vinegar or lemon-juice douche, or with natural yoghurt. Nystatin, miconazole or clotrimazole pessaries or vaginal cream are the usual treatment. Maintaining good personal hygiene and wearing loose-fitting clothes and cotton underwear may help prevent these infections.

Sexually transmitted diseases are a major cause of vaginal problems. Symptoms include a smelly discharge, painful intercourse and sometimes a burning sensation when urinating. Medical attention should be sought and male sexual partners must also be treated. For more details see Sexually Transmitted Diseases earlier. Besides abstinence, the best thing is to practise safer sex using condoms.

Pregnancy Pregnant women should take extra care when travelling, particularly in the first three months of pregnancy. Generally, it's best to avoid all vaccinations in those first three months as there's a theoretical risk of harm to the fetus, and of miscarriage. The best time to travel is during the middle three months when the risk of complications is less, the pregnancy is relatively well established and your energy levels are getting back to normal. Seek medical advice from your medical practitioner before travelling.

WOMEN TRAVELLERS
Women travellers should be ready to ignore stares, catcalls and unnecessary comments, although harassment is much less frequent than you might expect.

You still need to exercise common sense about where you go on your own. Think twice about going by yourself to isolated stretches of beach, lonely country areas or down empty city streets at night. Where there are crowds you are safer. It's highly inadvisable for a woman to hitchhike alone – and not a great idea even for two women together.

Topless bathing is OK on beaches in Catalunya and also at swimming pools. While skimpy clothing tends not to attract much attention in Barcelona and the coastal resorts, tastes in inland Catalunya tend to be somewhat conservative.

Organisations

The first stop for anyone seeking information on women's issues should be the Institut Català de la Dona (Map 4; ☎ 93 495 16 00), Carrer de Portaferrissa 1–3, Barcelona. They can point you in the right direction for: information on rape/assault counselling; marriage, divorce and related issues for long-termers; social activities, women's clubs and so on.

Also in Barcelona, Ca la Dona (Map 2; ☎ 93 412 71 61), Carrer de Casp 38, is the nerve centre of the region's feminist movement. It includes about 25 diverse women's groups and has been going since 1988.

On the subject of assault, the nationwide Comisión de Investigación de Malos Tratos a Mujeres (Commission of Investigation into the Abuse of Women) has a free 24-hour national emergency line for victims of physical abuse: ☎ 900 10 00 09. English may be in short supply, however.

GAY & LESBIAN TRAVELLERS

Gay and lesbian sex are both legal in Spain and the age of consent is 16 years, the same as for heterosexuals. Catalunya went a step further in October 1998 by introducing a law recognising de facto gay and lesbian couples (but not their right to marry or have children).

Barcelona has a busy gay scene but the region's gay capital is no doubt the saucily hedonistic Sitges, a major destination on the international gay party circuit. Gays take a leading role in the wild Carnaval celebrations there in February/March (see Festivals under Public Holidays & Special Events later in the chapter).

Entiendes, a gay magazine, sells for €3. *Mensual* (also €3) is a monthly gay guys' listings magazine with bars, hotels, saunas and so on for all of Spain. It is available in gay bookshops. *Nosotras* is a bi-monthly lesbian review.

An international gay guide worth tracking down is the *Spartacus Guide for Gay Men*, published by Bruno Gmünder Verlag,

Mail Order, PO Box 61 01 04, 10921 Berlin. It is not always terribly up to date, but it's a good start. The Spartacus list also includes the comprehensive *Spartacus National Edition España*, in English and German. Lesbians might try *Damron Women's Traveller 2001*, which is available on-line at Ⓦ www.damron.com.

The Barcelona-based Coordinadora Gai-Lesbiana has a good Web site with nationwide links at Ⓦ www.pangea.org/org/cgl. Here you can zero in on information ranging from bar, sauna and hotel listings through to contacts pages. Apart from Barcelona, you will find information on the rest of Catalunya and links to other parts of Spain. Other sources of listings are at Ⓦ www.gayinspain.com and also Ⓦ www.gaybarcelona.net.

Organisations

There are several gay organisations in Barcelona. Casal Lambda (Map 4; ☎ 93 412 72 72) at Carrer Ample 5 in the Barri Gòtic (Gothic Quarter) is a gay and lesbian social, cultural and information centre. Coordinadora Gai-Lesbiana (Map 1; ☎ 93 298 00 29, fax 93 298 06 18, Ⓔ cogailes@pangea.org), Carrer de Finlàndia 45, is the city's main coordinating body for gay and lesbian groups. Some of the latter, such as Grup de Lesbianes Feministes (☎ 93 412 77 01), are to be found at Ca la Dona (see Women Travellers earlier). There is a free gay helpline (which is also the number for Stop Sida, the AIDS helpline) on ☎ 900 60 16 01.

DISABLED TRAVELLERS

Some Spanish tourist offices in other countries can provide a basic information sheet with some useful addresses for disabled travellers and give details of accessible accommodation in specific places.

You'll find some accessible accommodation in main centres but it may not be in the budget category. Many hotels that claim to be accessible retain problem features.

The UK-based Royal Association for Disability & Rehabilitation (RADAR) publishes a useful guide called *European*

Holidays & Travel Abroad: A Guide for Disabled People, which provides a good overview of the facilities available to disabled travellers throughout Europe. Contact RADAR (☎ 020-7250 3222, ⓦ www .radar.org.uk), Unit 12, City Forum, 250 City Rd, London EC1V 8AS.

Another organisation worth calling is Holiday Care (☎ 01293-774535), 2nd floor, Imperial Buildings, Victoria Rd, Horley, Surrey RH6 7PZ. It produces an information pack on Spain for disabled people and others with special needs. Tips range from hotels with disabled access through to where you can hire equipment and find tour operators dealing with the disabled.

Organisations

In Catalunya ECOM (Map 3; ☎ 93 451 55 50, fax 93 451 69 04), Spain's federation of private organisations for the disabled, is at Gran Via de les Corts Catalanes 562, 08011 Barcelona. They can provide information on accommodation with disabled people's facilities and public and private transport options, as well as leisure time and holiday possibilities in and around Barcelona.

For more city information you could also try the Institut Municipal de Persones amb Disminució (Map 1; ☎ 93 291 84 00, fax 93 423 26 49), Carrer de Llacuna 161.

SENIOR TRAVELLERS

There are reduced prices for people aged over 60, 63 or 65 (depending on the place) at some attractions and occasionally on transport. You usually need to provide ID for proof of age. It is always worth asking. You should also seek information in your own country on travel packages and discounts for senior travellers, through senior citizens' organisations and travel agents.

TRAVEL WITH CHILDREN

You will generally have no problem taking your kids about with you in restaurants, hotels, cafes and the like, though few locals are inclined to take their *peques* (little ones) out for a night on the tiles.

Kids can open doors where adults alone never would. This is especially so where a language barrier impedes communication – cute kids doing the things that cute kids sometimes do can be a great ice-breaker.

Catalans have fewer qualms about keeping their children up late than people from more northerly climes. In summer especially, you'll see them at the local festes until the small hours. Taking children to cafes or snack bars that have outdoor tables (preferably in pedestrian zones) is no problem at all. Of course your wee bairn's body clock may not quite be up to it.

Most children don't like moving around too much but are happier if they can settle into places and make friends. It's easier on the parents too if you don't have to pack up all their gear and move on every day or two. Children are also likely to need extra time to acclimatise and extra care to avoid sunburn. Be prepared for minor health problems brought on by the change of diet or water or disrupted sleeping patterns.

Busy street life and the novelty of new places provide some distraction for most kids but they'll get bored unless some of the time is devoted to their favoured activities. The beaches are an obvious attraction.

Any adult deliberately found not taking their children to the Port Aventura amusement park (7km west of Tarragona; see the Costa Daurada & the South-West chapter) could probably be accused of unusual cruelty to minors. In Barcelona kids generally like L'Aquàrium (and the nearby Imax cinema), the Tibidabo fun park, the *funicular aereo* (cable car) and boat rides. Just a wander down La Rambla to gawk at all the street acts (clowns, living statues and the like) often scores high points with kids.

Bring some of the children's own toys, books etc and let them have time to get on with some of the activities they are used to back at home.

Nappies, creams, lotions, baby foods etc are as easily available in Spain as in any other western country, but if there's some particular brand you swear by it's best to bring it with you.

Children benefit from cut-price or free entry at many sights and museums. Those under four travel free on Spanish trains and those aged four to 11 normally pay 60% of the adult fare.

Lonely Planet's *Travel with Children* has lots of practical advice and first-hand stories from many Lonely Planet authors and others.

USEFUL ORGANISATIONS

The Instituto Cervantes, with branches in over 30 cities around the world, exists to promote the Spanish language and culture (it's not too hot on Catalan, however!). It's mainly involved in Spanish teaching and library and information services. The library at the London branch (☎ 020-7235 0353), 102 Eaton Square, London SW1W 9AN, has a wide range of reference books, literature, books on history and the arts, periodicals, over 1000 videos including feature films, language-teaching material, electronic databases and music CDs. In New York, the institute (☎ 212-689 4232) is at 122 East 42nd St, suite 807, New York, NY 10168. You can find further addresses on the institute's Web site at [W] www.cervantes.es.

Catalunya, together with the Balearic Islands, hopes to get a modest counterpart of the Instituto Cervantes off the ground – the Institut Ramon Llull. Although it would have branches in Barcelona and Palma de Mallorca only, the idea would be similar: to diffuse Catalan language and culture into the wider world. The Balearic Islands, once a possession of the Crown of Aragón, form a separate region but their inhabitants speak several dialects of Catalan.

DANGERS & ANNOYANCES

Catalunya is pretty safe territory. The main thing you have to be wary of is petty theft (which may of course not seem so petty to you if your passport, cash, travellers cheques, credit card and camera all go missing). However, with a few simple precautions you can minimise the risk and any worries.

Before you leave home, inscribe your name, address and telephone number *inside* your luggage and take photocopies of the important pages of your passport, travel tickets and other important documents. Keep the copies separate from the originals and ideally leave one set of copies at home.

In Case of Emergency

In general you can reach the Policía Nacional anywhere on ☎ 091, while the Guàrdia Urbana are on ☎ 092. Numbers for the Mossos d'Esquadra (☎ 088) and Guardia Civil (☎ 062) can vary from the norm in some areas.

You can often get the fire brigade *(bomberos)* on ☎ 080, but in some cases other local numbers are used. In most areas an ambulance can be reached on ☎ 061.

Remember that the national emergency number, ☎ 112, only *theoretically* gives you access to all emergency services throughout Catalunya. In reality, it seems that this number is still hit and miss in remoter areas.

These steps will make things easier if you do suffer a loss or theft.

Travel insurance against theft and loss is another good idea.

Theft & Loss

Downtown Barcelona is the main playground for pickpockets, bag-snatchers and the occasional mugger. The Costa Brava resorts and other tourist magnets like Figueres can also be a problem.

You are most at risk from theft when you first arrive somewhere with all your bags and are probably disoriented. Beware on Barcelona's public transport, at the train and bus stations and when looking for your hotel.

Carry valuables under your clothes if possible – not in a back pocket, a day pack or anything that could be snatched away easily – and keep your eyes open for people who get unnecessarily close to you on the streets and in public transport. Don't leave baggage unattended and avoid crushes. Also be cautious with people who come up to offer or ask you something (like the time or directions) or start talking to you for no obviously good reason. These could be attempts to distract you and make you an easier victim.

Anything left lying on the beach can disappear in a flash when your back is turned. At night avoid dingy, empty city alleys and

La Policía – Who's Who

Those of you used to the idea of the police being one single national corps of law enforcement folk will have to retune in Catalunya. There seems to be a different force for every occasion.

On the whole they are all courteous enough to the average law-abiding traveller with a problem or street direction quandary.

There are four main types of *policía*. Across Spain the Policía Nacional is the main civil force (these are the guys you need to see if you are robbed). The Guardia Civil also operates on a national level. Catalunya's own regional force is the Mossos d'Esquadra. Local urban police forces tend to be known as the Guàrdia Urbana, although you may come across the term used elsewhere in Spain – where they're usually called the Policía Local (aka Policía Municipal). In Spanish a *policía* also means a policeman, just as *guardia* means an individual Guardia Civil.

Guardia Civil

The main responsibilities of the green-uniformed members of the Guardia Civil are roads, the countryside, villages, prisons, international borders and some environmental protection.

The Guardia Civil was set up in the 19th century to quell banditry but soon came to be regarded as a politically repressive force that clamped down on any challenge to established privilege. Although its image has softened since responsibility for it has been switched from the defence ministry to the interior ministry, it's still a military body in some ways: most officers have attended military academy and members qualify for military decorations.

Policía Nacional

This force covers cities and bigger towns and is the main crime-fighting body because most crime happens on its patch. Those who wear uniforms are in blue. There is also a large contingent in plain clothes, some of whom form special squads dealing with drugs, terrorism and the like. Most of them will be found in large bunker-like police stations called *comisarías*, shuffling masses of paper and

back streets, or anywhere that just doesn't feel 100% safe.

You can also help yourself by not leaving anything valuable lying around your room, above all in any hostel-type place. Use a safe if one is available.

Remember that theft from cars, especially with foreign plates or of the hired variety, is far from uncommon. And it can happen in broad daylight even if you leave the car unattended for an hour or so! Always remove the radio and CD/cassette player and never leave any belongings visible when you leave the car. Better still, don't leave anything in an unattended car (admittedly often harder than it sounds).

Highway robbery, especially along the A-7 between the French border and Barcelona, is back in vogue. According to police reports, bands of Peruvians and Romanians dominate this trade. Cars parked in service stations along the highway are often targeted. Even while driving you are at risk. There have been cases of cars being stopped and emptied by these bandits, occasionally with violence or the threat of it. If you see people trying to wave you down, ignore them.

If anything valuable does go missing, you'll need to report it to the police and get a copy of the report if you want to make an insurance claim. If your passport has gone, contact your embassy or consulate for help in issuing a replacement (see Embassies & Consulates earlier in the chapter).

Terrorism

Although terrorists of the Basque Country's Euskadi ta Askatasuna (ETA; Basque Nation & Liberty) concentrate their efforts elsewhere, they don't mind carrying out the occasional operation in Catalunya. Between 1975 and 2000 a total of 48 people died at

La Policía – Who's Who

dealing with things like issuing passports, *documentos nacionales de identidad* (DNIs; national identity cards) and residence cards for foreigners who like Spain enough to opt for long-term entanglement with its bureaucracy. The Policía and Guardia Civil frequently find themselves treading on each other's patch.

Mossos d'Esquadra

Some of Spain's autonomous regions have their own police forces and Catalunya is one of them. The Mossos d'Esquadra are gradually raising their profile. In the late 1990s they took over highway patrol duties in the region from the Guardia Civil. Interestingly, the Mossos were first raised in the 18th century to combat anti-Madrid guerrillas operating in the Catalan countryside after defeat in the War of the Spanish Succession in 1714. Nevertheless, it seems extraordinary that a region of little more than six million people should require three police forces! Catalans would no doubt like to see at least the Guardia Civil removed altogether.

Guàrdia Urbana (Policía Local)

The Guàrdia Urbana are controlled by city and town councils and deal mainly with minor matters such as parking, traffic and bylaws.

Contacting the Police

In general the traveller will need to deal with the Policía Nacional for passport matters and petty crime such as theft. If you lose your passport or whatever and need a police statement for insurance purposes, these are your people.

Для traffic infringements, recovering towed cars and so on, go to the Guàrdia Urbana. It is unlikely you'll need to deal directly with either the Mossos d'Esquadra or the Guardia Civil, unless you get hauled over for a highway offence or happen to be a terrorist.

---

the hands of the separatists, the latest victim being a conservative Partido Popular (PP; People's Party) politician in September 2000. Since ETA broke its cease-fire in 1999, it has focused its campaign largely on conservative politicians. The problem for Spain is real although the chances of being caught up in the struggle are highly remote.

Annoyances

There isn't a whole lot to get annoyed about in Catalunya. On the whole most things work well, service is fairly prompt and people courteous. In Barcelona and other urban centres you will need to get used to a lot of racket from scooters, late night bars, intense traffic and the like. Elsewhere things range from tolerably vibrant to blissfully silent. Lager louts imported from beyond the Pyrenees can be a pain in the big seaside resorts.

LEGAL MATTERS

If you're arrested you will be allotted the free services of a duty solicitor *(abogado de oficio)*, who may speak only Catalan or Spanish. You're also entitled to make a phone call. If you use this to contact your embassy or consulate, the staff will probably be able to do no more than refer you to a lawyer who speaks your own language. If you are unfortunate enough to end up in court, the authorities are obliged to provide a translator.

Drugs

The only legal drug is cannabis and it's only legal in amounts for personal use, which means very small amounts. In the occasional bar people smoke the stuff openly, but the more liberal days of the late 1980s are long gone and discretion has become the better part of valour.

BUSINESS HOURS

Generally, Catalans work Monday to Friday from about 9 am to 2 pm and then again from 4.30 or 5 pm for another three hours. Shops and travel agencies are usually open these hours on Saturday too, though some may skip the evening session. In summer, many people work a *jornada intensiva* (intensive working day), starting as early as 7 am and finishing the day by 2 pm.

Big supermarkets, and department stores such as the nationwide El Corte Inglés chain, often stay open from about 9 am to 9 pm, Monday to Saturday. A few shops in tourist resorts open on Sunday in the summer. A lot of government offices don't bother opening in the afternoon on any day of the year.

Museums all have their own opening hours: major ones tend to open for something like normal Spanish business hours (with or without the afternoon break) but often have their weekly closing day on Monday.

For bank and post office hours see Exchanging Money under Money and Sending Mail under Post & Communications, respectively, earlier in the chapter.

PUBLIC HOLIDAYS & SPECIAL EVENTS

The two main periods when Catalans go on holiday are Setmana Santa (the week leading up to Easter Sunday) and, more noticeably, the month of August. Many tend to vacation in other parts of the region and are joined by plenty of Spaniards from elsewhere around the country and a growing foreign contingent. The highways on key weekends from mid-July to the end of August can be a nightmare of departing and returning holiday-makers.

Public Holidays

In Catalunya, as in the rest of Spain, there are 14 official holidays a year – some observed nationwide, some locally. When a holiday falls close to a weekend, people like to make a *puente* (bridge) – meaning they take the intervening day off too. On the odd occasion when a couple of holidays fall close together, they make an *acueducto*

(aqueduct)! Offices, banks and many shops close on holidays. Restaurants, bars and the like soldier on, as do most museums and other sights and attractions.

The seven national holidays are:

Any Nou/Año Nuevo (New Year's Day) 1 January – Plenty of parties in the discos and clubs on New Year's Eve (Cap d'Any/Noche Vieja) – expect to pay higher than usual prices. As the clock strikes midnight you are expected to eat a grape for each chime.

Divendres Sant/Viernes Santo (Good Friday) March/April – Although not, in general, celebrated with the verve it is accorded farther south in Spain, you get a taste of it in some places. In Barcelona, for instance, you can observe the procession from the Església de Sant Agustí in El Raval in the early afternoon of Good Friday. Accompanying the float bearing an image of the Virgin that is the centrepiece of the march (which then proceeds up La Rambla and on to Plaça de Catalunya) are solemn bands, members of various religious fraternities *(confraries)* dressed in robes and tall conical hoods. Most striking are the barefoot women penitents dressed in black and dragging heavy crosses and chains around their ankles. Easter celebrations take place all over Catalunya. On Palm Sunday, Vic holds its Mercat del Ram (Palm Sunday cattle market). The dramatised dance procession, or Moixiganga, during Holy Week in Sitges is worth catching. Other towns where the tradition of Easter processions is strong include: Badalona, Bossòst, Esterri d'Àneu, Girona, Tarragona and Vic. By far the most spectacular Easter celebration is the Dansa de la Mort (Dance of Death) held on Holy Thursday night in the small town of Verges.

Dia del Treball/Fiesta del Trabajo (Labour Day) 1 May – Labour Day once attracted big demonstrations in Barcelona. That is all but a memory nowadays – you'll probably hardly notice it's a holiday except for all the closed offices, banks and shops.

L'Assumpció/La Asunción (Feast of the Assumption) 15 August

Festa de la Hispanitat/Día de la Hispanidad (Spanish National Day) 12 October – The day off is appreciated, but no special celebrations mark this occasion in Catalunya.

La Immaculada Concepció/La Inmaculada Concepción (Feast of the Immaculate Conception) 8 December

Nadal/Navidad (Christmas) 25 December – This is a family time. Many celebrate with a big midday meal, although some prefer to eat on

Christmas Eve (Nit de Nadal/Nochebuena). In the run-up to Christmas it is customary in many places to build *pessebres* (Nativity scenes). A big one is set up in front of the cathedral in Barcelona. Markets dedicated to Santa Llúcia, where you can buy the figurines, moss and other ingredients to make your own one at home, spring up in towns across Catalunya at this time. *Pastorets*, or Nativity plays, are also staged in various towns (such as Mataró, Berga and El Vendrell). In the mountains, villagers tend to celebrate Christmas with bonfires.

In addition to these national holidays, the Generalitat adds the following holidays during the year:

Epifanía (Epiphany) or El Dia dels Reis/Día de los Reyes Magos (Three Kings' Day) 6 January – This is when children traditionally receive presents (generally they get little or nothing at Christmas). The night before is marked by colourful parades of the three kings in towns across the region.

Dilluns de Pasqua Florida (Easter Monday) April – Easter celebrations wind down in what for most people is a welcome extra day off work.

Dia de Sant Joan/Día de San Juan Bautista (Feast of St John the Baptist) 24 June – The evening before (Berbena de Sant Joan or Verbena de San Juan Bautista), the people of Barcelona hit the streets or hold parties at home to celebrate, with an evening of drinking, dancing, fireworks and bonfires. Bonfires can be seen in districts throughout Catalunya, for which reason the evening is also known as La Nit del Foc, or Fire Night. In Barcelona, Montjuïc lights up to a massive display of fireworks, while in the small north-western village of Isil, a dramatic torch-lit parade begins high up in the hills and ends when the torches are all flung together to form a bonfire in the town centre. The traditional pastry to eat on this summer solstice is a kind of dense candied cake known as *coca de Sant Joan*.

Diada Nacional de Catalunya 11 September – Catalunya's national day commemorates Barcelona's surrender to the Spaniards at the end

Of Giants, Dragons & Fire-Running

As befits a people of such independent traditions, Catalans get up to all sorts of unusual tricks at *festa* (festival) time. And festa time is a lot of the time!

Fire and fireworks play a big part in many Spanish festivals but Catalunya adds a special twist with the *correfoc* (fire-running), in which devil and dragon figures run through the streets spitting fireworks at the crowds (wear protective clothes if you intend to get close!). Correfocs are often part of the *festa major* – a town or village's main annual festival. Many of these are held from July through to the end of September.

Also usually part of the festa-major fun are the *sardana* (Catalunya's national round-dance), all sorts of costumed local dances, and *gegants*, splendidly attired and lifelike 5m-high giants who parade through the streets or dance in the squares to the sound of old-fashioned instruments. Giants usually come in male-female pairs: a medieval king and queen, a Muslim sultan and a Christian princess. Almost every town and village has its own – sometimes just one pair, sometimes five or six. They're usually accompanied by an entourage of grotesque 'dwarfs' (otherwise known as *capgrossos*, or bigheads).

On La Nit de Sant Joan, 23 June, big bonfires burn at crossroads and on town squares in a combined midsummer and St John's Eve celebration. Fireworks go on all night. But Catalunya's supreme fire festival is the Patum, a Corpus Christi (the Thursday following the eighth Sunday after Easter Sunday) celebration in the otherwise unexceptional Pyrenean foothill town of Berga. An evening of dancing and firework-spitting angels, devils, mule-like monsters, dwarfs, giants and men covered in grass culminates in a kind of mass frenzy of fire and smoke that has been likened to a medieval vision of hell. The main event happens on Corpus Christi though there are watered-down versions on the next two or three days.

of the War of the Spanish Succession in 1714. It is a relatively sober occasion, when small independence groups demand the predictable without anyone paying too much attention.

El Dia de Sant Esteve 26 December – The local equivalent of Boxing Day, it is a family occasion, much like Christmas Day, with festive lunches.

Finally, local governments add two holidays of their own. Some of the more interesting ones are included under Festivals in the next section. The following are celebrated in Barcelona:

Dilluns de Pasqua Granda May/June – The day after Pentecost Sunday.

Festes de la Mercè 24 September – This four-day burst of festivities begins shortly after the official close of summer and acts as a final round of pre-winter madness all over Barcelona, although the bulk of the activities takes place in the centre of town. It is a fun time to be in Barcelona and features a wild *correfoc* (fire-running; see the boxed text 'Of Giants, Dragons & Fire-running' earlier), *castellers* (human-castle builders), parades of gegants and capgrossos, musical events and loads of other activities and performances.

Festivals

Catalunya's calendar is rich in festivities of all sorts year round. Some fall on official holidays decided by local governments while others range from saints' days to more pagan knees-ups. They often involve a colourful display of traditional activities, dances and parades. Most towns celebrate a *festa major* (main festival) once a year. There is no shortage of arts and cultural festivals too. What follows is an introductory list of some of the more interesting festivals around the region.

Cavalcada dels Reis 5 January – The day preceding Epiphany (a public holiday) sees the three kings 'arrive' in Barcelona at Moll de la Fusta and then parade up into town (the route tends to change). As the kings parade around with floats, they hurl sweets to the kids in the crowd. Similar parades take place at towns all over Catalunya.

Festes dels Tres Tombs 17 January – A key part of the district festival of Sant Antoni in Barcelona, the Festival of the Three Circuits involves a parade of horsemen who march around Ronda de Sant Antoni to Plaça de Catalunya, down La Rambla and back up Carrer Nou de la Rambla. Sant Antoni Abat (St Anthony the Abbot) is the patron saint of muleteers. The procession is also staged at Vilafranca del Penedès, Igualada and Valls among others.

Festes de Santa Eulàlia February (Barcelona) – Coinciding with Carnaval (see the following entry), this is the feast of Barcelona's first patron saint. The Ajuntament organises all sorts of cultural events, from concerts through to performances by castellers and the appearance of *mulasses* (strange mule-like creatures) in the main parade.

Carnestoltes/Carnaval (Carnival) February/March – Several days of fancy-dress parades and merrymaking, usually ending on the Tuesday 47 days before Easter Sunday. The most popular Carnaval celebrations in Catalunya take place in Vilanova i la Geltrú. The festival kicks off on the Thursday before Shrove Tuesday with the *xatonada*, a feast with *xató* (a local spicy salad speciality) as its base. On Friday the carnival king arrives to declare the law of merrymaking that keeps the people happy for the weekend with masked balls and fancy-dress parades. In Barcelona there are parades and dancing for about 10 days. The celebrations are wildest in Sitges, where Carnaval marks the first stirrings of the party atmosphere that will grip the town from spring.

Dia de Sant Jordi 23 April – The day of Catalunya's patron saint, St George, and also the Day of the Book – men give women a rose, women give men a book; publishers launch new titles. In Barcelona La Rambla and Plaça de Sant Jaume (where the Generalitat building is open to the public) are filled with flower and book stalls.

Festa Major 11 May (Lleida) – This is held to celebrate the memory of Sant Anastasi. Lleida's big festival features parades of gegants and other characters around town, the most intimidating of whom is the Marraco, the town dragon. For gourmets, the big attraction of the festa is the Aplec del Cargol, or snail fest.

Patum May/June (Berga) – In a region where playing with fire seems to be the norm (witness the many occasions on which Catalan towns stage the crackling correfoc), Berga beats them all with this devilishly fiery celebration of Corpus Christi (the Thursday after the eighth Sunday after Easter Sunday). The fiery dance of some 40 devils armed to the teeth with spluttering fireworks in the main square is preceded by dances featuring gegants and capgrossos, angels and devils, charging *mules guites* (mule-like monsters equally well armed with fireworks) and a mock battle between Turcs and Cavellets (roughly Moors versus Christians).

L'Ou com Balla May/June (Barcelona) – A curious tradition with several centuries of history, the 'Dancing Egg' is an empty shell that bobs on top of the flower-festooned fountain in the cloister of the cathedral. This spectacle is Barcelona's way of celebrating Corpus Christi. Other dancing eggs can be seen on the same day in the courtyard of the Casa de l'Ardiaca and various other fountains in the Barri Gòtic.

Dia per l'Alliberament Lesbià i Gai 28 June (Barcelona) – Gay and lesbian festival and parade.

Festa Major de Gràcia Around 15 August (Barcelona) – Apart from the Festes de la Mercè, this is one of the biggest local festivals in Barcelona. More than a dozen streets in Gràcia are decorated by their inhabitants according to a certain theme as part of a competition for the most imaginative street of the year. Locals set up tables and benches to enjoy local feasts, but people from all over the city pour in to participate. In squares (particularly Plaça del Sol) and intersections all over the *barri* (quarter), bands compete for attention. Snack stands abound and numerous bars that open onto the streets to sell rivers of drink. Local residents who hope to get any sleep in this week tend to move to friends' places or leave town!

Festa Major 7–10 September (Solsona) – This is one of the town's two big annual get-togethers, the other being Carnaval. Along with the usual parades of gegants, a dragon and other town beasties, you can see the curious Catalan stick dancing *(ball dels bastons)*. These feature young people in stylised clashes with long poles. The dance is thought to have its routes in ritualised sword fights staged by the ancient Greeks. In some surrounding villages, this is the time of the *matança*, or pig slaughter (and subsequent sausage-making and feasting).

Festa de Sant Martin 11 November – Beyond the *comarca* (district) of Solsona, it is customary in many villages to celebrate the matança on this saint's day. Meals are generally accompanied by the new year's young wines.

Arts & Music Festivals

Barcelona plays host to several arts-oriented festivals in the course of the year. Not to be left out, various other towns around the region also get in on the act. Among the more important dates are:

Sonar June (Barcelona) – This is claimed to be Europe's biggest celebration of electronic music, where you can get into the latest house, hip-hop, trip-hop and eurobeat.

Festival del Grec Late June to August (Barcelona) – Many theatres shut down for the summer but into the breach steps this eclectic program of theatre, dance and music. Performances are held all over the city, not just at the amphitheatre on Montjuïc from which the festival takes its name.

Senglar Rock August (Montblanc) – Since 1998 this has been the biggest concert to bring together Catalan rock bands.

Mercat de Música September (Vic) – Several days of Latin rock featuring local and foreign acts.

BAM Around 24 September (Barcelona) – All the great (mostly) free music put on for the Festes de la Mercè is organised as Barcelona Acció Musical. Most of the performances take place in squares in the centre of town and/or on the waterfront.

International Fantasy Film Festival October (Sitges) – A celebration of off-the-wall cinema from around the world.

Festival de Músicas Contemporáneas October (Barcelona) – Mix of styles from jazz to electronic and beyond, first held in 1994 and since 2000 staged in L'Auditori.

Festival Internacional de Jazz de Barcelona Late October to late November (Barcelona) – Jazz and blues around the city.

ACTIVITIES

Catalunya offers one of the widest spectra of activities of any of Spain's regions. In the Pyrenees, for instance, you can go walking, mountain climbing, skiing, white-water rafting and horse-riding. On the coast, apart from enjoying some extremely pretty beaches, you can do some modest diving. Cycling and mountain-bike riding are fairly popular local pastimes.

Spanish tourist offices abroad may be able to give you some preliminary tips. Those within the region (starting with the regional office in Barcelona) can provide more detailed help.

Walking

Catalunya offers walkers plenty of scope for leg-stretching at pretty much all levels of difficulty. Options range from pretty coastal walks along tracts of the Costa Brava through to long high-altitude treks in the Pyrenees.

Catalunya's only national park, the Parc Nacional d'Aigüestortes i Estany de Sant Maurici, is laced with trails at many levels of difficulty.

Simply walking the country roads and paths between villages and towns, instead of taking the bus, can be highly enjoyable and a great way to meet the locals.

The best season for trekking in the Pyrenees is from mid-June to mid-September. Although still unpredictable, the weather is at its best then and most trails are free of snow and ice.

At lower altitudes in the foothills of the Pyrenees, along the coast and elsewhere throughout the region, the summer months can be trying because of the heat. You can walk in such areas pretty much year round, provided you are prepared for the weather.

For more detail, see the Moving Mountains special section in the Pyrenees chapter.

Cycling

Mountain biking is popular. There are kilometres upon kilometres of good and bad tracks and roads for biking in Catalunya. Tourist offices often have information on routes.

Skiing

Affordable, decent skiing is on offer all across the Catalan Pyrenees. It is true that Catalunya's pistes and resorts are not the mountains' top billing (superior skiing is available in Andorra and the neighbouring region of Aragón, and even on the French side of the Pyrenees) but you can certainly get in plenty of enjoyable snow action – at most degrees of difficulty – at the Catalan resorts.

For a resort-by-resort lowdown, see the Moving Mountains special section in the Pyrenees chapter.

Rafting, Canoeing & Hydrospeed

You can get some good white-water action in the Pyrenees. See the Moving Mountains special section in the Pyrenees chapter.

ASA ANDERSSON

Get seriously snowy in the rugged Catalan Pyrenees.

Diving & Snorkelling

Although it's no Red Sea, some of the rockier parts of Catalunya's Mediterranean coast – notably the Illes Medes off L'Estartit – offer the best diving in the country. You can organise snorkelling and diving trips (including rental of all the gear) on the spot. It is also possible to do PADI and other diving certificate courses here although the bulk of the operators cater more for passing tourists interested in doing one-off introductory dives. See also the Costa Brava chapter.

COURSES

A spot of study in Catalunya is a great way not only to learn something but also to meet people – locals as well as other travellers – and get more of an insight into the machinations of life in Catalunya than the average visitor is likely to have. Inevitably most people zero in on Barcelona.

Language

Branches of the Instituto Cervantes (see Useful Organisations earlier) can provide you with long lists of places that offer Spanish-language courses in Catalunya (and anywhere else in Spain for that matter).

Some Spanish embassies and consulates also have information on courses.

Universities and also private language schools offer courses and cater for a wide range of levels (from beginners up), course lengths, times of year, intensity and special requirements. Many courses have a cultural component as well as pure language. Costs vary widely but 40 hours' tuition over periods ranging from two weeks to a month can cost roughly €270. Many places can help organise accommodation with families, in student lodgings or in flats. Accommodation offers generally range from around €180 per month with no meals to about €360 for full board.

Considerations when choosing a course should be the intensity (*intensivo* means different things at different schools), class sizes, who the other students are likely to be and whether you want organised extracurricular social activities. It's also worth asking if your course will lead to any formal certificate of competence. The Diploma de Español como Lengua Extranjera (DELE; Diploma of Spanish as a Foreign Language) is recognised by Spain's Ministry of Education and Science.

It's also easy to arrange private classes in many places: check notice boards in universities, language schools and foreign cultural institutes, or small ads in the local press. Expect to pay around €12 per hour for individual private lessons.

It is also possible to do courses in Catalan. The Generalitat de Catalunya's Departament de Cultura produces a booklet, *226 Llocs per Aprendre Català*, which lists schools across the region where you can take Catalan courses. Ask at main provincial tourist offices or Generalitat bookshops (such as those in Barcelona and Girona).

For some more detailed information on language courses in Barcelona, turn to the Barcelona chapter.

Other Courses

Instruction in skiing, diving and other sports is available in the appropriate parts of the region. See the Pyrenees chapter for all but diving, which is covered in the Costa Brava chapter.

In Barcelona you can enrol in classes covering anything from contemporary dance to photography. Start your search at the CIAJ youth information service (Centre d'Informació i Assessorament per a Joves; Map 4; ☎ 93 402 78 00), at Carrer de Ferran 32 in the Barri Gòtic.

WORK

Although it is coming down, Spain's unemployment rate remains the highest in the EU. In Catalunya around 6% of the active population is without work.

Amid increasingly heated debate on immigration, calls for imported labour to do unpleasant tasks are growing louder. Such jobs range from factory work to fruit-picking and are generally so badly paid that they are unlikely to be attractive options. You could consider a few other ways of earning your keep (or almost) while you're here.

Nationals of EU countries, Norway and Iceland may work in Spain (and therefore Catalunya) without a visa, but for stays of more than three months they are supposed to apply within the first month for a *tarjeta de residencia* (residence card); for information on this laborious process, see Visas & Documents earlier in the chapter.

Virtually everyone else is supposed to get, from a Spanish consulate in their country of residence, a work permit and, if they plan to stay more than 90 days, a residence visa. These procedures are near to impossible unless you have a job contract lined up before you begin. In any case you should start the processes a long time before you aim to go to Spain. That said, quite a few people do work, discreetly, without bothering to tangle with the bureaucracy.

Language Teaching

This is the most obvious option, for which language-teaching qualifications are a big help. The region is carpeted in language schools. They're listed under 'Academias de Idiomas' in the yellow pages. Getting a job in one is harder if you're not an EU citizen. Some schools do employ people without work papers, usually at lower than normal rates. Giving private lessons is

euro currency converter €1 = 166 ptas

another avenue, but is unlikely to bring you a living wage straight away.

Language teachers unfortunately tend to abound as much as schools. Pay has remained stationery at fairly low levels for years. (Few earn more than €18 per hour of class time and many make considerably less.)

Sources of information on possible teaching work – in a school or private – include foreign cultural centres (the British Council, Alliance Française etc) in Barcelona, foreign-language bookshops, universities and language schools. Many have notice boards where you may find work opportunities or can advertise your own services.

Tourist Resorts

Summer work on the Mediterranean costas is another possibility, especially if you get in early in the season and are prepared to stay a while. Seasonal bar and restaurant work are possibilities, especially in the most boisterous of the coastal resorts, such as Salou and Lloret de Mar. A working knowledge of Spanish is pretty much indispensable.

Busking

A few travellers earn a crust (but not much more) busking. This is no more evident than along and near La Rambla in Barcelona. You might try this means in some of the bigger coastal resorts too.

ACCOMMODATION

Virtually all accommodation prices are subject to IVA, the Spanish version of value-added tax, at a rate of 7%. This is often included in the quoted price at cheaper places, but less often at more expensive ones. To check, ask: '¿Está incluido el IVA?' ('Is IVA included?').

Room prices given in this book include IVA unless stated otherwise.

Camping

More than 350 officially graded camp sites (càmpings) are spread across Catalunya. Some are well located in woodland or near beaches or rivers, but others are stuck away on the unattractive edges of towns and cities. Few are near town centres and they can be inconvenient if you are relying on public transport.

Sites are officially rated as luxury (L), 1st class (1a), 2nd class (2a) or 3rd class (3a). A few are classified as càmpings-masia, camping grounds attached to a farmhouse or similar country property.

The facilities generally range from reasonable to very good, though any site can be crowded and noisy at busy times. Even a 3rd-class site is likely to have hot showers, electrical hook-ups and a cafeteria. The best sites have heated swimming pools, supermarkets, restaurants, travel agencies, a laundry service, children's playgrounds and tennis courts. There is a range of sizes, some have a capacity of fewer than 20 tents and some stretch to more than 2000.

Camp sites usually charge per person, per tent and per vehicle – anywhere between €1.80 and €6 for each, although an average of €3.60 is typical. In some places you pay as much as €24 for a site (includes car and tent space) plus per person costs. Children usually pay a bit less than adults. Many sites are open year round, but quite a few close from around October to Easter. Some are crowded in July and August. In some cases charges drop in the low season.

The annual Càmpings – Guía, available in bookshops for €1.80, lists the region's grounds and their facilities and prices. It usually comes out around Easter. Tourist offices can always direct you to the nearest camping ground.

You sometimes come across a zona de acampada or área de acampada, a country site often used by local campers but with no facilities, no supervision and no charge.

With certain exceptions – such as many beaches and environmentally protected areas and a few municipalities that ban it – it is legal to camp outside camping grounds (although not within 1km of official ones!). Signs usually indicate where wild camping is not allowed. If in doubt you can always check with tourist offices. You'll need permission to camp on private land.

[continued on page 89]

Out to Eat in Catalunya

OLIVER STREWE

OLIVER STREWE

NEIL SETCHFIELD

Title Page: Barcelona offers a wonderful taste of Catalunya in its specialist food shops. (photograph: Oliver Strewe)

Top: A feast for the eyes at Mercat de la Boqueria, Barcelona

Middle: An ideal selection for Catalan *entremeses* (hors d'oeuvres)

Bottom: Chickens roasting at Los Caracoles in Barcelona: running since the 19th century, this place still heats up.

Food terminology throughout this book is given in Catalan/Castilian or Catalan alone, except in the few cases where the Castilian term is used in both languages. Rather than descend into the murky depths of linguistic polemics, the idea is to reflect what you are most likely to see/hear in the restaurants and bars of Catalunya.

When to Eat

Breakfast *(esmorzar/desayuno)* is generally a no-nonsense affair, taken at a bar on the way to work. Lunch *(dinar/comida)* is basically from 2 to 4 pm and is the main meal of the day. In the cities locals would rarely contemplate chomping into dinner *(sopar/cena)* before 9 pm. Most (but not all) kitchens close by midnight.

Habits change a little as you move around the region. In the mountains and inland, people tend to take their evening meals a little earlier – don't leave it too late to wander out for dinner. In central Barcelona and resorts used to dealing with foreigners, many places open for lunch and dinner at earlier hours preferred by people from more northern climes – you won't find any locals eating then though!

Where to Eat

Many bars and some cafes offer some form of solid sustenance. This can range from *entrepans/bocadillos* (filled rolls) and *tapes/tapas* (bar snacks) through to more substantive *raciones* (basically bigger versions of a tapa), and full meals in *menjadors/comedores* (sit-down restaurants) out the back. *Cerveseries/cervezerías* (beer bars), *tavernes/tabernas* (taverns), *tascas* (snack bars) and *cellers/bodegas* (literally 'cellars'; traditional wine bars) are just some of the kinds of place in this category.

For a full meal you will most frequently end up in a *restaurant/ restaurante*, but other names will pop out at you. A *marisquería* specialises in seafood, while a *mesón* (a 'big table') might indicate (but not necessarily!) a more modest eatery.

What to Eat

Breakfast A coffee with some sort of pastry *(pasta)* is the typical breakfast. You may get a croissant or some cream-filled number (such as a *canya*). Some people prefer a savoury start – you could go for a *bikini/sandwich mixto*, which is a toasted ham and cheese sandwich. A Spanish *tostada* is simply buttered toast (you might order something to go with it). The Catalan version, a *torrada*, is usually more of an open toasted sandwich with something on it besides butter (depending on what you ask for). Some people go for an all-Spanish favourite, *xurros amb xocolata/churros con chocolate*, a lightly deep-fried stick of plain pastry immersed in thick, gooey hot chocolate. They are sold at stands around town and for many are an early-morning, post-disco, pre-hangover cure.

JANE SMITH

Lunch & Dinner Many straightforward Spanish dishes are available here as elsewhere in the country. The traveller's friend is the *menú del día*, a set-price meal usually comprising three courses, with a drink thrown in. This is often only available for lunch and can range from around €5.50 to €30 at posh establishments.

A *plat combinat/plato combinado* is a simpler version still – a one-course meal consisting of basic nutrients – the 'meat-and-three-veg' style of cooking. You'll see pictures of this stuff everywhere. It's filling and cheap but has little to recommend it in culinary terms.

You'll pay more for your meals if you order a la carte but the food will be probably be better. The menu *(la carta)* begins with starters such as *amanides/ensaladas* (salads), *sopes/sopas* (soups) and *entremeses* (hors d'oeuvres). The latter can range from a mound of potato salad with olives, asparagus, anchovies and a selection of cold meats – almost a meal in itself – to simpler servings of cold meat, slices of cheese and olives.

The hungry Catalan, after a starter, will order a first then second course. The latter are often listed under headings such as: *pollastre/pollo* (chicken), *carn/carne* (meat), *mariscs/mariscos* (seafood), *peix/pescado* (fish), *arròs/arroz* (rice), *ous/huevos* (eggs) and *verdures/verduras* (vegetables). Meat may be subdivided into *porc/cerdo* (pork), *vedella/ternera* (beef), and *anyell/cordero* (lamb). Other good things to look out for include *oca* (goose) and *canalons* (Catalan cannelloni).

Desserts have a lower profile; *gelats/helados* (ice cream), fruit and flans (basically a creme caramel) are often the only choices in cheap places, although in better restaurants desserts can be a highlight. Sugar addicts should look out for a couple of local specialities such as sweet pizzas.

CATALAN CUISINE

Catalunya is geographically diverse and therefore provides a variety of fresh, high-quality seafood, meat, poultry, game, fruit and vegetables. These can come in unusual and delicious combinations: meat and seafood (a genre known as *mar i muntanya* – 'sea and mountain'), poultry and fruit, fish and nuts. Quality Catalan food tends to require a greater fiscal effort.

The essence of Catalan food lies in its sauces for meat and fish. These sauces may not be mentioned on menus as they're so ubiquitous. There are five main types: *sofregit* (fried onion, tomato and garlic); *samfaina* or *chanfaina* (sofregit plus red pepper and aubergine or courgette); *picada* (based on ground almonds, usually with garlic, parsley, pine or hazel nuts, and sometimes breadcrumbs); *allioli* (pounded garlic with olive oil, often with egg yolk added to make more of a mayonnaise); and *romesco* (an almond, tomato, olive oil, garlic and vinegar sauce, also used as a salad dressing).

JANE SMITH

Catalans find it hard to understand why other people put butter on bread when *pa amb tomàquet* – bread sliced then rubbed with tomato, olive oil, garlic and salt – is so easy.

JANE SMITH

The Catalan version of the pizza is the *coca*. There are many variations on this theme, savoury and sweet. The former can come with tomato, onion, pepper and sometimes sardines (a Lleida speciality). The sweet version, often almond-based, is more common and is a standard item at many a *festa* (festival; such as Sant Joan in June) throughout the year.

Wild mushrooms are a Catalan passion – people disappear into the forests in autumn to pick them. There are many, many types of *bolets*; the large succulent *rovellons* are a favourite.

The main centres of cheese production in Catalunya are in La Seu d'Urgell, the Cerdanya district and the Pallars area in the north-west. Although many traditional cheeses are disappearing you will still be able to find things like *formatge de tupí*, a goat's cheese soaked in olive oil.

You will also find all sorts of sausages, using pork meat above all as a base. Some generic names include *botifarra*, *fuet* (a thin, dried pork sausage) and *longanissa*. The names often seem to apply to very different sausages, depending on where you buy them. Some are spicier than others.

Of course fish and seafood are a major component of the region's cuisine. Curiously, only 15% of Catalunya's needs are fished in Catalan waters. Much of what ends up on Catalan tables comes from northern Spain, France, the UK and even as far off as South Africa (cod in particular in the latter case)!

Here are some typical Catalan dishes:

Starters

amanida catalana Catalan salad: almost any mix of lettuce, olives, tomatoes, hard-boiled eggs, onions, chicory, celery, green peppers and garlic, with fish, ham or sausage, and mayonnaise or an oil and vinegar dressing.

calçots amb romesco *Calçots* are a type of long onion, delicious as a starter with romesco sauce. Catalans sometimes get together for a *calçotada*, the local version of a BBQ!

escalivada Red peppers and aubergines (sometimes onions and toma-toes too), grilled, cooled, peeled, sliced and served with an olive oil, salt and garlic dressing.

esqueixada Salad of shredded salted cod *(bacallà)* with tomatoes, red peppers, onions, white beans, olives, olive oil and vinegar.

Arròs a la Catalana
Serves 2
400g of rice
100g of ham
250g of sausages
100g of lean pork meat
50g of bacon
2 artichokes
4 tomatoes
100g of peas
1 medium-sized onion
2 cloves of garlic
a tablespoonful of pine nuts
a tablespoonful of toasted almonds
fresh parsley
double the volume of the rice in hot meat broth or stock
salt

JANE SMITH

Chop the meat and toss into an earthenware casserole dish with sliced onion. Fry until the ingredients begin to brown, and then add the tomatoes (peeled and diced), the artichokes (peeled and sliced), and lightly fry on a low heat for a few minutes.

Add the rice, peas, hot broth and a pinch of salt. Crush the garlic with the parsley, pine nuts and almonds and toss the lot into the rice, which should be brought to the boil quickly. Once boiling, lower heat so as to cook through for about 20 to 25 minutes.

Main Dishes
arròs a la cassola or **arròs a la catalana** Catalan paella, cooked in an earthenware pot, without saffron.

arròs negre Rice cooked in cuttlefish ink and quite black. It sounds awful but is very good.

bacallà a la llauna Salted cod baked in tomato, garlic, parsley, paprika and wine.

botifarra amb mongetes Pork sausage with fried white beans.

cargols Snails, almost a religion in parts of Catalunya, often stewed with *conill* (rabbit) and chilli.

escudella A meat, sausage and vegetable stew, the liquid of which is mixed with noodles or rice and served as a soup, followed by the rest served as a main course known as *carn d'olla*. It's generally available in winter only.

espinacas a la catalana Spinach with raisins and pine kernels.

fideuá Similar to paella but using vermicelli noodles as the base, it is usually served with tomato and meat/sausage or fish. You should also receive a little side dish of allioli to mix in as you wish – if you don't, ask for it.

fricandó A pork and vegetable stew.

mandonguilles amb sipia Meatballs with cuttlefish, a subtly flavoured land-sea combination.

pollastre amb escamerlans Chicken with shrimps – another amphibious event.

sarsuela (zarzuela) Mixed seafood cooked in sofregit with seasonings – a Barcelona invention.

suquet de peix Fish, potato and tomato soup.

truita de botifarra Sausage omelette, a particularly Catalan version of the famous Spanish tortilla.

Desserts

crema catalana A cream custard with a crisp, burned-sugar coating.

mel i mató Honey and fresh cream cheese – simple but delicious.

music A serving of dried fruits and nuts, sometimes mixed with ice cream or a sweetish cream cheese and served with a glass of sweet muscatel wine.

Crema Catalana

Serves 4
1L of milk
300g of sugar
10 egg yolks
cinnamon
lemon peel
50g of potato or wheat starch
1 cup of milk
50g of sugar

Pour the litre of milk, 300g of sugar, cinnamon, lemon peel and egg yolks into a saucepan and heat, stirring constantly with a wooden spoon, till it becomes a creamy mix. Into another pan pour the cup of milk and starch. Stir on a low heat but don't allow to boil. Add the contents of the first pan and mix well. Pour into four bowls and allow to cool. When cold dust with the 50g of sugar. The trick then is that you need a kind of metal iron or blowtorch specifically designed to toast the sugar, leaving a golden caramelised surface.

DRINKS

From quenching your thirst to wetting your whistle, there are plenty of beverages to choose from in Catalunya.

Nonalcoholic

Clear, cold water from a public fountain or tap is a Spanish favourite – but check that it's *potable* (fit to drink). For tap water in restaurants, ask for *aigua de l'aixeta/agua de grifo*. *Aigua/agua mineral* (bottled water) comes in innumerable brands, either *amb/con gas* (fizzy) or sense/sin gas (still). A 1.5L bottle of agua mineral sense/sin gas can cost as little as €0.30 in a supermarket, but out and about you may be charged as much as €1.20 for the same.

Coffee Coffee in Spain is strong and slightly bitter. A cafè amb llet/café con leche (generally drunk at breakfast only) is about 50% coffee, 50% hot milk. Ask for grande or doble if you want a large cup, en got/en vaso if you want a smaller shot in a glass, or sombra if you want lots of milk. A café solo is an espresso (short black); cafè tallat/café cortado is an espresso (short black) with a little milk. For iced coffee, ask for cafè amb gel/café con hielo; you'll get a glass of ice and a hot cup of coffee, to be poured over the ice – which, surprisingly, doesn't all melt straight away!

Tea Catalans prefer coffee, but in the bigger towns and more tourist-ed locations it is increasingly possible to get hold of many different styles of tea and infusiones (herbal concoctions). Locals tend to drink tea black. If you want milk (llet/leche), ask for it to come separately (a parte) to avoid ending up with a cup of tea-flavoured watery milk.

Soft Drinks Suc de taronja/zumo de naranja (orange juice) is the main, freshly squeezed juice available. It's often served with sugar. To make sure you are getting the real thing, ask for the juice to be natural, otherwise you run the risk of getting a puny little bottle of runny con-centrate. Refrescos (soft drinks) include the usual international brands of soft drinks, local brands such as Kas, and granissat/granizado (iced fruit crush).

A batut/batido is a flavoured milk drink or milk shake. Orxata/hor-chata is a Valencian drink of Islamic origin, which is made from the juice of chufa (tiger nuts), sugar and water. It is sweet and tastes like soya milk with a hint of cinnamon.

Alcoholic

Wine Spain is a wine-drinking country and vi/vino (wine) accompanies almost every meal. Spanish wine is robust because of the sunny climate. It comes blanc/blanco (white), negre/tinto (red), or rosat/rosado (rosé). In general it is cheap, although there's no shortage of expensive wines. A €3 to €5 bottle of wine, bought from a supermarket or wine mer-chant, will be quite drinkable – and sometimes very good. The same money in a restaurant will get you considerably less (and sometimes nothing at all). Cheap vi de taula/vino de mesa (table wine) in cartons can sell for less than €1.80 a litre, but wines at that price can be pretty rank.

You can order wine by the glass (copa) in bars and restaurants. At lunch or dinner it is common to order a vi/vino de la casa (house wine) – usually by the litre or half litre. Or of course you can order by the bottle.

If your bottle is labelled DO (denominación de origen), you can be sure of reasonable quality. DO refers to those areas that have maintained con-sistent high quality over a long period. In Catalunya there are nine DO wine areas. Only some wines from Spain's premier wine-growing region, La Rioja, go one better – DOC, or *denominación de origen calificada*. These labels are indicative only. Some fine wines have no such tags.

Other categories of wine, in descending order, are: *denominación de origen provisional* (DOP), *vino de la tierra*, *vino comarcal*, and *vino de mesa* (ordinary table wine).

Vino joven is wine made for immediate drinking while *vino de crianza* has to have been stored for certain minimum periods. *Reserva* requires storage of at least three years for reds and two years for whites and rosés. *Gran reserva* is a title permitted for particularly good vintages. These wines must have spent at least two calendar years in storage and three in the bottle. They're mostly reds.

LPP

In Catalunya, the nine DO wines come from points all over the region, but the bulk of them comes from the Penedès area, which pumps out almost two million hectolitres a year. The other eight DO wine-growing areas (spread as far apart as the Empordà area around Figueres in the north and the Terra Alta zone around Gandesa in the south-west) together have an output of about half that produced in Penedès.

Most of the grapes grown are native to Spain and include the White Macabeo, Garnacha and Xarel.lo varieties, and the Black Garnacha, Monastrell and Ull de Llebre (Hare's Eye) varieties. Increasingly, foreign varieties are also being grown (such as Chardonnay, Riesling, Chenin Blanc, Cabernet Sauvignon, Merlot and Pinot Noir). While some reasonable reds and rosés are produced in Catalunya, the bulk of production in and beyond the Penedès area is white. And of these the best-known drops are *cava*, the regional version of champagne.

The two big names in bubbly are Freixenet and Codorníu, both of which have extensive export markets. Connoisseurs tend not to get too excited by the big boys, however, preferring the output of smaller and lesser known vintners. Possibly the biggest name in Penedès still wines is Miguel Torres – one of their stalwart reds is Sangre de Toro. Under Penedès Wine Country in the Around Barcelona chapter we provide some initial tips on wineries to visit in the Penedès area.

There is plenty of wine to look out for beyond Penedès. Raïmat, in the Costers del Segre DO area in Lleida province, produces some fine reds and a couple of notable whites. Good fortified wines come from around Tarragona and some nice fresh wines are also being produced in the Empordà area in the north, for instance by Cellers Santamaria and Cooperativa de Mollet de Perelada. Look out too for wines from the *comarca* (district) of El Priorat.

The Catalan regional government decided in 1998 to introduce a new, more generic label, *vinos de calidad producidos en una región determinada* (VCPRD; quality wines produced in a defined region), which would introduce more flexibility to compete with imports. The present DO rules make the mixing of grape varieties from various zones difficult.

As always, there is more to all this than meets the eye. Some of the bigger wine-makers were in favour of the change, but opponents were vociferous, claiming that smaller operators would be squashed in an avalanche of generic mediocrity. The Catalan wine industry has been on the boil for some time with court cases and polemics over dodgy competitive practices, shoddy cava production by big-name producers and so on. The VCPRD idea was also challenged in the courts which, apparently unmoved by cries that Catalunya's drinking product would suffer, decided the labelling could go ahead.

Wine-makers in favour of the new system say the ruling will not affect quality but rather give Catalan wine-makers the same kind of room to manoeuvre as that which Australian and Californian wine-makers have. For the moment, the old DO system is still in place.

If you want to get information on the Internet about Catalan wines and cava, try **W** www.interceller.com. From here, there are plenty of links to related subjects and individual wineries.

Beer The most common way to order *cervesa/cerveza* (beer) is to ask for a *canya*, which is a small draught beer *(cervesa/cerveza de barril)*. A larger beer (about 300mL) is sometimes called a *tubo* (which comes in a straight glass). A pint is a *jarra*. If you just ask for a cerveza you may get bottled beer, which is more expensive.

A small bottle of beer is called a *flascó/botellín*. The local brew is Estrella Damm (of which there are several variants, including the potent and flavoursome Voll Damm), while San Miguel, made in Lleida, is also widely drunk. The Damm company produces 15% of all Spain's beer, as does San Miguel. A 200mL bottle is a *quinto* (fifth of a litre) and 330mL is a *tercio* (third).

A *clara* is a shandy – a beer with a hefty dash of lemonade.

Other Drinks *Sangría* is a wine and fruit punch, sometimes laced with brandy. It's refreshing going down but can leave you with a sore head. You'll see jugs of it on tables in some restaurants.

The Catalan firewater is *ratafia*, a particularly Pyrenean drop tasting vaguely similar to Kahlua.

There is no shortage of imported and Spanish-produced top-shelf stuff – *coñac* (brandy) is popular. Local versions of gin include Larios. South American cocktails such as the Brazilian *caipirinha* and the Cuban *mojito* are especially popular – many bars in the bigger towns and resorts will whip these up for you.

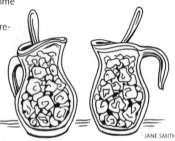

JANE SMITH

[continued from page 80]

Note that Camping Gaz is the only common brand of camping gas; screw-on canisters are hard to find.

Youth Hostels

The 26 member hostels of Catalunya's official youth hostel network, the Xarxa d'Albergs de Joventut, share a central booking service (Map 1; ☎ 93 483 83 63, fax 93 483 83 50, metro Rocafort), located at Turisme Juvenil de Catalunya, Carrer de Rocafort 116–122, Barcelona. Xarxa hostels are counted among the Spanish ones in the national youth hostel organisation, the Red Española de Albergues Juveniles (REAJ; Spanish Youth Hostel Network), the Spanish representative of Hostelling International (HI).

Nearly all hostels in Catalunya outside Barcelona are Xarxa (and REAJ/HI) hostels. Strikingly, most of those in Barcelona are not part of the Xarxa.

At Xarxa hostels you need an HI card. For information on getting one in Catalunya, see Hostel Cards under Visas & Documents earlier in this chapter. With only a few minor exceptions, all have the same price structure: if you're under 25 or have an ISIC, B&B is €10/11.45/13.55 in low/mid/high season; otherwise it's €13.25/15.10/16.90 respectively. Lunch or dinner costs €5.15 and sheets €2.10. For €1.80 you can stay in the hostel during the day. There's no cheaper rate for bed without breakfast. High and low seasons vary from hostel to hostel and are specified where hostels are mentioned in this chapter. The Christmas and Setmana Santa holidays and all long weekends are high season everywhere.

Those hostels (mostly in Barcelona) that are not part of the Xarxa will not appear in regional hostel directories.

Hostales, Pensiones & Hotels

Officially, *hoteles* are places with from one to five stars, *hostales* have one to three stars (officially the category of *hostal* no longer exists in Catalunya but no-one much seems to have taken any notice of that ruling) and *pensiones* have one or two stars. The star ratings refer to specific amenities offered rather than overall quality. The more stars a place has, by the way, the more tax they pay. Some successful budget establishments deliberately do what they can to keep their star rating down. In so doing their taxes remain low, they can keep prices down and so maintain a full house. A rise in charges caused by higher taxes might, some fear, leave them with fewer guests. You can deduce from all of this that the ratings are to be taken with a pinch of salt.

The regional directory, *Hoteles – Guía* (€4.85), lists all classes of accommodation – except those that for whatever reason do not have official recognition. This is frequently because they don't pay taxes or have otherwise managed to put themselves outside the regulations. There is a surprising number of these, some of which appear in this guide. That is because, whatever their quarrels with the taxman, they are worthwhile options to know about.

A *pensión* is basically a small private hotel, often family-run. In the case of one-stars you will often find they only have communal showers in the corridor.

Costs can vary from as little as €6/12 for a single/double room in basic places in less touristed towns through to €36/60 for better digs in Barcelona in high season. At worst, rooms will be bare and basic, small and without a window. They are, however, usually clean. Hostales are generally similar.

Establishments calling themselves hotels range from simple places, where a double room could cost as little as €36, up to wildly luxurious, five-star places where you could pay €360 or more. Even in the cheapest ones rooms are likely to have an attached bathroom and there'll probably be a restaurant.

Paradores de Turismo

In a special category are the *paradores de turismo*, a state-run chain of high-class hotels, often set in magnificent castles or mansions, that was established in 1928. In Catalunya there are seven, including medieval hill-top fortress complexes at Cardona and Tortosa. Less inspiring but located near one of the Costa Brava's more enchanting little beaches is the *parador* at Aiguablava. They are stylish places to stay if you have from €75 to €117 (depending on location and season) to spend for a double room. Occasional special offers, such as discounts of 35% for people aged 60 or more, can make them more affordable. You can book rooms at any parador in Catalunya through the Central de Reservas (Reservation Centre; ☎ 91 516 66 66, fax 91 516 66 57, W www.parador.es), Calle de Requena 3, 28013 Madrid.

Cases de Pagès

Rural tourism throughout Spain has taken off in recent years. What Spaniards call *casas rurales* are known in Catalunya as *residències-cases de pagès* (RCP). They are usually comfortably renovated country houses or farmhouses, with just a handful of rooms. Look for the RCP signs when seaing them out on the ground. Some have meals available, while at some you'll have to self-cater. A double room costs from around €18 to €48. Owners frequently rent the whole house out to groups for weekends or longer periods. Tourist offices can usually provide information or you can get hold of the annual guide, *Residències-Casa de Pagès – Guia* for €3.60. In the course of this guide they are referred to as *cases de pagès*.

Refugis

Refugis (*refugios* in Spanish) are mountain shelters for hikers and climbers and are quite liberally scattered around the Pyrenees. Accommodation, normally bunks squeezed into a dormitory, is usually on a first come, first served basis. In busy seasons (July and August in most areas) they can fill up quickly and you should try to book or arrive by mid-afternoon to be sure of a place. Prices per person range from nothing to €6.50 or so a night. Most have a bar and meals available and in many you can cook for yourself. Blankets are usually provided but you'll have to bring any further bedding yourself. See the Pyrenees chapter for more detailed information.

Apartments

In many places, especially along the coast and at ski resorts, you can rent self-catering apartments, or even houses and villas. On average you would be looking at starting rates of about €30 per night for two or three people in a simple one-bedroom apartment.

Apartments are worth considering if you plan to stay several days or more, in which case there will usually be discounts from the daily rate. Tourist offices can supply lists of apartments, villas and houses for rent.

Monasteries

It is possible to stay at some monasteries in Spain. Many orders have survived around the country and, with vocations not what they once were, renting out cells is one way of making a little extra cash. The Monestir de Montserrat (see the Around Barcelona chapter) is an obvious choice in Catalunya.

FOOD & DRINK

See the Out to Eat in Catalunya special section for an introduction to the delights awaiting your palate in this succulent region.

ENTERTAINMENT

Sitting over a coffee or a glass of wine in a plaza cafe and watching life go by is often entertainment enough in itself. The innumerable festes that spatter the Catalan calendar provide heaps of colourful spectacle.

Local papers often carry fairly thorough entertainment listings and in Barcelona you can pick up local 'what's on' guides (see Entertainment in the Barcelona chapter).

Bars, Discos & Clubs

Barcelona and the coastal resorts have plenty to keep you busy. Thursday to Saturday nights are the big ones for locals. The provincial capitals, especially Girona and Tarragona, both of which have student populations, don't do badly when school is in.

Most locals don't bother going out to bars until 10 pm or later. As they start closing from 2 am on, night owls drift on to clubs (which tend to go by the name of *discotecas*). There they remain from about 3 am until dawn. For the die-hards in Barcelona,

Known for its nightlife, you can booze
until breakfast in Barcelona.

it is possible to keep going even beyond
this hour.

Gay & Lesbian Venues Outside of Barcelona and Sitges (considered the gay capital of the Spanish costas), entertainment
venues specifically for gays and lesbians
are scarce. Still, in those two locations you
will find plenty to keep you occupied.

Music
Rock, Pop & Jazz The home-grown Spanish rock, pop and flamenco fusion scene is
big and in Barcelona especially you'll see
all sorts of performers. Jazz also gets a decent run in the city.

Flamenco Although it is possible to see
flamenco in Barcelona, it is not a big phenomenon in Catalunya, far removed from
the birthplace of this passionate music and
dance in southern Andalucía. This is strange
in some respects, because not a few stars of
flamenco have come from *gitano* (Romany)
families living in and around Barcelona.

Classical Music, Dance & Theatre
Again Barcelona is the main scene for a
range of theatre, classical music, opera and
so on. See the Barcelona chapter.

Cinema
Cinemas abound and films are inexpensive,
although foreign films are usually dubbed
into Spanish. Only in Barcelona will you
have a fair chance of seeing films in their
original languages with Spanish subtitles –
look for the letters 'v.o.' *(versión original)*
in listings.

SPECTATOR SPORTS
Football
Fútbol is as much a preoccupation in Catalunya as elsewhere. Catalans, like other
Spaniards, take the fate of their side very
seriously.

Almost any game in the Primera División
(First Division) will be worth attending, but
even more so if you can get to one in which
Barcelona (aka Barça) plays. Along with
arch-rivals Real Madrid, Barça is one of the
all-time top sides. Espanyol, also based in
Barcelona, runs a creditable second and can
put up a good fight in a local derby.

Bullfighting
Bullfights are held in Barcelona and other
towns around Catalunya, although the sport
(if such it can be called – some think of it
as a noble art while others condemn it as
cruel butchery) does not have the kind of
following here as in other parts of Spain.

Formula One, Motorbikes & Cycling
The Spanish Formula One motor-racing
Grand Prix is held at Montmeló (at the Cir-
cuit de Catalunya; **W** www.circuitcat.com),
about 20km north of Barcelona, usually in
May. One of three Spanish stages of the
World Motorcycle Championships is also
held here in June. See Montmeló in the
Around Barcelona chapter.

Spain's version of the Tour de France
cycle race is the three-week Vuelta a España,
usually held in September. At least part of the
route often passes through Catalunya.

SHOPPING
Barcelona is the main place for retail ther-
apy in Catalunya. Spanish and many foreign labels are represented in the clothing

department. Shoes and other leather goods are reasonable value. Designer stores purveying everything from candlesticks to sofas abound. Barcelona also has several interesting flea markets. See the Barcelona chapter for more details.

Around the rest of the region there is remarkably little that stands out. Of course, you will find the usual tourist-oriented stuff that you can get just about anywhere – there is a particular concentration in the busier parts of the Costa Brava and in the towns lining the highway into France out of the Val d'Aran. Of greater interest are the ceramics on sale in La Bisbal d'Empordà, a town halfway between Girona and the Costa Brava, particularly known for its pottery and tiles.

Getting There & Away

Catalunya is well connected to the rest of Spain and other European countries by air, rail and road. Ferries run to the Balearic Islands and Italy.

If you are coming from a major hub, it can even be cheaper to fly than travel overland – always check options before making assumptions.

Some good direct flights are available from North America. Those coming from Australasia have fewer choices and should watch out for deals including free internal European flights (see the Australia section under Air).

Insurance

See the Visas & Documents and Health sections in the Facts for the Visitor chapter for hints on travel insurance, something you should always consider.

AIR

Always reconfirm your onward flight or return bookings by the specified time: at least 72 hours before departure on intercontinental flights (on most European flights it is no longer necessary to reconfirm). Otherwise you risk missing your flight because it was rescheduled or you've been classified as a 'no-show'.

Airports & Airlines

There are three airports of any note in Catalunya, at Barcelona, Girona and Reus. Most people arrive at Barcelona. Some Costa Brava package charter flights (as well as some cheap scheduled flights) use Girona and others taking passengers to Tarragona or the southern resort town of Salou and the surrounding area arrive at the Reus aerodrome.

Several Spanish and many European and international carriers compete with the country's national airline, Iberia. Increasingly travellers are turning to the Web to look for flight deals and book tickets. Most airlines and many travel agents now operate interactive Web sites.

The high season for travel to Catalunya is July and August, as well as Easter and Christmas. Barcelona is busy year round.

Departure Tax

Airport taxes are factored into ticket prices, but fares are generally quoted without the taxes. These can range from about €19 to €65, depending on the destination.

Other Parts of Spain

Flying within Spain is generally not economical. Iberia (☎ 902 40 05 00) and its small franchise subsidiaries Iberia Regional-Air Nostrum (☎ 93 379 74 11) and Binter Mediterráneo cover all destinations. Ask about discounts and special rates. You get about 25% off flights departing after 11 pm (there are few of these). People under 22 or over 63 get 25% off *return* flights and another 20% off night flights.

A standard one-way fare between Madrid and Barcelona ranges from €73 to €98. Since 1999 Iberia Regional-Air Nostrum has been running a handful of direct flights between Girona and Madrid.

Competing with Iberia are Spanair (☎ 902 13 14 15) and Air Europa (☎ 902 40 15 01). Air Europa is the bigger of the two, with regular flights from Barcelona to Madrid, Palma de Mallorca, Málaga and a host of mainland Spanish destinations.

Between three and eight Air Europa flights connect Madrid with Barcelona daily. The cheapest one-way economy *(turista)* fare is €62.65. The return fare ranges from €72.50 to about €180. What you pay depends on when you fly and the conditions attached.

Canary Islands

From Barcelona, Iberia, Air Europa, Spanair and charters all fly to Tenerife and Las Palmas (Gran Canaria). Tourist-class return flights between Santa Cruz de Tenerife and Barcelona average around €169 to €211, although return charter fares can be as low as €114.

Air Travel Glossary

Alliances Many of the world's leading airlines are now intimately involved with each other, sharing everything from reservations systems and check-in to aircraft and frequent-flyer schemes. Opponents say that alliances restrict competition. Whatever the arguments, there is no doubt that big alliances are the way of the future.

Courier Fares Businesses often need to send urgent documents or freight securely and quickly. Courier companies hire people to accompany the package through customs and, in return, offer a discount ticket which is sometimes a bargain. However, you may have to surrender all your baggage allowance and take only carry-on luggage.

Fares Airlines traditionally offer 1st class (coded F), business class (coded J) and economy class (coded Y) tickets. These days there are so many promotional and discounted fares available that few passengers pay full fare.

Lost Tickets If you lose your airline ticket, an airline will usually treat it like a travellers cheque and, after inquiries, issue you with another one. Legally, however, an airline is entitled to treat it like cash and if you lose it then it's gone forever. Take very good care of your tickets.

Onward Tickets An entry requirement for many countries is that you have a ticket out of the country. If you're unsure of your next move, the easiest solution is to buy the cheapest onward ticket to a neighbouring country or a ticket from a reliable airline which can later be refunded if you do not use it.

Open-Jaw Tickets These are return tickets where you fly out to one place but return from another. If available, this can save you backtracking to your arrival point.

Overbooking Since every flight has some passengers who fail to show up, airlines often book more passengers than they have seats. Usually excess passengers make up for the no-shows, but occasionally somebody gets 'bumped' onto the next available flight. Guess who it is most likely to be? The passengers who check in late. If you do get 'bumped', you are normally offered some form of compensation.

Reconfirmation Some airlines require you to reconfirm your flight at least 72 hours prior to departure. Check your travel documents to see if this is the case.

Restrictions Discounted tickets often have various restrictions on them – such as needing to be paid for in advance and incurring a penalty to be altered or cancelled. Others are restrictions on the minimum and maximum period you must be away.

Round-the-World Tickets RTW tickets give you a limited period (usually a year) in which to circumnavigate the globe. You can go anywhere the carrying airlines go, as long as you don't backtrack. The number of stopovers or total number of separate flights is decided before you set off and they usually cost a bit more than a basic return flight.

Ticketless Travel Airlines are gradually waking up to the realisation that paper tickets are unnecessary encumbrances. On simple one-way or return trips, reservations details can be held on computer and the passenger merely shows ID to claim their seat.

Transferred Tickets Airline tickets cannot be transferred from one person to another. Travellers sometimes try to sell the return half of their ticket, but officials can ask you to prove that you are the person named on the ticket. On an international flight, tickets are compared with passports.

The UK

Most British travel agents are registered with ABTA (Association of British Travel Agents) and all agents that sell flights in the UK must hold an Air Travel Organiser's Licence (ATOL). If you have paid for your flight with an ABTA-registered or ATOL agent who then goes bust, the Civil Aviation Authority will guarantee a refund or an alternative under the ATOL scheme. Unregistered travel agents are riskier but sometimes cheaper.

STA Travel (☎ 020-7361 6161 for European flights, W www.statravel.co.uk), with several offices in London and others in Bristol, Cambridge, Leeds, Manchester and Oxford, is a reliable agent.

Trailfinders (☎ 020-7937 1234 for European flights) is similar. Its short-haul booking centre is at 215 Kensington High St, London W8 6RB. It also has agencies in Bristol, Birmingham, Glasgow, Manchester and Newcastle.

Usit Campus (☎ 0870 240 1010, W www.usitcampus.co.uk), 52 Grosvenor Gardens, London SW1W 0AG, is in much the same league and has several other branches in London and around the country.

The two flagship airlines linking the UK and Spain are British Airways (☎ 0845 773 3377, W www.britishairways.com), 156 Regent St, London W1R 5TA, and Spain's Iberia (☎ 0845 601 2854, W www.iberia.com), Venture House, 27–29 Glasshouse St, London W1R 6JU. Of the two, BA is more likely to have special deals. Cheaper alternatives abound, however.

From London's Luton airport you can fly to Barcelona with easyJet (☎ 0870 600 0000, W www.easyjet.com) for as little as UK£49 each way, plus UK£10 tax. In slow periods (such as winter weekdays), one-way prices can drop as low as UK£19 plus tax! Once fares approach the UK£99 mark (one way), look elsewhere. In Spain contact the company on ☎ 902 29 99 92.

A direct competitor is Go (☎ 0845 605 4321, W www.go-fly.com). Departures are from London Stansted (a 45-minute journey from London's Liverpool Street train station). If you comply with certain restrictions (easily done if you are planning to spend a week or more in Spain) you are looking at around UK£50 to UK£60 one way plus taxes to Barcelona. They sometimes have offers on return flights from Barcelona at around €73 (including taxes). Their number in Spain is ☎ 901 33 35 00.

A third cheapie airline, Buzz (☎ 0870 240 7070, W www.buzzaway.com), has one flight on Saturday and Sunday (daily flights from 1 July to 8 September) from Stansted to Girona for UK£50 each way.

Spanish Travel Services (☎ 020-7387 5337), 138 Eversholt St, London NW1 1BL, can get scheduled return flights with Iberia, BA, Air Europa and other airlines for as little as UK£90 in low season and around UK£150 in high season (including taxes).

The Charter Flight Centre (☎ 020-7565 6755), 15 Gillingham St, London SW1V 1HN, has return flights, valid for up to four weeks in low season, for around UK£130 (including taxes). Remember that if you miss a charter flight, you have lost your money.

Several times a year, usually around Easter and again in autumn (any time from September to November), various charter companies put on four- and five-day long-weekend fares to Barcelona and/or other Spanish destinations for silly prices: UK£49 return is not unheard of.

Continental Europe

Short hops can be expensive, but for longer journeys you can often find fares that beat the cost of overland alternatives.

France The student travel agency OTU Voyages (☎ 01 40 29 12 12, W www.otu.fr) has a central Paris office at 39 ave Georges-Bernanos and also branches around the country. usit Connections (☎ 01 42 44 14 00, W www.usitconnect.fr) is a safe bet for reasonable student and cut-price travel. They have four addresses in Paris, including 85 blvd St Michel, and more around the country. STA Travel's Paris agent is Voyages Wasteels (☎ 08 03 88 70 04).

Return flights from Paris to Barcelona with Iberia frequently cost under €305. Otherwise charter and discount flights can come in as low as €153 to €198.

Regional Airlines (☎ 91 401 21 36), aimed mainly at business travellers, links Barcelona (and Madrid) with Bordeaux in France, where you can get connecting flights to other French destinations. In France you can call them on ☎ 08 03 00 52 00. Air Littoral (☎ 08 03 83 48 34 in France) operates flights from Nice to Barcelona. Neither airline is cheap.

Germany In Berlin you could try STA Travel (☎ 030-311 09 50, W www.statravel.de) at Goethestrasse 73. They also have offices in Frankfurt-am-Main, including at Bockenheimer Landstrasse 133 (☎ 069-70 30 35), and in 16 other cities across the country.

High-season return flights from Frankfurt to Barcelona range from €201.50 with Sabena to €352 with Iberia. Taxes range from €20 to €27.50.

The Netherlands & Belgium Amsterdam is a popular departure point. The student travel agency NBBS Reizen (☎ 020-620 50 71, W www.nbbs.nl), Rokin 66, offers reliable and reasonably low fares. Compare them with the pickings in the discount flight centres along Rokin before deciding. NBBS has several branches throughout the city as well as in Brussels, Belgium.

The main hub for Virgin Express (☎ 02-752 05 05, W www.virgin-express.com) is Brussels. Up to seven flights a day connect with Barcelona (☎ 93 226 66 71). One-way fares can range from about €95 to €129.

Italy Centro Turistico Studentesco (CTS), with branches countrywide, is the best place for cheap fares. In Rome it is at Corso Vittorio Emauenele II 297 (☎ 06 687 26 72).

Portugal Only those in a tearing hurry will consider flying between Barcelona and Lisbon. Iberia, Air Europa and TAP do it for around €175 return in the high season.

The USA

Several airlines fly to Barcelona (usually with a stop and sometimes with a change of flight) including Iberia, BA and KLM.

Standard fares can be expensive. Discount and rock-bottom options from the USA include charter flights, stand-by and courier flights.

Stand-by fares are often sold at 60% of the normal price for one-way tickets. Whole Earth Travel (☎ 212-864 2000, ☎ 800 326 2009 toll free, W www.4standby.com), 325 W 38th St, Suite 1509, New York, NY 10025, is a specialist. One-way from the USA to Europe costs from US$159 (east coast) to US$239 (west coast) plus taxes. Whole Earth Travel has several other offices in the USA, including in Los Angeles (☎ 800 397 1098). In Europe they operate offices in Prague, Madrid and Rotterdam.

Otherwise, reliable travel agents include STA (☎ 800 781 4040, W www.sta.com) and Council Travel (☎ 800 2COUNCIL, W www.counciltravel.com). Both have offices in major cities.

Courier flights involve you accompanying a parcel to its destination. A New York–Madrid return on a courier flight can cost under US$300 in low season (more from the west coast). You may have to be a US resident and apply for an interview first. Most flights depart from New York. Now Voyager (☎ 212-431 1616) at Suite 307, 74 Varrick St, New York, NY 10013, is a courier flight specialist. The Denver-based Air Courier Association (☎ 303-278 8810) also does this kind of thing.

Iberia flies nonstop between Barcelona and New York, but often you can get better deals with other airlines if you are prepared to fly via other European centres.

The best-value low-season (November–December) fares from the east coast hover at around US$500 return (from New York). From Los Angeles you can expect to pay roughly US$150 more. In high season (June–August) you are looking at around US$700 and US$1200, respectively. Plenty of flights leave from other cities, usually connecting through New York. Fares from Chicago, for example, are comparable to those from Los Angeles. Flying from Barcelona you are looking at fares from €410 return (with Lufthansa, changing in Frankfurt) to €475 (Air Franca via Paris), plus tax (€64.50).

Air Europa (☎ 212-921 2381 or ☎ 888-2EUROPA) has flights to New York via Madrid, with occasional attractive offers.

If you can't find a good deal, consider a cheap transatlantic hop to London and stalking the discount flight centres there.

Canada

Scan the travel agents' ads in the *Globe & Mail*, *Toronto Star* and *Vancouver Sun*.

Travel CUTS (W www.travelcuts.com; known as Voyages Campus in Quebec), Canada's main student travel organisation, has offices in Toronto (☎ 416-977 0441), 74 Gerrard St E, and Montreal (☎ 514-398 0647), Université McGill, 3480 rue McTavish.

For courier flights originating in Canada, contact FB On Board Courier Services (☎ 514-631 2077 in Toronto).

Iberia has direct flights to Barcelona from Toronto and Montreal. Other major European airlines offer competitive fares to Barcelona via other European capitals. Low-season fares from Montreal start at around C$900, and from around C$1300 from Vancouver. In the high season you are looking (usually) at C$1200 and C$1700, respectively, although good deals crop up in Montreal.

Australia

STA Travel (Australia-wide fast fares on ☎ 1300 360 960, W www.statravel.com.au) and Flight Centre (Australia-wide ☎ 1310 362 665, W www.flightcentre.com.au) are major dealers in cheap air fares, although heavily discounted fares can often be found at your local travel agent. The Saturday editions of the Melbourne *Age* and the *Sydney Morning Herald* have many advertisements offering cheap fares to Europe.

There are no direct flights from Australia to Spain. You will have to fly to another European city via Asia and change flights (and possibly airlines).

Low-season return fares to Barcelona start from around A$1749, flying Qantas/British Airways via London or Egypt Air via Cairo. Return fares in the high season start from A$2019 with Egypt Air or A$2349 with Qantas/British Airways. Other

airlines offer side trips to Barcelona from Frankfurt or Paris for around the same price.

For courier flights try Jupiter (☎ 02-9317 2230), 3/55 Kent Rd, Mascot, Sydney 2020.

New Zealand

STA Travel and Flight Centre are popular agents. A RTW (round-the-world) ticket can be good value from New Zealand as they are often cheaper than a return in the high season. Low-season Air New Zealand/KLM return fares start from around NZ$2499.

LAND

There are plenty of options for reaching Catalunya by land. Bus is generally the cheapest choice, but over long distances services are often less frequent and considerably less comfortable than the train.

If you are travelling overland to Spain check whether you require visas to the countries through which you intend to pass.

Bus

Other Parts of Spain Buses run to most large Spanish cities from various points in Catalunya. The central arrival/departure point is Barcelona, but you can pick up long-distance Spanish services in many towns along the way. Services also depart from main centres like Lleida and Tarragona.

A plethora of companies operates to different parts of the country, although many come under the umbrella of Enatcar. For schedule information call ☎ 93 245 88 56.

In Barcelona, services arrive at and leave from Estació del Nord. They include the following (where frequencies vary, the lowest figure is usually for Sunday):

departure	buses daily	hours	cost (€)
Almería	2	12¾–13½	42.90
Burgos	2–4	7½	30.15
Granada	3	13–14¼	47.70
Madrid	11–18	7–8	20.50
Salamanca	3	11½	38.70
Seville	1–2	16	55
Valencia	5–10	4½	17.50
Vigo	1–2	15½	41.20
Zaragoza	11	4½	10

The UK Eurolines (☎ 0870 514 3219, fax 01582-400694, W www.gobycoach.com), at 4 Cardiff Road, Luton LU1 1PP, runs buses to Barcelona from Victoria Coach Station on Saturday, Monday (leaving at 11 am; connection to Alicante) and Wednesday (9.30 pm). The trip takes 24 to 26 hours. The one-way and return fares are, respectively, UK£65 and UK£99 (UK£63 and UK£95 for those under 26 and senior citizens). The standard adult one-way fare going the other way is €84. Fares drop in the low season.

You usually have the option of getting off at several points along the way to Barcelona (such as Girona).

France Eurolines can be found at the bus station in Paris (☎ 01 49 72 51 51, W www .eurolines.com), 28 ave du Générale de Gaulle and (☎ 01 43 54 11 99), rue St Jacques 55, off blvd St Michel. Other French cities also have offices. UK passengers may have to change buses in Paris. From Paris you pay €62 (under 26) or €79.50; from Barcelona it costs €72 .

Andorra La Hispano Andorrana (☎ 82 13 72) runs five to eight buses daily from Andorra la Vella to La Seu d'Urgell (€2.10, 30 minutes).

Alsina Graells (☎ 82 73 79) has up to seven buses daily between Barcelona's Estació del Nord and Andorra la Vella's bus station on Carrer de Bonaventura Riberaygua (€14.70 to €16.40, four hours).

Novatel Autocars (☎ 86 48 87, e novatel@ andornet.ad) has three runs daily (€21.10) between Andorra la Vella's bus station and Barcelona's El Prat airport. Eurolines (☎ 86 00 10) has four services daily (€16.90) between Andorra (departing from the car park of Hotel Diplomátic) and Barcelona's Estació d'Autobusos de Sants (which is next to the Estació Sants train station). Three of these originate from/continue to El Prat airport (€19.90).

Other International Services Eurolines/ Julià Via (☎ 93 490 40 00) also has services at least three times weekly to Amsterdam, Brussels, Florence, Geneva, Milan, Montpellier, Nice, Perpignan, Rome, Toulouse, Venice and Zürich, and twice a week to several cities in Morocco. Most international services arrive at and leave from Estació d'Autobusos de Sants.

Train

The *Thomas Cook European Timetable* has a complete listing of train schedules. It is updated monthly and available from Thomas Cook offices and agents worldwide.

On overnight hauls you can book a *litera* (couchette) for around UK£10 to UK£15 for most international trains. In 1st class there are four bunks per cabin and in 2nd class there are six bunks.

It is always advisable, and sometimes compulsory, to book seats on international trains to and from Spain.

The main train line leading into Catalunya from the north crosses from France by the Mediterranean. This line proceeds south to Barcelona via Figueres and Girona.

Other Parts of Spain Two main lines enter Catalunya from the rest of Spain. One comes from Valencia in the south to Tarragona and on up to Barcelona (continuing north through Catalunya into France). The other comes from the west (Madrid etc) with a first major stop at Lleida. From there the direct main line takes you on to Barcelona but it is possible (often with a change of train) to make for other destinations instead, such as Tarragona.

Information It's advisable to book at least a day or two ahead for most long-distance trains, domestic or international.

For information on all national Red Nacional de los Ferrocarriles Españoles (RENFE) train services, call ☎ 902 24 02 02 or have a look at its Web site at W www .renfe.es (where you can book on-line).

Train timetables are posted at the main stations. Impending arrivals *(arribades/ llegadas)* and departures *(sortides/salidas)* appear on big electronic boards and TV screens. Timetables for specific lines are generally available free of charge.

Eurail, Inter-Rail, Europass and Flexi-pass tickets are valid on the RENFE network throughout Spain.

Types of Train in Spain A host of different train types coasts the wide-gauge lines of the Spanish network. A saving of a couple of hours on a faster train can mean a big hike in the fare.

Most long-distance *(largo recorrido)* trains have 1st and 2nd classes. The cheapest and slowest of these are the *regionales*, generally all-stops jobs between provinces within one region (although a few travel between regions). If your train is a *regional exprés* it will make fewer stops.

All trains that run for more than 400km are denominated Grandes Líneas services – just a fancy way of saying long distance. Among these are *diurnos* and *estrellas*, the standard interregional trains. The latter is the night-time version of the former.

Faster, more comfortable and expensive are the Talgos (Tren Articulado Ligero Goicoechea Oriol). They make only major stops and have such extras as TVs. The Talgo Pendular is a sleeker, faster version of the same thing that picks up speed by leaning into curves.

Some Talgos and other modern trains are used for limited-stop trips between major cities. These services are known as Inter-City (and when they're really good as InterCity Plus!).

A classier derivative is the Talgo 200, a Talgo Pendular using the standard-gauge, high-speed Tren de Alta Velocidad Española (AVE) line between Madrid and Seville on part of the journey to such southern destinations as Málaga, Cádiz and Algeciras.

The most expensive way to go is to take the high-speed AVE train itself along the Madrid-Seville line (another line between Madrid and Barcelona, which would link up with the French TGV, is currently under construction).

A high-speed AVE train on standard Spanish track, known as Euromed, connects Barcelona with Valencia and Alicante.

Autoexpreso and Motoexpreso wagons are sometimes attached to long-distance services for the transport, respectively, of cars and motorbikes.

A *trenhotel* is an expensive sleeping-car train. There can be up to three classes on these trains, ranging from *turista* (for those sitting or in a couchette) to *preferente* (sleeping car) and *gran clase* (sleeping in sheer bloody luxury).

Train Passes It is not worth buying a Eurail or Inter-Rail pass for travel only within Catalunya (or even Spain), since train fares are reasonably cheap. Several national passes are available from RENFE in Spain.

With a Euro<26, GO25 or ISIC student card you can get reductions on rail tickets (see Costs & Discounts later in this section), or you can buy an ExploreRail card. This allows the holder unlimited 2nd-class train travel across Spain, except on the AVE and Euromed. You can also upgrade to 1st class by paying the difference. It is valid for seven, 15 or 30 days, and costs €114.50/138.50/180.75, respectively – a bargain for anyone contemplating serious rail travel in Spain. You can include *rodalies/cercanías* trains (local networks around main cities) by paying €132.50/168.70/222.90, respectively. The card is sold by authorised travel agencies, including usit Unlimited (☎ 902 25 25 75, W www.unlimited.es) at Carrer de Rocafort 116–122 in Barcelona (metro Rocafort).

The Tarjeta Dorada is a senior citizens' pass (you must be over 60 and a resident in Spain) issued by RENFE for €3. The card allows 25% off rail fares from Friday to Sunday and up to 40% off during the week.

RENFE also issues a Tarjeta Turística, also known as a Spain Flexipass. It is for non-European residents and is valid for three to 10 days' travel within a two-month period on all Spanish trains. In 2nd class, a three/10-day pass costs US$155/365. The Flexipass is sold by travel agents outside Europe and at a few main stations and RENFE offices in Spain.

Costs & Discounts The variety of possible fares is even more astounding than the number of train types. All fares quoted should be considered a rough sample of basic 2nd-class fares on the diurnos and estrellas (the cheapest fares).

On regionales and some of the faster long-distance trains (diurnos, InterCitys and Talgos), you have the easy choice of 1st- or 2nd-class seats (a regional exprés will generally cost a little more as you are paying for the privilege of arriving more quickly). The evening trains (estrellas) offer 1st- and 2nd-class seats, couchettes and in some cases *camas* (sleeping compartments).

If you buy a return ticket you can get a 20% discount (25% if the return is on the same day). Children under four travel free; children aged four to 11 get 40% off. Reductions are possible for holders of some youth passes, such as the Euro<26 card (also known as Carnet Jove in Catalunya) which allows a 20% discount.

Trains run from Barcelona to most Spanish cities. The trip to Madrid can take 6½ to 9½ hours and a basic 2nd-class fare costs €30.75. The Talgo (which is quickest) costs €39.75.

The high-speed Euromed service connects Barcelona with Valencia (three hours) five times daily, and with Alicante (4¾ hours) three times daily. The respective turista/preferente (2nd/1st-class) fares are €30.75/44.75 to Valencia and €41/59.75 to Alicante.

A stylish new train known as Arco runs between Portbou (close to the French border in the far north-east of Catalunya) and Alicante. It takes only 20 minutes more than Euromed to reach Valencia from Barcelona, and 35 minutes more to Alicante. The fares are €25.90/33.75 (turista/preferente) to Valencia and €35/46 to Alicante. It runs up to four times daily to Valencia and twice daily to Alicante.

Other examples of 2nd-class travel in diurno/estrella trains from Barcelona include:

to	hours	one way (€)
Granada	12½	38.60
Pamplona	6½–10	26.50
San Sebastián	8¼–10	30.15
Zaragoza	3½–4½	17.50

Fines If you board a train without a ticket, you are to some degree at the mercy of the inspector. You may simply be obliged to buy a full one-way ticket for your journey, but you could just as easily be told to cough up double. If you are in real trouble you will be forced off the train and be made liable to a fine of up to €512!

The UK Your choices from London are limited by the options in Paris, where you must change trains. Trains run from Charing Cross or Victoria station to Paris (via ferry or hovercraft from Dover to Calais or Folkestone to Boulogne), or from Waterloo (with Eurostar). You arrive at Gare du Nord and must proceed to Gare d'Austerlitz (take the RER B to St Michel and change there for the RER C to Austerlitz), Gare de Montparnasse (Metro 4) or Gare de Lyon (RER B to Châtelet and then RER A for Gare de Lyon). See also the section on France below.

The one-way/return fares to Barcelona are UK£90/143 (more if you use the Eurostar), and tickets are valid for two months. Those aged under 26 can get Wasteels or BIJ (Billet International de Jeunesse) tickets for UK£68/121.

Children qualify for discounts and those over 60 can get a Rail Europe Senior Railcard (valid only for trips that cross at least one border). You pay UK£5 for the card but you must already have a Senior Railcard (UK£18), which is available to anyone who can prove they are over 60 (you are not required to be a UK resident). The pass entitles you to roughly 30% off standard fares.

For information on all international rail travel (including Eurostar services) contact Rail Europe Travel Centre (☎ 0870 584 8848, ⓦ www.raileurope.co.uk) at 179 Piccadilly, London W1V 0BA. For Eurostar you can also make enquiries and buy tickets at Waterloo station, from where the trains depart.

France The only truly direct train to Barcelona is the *trenhotel* sleeper-only job. It leaves Gare d'Austerlitz at 8.47 pm daily and arrives at 8.53 am or 9 am (stopping at Dijon, Figueres, Girona and Barcelona's

Estació Sants). The standard one-way fare in a couchette is €115.40. Going the other way, the trenhotel leaves Estació Sants at 8.05 pm and arrives at 8.14 am in Paris. The couchette costs €101.80. Reservations on this train can be made in Barcelona by calling ☎ 93 490 11 22.

Otherwise, the cheapest and most convenient option to Barcelona is the 9.47 pm from Gare d'Austerlitz, changing at Latour-de-Carol and arriving in Estació Sants at 11.27 am. A reclining seat costs €75 one way, or €85.70 in a 2nd-class couchette. There is an alternative train with a change at Portbou (on the coast). Those under 26 get a 25% reduction. Note also that fares rise in July and August.

Up to three TGVs (Trains de Grande Vitesse; high-speed trains) also put you on the road to Barcelona (leaving from Paris Gare de Lyon), with a change of train at Montpellier or Narbonne. Prices and timetables vary, so check the latest details. A direct Talgo service also connects Montpellier with Barcelona (€39 in 2nd class, 4½ hours). A couple of other slower services (with a change of train at Portbou) also make this run. All stop in Perpignan.

When appropriate track is eventually laid, Barcelona will be linked to the French TGV network.

From Estació Sants, eight to 10 trains daily run to Cerbère (2½ hours) and four to five to Latour-de-Carol (3½ hours), with several onward connections to Montpellier and Toulouse, respectively.

Check W www.sncf.com and W www.tgv.com for more information or contact Rail Europe (for details see under The UK).

Other European Services Direct overnight trains from Estació Sants also run to Zürich (13 hours) and Milan (12¾ hours), from three to seven days a week, depending on the season. These trains meet connections for numerous other cities.

Car & Motorcycle
From the UK, you can transport your car to France by ferry (Dover to Calais) or by Eurotunnel train (Folkestone to Calais). With your foot flat on the floor through France, you may save a little time over the direct Spain ferries (see later). Whether or not it is cheaper depends on the French toll roads you take, how much juice your vehicle burns and mechanical problems en route.

Instead of driving across France, you can opt for a P&O European Ferries (☎ 0870 242 4999, W www.poef.com) ship from Portsmouth to Bilbao or a Brittany Ferries (☎ 0870 536 0360, W www.brittanyferries.co.uk) vessel from Plymouth to Santander. Sailings are generally a couple of times a week and take anything from 24 to 33 hours. You then have to calculate driving time to reach Catalunya (reckon on six or seven hours).

Roads in Spain are generally good and improving all the time. The main motorway link from France in Spain is the A-7 *autopista* (toll road) that enters Catalunya from France just north of La Jonquera. In France the highway is A-9. The A-7 proceeds south to Barcelona via Girona and heads on south to Valencia via Tarragona. It continues on down the Spanish coast. The other main toll-road entrance into Catalunya is the A-2 from Zaragoza.

If you don't want to pay tolls and don't mind travelling more slowly, the French N-9 runs parallel to the A-9 into Catalunya, where it changes name to the N-II. The N-II then proceeds south to Barcelona via Girona and then the coast. It picks up again at St Vicenç dels Horts, north-west of Barcelona and cuts a path across to Lleida, from where it follows the A-2 to Zaragoza. From there onto Madrid the N-II takes over and the toll road ends. The A-7 on its continuation from Barcelona south into Valencia and beyond is also accompanied by a national road, the heavily used and occasionally dangerous N-340.

So much for the main and boring access roads to Catalunya. Those approaching from France could take one of a number of much more imaginative routes, especially across the Pyrenees. They include: the winding coast road (the N-114 in France, becoming the N-260 in Catalunya); the D-115 (C-38/C-26 in Catalunya) road that leads to Camprodon; the several roads connecting Puigcerdà with the area around the Catalan enclave of Llívia in France; the road through Andorra to La Seu d'Urgell (the N-145 in Catalunya) or N-125 (N-230 in Catalunya) that comes down to Vielha from France.

Several interesting minor roads connect Catalunya with its other two neighbouring regions, Aragón and Valencia. The N-232 from the enchanting town of Alcañiz in Aragón becomes the N-420 on its way to Gandesa and Reus in Catalunya. A little farther south, the T-330 provincial road that hits Arnes on the border with Aragón becomes the A-231 on the picturesque route to Valderrobres.

An interesting Web site loaded with advice for people planning to drive in Europe is W www.ideamerge.com/motoeuropa. If you want help with route planning, try out W www.euroshell.com.

For information on road rules, see the Getting Around chapter.

Paperwork & Preparations Proof of ownership of a private vehicle should always be carried (Vehicle Registration Document for UK-registered cars) when driving through Europe.

Third-party motor insurance is a minimum requirement and it is compulsory to have a Green Card, an internationally recognised proof of insurance, which can be obtained from your insurer. Also ask your insurer for a European accident statement form, which can simplify matters in the event of an accident. Never sign statements you can't read or understand: insist on a translation and sign that only if it's acceptable.

A European breakdown assistance policy such as the AA Five Star Service or RAC Eurocover Motoring Assistance is a good investment.

Every vehicle travelling across an international border should display a nationality plate of its country of registration. Two warning triangles (to be used in the event of a breakdown) are compulsory in Spain. Recommended accessories are a first-aid kit, a spare bulb kit and a fire extinguisher.

If the car is from the UK or Ireland, remember to have the headlights adjusted for driving in continental Europe.

For information on driving licences turn to the Visas & Documents section of the Facts for the Visitor chapter.

In the UK, you can get more information from the RAC (☎ 0870 572 2722) or the AA (☎ 0870 600 0371).

Rental Many people opt to get to Catalunya by other means, then rent a car once they arrive. Prebooking a car through a multinational agency – such as Hertz, Avis, Budget Car or Europe's largest rental agency, Europcar – before leaving home will enable you to find the best deals. Prebooked and prepaid rates are generally cheaper and it may be worth your while looking into fly-drive combinations and other programs. You simply pick up the vehicle on arrival and return it to a nominated point at the end of the rental period. Ask your travel agent for information or contact one of the major rental agencies.

Holiday Autos sometimes has good rates for which you need to prebook; its main office is in the UK (☎ 0870 400 0099, W www.holidayautos.com).

Another possibility if you don't know when you want to rent is to call home from Spain and make a reservation through an agent there. This way you get the benefits of booking from home.

No matter where you rent, make sure you understand what is included in the price (unlimited kilometres, tax, insurance, collision damage waiver etc) and what your liabilities are. The minimum rental age in Spain is 21 years. A credit card is usually required.

For more details of rental rates and options within Catalunya see Car & Motorcycle in the Getting Around chapter and Getting Around in the Barcelona chapter.

Purchase Only residents may legally purchase vehicles in Spain (see Car & Motorcycle in the Getting Around chapter).

Otherwise, the UK is probably the best place to buy a vehicle for travelling in Europe, as second-hand prices are good. But bear in mind that you will be getting a left-hand drive car (ie, the steering wheel will be on the right). If you want a right-hand drive car and can afford to buy a new one, prices are relatively low in Belgium, the Netherlands and Luxembourg.

SEA
Balearic Islands
Regular ferry and high-speed vessels run from Barcelona to the Balearic Islands. See the Barcelona chapter for more details.

Italy
After a 15-year absence, the so-called *canguro* shipping run between Barcelona and Genoa was relaunched in September 1998. It is operated by Grimaldi and runs three times a week. See the Barcelona chapter for details.

ORGANISED TOURS
Quite a few companies offer tours to Catalunya. Spanish tourist offices provide lists of tour operators. What follows is only a brief guide to the kind of options available.

The UK
Short Breaks A range of companies offers short trips to Barcelona and elsewhere. You could try a couple of the big ones, like Mundicolor (☎ 020-7828 6021) or Magic of Spain (☎ 020-8748 4220).

Walking Holidays Explore Worldwide (☎ 01252-760000, W www.explore.co.uk), 1 Frederick St, Aldershot, Hants GU11 1LQ, is a company that can take you trekking in the Pyrenees. It has offices worldwide. Headwater (☎ 01606-813333, W www.headwater.com), 146 London Rd, Northwich, Cheshire CW9 5HH, organises week-long walking holidays.

Cycling Holidays Bolero International Holidays does cycling holidays through France to the Costa Brava from UK£184 to UK£304. The company can be contacted through European Bike Express (☎ 01642-251440), 31 Baker St, Middlesbrough, Cleveland TS1 2LF.

Tastebud Tours If you fancy learning how to whip up a *fideuá* or *crema catalana*, ask Mundicolor (see Short Breaks earlier) about their gastronomy and cooking-lesson trips. If drinking is more your thing, Arblaster & Clarke Wine Tours (☎ 01730-893344) might have something for you. They generally do one trip a year (around November), staying a couple of nights each in Barcelona and Tarragona and touring the Penedès and Priorat wine regions, with tastings and meals accompanied by wine guides. You're looking at about UK£800 per person staying in four-star accommodation.

Self-Catering Several operators can offer self-catering packages in villas, cottages and apartments. Individual Travellers Spain (☎ 0870 077 3773), Manor Court Yard, Bignor, Pulborough RH20 1QD, has plenty of options.

The USA
A plethora of operators run tours from the USA. Spanish Heritage Tours (☎ 800 456 5050), 116–47 Queens Blvd, Forest Hills, NY 11375, is a reputable mainstream operator that can organise a broad array of tour options.

Escapade Vacations (☎ 800 223 7460), 630 Third Ave, New York, NY 10017, offers a range of tours, from coach trips staying in *paradores* (see Accommodation in the Facts for the Visitor chapter) to more flexible 'plan-it-yourself' packages.

Alta Tours (☎ 800 338 4191, W www.altatours.com), 870 Market St, Suite 784, San Francisco, CA 94102, specialises in

Warning
The information in this chapter is vulnerable to change: prices for international travel are volatile, routes are introduced and cancelled, schedules change, special deals come and go and visa requirements are amended. Before you part with your cash, you should get as much information as you can. This chapter is no substitute for your own research.

customised itineraries for individuals and groups. Saranjan Tours (☎ 800 858 9594), PO Box 292, Kirkland, WA 98033, does everything from city breaks to walking trips in the Pyrenees.

Australia

You can organise tours of Spain through the following operators:

Ibertours Travel (☎ 03-9670 8388, W www .ibertours.com.au) 1st floor, 84 William St, Melbourne, Vic 3000

Spanish Tourism (☎ 03-9670 7755, W sales@ spanishtourism.com.au) Level 2, 221 Queen St, Melbourne, Vic 3000

Ya'lla Tours (☎ 03-9646 0277, W www.yallatours .com.au) Level 1, 40 Beach St, Port Melbourne, Vic 3207

Getting Around

AIR
There are no direct flights between cities in Catalunya.

BUS
Unless you have your own wheels, bus is the only way to get around parts of Catalunya. Much of the Pyrenees and the entire Costa Brava are served only by buses, as train services are limited to important railheads such as Girona, Figueres, Lleida, Ripoll and so on. If there is a train then take it – they're generally a more comfortable and convenient option.

Various bus companies operate across the region. Alsina Graells (☎ 93 265 65 92 in Barcelona) runs buses from Barcelona to destinations west and north-west, such as Vielha, La Seu d'Urgell and Lleida. SARFA (☎ 93 265 65 08 in Barcelona, W www .sarfa.es) is the main operator on and around the Costa Brava, and connects with Barcelona. TEISA (☎ 972 20 48 68) is a company that covers a large part of the eastern Catalan Pyrenees from Girona and Figueres. Hispano-Igualadina (☎ 93 488 26 21) covers much of central Catalunya. You will also come across many other companies that serve towns and villages within a fairly limited area.

Services can be frequent on weekdays but between smaller towns they often drop to a few or even none on Sundays and public holidays. If you are depending on buses to get around, always keep this in mind, as it is easy to get stuck in places at the weekend.

On the Buses

To give you an idea of the cost and time involved for making bus journeys around Catalunya, a few sample one-way trips follow. Frequencies given are for weekdays in summer. On the Costa Brava, for instance, services drop drastically in winter. Further information appears in the destination chapters in the course of the guide.

from	to	daily	cost (€)	hours
Barcelona	Cadaqués	2–5	14.30	2¼
Barcelona	Figueres	6	10.50	2¼
Barcelona	Girona	3–7	8.75	1¼
Barcelona	La Seu d'Urgell	4–5	14.90	3½
Barcelona	Lleida	10+	13.20	2¼–2¾
Barcelona	Olot	2–4	11.20	up to 2½
Barcelona	Palafrugell	7–13	9.85	2
Barcelona	Puigcerdà	2	11.90	3
Barcelona	Solsona	4	9.25	2
Barcelona	Tarragona	9	6.95	1½
Barcelona	Tossa de Mar	10	6.45	1¼
Barcelona	Vielha	1	22.45	up to 7
Girona	Cadaqués	3	6.30	1½
Girona	Palafrugell	10+	3.30	1
La Seu d'Urgell	Puigcerdà	2–3	4	1
Lleida	La Seu d'Urgell	2	6.95	2½
Lleida	Tarragona	6	3.70	2
Lleida	Vielha	2	9.25	2¾

TRAIN
The easiest way of getting from Barcelona down the coast towards Valencia and up as far as Blanes is by train. Many destinations of interest surrounding the capital are also most easily reached by train. The main cities and towns, including Figueres, Girona, Tarragona, Lleida, Vic, Manresa, Ripoll and Puigcerdà, are generally more accessible by train from the capital than by bus. Travelling between them can be another story, and often you will find buses more direct.

On occasion, a combination of train and bus is the best way to get where you're headed. To reach many spots on the Costa Brava it is often quickest to catch a train to Girona or Figueres and catch a bus from there. The same goes for the Pyrenees. Trains can get you to useful railheads such as Manresa, Vic, Ripoll and Puigcerdà, from where you would need to pick up a bus to head farther afield.

You can use the long-distance trains, fanning out from Barcelona across Spain to distant objectives such as Madrid or Valencia, but they are generally more expensive than the regional services. These regional services are divided into three types in Catalunya. The slowest all-stops ones are called Regionals. Making fewer stops are the Deltas, while Catalunya Exprès trains are the fastest (and about 15% dearer than

the others). From Barcelona, regional trains depart from Estació Sants; many also stop at Catalunya and/or Passeig de Gràcia.

Rodalies (*cercanías* in Castilian) trains are a more reliable way to get to some destinations not too far out from Barcelona (such as the airport, Sitges, Manresa and the like). They run on a fixed-fare, six-zone system. These trains almost always stop at several stations with metro connections: Estació Sants, Catalunya, Passeig de Gràcia, Arc de Triomf and Clot.

CAR & MOTORCYCLE
If bringing your own car, remember to have your insurance and other papers in order (see Paperwork & Preparations under Car & Motorcycle in the Getting There & Away chapter).

Touring Catalunya with your own wheels allows you a flexibility that public transport just doesn't provide. There are some drawbacks, however, and it is worth making judicious use of trains and buses too. You could decide to base yourself in one of the cities and make day excursions by public transport, saving wear and tear on your car and nerves. From Barcelona, for instance, it is generally easier and less hassle to use trains or buses to reach places Such as Sitges, Tarragona, Girona, Figueres and Lleida.

If you prefer to tour and want to get off

Making Tracks

Some sample one-way, 2nd-class train fares and times follow. Bear in mind that times vary considerably depending on what kind of train you end up on and the number of stops made. Ticket prices also fluctuate, depending on the kind of train you catch.

from	to	daily	cost (€)	hours
Barcelona	Figueres	20	7.80	2¼
Barcelona	Girona	20	5.50	1½
Barcelona	Sitges	30+	2	½
Barcelona	Lleida	20+	from 7.60	2–4
Barcelona	Tarragona	40	4	1–1½
Barcelona	Ripoll	12	4.85	2
Lleida	Tarragona	10	4	1¼
Lleida	La Pobla de Segur	3	4	2
Ripoll	Puigcerdà	5	2.55	1¼

euro currency converter 1000ptas = €6.01

the beaten track it's time to get the keys into the ignition.

The main toll roads that cross parts of Catalunya are generally fast and not too busy with traffic. They include the A-2 and A-7 (see Car & Motorcycle in the Getting There & Away chapter for more details), which run from Barcelona to Lleida (and beyond) and the French border south to Valencia via Girona, Barcelona and Tarragona. In addition, the C-32 runs south-west from the capital along the coast via Sitges, linking up with the A-7 outside Vendrell, the C-58/C-16 runs from Barcelona to Manresa and the C-31/C-32 runs north-east along the coast from Barcelona to just short of Blanes. Tolls are not excessively cheap, although they have come down a little in recent years. To use the C-58/C-16 from Barcelona to Manresa, for instance, costs €2.60 on weekdays and €4.60 on weekends and public holidays.

Because of the region's geography, especially in the Pyrenees, most of the main regional and provincial roads run roughly north to south. Apart from the A-2 and the N-II from Barcelona to Lleida and on into Aragón, the two big exceptions are the N-260/C-26/N-152, which is otherwise known as the Eix Pirenaica (Pyrenees Highway; literally 'axis') and the more recently opened C-25 or Eix Transversal, a cross-Catalan expressway. The former starts at Portbou on the French border by the Mediterranean Sea, drops south to Figueres and then winds its way westwards through the mountains, passing Olot, Ripoll, Puigcerdà, La Seu d'Urgell and Sort and El Pont de Suert, from where it proceeds across the Ara-gonese Pyrenees. The latter starts 11km south of Girona off the A-7, passes through Vic and Manresa and hooks up with the N-141 just short of Cervera, where it flows into the N-II. Making east to west progress anywhere in the area north of the N-II is fascinating but slow-going.

The worst areas for dense traffic are Barcelona and its satellite towns, especially on Sunday evenings (approaching Barcelona) and peak times on weekdays. The N-II along the coast north-east of the capital is often busy and the N-340 and other coast roads south as far as the Delta de l'Ebre (Ebro in Castilian) are also pretty heavily choked.

Road Maps & Atlases

See under Maps in the Facts for the Visitor chapter for information on road maps. Note that, in a spurt of Catalan national pride, many regional road numbers have been changed since March 2001. Increasingly they begin with C and the new numbers bear no relation to the old ones. Inevitably there will be disparities for some time between available road maps and the new reality on the ground. You may also find that some road signs still need to catch up. We have used the updated road names throughout the guide. The latest information can be gleaned at W www.gencat.es/ptop/program/codific/index.htm.

Road Rules

In built-up areas the speed limit is 50km/h, which rises to 100km/h on major roads and up to 120km/h on *autovías* and *autopistas* (toll-free and tolled dual-lane highways, respectively). Cars towing caravans are restricted to a maximum speed of 80km/h. The minimum driving age is 18.

Motorcyclists must use headlights at all times and wear a crash helmet if riding a bike of 125cc or more. The minimum age for riding bikes and scooters of 80cc and over is 16 and for those 50cc and under the minimum age is 14. A licence is required.

Spanish truck drivers often have the courtesy to turn on their right indicator to show that the way ahead of them is clear for overtaking (and the left one if it is not and you are attempting this manoeuvre).

Vehicles already on roundabouts have right of way.

The blood-alcohol limit is 0.05% (0.03% for drivers with less than two years' experience and professional drivers) and breath-testing is occasionally carried out. If fitted, rear seat belts must be worn. Fines for many traffic offences, including driving under the influence of alcohol, range from €301 to €602.

Nonresident foreigners can be fined up to

€301 on the spot, although you can get 20% off normal fines if you settle immediately. You can contest the fine in writing (and in English) within 10 days, but don't hold your breath for a favourable result.

Petrol

In Spain *benzina/gasolina* is pricey but generally cheaper than in its major EU neighbours (including France, Germany, Italy and the UK). About 30 companies, including several foreign operators, run petrol stations in Spain, but the two biggest are the home-grown Repsol and Cepsa.

Prices vary (up to €0.02 per litre) between service stations *(benzineras/gasolineras)* and fluctuate with oil tariffs and tax policy. Diesel *(gasoil/gasóleo)* costs €0.69 per litre. Lead-free *(sense plom/sin plomo*; 95 octane) costs €0.84 per litre and a 98 octane variant (also lead-free) that goes by various names, costs up to €0.93 per litre. Super, which costs €0.90 per litre, will be phased out by January 2002. You can pay with major credit cards at many service stations. Petrol is about 15% cheaper in Andorra.

Road Assistance

The head office of the Real Automóvil Club de España (RACE; ☎ 900 20 00 93) is at Calle de José Abascal 10 in Madrid. For RACE's 24-hour, nationwide emergency breakdown assistance, you can try calling ☎ 900 11 22 22. The Catalan version of the RACE is the Reial Automòbil Club de Catalunya (RACC; ☎ 902 30 73 07), with headquarters in Barcelona at Avinguda Diagonal 687. Their assistance number is ☎ 902 10 61 06.

As a rule, holders of motoring insurance with foreign organisations such as the RAC, AA (UK) or AAA (USA) will be provided with an emergency assistance number to use while travelling in Spain, so in general you should not require the above numbers. Whichever numbers you use, in Catalunya you may well be assisted by the RACC. If you plan on a long stay in Catalunya, you may want to take out local insurance with the RACC, which is quite possible for cars registered abroad.

City Driving

Driving in the bigger Spanish centres such as Barcelona can be nerve-racking at first. Road rules and traffic lights are generally respected but the pace and jostling take a little getting used to. The quietest time is between about 2 and 5 pm, when most locals are either eating or snoozing. Outside Barcelona you may also get flustered in Tarragona, Girona, Lleida, Sitges and some of the other coastal towns in high summer.

Parking can be difficult. Where possible, avoid leaving luggage and valuables in unattended vehicles. If you must leave luggage in vehicles, you should probably use paid car parks (an average €1.20 per hour). All the main town centres operate a restricted parking system and, although many locals ignore the fines, you risk your car being towed away if you double-park or if you leave your vehicle in a designated no-parking zone. Recovering the vehicle can cost €60 to €100.

Rental

If you haven't organised a rental car from abroad, local firms such as Julià Car, Ronicar and Vanguard (all in Barcelona) are generally cheaper than the big international names. From these, a typical small car like a Ford Ka or Fiat Punto should cost from around €17 per day plus €0.15 per km, plus IVA. For unlimited kilometres, they're around €109 for three days or €211 per week, plus IVA. You pay insurance on top, which can come to around €9 per day. Special low weekend rates (from Friday lunchtime or afternoon to Monday morning) are worth looking into.

Another option is to book a car on the Web with easyRentacar, run by the budget airline easyJet. For more details on this and a list of car-rental outlets in Barcelona, see Getting There & Away in the Barcelona chapter.

Purchase

Only people legally resident in Spain may buy vehicles there. One way around this is to have a friend who is a resident put the ownership papers in their name.

Car-hunters need a reasonable knowledge of Spanish to get through paperwork and understand dealers' patter. Trawling around showrooms or looking through classifieds can turn up second-hand small cars in good condition from around €1800. The annual cost of third-party insurance on such a car, with theft and fire cover and national breakdown assistance, comes in at between €240 and €300 (with annual reductions if you make no claims).

Vehicles of five years and older must be submitted for roadworthiness checks, known as Inspección Técnica de Vehículos (ITV). If you pass, you get a sticker for two years. After 10 years you have to do it annually. Check that this has been done when buying: the test costs about €24.

You can get second-hand 50cc *motos* (motorcycles) for anything from €240 to €605.

Warning

If you drive a foreign or rental car to and around Barcelona, take extra care. Groups of delinquents are known to zero in on them occasionally. They get you to pull over indicating you have a problem with a tyre or whatever. While you and one of them are busy examining the problem, the guy's sidekick is busy emptying your car.

BICYCLE

Bicycle rental, while not as common as you might hope, is still possible in many areas of Catalunya. This is especially true of mountain bikes *(bicicleta tot terreny/ bici todo terreno)*. There are quite a few bicycle-hire outlets in Barcelona itself (see under Getting Around in the Barcelona chapter).

If you plan to bring your own bike, check with the airline about any hidden costs and also how you will have to disassemble or pack it.

You should travel light on a cycle tour but bring tools and some spare parts, including a puncture-repair kit and a spare inner tube. Panniers are essential to balance your possessions on either side of the bike frame. A bike helmet is a good idea, as are a solid bike lock and chain to prevent theft.

Cycle-touring across Catalunya is quite possible, although you need to be in good shape in the Pyrenees.

UK-based cyclists planning to tour might want to contact the Cyclists' Touring Club (CTC; ☎ 01483-417217), Cotterell House, 69 Meadrow, Godalming, Surrey GU7 3HS. It can supply information to members on cycling conditions and itineraries in Catalunya as well as cheap insurance. Membership costs UK£25 per annum.

If you get tired of pedalling it is possible to take your bike on the train. You have to be travelling overnight in a sleeper or *litera* (couchette) to have the (dismantled) bike accepted as normal luggage. Otherwise, it can only be sent separately as a parcel. Some regional trains have space for bicycles – ask before buying tickets. Bikes are permitted on most rodalies/cercanías trains. It's often possible to take your bike on a bus (usually you'll just be asked to remove the front wheel).

The European Bike Express is a bus service that enables cyclists to travel with their machines. It runs in summer (April to October) from north-eastern England to Spain, with pick-up/drop-off points en route. The one-way/return fare costs UK£99/169 (UK£159 return for CTC members). Phone ☎ 01642-251440 in the UK for details.

HITCHING

Hitching is never entirely safe and we don't recommend it. Travellers who decide to hitch should understand that they are taking a small but potentially serious risk. Hitching on autopistas is illegal and it is unlikely anyone will stop for you. Your chances of getting a ride increase on the busier national roads, such as the N-II heading northwards from Barcelona along the coast and then inland to Girona. On the myriad network of smaller provincial roads that dominate the Pyrenees and much of inland Catalunya you may also get lucky, although traffic can be scarce on some back roads.

If starting in Barcelona or another large centre you need to head for the city outskirts, or preferably a smaller town on your route, before sticking your thumb out.

LOCAL TRANSPORT

All cities and major towns have a reasonable local bus service. Generally you won't need to use them, as the towns are compact, with sights, hotels, restaurants and long-distance transport stations within walking distance of each other. The only exception is Barcelona, which also has an extensive metro and train system to help whisk you around the city.

Buses and trains connect El Prat airport with downtown Barcelona (see Getting Around in the Barcelona chapter).

ORGANISED TOURS

It is possible to get onto guided city tours in some of the main centres, especially Barcelona. They can be illuminating but you can generally get around any of the towns under your own steam with no difficulty. From Barcelona and resorts along the coast you can join tours to various parts of the region. Again, they can save you hassle but it is pretty easy to get around these areas yourself.

Other possibilities include walking and adventure packages. Operators scattered across the small towns of Catalunya propose walking trips of a week or so, staying in camping grounds or refuges, in the Pyrenees and elsewhere. To start your search ask at the Palau Robert regional tourist office in Barcelona (see under Information in the Barcelona chapter) for a booklet called *Activity Holidays*, which contains details of numerous such organisations and their tours.

Barcelona

postcode 08080 • pop 1.5 million

If extreme Catalan nationalists were ever to see their desires realised and an independent state of Catalunya were created, they would have in Barcelona a capital to do it proud. All the cards are in order. Like any self-respecting European metropolis it has a good 2000 years of history. Industrious, dynamic and vibrant, Barcelona has known good and not-so-good times. Today it is in its element as the preferred monthly flavour of many a Euro-jetsetter and with a sizable amount of fans over the pond. Showing all the classic signs of a capital, it is expanding octopus-like into its own hinterland, devouring villages and spawning high-rise dormitory suburbs.

Controversial urban renovation programs that began in preparation for the 1992 Olympics and continue apace today have changed the face of the city centre. Like it or not (and not everyone does), Barcelona has shown itself in a hurry to plunge into the vanguard of urban Europe.

Although it ain't Rome or Paris, Barcelona has a respectable menu of sights for the curious visitor, and also a couple of aces, altogether missing from the others' decks.

Start with the sea. Not only is Barcelona one of the most dynamic ports on the Mediterranean, it also has a string of reasonable beaches (and plenty more farther up and down the coast beyond the city). Just in from the port is the tangled jumble of the Barri Gòtic (Gothic Quarter), which combines the fascination of history with an admirable determination on the part of many of its citizens to have a good time in a swarm of cafes, bars and restaurants.

Beyond this core spreads the 19th- and early-20th-century expansion of the city, sprinkled with the architectural delights of Modernisme, exemplified by Antoni Gaudí's La Sagrada Família. There's plenty more. You'd need a week to even begin to get a serious feel for the place.

Highlights

- Rambling along La Rambla, Spain's most famous street
- Exploring the Barri Gòtic, a classic medieval quarter
- Inspecting the Museu Picasso, the country's best collection of this major modern artist's work
- Marvelling at La Sagrada Família, Spain's most original 'work-in-progress'
- Embarking on a day out on Montjuïc, the hill of parks, museums and Olympic stadiums
- Tucking into a first-class Catalan meal at the city's finer restaurants
- Quaffing an absinthe or two in Bar Marsella
- Sipping *cava* (Catalan 'champagne') at El Xampanyet
- Dancing the night away at stylish Otto Zutz
- Following the Modernista trail of architecture

FRANCE
ANDORRA
Girona
Lleida
Barcelona
BARCELONA
Barcelona Metro p145
Map 1 Barcelona pp146-7
Map 2 L'Eixample & Gràcia pp148-9
Map 3 Central Barcelona pp150-1
Map 4 Ciutat Vella pp152-3
Tarragona
MEDITERRANEAN SEA

HISTORY

Barcelona was probably founded by the Carthaginians in about 230 BC, taking the surname of Hamilcar Barca, Hannibal's father. Roman Barcino (Barcelona) covered

111

BARCELONA

an area within today's Barri Gòtic and was overshadowed by Tarraco (Tarragona), 90km to the south-west. Under the Visigoths, and then the Muslims (from AD 713), Barcelona remained a modest place.

By the 12th and 13th centuries all of Catalunya was entering a golden age, during which it created a substantial Mediterranean empire. Barcelona's trading wealth paid for the great Gothic buildings that still bejewel the city.

The Casp Agreement (1412) marked the beginning of decline for Barcelona, as it was increasingly marginalised on the fringe of Aragonese and later Castilian affairs. Siege in the War of the Spanish Succession ended in defeat in 1714, at which point any vestige of Catalan autonomy disappeared.

Barcelona suffered but by the mid-19th century had recovered much of its self-confidence as it led the way in Spain's hopelessly delayed introduction to the industrial age. The late 19th century brought urban expansion with the creation of L'Eixample (Enlargement), some worldwide publicity with the 1888 Universal Exhibition and a revival of Catalan consciousness with the so-called Renaixença (Renaissance).

In the wake of WWI, however, massive strikes and violent clashes between right and left became the order of the day, culminating in civil war in 1936. In 1937 Barcelona became the Republican capital, which it remained until the last days of the war. The city fell to the Nationalists on 25 January 1939. Up to 35,000 people were shot in the ensuing purge, and the executions continued into the 1950s.

Some 750,000 immigrants flooded into Barcelona in the 1950s and 1960s, the majority of whom came to form great pockets of Spanish-speaking population in the poorer working-class districts of the city.

Barcelona was transformed by the successful 1992 Olympics, which spurred a burst of public works and brought new life to areas like Montjuïc, where the major events were held. The once-shabby waterfront has been regenerated. Enormous urban redevelopment projects are ongoing and the city seems more ebullient than ever.

ORIENTATION

Barcelona's coastline runs roughly from north-east to south-west, with many streets parallel or perpendicular to it.

The focal axis is La Rambla, a 1.25km boulevard running north-west and slightly uphill from Port Vell (Old Harbour) to Plaça de Catalunya.

The Ciutat Vella (Old City), which surrounds La Rambla, is divided into three parts, the Barri Gòtic (the city's ancient core), La Ribera to the north-east and El Raval to the south-west. L'Eixample, the grid of straight streets into which Barcelona grew in the 19th century, starts at Plaça de Catalunya, from where it radiates outwards.

Two good landmarks for orientation are the hills of Montjuïc and Tibidabo. Montjuïc, the lower of the two, begins about 700m south-west of the bottom (south-eastern end) of La Rambla. Tibidabo, with its landmark TV tower and golden Christ statue, is 6km north-west of the top (north-western end) of La Rambla. It's the high point of the range of wooded hills forming a backdrop to the city.

Maps

Tourist offices hand out free city and transport maps that are OK but Lonely Planet's *Barcelona City Map* is better and includes an index of streets and sights. If you can't find it, try the Michelin No 40 *Barcelona* map (€5.75). Together with a comprehensive street index (Michelin No 41) the price is €7.25.

INFORMATION
Tourist Offices

The Oficina d'Informació de Turisme de Barcelona (Map 3; ☎ 906 30 12 82 from within the country, ☎ 00 34 93 304 34 21 from abroad) at Plaça de Catalunya 17-S (underground) concentrates on city information, and staff can also book accommodation. It opens 9 am to 9 pm daily.

In the Ajuntament (town hall; Map 4) on Plaça de Sant Jaume there is another information office with similar hours.

The regional tourist office (Map 2; ☎ 93 238 40 00) is in the Palau Robert, Passeig de

Strange medieval knights on the roof of La Pedrera, Barcelona?

Flying the Catalan flag

Gaudí's playful tiling on the Banc de Trenadis, Parc Güell, Barcelona

Tiled ceiling, Parc Güell

Flamboyant mosaic on Casa de les Punxes, Barcelona

Gegants (giants) at Barcelona's pre-winter Festes de la Mercè

Another *gegant* on parade

Dancing in the street during the Festes de la Mercè, Barcelona

For the best in Barcelona's festival entertainment, just follow your nose!

Gràcia 107. It opens 10 am to 7 pm Monday to Saturday, and 10 am to 2.30 pm Sunday. It has a host of material, audiovisuals, a bookshop and a branch of Turisme Juvenil de Catalunya.

Turisme de Barcelona in Estació Sants (Map 1) covers Barcelona only. It opens 8 am to 8 pm daily (from October to May it closes at 2 pm weekends and holidays).

There's also a tourist office (☎ 93 478 05 65) in the airport's EU arrivals hall, open 9.30 am to 8 pm Monday to Saturday, and 9.30 am to 3 pm Sunday (about 30 minutes later in summer). It has information on all of Catalunya. The office (☎ 93 478 47 04) at the international arrivals hall opens the same hours.

Another useful office for information on events (and tickets) is the Palau de la Virreina arts-entertainment and ticket information office (Map 4; ☎ 93 301 77 75) at Rambla de Sant Josep 99.

You can find out about accommodation at W www.barcelona-on-line or on ☎ 93 304 32 32.

A couple of general information lines worth bearing in mind are ☎ 010 and ☎ 012. The former is for Barcelona and the latter for all of Catalunya (run by the Generalitat). You sometimes strike English-speakers although for the most part operators are Catalan/Castilian bilingual. They can often answer quite obscure questions.

Foreign Consulates

Most of the consulates in Barcelona are open 9 or 10 am to 1 or 2 pm weekdays. Some are marked on the maps. See also Consulates in Barcelona in the Facts for the Visitor chapter.

Money

Barcelona abounds with banks, many with ATMs, including several around Plaça de Catalunya and more on La Rambla and on Plaça de Sant Jaume in the Barri Gòtic.

The exchange offices that you see along La Rambla and elsewhere are open for longer hours than banks but generally offer poorer rates.

American Express (AmEx; Map 2; ☎ 93

415 23 71, ☎ 93 217 00 70) at Passeig de Gràcia 101 (the entrance is on Carrer del Rosselló) has a machine giving cash on AmEx cards. The office opens 9.30 am to 6 pm weekdays and 10 am to noon Saturday. There is another branch at Rambla dels Caputxins 74 (Map 4), which opens 9 am to midnight daily, April to September; 9 am to 8.30 pm weekdays and 10 am to 7 pm Saturday (closed for lunch 2 to 3 pm), the rest of the year.

Post & Communications

The main post office (correus/correos; Map 4; ☎ 902 19 71 97) is on Plaça d'Antoni López, opposite the north-eastern end of Port Vell. It opens for stamp sales, poste restante (window Nos 7 and 8) and information 8 am to 9.30 pm Monday to Saturday.

The post office also has a public fax service, as do many shops and offices around the city.

Another useful post office is at Carrer d'Aragó 282 (Map 2), just off Passeig de Gràcia, which opens 8.30 am to 8.30 pm weekdays, and 9.30 am to 1 pm Saturday. Other district offices tend to open 8 am to 2 pm weekdays only.

AmEx (see Money earlier) offers a free mail-holding service for those with an AmEx card or travellers cheques.

There are telephone and fax offices at Estació Sants (open 8.30 am to 9.30 pm daily except Sunday) and Estació del Nord.

Email & Internet Access Dozens of places, ranging from cafes to computer stores, offer Internet access. It is a rapidly changing scene and prices are falling fast. Some options include:

easyEverything (Map 3) Ronda de la Universitat 35. With 300 terminals and some ridiculous offers (such as six hours on-line for €1.20 if you start between 6 am and 9 am), this place, run by the Greek businessman who set up the UK-based budget airline easyJet, opens 24 hours a day and you can fuel up on coffee and doughnuts. There is another branch is at La Rambla 31 (Map 4).

Conéctate (Map 2; ☎ 93 467 04 43) Carrer de Pau Claris 134. This is a similar place, also open for

24 hours, with net time at a flat rate of €1.20 per hour. It has replaced what was not a bad cinema.
Café Interlight (Map 2; ☎ 93 301 11 80) Carrer de Pau Claris 106. They charge €1.50 per hour and open 9 am (noon at weekends) to 10 pm.

Travel Agencies
usit Unlimited (Map 3; ☎ 93 412 01 04), at Ronda de la Universitat 16, sells youth and student air, train and bus tickets. It has a branch in the Turisme Juvenil de Catalunya office (Map 1) at Carrer de Rocafort 116–122. Viajes Wasteels at Catalunya metro station (Map 3) has similar youth and student fare. Halcón Viatges is a reliable chain of travel agencies that sometimes has good deals. Its branch at Carrer de Pau Claris 108 (Map 2) is one of 28 around town. Its national phone reservation number is ☎ 902 30 06 00.

Bookshops
Many newsstands, especially on La Rambla, carry a wide range of foreign newspapers. Here's a selection of Barcelona's many good bookshops:

La Rambla
Llibreria & Informaciò Cultural de la Generalitat de Catalunya (Map 4; ☎ 93 302 64 62) Rambla dels Estudis 118. A good first stop for books and pamphlets on all things Catalan, although a lot of it is highly specialised and technical.
Llibreria de la Virreina (Map 4; ☎ 93 301 77 75) Palau de la Virreina, Rambla de Sant Josep 99. An assortment of art/architecture and art history books, many with at least some relevance to Barcelona.

Barri Gòtic & El Raval
Antinous (Map 4; ☎ 93 301 90 70) Carrer de Josep Anselm Clavé 6. Good gay bookshop-cafe.
Documenta (Map 4; ☎ 93 317 25 27) Carrer del Cardenal Casañas 4. Stocks novels in English and French; also sells maps.
Próleg (Map 4; ☎ 93 319 24 25) Carrer de la Dagueria 13. Women's bookshop.

L'Eixample
Altaïr (Map 3; ☎ 93 342 71 71) Gran Via de les Corts Catalanes 616. Great travel bookshop with maps, guides and travel literature.

Come In (Map 2; ☎ 93 453 12 04) Carrer de Provença 203. Specialist in English-teaching books; also has plenty of novels and books on Spain, in both English and French.
Librería Francesa (Map 2; ☎ 93 215 14 17) Passeig de Gràcia 91. Lots of novels and guidebooks in French.

Cultural Centres
There are English-language libraries at the British Council (Map 1; ☎ 93 241 99 77) at Carrer d'Amigó 83, as well as at the Institute of North American Studies (Map 2; ☎ 93 200 24 67), Via Augusta 123. Institut Français de Barcelona (Map 2; ☎ 93 209 59 11) at Carrer de Moià 8 puts on films, concerts and exhibitions.

Gay & Lesbian Information
Casal Lambda (Map 4; ☎ 93 412 72 72) at Carrer Ample 5 in the Barri Gòtic is a social, cultural and information centre for gays and lesbians. Coordinadora Gai-Lesbiana (Map 1; ☎ 93 298 00 29, fax 93 298 06 18, e cogailes@pangea.org), Carrer de Finlàndia 45, is the city's main coordinating body for gay and lesbian groups. Some of the latter, such as Grup de Lesbianes Feministes, are to be found at Ca la Dona (Map 2; ☎ 93 412 71 61), Carrer de Casp 38. There is a free gay helpline (which is also the number for Stop Sida, the AIDS helpline) on ☎ 900 60 16 01.

Photography
There are plenty of places to have films developed. Panorama Foto, which has seven branches around town, including one at Passeig de Gràcia 2 (Map 3), will develop most photos, including slides, within an hour.

Laundry
Self-service laundries are a rarity indeed. One is Lavomatic (Map 4), Carrer del Consolat de Mar 43–45. A 7kg load costs €3.50 and drying costs €0.65 for five minutes.

Wash'N Dry (Map 2), on the corner of Carrer de Torrent de l'Olla and Carrer Ros de Olano in Gràcia, charges €4.25 for an 8kg load and €0.60 for six minutes' drying time. It opens 7 am to 10 pm.

Lost Property

The city's main lost property *(objetos perdidos)* office (☎ 010) is in the Ajuntament (Map 4) at Carrer de la Ciutat 7. If you leave anything in a taxi, you can call ☎ 93 223 40 12 to see if it's been handed in. If you leave anything in the metro, try the Centre d'Atenció al Client (Map 3; ☎ 93 318 70 74) at the Universitat stop.

Medical Services

Hospitals with an emergency service include Hospital de la Creu Roja (Map 1; ☎ 93 300 20 20), Carrer del Dos de Maig 301, and Hospital de la Santa Creu i Sant Pau (Map 1; ☎ 93 291 90 00), Carrer de Sant Antoni Maria Claret 167.

For an ambulance, call ☎ 061, ☎ 93 329 97 01 or ☎ 93 300 20 20; for emergency dental help, contact ☎ 93 277 47 47.

There's a 24-hour pharmacy at Carrer d'Aribau 62 (Map 3) and another at Passeig de Gràcia 26 (Map 2). A third, Farmàcia Saltó (Map 1; ☎ 93 339 63 32), is somewhat out of the centre at Avinguda de Madrid 222. Otherwise, for information about on-duty chemists, call ☎ 010.

Emergency

The general EU standard emergency number is ☎ 112. You can reach all emergency services on this number and occasionally even get multilingual operators.

Barcelona abounds with different kinds of police (see the boxed text 'La Policía – Who's Who' in the Facts for the Visitor chapter). The Guàrdia Urbana (city police; Map 4; ☎ 092) has a station at La Rambla 43, opposite Plaça Reial. If you need to report the theft or loss of your passport and other belongings, head to the *comisaría* (police station) of the Policía Nacional (Map 3; ☎ 091), Carrer Nou de la Rambla 80. There's usually an English-speaker on duty.

Dangers & Annoyances

The Barri Xinès (literally 'Chinese Quarter', a curious term that means 'red-light district' but has nothing to do with the presence or otherwise of Chinese people), the lower end of La Rambla and the area around Plaça Reial, although much cleaned up in recent years, remain dodgy – watch your wallet.

LA RAMBLA (Map 4)

Head to Spain's most famous street for a first taste of Barcelona's atmosphere. Flanked by narrow traffic lanes, the middle of La Rambla is a broad, pedestrian boulevard, lined with cafes and restaurants and crowded beyond midnight every day with a cross section of Barcelona's permanent and transient population.

La Rambla gets its name from a seasonal stream *(raml* in Arabic) that once ran here. It was outside the city walls until the 14th century and built up with monastic buildings and palaces in the 16th to 18th centuries. Unofficially it's divided into five sections with their own names.

Rambla de Canaletes

A block off to the east of this first stretch at the northern end of La Rambla, along Carrer de la Canuda, is Plaça de la Vila de Madrid, with a sunken garden where some **Roman tombs** have been exposed.

Rambla dels Estudis

This second stretch of La Rambla, from below Carrer de Santa Anna to Carrer de la Portaferrissa, is also called Rambla dels Ocells (birds) because of its twittering **bird market**.

Rambla de Sant Josep

This section from Carrer de la Portaferrissa to Plaça Boqueria is lined with **flower stalls**, which give it the alternative name Rambla de les Flors. The **Palau de la Virreina**, at Rambla de Sant Josep 99, is a grand 18th-century rococo mansion housing an arts information office run by the Ajuntament (for details see under Tourist Offices earlier).

The next building down is La Rambla's most colourful: the **Mercat de la Boqueria**, a bustling covered food market. Plaça Boqueria, where four side streets meet just north of Liceu metro station, is where you'll get the chance to walk all over a Miró – the colourful **Mosaïc de Miró** in the pavement, with one tile signed by the artist.

In the **Museu de l'Eròtica**, at No 96, you can observe how people have been enjoying themselves since ancient times – including lots of Karma Sutra and porn flicks from the 1920s. The centre opens 10 am to midnight daily and admission costs €6.

Rambla dels Caputxins

Also called Rambla del Centre, this stretch runs from Plaça Boqueria to Carrer dels Escudellers. On the western side is the **Gran Teatre del Liceu**, Barcelona's famous 19th-century opera house which reopened in 1999, five years after its destruction in a fire.

On the eastern side of Rambla dels Caputxins, farther south, is the entrance to the Plaça Reial (see under Barri Gòtic later). Just below this point, La Rambla becomes seedier, with a few strip clubs and peep shows reflecting this section's former status as Barcelona's chief red-light area.

Rambla de Santa Mònica

The final stretch of La Rambla widens out to approach the Monument a Colom (Columbus monument) overlooking Port Vell. On the eastern side, at the end of narrow Passatge de la Banca, is the **Museu de Cera** (Wax Museum), which has tableaux of a *gitano* (Romany) cave, a bullring medical room and a hall of horror as well as wax figures of Cleopatra, Franco etc – it's not bad as wax museums go. It opens 10 am to

---

Barcelona's Museums

Every Barcelona museum has its own concoction of opening days and hours, sometimes with seasonal variations. Many have a range of prices too, with students and pensioners often paying half-price and those under 16 getting in for free. Some museums are free to everyone on the first Sunday of the month and/or half-price on nonholiday Wednesdays. Where only one price is given in this chapter, that's the normal full adult price.

1.30 pm and 4 to 7.30 pm weekdays, and 11 am to 2 pm and 4.30 to 8.30 pm weekends and holidays. Admission costs €6.65.

Monument a Colom (Map 3)

The bottom of La Rambla, and the harbour beyond it, are supervised by the tall Columbus Monument, built in the 1880s. You can ascend by lift (€1.50) from 9 am to 8.30 pm daily, June to September. It opens 10 am to 7.30 pm daily (with a break from 2 to 3.30 pm weekdays), in April and May; and to 6.30 pm, the rest of the year.

Museu Marítim (Map 3)

West of the Monument a Colom on Avinguda de les Drassanes stand the **Reials Drassanes** (Royal Shipyards), a rare work of nonreligious Gothic architecture. The buildings now house the Museu Marítim (Maritime Museum) – which, together with its setting, forms a fascinating tribute to the seaborne contacts that have shaped Barcelona's history.

The shipyards, first built in the 13th century, gained their present form (a series of long bays divided by stone arches) a century later. Extensions in the 17th century made them big enough to accommodate the building of 30 galleys. In their shipbuilding days (up to the 18th century) the sea came right up to them.

Inside is an impressive array of boats, models, maps, paintings and more, with sections devoted to ships' figureheads, Columbus and Magellan, and 16th-century galleys (the full-scale replica of Don Juan of Austria's royal galley from the Battle of Lepanto is a highlight).

The museum opens 10 am to 7 pm daily and admission costs €4.85 (€3.65 for students and seniors). Admission is free after 3 pm on the first Saturday of the month.

BARRI GÒTIC (Map 4)

The Gothic Quarter, east of La Rambla, is a classic medieval warren of narrow, winding streets, quaint little plazas and wonderful structures from Barcelona's golden age. Most of the city's best budget accommodation is here and plenty of good bars, cafes and restaurants. Few of its great buildings date from after the early 15th century.

The area stretches from La Rambla in the west to Via Laietana in the east and roughly from Carrer de la Portaferrissa in the north to Carrer de la Mercè in the south.

Plaça de Sant Jaume

This square at the eastern end of Carrer de Ferran has been Barcelona's political hub on and off since the 15th century. Facing each other across it are the **Palau de la Generalitat** (the seat of Catalunya's government) on the northern side and the **Ajuntament** on the southern side. Both have fine Gothic interiors, which the general public can only enter at limited times. The Palau de la Generalitat, founded in the early 15th century, opens only on 23 April, the Dia de Sant Jordi (St George's Day; Catalunya's patron saint), when it's decked out with roses and also very crowded, and on 24 September, the beginning of Festes de la Mercè. At any time, however, you can admire the original Gothic main entrance on Carrer del Bisbe Irurita.

The only exterior feature of the Ajuntament still worthy of note is the disused Gothic entrance on Carrer de la Ciutat. From 10 am to 2 pm at the weekend you can tour the inside to visit, above all, the Saló de Cent, a fine arched hall created in the 14th century (but since remodelled) for the medieval city council, the Consell de Cent.

Catedral & Around

You can reach Barcelona's cathedral, one of its most magnificent Gothic structures, by following Carrer del Bisbe Irurita northwest from Plaça de Sant Jaume. The narrow old streets around the cathedral are traffic-free but dotted with buskers.

On your way to the cathedral, at the northern end of Carrer del Bisbe Irurita poke your head into the courtyards of the 16th-century **Casa de l'Ardiaca** (Archdeacon's House) and the 13th-century **Palau de Bispat** (Bishop's Palace). On the outside of both buildings at the very end of Carrer del Bisbe Irurita you can make out the bottom parts of the rounded **Roman towers** that

guarded a Roman gate here. The lower part of the Casa de l'Ardiaca's north-western wall was part of the **Roman walls**.

The best view of the cathedral is from Plaça de la Seu beneath its main **north-western facade**. Unlike most of the building, which dates from between 1298 and 1460, this facade was not created until the 1870s, though it is closely based on a 1408 design. It is unusual in that it reflects northern European Gothic styles rather than the sparer, Catalan version of the Gothic style.

The interior of the cathedral is a broad, soaring space divided into a central nave and two aisles by lines of elegant, thin pillars. The cathedral was one of the few churches in Barcelona spared by the anarchists in the Civil War, so its ornamentation, never overly lavish, remains intact.

In the first chapel on the right from the north-western entrance, the main Crucifixion figure above the altar is the **Sant Crist de Lepant**, which is said to have been carried on the prow of the Spanish flagship at the battle of Lepanto. Farther along this same wall, past the south-western transept, are the wooden **coffins** of Count Ramon Berenguer I and Almodis, his wife, the founders of the 11th-century Romanesque predecessor of the present cathedral.

The **crypt** beneath the main altar contains the tomb of Santa Eulàlia, one of Barcelona's patron saints and a good Christian lass of the 4th century, who suffered terrible torture and death at the hands of the pagan Romans.

You can visit the cathedral's **roof** and tower by an *ascensor* (lift), which ascends every 30 minutes from 10.30 am to 12.30 pm and 4.30 to 6.30 pm Monday to Saturday, from the Capella de les Animes del Purgatori near the north-eastern transept. Tickets cost €1.20.

From the south-western transept, exit to the lovely **claustre** (cloister), with its trees, fountains and flock of geese (there have been geese here for centuries). One of the cloister chapels commemorates 930 priests, monks and nuns martyred in the Civil War.

The interior of the cathedral opens 8.30 am to 1.30 pm and 4 to 7.30 pm (5 to 7.30 pm weekends).

Opposite the south-eastern end of the cathedral, narrow Carrer del Paradis leads back down towards Plaça de Sant Jaume. Inside No 10 are four columns of Barcelona's main **Temple Romà d'Augustí** (Roman Temple of Augustus), built for emperor worship in the 1st century AD. If the door is open, pop in. Mornings are the best bet and admission is free.

Plaça del Rei & Around

Just a stone's throw east of the cathedral, Plaça del Rei is the former courtyard of the Palau Reial Major, the palace of the counts of Barcelona and monarchs of Aragón.

Museu d'Història de la Ciutat Most of the tall, centuries-old buildings surrounding Plaça del Rei are now open to visitors as the city's history museum. This is one of Barcelona's most fascinating museums, combining large sections of the palace with a subterranean walk through Roman and Visigothic Barcelona.

The entrance to the museum is through the **Casa Padellàs** on Carrer del Veguer just south of Plaça del Rei. Casa Padellàs, built for a 15th-century noble family, has a courtyard typical of Barcelona's Gothic mansions. Below ground is a remarkable walk through excavated Roman and Visigothic Barcelona – complete with sections of a Roman street, Roman baths and remains of a Visigothic basilica. You emerge from this part of the museum at a hall and ticket office set up on the northern side of the Plaça del Rei. To your right is the Saló del Tinell and to the left ahead of you is the Capella Reial de Santa Àgata. The **Saló del Tinell** was the royal palace's throne hall, a masterpiece of strong, unfussy Catalan Gothic, built in the mid-14th century with wide, rounded arches holding up a wooden roof. The **Capella Reial de Santa Àgata**, also dating from the 14th century, whose spindly bell tower rises from the north-eastern side of Plaça del Rei, was the palace's chapel.

Head into Plaça del Rei down the fan-shaped stairs and bear left to the entrance to the multitiered **Mirador del Rei Martí** (King Martin's Lookout Tower), built in 1555.

It is part of the museum and leads you to the gallery above the square. You can also climb to the top of the tower, which dominates Plaça del Rei and affords excellent views over the city.

The museum opens 10 am to 2 pm and 4 to 8 pm Tuesday to Saturday, and 10 am to 2 pm Sunday. Admission costs €3 and is free for the evening session on the first Saturday of the month. You pay an extra €1.20 to watch a 3-D video that traces, in entertaining fashion, the history of the city – before you commence your visit proper.

Palau del Lloctinent The south-western side of Plaça del Rei is taken up by the Palau del Lloctinent (Viceroy's Palace), built in the 1550s as the residence of the Spanish viceroy of Catalunya.

Museu Frederic Marès A short distance down Carrer dels Comtes is the Museu Frederic Marès, in another part of the Palau Reial Major. Marès was a rich 20th-century Catalan sculptor, traveller and obsessive collector. He specialised in medieval Spanish sculpture, huge quantities of which are displayed on the ground and 1st floors – including some lovely polychrome wooden sculptures of the Crucifixion and the Virgin. The top two floors hold a mind-boggling array of knick-knacks, from toy soldiers and cribs, scissors and 19th-century playing cards to early still cameras, pipes and fine ceramics. There is also a room that once served as Marès' study and library, now crammed with his sculptures.

The museum opens 10 am to 7 pm (to 5 pm Tuesdays, Thursdays, to 2 pm Sundays and holidays) daily except Monday. Admission costs €2.40 but is free on the first Sunday of the month.

Roman Walls

From Plaça del Rei it's worth a little detour to see the two best surviving stretches of Barcelona's Roman walls. One is on the south-western side of Plaça de Ramon Berenguer el Gran, with the Capella Reial de Santa Àgata atop it. The other is a little farther south, by the northern end of Carrer del Sotstinent Navarro. Both stretches date from the 3rd and 4th centuries, when the Romans rebuilt their walls after the first attacks by Germanic tribes from the north.

Plaça de Sant Josep Oriol & Around

This small plaza not far off La Rambla is the prettiest in the Barri Gòtic. Its bars and cafes attract buskers and artists and make it a lively place to hang out for a while. The plaza is dominated by the **Església de Santa Maria del Pi**, a Gothic church built from the 14th to 16th centuries, open 8.30 am to 1 pm and 4.30 to 9 pm daily (9 am to 2 pm and 5 to 9 pm Sunday and holidays). The beautiful rose window above its entrance on Plaça del Pi is claimed to be the world's biggest. The inside of the church was gutted by fire in 1936 and most of the stained glass is modern.

The area between Carrer dels Banys Nous and Plaça de Sant Jaume is known as the Call and was Barcelona's **Jewish quarter** – and centre of learning – from at least the 11th century until 1424.

Plaça Reial & Around

Just south of Carrer de Ferran, near its La Rambla end, is Plaça Reial, an elegant shady square surrounded by eateries, bars, nightspots and budget accommodation. The plaza's 19th-century neo-classical architecture looks as if it would be at home in some Parisian quarter but before its 1980s cleanup this area had a fearsome reputation for poverty, crime and drugs.

The plaza still has a restless atmosphere, with respectable tourists, ragged buskers and down-and-outs coming face to face. Don't be put off but watch your bags and pockets. The lampposts by the central fountain are Gaudí's first known works.

This southern half of the Barri Gòtic is imbued with the memory of Picasso, who lived as a teenager with his family on Carrer de la Mercè, had his first studio on Carrer de la Plata and was a regular visitor to a brothel at Carrer d'Avinyò 27, which may have inspired his 1907 painting *Les Demoiselles d'Avignon*.

EL RAVAL

West of La Rambla, the Ciutat Vella spreads to Ronda de Sant Antoni, Ronda de Sant Pau and Avinguda del Paral.lel, which together trace the line of Barcelona's 14th-century walls. Known as El Raval, the area contains one of the city's most dispiriting slums, the seedy red-light zone and drug-abusers' haunt of the Barri Xinès. Take care in this area.

Museu d'Art Contemporàni de Barcelona (MACBA) & Around (Map 3)

One of the more upbeat parts of El Raval is the Plaça dels Àngels in the north of the area. Here the vast, white Museu d'Art Contemporàni de Barcelona (MACBA) opened in 1995. Artists frequently on show include Antoni Tàpies, Joan Brossa, Paul Klee, Alexander Calder and Miquel Barceló. It opens 11 am to 7.30 pm weekdays except Tuesday, 10 am to 8 pm Saturday, and 10 am to 3 pm Sunday and holidays. Admission costs €4.70 or €2.10 on nonholiday Wednesdays.

On Carrer de Montalegre behind the museum is the **Centre de Cultura Contemporània de Barcelona**, a complex of auditoriums and exhibition and conference halls created in the early 1990s from an 18th-century hospice. The big courtyard, with a vast glass wall on one side, is spectacular. Exhibitions are regularly held here.

Across Plaça dels Àngels from the MACBA, the former 16th-century Dominican **Convent dels Àngels** has been restored and is used for temporary exhibitions.

Antic Hospital de la Santa Creu (Map 4)

Two blocks south-east of Plaça dels Àngels is an architectural masterpiece from another age. Founded in the early 15th century as the city's main hospital, the Antic Hospital de la Santa Creu today houses the Biblioteca de Catalunya (Catalunya's national library) and the Institut d'Estudis Catalans (Institute of Catalan Studies). Take a look inside the library to admire some fine Catalan Gothic construction.

BARCELONA

Palau Güell (Map 4)

A few steps off La Rambla at Carrer Nou de la Rambla 3–5, the Palau Güell is the only Gaudí house completely open to the public in Barcelona and one of the few Modernista buildings in the Ciutat Vella. Gaudí built it in the late 1880s for his most important patron, the industrialist Eusebi Güell, as a guest wing and social annexe to Güell's main mansion on La Rambla. The Palau Güell lacks some of Gaudí's later playfulness but is still a characteristic riot of styles – Art Nouveau, Gothic, Islamic – and materials. After the Civil War it was occupied by the police and political prisoners were tortured in its basement.

Features to look out for include the carved wooden ceilings and fireplace, the stonework, the use of mirrors, stained glass and wrought iron, and the main hall which stretches up three storeys and has a dome reaching right up to the roof. There's little colour until you come out on the roof with its spectacularly tiled and fantastically shaped chimney pots. Palau Güell opens 10 am to 1.30 pm and 4 to 6.30 pm Monday to Saturday. Admission costs €2.40 (students €1.20) and tours usually start on the hour.

Ruta del Modernisme

Modernisme enthusiasts should consider picking up a Ruta del Modernisme ticket at the Casa Amatller before forking out for individual sights. The €3.65 (€2.40 for students and seniors) ticket is valid for 30 days and is astoundingly good value. It entitles you to half-price admission to the following sights: Palau Güell, Palau de la Música Catalana, La Pedrera, La Sagrada Família, Fundació Antoni Tàpies, Casa Museu Gaudí (in Parc Güell), Museu de la Música, Museu de Zoologia and the Museu Nacional d'Art Modern de Catalunya. Of the buildings comprising the Manzana de la Discòrdia, all in private hands, you can enter the foyer of Casa Amatller to pick up this ticket but that's it. For more information call ☎ 93 488 01 39. Casa Amatller opens 10 am to 7 pm (to 2 pm Sunday).

LA RIBERA

La Ribera is the area of the Ciutat Vella northeast of the Barri Gòtic, from which it's divided by noisy Via Laietana, driven through the city in 1907. La Ribera has intriguing, narrow streets, some major sights and good bars and restaurants, and lacks the seedy character of some parts of the Barri Gòtic.

Palau de la Música Catalana (Map 3)

This concert hall at Carrer de Sant Pere més alt 11 is one of the high points of Modernista architecture. It's not exactly a symphony, more a series of crescendos in tile, brick, sculptured stone and stained glass. Built between 1905 and 1908 by Lluís Domènech i Montaner for the Orfeó Català musical society, with the help of some of the best Catalan artisans of the time, it was conceived as a temple for the Catalan Renaixença.

You can see some of its splendours – such as the main facade with its mosaics, floral capitals and cluster of sculpture representing Catalan popular music – from the outside and glimpse lovely tiled pillars inside the ticket office entrance on Carrer de Sant Francesc de Paula. But best is the richly colourful auditorium upstairs, with its ceiling of blue and gold stained glass and, above a bust of Beethoven, a towering sculpture of Wagner's Valkyries (Wagner was No 1 in the Renaixença charts).

To see this, you need to attend a concert or join a guided tour. Tours, which take 50 minutes, begin every 30 minutes from 10 am to 3.30 pm daily. You can buy tickets from Les Muses del Palau shop at Carrer de Sant Pere més alt 1 up to a week in advance. They cost €4.25. For information call ☎ 93 268 10 00 or ☎ 93 295 72 00.

Museu Picasso (Map 4)

This, Barcelona's most visited museum, occupies three of the many fine medieval stone mansions on narrow Carrer de Montcada (Nos 15–19).

The museum is strongest on the artist's Barcelona periods. It shows clearly how the young Picasso learned to handle a whole spectrum of subjects, styles and treatments before going on to develop his own forms of expression.

On the 1st floor are 1890s paintings from Barcelona, Madrid and Málaga. The 2nd floor starts with work from 1900 to 1904 from Barcelona and Paris, and has more impressionist-influenced paintings such as *Waiting* and Blue Period canvases such as *The Defenceless*. There's also the haunting *Portrait of Senyora Canals* (1905) from the following Pink Period.

Among the later works, all created in Cannes in 1957, is a complex technical series, *Las Meninas*. These consist of studies on Diego Velázquez's masterpiece of the same name (which hangs in the Museo del Prado in Madrid).

The museum opens 10 am to 8 pm Tuesday to Saturday and holidays, and 10 am to 3 pm Sunday. Admission costs €4.40 or is free on the first Sunday of each month.

Museu Tèxtil i d'Indumentària (Map 4)

The Textile and Costume Museum is in the 14th-century Palau dels Marquesos de Llió at Carrer de Montcada 12. Its 4000 items range from 4th-century Coptic textiles to 20th-century local embroidery. The highlight is the large collection of clothing dating from the 16th century to the 1930s. The museum opens 10 am to 8 pm Tuesday to Saturday, and 10 am to 3 pm Sunday and holidays. Admission costs €2.40 (€4.25 combined with the Museu Barbier-Mueller d'Art Precolombí next door) or is free on the first Saturday of each month.

Museu Barbier-Mueller d'Art Precolombí (Map 4)

Occupying the Palau Nadal at Carrer de Montcada 14, this museum holds one of the most prestigious collections of pre-Colombian art in the world. The artefacts from South American 'primitive' cultures come from the collections of the Swiss businessman Josef Mueller (who died in 1977) and his son-in-law Jean-Paul Barbier, who directs the Musée Barbier-Mueller in Geneva. It opens 10 am to 8 pm Tuesday to Saturday, and 10 am to 3 pm

Sunday and holidays. Admission costs €3 (€4.25 combined with the Museu Tèxtil i d'Indumentària) or is free on the first Saturday of each month.

Along Carrer de Montcada (Map 4)

Several other mansions on the street are now commercial art galleries where you're welcome to browse (they often stage exhibitions). The biggest is **Galeria Maeght** at No 25 in the 16th-century Palau dels Cervelló.

Església de Santa Maria del Mar (Map 4)

Carrer de Montcada opens at its southeastern end into **Passeig del Born**, a plaza where jousting tournaments took place in the Middle Ages and which was Barcelona's main square from the 13th to 18th centuries. At its south-western end stands one of Barcelona's finest Gothic churches, Església de Santa Maria del Mar. Built in the 14th century, Santa Maria was lacking in superfluous decoration even before anarchists gutted it in 1909 and 1936. This austerity only serves to highlight its fine proportions, purity of line and sense of space. It opens 9 am to 1.30 pm and 4.30 to 8 pm daily. Evening concerts are sometimes held here.

PARC DE LA CIUTADELLA (Map 3)

East of La Ribera and north of La Barceloneta, Parc de la Ciutadella is perfect if you need a bit of space and greenery, but it also has some more specific attractions.

After the War of the Spanish Succession, Felipe V built a huge fort (La Ciutadella) to keep watch over Barcelona. It became a much loathed symbol of everything Catalans hated about Madrid and was later used as a political prison. Only in 1869 did the government allow its demolition. The site was turned into a park and used as the main site for the Universal Exhibition of 1888. It opens 8 am to 8 pm daily (to 9 pm from April to September).

The single most impressive object in the park is the monumental **Cascada** near the Passeig de les Pujades entrance, created

1875–81 by Josep Fontsère, with the help of the young Gaudí. It's a dramatic combination of classical statuary, rugged rocks and thundering water.

South-east of here, in the fort's former arsenal, are the **Museu Nacional d'Art Modern de Catalunya** and the **Parlament de Catalunya**, where the Generalitat meets. The art gallery, despite its title, is devoted to Catalan art from the mid-19th century to the 1920s, the era of Modernisme and its classicist antithesis, Noucentisme. Look for works by the two leading lights of Modernista art, Ramon Casas and Santiago Rusiñol. The museum opens 10 am to 7 pm Tuesday to Saturday, and 10 am to 2.30 pm Sunday and holidays. Admission costs €3.

At the southern end of the park is the large **Parc Zoològic** (zoo), best known for its albino gorilla called Floquet de Neu (Copito de Nieve in Spanish; Snowflake), who was orphaned by poachers in Africa in the 1960s. It opens 10 am to 7.30 pm daily (to 5 pm in winter). Admission costs €9.35.

Along the Passeig de Picasso side of the park are several buildings constructed for, or just before, the Universal Exhibition. These include two arboretums, the specialised **Museu de Geologia** and the **Museu de Zoologia** or Castell dels Tres Dragons. The latter opens 10 am to 2 pm Tuesday to Sunday, and to 6.30 pm Thursday. Admission costs €2.40. The contents of this museum are less interesting than the building itself, by Lluís Domènech i Montaner, who put medieval castle trimmings on a pioneering steel frame.

North-west of the park along Passeig de Lluís Companys is the imposing Modernista **Arc de Triomf** (Map 1), with unusual, Islamic-style brickwork.

PORT VELL (Map 3)

Barcelona's old port at the bottom of La Rambla, once such an eyesore that it caused public protests, has been transformed since the 1980s into an attractive and people-friendly environment with some excellent leisure facilities.

For a view of the harbour (Map 4) from the water, you can take a **golondrina** (excursion boat; ☎ 93 442 31 06) from Moll de

les Drassanes in front of the Monument a Colom. A 35-minute trip to the breakwater *(rompeolas)* and lighthouse *(faro)* on the seaward side of the harbour costs €3.20; a one-hour trip (on a glass-bottom catamaran) to Port Olímpic costs €5.45. North-east from the golondrina quay stretches the palm-lined promenade **Moll de la Fusta**. At the end of it you will find other modest little boats that will take you for a 30-minute spin around the harbour for €2.15. Also moored at Moll de la Fusta is the *Santa Eulàlia*, a three-mast sailing vessel originally built in 1918 and now fully restored by the Museu Marítim. You can climb aboard to inspect it from 11 am to 5.30 pm daily (to 7.30 pm from April to September).

At the centre of the redeveloped harbour is the **Moll d'Espanya**, a former wharf linked to Moll de la Fusta by a wave-shaped footbridge, **Rambla de Mar**, which rotates to let boats enter the marina behind it. At the end of Moll d'Espanya is the glossy Maremàgnum shopping and eating complex, but the major attraction is **L'Aquàrium** (☎ 93 221 74 74) behind it. It's claimed to be Europe's biggest aquarium and to have the world's best Mediterranean collection. One highlight is the 80m-long shark tunnel. Admission costs a steep €8.75 (€5.75 for children aged four to 12 and seniors). It opens 9.30 am to 9 pm (to 11 pm in July and August). Beyond L'Aquàrium is the Imax Port Vell big-screen cinema.

The **cable car** *(telefèric* or *funicular aereo)* strung across the harbour to Montjuïc provides another view of the city. You can get tickets at Miramar (Montjuïc; Map 1) and the Torre de Sant Sebastià (La Barceloneta; Maps 1 & 3). Access to the Torre de Jaume I, halfway along, was suspended at the time of writing. Miramar to Sant Sebastià costs €7.25 return (€6.05 one way). The cable car runs 10.30 am to 7 pm daily (to 5.30 pm in winter).

LA BARCELONETA & PORT OLÍMPIC

It used to be said that Barcelona had 'turned its back on the sea', but an ambitious Olympics-inspired redevelopment program has returned to life a long stretch of coast north-east of Port Vell.

La Barceloneta is an old sailors' quarter now mostly composed of dreary five- and six-storey apartment blocks and seafood restaurants. In the Palau de Mar building facing the harbour is the **Museu d'Història de Catalunya** (History of Catalunya Museum; Map 3). It's an almost Disneyesque sort of place – it incorporates lots of technological wizardry, with audiovisuals and interactive information points galore. Nearly all the labelling is in Catalan but you can request a returnable explanatory booklet in several languages, including English. Covering the region's prehistory, and history to 1980, the museum has re-creations including a Roman house and a Civil War air-raid shelter. The museum opens 10 am to 7 pm (to 8 pm Friday and Saturday) Tuesday to Saturday, and 10 am to 2.30 pm Sunday and holidays. Admission costs €3.

The city's fishing fleet ties up along the Moll del Rellotge, south of the museum. On La Barceloneta's seaward side are the first of Barcelona's **beaches**, now cleaned up and popular on summer weekends. **Passeig Marítim de la Barceloneta** (Map 1), a 1.25km promenade from La Barceloneta to Port Olímpic (an area formerly full of railway sidings and warehouses) is pleasant.

Port Olímpic (Map 1) was built for the Olympic sailing events and is now surrounded by bars and restaurants. An eye-catcher on the approach from La Barceloneta is the giant copper *Peix* (Fish) sculpture by Frank Gehry. To the north-east are more beaches.

L'EIXAMPLE (Map 2)

L'Eixample (Enlargement), Barcelona's 19th-century answer to overcrowding in the medieval city, stretches 1km to 1.5km north, east and west of Plaça de Catalunya.

Work on L'Eixample began in 1869, following a design by the architect Ildefons Cerdà, who specified a grid of wide streets with plazas formed by their cut-off corners. Cerdà also planned numerous green spaces but these didn't survive the intense demand for L'Eixample real estate.

How Do You Like Them Apples?

Despite the Catalanisation of most Barcelona names in recent decades, the Manzana de la Discordia has kept its Spanish name to preserve a pun on *manzana*, which means both 'block' and 'apple'. According to Greek myth, the original Apple of Discord was tossed on to Mt Olympus by Eris (Discord) with orders that it be given to the most beautiful goddess, sparking jealousies that helped start the Trojan War. The pun won't transfer into Catalan, in which block is *illa* and apple is *poma*.

L'Eixample has been inhabited from the start by the city's middle classes, many of whom still think it's the best thing about Barcelona. Along its grid of straight streets are the majority of the city's most expensive shops and hotels, plus a range of eateries and several nightspots. The main sightseeing objective is Modernista architecture, the best of which – apart from La Sagrada Família – is clustered on or near L'Eixample's main avenue, Passeig de Gràcia.

Manzana de la Discordia

The so-called 'Apple (read Block) of Discord' on the western side of Passeig de Gràcia, between Carrer del Consell de Cent and Carrer d'Aragó, gets its name from three houses remodelled in a highly contrasting manner between 1898 and 1906 by three of the leading Modernista architects.

At No 35, on the corner of Carrer del Consell de Cent, is **Casa Lleo Morera**, Lluís Domènech i Montaner's contribution, with Art Nouveau carving outside and a bright, tiled lobby in which floral motifs predominate. You can no longer visit the 1st floor, which is giddy with swirling sculptures, rich mosaics and whimsical decoration.

At No 41, **Casa Amatller** by Josep Puig i Cadafalch, combines Gothic window frames with a stepped gable borrowed (deliberately) from urban architecture of the Netherlands. The pillared entrance hall and the staircase lit by stained glass are like the inside of a romantic castle. You can wander around the ground floor and pick up a Ruta del Modernisme ticket here (see the boxed text earlier).

Next door at No 43 is **Casa Batlló**, one of Barcelona's gems. Of course it's by Gaudí. The facade, sprinkled with bits of blue, mauve and green tile and studded with wave-shaped window frames and balconies, rises to an uneven, blue tiled roof with a solitary tower. The roof represents, according to some, Sant Jordi (St George) and the dragon. If it's not a dragon, it could just as easily be an exotic, scaly deep-sea fish. You might fluke your way into the foyer (but not beyond) if either of the entrances is open.

While in this area you may want to pop into the **Museu del Parfum**, Passeig de Gràcia 39 in the Regia store. It contains everything from ancient scent receptacles to classic eau de Cologne bottles. It opens 10 am to 8.30 pm weekdays; 10.30 am to 2 pm and 5 to 8.30 pm Saturday.

Fundació Antoni Tàpies

Around the corner from the Manzana de la Discòrdia, at Carrer d'Aragó 255, this is both a pioneering Modernista building of the early 1880s and home to the major collection of a leading 20th-century Catalan artist. The building, designed by Domènech i Montaner, combines a brick-covered iron frame with Islamic-inspired decoration. Antoni Tàpies, whose experimental art has often carried political messages (he opposed Francoism in the 1960s and 1970s) launched the Fundació in 1984 to promote contemporary art, donating a large collection of his own work. Only about 14 of his works are permanently on show, except from July to September when the downstairs levels are filled with more works. During the rest of the year these levels host displays of contemporary artists.

The Fundació opens 10 am to 8 pm Tuesday to Sunday and admission costs €4.25 (students €2.15).

La Pedrera

Back on Passeig de Gràcia, at No 92, is another Gaudí masterpiece, built between 1905 and 1910 as a combined apartment and office block. Formally called the Casa Milà after the businessman who commissioned it, it's better known as La Pedrera (Quarry) because of its uneven grey stone facade, which ripples around the corner of Carrer de Provença. The wave effect is emphasised by elaborate wrought-iron balconies.

The Fundació Caixa Catalunya office (☎ 93 484 59 95) has opened the place up to visitors, organising it as the Espai Gaudí (Gaudí Space) and guiding visitors through the building and up onto the roof, with its giant chimneypots looking like multicoloured medieval knights. One floor below the roof, where you can appreciate Gaudí's taste for McDonald's M-style arches, is a modest museum dedicated to his work. You can see models and videos dealing with each of his buildings.

Downstairs on the next floor you can inspect an apartment (El Pis de la Pedrera). It is fascinating to wander around this elegantly furnished home, done up in the style that a well-to-do family might have enjoyed at the turn of the last century.

La Pedrera opens 10 am to 8 pm daily. Guided visits take place at 6 pm (11 am weekends and holidays). From July to September, the place is opened up on Friday and Saturday evenings (9 pm to midnight). You can elect to pay €3.65 just to see the Espai Gaudí and the roof terrace *or* the apartment. It is worth paying the full €6.05 to see both if you have failed to purchase a Ruta del Modernisme ticket.

Palau del Baró de Quadras & Casa de les Punxes

Within a few blocks north and east of La Pedrera are two of Puig i Cadafalch's major buildings. The nearer is the Palau del Baró de Quadras at Avinguda Diagonal 373, created between 1902 and 1904 with detailed neo-Gothic carvings on the facade and fine stained glass. It houses the **Museu de la Música**, with a collection of international instruments from the 16th century to the present. It opens 10 am to 2 pm Tuesday to Sunday (until 8 pm on Wednesday from late September to late June). Admission costs €2.45.

The Casa Terrades is on the other side of Avinguda Diagonal, 1½ blocks east at No 420. This apartment block of 1903–05, resembling a castle in a fairy tale, is better known as the Casa de les Punxes (House of the Spikes) because of its pointed turrets.

La Sagrada Família

If you have time for only one sightseeing outing in Barcelona, this should probably be it. La Sagrada Família inspires awe by its sheer verticality and, in the true manner of the great medieval cathedrals it emulates, it's still not even half-built, after more than 100 years. If it's ever finished, the topmost tower will be more than half as high again as those standing today.

The Temple Expiatori de la Sagrada Família (Expiatory Temple of the Holy Family) was the project to which Gaudí dedicated his life. It stands in the east of L'Eixample and opens to visitors daily from 9 am. From April to the end of August it closes at 8 pm; in March, September and October at 7 pm; from November to February at 6 pm. The admission charge of €5.15 for everybody (the money goes towards the building program) includes a good museum in the crypt.

The entrance is by the south-western facade fronting Carrer de Sardenya and Plaça de la Sagrada Família. Inside is a bookstall where you can buy one of several guides if you want a detailed account of the church's sculpture and symbolism. To get your bearings, you need to realise that this facade, and the opposite one facing Plaça de Gaudí, each with four skyscraping towers, are at the *sides* of the church. The main facade, as yet unbuilt, will be at the south-eastern end, on Carrer de Mallorca. The 170m central tower will be above the crossing, halfway between the two existing facades.

Nativity Facade This, the north-eastern facade, is the building's artistic pinnacle, mostly done under Gaudí's personal supervision and much of it with his own hands. You can climb high up inside some of the four towers by a combination of lifts (€1.20; when they're working) and narrow spiral staircases; a vertiginous experience. The

towers are destined to hold tubular bells capable of playing complex music at great volume. Their upper parts are decorated with mosaics spelling out *'Sanctus, Sanctus, Sanctus, Hosanna in Excelsis, Amen, Alleluia'*.

Beneath the towers is a tall, three-part portal on the theme of Christ's birth and childhood. It seems to lean outward as you stand beneath looking up. Gaudí used real people and animals as models for many of the sculptures.

The three sections of the portal represent, from left to right, Hope, Charity and Faith. Amid the forest of sculpture on the Charity portal, you can make out, low down, the manger surrounded by an ox, an ass, the shepherds and kings, with angel musicians above. Directly above the blue stained-glass window is the Archangel Gabriel's Annunciation to Mary. At the top is a green cypress tree, a symbolic refuge from a storm for the white doves of peace dotted over it.

Interior The semicircular apse wall at the north-western end of the church was the first part to be finished (in 1894). Access is now blocked by construction work in the transept. In the nave the roof is held up by unique treelike pillars whose top branches spread out to share the load. The main Glory Facade on the south-eastern end will, like the north-eastern and south-western facades, be crowned by four towers – the total of 12 representing the 12 apostles. Further decoration will make the whole building a microcosmic symbol of the Christian church, with Christ represented by the massive 170m central tower above the transept and the five remaining planned towers symbolising the Virgin Mary and the four Evangelists.

Passion Facade This south-western facade, on the theme of Christ's last days and death, has been constructed since the 1950s with, like the Nativity Facade, four needling towers and a large, sculpture-bedecked portal. The sculptor, Josep Subirachs, has not attempted to imitate Gaudí's work but has produced strong images of his own. The sculptures, on three levels, form an S-shaped

Gaudí – God's Architect

The idea for La Sagrada Família came from a rich publisher, Josep Marià Bocabella i Verdaguer, the man behind the emergence of an arch-conservative society dedicated to Sant Josep (St Joseph). Pope Pius IX was exhorting the Catholic world to renew devotion to Jesus, Mary and Joseph, the Holy Family, or *La Sagrada Família*. And so Bocabella had an inspired idea. What decadent, liberal Barcelona needed was a great church raised to the Holy Family. The society raised the cash and the first stone of a neo-Gothic structure was laid in 1882. The original architect soon quit, and into the breech stepped Antoni Gaudí in 1884.

He was given a free hand. He conceived a structure that drew on Gothic roots, and embellished it with his own very particular spin.

Gaudí was already a successful architect. Up to 1910 he worked on numerous buildings in Barcelona and elsewhere but by 1916 he was consumed by this almost mystical project. Outside interest and funds waned, however, and Gaudí invested all he had – not only in the building but in nurturing a skilled artisan workforce. He died a poor man when run over by a tram in 1926.

Gaudí stuck to the basic Gothic cross-shaped ground plan with an apse but eventually devised a temple 95m long and 60m wide, able to seat 13,000 people, with a central tower 170m high and another 17 of 100m or more. With his characteristic dislike for straight lines (there are none in nature, he said), Gaudí gave his towers swelling outlines inspired by the weird peaks of Montserrat, and encrusted them with a tangle of sculpture that seems an outgrowth of the stone.

At Gaudí's death only the crypt, the apse walls, one portal and one tower had been finished. Three more towers were added by 1930 – completing the north-eastern (Nativity) facade – but in 1936 anarchists burned and smashed everything they could in La Sagrada Família, including the workshops, models and plans.

Work restarted in 1952 using restored models and photographs of drawings, with only limited guidance on how Gaudí had thought of solving the huge technical problems of the building. Between 1954 and 1976 the south-western (Passion) facade, with four more towers, was completed,

---

sequence starting with the Last Supper at bottom left and ending with Christ's burial at top right. A lift (€1.20) takes you close to the top of the far right tower and you can walk back down to the bottom.

Museu Gaudí With the same opening hours as the church, the museum (in the crypt) includes interesting material on Gaudí's life and other work, as well as models, photos and other material on La Sagrada Família. You can see a good example of his plumb-line models, which showed him the stresses and strains he could get away with in construction.

GRÀCIA (Map 2)

Gràcia is the area north of the middle of L'Eixample. Once a separate village, then in the 19th century an industrial *barrio* (district) famous for its republican and liberal

ideas, it became fashionable among radical and bohemian types in the 1960s and 1970s. Although now more sedate and gentrified, it retains much of its style of 20 years ago, with a mixed-class population. An evening wander lets you savour the atmosphere of Gràcia's narrow streets, small plazas and the bars and restaurants lining them. Diagonal and Fontana are the nearest metro stations to central Gràcia.

The liveliest plazas are **Plaça del Sol**, **Plaça de Rius i Taulet** with its clock tower, and **Plaça de la Virreina** with the 17th-century Església de Sant Josep. Three blocks north-east of Plaça de Rius i Taulet there's a big covered **market**. West of Gràcia's main street, Carrer Gran de Gràcia, at Carrer de les Carolines 22, stands **Casa Vicenç**, an early Gaudí house that is turreted and vaguely *mudéjar* (a decorative Muslim style of architecture).

Gaudí – God's Architect

with only some decorative detail work outstanding. The nave, started in 1978, has been roofed over and is coming along nicely.

Controversy has dogged the building. Some say the quality of the new work and its materials – concrete has been used instead of stone – are inferior, while others claim that the shell should have been left as a monument to Gaudí. The chief architect, Jordi Bonet, and his supporters argue that their task is a sacred one: this is a church intended to atone for sin and appeal for God's mercy on Catalunya. The way things are going, it might be finished by the 2020s, which seems like a truly medieval construction timetable.

Gaudí's own story is far from over. The rector of La Sagrada Família, Lluís Bonet Armengol (the chief architect's brother), is promoting Gaudí's beatification. In March 2000 the Vatican decided to proceed with the examination of the case for canonising him. Even before becoming a saint, Gaudí has started attracting pilgrims, as devotees come to pray at his tomb in the crypt of La Sagrada Família. Bonet Armengol claims Gaudí's contemporaries 'knew he was God's Architect'.

In 2002 Barcelona intends to squeeze every tourist euro it can out of the 150th anniversary of Gaudí's birth. The city has already dubbed it the 'year of architecture and Gaudí'.

ÅSA ANDERSSON

MONTJUÏC (Map 1)

Montjuïc, the hill overlooking the city centre from the south-west, is home to some of Barcelona's best museums and leisure attractions, some fine parks and the main group of 1992 Olympics sites. It's well worth a day or two of your time.

The name Montjuïc (Jewish Mountain) indicates that there was once a Jewish settlement here. Before Montjuïc began to be turned into parks in the 1890s, its woodlands had long provided food-growing and breathing space for the people of the cramped Ciutat Vella. Montjuïc also has a darker history: its castle was used by the Madrid government to bombard the city after political disturbances in 1842 and as a political prison right up to the Franco era. The first main burst of building on Montjuïc came in the 1920s, when it was chosen as the stage for Barcelona's 1929 World

Exhibition. The Estadi Olímpic, the Poble Espanyol and some museums all date from this time. Montjuïc got a face-lift and further new buildings for the 1992 Olympics.

Abundant roads and paths, with occasional escalators, plus buses and even a chairlift allow you to visit Montjuïc's sights in any order you choose. The five main attractions – the Poble Espanyol, the Museu Nacional d'Art de Catalunya, the Estadi Olímpic, the Fundació Joan Miró and the views from the castle – would make for a full day's sightseeing.

Getting There & Away

You *could* walk from Ciutat Vella (the foot of La Rambla is 700m from the eastern end of Montjuïc). Local bus Nos 50 and 61 make their way up here from Plaça d'Espanya and other parts of town. The Bus Turístic (see Getting Around later in this chapter) also makes several stops on Montjuïc. Or you could hop on one of those silly little road trains, which leave from the same spot as the bus and create havoc for normal traffic trying to get up the same hill!

Another way of saving your legs is the funicular railway from the Paral.lel metro station to Estació Parc Montjuïc. This runs 11 am to 10 pm daily, mid-June to mid-September; 10.45 am to 8 pm during the Christmas and Easter holiday periods; and 10.45 am to 8 pm Saturday, Sunday and holidays only, the rest of the year. Tickets cost €1.65/2.40 one way/return.

From Estació Parc Montjuïc, the Telefèric de Montjuïc chairlift will carry you yet higher, to an upper entrance of the now closed Parc d'Atraccions (Mirador stop) and then to the castle (Castell stop). This runs 11.30 am to 9.30 pm daily, mid-June to the end of September; 11 am to 2.45 pm and 4 to 7.30 pm in October and the Christmas and Easter holiday periods; 11 am to 2.45 pm and 4 to 7.30 pm Saturday, Sunday and holidays only, the rest of the year. Tickets cost €3/4.25 one way/return.

Another option is the cable car or telefèric aereo, which runs between Miramar and Sant Sebastià (La Barceloneta). For details, see Port Vell earlier.

Around Plaça d'Espanya

The approach to Montjuïc from Plaça d'Espanya gives you the full benefit of the landscaping on the hill's northern side and allows Montjuïc to unfold for you from the bottom up. On Plaça d'Espanya's northern side is the big **Plaça de Braus Les Arenes** bullring, built in 1900 but no longer used for bullfights. The Beatles played here in 1966. Behind the bullring is the **Parc Joan Miró**, created in the 1980s, and worth a quick detour mainly for Miró's giant, highly phallic sculpture *Dona i Ocell* (Woman and Bird) in the north-western corner.

Fountains & Museu Nacional d'Art de Catalunya

Avinguda de la Reina Maria Cristina, lined with modern exhibition and congress halls, leads from Plaça d'Espanya towards Montjuïc. On the hill ahead of you is the Palau Nacional de Montjuïc and stretching up a series of terraces below it are Montjuïc's fountains, starting with the biggest, **La Font Màgica**. These come alive with a (free) music-and-light show on summer evenings. The regular show lasts about 15 minutes and takes place every 30 minutes from 9.30 to 11.30 pm Thursday to Sunday, June to September; and 7 to 9 pm Friday and Saturday, the rest of the year.

The Palau Nacional, built in the 1920s for displays in the World Exhibition, houses the **Museu Nacional d'Art de Catalunya**. The museum's Romanesque section consists mainly of 11th- and 12th-century murals, woodcarvings and painted altar frontals (low-relief wooden panels that were forerunners of the elaborate altarpieces adorning later churches). These works, gathered from decaying country churches in northern Catalunya early in the 20th century, probably constitute Europe's greatest collection of Romanesque art. The museum's other main section is devoted to Gothic art and expansion is planned to include paintings dating back to up to the 17th century.

The first thing you see as you enter the Romanesque section is a remake of the apse of the church of Sant Pere de la Seu d'Urgell, dominated by a beautiful fresco from the early 12th century. In this first hall (Àmbit I) there are coins from the early days of the *comtes* (counts) of Barcelona, capitals from columns used in Muslim monuments and some finely decorated altar frontals.

In Àmbit III, the frescoes from the Església de Sant Pere in Àger (see the Central Catalunya chapter) stand out (item No 31). The depiction of Christ on wood from the church of Sant Martí de Tost (No 47 in Àmbit IV) is in a near-perfect state of preservation. One of the star attractions is the fresco of Mary and the Christ Child from the apse of the church of Santa Maria de Taüll (No 102 in Àmbit VII; see under Parc Nacional d'Aigüestortes i Estany de Sant Maurici & Around in the Pyrenees chapter).

The museum opens 10 am to 7 pm Tuesday to Saturday (to 9 pm Thursday), and 10 am to 2.30 pm Sunday and holidays.

Admission costs €4.85 and is free on the first Thursday of the month.

Poble Espanyol

This 'Spanish Village' in the north-west of Montjuïc, a 10-minute walk from Plaça d'Espanya or the Museu Nacional d'Art de Catalunya, is both a tacky tourist trap and an intriguing scrapbook of Spanish architecture. Built for the Spanish crafts section of the 1929 exhibition, it's composed of plazas and streets lined with surprisingly good copies of typical buildings from all the country's regions.

You enter from Avinguda del Marquès de Comillas, beneath a towered medieval gate from Ávila. Inside, to the right, is an information office with free maps. Straight ahead from the gates is a *plaza mayor* (town square), surrounded with mainly Castilian and Aragonese buildings. Elsewhere you'll find an Andalucian barrio, a Basque street, Galician and Catalan quarters and even, at the eastern end, a Dominican monastery. The buildings house dozens of mid-range to expensive restaurants, cafes, bars, craft shops and workshops, and a few souvenir shops.

The Poble Espanyol opens from 9 am daily (to 8 pm Monday, to 2 am Tuesday to Thursday, to 4 am Friday and Saturday, and until midnight on Sunday). Admission costs €5.90 (students and children aged seven to 14 €3.35). A combined ticket with Galería Olímpica (see under Anella Olímpica later) costs €7.25. After 9 pm from Sunday to Thursday, it's free. At night, the restaurants, bars and discos become a lively corner of Barcelona nightlife. For more information or a guided tour, call ☎ 93 325 78 66.

Museu Etnològic & Museu d'Arqueologia

Down the hill east of the Museu Nacional d'Art de Catalunya, these museums are worth a visit if their subjects interest you, but neither is very excitingly presented and most explanatory material is in Catalan.

The Museu Etnològic on Passeig de Santa Madrona puts on extensive temporary exhibitions covering a range of cultures from other continents. It opens 10 am to 3 pm (to 7 pm Tuesday and Thursday in winter), daily except Monday. Admission costs €2.40 and is free on the first Sunday of the month.

The Museu d'Arqueologia, at the corner of Passeig de Santa Madrona and Passeig de l'Exposició, concentrates on ancient Catalunya, although with material from other parts of Spain thrown in. Items range from copies of pre-Neanderthal skulls to lovely Carthaginian necklaces and jewel-studded Visigothic crosses. There's good material on the Balearic Islands (rooms X to XIV) and Empúries, or Emporion, the classical city on the Costa Brava (rooms XV and XVI). It opens 9.30 am to 7 pm Tuesday to Saturday, and 10 am to 2.30 pm Sunday. Admission costs €2.40.

Anella Olímpica

The 'Olympic Ring' is the group of sports installations where the main events of the 1992 Olympics were held, on the ridge above the Museu Nacional d'Art. Westernmost is the **Institut Nacional d'Educació Física de Catalunya (INEFC)**, a kind of sports university, designed by the best-known contemporary Catalan architect, Ricardo Bofill. Past a circular arena, the Plaça d'Europa, with the Torre Calatrava telephone tower behind it, is the **Piscines Bernat Picornell** building, where the swimming and diving events were held; it's now open to the public (see Swimming later in the chapter).

Next comes a pleasant little park, the Jardí d'Aclimatació, followed by the **Estadi Olímpic**, the main stadium of the games. It opens 10 am to 6 pm daily and admission is free; enter at the northern end. If you saw some of the Olympics on TV, the 65,000-capacity stadium may seem surprisingly small. So may the Olympic flame-holder rising at the northern end, into which a long-range archer spectacularly deposited a flaming arrow in the opening ceremony. The stadium was opened in 1929 but completely restored for 1992. At the southern end of the stadium (enter from the outside) is the **Galería Olímpica**, which has an exhibition, including videos, on the 1992 games. It opens 10 am to 1 pm and 4 to

BARCELONA

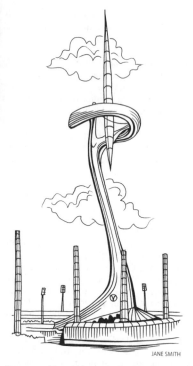

JANE SMITH

Space-age Torre Calatrava takes the design of communication transmitters to a new level.

6 pm (to 8 pm in summer) weekdays, and 10 am to 2 pm on holidays. Admission costs €2.40.

West of the stadium is the **Palau Sant Jordi**, a 17,000-capacity indoor sports, concert and exhibition hall opened in 1990 and designed by the Japanese architect Arata Isozaki.

Cementiri del Sud-Ouest

On the hill south of the Anella Olímpica you can see the top of a huge cemetery, the Cementiri del Sud-Ouest or Cementiri Nou, which extends right down the southern side of the hill. Opened in 1883, it's an odd combination of elaborate architect-designed tombs for rich families and small niches for the rest. It contains the graves of numerous Catalan artists and politicians.

Fundació Joan Miró

Barcelona's gallery for the greatest Catalan artist of the 20th century, Joan Miró, is 400m north of Estadi Olímpic.

Miró gave 379 paintings, sculptures and textile works, and almost 5000 drawings, to the collection but only a selection of these is displayed at any one time. The displays tend to concentrate on Miró's more settled last 20 years, but there are some important exceptions. The ground-floor Sala Joan Prats shows the younger Miró, under surrealist influence, moving away from his *relative* rea-lism, and then starting to work towards his own recognisable style. This section also includes the 1939–44 Barcelona Series of tortured lithographs – Miró's comment on the Spanish Civil War.

The Sala Pilar Juncosa, upstairs, also displays works from the 1930s and 1940s. Another interesting section is devoted to the 'Miró Papers', which include many preparatory drawings and sketches, some on bits of newspaper or cigarette packets. 'A Joan Miró' is a collection of work by other contemporary artists, donated in tribute to Miró.

The Fundació has a contemporary art library open to the public, a good specialist art bookshop and a cafe. It also stages exhibitions and recitals of contemporary art and music. The gallery opens 10 am to 7 pm (an hour longer each day in the summer months; to 9.30 pm Thursday year round) Tuesday to Saturday, and 10 am to 2.30 pm Sunday and holidays; admission costs €4.85.

Castell de Montjuïc & Around

The south-eastern part of Montjuïc is dominated by the *castell* (castle). Near the bottom of the ruined remains of what was the Parc d'Atraccions (Amusement Park) are the Estació Parc Montjuïc telefèric/funicular station and the ornamental **Jardins de Mossèn Jacint Verdaguer**. The one-time amusement park is destined to become part of a larger botanical garden.

From the **Jardins del Mirador** opposite the Mirador telefèric station there are fine views over the port of Barcelona.

The Castell de Montjuïc dates in its present form from the late 17th and 18th centuries. For most of its existence it has been used to watch over the city and as a political prison and killing ground. Anarchists were executed here around the turn of the 20th century, fascists during the Civil War and Republicans after it – most notoriously Lluís Companys in 1940. The army finally handed it over to the city in 1960. The castle is surrounded by a network of ditches and walls, and today houses the fusty old **Museu Militar** with a section on Catalan military history, plus old weapons, uniforms, maps and castle models. The museum opens 9.30 am to 7.30 pm daily except Monday and admission costs €1.20. Best of all are the excellent views from the castle area of the port and city below.

Towards the foot of this part of Montjuïc, above the thundering traffic of the main road to Tarragona, the **Jardins de Mossèn Costa i Llobera** have a good collection of tropical and desert plants and open 10 am to sunset; admission is free.

PARC GÜELL (Map 1)

North of Gràcia and about 4km from Plaça de Catalunya, Parc Güell is where Gaudí turned his hand to landscape gardening. It's a strange, enchanting place where his passion for natural forms really took flight, to the point where the artificial almost seems more natural than the natural.

Parc Güell originated in 1900 when Count Eusebi Güell bought a tree-covered hillside (then outside Barcelona) and hired Gaudí to create a miniature garden city of houses for the wealthy, in landscaped grounds. The project was a commercial flop and was abandoned in 1914 but not before Gaudí had created 3km of roads and walks, steps and a plaza in his inimitable manner, plus two gatehouses. In 1922 the city bought the estate for use as a public park.

The park opens 9 am to 9 pm daily, June to September; to 8 pm April, May and October; to 7 pm March and November; and to 6 pm in other months. Admission is free. It's extremely popular, and its quaint nooks and crannies are irresistible to photographers.

The steps up from the entrance, guarded by a mosaic dragon/lizard, lead to the **Sala Hipóstila**, a forest of 84 stone columns (some of them leaning), intended as a market. To the left curves a gallery whose twisted stonework columns and roof give the effect of a cloister beneath tree roots – a motif repeated in several places in the park. On top of the Sala Hipóstila is a broad open space whose centrepiece is the **Banc de Trenadis**, a tiled bench curving sinuously around its perimeter.

The spired house to the right is the **Casa Museu Gaudí**, where Gaudí lived for most of his last 20 years (1906–26). It contains furniture by him and other memorabilia. It opens 10 am to 8 pm daily, May to September; to 7 pm March, April and October; and to 6 pm the rest of the year. As a rule it opens only 10 am to 2 pm Sunday and may close between 2 and 4 pm in the low season. Admission costs €2.40.

Much of the park is still wooded but full of pathways. The best views are from the cross-topped **Turó del Calvari** in the southwestern corner.

Getting There & Away

The simplest way to Parc Güell is to take the metro (line 3) to Lesseps, then walk for 10 to 15 minutes: follow the signs northeast along Travessera de Dalt then turn left up Carrer de Larrard, which brings you almost to the park's two Hansel and Gretel-style gatehouses on Carrer d'Olot.

TIBIDABO (Map 1)

Tibidabo (542m) is the highest hill in the wooded range that forms the backdrop to Barcelona. It's a good place for some fresh air (it's often a few degrees cooler than in the city) and, if the air's clear, for views over the city and inland as far as Montserrat. Tibidabo gets its name from the devil who, trying to tempt Christ, took him to a high place and said: *'Haec omnia tibi dabo si cadens adoraberis me'* ('All this I will give you if you will fall down and worship me').

Getting There & Away

First, get an FGC suburban train to Avinguda del Tibidabo from Catalunya station

Saint's Patron

Should the Vatican one day decide to elevate the eccentric artist to sainthood, pilgrims who come to give thanks for St Gaudí's intercession might do well to spare a thought for the man who made much of what we enjoy today possible.

Gaudí was no doubt an architect with extraordinary gifts but he had to work for a living. Like so many artists of lasting talent, he needed a patron. He got one.

Eusebi Güell i Bacigalupi (1846–1918) was the son of one of Catalunya's most successful industrialists, Joan Güell i Ferrer. The latter had made a small fortune in Cuba (a Spanish colony where Catalans were particularly busy and agricultural slave labour made the economy go around), which he then used to lay the foundations of some of Barcelona's earliest heavy industry. Eusebi inherited this on his father's death in 1872. He had already received a broad education in Barcelona, France and Britain and was one of those rare combinations, a cultured magnate. He would go on to preside over a thriving textiles empire, alongside other interests ranging from banking and wine production to Catalunya's first cement plants.

Güell first discovered Gaudí in Paris, or rather in a shop window designed by Gaudí for a Catalan glove-maker at the Paris Universal Exhibition in 1878. Güell liked what he saw and soon found in Gaudí an aesthetic soul mate. Often Güell had a substantial say in how he wanted Gaudí to proceed on the many projects with which he entrusted the architect in the following decades. Both were driven, albeit perhaps in differing degrees, by a conservative desire for the resurrection of sound Christian principles and Catalan nationalism. These deeply felt principles found their expression in the buildings Gaudí created and Güell (in so many cases) commissioned. With Güell's death, Gaudí lost not only his main backer, but one of the few people who understood him and his work.

---

on Plaça de Catalunya, a 10-minute ride for €1. Outside Avinguda del Tibidabo station, hop on the *tramvia blau,* Barcelona's last surviving tram, which runs up between fancy turn-of-the-20th-century mansions to Plaça del Doctor Andreu (€1.80/2.60 one way/return). The tram runs every 15 or 30 minutes from 9 am to 9.30 pm daily in summer; and on Saturday, Sunday and holidays, the rest of the year. On other days a bus (€1) serves the route at similar times. From Plaça del Doctor Andreu, the Tibidabo funicular railway climbs through the woods to Plaça de Tibidabo at the top of the hill (€1.80/2.40 one way/return), every 15 to 30 minutes from 7.15 am to 9.45 pm daily. If you're feeling active, you can walk up or down through the woods instead. The funicular only operates when the Parc d'Atraccions is open.

The cheaper alternative is bus No T2, the 'Tibibús', from Plaça de Catalunya to Plaça de Tibidabo (€1.40). This runs every hour from 10.30 am daily, late June to early

September; and every 30 minutes from 10.30 am on Saturday, Sunday and holidays year round. The last bus down leaves from Tibidabo 30 minutes after the Parc d'Atraccions closes.

Temple del Sagrat Cor

The Church of the Sacred Heart, looming above the top funicular station, is Barcelona's answer to Paris' Sacré Coeur. It's equally visible and even more vilified by aesthetes. A tall grey neo-Gothic structure, topped by a giant bronze statue of Christ and completed in 1930, it rests upon a brownstone crypt with Modernista touches. Visiting times are 8 am to 7 pm daily, but the lift to the roof of the top part (€1.20) operates from 10 am to 2 pm and 3 to 7 pm only.

Parc d'Atraccions

The reason most Barcelonins come up to Tibidabo is for some thrills (but hopefully no spills) in this funfair (☎ 93 211 79 42), close to the top funicular station. Admission costs €4.25 plus extra for each ride, or €15 with access to all rides – including seven minutes in the Hotel Krueger, a house of horrors inhabited by actors playing out their Dracula, Hannibal Lecter and other fantasies. The funfair's opening times change with the season, so check with a tourist office: in summer it's usually open from noon until late at night daily; in winter it may open on Saturday, Sunday and holidays only (from about noon to 7 pm).

Torre de Collserola

The 288m Torre de Collserola telecommunications tower (☎ 93 406 93 54 for information) was built between 1990 and 1992. The external glass lift to the visitors observation area, 115m up, is as hair-raising as anything at the Parc d'Atraccions. From the top they say you can see for 70km on a clear day. It opens 11 am to 2.30 pm and 3.30 to 6 pm Wednesday to Friday and 11 am to 6 pm weekends and holidays; these hours may be extended to 8 pm in summer. It closes in January. The ride up costs €3.

CAMP NOU (Map 1)

Hard on the heels of the Museu Picasso as one of Barcelona's most visited museums, comes the **Museu del Futbol Club Barcelona** at the club's giant Camp Nou stadium, 3.5km west of Plaça de Catalunya. Barça, as it's known, is one of Europe's top football (soccer) clubs, having carried off the Spanish championship a couple of dozen times and the European Cup more than once. The many world greats who have worn Barça's blue and red stripes include Johann Cruyff and Diego Maradona.

Camp Nou, built in the 1950s and enlarged for the 1982 World Cup, is one of the world's biggest stadiums (holding 120,000 people) and the club has a world record membership of 110,000. Football fans who can't get to a game should find the museum, on the Carrer d'Aristides Maillol side of the stadium, worthwhile. The best bits are the photo section, the goal videos and the visit to high-up seats overlooking the pitch.

The museum opens 10 am to 6.30 pm

Monday to Saturday (Tuesday to Saturday, from October to March) and 10 am to 2 pm Sunday and holidays. Admission costs €3.

PEDRALBES (Map 1)

Pedralbes is a wealthy residential area situated north of Camp Nou, with some worthwhile attractions.

Palau Reial de Pedralbes

Right by Palau Reial metro station, across Avinguda Diagonal from the main campus of the Universitat de Barcelona, is the entrance to the **Jardins del Palau Reial**, a verdant park open daily. In the park is the Palau Reial de Pedralbes, an early 20th-century building that has served as a residence for Gaudí's patron, and hosted Eusebi Güell, King Alfonso XIII, the president of Catalunya and General Franco. Today it houses the **Museu de Ceràmica**, with a good collection of Spanish ceramics from the 13th to 19th centuries, including works by Picasso and Miró, and the **Museu de les Arts Decoratives**, with an eclectic assortment of furnishings, ornaments and knick-knacks dating as far back as the Romanesque period. Both museums open 10 am to 6 pm Tuesday to Saturday (to 3 pm Sunday) and admission costs €4.25 for both.

Museu-Monestir de Pedralbes

This peaceful old convent, now a museum of monastic life also housing part of the Thyssen-Bornemisza art collection, stands at the top of Avinguda de Pedralbes. Founded in 1326, the convent still houses a community of nuns who inhabit separate closed quarters. The architectural highlight is the large, elegant, three-storey cloister, a jewel of Catalan Gothic built in the early 14th century.

The Col.lecció Thyssen-Bornemisza (entry from the ground floor), quartered in the (painstakingly restored) one-time dormitories of the nuns and the Saló Principal, is part of a wide-ranging art collection acquired by Spain in 1993. Most of it went to the Museo Thyssen-Bornemisza in Madrid; what's here is a select group ranging from the 14th to the 18th centuries by European (above all Italian) painters, including masters such as Canaletto, Titian, Tintoretto, Rubens, Zurbarán and Velázquez.

The museum entrance is on Plaça del Monestir, a divinely quiet corner of Barcelona and opening hours are 10 am to 2 pm (the church closes at 1 pm) Tuesday to Sunday. Admission costs €4.85 or €3.65 only for either the monastery *or* the Thyssen-Bornemisza collection.

The easiest way here is by suburban FGC train to Reina Elisenda (the end of the line) from Catalunya station and then a walk (about 10 minutes) or take one of the buses running along Passeig de la Reina Elisenda de Montcada (such as Nos 22, 64 and 75).

SWIMMING

The Olympic pool on Montjuïc (Map 1), the Piscines Bernat Picornell (☎ 93 423 40 41), opens to the public from 7 am to midnight weekdays, to 9 pm Saturday, and 7.30 am to 4.30 pm Sunday. It costs €7.25, which includes use of the good gym. Access to the outdoor pool alone costs €3.95 in summer only. This pool opens 10 am to 6 pm (9 am to 9 pm in summer) Monday to Saturday, and 10 am to 2.30 pm (9 am to 8 pm in summer) Sunday.

LANGUAGE COURSES

Some of the best-value Spanish-language courses are offered by the Universitat de Barcelona, which runs intensive courses (40 hours' tuition over periods ranging from two weeks to one month; €272) all year. Longer Spanish courses, and courses in Catalan, are also available. For more information you can ask at the university's information *(informació)* office (Map 3) at Gran Via de les Corts Catalanes 585. It opens 9 am to 2 pm weekdays. Otherwise, try (for Spanish) its Instituto de Estudios Hispánicos (☎ 93 403 55 19, fax 93 403 54 33) or (for Catalan) its Servei de Llengua Catalana (☎ 93 403 54 77, fax 93 403 54 84), both in the same building as the information office.

The university-run Escola Oficial d'Idiomes de Barcelona (Map 3; ☎ 93 324 93 30, fax 93 934 93 51) at Avinguda de les Drassanes s/n is another place offering economical summer Spanish courses (80 hours), as well as longer part-time courses in Spanish and Catalan.

Advertisements for courses and private tuition are posted at the university, Come In bookshop (Map 2) at Carrer de Provença 203, and the British Council (Map 1).

ORGANISED TOURS
Bicycle Tours

Un Menys bicycle shop (Map 4; ☎ 93 268 21 05), Carrer de la Espartería 3, organises bicycle tours around the old centre of town, La Barceloneta and Port Olímpic. Daytime tours take place on Saturday and Sunday, starting at the shop at 10 am and finishing at 12.30 pm. The cost (€15) includes a stop for a drink in Port Vell. The night version starts at 8.30 pm on Tuesday and Saturday, and finishes at midnight. The €36.15 price tag includes a drink stop and a meal along the waterfront at La Barceloneta.

Other Tours

The Bus Turístic (see the Getting Around section later in this chapter) is better value than conventional tours for getting around the sights, but if you want a guided trip, try Julià Tours (Map 3; ☎ 93 317 64 54), Ronda de la Universitat 5, and Pullmantur (Map 2; ☎ 93 318 02 41), Carrer del Bruc 645. Both companies do daily city tours by coach, plus out-of-town trips to Montserrat, Vilafranca del Penedès, the Costa Brava and Andorra. Their city tours cost about €29 for a half-day, €64 per full day.

A walking tour of the Ciutat Vella on Saturday and Sunday mornings departs from the Oficina d'Informació de Turisme de Barcelona (Map 3) on Plaça de Catalunya (English at 10 am; Spanish and Catalan at noon). The price is €6.

For other guide services and tailor-made tour options, get in touch with the Barcelona Guide Bureau (☎ 93 310 77 78, fax 93 268 22 11).

SPECIAL EVENTS

See Public Holidays & Special Events in the Facts for the Visitor chapter for Barcelona highlights.

PLACES TO STAY – BUDGET
Camping

The nearest camp site is the big *Cala Gogó* (☎ /fax 93 379 46 00, *Carretera de la Platja s/n)*, 9km south-west of the centre at El Prat de Llobregat, near the airport. It opens mid-March to mid-October and charges €20.50 for a site, car and two people. Bus No 65 from Plaça d'Espanya takes you there, or catch RENFE train from Plaça de Catalunya to El Prat, then a 'Prat Platja' bus.

Some better (but still vast) sites a few kilometres farther out, to the south-west on the coastal C-31 road, the Autovía de Castelldefels are reachable by bus No L95 from the corner of Ronda de la Universitat and Rambla de Catalunya. They include (with prices for a car, a tent and two people):

El Toro Bravo (☎ 93 637 34 62) Carretera C-31, Km 11, Viladecans – open all year, though it's a tad shabby (€20.50).

Filipinas (☎ 93 658 28 95) Carretera C-31, Km 12, Viladecans – open all year, this is one of the best value-for-money places (€20.50).

La Ballena Alegre (☎/fax 93 658 05 04) Carretera C-31, Km 12.4, Viladecans – open from April to the end of September, and also good (€25.90).

Eleven kilometres north-east of the city, *Camping Masnou* (☎ 93 555 15 03, *Camí Fabra 33, El Masnou)* opens year round. It's 200m from El Masnou train station – reached by suburban *rodalies/cercanías* (local) trains from Catalunya station on Plaça de Catalunya – and charges €16.50 for a car, tent and two people.

All are inconvenient if you want late nights in Barcelona, because the only way back late at night is by taxi.

Youth & Backpacker Hostels

Barcelona has four Hostelling International (HI) hostels and several non-HI hostels. All require you to rent sheets (€0.90 to €2.10) if you don't have any, and some lock their gates in the early hours so aren't suitable if you plan to party until late. Except at the Kabul, which doesn't take bookings, it's advisable to call ahead in summer. Most have washing machines.

The non-HI *Youth Hostel Kabul (Map 4; ☎ 93 318 51 90, fax 93 301 40 34, Plaça Reial 17)* is in the Barri Gòtic. It's a rough-and-ready place but does have, as its leaflets say, a 'great party atmosphere' and no curfew. The price is €12, plus €6 key deposit. Safes are available for valuables. There's room for 130 people in bare bunk rooms holding up to 10 each.

The biggest and most comfortable hostel is the 183-place *Alberg Mare de Déu de Montserrat (Map 1; ☎ 93 210 51 51, fax 93 210 07 98, Passeig de la Mare de Déu del Coll 41–51)*. It's 4km north of the centre, a 10-minute walk from Vallcarca metro or a 20-minute ride from Plaça de Catalunya on bus No 28, which stops almost outside the gate. The main building is a former private mansion with a mudéjar-style lobby. Most rooms sleep six. A hostel card is needed: if you're under 25 or have an ISIC card, B&B costs €11.45; otherwise you pay €15.10. The hostel is in HI's International Booking Network (IBN). You can also book through the central booking service of Catalunya's official youth hostels organisation, the Xarxa d'Albergs de Joventut (☎ 93 483 83 63, fax 93 483 83 50). The other Barcelona hostels, even the HI ones, are not in the Xarxa.

Alberg Juvenil Palau (Map 4; ☎ 93 412 50 80, Carrer del Palau 6) in the Barri Gòtic has a friendly atmosphere and just 40 places in separate-sex bunk rooms. The cost is €9.65, including breakfast.

Hostal de Joves (Map 1; ☎ 93 300 31 04, Passeig de les Pujades 29) faces the northern end of Parc de la Ciutadella, a few minutes' walk from the Arc de Triomf metro station. It has 68 bunk places in small, rather grim dorms. The price is €9.05, including breakfast.

Another handy but spartan place, off Carrer de la Boqueria, is *Albergue Arco (Map 4; ☎ 93 301 31 93, Carrer de l'Arc de Santa Eulàlia 1)*. It is open 24 hours a day and a bed in a separate-sex dorm costs €8.45.

Alberg Pere Tarrès (Map 1; ☎ 93 410 23 09, fax 93 419 62 68, Carrer del Numància 149), 1km north of Estació Sants, has 92 places in dorms of four to eight bunks. B&B costs from €9 to €12, depending on age and whether you have a hostel card. The gates are shut from 11 am to 3 pm and from 11 pm to 8.30 am (they're opened briefly to let guests in at 2 am).

The small and distant *Alberg Studio* (Map 1; ☎ 93 205 09 61, fax 93 205 09 00, Carrer de la Duquessa d'Orleans 58), off Passeig de la Reina Elisenda de Montcada, 4km north-west of Plaça de Catalunya, opens only from 1 July to 30 September, and has 50 places. It stays open 24 hours and charges €10.25. FGC trains run to the nearby Reina Elisenda station from Catalunya station.

Hostales, Pensiones & Hotels

Barcelona is flavour of the decade, so competition for rooms can be fairly intense. Many of the places below are often full, so you may want to let your fingers do the walking.

Bathrooms are often in the corridor and shared at these places. Prices sometimes fall a little in the low season or if you stay for a week or more.

La Rambla At the top of La Rambla, *Pensión Noya* (Map 4; ☎ 93 301 48 31, Rambla de Canaletes 133), above Restaurante Nuria, has 15 smallish but clean rooms (shower and toilet in the corridor) which cost €18.10/36.20 for singles/doubles in the high season. Front rooms overlooking La Rambla can be noisy.

Barri Gòtic This central, atmospheric area has many of the better budget places. A few of those listed below are not strictly speaking in the Barri Gòtic, but within a couple of minutes' walk of it.

Hostal Lausanne (Map 4; ☎ 93 302 11 39, Avinguda del Portal de l'Àngel 24) is a good spot, with security and helpful staff. Popularity has made prices sneak up, but on balance this remains a great place to stay. Clean doubles without a bathroom cost €33.15. Getting a single seems impossible.

An excellent deal is *Hostal Campi* (Map 4; ☎ 93 301 35 45, fax 93 301 41 33, Carrer de la Canuda 4). Rooms without bathroom cost €16.30/30.15. A little pricier, the

best rooms are the doubles (with shower and toilet), which are extremely roomy and bright and cost €36.15.

Hostal-Residencia Rembrandt (Map 4; ☎/fax 93 318 10 11, Carrer de la Portaferrissa 23), is extremely popular so it's wise to book ahead. The rooms are good and cost €18.10/30.15 without a bathroom, or €24.10/42.20 with.

Hostal Galerias Maldà (Map 4; ☎ 93 317 30 02, Carrer del Pi 5), upstairs in the arcade, is a rambling family house with 21 rooms, some of them huge. It's one of the cheapest places in town, at €9/18.10, and has one great single that's set in a kind of tower.

Hostal Fontanella (Map 3; ☎/fax 93 317 59 43, Via Laietana 71) is a friendly, immaculately clean place, with 10 (in some cases smallish) rooms costing €18.10/30.15 or €24/41.60 with bathroom.

Pensión Fernando (Map 4; ☎ 93 301 79 93, Carrer de l'Arc del Remedio 4), is on Carrer de Ferran, in spite of the address. You have the option of dorms here, at €13.90 per person (if you get lucky you'll be in a room with its own shower and toilet). At least one of these rooms is designed for wheelchair access too. There are lockers in the dorm rooms (which start at four beds). Otherwise, you can take a double or triple for €42.20/51.20. You can catch some rays on the roof.

If you want a nice double on one of the area's main squares, head to *Pensión Villanueva* (Map 4; ☎ 91 301 50 84, Plaça Reial 2). Prices start at €15.10/21.10 for basic singles/doubles and range up to €45.20 for the best rooms: spacious doubles with bathroom looking onto the square.

Hotel Barcelona House (Map 4; ☎ 93 301 82 95, fax 93 412 41 29, Carrer dels Escudellers 19) is a newish place in the middle of the Gothic action. It has reasonable, comfortable rooms. The doubles are quite OK at €52.25, while the singles are less inspiring for €22.60.

Hostal Levante (Map 4; ☎ 93 317 95 65, Baixada de Sant Miquel 2), off Plaça de Sant Miquel, is a large, bright place with rooms of all shapes and sizes. Smallish singles start at €21.10, while doubles without/with bathroom go for €33.15/39.20. Try for the room with the balcony. These people have some apartments nearby too, which can work out well for groups of four or more – ask at the reception.

Casa Huéspedes Mari-Luz (Map 4; ☎ 93 317 34 63, Carrer del Palau 4) is another fine budget option. The bright, sunny rooms with wooden beams in the ceiling are well maintained and the management is chirpy. The place has a genuinely social atmosphere. There are rooms sleeping four or more at €12 per person, and doubles for €33.15 or €34.95.

Lone travellers have a hard time of it in many Barcelona digs, but *Pensión Alamar* (Map 4; ☎ 93 302 50 12, Carrer de la Comtessa de Sobradiel 1) seems to specialise in them. It has only one double among the 13 small but well kept rooms. You pay €15.10 per person, which is fair.

Moving a little farther towards the waterfront, *Hostal El Cantón* (Map 4; ☎ 93 317 30 19, Carrer Nou de Sant Francesc 40) is another good low-budget bet. You'll pay €12.05/24.10/34.35 for singles/doubles/triples without bathroom. With bathroom, you are looking at €15.70/34.95/47. Some rooms are spacious with a sparkling new bathroom, fan, fridge and balcony.

El Raval A bit of an oasis on the fringe of the Barri Xinès is *Hotel Peninsular* (Map 4; ☎ 93 302 31 38, fax 93 412 36 99, Carrer de Sant Pau 34). Once part of a convent, it has a plant-draped atrium extending the full height and most of the length of the hotel. The 80 rooms are clean and (mostly) spacious but otherwise nothing particularly special. Prices start at €21.10/36.15 for rooms without or €30.15/45.20 with bathroom.

A much better option, but one that is perenially full and nudging up into the mid-range price bracket, is *Hostal Mare Nostrum* (Map 4; ☎ 93 318 53 40, fax 93 412 30 69, Carrer de Sant Pau 2). Bright doubles without/with bathroom cost €45.20/54.10 plus IVA. It has a couple of singles for €35.25.

La Ribera At *Pensión Lourdes* (Map 4; ☎ 93 319 33 72, Carrer de la Princesa 14) there are about 20 clean singles/doubles which cost €21.10/28.35. Doubles with bathroom cost €40.40.

L'Eixample A few cheapies are spread strategically across this upmarket part of the city north of Plaça de Catalunya.

Hostal Goya (Map 2; ☎ 93 302 25 65, fax 93 412 04 35, Carrer de Pau Claris 74) has 12 nice, good-sized rooms at €18.70/27.15. Doubles with shower and toilet cost €33.75.

You should check out *Hostal Oliva* (Map 2; ☎ 93 488 01 62, fax 93 488 17 89, Passeig de Gràcia 32) just for the quaint old lift, which you'll want to take up to the 4th floor. The rooms are basically well kept, but some of those without a bathroom have little space for anything but the bed. Rooms cost €24.10/37.35, doubles with bathroom cost €43.40.

In a leafier location is *Hostal Neutral* (Map 2; ☎ 93 487 63 90, fax 93 487 68 48, Rambla de Catalunya 42). Doubles with bathroom cost €39.35; those without cost €32.90. There are no singles.

PLACES TO STAY – MID-RANGE

All rooms in this range have private bathrooms.

La Rambla

Hotel Continental (Map 4; ☎ 93 301 25 70, fax 93 302 73 60, Rambla de Canaletes 138) has 35 pleasant, well decorated rooms, all with cable TV, microwave, fridge, safe and fan. Room rates, including a good breakfast, start at €41.60/54.25 in summer and rise for doubles with Rambla views. Seems OK to us, but some readers have reported being disappointed.

Hotel Cuatro Naciones (Map 4; ☎ 93 317 36 24, fax 93 302 69 85, La Rambla 40) has adequate rooms for €45.15/64.50, including breakfast and IVA. It was built in 1849 and was once (a long time ago) Barcelona's top hotel. Buffalo Bill preferred it to a wagon when he was in town back in 1889.

BARCELONA

Hotel Oriente (Map 4; ☎ 93 302 25 58, fax 93 412 38 19, La Rambla 45) is one of the city's oldest grand hotels, built in 1842 around the cloister of a Franciscan monastery. It has a fine sky-lit restaurant and other public rooms, but staff can be off-hand. The bedrooms are slightly past their prime but still comfortable, with tiled floors and bathrooms, safes and TV. Rooms, pushing the limits of mid-range pricing, cost €64.50/103.15 plus IVA.

Barri Gòtic

Hotel Roma Reial (Map 4; ☎ 93 302 03 66, fax 93 301 18 39, Plaça Reial 11) has decent rooms which cost €36.15/54.25 in the high season.

At *Hotel Jardi (Map 4; ☎ 93 301 59 00, Plaça de Sant Josep Oriol 1)* doubles with a balcony over the lovely square cost around €48. At the time of writing some rooms were being refurbished, including the singles. It is a good little hotel and may well be much better when the work is finished.

Hotel Nouvel (Map 4; ☎ 93 301 82 74, fax 93 301 83 70, Carrer de Santa Anna 18–20) has some elegant Modernista touches and good rooms with air-con and satellite TV for €62.05/94.90 plus IVA. Prices include breakfast.

El Raval

Hotel Mesón de Castilla (Map 3; ☎ 93 318 21 82, fax 93 412 40 20, Carrer de Vall-donzella 5) has some lovely Modernista decoration, including stained glass and murals in its public rooms, and Gaudí-esque window mouldings. It also has 56 good, quaintly decorated rooms which cost €69.90/89.20 plus IVA, with breakfast included.

Hotel España (Map 4; ☎ 93 318 17 58, fax 93 317 11 34, Carrer de Sant Pau 9–11) is famous for its two marvellous dining rooms designed by Domènech i Montaner. One has big sea-life murals by Ramon Casas, the other has floral tiling and a wood-beamed roof. The 60-plus simple but comfortable rooms cost €34.35/65.10, including breakfast.

L'Eixample

A fine choice for a bit of old-fashioned style is *Hotel Gran Via (Map 2; ☎ 93 318 19 00, fax 93 318 99 97, Gran Via de les Corts Catalanes 642)*, with 53 good-sized rooms at €60.25/84.35 plus IVA and a big, elegant lounge opening onto a roof terrace. Breakfast is available for €6.65.

PLACES TO STAY – TOP END

Someone has neglected to tell these people that inflation in Spain is running at under 3%. In a little more than two years some hotels have lifted their official rates by as much as 50%! If you get lucky and turn up when businesspeople aren't in town, you can get some good offers – always ask. You must add 7% IVA to the rates below, except where otherwise indicated.

La Rambla

The top hotel on La Rambla is elegant *Le Meridien (Map 4; ☎ 93 318 62 00, fax 93 301 77 76)* at No 111. Its top-floor presidential suite is where the likes of Michael Jackson, Madonna and Julio Iglesias stay. Standard rooms cost €228.95/253.05 but occasionally it puts on specials at €156.65 per room (single or double use).

Barri Gòtic

Hotel Suizo (Map 4; ☎ 93 310 61 08, fax 93 310 40 81, Plaça de l'Àngel 12) is old on the outside but quite modern within and has a restaurant and snack bar. Rooms are comfortable, if unspectacular, and cost €85.85/111.45.

Hotel Colón (Map 4; ☎ 93 301 14 04, fax 93 317 29 15, Avinguda de la Catedral 7) is a better choice (if you can afford it) for its location facing the cathedral. The 146 comfortable and elegant rooms cost €105.45/158.45.

El Raval

Hotel San Agustín (Map 4; ☎ 93 318 16 58, fax 93 317 29 28, Plaça de Sant Agustí 3) has some character, if only because of its location on a quiet square. Rooms, all with air-con, heating and satellite TV, cost €75.30/105.45, including breakfast.

L'Eixample

Hotel Balmes (Map 2; ☎ 93 451 19 14, fax 93 451 00 49, Carrer de Mallorca 216) is a good, modern hotel with white bricks much in evidence in the interior. Average-sized rooms with air-con, tiled bathrooms and satellite TV are comparatively good value at €87.35/147.

Hotel Majèstic (Map 2; ☎ 93 488 17 17, fax 93 488 18 80, Passeig de Gràcia 70) is a sprawling, comfortable place with a nice line in modern art on the walls and a rooftop swimming pool. The 300-plus rooms, with air-con and satellite TV, cost up to €180.75/216.90.

Comtes (or Condes) de Barcelona Hotel (Map 2; ☎ 93 488 22 00, fax 93 488 06 14, Passeig de Gràcia 73–75) is one of Barcelona's best hotels. It has two separate buildings facing each other across Carrer de Mallorca. The older one occupies the Casa Enric Batló, built in the 1890s but now stylishly modernised. The air-con, soundproofed rooms have marble bathrooms. Rooms start at €174.70/186.75.

Hotel Ritz (Map 2; ☎ 93 318 52 00, fax 93 318 01 48, Gran Via de les Corts Catalanes 668) is the city's top choice for old-fashioned elegance, luxury, individuality and first-class service. It's been going since 1919. Room rates (regardless of whether you constitute a single or double occupancy) start at €271.10. A one-bedroom suite with tiled step-down 'Roman bath' costs €843.40.

One of the classiest addresses in town is *Hotel Claris (Map 2; ☎ 93 487 62 62, fax 93 487 87 36, Carrer de Pau Claris 150)*. Of course you pay for the pleasure, to the tune of €216.90/258.45. Suites cost up to €753. Breakfast will cost you another €16.90.

Port Olímpic

Barcelona's most fashionable, if rather impersonal, lodgings are at *Hotel Arts Barcelona (Map 1; ☎ 93 221 10 00, fax 93 221 10 70, Carrer de la Marina 19–21)*, in one of the two sky-high towers that dominate Port Olímpic. It has over 450 rooms and charges from €301.20 for a double.

PLACES TO EAT

Barcelona is packed with good places to eat. See the Out to Eat in Catalunya special section for some background, menu tips and other information.

PLACES TO EAT – BUDGET
La Rambla

Cafè de l'Òpera (Map 4; ☎ 93 317 75 85, La Rambla 74), opposite the Gran Teatre del Liceu, is La Rambla's most interesting cafe, with elegant 1920s decor. It gets busy at night, but is quieter for morning coffee and croissants.

Barri Gòtic

This area is peppered with good eateries, some of them excellent value. All items listed are on Map 4.

Pastry Shops & Coffee Bars Tempting pastry and/or chocolate shops, often combined with coffee bars, abound. They are especially concentrated along Carrer de la Llibreria and Baixada de la Llibreteria, north-east of Plaça de Sant Jaume. Among the least resistible are *Santa Clara (Carrer de la Llibreteria 21)* and *La Colmena*, on the corner of Baixada de la Llibreteria and Plaça de l'Àngel.

Xocolateria La Xicra (Plaça de Sant Josep Oriol 2) has great cakes, various coffees and teas, and *xocolata* (hot chocolate; €1.50) so thick it's listed on the menu under *postres* (desserts). Nearby, two other good places to sit down for a coffee and croissant are *Granja La Pallaresa (Carrer de Petritxol 11)* and *Croissanterie del Pi (Carrer del Pi 14)*.

A great little place to sip a wide variety of teas and herbal infusions is *Salterio (Carrer de Sant Domènec del Call 4)*, just in off Carrer de Ferran.

Takeaway Felafel & Kebabs On the corner of Plaça Reial and Carrer de Colom, *Disco-Bar Real* has a takeaway counter doing good felafel for €1.50. *Buen Bocado (Carrer dels Escudellers 31)* has felafel for €1.80 and doner kebabs for €2.60. It opens evenings only, until 2 am. The nameless *felafel & kebab takeaway*, on Carrer dels Escudellers just north of Carrer dels Obradors, charges a tad less.

For the Israeli version of the same thing, head for *Maoz (Carrer de Ferran 13)*. You add the fillings here yourself, which means you can end up with a big, tasty felafel sandwich for just €2.75.

Restaurants A popular self-service vegetarian restaurant, *Self-Naturista* (☎ 93 318 26 84, Carrer de Santa Anna 13), has a four-course lunch *menú del día* (set-price meal) for €5.85. Main courses don't cost more than €4.25.

Carrer de la Mercè, running south-west from the main post office, is a good place to hunt around for great little northern Spanish *tascas* (bars) and *sidrerías* (cider houses). Most of these are run by immigrants from Galicia and Asturias. *Tasca El Corral*, at No 19, and *Sidrería La Socarrena*, at No 21, are both worth checking out but there are many others. *Bar Celta*, No 16, is cheap – you can fill up on tapas for under €6.

A cross between a cafe of a century ago and a hippy hang-out, *La Cereria* (☎ 93 301 85 10, Baixada de Sant Miquel 3–5) is a cooperative that offers some tasty vegetarian cooking, great desserts and low prices. The fruit shakes are good too.

La Verónica (☎ 93 412 11 22, Carrer d'Avinyò 20) shines out like a beacon around here; its red decor and bright white lighting are hard to miss. It serves reasonable pizzas at affordable prices in an atmosphere that could be described as fashionably camp. There is a lunch *menú* for €6.

International Cuisine Just in off La Rambla, *The Bagel Shop* (☎ 93 412 48 38, Carrer de la Canuda 25), is the only place in town where your lox and cream cheese bagel will be the genuine article. It also opens for Sunday hangover breakfast (not bad at €4.25).

Sushi-Ya (☎ 93 412 72 49, Carrer d'En Quintana 4) is a simple place for cheap Japanese food. The sushi set meal costs €7.10, which is hard to argue with in terms of price and you can take food away. Don't

expect top Japanese cuisine, but it makes an affordable change.

Wagamama (Carrer dels Escudellers 39) is a cool place to get into good noodle dishes (up to €5.45) until 1 am daily. It also does weird and wonderful salads and mixed fruit drinks.

El Raval

These places are all on Map 4. *Restaurant Els Tres Bots (Carrer de Sant Pau 42)* is grungy but cheap, with a *menú* for €5.30. Along the same street at No 31, *Restaurante Pollo Rico* has a downstairs bar where you can get a quarter chicken, an omelette or a veal steak with chips, bread and wine, from €3. There's a more salubrious but only slightly more expensive upstairs restaurant.

Bar Kasparo (☎ 93 302 20 72, Plaça de Vicenç Martorell 4) is a relaxed Australian-run place where you can get great mixed salads and other healthy light food – perfect in summer on this quiet pedestrianised square.

Another hip little establishment is *Ra* (☎ 93 301 41 63, Plaça de la Gardunya), which looks like a beach bar that got lost and ended up in the car park. It offers a vaguely vegetarian menu, with a couple of meat options thrown in. The food is OK but unexceptional. It is, however, cheap (*menú* for €6) and the atmosphere decidedly groovy. It opens Monday to Saturday.

The charming *El Convent* (☎ 93 302 31 12, Carrer de Jerusalem 3), elegantly lodged in what was once a religious institution, offers a good *menú* for €5.85. The *ensalada de arroz con gambitos* (rice salad with shrimps) is a tasty first course.

La Ribera

Comme-Bio aka *La Botiga* (Map 4; ☎ 93 319 89 68, Via Laietana 28) is a modern, chemical-additive-free vegetarian restaurant and whole-food shop. Its good, four-course *menú* (€6.80) includes a help-yourself salad bar. Many a-la-carte dishes, including pizzas and spinach-and-Roquefort crepes, cost around €5.45, or you can go for a set dinner menu for €11.15. There's another branch at Gran Via de les Corts Catalanes 603 (Map 3).

Lluna Plena (Map 4; ☎ 93 310 54 29, Carrer de Montcada 2) is a bare-brick, cellar-style place with good Catalan and Spanish food. It gets packed due to its four-course, €6.35 lunch *menú*. It closes on Sunday night and Monday.

Restaurant L'Econòmic (Map 3; ☎ 93 319 64 94, Plaça de Sant Agustí Vell 13) is a popular local hang-out where a full set lunch comes in at €6, unless you want to try the classier €18.10 version.

Can Paixano (Map 4; ☎ 93 310 08 39, Carrer de la Reina Cristina 7) is a fine old champagne bar, tucked away amid the bright tacky lights of cheap electronics stores that are vaguely reminiscent of shops in South-East Asia. Munch on tapas at the two bars (there are no tables) while sipping elegant little glasses of bubbly rosé. It's a hugely popular spit and sawdust establishment. It closes on Sunday and holidays.

L'Eixample
A good place to start a visit to L'Eixample is at the top cafeteria at *El Corte Inglés* department store on Plaça de Catalunya (Map 3). It's reasonably priced and has tremendous views.

Tapas, Snacks & Coffee You'll find a number of glossy but informal tapas places near the bottom end of Passeig de Gràcia (Map 2). At No 24 is *Quasi Queviures (Qu Qu)* (☎ 93 317 45 12), with a wide choice including sausages and hams, pâtés and smoked fish. Many tapas cost over €2.40, but portions are decent. At No 28 is *Ba-Ba-Reeba* (☎ 93 302 21 29), which is similar but less Catalan.

Lizarran (Map 2; Carrer de Mallora 257) is a lively spot serving reasonable tapas. It is part of a chain but, as chains go, the quality isn't bad.

Restaurants A block east of Passeig de Gràcia, *L'Hostal de Rita* (Map 2; ☎ 93 451 87 07, Carrer d'Aragó 279), is an excellent medium-priced restaurant. The €6 four-course lunch *menú* is a good deal. A-la-carte main courses cost €4.25 to €6.05. Expect to queue.

Gràcia
Bar Candanchu (Map 2; ☎ 93 237 73 62, Plaça de Rius i Taulet 9) has a restaurant with many *plats combinats* (literally 'combined plate'; large serving of meat/seafood/ omelette with trimmings) and paella for €7.55. *Mario Pizza*, on the same square, does pizzas for €5.45 to €6.65.

A good homy Lebanese place is *Sannin* (Map 1; ☎ 93 285 00 51, Carrer de l'Encarnació 44). A full meal of old faves such as doner kebabs, hummus, tabbouleh, dessert and drinks will not cost you much more than €9.

Restaurant Chains
There are a few local restaurant chains where you can get a quick, decent snack or meal with minimum effort. *Bocatta* and *Pans & Company* both do hot and cold baguettes with a range of fillings. *Pastafiore* does a fast impression of Italian food. Some of these places have been marked on the maps – you'll see plenty of them around.

Self-Catering
There's great fresh food of all types at the *Mercat de la Boqueria* on La Rambla (Map 4), open 8 am to 8 pm Monday to Saturday. In La Ribera (Map 6), *Mercat de Santa Caterina*, which has been temporarily shifted to Passeig de Lluís Companys (Map 3), is another good shopping choice. In Gràcia there's a big covered *food market* at the corner of Travessera de Gràcia and Carrer de la Mare de Déu dels Desemparats (Map 2).

Champion (Map 4), near the northern end of La Rambla, is a convenient central supermarket.

PLACES TO EAT – MID-RANGE
Opening your purse wide will improve your options greatly. At the places listed below you can expect to pay anything from €12 to €21 for a full evening meal with all the trimmings.

Plaça de Catalunya
Café Zurich (Map 4; ☎ 93 317 91 53, Carrer de Pelai 39), actually right on the

square, has been resuscitated after years of closure. It is an old-style cafe, great for the morning paper but a little more expensive than the average cafe.

Barri Gòtic

A Basque favourite is **Irati** (Map 4; ☎ 93 302 30 84, Carrer del Cardenal Cassañes 17). Its lunch menú costs €9, or you can enjoy the great tapas and a glass of beer, or six (but watch how your debts mount!). It closes on Sunday night and Monday.

Can Culleretes (Map 4; ☎ 93 317 30 22, Carrer d'En Quintana 5) is Barcelona's oldest restaurant, founded in 1786. It's still going strong, with old-fashioned decor and good Catalan food. A three-course menú, including half a bottle of wine, will cost around €15. It closes on Sunday night and Monday.

Les Quinze Nits (Map 4; ☎ 93 317 30 75, Plaça Reial 6) is a stylish, bistro-like restaurant, on the borderline between smart and casual, with a long menu of good Catalan and Spanish dishes at reasonable prices. Three courses with wine and coffee typically come to about €15. The problem is you almost always have to queue for ages and, while the place is good, it is not *that* good!

La Fonda Escudellers (Map 4; ☎ 93 301 75 15, Carrer dels Escudellers 10) is run by the same people as Les Quinze Nits and has a similar ambience and standards. You will be directed efficiently from the entrance to one of the three floors, and the food is better than in many places around town that charge double.

El Paraguayo (Map 3; ☎ 93 302 14 41, Carrer del Parc 1) is a great place for succulent slabs of meat bigger than your head. Try the entraña; the word means 'entrails' but the meal is in fact a juicy slice of prime beef folded over onto itself and accompanied by a herb sauce. The dulce de leche (a South American version of caramel) is to die for. Expect to pay around €12 per head. It closes on Monday.

El Raval

Urban revival is bringing new life into this area, one of the poorest quarters of old Barcelona. Several tempting places have popped up, attracting a hip, young clientele.

Salsitas (Map 4; ☎ 93 318 08 40, Carrer Nou de la Rambla 22) is the place to go for your post-binge brunch a la East Village. Eggs Benedict anyone? It opens from the unlikely time of 8 am to 1 pm on weekend mornings.

At **Rita Blue** (Map 4; ☎ 93 412 34 38, Plaça de Sant Agustí 3) be prepared to wait at the bar of this pleasant designer restaurant with a whiff of New York in the air. The food is a tempting mix of Mediterranean dishes with a hint of the exotic. For instance, you could order Mexican fajitas with tandoori chicken. The lighting is perfect and the service efficient. Expect to pay up to €18 per head. It opens all week, but for dinner only at weekends.

Poble Sec

The recently renovated **Restaurant Elche** (Map 3; ☎ 93 441 30 89, Carrer de Vila i Vilà 71) does some of Barcelona's best paella and good fideuá (noodle paella). Several varieties are on offer, mostly costing around €8 to €11 per person (minimum of two people).

La Ribera

For a bit of a splurge on superb, mainly Catalan and French cooking, you can't do much better than **Senyor Parellada** (Map 4; ☎ 93 310 50 94, Carrer de l'Argenteria 37), an informally chic restaurant. Main courses start at around €12. You might start with carpaccio de salmó (thin strips of garnished uncooked salmon), followed by anec amb figues (duck with figs). Book for dinner.

You'll struggle to get into **L'Ou Com Balla** (Map 4; ☎ 93 310 53 78, Carrer dels Banys Vells 20) without a reservation. It presents a sometimes exquisite choice of local, sort-of-Moroccan and more-or-less French dishes in an inviting space with low lighting and well chosen ambient music. A meal can cost about €21. It opens for dinner only.

International Cuisine With its Malaysian and Indonesian cooking **Restaurante Bunga Raya** (Map 4; ☎ 93 319 31 69, Carrer dels Assaonadors 7) makes a nice change. It has a *menú* for €10.85 and closes on Monday.

L'Eixample

Centro Asturiano (Map 2; ☎ 93 215 30 10, Passeig de Gràcia 78) is a great little club tucked away up on the 1st floor. It opens its doors to the lunch-time rabble for the solid €7.25 *menú*. The open-air interior patio is a wonderful spot to eat but you can go inside too. It closes on Sunday.

International Cuisine At *Thai Gardens (Map 2; ☎ 93 487 98 98, Carrer de la Diputació 273)* you can pop in for a limited lunch *menú* for €9 or try the more extensive evening spread for €27.15. It closes on Sunday.

Gràcia

Taverna El Glop (Map 2; ☎ 93 213 70 58, Carrer de Sant Lluís 24) is a rustic spot specialising in *torrades* (open toasted sandwiches), grilled meats and salads. Locals say it's a bit passé, and it has taken to opening branches elsewhere in town but the food remains good. A meal with drinks costs €15 to €18. It closes on Monday.

La Singular (Map 2; ☎ 93 237 50 98, Carrer de Franciso Giner 50) does fantastic salads (with salmon, tuna or pâté) as big first courses. Throw in a second course of meat (such as pork in almond sauce) with wine and dessert and you'll be looking at €15 per head. It closes on Wednesday.

Port Vell & La Barceloneta

Fronting the Palau de Mar is a line of al fresco dining options mostly specialising in (finer) seafood. One of the best is *La Gavina (Map 3, ☎ 93 221 05 95)*, where you can expect to pay around €24 per head for a full meal with wine. When on form, their fideuá is scrummy.

Restaurant Set (7) Portes (Map 4; ☎ 93 319 30 33, Passeig d'Isabel II 14) is a classic, founded in 1836. The old-world atmosphere is reinforced by the decor of wood panelling, tiles, mirrors and plaques naming some of the famous – such as Orson Welles – who have eaten here. Paella (€8.90 to

€13.45) is the speciality. It's near-essential to book.

La Barceloneta has some good seafood restaurants. One of the best along the strip is *Puda Can Manel (Map 3; ☎ 93 221 50 13, Passeig de Joan de Borbó 60–61)*. The paella is fine at €8.45 per head, but the *crema catalana* (cream custard dessert) is not so hot. All up you will pay around €21 per head. It closes on Monday.

Port Olímpic

The harbour here is lined on two sides by dozens of restaurants and tapas bars, extremely popular in spring and summer. They are not cheap and mostly rely on the frenetic portside activity for atmosphere. One of the more economical places is *La Taverna del Cel Ros (Map 1; ☎ 93 221 00 33)*, which does a reasonable fideuá for €8.30. It closes on Thursday. The irritating thing around here is the touting waiters – seriously good eateries don't need to tout for business.

PLACES TO EAT – TOP END
Barri Gòtic

Els Quatre Gats (Map 4; ☎ 93 302 41 40, Carrer de Montsió 3 bis) was a turn-of-the-20th-century artists' lair, now reincarnated as a fairly expensive restaurant with somewhat dismissive service. Starters/snacks such as *esqueixada* (salted cod salad), cost close to €6, and main courses cost close to €18. Just have a drink if you only want to sample the atmosphere. It closes for Sunday lunch.

Les Quatre Barres (Map 4; ☎ 93 302 50 60, Carrer d'En Quintana 6) serves up excellent Catalan food – costing €18 or €24 for a meal with drinks. It offers a set lunch for €8.35. It closes all day Sunday and Monday night.

Los Caracoles (Map 4; ☎ 93 302 31 85, Carrer dels Escudellers 14) started life as a tavern in the 19th century and is one of Barcelona's best-known restaurants – although it's now frequented by tourists rather than by the celebrities whose photos adorn its walls. It's still good and lively and offers a big choice of seafood, fish, rice and meat. Try the snails.

El Raval

Casa Leopoldo (Map 4; ☎ 93 441 30 14, Carrer de Sant Rafael 24) was long a well hidden El Raval classic. Since the Rambla del Raval was crashed through this down-at-heel part of town it has somehow become easier to find! You can eat well a la carte or choose a special set menu for €33.15.

La Ribera

Cal Pep (Map 4; ☎ 93 310 79 61, Plaça de les Olles 8) has great tapas and a small dining room with good seafood where a three-course Catalan meal with drinks will cost around €21. It closes on Sunday, holidays and at lunchtime on Monday.

L'Eixample

You could easily miss *Tragaluz (Map 2; ☎ 93 487 01 96, Passatge de la Concepció 5)*, but don't. It serves inventive Mediterranean cuisine (with an Italian leaning) and mouth-watering desserts – try the *tarta de manzana con helado de dulce de leche* (apple pie with caramel ice cream). A meal with wine costs about €30 per head.

Barcelona's first Japanese restaurant is still one of its best. *Yamadori (Map 3; ☎ 93 453 92 64, Carrer d'Aribau 68)* will set you back about €30. It closes on Sunday.

Gràcia

The shellfish at *Botafumeiro (Map 2; ☎ 93 218 42 30, Carrer Gran de Gràcia 81)* are reputedly as good as they get in all Barcelona. You'd hope so, as you'll pay the best part of €60 per head here.

ENTERTAINMENT

Barcelona's entertainment bible is the weekly Spanish-language magazine *Guía del Ocio* (€0.75), which comes out on Thursday and lists almost everything that's on in the way of music, film, exhibitions, theatre and more. You can pick it up at most newsstands. An alternative is *La Agenda de Barcelona* (€1.40).

Bars

Barcelona's bars run the gamut from wood-panelled wine cellars to bright waterfront places and trendy designer haunts. Most are at their liveliest from about 10 pm to 2 or 3 am, especially from Thursday to Saturday, as people get into their night-time stride.

Barri Gòtic All these places are on Map 4. *Glaciar (Plaça Reial 3)* gets busy with a young crowd of foreigners and locals in the evening and stays open until 2 or 3 am.

Tiny *Bar Malpaso (Carrer d'En Rauric)*, just off Plaça Reial, is packed at night with a young, casual crowd and plays great Latin and African music – it takes a while to get into gear. Another hip low-lit place with a more varied, gay-leaning clientele is *Schilling (Carrer de Ferran 23)*. Mixed drinks cost about €4.25 at both.

A few yards closer to the waterfront you can raise the red lantern at *Shanghai (Carrer de N'Aglá 9)*, a humming but cosy place for a beer, or sake.

Thiossan (Carrer del Vidre 3) is a cool Senegalese haunt where you can get a bite to eat or just sit in mellow content listening to the African rhythms and allowing soothing ales to do their work.

Zoo (Carrer dels Escudellers 33) is a busy little watering hole in the heart of the Barri Gòtic. It will cater to foreigners' desires for *sangría* (wine and fruit punch) but the place gets a few locals in too.

Dot (Carrer Nou de Sant Francesc 7) is generally open until about 3 am (a little later on Friday and Saturday) and each night the musical theme changes, from 'easy listening' to 'space funk' on Friday and drum 'n' bass on Saturday.

El Raval Don't miss *Bar Marsella (Map 4; Carrer de Sant Pau 65)*, which opened its doors in 1820 and still specialises in *absenta* (absinthe), a hard-to-find beverage (because of its supposed narcotic qualities).

Another good place is *Casa Almirall (Map 3; Carrer de Joaquím Costa 33)*, which has been going since the 1860s; it's dark and intriguing (although less so since it was spruced up in early 2000), with Modernista decor and a mixed clientele.

[continued on page 157]

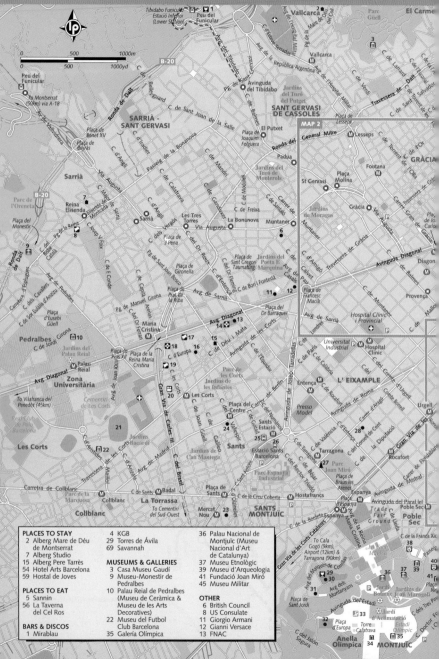

MAP 1 - BARCELONA

MAP 1 - BARCELONA

PLACES TO STAY
2 Alberg Mare de Déu de Montserrat
7 Alberg Studio
15 Alberg Pere Tarrès
54 Hotel Arts Barcelona
59 Hostal de Joves

PLACES TO EAT
5 Sannin
56 La Taverna del Cel Ros

BARS & DISCOS
1 Mirablau

4 KGB
29 Torres de Ávila
69 Savannah

MUSEUMS & GALLERIES
3 Casa Museu Gaudí
9 Museu-Monestir de Pedralbes
10 Palau Reial de Pedralbes (Museu de Ceràmica & Museu de les Arts Decoratives)
22 Museu del Futbol Club Barcelona
35 Galería Olímpica

36 Palau Nacional de Montjuïc (Museu Nacional d'Art de Catalunya)
37 Museu Etnològic
39 Museu d'Arqueologia
41 Fundació Joan Miró
45 Museu Militar

OTHER
6 British Council
8 US Consulate
11 Giorgio Armani
12 Gianni Versace
13 FNAC

OTHER (CONTINUED)
14 L'Illa de Diagonal
   Shopping Complex
16 Ronicar
17 Netherlands Consulate
18 El Corte Inglés
19 Australian Consulate
20 Renoir-Les Corts Cinema
21 Camp Nou
23 Coordinadora Gai-Lesbiana
24 Farmàcia Saltó
25 Estació d'Autobusos de Sants
26 Aerobús Stop
27 Dona i Ocell Sculpture
28 Turisme Juvenil de Catalunya;
   Xarxa d'Alberg de Catalunya;
   usit Unlimited
30 Poble Espanyol
31 Tennis Municipal Pompeia
32 Institut Nacional d'Educació
   Física de Catalunya (INEFC)

OTHER (CONTINUED)
33 Piscines Bernat Picornell
34 Palau Sant Jordi
38 Teatre Mercat de les Flors
40 Teatre Grec
42 Estació Parc Montjuïc
   (Funicular & Telefèric)
43 Terminus for Bus Nos 50 & 61
44 Castell (Telefèric)
46 Estació Mirador (Telefèric)
47 Telefèric (Funicular Aereo)
48 Barcelona-Genoa Ferry Dock
49 Ferry Terminal;
   Trasmediterránea
50 Torre de Jaume I
51 World Trade Center
52 Torre de Sant Sebastià
54 Peix Sculpture
55 Torre Mapfre
57 Scenic Bike Hire
58 Icària–Yelmo Cinema
60 Palau de Justicia
61 Arc de Triomf; easyRentacar
62 Estació del Nord
63 L'Auditori
64 Teatre Nacional de Catalunya
65 Plaça de Braus Monumental
66 Els Encants Vells Flea Market
67 Centre Comercial
   de les Glòries
68 Institut Municipal de
   Persones amb Disminució
70 Hospital de la Creu Roja
71 Hospital de la Santa
   Creu i Sant Pau

MAP 2 - L'EIXAMPLE & GRÀCIA

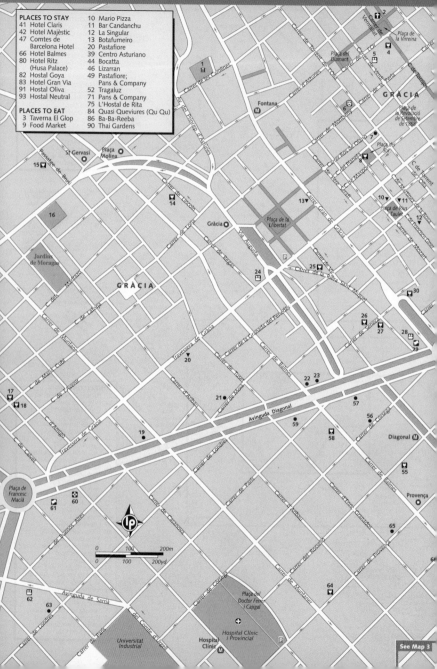

PLACES TO STAY
41 Hotel Claris
42 Hotel Majèstic
47 Comtes de
   Barcelona Hotel
66 Hotel Balmes
80 Hotel Ritz
   (Husa Palace)
82 Hostal Goya
83 Hotel Gran Via
91 Hostal Oliva
93 Hostal Neutral

PLACES TO EAT
3 Taverna El Glop
9 Food Market
10 Mario Pizza
11 Bar Candanchu
12 La Singular
13 Botafumeiro
20 Pastafiore
39 Centro Asturiano
44 Bocatta
46 Lizarran
49 Pastafiore;
   Pans & Company
52 Tragaluz
71 Pans & Company
75 L'Hostal de Rita
84 Quasi Queviures (Qu Qu)
86 Ba-Ba-Reeba
90 Thai Gardens

GRÀCIA

Plaça de
la Virreina

Plaça del
Diamant

Fontana

Plaça de
la Revolució
de Setembre
de 1868

St Gervasi

Plaça
Molina

Plaça del
Sol

GRÀCIA

Jardins
de Moragas

Gràcia

Plaça de la
Llibertat

Plaça de Rius
i Taulet

Travessera de Gràcia

Avinguda Diagonal

Diagonal M

Plaça de
Francesc
Macià

Provença M

Avinguda de Sarrià

Universitat
Industrial

Plaça del
Doctor Ferrer
i Caigal

Hospital Clínic
i Provincial

Hospital
Clínic M

See Map 3

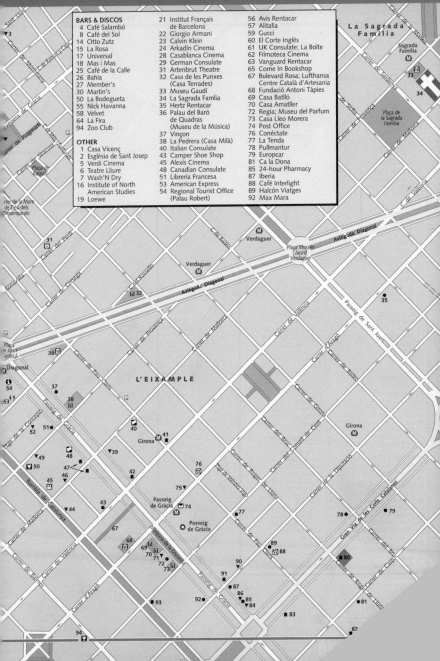

BARS & DISCOS
4 Café Salambó
8 Café del Sol
14 Otto Zutz
15 La Rosa
17 Universal
18 Mas i Mas
25 Café de la Calle
26 Bahía
27 Member's
30 Martin's
55 La Bodegueta
55 Nick Havanna
58 Velvet
64 La Fira
94 Zoo Club

OTHER
1 Casa Vicenç
2 Església de Sant Josep
5 Verdi Cinema
6 Teatre Lliure
7 Wash'N Dry
16 Institute of North
   American Studies
19 Loewe

21 Institut Français
   de Barcelona
22 Giorgio Armani
23 Calvin Klein
24 Arkadin Cinema
28 Casablanca Cinema
29 German Consulate
31 Artenbrut Theatre
32 Casa de les Punxes
   (Casa Terrades)
33 Museu Gaudí
34 La Sagrada Famlia
35 Hertz Rentacar
36 Palau del Baró
   de Quadras
   (Museu de la Música)
37 Vinçon
38 La Pedrera (Casa Milà)
40 Italian Consulate
43 Camper Shoe Shop
45 Alexis Cinema
48 Canadian Consulate
51 Librería Francesa
53 American Express
54 Regional Tourist Office
   (Palau Robert)

56 Avis Rentacar
57 Alitalia
59 Gucci
60 El Corte Inglés
61 UK Consulate; La Boîte
62 Filmoteca Cinema
63 Vanguard Rentacar
65 Come In Bookshop
67 Bulevard Rosa; Lufthansa
   Centre Català d'Artesania
68 Fundació Antoni Tàpies
69 Casa Batlló
70 Casa Amatller
72 Regia; Museu del Parfum
73 Casa Lleo Morera
74 Post Office
76 Conéctate
77 La Tenda
78 Pullmantur
79 Europcar
81 Ca la Dona
85 24-hour Pharmacy
87 Iberia
88 Café Interlight
89 Halcón Viatges
92 Max Mara

MAP 3 - CENTRAL BARCELONA

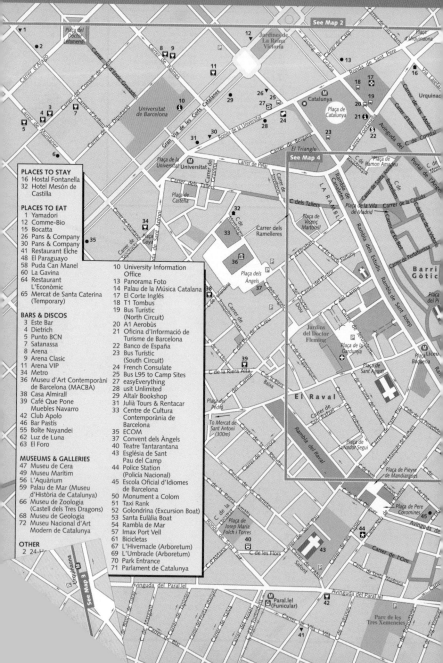

PLACES TO STAY
16 Hostal Fontanella
32 Hotel Mesón de
   Castilla

PLACES TO EAT
1 Yamadori
12 Comme-Bio
15 Bocatta
26 Pans & Company
30 Pans & Company
41 Restaurant Elche
58 El Paraguayo
58 Puda Can Manel
60 La Gavina
64 Restaurant
   L'Econòmic
65 Mercat de Santa Caterina
   (Temporary)

BARS & DISCOS
3 Este Bar
4 Dietrich
6 Punto BCN
7 Satanassa
8 Arena
9 Arena Clasic
11 Arena VIP
34 Metro
36 Museu d'Art Contemporàni
   de Barcelona (MACBA)
38 Casa Almirall
39 Café Que Pone
   Muebles Navarro
42 Club Apolo
48 Bar Pastís
55 Boîte Nayandei
62 Luz de Luna
63 El Foro

MUSEUMS & GALLERIES
47 Museu de Cera
49 Museu Marítim
56 L'Aquàrium
59 Palau de Mar (Museu
   d'Història de Catalunya)
66 Museu de Zoologia
   (Castell dels Tres Dragons)
68 Museu de Geologia
72 Museu Nacional d'Art
   Modern de Catalunya

OTHER
2 24-H

10 University Information
   Office
13 Panorama Foto
14 Palau de la Música Catalana
17 El Corte Inglés
18 T1 Tombus
19 Bus Turístic
   (North Circuit)
20 A1 Aerobús
21 Oficina d'Informació de
   Turisme de Barcelona
22 Banco de España
23 Bus Turístic
   (South Circuit)
24 French Consulate
25 Bus L95 to Camp Sites
27 easyEverything
28 usit Unlimited
29 Altaïr Bookshop
31 Julià Tours & Rentacar
33 Centre de Cultura
   Contemporània de
   Barcelona
35 ECOM
37 Convent dels Àngels
40 Teatre Tantarantana
43 Església de Sant
   Pau del Camp
44 Police Station
   (Policia Nacional)
45 Escola Oficial d'Idiomes
   de Barcelona
50 Monument a Colom
51 Taxi Rank
52 Golondrina (Excursion Boat)
53 Santa Eulàlia Boat
54 Rambla de Mar
57 Imax Port Vell
61 Bicicletas
67 L'Hivernacle (Arboretum)
69 L'Umbracle (Arboretum)
70 Park Entrance
71 Parlament de Catalunya

MAP 4 - CIUTAT VELLA

MAP 4 - CIUTAT VELLA

PLACES TO STAY
3 Pensión Noya
9 Le Meridien
13 Hostal Mare Nostrum
14 Hotel San Agustín
20 Hotel Peninsular
21 Hotel España
23 Hotel Oriente
32 Hostal El Cantón
43 Alberg Juvenil Palau
44 Casa Huéspedes Mari-Luz
46 Hostal Levante
48 Pensión Alamar
55 Hotel Roma Reial
63 Hotel Barcelona House
64 Hotel Cuatro Naciones
65 Youth Hostel Kabul
68 Pensión Villanueva
83 Albergue Arco
84 Pensión Fernando
95 Hotel Suizo
109 Hotel Jardi
110 Hostal Galerias Maldà
115 Hostal-Residencia
    Rembrandt
117 Hostal Campi
119 Hotel Continental
121 Hotel Nouvel
123 Hostal Lausanne
126 Hotel Colón
132 Pensión Lourdes

PLACES TO EAT
1 Café Zurich
4 Pastafiore
5 Bar Kasparo
7 Pans & Company
8 Champion Supermarket
11 Ra
12 El Convent
15 Rita Blue
16 Casa Leopoldo
18 Restaurante Pollo Rico
19 Restaurant Els Tres Bots
29 Salsitas
38 Bar Celta
39 Tasca El Corral
40 Sidrería La Socarrena
45 La Cereria
47 La Verónica
49 Felafel & Kebab Takeaway
52 Pans & Company
58 Wagamama
59 Buen Bocado
60 Los Caracoles
62 La Fonda Escudellers

67 Disco Bar-Real
71 Les Quinze Nits
72 Maoz
73 Cafè de l'Òpera
74 Les Quatre Barres
75 Sushi-Ya
79 Irati
81 Can Culleretes
86 Salterio
90 Bocatta
92 Santa Clara
96 La Colmena
107 Croissanterie del Pi
108 Xocolateria La Xicra
112 Granja La Pallaresa
118 Bocatta
120 Self-Naturista
122 The Bagel Shop
124 Els Quatre Gats
125 Pans & Company
127 Comme-Bio (La Botiga)
128 Lluna Plena
129 Restaurante Bunga Raya
133 Senyor Parellada
134 L'Ou Com Balla
141 Cal Pep
146 Restaurant Set (7) Portes
147 Can Paixano

BARS & DISCOS
6 L'Ovella Negra
17 Bar Marsella
30 London Bar
31 Moog
42 Harlem Jazz Club
50 Shanghai
51 Bar Malpaso
53 Sidecar
54 Karma
56 Thiossan
57 Zoo
61 Dot
66 Jamboree
69 Barcelona Pipa Club
70 Glaciar
82 Schilling
135 El Xampanyet
138 Miramelindo
139 El Copetín
140 Mudanzas
144 La Vinya del Senyor

MUSEUMS & GALLERIES
77 Museu de l'Eròtica
97 Museu d'Història de la Ciutat;
   Casa Padellàs

102 Museu Frederic Marès
130 Museu Picasso
131 Museu Tèxtil i d'Indumentària;
    Museu Barbier-Muellerd'Art
    Precolombí
137 Galeria Maeght

OTHER
2 FNAC
10 Palau de la Virreina
22 Gran Teatre del Liceu
24 Guàrdia Urbana Station
25 Tablao Cordobés
26 easyEverything
27 Teatre Principal
28 Palau Güell
33 Casal Lambda
34 Antinous
35 Harbour Boat Rides
36 Universitat Pompeu Fabra
37 Església de la Mercè
41 Main Post Office
76 American Express
78 24-Hour Pharmacy
80 Documenta Bookshop
85 CIAJ Youth Information
   Centre
87 Palau de la Generalitat
88 Ajuntament (Town Hall)
89 Centre d'Informació de
   Turisme de Barcelona
91 Temple Romà d'Augustí
93 Església de Sants Just
   i Pastor
94 Próleg Bookshop
98 Capella Reial de
   Santa Àgata
99 Saló del Tinell
100 Mirador del Rei Martí
101 Palau del Lloctinent
103 Casa de l'Ardiaca
104 Capella de Santa Llúcia
105 Església de Sant Sever
106 Palau de Bisbat
111 Quera Bookshop
113 Institut Català de
    la Dona
114 Llibreria & Informaciò
    Culturalde la Generalitat
    de Catalunya
116 Roman Tombs
136 Palau de Dalmases
142 Un Menys
143 Església de Santa Maria
    del Mar
145 Lavomatic

The wave-shaped Rambla de Mar footbridge in Barcelona rotates to let boats enter the marina.

Dining alfresco in Plaça Reial

The city's beaches are a great place to unwind.

A taste of the modern at glossy Maremàgnum

Meet the Generalitat at the imposing Parlament de Catalunya in Parc de la Ciutadella.

Gaudí's fairy-tale Casa Batlló

The soaring towers of La Sagrada Família

The classic Cascada fountain

[continued from page 144]

Bar Pastís *(Map 3; Carrer de Santa Mònica 4)* is a tiny old bar with a French cabaret theme (lots of Piaf in the background).

L'Ovella Negra *(Map 4; Carrer de les Sitges 5),* or The Black Sheep, is a noisy, fun, barn-like tavern with a young crowd.

Café Que Pone Muebles Navarro *(Map 3; Carrer de la Riera Alta 4–6)* is an art gallery-cum-lounge-cum-bar (whose name means 'Cafe Where the Sign Says Navarro Furniture'). It's an odd place but worth a look and it does great cheesecake. It opens until midnight, and closes Monday.

If by 2.30 am, when all or most of these places have shut their doors, you still need a drink and don't want a club or disco, your best bet (except on Sunday) is the **London Bar** *(Map 4; Carrer Nou de la Rambla 36).* It opens until 5 am and occasionally stages some off-the-wall music acts; a bottled beer costs about €3.

La Ribera All these places are on Map 4. **El Xampanyet** *(Carrer de Montcada 22)* is the city's best-known cava bar – a small, cosy place with tiled walls and good tapas as well as cava by the glass.

Next door at No 20, the baroque magnificence of the **Palau de Dalmases** is matched only by the plush luxury inside. The snag is the price – a glass of no-name wine will cost €6!

Along and near Passeig del Born, which links the Església de Santa Maria del Mar and the former fresh-produce market Mercat del Born, you'll find stacks of bars. Worth a try are **El Copetín**, at No 19, for cocktails, and **Miramelindo**, at No 15, a spacious tavern where you can actually hear yourself talk as well as drink.

Mudanzas *(Carrer de la Vidrieria 15)* has been around for a lot longer. It's a popular little bar and you can often hear live music here. Around the corner, shady Plaça de les Olles is a charming little hideaway square in summer when the *terrasses* are in operation.

In a class of its own is the nearby wine bar **La Vinya del Senyor**, on Plaça de Santa Maria del Mar. Come here to taste a selection of wines and cavas, accompanied by simple snacks.

L'Eixample In general the 19th-century expanse that is L'Eixample is not a good place to go looking for nightlife. One or two options are worthwhile, however.

La Bodegueta *(Map 2; Rambla de Catalunya 100)* is a classic wine cellar. Bottles and barrels line the walls and stools surround marble tables.

La Fira *(Map 2; Carrer de Provença 171)* is a designer bar with a difference. You enter through a hall of distorting mirrors and inside you'll find that everything is fairground paraphernalia. It sounds corny but the atmosphere is fun.

Gràcia Two lively bars on Plaça del Sol (Map 2) are **Café del Sol** at No 16 and **Mirasol**, opposite at No 4. The former has a vaguely bohemian crowd, tapas, and tables outside.

Café Salambó *(Map 2; Carrer de Torrijos 51)* is a gentle designer haunt imitating a village bar, with benches at low tables. It has an upper level with pool tables and there's food too – €7 for a three-course *menú*.

Montjuïc The Poble Espanyol (Map 1) has several bars that get lively. The most original is **Torres de Ávila** inside the tall entrance towers themselves. Created by the top designer Javier Mariscal (he was responsible for the Olympics mascot 'Kobi' in 1992), it has several levels and all sorts of surreal touches, including an egg-shaped room and glass lifts that you fear will shoot you through the roof. It opens 10 pm to 4 am and admission costs €6.

Western Gràcia/Avinguda Diagonal
The area around Carrer de Marià Cubí gets busy with locals at the weekend. It's a little on the *pijo* (well-off kid) side but can be fun all the same. And it's not likely to be filled with tourists! Don't bother earlier in the week as the area tends to be dead.

Mas i Mas *(Map 2; Carrer de Marià Cubí 199)* is one of the area's best-known drinkeries. Another must is **Universal**, across the road at No 182. It opens until 4.30 am Monday to Saturday.

Live Music
There's a good choice of live music most nights of the week and many venues double as bars or clubs. In the latter case, if you paid to get in to see an act, the dancing afterwards will come free. Starting times are rarely before 10 pm, more often around midnight. Admission ranges from free to €9 or so – the higher prices often include a drink.

To see big-name acts, either Spanish or from abroad, you will probably pay more. They often perform at venues such as the 17,000-capacity **Palau Sant Jordi** (Map 1) on Montjuïc or the **Teatre Mercat de les Flors** (Map 1), at the foot of Montjuïc.

Barri Gòtic These places are all on map 4. **Barcelona Pipa Club** (Plaça Reial 3) occasionally has jazz from Thursday to Saturday at around midnight; usually costing €6 plus drinks. It's like someone's apartment inside and stays open until 2 or 3 am.

Harlem Jazz Club (Carrer de la Comtessa de Sobradiel 8) is a stalwart stop on the Barcelona jazz circuit, although it sometimes gets in other acts too, including some rock and Latin.

Jamboree (Plaça Reial 17) offers varied jazz and funk most nights. Admission costs up to €12 (which generally includes a drink).

Sidecar (Carrer de les Heures 4–6), just off Plaça Reial, presents pop and rock bands of various denominations several nights a week, usually starting at about 11 pm and winding up by about 3 am. Admission costs up to €6.

La Ribera At **El Foro** (Map 3; Carrer de la Princesa 53) you'll find jazz, tango and other music sessions from Wednesday through to the weekend, usually kicking off at 11 pm.

Poble Sec The place for world music – chiefly African, Latin and Spanish – is **Club Apolo** (Map 3; Carrer Nou de la Rambla 113). Bands play several nights a week at

around 10.30 pm (€12 for big-names), followed by live salsa or (on Friday and Saturday) a disco.

Western Gràcia/Avinguda Diagonal
Several nights a week at midnight **La Boîte** (Map 2; Avinguda Diagonal 477), underneath the UK consulate, offers jazz or blues, with the occasional jam session. Admission costs €7.25 to €15.

Clubs & Discos
Barcelona's discos come alive from about 2 or 3 am until 5 or 6 am, and are best on Friday and Saturday nights. Some have live bands, often starting about midnight, to fill the place before the real action begins. Cover charges range from nothing to as much as €18. The price depends partly on how busy the place is and whether the bouncers like your look. If you go early, you'll often pay less. Drinks are expensive – anything up to €4.85 for a beer.

Barri Gòtic **Jamboree** (see under Live Music earlier) becomes a crowded dance scene from around 1.30 am, after the live stuff finishes. It has two spaces – one for Latin rhythms, one for rock – until 5 am or so. Admission ranges from free to €9.

Karma (Map 4; Plaça Reial 10) is a young, student-type basement place with good music, open from around 11 pm to 4 am. Admission usually costs €6, which covers a drink.

El Raval A fun disco, **Moog** (Map 4; Carrer de l'Arc del Teatre 3) has Latin and dance hits from as far back as the 1970s upstairs, and strobe lights and techno downstairs. It opens until about 7 am at weekends and admission costs €6 (as do the mixed drinks!).

La Ribera For a sassy place try **Luz de Luna** (Map 3; Carrer del Comerç 21), where early in the week you can sip on piña coladas and other South American mixes and dance on the luridly decorated dance floor. Midweek, it fills up from around 2 am but closes by about 4 am. On Friday and Saturday you can shake and wiggle until

6 am. Admission costs between €6 and €12 and cocktails cost around €3.65.

Port Vell A bevy of bars and discos open in the Maremàgnum complex (Map 3) until the wee hours. In July and August, most of the action is here and spreads along the waterfront. One of the places to watch for is *Boîte Nayandei*.

L'Eixample A big 1980s 'designer bar', *Nick Havanna (Map 2; Carrer del Rosselló 208)* has a video bank at one end of the dance space as well as glass-backed urinals flushed by veritable cascades of water. It opens nightly from 11 pm to 4 or 5 am, often with bands or salsa/merengue classes at midnight. Admission is free but drink prices are cheeky.

Satanassa (Map 3; Carrer d'Aribau 27) is an 'antidesign' haunt of mixed crowds (with a notable gay leaning), with gaudy erotic murals. It opens from about 11 pm to 4 or 5 am and admission is free.

Velvet (Map 2; Carrer de Balmes 161) is a smallish designer bar and disco inspired by the film *Blue Velvet*, with 1960s music. It is busy with a fairly straight crowd. Admission is free.

Zoo Club (Map 2; Carrer de Balmes 51) is relatively new on the Barcelona scene. The standard fare is house but it's an accessible club that attracts a heterodox clientele. It opens at 11.30 pm and keeps hopping until 5 am from Wednesday to Saturday nights. Admission generally costs €12.

Around Avinguda Diagonal West of Via Augusta, *Otto Zutz (Map 2; Carrer de Lincoln 15)*, is for beautiful people (bouncers will decide how beautiful you are) and those who favour wearing black. Admission costs between €6 and €12 and a beer costs €4.85.

Gràcia Maintaining a hard-rock warehouse-type scene *KGB (Map 1; Carrer de Ca l'Alegre de Dalt 55)* stays open until 8 am for tireless all-nighters.

Tibidabo A bar with great views, *Mirablau (Map 1; Plaça del Doctor Andreu)* has a

small disco floor that keeps going until about 5 am.

El Clot At *Savannah (Map 1; Carrer de la Muntanya 16)* there's good dance music – to midnight on Sunday, to 3 am Tuesday to Thursday and to 5 am Friday and Saturday.

Gay & Lesbian Venues

Bars & Cafes Three good gay bars, virtually one on top of the other, are *Punto BCN (Map 3; Carrer de Muntaner 63–65)*, *Dietrich (Map 3; Carrer del Consell de Cent 255)* and *Este Bar (Map 3; Carrer del Consell de Cent 257)*. Punto BCN is a relaxed place to meet a 30-something-plus crowd, while Este Bar is perhaps a tad more self-conscious. Dietrich is more of a theatre cafe, often with very camp entertainment. It is a big, friendly space and open until about 3 am. This local concentration of bars (and some clubs – see later) has earned this part of town the sobriquet of 'Gaixample'.

Café de la Calle (Map 2; Carrer de Vic 11) is a cosy meeting place for lesbians and gay men. *Antinous (Map 4; Carrer de Josep Anselm Clavé 6)* is a gay bookshop-cafe.

A good lesbian bar is *Bahía (Map 2; Carrer de Seneca 12)*, open until about 2.30 am. Another nearby is *Member's (Map 2; Carrer de Seneca 3)*. Both are open to all-comers. More exclusively lesbian is *La Rosa (Map 2; Passatge de Brusi 39)*.

Clubs & Discos The two top gay discos are *Metro (Map 3; Carrer de Sepúlveda 185)* near Plaça de la Universitat, and *Martin's (Map 2; Passeig de Gràcia 130)*. Metro attracts some lesbians and straight folk as well as gay men; it's packed for its regular Monday-night cabarets. Martin's is for gay men only. Both are open from midnight to 5 am and have dark rooms.

Popular with a young, cruisy gay crowd is *Arena (Map 3; Carrer de Balmes 32)*. It has a dark room, opens at midnight and closes around 5 am. Around the corner, *Arena Clasic (Map 3; Carrer de la Diputació 233)* is a little more sedate. *Arena VIP (Map 3; Gran Via de les Corts Catalanes 593)* is a more mixed mainstream place with a gay flavour. It opens at midnight and you will probably leave about dawn.

Classical Music & Opera

Guía del Ocio has ample listings, but the monthly *Informatiu Musical* leaflet has the best coverage of classical music (as well as other genres). You can pick it up at tourist offices and the Palau de la Virreina arts information office (Map 4; ☎ 93 301 77 75) at Rambla de Sant Josep 99, which also sells tickets for many events. Recitals take place all over the city and beyond, in theatres, museums, monasteries and so on.

At Barcelona's grand opera house, ***Gran Teatre del Liceu*** *(Map 4; ☎ 93 485 99 13, La Rambla 51–59)*, you can attend opera, world-class dance, and classical music concerts. Tickets can cost anything from €3 to €67. You need to book ahead and can do so through ServiCaixa on ☎ 902 33 22 11. Take a peek at the Liceu's Web site at W www.liceubarcelona.com.

The chief venue for classical and choral music is ***Palau de la Música Catalana*** *(Map 3; ☎ 93 295 72 00, Carrer de Sant Pere més alt 11)* in La Ribera, which has a busy and wide-ranging program.

In the late 1990s, Barcelona's impressive new home for serious music lovers, ***L'Auditori*** *(Map 1; ☎ 93 247 93 00, Carrer de Lepant 50),* swung into action. It puts on plenty of orchestral, chamber, religious and other musical events throughout the year.

The easiest way to get hold of tickets for most of the above venues and other theatres throughout the city is through the Caixa de Catalunya's Tel-Entrada service on ☎ 902 10 12 12, or on the Internet at W www .telentrada.com. There's also a ticket office *(venta de localidades)* on the ground floor of El Corte Inglés (Map 3) on Plaça de Catalunya and another at the FNAC store (Map 4) on the same square.

Cinemas

Foreign films, shown with subtitles and original soundtrack rather than dubbed, are marked 'v.o.' *(versión original)* in film listings. Cinemas to check for these (all on Map 2 except where indicated) include:

Alexis (☎ 93 215 05 06) Rambla de Catalunya 90
Arkadín (☎ 93 405 22 22) Travessera de Gràcia 103
Casablanca (☎ 93 218 43 45) Passeig de Gràcia 115
Icària-Yelmo (Map 1; ☎ 93 221 75 85) Carrer de Salvador Espriu 61
Renoir-Les Corts (Map 1; ☎ 93 490 55 10) Carrer de Eugeni d'Ors 1
Verdi (☎ 93 237 05 16) Carrer de Verdi 32
Filmoteca (☎ 93 410 75 70) Avinguda de Sarrià 3. This cinema specialises more in film seasons that concentrate on particular directors, styles and eras of film.

A ticket usually costs €3.65 to €4.55 but most cinemas have a weekly *día del espectador* (viewer's day; often Monday or Wednesday) when they charge €2.45 to €3.65.

Theatre

Theatre is nearly all in Catalan or Spanish (*Guía del Ocio* specifies which). For all that's happening in theatre, head for the information office in Palau de la Virreina. Look for the many leaflets and the monthly listings guide, *Teatre BCN*.

Teatre Lliure *(Map 2; ☎ 93 218 92 51, Carrer de Montseny 47)* in Gràcia is dedicated to theatre in Catalan. ***Artenbrut*** *(Map 2; ☎ 93 457 97 05, Carrer del Perill 9–11)* concentrates more on new and rising directors. Performances are usually in Catalan and occasionally in Castilian.

Teatre Tantarantana *(Map 3; ☎ 93 285 79 00, Carrer de les Flors 22),* apart from staging all sorts of contemporary theatre, also puts on kids' shows such as pantomimes and puppet shows. These shows start at 6 pm.

Originally destined to become *the* home of Catalan theatre, Ricard Bofill's ultra-neo-classical ***Teatre Nacional de Catalunya*** *(Map 1; ☎ 93 306 57 06, Plaça de les Arts 1)* opened its doors in 1997. So far it has put on a mixed bag of not-always-exciting theatre but it is worth keeping an eye on the program.

Dance

Sardana The *sardana*, Catalunya's national dance, is danced every week – except sometimes in August – on Plaça de la Seu

(Map 4) in front of the cathedral at 6.30 pm Saturday and noon Sunday. These are not shows for tourists but feature ordinary Catalans doing something they enjoy.

Flamenco Although quite a few important flamenco artists grew up in the gitano barrios of Barcelona, seeing good performances of this essentially Andalucian dance and music is not always easy here. A few *tablaos* (tourist-oriented flamenco performances) are scattered about. If this is the only way you can see it, perhaps it's better than nothing – and occasionally they attract class acts. *El Tablao de Carmen (Map 1; ☎ 93 325 68 95, Carrer dels Arcs 9)* is in the Poble Espanyol, while *Tablao Cordobés (Map 4; ☎ 93 317 66 53)* is at La Rambla 35. Book ahead.

SPECTATOR SPORTS
Football
Barcelona Football Club has not only one of Europe's best teams, Barça, but also one of its best stadiums, the 120,000-capacity Camp Nou (Map 1). Tickets, available at the stadium and through some banks, cost from around €18 to €48. For more information, call ☎ 93 496 36 00. The city's other club, Espanyol, based at the Estadi Olímpic on Montjuïc (Map 1), traditionally plays second fiddle (in the top division) to Barça.

Bullfights
Death in the Afternoon is not a favourite Catalan theme but fights take place on Sunday afternoons in summer at the Plaça de Braus Monumental (Map 1), on the corner of Gran Via de les Corts Catalanes and Carrer de la Marina. The 'fun' usually starts at 6 pm. Tickets are available at the arena from 10.30 am to 2 pm and 6 to 7 pm Wednesday to Saturday, and from 10 am Sunday, or by calling ☎ 902 33 22 11. Prices range from €15 to €73.

SHOPPING
There are enough chic (and expensive) boutiques and trendy shops to keep the fashion-conscious happy (or worried) for weeks.

Most of the mainstream stores can be found on a shopping 'axis' that looks something like the hands of a clock set at a quarter to five. From the waterfront it leads up La Rambla through Plaça de Catalunya and on up Passeig de Gràcia. At Avinguda Diagonal you turn left. From here as far as Plaça de la Reina Maria Cristina (especially the final stretch from Plaça de Francesc Macià), the Diagonal is jammed with places where you can empty your bank account. The T1 Tombbus service (see under Getting Around) has been laid on for the ardent shopper.

The best shopping areas in central Barcelona are Passeig de Gràcia and the streets to its south-west (including the Bulevard Rosa arcade, just north of Carrer d'Aragó; Map 2), and Barri Gòtic (Map 4) streets such as Carrer de la Portaferrissa, Carrer de la Boqueria, Carrer del Call, Carrer de la Llibreteria and Carrer de Ferran, and around Plaça de Sant Josep Oriol.

Department store bargain-hunters should note that the winter sales officially start on or around 10 January and their summer equivalents on or around 5 July.

Art Galleries
Along Carrer de Montcada (Map 4) are several galleries, the biggest being Galeria Maeght at No 25. You'll also find half a dozen small galleries and designer stores on Carrer del Doctor Dou, Carrer d'Elisabets and Carrer dels Àngels (all on Map 4).

The classiest concentration of galleries – about a dozen of them – is on the short stretch of Carrer del Consell de Cent between Rambla de Catalunya and Carrer de Balmes (Map 2).

Clothing & Fabrics
If you are after international fashion, Avinguda Diagonal is the place to look. Calvin Klein (Map 2) is at No 484, Giorgio Armani at Nos 490 (Map 2) and 620 (Map 1), Gianni Versace (Map 1) at No 606 and Gucci (Map 2) at No 415. Max Mara fans will want to head for Passeig de Gràcia 23 (Map 2).

Loewe (Map 2), at Avinguda Diagonal 570, is one of Spain's leading and oldest fashion stores, founded in 1846. There's another branch in the Modernista Casa Lleo Morera (Map 2) on Passeig de Gràcia.

Zara is another well known local name for women's fashion. It is a chain and you'll find several branches across town, including in L'Illa del Diagonal shopping complex (Map 1).

Crafts

If you want to take a look at high-quality Catalan crafts *(artesania)* to perhaps get some inspiration for future shopping expeditions, pop into the Centre Català d'Artesania (Map 2; ☎ 93 467 46 60) at Passeig de Gràcia 55.

Design

Vinçon (Map 2), Passeig de Gràcia 96, has the slickest designs in furniture and household goods, both local and imported.

Markets

The large Els Encants Vells (The Old Charms; Map 1) flea market (also known as the Fira de Bellcaire) is held every Monday, Wednesday, Friday and Saturday from 8 am to 7 pm (8 pm in summer) next to Plaça de les Glòries Catalanes.

In the Barri Gòtic, there's a crafts market in Plaça de Sant Josep Oriol (Map 4) on Thursday and Friday, an antiques market in Plaça Nova on Thursday (Map 4), and a coin and stamp collectors' market in Plaça Reial on Sunday morning (Map 4). On the western edge of El Raval, the Mercat de Sant Antoni (Map 3) dedicates Sunday morning to old maps, stamps, books and cards.

Shoes

There's a gaggle of relatively economical shoe shops on Avinguda del Portal de l'Àngel, off Plaça de Catalunya (Maps 3 & 4).

Camper (Map 2), Carrer de València 249, something of a classic shoe merchant in Spain, has a good range.

GETTING THERE & AWAY

For some agencies offering cheap air fares and youth and student train and bus tickets, see Travel Agencies earlier in this chapter.

Air

The airport (☎ 93 298 38 38) is 14km south-west of the centre at El Prat de Llobregat. Barcelona is a big international and domestic destination, with direct flights from North America as well as many European cities.

Tickets can be bought at almost any travel agency. Iberia (Map 2; ☎ 902 40 05 00) is at Passeig de Gràcia 30; Spanair (☎ 902 13 14 15, 24 hours) and Air Europa (☎ 902 40 15 01) are at the airport. Other airline numbers include Alitalia (☎ 902 10 03 23), Delta Airlines (☎ 93 412 43 33), easyJet (☎ 902 29 99 92), KLM (☎ 93 379 54 58), Lufthansa (☎ 93 487 03 52) and TWA (☎ 93 215 84 86).

For more information on flights and air fares, see under Air in the Getting There & Away chapter.

Bus

The main intercity bus station *(estació d'autobusos)* is the modern Estació del Nord at Carrer d'Alí Bei 80, 1.5km north-east of La Rambla and 1½ blocks from the Arc de Triomf metro (Map 1). Its information desk (☎ 93 265 65 08) opens 7 am to 9 pm daily.

A few services – most importantly some international buses and the few buses to Montserrat – use Estació d'Autobusos de Sants beside Estació Sants train station (Map 1).

For information on fares and journey times to international and Spanish destinations turn to the Getting There & Away chapter. For buses around Catalunya, see the Getting Around and destination chapters.

Train

The main international and domestic station is Estació Sants, on Plaça dels Països Catalans, 2.5km west of La Rambla (Map 1).

Other useful stations for long-distance and regional trains are Catalunya on Plaça de Catalunya (Map 3), and Passeig de Gràcia, on the corner of Passeig de Gràcia and Carrer d'Aragó (Map 2), 10 minutes' walk north of Plaça de Catalunya.

It's advisable to book at least a day or two ahead for most long-distance trains, domestic or international. You can get information and book tickets directly at Estació Sants. There's a RENFE information and booking office in Passeig de Gràcia station, open 7 am to 10 pm daily (9 pm Sunday).

For details on getting to Barcelona by rail from international and Spanish destinations, see the Getting There & Away chapter. For journeys within Catalunya, see the Getting Around chapter.

Car & Motorcycle
For general information on driving around Catalunya, see the Getting Around chapter. A popular option is to hire a Mercedes Class A or Smartcar with easyRentacar. The Web site W www.easyrentacar.com is where you can book this. The car pick-up and drop-off point is at Passeig de Lluís Companys (the underground parking area below the boulevard – the entrance is at the northern end near the Arc de Triomf; Map 1) and it opens from 7 am to 11 pm. Rates depend on demand and how far in advance you book – the further the better. You can be looking at UK£9 per day plus a UK£5 preparation charge and 5p per kilometre over the first 100km. The vehicles are tiny and, worse, bear enormous easyRentacar banners – which is a bit like screaming out: Pick Me! – but the deal can work out quite cheaply.

Other rental outlets in Barcelona include:

Avis (Map 2; ☎ 902 13 55 31, ☎ 93 237 56 80) Carrer de Córsega 293–295
Europcar (Map 2; ☎ 902 10 50 30) Gran Via de les Corts Catalanes 680
Hertz (Map 2; ☎ 902 40 24 05, ☎ 93 270 03 30) Carrer d'Aragó 382–384
Julià Car (Map 3; ☎ 93 402 69 00) Ronda de la Universitat 5
National/Atesa (Map 3; ☎ 902 10 01 01, ☎ 93 323 07 01) Carrer de Muntaner 45
Ronicar (Map 1; ☎ 989 06 34 73) Carrer d'Europa 34–36
Vanguard (Map 2; ☎ 93 439 38 80) Carrer de Londres 31

Avis, Europcar, Hertz and several other big companies also have desks at the airport, Estació Sants train station and Estació del Nord bus terminus.

Boat
Balearic Islands Passenger and vehicular ferries to the Balearic Islands, operated by Trasmediterránea, dock at Moll de Barcelona wharf in Port Vell (Map 1). Information and tickets are available from Trasmediterránea (☎ 902 45 46 45) or from travel agencies.

Scheduled services are: Barcelona to Palma (eight hours, seven to 21 services weekly); Barcelona to Maó (nine hours, two to eight services weekly); Barcelona to Ibiza city (9½ hours or 14½ hours via Palma, three to six services weekly). The standard one-way fare to any of the islands is €41.70 for a 'Butaca Turista' (seat). You can also get sleeping berths and transport vehicles. In summer, Trasmediterránea also operates a 'Fast Ferry' service to Palma (€54.20, 4¼ hours, up to eight services a week).

Italy There are departures from Barcelona to Genoa on Tuesday, Thursday (both at 10 pm) and Sunday (2 am). Going the other way, departures are on Monday (10 pm), Wednesday and Friday (both at 9 pm). An airline-style seat costs from €58.40 one way in the low season to €86.30 in the high season. A car costs anywhere from €83.20 to €132.25 one way, depending on the size of the vehicle and time of year. The trip lasts about 17 hours.

In Genoa, Grimaldi (☎ 010 58 93 31, fax 010 550 92 25) is at Via Fieschi 17/17a. The ferry terminal is at Via Milano (Ponte Assereto). You can book direct by phone, through a travel agency, at the docks (if there is space) or online at W www .grimaldi.it. In Barcelona, where you can book through any travel agency, the boat docks at Moll de Ponent (Map 1).

GETTING AROUND
The metro is the easiest way to get around. For some trips you need buses or FGC suburban trains. The main tourist office on Plaça de Catalunya gives out the comprehensive *Guia d'Autobusos Urbans de Barcelona*, with a metro map and all bus routes. For public transport information, you can call ☎ 010 or ☎ 93 412 00 00, or

☎ 93 205 15 15 for FGC trains only. For information on disabled facilities call ☎ 93 486 07 52.

TMB, the public transport authority, runs four Centres d'Atenció al Client (customer service centres): in Estació Sants train station and at Universitat, Diagonal and Sagrada Família metro stops.

Tickets & Targetas

In 2001, Barcelona's public transport fare system, put under the control of the Autoritat del Transport Metropolità (ATM), was overhauled and a zone system introduced covering Barcelona and 200 surrounding municipalities. Tickets were made valid on all forms of transport (except a handful of special services): buses, metro, FGC trains and RENFE's rodalies/cercanías trains. Six zones were established but for most visitors a Zona 1 ticket will always be sufficient. A single ride ticket costs €0.97.

Targetas are multiple-trip transport tickets and offer worthwhile savings. They are sold at most city-centre metro stations. Targeta T-10 (€5.35) gives you 10 rides and you can change from metro to bus to suburban train once within one hour and 15 minutes from the time you validate the ticket. Targeta T-DIA (€4.05) gives unlimited travel for a day. The T-3 and T-5 tickets give unlimited travel on metro, FGC and bus for three (€10.25) and five days (€15.70), respectively. Similar tickets inclusive of the ride in from the airport on the airport bus cost €11.45/16.90. The Targeta T-50/30 is for 50 trips within 30 days and costs €22.30. The T-Mes is a monthly pass for unlimited use of transport and costs €35.10. For this you will need a photopass, which you can arrange at the Centres d'Atenció al Client (Map 3; ☎ 93 318 70 74) at the Universitat metro stop.

To/From the Airport

Rodalies trains run from the airport (in Zona 1) to Estació Sants (Map 1) and Catalunya station on Plaça de Catalunya (Map 3) every 30 minutes from 6.13 am to 10.41 pm daily. It takes 16 minutes to Estació Sants and 21 minutes to Catalunya. Departures from

Estació Sants to the airport are from 5.43 am to 10.13 pm; from Catalunya they're five minutes earlier.

The A1 Aerobús service runs from the airport to Plaça de Catalunya via Estació Sants every 15 minutes from 6 am to midnight weekdays (from 6.30 am at weekends and holidays). Departures from Plaça de Catalunya are from 5.30 am to 11.15 pm weekdays (6 am to 11.20 pm at weekends and holidays). The trip takes about 40 minutes – depending on traffic – and costs €3.20.

A taxi to/from the centre, a 30-minute ride, costs about €15.

Bus

Buses run along most city routes every few minutes from 5 or 6 am to 10 or 11 pm. Many routes pass through Plaça de Catalunya and/or Plaça de la Universitat (both on Map 3). After 11 pm, a reduced network of yellow *nitbusos* (night buses) runs until 3 or 5 am. All night-bus routes pass through Plaça de Catalunya and most run every 30 to 45 minutes.

Bus Turístic This bus service covers two circuits (24 stops) linking virtually all the major tourist sights. Tourist offices, TMB offices and many hotels have leaflets explaining the system. Tickets, available on the bus, cost €13.25 for one day of unlimited rides, or €16.90 for two consecutive days. Buses run from 9 am to 7.45 pm and the frequency varies from 10 to 30 minutes, depending on the season.

Tombbus The T1 Tombbus route has been thought out for shoppers and runs regularly from Plaça de Catalunya up to Avinguda Diagonal, along which it proceeds west to Plaça de Pius XII (Map 1), where it turns around. On the way you pass such landmarks as El Corte Inglés (several of them), Bulevard Rosa and FNAC. Tickets are €1.10.

Train

FGC Suburban Trains Suburban trains, run by the Ferrocarrils de la Generalitat de Catalunya (FGC), include a couple of useful city lines. One heads north from Plaça de Catalunya. A branch of it will get you to Tibidabo and another within spitting distance of the Monestir de Pedralbes.

The other FGC train line heads to Manresa from Plaça d'Espanya and is less likely to be of use (except for the trip to Montserrat).

These trains run from 5 am to 11 or 11.30 pm Sunday to Thursday, and 5 am to 2 am on Friday and Saturday.

Rodalies/Cercanías These RENFE-run local trains serve towns around Barcelona, as well as the airport.

Metro

The metro has five lines, numbered and colour-coded, and is easy to use. Tickets are available from machines and staffed booths at most stations. At interchange stations, you just need to work out which line and direction you want. The metro runs from 5 am to 11 pm Monday to Thursday; 5 am to 2 am on Friday, Saturday and the day before public holidays; 6 am to midnight on Sunday; 6 am to 11 pm on other holidays; and 6 am to 2 am on holidays immediately preceding another holiday. Line 2 has access for the disabled and some stations on other lines have lifts.

Car & Motorcycle

An effective one-way system makes traffic flow fairly smoothly, but you'll often find yourself flowing the way you don't want to go, unless you happen to have an adept navigator and a map that shows one-way streets.

Parking can also be tricky, and expensive if you choose a parking garage. It's better to leave your car alone while you're here and use Barcelona's public transport.

Taxi

Taxis charge a €1.80 minimum charge plus meter charges. These work out to about €0.64 per kilometre (€0.18 more from 10 pm to 6 am weekdays and all day Saturday, Sunday and holidays). A further €1.80 is added for all trips to/from the airport, and €0.75 for luggage bigger than 55cm x 35cm x 35cm. The trip from Estació Sants to Plaça de Catalunya, about 3km, costs roughly €4.25. You can call a taxi on ☎ 93 225 00 00, ☎ 93 330 03 00, ☎ 93 266 39 39 or ☎ 93 490 22 22. General information is available on ☎ 010.

Radio Taxi Móvil (☎ 93 358 11 11) has disabled-adapted taxis.

Bicycle

Several outlets rent out bicycles. Un Menys (Map 4; ☎ 93 268 21 05), Carrer de l'Esparteria 3, charges €12 for a whole day, €9 for half a day or €3.65 an hour. Scenic (Map 1; ☎ 93 221 16 66), Carrer de la Marina 22, charges €4.60 an hour or €18.15 for a whole day. Another option is the car park and bicycle rental place (look for the Bicicletas sign) at Passeig de Picasso 40 (Map 3; ☎ 93 319 18 85). They rent out cycles for €2.45 an hour or €12.10 per day. There are several other rental outlets in the vicinity.

Around Barcelona

The mountain and monastery at Montserrat and the Penedès wine-growing area are within easy day-trip distance of Barcelona.

So too are the hedonistic beachside playground of Sitges, south of the city and gay capital of the Spanish *costas* (coasts), and several waterfront locations north of the city – with great long beaches that are cleaner and less crowded than those in central Barcelona.

From Montserrat you could continue northwards to the Pyrenees, and from Sitges you can proceed down the Costa Daurada to Tarragona and southern Catalunya.

From Vilafranca del Penedès the highway west enters the lovely Conca de Barberà area, dominated by the great Monestir de Poblet (Poblet Monastery). From there the highway sweeps you westwards to Lleida.

THE OUTSKIRTS
Jardins del Laberint d'Horta

Laid out in the late 18th century by Antoni Desvalls, Marquès d'Alfarras i de Llupià, this carefully manicured park remained a private family idyll until the 1970s, when it was opened to the public. The gardens take their name from a labyrinth in their centre but other paths take you past an artificial lake *(estany)*, waterfalls, a neo-classical pavilion and a false cemetery.

The gardens open 10 am to sunset daily and admission costs €1.50. Take the metro (line 3) to Montbau, from where you have about a 15-minute walk eastwards along the Ronda de Dalt highway to the gardens, on Carrer dels Germans Desvalls s/n.

Colònia Güell

Apart from La Sagrada Família, Gaudí's last grand project was to build a church for a Utopian workers' complex outside Barcelona at Santa Coloma de Cervelló. Work on the crypt started in 1908 and proceeded for eight years, at which point interest in the whole idea fizzled. The crypt still serves as a working church.

Highlights

This structure is an important part of Gaudí's oeuvre, little visited by tourists and yet a key to understanding what the master had in mind for La Sagrada Família, his magnum opus. The mostly brick-clad columns that support the ribbed vaults in the ceiling are inclined at all angles in much the way you might expect trees in a forest to lean (reminiscent also of Parc Güell, which Gaudí was working on at around the same time). Gaudí had worked out the angles in such a way that their load would be transmitted from the ceiling to the earth without the help of extra buttresses.

The easiest way there is to take an FGC train (No S3; €0.90) from Plaça d'Espanya

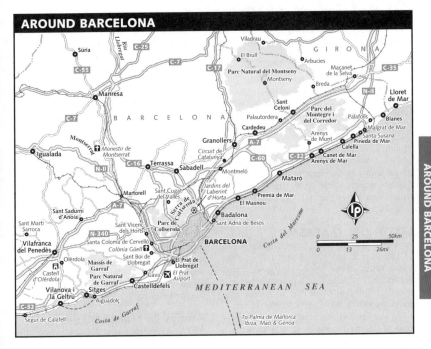

AROUND BARCELONA

and get off at Molí Nou station, the last stop (train No S33 leaves about hourly, usually at a quarter past the hour, for Santa Coloma station, one farther on). When you reach the station, exit by the underpass and turn right (north) up the BV-2002 road towards Santa Coloma de Cervelló. It's a 15-minute walk.

Alternatively, you could get off the train one stop earlier at Sant Boi de Llobregat and catch bus No L76 right to Santa Coloma, but this will end up taking longer.

The Colònia Güell opens 10 am to 1.15 pm and 4 to 6 pm daily (mornings only on Thursday and holidays); if in doubt call ahead on ☎ 93 640 29 36. Admission costs €0.60.

Catalunya en Miniatura
Only a few kilometres of narrow, winding road separate Santa Coloma de Cervelló from Torrelles de Llobregat, home to Catalunya en Miniatura, where you can see La Sagrada Família in mini-form, alongside other architectural highlights from around

the region. They say it took modellers 13,000 hours to reproduce La Sagrada Família.

The place opens 10 am to 7 pm daily (call ☎ 93 689 09 60 to confirm). If you are driving, take the N-II out of Barcelona and exit on the BV-2005. Otherwise, hourly buses (No L62) with the Soler i Sauret company leave from the corner of Travessera de les Corts and Riera Blanca (near the Camp Nou football stadium) at a quarter to the hour (€1.45, one hour). The nearest metro station to the bus stop is Collblanc.

Sant Cugat del Vallès
When the marauding Muslims tramped through the one-time Roman encampment turned Visigothic monastery of Sant Cugat del Vallès in the 8th century, they razed the lot to the ground. These things happen, and so after the Christians got back in the saddle, work on a new monastic complex stoically began. What you see today is a combination of Romanesque and Gothic

buildings. The lower floor of the cloister is a fine example of Romanesque and the principal reason for making the effort to come here. The mostly Gothic church and upper storey of the cloister are also worth some quiet contemplation. The monastery opens 9 am to noon and 4 to 8 pm daily.

Take the FGC train from Plaça de Catalunya (No S1, S2, S5 or S55) to Sant Cugat del Vallès (€1.75, 25 minutes). If you go on the second or fourth Sunday of the month, you may catch a *clàssic tren*, a vintage electric job from the 1920s that will take you up to the sound of live jazz or classical music. Tickets are the same price as for normal trains. For more information call FGC on ☎ 93 205 15 15.

COSTA DEL MARESME

As Barcelona's suburbs peter out north-east of the city, a string of coastal dormitory towns takes up the baton. This is the Costa del Maresme – which you probably haven't heard of (but don't feel bad, as no-one else much outside Catalunya has either).

At the far end the heavy tourist concentration begins – mostly people who have been sold packages here and told they were going to the Costa Brava (close but no cigar). In the earlier stages the scene is more local. The one abiding theme is long, broad, sandy beaches. The backdrop is frequently far from inspiring, though not bad on occasion.

The fun thing is that any of these places is an easy commute by regular *rodalies* (local) trains from central Barcelona. Indeed, depending on where you are staying in the big B, it is as easy to get to these beaches as it is to those in the metropolis! Trains as far as Mataró leave Barcelona every eight to 15 minutes, stopping at Badalona, El Masnou and elsewhere en route. From then on, as far as Blanes, frequency drops – about 30 trains a day run to Blanes. The trip to Blanes, the longest on this run, takes one hour 23 minutes and is generally a much better option than struggling through clogged traffic on the N-II. For information about Blanes see the Costa Brava chapter.

It is odd to think that so many tourists take the trouble to be parachuted in here,

when they could base themselves in Barcelona and trundle out for the beaches whenever it takes their fancy. But then they might miss out on the all-night sessions in the local German *Kneipen* (taverns), English pubs and Dutch cafes.

Badalona to Mataró

You could hop off the train as early as **Badalona** although there is little difference in beach quality between here and the northernmost strands of Barcelona. **El Masnou** also has a reasonable beach but the area is heavily built-up. Still, it's quite sprightly on a sunny summer morning. The situation doesn't change much as you head towards Mataró – the beaches succeed one another in orderly fashion, each as clean and wide as the next. **Mataró** is scarred by industry and not an overly attractive place, although again the beaches are fine. At the end of the day, if you just want a quick escape from Barcelona and a decent sandy beach, any of these places will do.

Arenys de Mar to Blanes

The first big town after Mataró is not a bad bet if you'd like to make a bit of an excursion of it. Arenys de Mar boomed in the late 18th century when trade with the Americas was opened up to Catalunya. The old town is an agreeable pedestrian zone that you might feel inclined to explore after your session on the beach. From the train station head a few streets north-east and then turn inland up Baixada de Santa Anna. You will shortly find yourself in the town centre, which with its cathedral, museums, eateries and cafes makes for a nice stroll in a tourist-free environment.

Just a couple of kilometres *before* Arenys is **Caldes d'Estrac**, known to locals as Caldetes. This is one of the few points along the Costa de Maresme where the beach is out of sight of the railway line. There are a few reasonable little restaurants here too.

From Arenys de Mar the railway and N-II coast road push on towards the next big town, Calella. If you are driving, shortly before you reach Calella, and just after Sant Pol de Mar, you'll notice a sign for Camping

Roca Grossa. Pull off the main road on the seaward side, park your steed and head down to one of three delicious little cliff-backed coves.

At **Calella** you can, as in Arenys, just make out the old centre of town. Again the beaches are fine and on some you'll find pleasant little beach bars. In the minds of many, this is where the Costa Brava begins. All the usual souvenir stands, English breakfasts and German Kneipen are here to welcome the charter plane-loads. The beaches continue up the coast. The one at **Pineda de Mar** actually has a leafy backdrop in parts, and the strip just near the **Santa Susanna** train station is not bad. **Malgrat de Mar** has wall-to-wall hotels, bars and souvenir shops, and marks the end of the Maresme *comarca* (district). Across the Tordera stream is Blanes, where we can say the Costa Brava begins (see the Costa Brava chapter).

Palafolls

There is precious little reason for coming to this inland town near Malgrat de Mar unless you have pesky kids in tow and they demand you take them to... Marineland-Catalunya. As well as lots of water, slippery dips and other aquatic diversions, the kiddies can get in some animal fun too. Distributed about extensive grounds are everything from dolphins and sea lions through to turtles and pelicans. Marineland (☎ 93 765 48 02) opens 10 am to 7 pm daily from Easter to the end of October. Admission costs €13.85/8.15 for adults/children. Tour operators in central Calella sell tickets that include free local bus travel.

Parc del Montnegre i del Corredor

Sick of sand and pints? Take a hike. This park is a modest one but heavily wooded, especially with pines and cork, and is easily accessible. Made up of two ranges, the Serra del Montnegre and the Serra del Corredor, the park is almost split in two by the B-511 road that connects Arenys de Mar on the coast with Sant Celoni (see Inland later in this chapter) on the A-7. The A-7 road passes through the unprepossessing hamlet of Vallgorguina, where the park's information office (☎ 93 867 94 52) is located at Carrer de l'Església 13. It opens 9 am to 1 pm weekdays.

The GR92 long-distance trail north to Portbou passes along the length of the park. Some of the other trails are (perhaps unfortunately) driveable forest tracks – for instance you can drive from Vallgorguina to Calella via the church of Sant Martí del Montnegre. If you are driving around here at the weekend, and fancy a hearty country lunch, stop in at the sprawling *Masia Tasca i Vins* (☎ 93 744 00 07), a 15th-century country house south of the A-7 along the B-511 to Vallgorguina. Meats and *torrades* (open toasted sandwiches) are the speciality; main courses cost about €9.

MONTSERRAT

postcode 08199 • pop 161 • elevation 725m
Montserrat (Serrated Mountain), 50km north-west of Barcelona, is an amazing 1236m mountain of truly weird rock pillars, shaped by wind, rain and frost from a conglomeration of limestone, pebbles and sand that once lay under the sea. With the historic Benedictine Monestir de Montserrat, one of Catalunya's most important shrines, perched at 725m on its side, it makes a great outing from Barcelona.

The most dramatic approach is by the cable car that swings high across the Llobregat valley from Montserrat-Aeri station, served by regular trains from Barcelona. From the mountain, on a clear day, you can see as far as the Pyrenees, Barcelona's Tibidabo hill and even, if you're lucky, Mallorca. It can be a lot colder on Montserrat than in Barcelona.

Orientation & Information

The cable car from Montserrat-Aeri arrives on the mountain just below the monastery. Just above the cable-car station is a road, and to the left is the information office (☎ 93 877 77 77), open 10 am to 6 pm daily, with a good free leaflet/map about the mountain and monastery. Past here, a minor road doubles back up to the left to the lower station of the Funicular de Sant Joan. The main road curves round and up to the right, passing the blocks of the Cel.les de Montserrat (see Places to Stay & Eat), to enter Plaça de Santa Maria at the centre of the monastery complex.

Monestir de Montserrat

The monastery was founded in 1025 to commemorate a 'vision' of the Virgin on the mountain. Wrecked by Napoleon's troops in 1811, then abandoned as a result of anticlerical legislation in the 1830s, it was rebuilt from 1858. Today there is a community of about 80 monks. Pilgrims come from far and wide to venerate La Moreneta (Black Virgin), a 12th-century, Romanesque wooden sculpture of Mary with the infant Jesus that has been Catalunya's official patron since 1881.

The two-part **Museu de Montserrat** on Plaça de Santa Maria has an excellent collection ranging from an Egyptian mummy and Gothic altarpieces to art by El Greco, Caravaggio, Monet, Degas, Picasso and many others. It opens 10 am to 6 pm (9.30 am to 6.30 pm at the weekend and holidays) and admission costs €3.65 (students €2.45).

From Plaça de Santa Maria you enter the courtyard of the 16th-century **basilica**, the monastery's church. The basilica's facade, with its carvings of Christ and the 12 Apostles, dates from between 1900 and 1901, despite its 16th-century Plateresque style. Opening times when you can file past the image of La Moreneta, high above the basilica's main altar, vary according to season. Roughly, hours are 8 to 10.30 am and 12.15 to 6.30 pm. The church opens from 8 am on Sunday and holidays and from 9 am on other days. It remains open until 8 pm in summer (July to September) but tends to close earlier during the rest of the year. Follow the signs to the Cambril de la Mare de Déu, to the right of the main basilica entrance.

The **Montserrat Boys' Choir**, or Escolania, reckoned to be Europe's oldest music school, sings in the basilica at 1 and 7.10 pm Monday to Saturday (1 pm only on Sunday), except in July. It is a rare (if brief) treat as the choir does not often perform outside

Montserrat – five concerts a year and a world tour every two. The Escolania has sung hymns since the 13th century, although through much of the 19th century all activity came to a halt after French troops sacked the monastery in 1811. The 40 to 50 *escolanets*, aged between 10 and 14, go to boarding school at Montserrat and must endure a two-year selection process to join the choir.

On your way out have a look in the room across the courtyard from the basilica entrance, filled with gifts and thank-you messages to the Montserrat Virgin from people who give her the credit for all manner of happy events. The souvenirs range from plaster casts to wedding dresses.

The Mountain

You can explore the mountain above the monastery by a web of paths leading to some of the peaks and to 13 empty and rather dilapidated hermitages. The **Funicular de Sant Joan** (€3.50/5.60 one way/return) will carry you up the first 250m from the monastery in seven minutes (departures every 20 minutes; last one down at 6 pm). If you prefer to walk, the road past the funicular's bottom station will lead you up and around to its top station in about one hour (3km).

From the Sant Joan top station, it's a 20-minute stroll (signposted) to the **Sant Joan hermitage**, with fine westward views. More exciting is the hour's walk north-west along a path marked with occasional blobs of yellow paint to Montserrat's highest peak, **Sant Jeroni** (1236m), from which there's an awesome sheer drop on the northern side. The walk takes you across the upper part of the mountain, with a close-up experience of some of the weird rock pillars. Many of them have been given names: on your way to Sant Jeroni look over to the right for La Prenyada (Pregnant Woman), La Mòmia (Mummy), L'Elefant (Elephant), the phallic Cavall Bernat and El Cap de Mort (Death's Head).

Places to Stay & Eat

For accommodation options call the information office (☎ 93 877 77 77). A small camping ground 300m along the road past the lower Sant Joan funicular station opens from Setmana Santa (Holy Week, the week leading up to Easter Sunday) to October. The cheapest rooms are in the *Cel.les de Montserrat*, which has three blocks of simple apartments for two to 10 people. A two-person apartment costs up to €36 in the high season. You must stay for a minimum of two days (a week in July and August). Overlooking Plaça de Santa Maria is the comfortable *Hotel Abat Cisneros*, with rooms from €40.55/70.20 in the high season.

The *Snack Bar* near the top cable-car station has straightforward meals, *bocadillos* (filled rolls) and snacks, as does *Bar de la Plaça* in the Abat Oliva cel.les building. *Cafeteria Self-Service* near the car park has a set lunch menu at €8 and in the restaurant downstairs you can eat a la carte or opt for the set lunch at €10.60. The views are great. *Hotel Abat Cisneros* has a four-course set meal for €17.50.

Getting There & Away

Bus A daily bus with the Julià company leaves for the monastery from Estació d'Autobusos de Sants in Barcelona at 9 am (plus 8 am in July and August) for a return fare of €8.45. It takes about 45 minutes and returns at 5 pm.

Train & Cable Car The alternative is a trip by train and cable car. FGC trains run from Plaça d'Espanya station in Barcelona to Montserrat-Aeri up to 18 times daily; get the R5 train. Return tickets for €11.50 include the cable car between Montserrat-Aeri station and the monastery, and the whole trip takes a little over an hour. The price for the cable car alone is €3.80/5.75 one way/return. The cable car goes about every 15 minutes, from 9.25 am to 1.45 pm and 3 to 6.45 pm Monday to Saturday.

FGC offers various all-in-one tickets. Return tickets for €16.90 include the train, cable car to/from Montserrat-Aeri, two metro rides and unlimited use of the funiculars. For €24.70 you can have all this, plus museum entrance and a modest dinner at the self-service restaurant.

There is talk of building a new *cremallera*,

An Old Oak Tree

When, back in 1498, Javier Codorníu bought the land that he would turn into the first vineyards of Sant Sadurní d'Anoia, the single greatest feature of his purchase was a 100-year-old oak tree.

In the following centuries a good number of the surrounding country's business deals were solemnly sworn in the shade of the grand old tree. It is said that in those days a witnessed handshake was as cast iron a guarantee as anyone could expect.

By the time the first *cava* was bottled in 1872, the tree had become the symbol of the Raventós i Blanc family that now ran the winery, and also of the Can Codorníu farm. For Manuel Raventós, the grandson of the original producer of the farm's cava, protecting the ancient oak has taken priority even over the business of wine-making. After about 600 years, the grand old oak tree of Can Codorníu is not only in good health, it's even growing!

AROUND BARCELONA

an electric narrow-gauge, cog-wheel railway line, up the hill from Monistrol. One of these steep incline lines ran from 1892 to 1957 and planners hope the new one will cut down car and bus traffic to what is, with 2.5 million visitors a year, Catalunya's second most visited spot.

From Montserrat-Aeri, trains continue north to Manresa, from where there are three trains daily going west to Lleida and one or two Alsina Graells buses daily going north to Berga, Guardiola de Berguedà, Puigcerdà and (except on Sunday) La Seu d'Urgell.

Car & Motorcycle The most straightforward route by car from Barcelona is to get on to the C-58 and take the Montserrat exit, which will lead you to Monistrol de Montserrat. From there a road snakes about 7km up the mountain to the monastery.

PENEDÈS WINE COUNTRY

Some of Spain's best wines come from the area centred on the towns of Sant Sadurní d'Anoia and Vilafranca del Penedès. Sant

ASA ANDERSSON

Try a *copa* of *cava*, Catalunya's
bubbly beverage.

Sadurní d'Anoia, a half-hour train ride west of Barcelona, is the capital of *cava*, Spanish 'champagne'. Vilafranca del Penedès, 12km farther down the track, is the heart of the Penedès DO, which produces noteworthy light, still whites. A number of wineries open their doors to visitors and there'll often be a free glass or two included in the tour, and plenty more for sale. It's a little ad hoc and often you need to call ahead to arrange a visit.

Simply touring the area in the hope of stumbling across wineries is unlikely to yield results. See the Vilafranca del Penedès section for tips on where to gather information before embarking on a wine excursion.

Getting There & Away
Up to three rodalies trains an hour run from Estació Sants in Barcelona to Sant Sadurní (€2.05, 40 minutes) and Vilafranca (€2.50, 50 minutes). By car, take the A-2, then the A-7 and follow the exit signs. From Sitges, both places are a short drive inland, or a longer train journey involving a change at Coma-ruga. Two or three buses a day connect Vilafranca with Sitges too.

Sant Sadurní d'Anoia
postcode 08770 • pop 9343

A hundred or so wineries around Sant Sadurní produce 140 million bottles of cava a year – something like 85% of the national output. Cava is made by the same method as French champagne and is gaining ground in international markets. If you happen to be in town in October, you may catch the Mostra de Caves i Gastronomia, a cava and food-tasting fest that has been held annually since 1997 – this is an opportunity to taste the products of a lot of competition cavas.

Vilafranca del Penedès
postcode 08720 • pop 27,818

Vilafranca is larger than Sant Sadurní and much more interesting. It is a busy place with a couple of attractions.

Information The tourist office (☎ 93 892 03 58, e turisme@ajvilafranca.es) on Plaça de la Vila opens 9 am to 1 pm and 4 to 7 pm Tuesday to Friday, and 10 am to 1 pm on Saturday. In summer it also opens 5 to 8 pm on Saturday and 10 am to 1 pm on Sunday. This is a good place to look for information on wineries. Staff can direct you to several places aside from the big boys so you can see how wine and cava are made and get a glass or two at the end. They also sell a booklet called *L'Alt Penedès* (€4.85) that lists most of the area's wineries that are open to the public.

For information on wineries and wines in the area, you could approach Penedès Denominació d'Origen (☎ 93 890 48 11, fax 93 890 47 54), Plaça de l'Agora. Located near the A-7 motorway on the way to Tarragona, this is an association of all DO wineries in the region. Another place to get more of a handle on the area's wines is the Celler Cooperatiu Vilafranca del Penedès (☎ 93 817 10 35), Camí de les Clotes s/n. Take the road for San Martí Sarroca and watch out for the signs – it's a couple of kilometres from the town centre.

Things to See A block north of the tourist office, the mainly Gothic **Basílica de Santa Maria** faces the combined **Museu de**

Vilafranca and **Museu del Vi** (wine museum) across Plaça de Jaume I. The museum, a fine Gothic building, covers local archaeology, art, geology and bird life, and also has an excellent section on wine, at the end of which you're treated to a free *copa* (glass). It opens 10 am to 2 pm and 4 to 7 pm (9 am to 9 pm in summer) Tuesday to Saturday; and 10 am to 2 pm on Sunday and holidays. Admission costs €2.45. A statue on Plaça de Jaume I pays tribute to Vilafranca's famous *castellers* (human-castle builders).

Special Events Vilafranca's *festa major* (main festival), lasting about 10 days in the last week of August and spilling over into September, is dotted with processions and exhibitions of traditional dance, music and the like. The feast day of Sant Felix, in whose honour the festa is celebrated, is on 30 August and from 29 to 31 August the festa is at its busiest, with castells, processions and fireworks. The last day features a *correfoc* (fire-running).

Places to Stay & Eat Being so close to Barcelona and Sitges, there is no real need to stay. If you get stuck, Vilafranca is home to a trio of uninspiring *hostales* (budget hotels), among them **Habitacions Jordina** (☎ 93 890 29 92, Avinguda de Tarragona 32), where you will pay €12.05/21.10 for a single/double. On the food front a popular local choice is the **Taverna de l'Ateneu** (☎ 93 890 08 17, Carrer de l'Ateneu 18). Meat main courses cost from €4.80 to €10.25, or try the *fideuá amb peix* (noodle paella with fish) for €7.25. Another rustic option is **La Bota del Racó** (☎ 93 890 42 17, Plaça de l'Estació 5), where you'll pay around €18 for a meal.

Visiting Wineries

You need your own transport to tour the area. As already hinted, you should not expect

VILAFRANCA DEL PENEDÈS

1 Museu de Vilafranca; Museu del Vi
2 Basílica de Santa Maria
3 Tourist Office
4 Capella de Sant Joan
5 Habitacions Jordina
6 Taverna de l'Ateneu
7 La Bota del Racó
8 Train Station
9 Bus Station

to wander into any old winery you pass. Many open their doors to the public only at limited times during the weekend, if at all. The more enthusiastic ones will show you around, give you an idea of how wines and/or cava are made and finish off with a glass or two. Since cava is the area's single biggest product, it makes sense that many of the wineries that open to the public specialise in bubbly rather than in still wines.

The following list is by no means exhaustive but should get you started:

Freixenet (☎ 93 891 70 00, W www.freixenet.es) This is the best-known cava company (although not everyone agrees its bubbly is the best), based next to the train station in Sant Sadurní d'Anoia at Carrer de Joan Sala 2. It is one of about 20 wineries in Sant Sadurní itself that occasionally open to visitors, though many require you to book ahead. Free tours are given at 9, 10 and 11.30 am and 3.30 and 5 pm, Monday to Thursday (also Friday morning, Saturday and Sunday in December).

Codorníu (☎ 93 818 32 32, W www.codorniu.es) Bottled for the first time in 1872, Codorníu remains one of the best cavas around (see the boxed text 'An Old Oak Tree'). The Codorníu headquarters, a modernist building at the entry to Sant Sadurní town by road from Barcelona, opens for free visits 9 am to 5 pm Monday to Friday, and 9 am to 1 pm at the weekend.

Torres (☎ 93 817 74 87) Three kilometres northwest of the centre of Vilafranca, on the BP-2121 road near Pacs del Penedès, is the area's premier winery. The Torres family tradition reaches back to the 17th century but the company, in its present form, was founded in 1870. Torres revolutionised Spanish wine-making in the 1960s by introducing temperature-controlled stainless-steel apparatus and French grape varieties to produce much lighter wines than the traditional heavy Spanish plonk. One of the biggest names in global wine production, the Torres enterprise no longer restricts itself to home territory, with wineries in California and Chile and plans for a foray into China – that famous wine-drinking nation! Red and white wines of all qualities are produced, using many grape varieties, including: Chardonnay, Sauvignon Blanc, Merlot, Cabernet Sauvignon, Pinot Noir and more local varieties such as Parellada, Garnacha and Tempranillo. Torres opens for visits 9 am to 6 pm Monday to Saturday, and 9 am to 1 pm on Sunday and holidays.

Blancher (☎ 93 818 32 86) Just off Sant Sadurní's main road, La Rambla de la Generalitat, at Plaça del Pont Romà 5, this rather huge place has been going since 1955. Visits will lead you around the plant and there is also a small museum. There are hourly tours from 10.30 am to 1.30 pm at the weekend. During the week you need to call ahead.

Nadal (☎ 93 898 80 11) Nadal is just outside the hamlet of El Pla del Penedès, about 8km north of Vilafranca, off the C-15. It has been producing cava since 1943. The centrepiece of the place is a fine *masia* (country farmhouse), where you can join organised visits to be acquainted with vine growing, the harvest and the whole process of producing the sparkling wine. A tasting rounds off each visit. You can join in at 10 and 11 am, noon and 4, 5 and 6 pm Monday to Friday, and 10.30 am and 12.30 pm on Saturday.

Mas Tinell (☎ 93 817 05 86) Here is a good drop that ended up on the table for the Infanta Cristina's wedding. Mas Tinell, just outside Vilafranca on the road to Sant Martí Sarroca, also produces some still wines and is technically open to visitors from 9 am to noon and 3 to 6 pm Monday to Saturday, though they prefer you to call ahead.

Caves Romagosa Torné (☎ 93 899 13 53) This vineyard is farther up the road from Mas Tinell, at Finca La Serra on the road to Sant Martí Sarroca. Again, although it produces other wines, cava is the star. It opens 9 am to 1 pm and 4 to 8 pm Monday to Saturday, and 10 am to 2 pm on Sunday and holidays. If you come here try to visit **Sant Martí Sarroca**, as atop the rise just out of this humdrum modern town are a fine Romanesque church and castle. A little way down the hill are a few enticing dining options too.

Cava San Martín (☎ 93 898 82 74) Just off the C-15, about 10km north of Vilafranca, this small, friendly outfit produces several varieties of wine, including whites, reds and rosés; though again, it is most proud of its bubbly. It's best to call ahead.

Masia Pere Rius (☎ 93 891 82 74) This cute little masia, which lies just outside La Múnia on the B-212 about 5km south-west of Vilafranca, shows how cava is made and will invite you to taste some of the wines as well as the bubbly. It opens 10 am to 8 pm Monday to Saturday, and 10 am to 3 pm on Sunday and holidays.

Caves Ramon Canals Canals (☎ 93 775 54 46) In Castellví de Rosanes, just off exit 25 from the A-7 south from Barcelona, this cellar opens for visits on Saturday and Sunday morning. You have to call ahead.

Cava Martín Soler (☎ 93 898 82 20) Here at Puigdàlber, 8km north of Vilafranca, is another attractive masia surrounded by vineyards. It produces only various kinds of cava and opens for visits 9 am to 1 pm and 2.30 to 7 pm Monday to Friday, and 10 am to 2 pm at the weekend and holidays.

OLÈRDOLA

Occupying a high point between Penedès country and the coast north-west of Sitges, the Castell d'Olèrdola is an interesting archaeological site that has bits of everything from Iberian times to the Middle Ages. You can wander around the slight remains of Iberian and medieval homes, inspect part of the Roman and medieval wall and then proceed uphill to the Romanesque church, which incorporates an entrance topped by a pre-Romanesque horseshoe arch. The peak of the hill is dominated by the ruins of a Roman watchtower and its medieval successor. Just in from the entrance to the site is a modest Museu d'Arqueologia, with displays detailing Olèrdola's long history.

The castle and museum open 10 am to 2 pm and 3 to 8.30 pm daily except Monday (3 to 6 pm from mid-September to mid-March and 3 to 8 pm from mid-March to mid-June). Admission costs €1.80. You need a car to get to Olèrdola.

COSTA DE GARRAF
Castelldefels
postcode 08860 • pop 33,100
Just 18km south-west of Barcelona, this is the first point of (vague) interest on the Costa de Garraf, which serves as an appetiser on your way down to the Costa Daurada.

Castelldefels' 10km-long beach is broad and sandy, attracting lots of local and some more distant punters. The much-restored castle, after which the place is named, was the International Brigade's headquarters during the Civil War.

On the coastal road from Castelldefels westwards to Sitges you'll enjoy some pretty vistas but probably in company, as the traffic can be intense and for some reason drivers of many a lumbering lorry seem to have a particular yearning to take in the cliff-side views.

Inland stretches the **Garraf massif**, which has been declared a local park. Regular rodalies trains run here from Barcelona.

Sitges
postcode 08870 • pop 17,600
Sitges, 35km south-west of Barcelona and barely a half-hour away by train, attracts everyone from jet-setters to young backpackers, honeymooners to weekending families, and Barcelona night owls to an international gay crowd. The beach is long and sandy, the nightlife thumps till breakfast and there are lots of groovy boutiques if you need to spruce up your wardrobe. In winter Sitges can be dead, but it wakes up with a vengeance for Carnaval in February, when the gay crowd puts on an outrageous show.

Sitges has been fashionable in one way or another since the 1890s, when it became an avant-garde art-world hang-out. It has been one of Spain's most anticonventional, anything-goes resort since the 1960s. One thing it isn't is cheap. You'll struggle to find a room for under €30, food is pricey and a mixed drink can easily set you back €6.

Orientation The main landmark is the Església de Sant Bartomeu i Santa Tecla parish church, atop a small, rocky elevation that separates the 2km-long main beach to the south-west from the smaller, quieter Platja de Sant Sebastià to the north-east. The old part of town climbs gently inland from the church area, with the train station some 500m back at the top of Avinguda d'Artur Carbonell.

Information The tourist office (☎ 93 894 42 51, W www.sitgestur.com, Carrer de Sínia Morera 1) opens 9 am to 9 pm daily, July and August; 9 am to 2 pm and 4 to 6.30 pm Monday to Friday and 10 am to 1 pm Saturday, the rest of the year. To book accommodation in advance you can also call (from within Spain) ☎ 902 10 34 28.

You can occasionally pick up a free map of gay-oriented bars, hotels, restaurants and shops, the *Plano Gay de Sitges*, at several

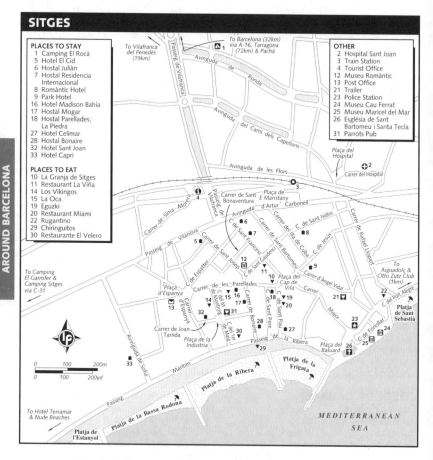

SITGES

PLACES TO STAY
1 Camping El Rocà
5 Hotel El Cid
6 Hostal Julián
7 Hostal Residencia Internacional
8 Romàntic Hotel
9 Park Hotel
16 Hotel Madison Bahía
17 Hostal Mogar
18 Hostal Parellades; La Piedra
27 Hotel Celimar
28 Hostal Bonaire
32 Hotel Sant Joan
33 Hotel Capri

PLACES TO EAT
10 La Granja de Sitges
11 Restaurant La Viña
14 Los Vikingos
15 La Oca
19 Eguzki
20 Restaurant Miami
22 Rugantino
29 Chiringuitos
30 Restaurante El Velero

OTHER
2 Hospital Sant Joan
3 Train Station
4 Tourist Office
12 Museu Romàntic
13 Post Office
21 Trailer
23 Police Station
24 Museu Cau Ferrat
25 Museu Maricel del Mar
26 Església de Sant Bartomeu i Santa Tecla
31 Parrots Pub

spots around town including Parrots Pub on Plaça de la Industria.

A gaggle of banks and ATMs lurks on and around Plaça del Cap de Vila in the old town. The post office (correus/correos) is on Plaça d'Espanya. The Policía Local (☎ 93 811 76 25) have a station on Plaça d'Ajuntament behind the parish church. The Hospital Sant Joan (☎ 93 894 00 03), Carrer del Hospital, is in the upper part of town near the train station.

Museums The Museu Cau Ferrat on Carrer de Fonollar was built in the 1890s as a house-cum-studio by Santiago Rusiñol, a co-founder of Els Quatre Gats in Barcelona, and the man who attracted the art world to Sitges. In 1894 Rusiñol reawakened the public to the then unfashionable work of El Greco by parading two of the Cretan's canvases from Sitges train station to Cau Ferrat. They are now on show in the museum along with the remainder of Rusiñol's large art and crafts collection, which includes paintings by the likes of Picasso, Ramon Casas (another of the 'four cats') and Rusiñol himself. The interior of the house, with its exquisitely tiled walls and lofty arches, is enchanting.

Next door is the **Museu Maricel del Mar**, with art and handicrafts from the Middle Ages to the 20th century. The museum is part of the Palau Maricel, a stylistic fantasy built around 1910 by Miquel Utrillo (yet another 'cat').

The **Museu Romàntic** at Carrer de Sant Gaudenci 1, housed in a late-18th-century mansion, re-creates with its furnishings and dioramas the lifestyle of a 19th-century Catalan landowning family. The museum also has a collection of several hundred antique dolls, most of which are incredibly ugly – they say the ones with teeth were worth more than the average doll but they look positively demonic. You have to join a guided tour lasting about 40 minutes, which starts on the hour and may or may not cater to your language, depending on numbers.

All three museums open 10 am to 1.30 pm and 3 to 6.30 pm Tuesday to Friday, 10 am to 7 pm on Saturday, and 10 am to 3 pm on Sunday. Admission to each costs €3, or you can get an all-in ticket for €5.45.

Beaches The main beach is divided by a series of breakwaters into sections with different names. A pedestrian promenade runs its whole length. In high summer, especially at the weekend, the end nearest the parish church gets jam-packed. Crowds thin out slightly towards the south-western end. Sitges also has two nude beaches – one exclusively gay – about a 20-minute walk beyond the Hotel Terramar at the far end of the main beach; to reach them, walk along the coast past a sewage plant, over a hill and a short distance along the railway.

Special Events Carnaval in Sitges, at the end of February, is a week-long riot of the extrovert, ambiguous and exhibitionist, capped by an extravagant gay parade on the last night. June sees the Sitges International Theatre Festival, with a strong experimental leaning.

Around the same time, the Corpus Cristi celebrations are marked by the creation of floral 'carpets' in the streets of central Sitges. These can be of incredible complexity

and generally consist of g⌣ or depictions of biblical alle⌣ is transitory, and the carpets a⌣ when the religious procession pass⌣ them.

Sitges' festa major in late August featur⌣ a huge firework display on 23 August. Early October is the time for Sitges' International Fantasy Film Festival. Festival information is available from the tourist office.

Places to Stay Sitges has over 50 hotels and hostales but many close from around October to April, and then are full in July and August.

If you haven't booked ahead, it's not a bad idea (especially if you arrive late in the day) to ask the tourist office to ring around for you.

Camping In the upper part of town north of the train station and 1km from the beach, is *Camping El Rocà (☎ 93 894 00 43, Avinguda de Ronda s/n)*. It has space for 600 people and charges €4.20 per person, per car and per tent. It opens from April to September. *Camping El Garrofer (☎ 93 894 17 80)* and *Camping Sitges (☎ 93 894 10 80)* are out of town off the C-31 (follow the signposts).

Hostales A friendly place, popular with travellers is *Hostal Parellades (☎ 93 894 08 91, Carrer de les Parellades 11)*, which has singles without bathroom for €16.30 and doubles with bathroom for €31.95.

Hostal Julià (☎ 93 894 03 06, Avinguda d'Artur Carbonell 2), near the train station and tourist office, has garish wallpaper but good-sized rooms, with shared bathrooms, for €28.20/36.15. Close by, *Hostal Residència Internacional (☎ 93 894 26 90, Carrer de Sant Francesc 52)* has eight sizable and clean doubles for €30.15 (€31.15 with shower).

One place open all year is the quirky *Hostal Bonaire (☎ 93 894 53 26, Carrer de Bonaire 31)*, where singles/doubles with bathroom cost €30.15/31.15.

Hostal San Joan (☎ 93 894 13 50, Carrer de Joan Tarrida 16) is not a bad choice.

AROUND BARCELONA

*metric designs
ries. Beauty
trampled
's over*

l quiet, have
€30.15/50.

e is **Hotel El**
94 63 35, Car-
:re reasonable,
50.60.
/fax 93 894 00
des 31–33) has
friendly man...   en-suite singles/
doubles/triples   for   €47.60/59.05/71.10
(prices drop by a third or more in the low
season). All 25 rooms have exterior windows. **Park Hotel** (☎ 93 894 02 50, fax 93
894 08 93, Carrer de Jesús 12–14) is
slightly better with rooms at €53.65/75.90.

The **Romàntic Hotel** (☎ 93 894 83 75,
fax 93 894 81 67, Carrer de Sant Isidre 33)
comprises three adjoining 19th-century villas, sensuously restored in period style, with
a leafy dining courtyard. It's popular with
gay visitors, though not exclusively so.
There are about 60 rooms with shower costing up to €77.30.

On the seafront near the parish church,
Hotel Celimar (☎ 93 811 01 70, fax 93 811
04 03, Passeig de la Ribera 20) has rooms
for €64.80 to €106.95 plus IVA. **Hotel
Capri** (☎ 93 811 02 67, fax 93 894 51 88,
Avinguda de Sofia 13–15) is a good family-
run place with doubles at €87.35 plus IVA.

Places to Eat You'll be lucky to find a
menú (fixed-price meal) for less than €7.
The self-service **Los Vikingos** (☎ 93 894 96
87, Carrer del Marques de Montroig 7–9),
in the thick of the action, does tolerable
pasta, pizza and seafood dishes from €5.15.
La Oca (☎ 93 894 79 36, Carrer de les Parellades 41) is popular for its pizzas from
€4.40 and grilled chicken at €2.35 for a
quarter of a bird. The best thing about **La
Piedra** (Carrer de les Parellades 7) is the
big terrace out the back. The food's OK but
nothing marvellous.

Carrer de Sant Pau has a string of good
restaurants including the Basque **Eguzki**
(☎ 93 811 03 20) at No 3, which has good
tapas and a mixed menu of seafood and
meat main courses from €6 to €11.
Restaurant Miami (☎ 93 894 02 06) at No

11 has a decent four-course *menú* for
€11.30. It closes on Tuesday.

La Granja de Sitges (☎ 93 811 02 85,
Carrer de les Parellades 4) is a lively tapas
spot. **Restaurant La Viña** (☎ 93 894 05 52,
Carrer de Sant Francesc 11) also has a
range of generous tapas starting at around
€3. It closes on Thursday.

Restaurante El Velero (☎ 93 894 20 51,
Passeig de la Ribera 38) is a fairly classy
fish and seafood joint with most main
courses at €9 or more. They close on Sunday evening and Wednesday. For real seaside dining you could munch away on
expensive tapas at the two *chiringuitos*
(food stalls) on Passeig de la Ribera.

A calmer area to eat is over on Platja de
Sant Sebastià, where **Rugantino** (☎ 93 894
78 09, Carrer del Port Alegre 21) serves
pizza, pasta, meat and vegetarian dishes
from around €5.50. They close on Monday
evening, except during the summer months.

Entertainment Much of Sitges' nightlife happens on one short pedestrian strip
packed with humanity right through the
night in summer: Carrer del 1er de Maig,
Plaça de la Industria and Carrer del Marques de Montroig, all in a short line off the
seafront Passeig de la Ribera.

Carrer del 1er de Maig – or Calle del
Pecado (Sin Street) – vibrates to the volume
of 10 or so disco-bars all trying to outdo each
other in decibels. They start to fill at around
midnight. Plaça de la Industria and Carrer del
Marques de Montroig have the bars and
cafes where people sit, drink and watch other
people. All you have to do is cruise along,
see what takes your fancy and try not to bust
your budget (more easily said than done).

If you're in need of a change of location,
head around the corner to Carrer de les Parellades, Carrer de Bonaire or Carrer de Sant
Pere, where you'll find more of the same.
Carrer de Sant Bonaventura has a string
of gay bars, mostly behind closed doors.
Trailer (Carrer d'Àngel Vidal 36) is a popular gay disco.

Some distance from the centre of town
are some of the big discos, like **Pachá** (☎ 93
894 22 98), in Vallpineda, and the local

branch of Barcelona's *Otto Zutz* club in Aiguadolç, where you will also find other bars along the waterfront.

Getting There & Away Four rodalies trains an hour, from about 6 am to 10 pm, run from Barcelona Estació Sants to Sitges (€2.05, 30 minutes). They go on to Vilanova i la Geltrú. Three trains a day leave Sitges for Tarragona (one hour), where you can change for Port Aventura, Valencia and beyond.

The best road from Barcelona is the C-32 toll road. More scenic is the C-31, which hooks up with the C-32 after Castelldefels, but it is often busy and slow. At the weekend it is jammed with Barcelonins on day- or even just lunch-excursions – take the train!

Getting Around In Sitges itself, the traffic usually makes it quicker to walk than drive. For taxis call ☎ 93 894 35 94 or ☎ 93 894 13 29.

Vilanova i la Geltrú
postcode 08800 • pop 45,864
Only six minutes west from Sitges by the train from Barcelona, Vilanova is a large industrial and fishing town sprawling inland from its trio of beaches. It lacks the glamour and clamour of its eastern neighbour, but its beaches are fine and the town boasts a few worthwhile museums. The tourist office (☎ 93 815 45 17), Passeig del Carme, opens 10 am to 1.30 pm and 5 to 8 pm Tuesday to Saturday, and morning only on Sunday.

Things to See Along the main strand, Platja de Ribes Roges, is a modern **sculpture of Pasiphae** and the white bull she fell in love with in the Greek myth of the Minotaur, who was the result of this unnatural union.

Among the gaggle of museums, the **Museu del Ferrocarril** (Railway Museum; ☎ 93 815 84 91) is located in the 19th-century installations for the maintenance of steam trains, next to the train station on Plaça d'Eduard Maristany. It is claimed that the collection of steam locomotives is the biggest in Europe, and it attracts kids of all ages. All aboard from 10 am to 3 pm (until 7 pm on Saturday) daily; 4.30 to 8.30 pm

daily except Monday, plus 10 am to 1 pm at the weekend, July and August. Admission costs €3.95.

Biblioteca-Museu Víctor Balaguer (☎ 93 815 42 02), across from the Museu del Ferrocarril, is named after the 19th-century writer and collector behind the revival of the Jocs Florals, a literary competition designed to help resuscitate the Catalan language. The collection ranges from ancient Egyptian items (including a mummified child) to pre-Colombian and Oriental art objects, and includes a section devoted to 19th- and 20th-century painting and sculpture,

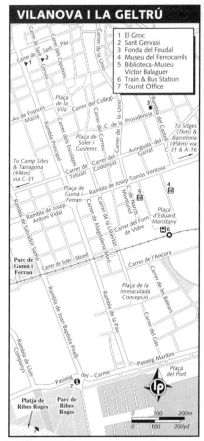

most of it Catalan. It opens 10 am to 1.30 pm and 4.30 to 7 pm (6 to 8.30 pm on Saturday and mornings only on Sunday) and closes on Monday. Admission costs €3.65.

Special Events Vilanova i la Geltrú also likes to party occasionally. Carnaval in February lasts for 13 days – Vilanova was one of the few Spanish cities to defy the ban on this festival during the Franco years. The city celebrates its festa major on 5 August.

Places to Stay & Eat Three camping grounds are located out of town, one on the road inland to Arboç and the others on the C-246 road to Tarragona. In town itself, about the cheapest option for putting your head down is at the hostal *Fonda del Feudal* (☎ 93 893 19 30, Rambla del Castell 46), where a double room costs €33.15. A couple of other hostales in town and a handful of more expensive hotels along the waterfront road, the Passeig Marítim, complete the picture. Apartments are also available.

Vilanova's contribution to Catalan cuisine is *xató*, a sauce with almonds and hazelnuts used on various dishes, particularly seafood. With a little luck you may get to try it at some of the town's eateries. For inexpensive home cooking try *Sant Gervasi* (☎ 93 893 86 78, Carrer de Sant Gervasi 33), open Monday to Saturday. You'll pay less than €18 for a full meal. For something a little more fanciful, head to *El Groc* (☎ 93 814 17 37, Rambla Principal 3), where you can eat seafood and other dishes with an international touch. Reckon on spending about €24. It closes on Sunday night and Monday.

Getting There & Away The town is just down the rodalies line 2 from Sitges. From Barcelona the fare is €2.05. In summer boats commute three or four times daily between Vilanova and Aiguadolç (at the north-eastern extremity of Sitges). Contact the Vilanova tourist office for details.

INLAND

The inland area immediately beyond the Collserola hills is a curious mix of industry, suburban dormitory sprawl and little corners of greenery and history tucked away in the folds of the landscape.

Terrassa
postcode 08223 • pop 158,000
About 25km north-west of Barcelona, this town is, along with its neighbour **Sabadell**, the heartland of the Catalan textile industry. The two towns together count well over 300,000 inhabitants, the grand majority of whom live in uninspiring tower blocks arranged seemingly randomly over a great expanse of the Vallès Occidental comarca of which the towns are joint capitals.

The locals say that Japanese universities send architecture and town-planning students to one or the other (it depends on who is telling you the story) to study how *not* to build a town. Believe it or not, a keen sense of rivalry reigns between the two towns.

Terrassa has been inhabited since the ancient days of the Iberians and was long known as Égara. There is some evidence that churches were built here prior to the Muslim invasion, after which the sources are silent on the fate of the town for three centuries. It then became a separate bishopric from Barcelona, and from the Middle Ages on was known for the production of fabrics.

The tourist office (☎ 93 739 70 19) is in the centre of town at Raval de Montserrat 14.

If you scoot by along the C-58 and see the marshalled columns of apartments, you may find it hard to believe that amid them is a unique architectural gem – a trio of pre-Romanesque churches set in a peaceful garden above a dry riverbed turned into a park. The Esglésies de Sant Pere are actually dedicated to Sant Pere, Sant Miquel and Santa Maria, and their oldest elements date from the 9th and 10th centuries.

Of the three, the most intriguing church is Sant Miquel – a simple square-based building in which columns of all shapes and sizes retrieved from earlier Visigothic and Roman structures have been used to support the ceiling. Santa Maria contained some of the most striking art, including a vivid Romanesque fresco and a Gothic altarpiece by Jaume Huguet. The largest of the three churches and still in use today is Sant Pere. The complex opens 10 am to 1.30 pm and 4 to 7 pm Tuesday to Saturday, and 11 am to 2 pm on Sunday. Admission is free.

A little south down the river stands the **Castell de Vallparadís**, a 12th-century castle. About a five-minute walk to the west across the 17th-century bridge, **Pont de Sant Pere**, is the historic centre of town. It's pleasant without being wildly moving. However, you should make a little time to visit the **Casa Alegre de Sagrera** on Carrer de la Font Vella, a fine late-18th-century mansion given a Modernista overhaul 100 years later. Opening times for the castle and mansion are the same as for the churches and admission is free.

Terrassa is on rodalies train line 4 between Manresa and Sant Vicenç de Calders. There are regular trains from Barcelona taking 40 to 45 minutes from Estació Sants; tickets cost €2.05.

Martorell
postcode 08760 • pop 16,653
If you're into fine medieval bridges, consider a quick excursion to Martorell, otherwise known as the home of Seat, the national car factory (now owned by Volkswagen). The Roman foundations of the original bridge that carried the Via Augusta across the Riu Llobregat are still visible; upon them a remarkable Gothic bridge, Pont del Diable (Devil's Bridge), was later raised. It has since been restored in parts and at one end the original Roman arched entrance still stands. Take a rodalies train on line 4 (€1.55, 28 minutes) from Estació Sants, and the bridge is a couple of minutes walk directly in front of you.

Montmeló
Opened in 1991 just outside town, the Circuit de Catalunya Formula One racetrack (☎ 93 571 97 00, W www.circuitcat.com), is the only vague attraction here. As a rule you can only pop along for a visit if race events (which take all shapes and sizes during the year) are being held; call to find out. The Formula One Grand Prix is generally held here in May, followed by a stage of

the World Motorcycling Championships in June.

The trick is getting here. Rodalies trains from Barcelona call in regularly (€1.55, 30 minutes) but you would still need a taxi (about €6) to reach the track. Eventually RENFE will build a train station at the track entrance.

Granollers
postcode 08400 • pop 51,873
Not an awful lot will draw you to Granollers, which is yet another satellite town. The main reason for making the effort is to sit down to a meal at the *Fonda Europa* (☎ 93 870 03 12, Carrer de Anselmo Clavé 1). The cooking is robust and the atmosphere has an elegant touch, especially if you can get a seat upstairs. Expect to shell out around €24 a head.

Rodalies trains on line 2 call in frequently from Barcelona. The trip takes about 30 minutes and costs €1.55.

Sant Celoni
postcode 08470 • pop 11,957
If you want the region's most prized culinary experience, head farther up the rodalies line 2 from Granollers to this otherwise nondescript town. Apart from being a possible starting point for excursions into the Parc Natural del Montseny, it is home to Racó de Can Fabes (☎ 93 867 28 61, Carrer de Sant Joan 6). Run by Santi Santamaría, one of only three chefs in Spain to have been consistently awarded three Michelin stars, this is as fine as dining will probably get during your stay in Catalunya. You can easily part with €60 for the pleasure. See under Parc Natural del Montseny for Getting There & Away information.

Parc Natural del Montseny
This surprising natural park lies roughly halfway between Barcelona and Girona, and its southern boundary is about 5km north of Sant Celoni. Covering more than 17,000 hectares, the park was declared a world biosphere reserve by Unesco in 1978.

At lower levels it is rich in forest, including several types of pine and oak, giving way to scrub higher up. The highest peak is the Turó del Home (1706m), about 10km north-east of Sant Celoni, with the Agudes range nearby. Farther north, the Matagalls peak (1697m) offers some wonderful views as far as the Pyrenees. These summits abruptly jut out of the surrounding territory, making them seem still higher than they really are. For information, call or visit the park office (☎ 93 847 51 02) at Font Martina, a water fountain along a back road that links La Costa del Montseny and Santa Fe del Montseny. It opens 9 am to 4 pm Monday to Friday, and 10 am to 2 pm weekends and holidays. You can also get information at the Sant Celoni tourist office (☎ 93 867 04 25), in the centre of town at Plaça de la Vila s/n.

The GR5 long-distance path crosses the park from west (at Aiguafreda) to southeast (near Campins), and various treks around the park and to the peaks are possible. The park office has information on walking trails. You will also find some mountain-biking options.

Those with their own wheels can actually drive all the way to the Turó del Home but walkers will get greater satisfaction from yomping up. Get a hold of Editorial Alpina's *Montseny Mapa i Guia Excursionista* (1:40,000). Several approaches to the Turó del Home are possible but the most direct (and steepest) starts at the Font Martina. You can park your car here or, if walking, approach along the signposted GR5 trail about 1½ hours west from the town of Montseny. This brings you to the asphalt road that leads to the Turó del Home. Follow it north a few hundred metres until you reach a bend that makes a junction with a dirt trail. That trail is marked GR5.2 and is the track you need to follow for about two hours (for moderately fit hikers) to reach the peak. You pass one house and reach another within about 25 minutes heading north-west along the trail. At the second house you cut north and hit the walking track that leads up to the peak – keep a lookout for the GR5.2 signs. The vegetation thickens for a while about halfway up but then reduces to scrub and your objective

remains in sight for most of the time. Although the change in altitude from the Font Martina is around 800m, the walk is not overly taxing. The views from the often wind-whipped top are far-reaching. If time allows, you can spend another hour or so walking to Les Agudes (about 1.5km northeast). Another good two-hour walk is from the Hostal Sant Marçal (see Places to Stay & Eat) west to Matagalls.

Places to Stay & Eat Several camping grounds dot the area. One of the handiest is the leafy *Fontmartina* (☎ 93 847 51 63), where you pay €2.40 per person and €1.75 per tent space. It's on the BV-5119 road (follow the signs for Turó del Home). There's also a handful of *cases de pagès* (country houses with rooms to let), including three or four in and around Montseny.

Viladrau is a pretty little village on the northern edge of the park, with several hotel options. *Hostal Bofill* (☎ 93 884 90 12, Carrer de Sant Marçal 2) has spacious, characterful rooms but the somewhat surly owners insist on you taking half-board *(media pensión)*, which comes to €25.30/ 37.95 for a single/double. *La Coromina* (☎ 93 884 92 64, fax 93 884 81 60, Carretera de Vic s/n), if you can afford it, is a much better choice. Once a family's country retreat, this enchanting little place offers tastefully decorated rooms, some with wood panelling and windows looking onto the rear garden. The breakfast/dining area has the air of an English tearoom. Rooms cost €51.85/66.30 (plus IVA and €6.05 per head for breakfast, which is reasonable).

Easily the most enchanting place of all is the *Hostal Sant Marçal* (☎ 93 847 30 43, e tellhotels@arquired.es), set in an 11th-century former monastery just behind the rustic little Romanesque church of the same name. The exquisitely maintained rooms and common areas, all in solid stone and timber, ooze warmth. The spot is ideally located about 10km into the natural park from Viladrau on the road to Sant Celoni via Santa Fe del Montseny. The only obstacle, especially if (as is recommended) you decide to dine here on Catalan specialities, is the cost, which can (for room and half-board) run up to €85 per person plus IVA.

Many of the park's hotels have restaurants. Just outside the town of Arbúcies, on the eastern edge of the park and the GI-543 road heading for Viladrau, is *Restaurant Corbadora* (☎ 972 86 08 00). This big, barn-like place has a bucolic feel and offers giant servings of entrecote cooked in a cheese and green pepper sauce for around €12.

Getting There & Away You can reach several points on the park's boundaries with little trouble, but there are no real transport options inside the park. Frequent rodalies trains run from Barcelona to Sant Celoni and Palautordera (the previous stop), from where there are sometimes local buses to Montseny. La Hispano Hilariense (☎ 972 24 50 12) has a daily bus (two at the weekend) between Barcelona and Arbúcies via Sant Celoni. It leaves Barcelona (from Plaça del Palau) at 7.15 pm Monday to Friday, at 9 am and 5.15 pm on Saturday, and 9.15 pm on Sunday. The trip takes about 1¼ hours and costs €7.60 (€8.70 at the weekend).

Costa Brava

Josep Pla, an icon in Catalunya's literary pantheon of the 20th century, thought they should call this stretch the Costa del Coral – the Coral Coast. Indeed for centuries daring coral divers roamed the length of the coast in the search for the prized red coral that even now survives (at great depth and in small quantities). Pla's sentiments went unheeded and in 1905 another name was coined: Costa Brava – the Rugged Coast.

Stretching from Blanes, 60km north-east of Barcelona, to the French border, the coast ranks up there with the Costa Blanca and Costa del Sol as one of Spain's three great holiday *costas*. But for all the discos, concrete megaliths, English breakfasts and *Konditoreien* (German cake shops), much of the coast has remained untamed. Sheer cliffs, crystal clear water, sand and pebble beaches accessible only on foot, enchanting coastal towns, diving, wild and woolly coastal walking paths and high winding drives combine to make much of this coast a joy. There is always some hidden *cala* (a small beach on an inlet) to discover.

The country varies with astounding rapidity. The southern half of the coast, hilly and pine-covered, gives way to several flatter stretches before reaching the lunar-looking Cap de Creus peninsula. Beyond, on the final stretch to the French frontier, the terraced contours of the green hills appear as so many natural stadiums looking seawards.

Inland, the story also changes. Rolling hills, sunflower fields and the deep green carpets of grass and wheat in spring, unfold like a patchwork quilt before you. Sprinkled in among it all is a series of warm stone villages, monasteries and castles. Farther inland again stands the proud medieval city of Girona (Gerona in Castilian), and Figueres (Figueras), famous for its bizarre Teatre-Museu Dalí, the foremost of a series of sites associated with the eccentric surrealist artist Salvador Dalí.

The Costa Brava does get packed in the second half of July and August – you should

Highlights

- Swimming the limpid waters of the stunning little Costa Brava beaches around Palafrugell
- Exploring the medieval town of Girona
- Marvelling at the extravagance of Dalí in Figueres, Port Lligat and Castell de Púbol
- Walking along the northern Costa Brava and up to the Monestir de Sant Pere de Rodes
- Diving off the Illes Medes
- Pottering about in the medieval stone villages of Besalú, Peratallada and Pals
- Savouring a romantic dinner overlooking the water in Cadaqués
- Taking in summertime classical concerts at the Peralada castle
- Embracing the sunset at Tossa de Mar

ring ahead to avoid a lengthy room search in many places. June and September are a pleasant couple of degrees cooler than July and August, while May and October can be nicely warm. Sea temperatures hold up well through September. Beware however – in the north (Cap de Creus and upwards) in particular you must be prepared for anything. When the howling *tramuntana* (north wind) blows, whipping up the sea into an oceanic

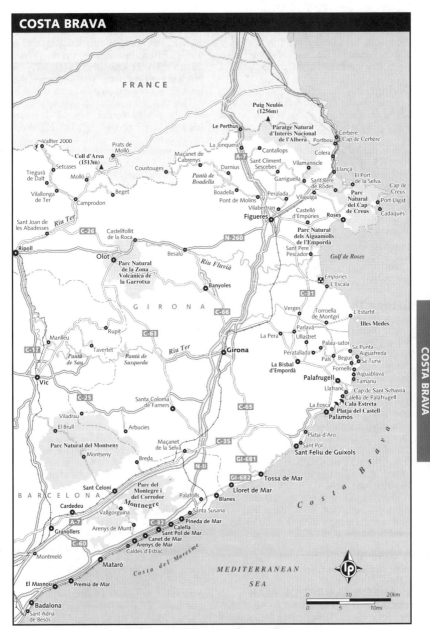

COSTA BRAVA

FRANCE

Puig Neulós
(1256m)

Le Perthús

Paratge Natural
d'Interès Nacional
de l'Albera

Portbou
Cerbère
Cap de Cerbère

La Jonquera
A-7

Cantallops

Colera

Vilamaniscle

Vallter 2000

Prats de
Molló

Maçanet de
Cabrenys

Sant Climent
Sescebes

Llançà

El Port
de la Selva

Setcases
Coll d'Area
(1513m)

Coustouges

Darnius

Garriguella

Sant Pere
de Rodes

Cap de
Creus

Tregurà
de Dalt

Molló

Pantà de
Boadella

Peralada

Sant Pere

Port Lligat

Vilallonga
de Ter

Beget

Boadella

Vilajuïga

Parc
Natural
del Cap
de Creus

Cadaqués

Camprodon

Pont de Molins

Vilabertran

Castelló
d'Empúries

Sant Joan de
les Abadesses

Riu Ter

Figueres

Roses

Ripoll

C-26

Castellfollit
de la Roca

Besalú

Riu Fluvià

N-260

Parc Natural
dels Aiguamolls
de l'Empordà

Olot

Parc Natural
de la Zona
Volcànica de
la Garrotxa

Sant Pere
Pescador

Golf de Roses

Banyoles

Empúries
L'Escala

GIRONA

C-66

C-31

Verges

Torroella
de Montgrí

L'Estartit

Illes Medes

Manlleu

Rupit

C-63

Tavertet

Parlavà

Ullastret

La Pera

Palau-sator

Sa Punta
Aiguafreda

C-17

Pantà
de Sau

Pantà de
Susqueda

Riu Ter

GIRONA

Peratallada

Pals

Begur

Sa Tuna

La Bisbal
d'Empordà

Fornells

Aiguablava

Vic

Palafrugell

Tamariu

C-25

Llafranc

Cap de Sant Sebastià
Calella de Palafrugell

Viladrau

Santa Coloma
de Farners

C-65

La Fosca
Cala Estreta
Platja del Castell

El Brull

Arbúcies

Palamós

Parc Natural del Montseny

Maçanet
de la Selva

C-35

Platja d'Aro

Montseny

Breda

GI-681

Sant Pol

N-II

Sant Feliu de Guíxols

BARCELONA

Sant Celoni

Parc del
Montegre i
del Corredor
Montnegre

Palafolls

GI-682

Tossa de Mar

Cardedeu

Vallgorguina

Palafolls

Blanes

Lloret de Mar

Costa Brava

Granollers

A-7

Arenys de Munt

C-32

Santa Susana

Pineda de Mar

Montmeló

C-60

Calella

Sant Pol de Mar

Canet de Mar

Arenys de Mar

Caldes d'Estrac

Mataró

Costa del Maresme

MEDITERRANEAN

El Masnou

Premià de Mar

SEA

Badalona
Sant Adrià
de Besòs

0   10   20km

0   5   10mi

COSTA BRAVA

frenzy and making the simplest operations, like closing doors and windows, a challenge,. you simply have to sit it out. It is fair to say that the weather is far less predictable on the Costa Brava than south of Barcelona.

Diving

The ruggedness of the Costa Brava continues under the sea to provide some of the best diving in Spain. In some spots remarkable crimson coral, an increasingly rare item in the Mediterranean, still thrives. Approved tourist diving centres with certified instructors operate at a dozen or more places. The Illes Medes off L'Estartit are a group of protected islets with probably the most diverse sea life along the Spanish coast. Other top diving spots include the Illes Formigues, rocky islets off the coast between Palamós and Calella de Palafrugell with waters down to 45m, and Els Ullastres, three underwater hills off Llafranc with some sheer walls and depths to 54m.

Getting There & Away

Direct buses from Barcelona go to most towns on and near the Costa Brava. The railway between Barcelona and the coastal border town of Portbou runs inland most of the way, through Girona and Figueres. From Girona and Figueres there are fairly good bus services to the coast. The main (but by no means only) bus company operating along and around the coast is SARFA.

In summer, you could take an alternative approach to the southern Costa Brava from Barcelona by a combination of suburban *rodalies* (local) train and boat (for more information see Getting There & Away in the Tossa de Mar section).

The A-7 toll road and the toll-free N-II highway both run from Barcelona via Girona and Figueres to the French border a few kilometres north of La Jonquera. The C-32 toll road follows the N-II up the coast as far as Blanes. Other roads run up the coast and inland to Girona and Figueres.

BLANES & LLORET DE MAR

It is difficult to know what to say about these two towns. Blanes marks the southern

tip of the Costa Brava and its beaches are really quite OK. The main beach at Lloret de Mar, an extensive, fine sandy stretch, is also excellent. Between the two is a series of attractive beaches that can mostly be reached easily on foot. Both towns are also backed by hills and pine and cork trees.

However, both places have been built up in willy-nilly fashion since the 1960s to create a package holiday behemoth. Hundreds of thousands of sun-and-sea tourists cram into Lloret de Mar, one of the biggest coastal resorts in Spain, in summer. Hotels, apartments, bars, tacky stores, discos, casinos, supermarkets, malls, car parks – endless ranks of concrete slabs – cater to the annual invasion. By night, Lloret lights up like a Christmas tree in what could pass for an attempt to emulate Las Vegas. Through it all, vast crowds from all over Europe slope around in search of amusement. Not a few find it in booze, drugs and (they hope) summertime sex. It is quite remarkable that the authorities manage to keep the place clean and liveable for those Catalans who choose to reside here (if you can get a flat in the quieter hilly parts it really isn't too bad!).

A handful of monuments and narrow lanes at the centre of each location remind you that both places were once small towns with a long history.

There isn't a lot of point in making accommodation suggestions – it's difficult to know where to begin. If this is really your thing, you are better off organising a package deal – the lodging will come out cheaper that way. A good upper level place, however, is *Hotel Rigat Park* (☎ 972 36 52 00, fax 972 37 04 11, Avinguda d'America s/n), on Platja Fanals. The many rooms cost from €78.10 to €150.25 and have all mod cons. The setting amid pine trees is a big plus.

On the food front, there are a few places in among the fast-food chains and low-quality adulterated stuff laid on for those who don't want to wander too far from their home habits. *Les Petxines* (☎ 972 36 41 27, Passeig de Mossen Jacint Verdaguer 16) is reasonable for a bit of a quality splurge. The rice dishes are among the better options and you are likely to spend about €36.

Frequent rodalies trains get you as far as Blanes. To continue the 6km to Lloret there are local buses or you can get a taxi. SARFA buses also run to Lloret from Barcelona (€6, one hour), Girona and Tossa de Mar.

TOSSA DE MAR
postcode 17320 • pop 4016
Curving round a boat-speckled bay guarded by a headland crowned with medieval defensive walls and towers, Tossa de Mar is a white village of crooked, narrow streets onto which tourism has tacked a larger, modern extension of straighter, wider ones.

In July and August it's hard to reach the water's edge without tripping over oily limbs, but it is heaven compared with Lloret de Mar, just 12km to the south-west.

Tossa was one of the first places on the Costa Brava to attract foreign visitors – a small colony of artists and writers gravitated towards here in the 1930s. The French painter Marc Chagall spent the summer of 1934 in Tossa and dubbed it the 'Blue Paradise'.

Orientation & Information
The bus station is beside the GI-682 road where it leaves Tossa for Lloret de Mar. It

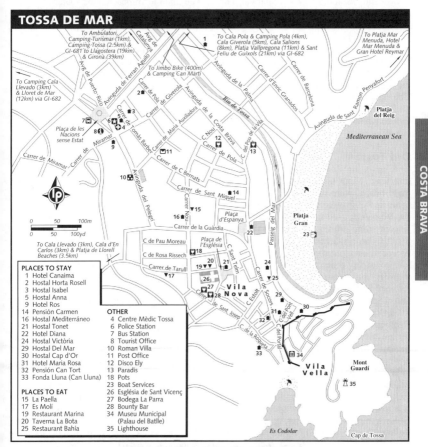

TOSSA DE MAR

To Ambúlatori,
Camping-Turismar (1km),
Camping-Tossa (2.5km),
GI-681 to Llagostera (19km)
& Girona (39km)

To Jimbo Bike (400m)
& Camping Can Martí

To Camping Cala
Llevadó (3km)
& Lloret de Mar
(12km) via GI-682

To Cala Pola & Camping Pola (4km),
Cala Giverola (5km), Cala Salions
(8km), Platja Vallpregona (11km) & Sant
Feliu de Guíxols (21km) via GI-682

To Platja Mar
Menuda, Hotel
Mar Menuda &
Gran Hotel Reymar

Avinguda de Catalunya
Avinguda de Ferran Agulló
Av. de Puerto Rico
Carrer de Pola de Giverola
Avinguda de la Palma
Carrer d'Enric Granados
Carrer de Barcelona
Riu de Tossa
Avinguda de la Costa Brava
Avinguda de Sant Ramon Penyafort
Carrer de Pomàs Barber
Carrer de Maria Auxiliadora
C Nou Tossa
Avinguda del Pou de la Vila

Plaça de les
Nacions
sense Estat

Platja
del Reig

Mediterranean Sea

Carrer de Miramar
Carrer de Miramar

Avinguda del Pelegrí

Carrer de Pola

Carrer de C Bernats

Carrer de Sant Miquel

Plaça
d'Espanya

Platja
Gran

Carrer Nou

Carrer de la Guàrdia

C de Pau Moreau
C de Rosa Rissech

Plaça de
l'Església

C Sant Telm

Passeig del Mar

Carrer de Tarull

Vila
Nova

Vila
Vella

C Estolt
Carrer de Socors
C del Portal
C de la Roqueta
C del Front Vell
C. de Sant Josep

Mont
Guardí

Es Codolar

Cap de Tossa

0   50   100m
0   50   100yd

To Cala Llevadó (3km), Cala d'En
Carlos (3km) & Platja de Llorell
Beaches (3.5km)

PLACES TO STAY
1   Hotel Canaima
2   Hostal Horta Rosell
3   Hostal Isabel
5   Hostal Anna
9   Hotel Ros
14 Pensión Carmen
16 Hostal Mediterráneo
21 Hostal Tonet
22 Hotel Diana
24 Hostal Victòria
29 Hostal Del Mar
30 Hostal Cap d'Or
31 Hotel Maria Rosa
32 Pensión Can Tort
33 Fonda Lluna (Can Lluna)

PLACES TO EAT
15 La Paella
17 Es Molí
19 Restaurant Marina
20 Taverna La Bota
25 Restaurant Bahía

OTHER
4   Centre Mèdic Tossa
6   Police Station
7   Bus Station
8   Tourist Office
10 Roman Villa
11 Post Office
12 Disco Ely
13 Paradis
18 Pots
23 Boat Services
26 Església de Sant Vicenç
27 Bodega La Parra
28 Bounty Bar
34 Museu Municipal
     (Palau del Batlle)
35 Lighthouse

COSTA BRAVA

fronts onto a roundabout with the unmistakably Catalan name Plaça de les Nacions sense Estat (Stateless Nations' Plaza).

Almost next door, at Avinguda del Pelegrí 25, is the tourist office (☎ 972 34 01 08), open 9 am to 9 pm Monday to Saturday and 10 am to 1 pm Sunday, June to August. Opening hours are reduced during the rest of the year.

The main beach, Platja Gran, and the older part of town, are a 10-minute walk to the south-east.

You'll find banks, many with ATMs, along streets like Avinguda de la Costa Brava and around Plaça d'Espanya. The post office *(correus/correos)* is on Carrer de Maria Auxiliadora, one block east of Avinguda del Pelegrí.

The police station (☎ 972 34 01 35) is at Avinguda del Pelegrí 14. The Centre Mèdic Tossa (☎ 972 34 14 48), Avinguda del Pelegrí 16, is a private-practice medical clinic. The state clinic is the Ambulatori (☎ 972 34 18 28) in the Casa del Mar at Avinguda de Catalunya s/n, about 1km north-west of the old town.

Old Tossa

The walls and towers on the pine-dotted headland, Mont Guardí, at the end of the main beach, were built in the 12th to 14th centuries. The area they girdle is known as the **Vila Vella** (old town), a quaint sprinkling of stone houses. You can walk up on Mont Guardí, where there are also vestiges of a castle, a Gothic church and a *far* (lighthouse), at any time of the day or night.

In the lower part of the Vila Vella is the interesting **Museu Municipal** in the 14th- and 15th-century Palau del Batlle, open 10 am to 10 pm daily, mid-June to mid-September. The rest of the year it opens 10 am to 1 pm and 3 to 6 pm Tuesday to Sunday. Admission costs €3. In the museum are mosaics and other finds from a **Roman villa** off Avinguda del Pelegrí, and Tossa-related art including Chagall's *El Violinista*. Behind the musician in question, a Tossa window opens onto a landscape of Chagall's Belarus birthplace. Wander up around the town within the walls. If you are not tempted

by the handful of bars and restaurants, some with enchanting views back down on the Vila Nova and beach, the views alone out to sea and down the rocky south-west coast should do the trick – the sunsets here are just what a romantic is looking for!

The so-called **Vila Nova** (new town) is actually the part of the old town that stands outside of the walled Vila Vella. Much of its tangle of lanes dates from the 18th century. The real new town stretches a lot farther north, north-west and north-east.

Beaches & Coves

The main town beach, **Platja Gran**, tends to be busy. Farther along the same bay are the little **Platja del Reig** and **Platja Mar Menuda** at the end of Avinguda de Sant Ramon Penyafort, which tends to be less crowded. The coast north-east and south-west of Tossa has rocky coves, some with small beaches (sometimes sandy, more often stony). You can walk cross-country from Tossa to the small **Cala Llevadó** and **Cala d'En Carlos** beaches, 3km south-west, or the longer **Platja de Llorell** (3.5km), or drive down to Platja de Llorell from the GI-682. To the north-east, you can walk down from the GI-682 to small beaches like **Cala Pola** (4km), **Cala Giverola** (5km), **Cala Salions** (8km) and **Platja Vallpregona** (11km). In summer (May to September), glass-bottomed boats run to some of these north-eastern beaches from Platja Gran, calling in at a few sea caves (about €6.60 return, hourly).

Places to Stay – Budget

Tossa has over 80 hotels, *hostales* (budget hotels) and *pensiones* (guesthouses). You'll find plenty of them open from Setmana Santa (Holy Week, the week leading up to Easter Sunday) to October but only a handful outside those months. Some of the best-value places get booked up weeks, even months, ahead for high summer.

Camping There are five camping grounds around Tossa, each holding between 800 and 1700 people, but you're unlikely to find any of them open between mid-October and Setmana Santa. Nearest to town is *Camping*

Can Martí (☎ *972 34 08 51)* on Rambla Pau Casals, 1km back from the beach. Two people with a car and tent pay €18.20. *Camping Turismar* (☎ *972 34 04 63)* and *Camping Tossa* (☎ *972 34 05 47)* are respectively about 1km and 2.5km farther out, on the GI-681. *Camping Pola* (☎ *972 34 10 50, fax 972 34 13 58)*, 4km out on the GI-682, is well sited in a shady valley that leads to a picturesque cove. *Camping Cala Llevadó* (☎ *972 34 03 14)* is 3km out on the GI-682 to Lloret de Mar. You can expect to pay between €17 and €21 for two people, a car and a tent at all these camp sites.

Pensiones & Hostales In July and August it's easier to find rooms in the streets just down from the tourist office and bus station than in the older part of town or on the seafront. Even so, you might want to start looking in the more atmospheric older area. In busy times the lone traveller will have a hard time, generally being obliged to pay the full cost of double rooms.

Fonda Lluna (☎ *972 34 03 65, Carrer de la Roqueta 20)*, also called *Can Lluna*, is good value at €12/24 for small single/double rooms with bathroom, and breakfast included.

Pensión Can Tort (☎ *972 34 11 85, Carrer del Portal 1)* has sizable doubles with breakfast for €36 with bathroom. Prices drop in July and further in other months. It opens April to the end of October. *Hostal Tonet* (☎/fax *972 34 02 37, Plaça de l'Església s/n)*, where doubles with bathroom cost up to €36 plus IVA, is open year round.

A dozen or so pensiones and hostales lie scattered about within three blocks of the tourist office. *Hotel Ros* (☎ *972 34 02 11, Avinguda del Pelegrí 27)*, right by the tourist office, has good rooms with bathroom for up to €33 for a double. Comparable places include *Hostal Isabel* (☎ *972 34 03 36, Carrer de Sant Vicenç 3)*; *Hostal Anna* (☎ *972 34 06 44, Carrer de Tomàs Barber s/n)*; and *Hostal Horta Rosell* (☎ *972 34 04 32, Carrer de Pola 29)*.

A few blocks towards the old town, *Pensión Carmen* (☎ *972 34 05 26, Carrer de Sant Miquel 8)*, with signs also saying

Pensión Pepi and, for good measure, *Pensión Carmen-Pepi*, has decent rooms (doubles only), with shower, for €29.75. The place is built around a charming courtyard.

A decent beachfront *hostal* is *Hostal Del Mar* (☎ *972 34 00 80, Passeig del Mar 13)* with rooms for about €24/33. The owners have another place, *Hostal Mediterráneo* (☎ *972 34 00 99, Carrer Nou 3)*, back in from the beach. The front part is a refurbished centuries-old house with exposed timber beams in the ceiling and some charm. Doubles only cost €33, although in June you'll get them for less and they may do a deal on single occupation.

Hotel Maria Rosa (☎ *972 34 02 85, Carrer del Pont Vell 4)* is a meticulously well kept little house where smallish but welcoming rooms cost €33.

Hotel Canaima (☎ *972 34 09 95, Avinguda de la Palmas 24)* has been largely renovated and offers spotless and spacious rooms for up to €22.70 per person.

Places to Stay – Mid-Range & Top End

On the beachfront, *Hostal Victòria* (☎ *972 34 01 66, Passeig del Mar s/n)* is plain but adequate and rooms cost €21/26.45 for singles/doubles in slow months but €70.90 for a double and half-board *(media pensión)* in the busy period.

The more attractive, *Hostal Cap d'Or* (☎/fax *972 34 00 81, Passeig de la Vila Vella 1)*, in front of the old town walls, charges €28.40/56.80 including breakfast.

Hotel Diana (☎ *972 34 18 86, fax 972 34 11 03, Plaça d'Espanya 6)* is a relaxed, small-scale, older hotel fronting Platja Gran. It has a Gaudí fireplace in the lounge and offers doubles costing €90.75 with sea views or €78.15 looking onto the square.

On Platja Mar Menuda, the 40-room *Hotel Mar Menuda* (☎ *972 34 10 00, fax 972 34 00 87)* has high standards of comfort and service at €82.35 for doubles with breakfast plus IVA. From mid-July to mid-August it offers half-board only at €63.10 per person (plus IVA).

The 166-room *Gran Hotel Reymar* (☎ *972 34 00 00, fax 972 34 15 04)* on Mar

COSTA BRAVA

Menuda beach is the top place in town, with doubles costing €168.30 plus IVA in July and August. It closes from November to April.

Places to Eat

Tossa has a lot of bland, overpriced eateries. The alfresco restaurants lining Carrer del Portal are nicely situated and do some good fish and seafood, but are expensive for what you get.

Restaurant Bahía (☎ 972 34 03 22, Passeig de Mar 19) does some of the better food along the Tossa waterfront, with a set *menú del día* (fixed-price meal) for €11.60.

On Carrer de Tarull, beside the church in the old town, *Restaurant Marina (☎ 972 34 07 57)* at No 6 offers a fairly good *menú* for €8.40 and also does some economical specials such as chicken, chips, salad and beer for €3. *Taverna La Bota (☎ 972 34 16 60)* next door has a simpler *menú* for €7.20. It has a nice garden.

Es Molí (☎ 972 34 14 14, Carrer de Tarull 5), farther up the same street, serves up classier local cooking, including good prawns and *fideuá* (noodle paella), and has a tranquil, shady garden patio. There are *menús* for €16.20 and a gourmet version for €28.95.

La Paella (Carrer Nou 12) is not a bad little eatery, where a *menú* costs €7.80 and *raciones* (a large portion of tapas) around €4.80.

Entertainment

The old town's lively bars, some with music, are mostly gathered along and near Carrer de Sant Josep. *Bodega La Parra (Carrer de Sant Josep 26)* is one that manages to maintain an old-fashioned wine-cellar atmosphere. *Bounty Bar (Carrer de l'Església 6)*, around the corner, is a lively little watering hole while *Pots*, on the corner of Carrer Nou and Carrer de Rosa Rissech, is a barn of a place that certainly grabs attention. *Disco Ely* off Avinguda de la Costa Brava is currently the in place to carry on at later. Otherwise you could try *Paradis (Carrer del Pou de la Vila 12–14)*, which opens for dancing on Friday and Saturday.

Getting There & Away

Bus SARFA runs buses to/from Barcelona's Estació del Nord up to 10 times daily. The trip costs €6.40 and takes 1¼ hours.

There are fairly frequent buses to/from Lloret de Mar (€1): in summer they go every 30 minutes from 8.45 am to 8.45 pm.

In July and August one all-stops bus leaves for Sant Feliu de Guíxols at 10.40 am daily, returning at 7 pm (€2.50). From Sant Feliu there are SARFA buses to Girona, Palafrugell, Torroella de Montgrí and L'Escala (most several times daily). In June, July or August you can also reach Sant Feliu by one of the six daily boats from Tossa (see later in this section).

Two or three buses daily run direct between Tossa and Girona in July and August; otherwise there's one daily on school days at 7.30 pm (€3.25). Year round there are more frequent connections to Girona from Lloret de Mar.

Car & Motorcycle From Barcelona, the C-32 toll road, which takes you almost to Blanes, saves a weary trudge on the toll-free N-II. To the north, the 23km stretch of the GI-682 to Sant Feliu de Guíxols is a great drive, winding its way up, down and around picturesque bays. Rose Macaulay, author of *Fabled Shore* (1950), 'met only one mule cart, laden with pine boughs, and two very polite *guardias civiles*' on this road.

Boat In June, July and August three boat services offer a scenic way of reaching Tossa, or of taking an outing from it. Cruce-tours (☎ 972 37 26 92), Viajes Marítimos (☎ 608 93 64 76) and Dolfi-Jet (☎ 972 37 19 39) run several times daily between Blanes, Lloret de Mar and Tossa (one to 1½ hours), with stops at a few in-between points. A few of the services continue to/from Calella, 12km south of Blanes (*not* Calella de Palafrugell farther north), and/or Palamós, north of Tossa, again with intermediate stops (including Sant Feliu de Guíxols). You could catch one of the frequent suburban rodalies trains from Barcelona's Catalunya station to Calella or Blanes, then transfer to the boat. A return boat ticket to Tossa is generally

€11.70 from Calella or €8.10 from Sant Feliu de Guíxols. In many places the boats simply pull up at the beach (in Tossa, at Platja Gran) and tickets are sold at a booth there.

Getting Around
Jimbo Bike (☎ 972 34 30 44), Avinguda de Pau Casals 12, rents out mountain bikes for €18 a day or €3 an hour.

SANT FELIU DE GUÍXOLS
postcode 17220 • pop 17,071
A snaking road hugs the spectacular ups and downs of the Costa Brava for the 21km from Tossa de Mar to Sant Feliu de Guíxols. Along the way are several enticing little inlets and largely hidden beaches. One, known as **La Cala del Senyor Ramon**, is signposted and is a delightful little sandy, half-moon beach surrounded by high rocky walls. Leave the car where you can on the road and follow the track down. *Camping Pola* (☎ 972 34 10 50, fax 972 34 13 58), at Km 27, is a tempting place to stay down by another of these little beaches. It opens mid-May to mid-October and charges around €23.45 for a car and tent space and another €4.80 per person from July to August. Prices drop to €15.20 and €3, respectively, at other times.

Sant Feliu itself has an attractive waterside promenade and a handful of curious leftovers from its long past, the most important of them being the so-called **Porta Ferrada**, a wall and entrance which is all that remains of the 10th-century Monestir de Sant Benet. The town boasts a busy commercial port and hinterland cork industry, although tourism plays a big part here. A couple of nice enough beaches can be found either side of the town but it is all rather too busy. With around 40 hotels and hostales there is no shortage of places to stay either but the place has neither the beauty of other Costa Brava localities nor the thumping disco-by-sea power that some are in search of. Better to move on really.

In September Sant Feliu de Guíxols stages the Festival Internacional de Música de la Porta Ferrada, an annual celebration of classical music that has been going since 1962.

SARFA buses run here frequently (especially in summer) between Barcelona and Palafrugell (€8.90).

PLATJA D'ARO & PALAMÓS
These two spots mark the two ends of one of the Costa Brava's party spots. The beaches are not bad, the high rises are standard issue and the nightlife is busy. The area tends to attract more Spanish tourism than foreign and for that reason can be a vaguely interesting take on the whole costa holiday phenomenon. A great deal more than that cannot be said. Again, the area is crawling with hostales, hotels and apartments and mostly poor-quality restaurants. Both of these places are stops on the frequent Barcelona-Palafrugell SARFA bus route.

If you should end up in Palamós and wonder how it could have happened, all is not lost. Not too far north of the town lies salvation. **Platja del Castell** is one of the relatively untouched strands along this strip of the coast. Local citizens have been campaigning since the early 1990s to have the area protected. Unsealed roads lead to it just a couple of kilometres north of the town – you'll need to ask directions.

If you are prepared to explore a little more, pass the camping ground and follow the GR-92 road towards Cap Roig and the Sant Sebastià lighthouse. After the turn-off for Cala Canyers you reach some pine trees where you have to leave any wheeled vehicles and continue on foot to the utterly charming **Cala Estreta**. The water is pure and the sand clean. You'll need footwear though, because the rocks in the water are home to some prickly sea critters. Other pretty spots you can reach on foot from here are **Roca Bona** and **Cap de Planes**.

PALAFRUGELL & AROUND
postcode 17200 • pop 17,564
The 21km reach of coast from Sant Feliu de Guíxols to Palamós is unattractively built up all the way, but north of Palamós begins one of the most beautiful stretches of the Costa Brava. The town of Palafrugell, 5km

inland, is the main access point for a cluster of attractive beach spots.

East of Palafrugell are Calella de Palafrugell, Llafranc and Tamariu, once fishing villages squeezed into small bays and now three of the Costa Brava's most charming, low-key and low-rise resorts. Even in July and August they remain relatively laid-back, although accommodation is on the expensive side (Palafrugell itself has some cheaper rooms). Begur, 7km north-east of Palafrugell, is an interesting village, with a cluster of less developed beaches nearby.

Palafrugell

Palafrugell, a pleasant enough if vaguely chaotic town, is the main transport, shopping and service hub for the area.

Orientation & Information The C-66 Palamós-Girona road passes through the western side of Palafrugell, a 10-minute walk from the central square, Plaça Nova. The tourist office (☎ 972 30 02 28) is at Carrer del Carrilet 2 beside the C-66. It opens from at least 10 am to 1 pm and 5 to 7 pm Monday to Saturday, and 10 am to 1 pm Sunday and holidays; and 9 am to 9 pm Monday to Saturday, July and August.

The SARFA bus station, Carrer de Torres Jonama 67–9, is five minutes' walk from the tourist office and 10 minutes from Plaça Nova. Banks, many with ATMs, telephones and shops cluster on and around Plaça Nova. The post office is at Carrer de Torres Jonama 16. The local police (☎ 092 or ☎ 972 61 31 01) are at Avinguda de Josep Pla s/n.

Museu del Suro The Museu del Suro, dedicated to the important local cork industry, is one block east of Carrer de Pi i Margall at Carrer de la Tarongeta 31. It opens 5 to 9 pm Tuesday to Saturday, plus 10 am to 1 pm in summer (10.30 am to 1.30 pm on Sunday). Admission is free.

Places to Stay A block west of Plaça Nova, *Fonda L'Estrella (☎ 972 30 00 05, Carrer de les Quatre Cases 13–17)*, is a pleasant, cool, old-fashioned house where singles/doubles with shared bathrooms cost

€15.60/28.85. It closes from November to April.

Two blocks in the opposite direction from the square, *Residència Familiar (☎ 689 26 95 38, Carrer de Sant Sebastià 29)* is ordinary but good and clean with doubles costing up to €27.65. The good *Hostal Platja (☎ 972 30 05 26)* across the street at No 34 has a nice courtyard, and rooms with bathroom for €19.25/36. It opens year round.

Getting There & Away SARFA (☎ 972 30 06 23) runs buses to/from Barcelona's Estació del Nord (€9.85, two hours) seven to 13 times daily and to/from Girona (€3.30, one hour) up to 15 times daily. SARFA also has a few daily services north to Begur, Torroella de Montgrí, L'Escala and Figueres (1½ hours), and, in July and August only, two buses daily to Lloret de Mar and Tossa de Mar (two hours).

Calella de Palafrugell

The southernmost of the three Palafrugell resorts, Calella is also the most spread out. Its low buildings are strung Aegean-style around a bay of rocky points and small beaches, with a few fishing boats still hauled up on the sand. The tourist office (☎ 972 61 44 75), down near the seafront at Carrer de les Voltes 4, opens 10 am to 1 pm and 5 to 8 pm Monday to Saturday, and from 10 am to 1 pm Sunday and holidays (April to October).

Things to See & Do Apart from plonking yourself on one of the beaches, you can stroll along nice coastal footpaths north-east to Llafranc (20 or 30 minutes), or south to Platja del Golfet beach close to Cap Roig (about 40 minutes). Atop Cap Roig, the **Jardí Botànic de Cap Roig**, a beautiful garden of 1200 Mediterranean species, is set around the early 20th-century castle/palace of Nikolai Voevalsky, a tsarist colonel who fled the Russian Revolution. The garden opens 8 am to 8 pm daily in summer and 9 am to 6 pm in winter. Admission costs €1.80.

Special Events Calella stages probably the Costa Brava's biggest summer *cantada*

Perched high on the 'serrated mountain' is the Monestir de Montserrat.

Monumental *castellers* (human-castle builders)

A quieter side of Sitges, Costa de Garraf

Cadaqués is set around a rocky bay on the Costa Brava, surrounded by beautiful blue waters.

Take a dip at the utterly charming Cala Estreta on the Costa Brava.

de havaneres sing-song. Havaneres are strangely melancholy songs from the Caribbean that became popular among Costa Brava sailors in the 19th century, when Catalunya maintained busy links with Cuba. Havaneres are traditionally accompanied by the drinking of *cremat*, a rum, coffee, sugar, lemon and cinnamon concoction that you set alight briefly before quaffing. Traditionally, Calella's cantada used to be held in July but it has become such a popular event that it is repeated each Monday evening (from about 10 pm) throughout the summer and to the end of September.

Places to Stay & Eat In the village, *Camping Moby Dick (☎ 972 61 43 07, Carrer de la Costa Verde 16–28)* has room for 470 people. *La Siesta Camping (☎ 972 61 51 16)* has a shady site by the Palafrugell road 1.25km back from the beach, with space for 2000. Both open from April to September. Moby Dick charges €14.15 plus IVA for two people, a tent and a car; at La Siesta it's €21.20 plus IVA.

Hostería del Plancton (☎ 972 61 50 81, Carrer de Codina 12) – follow the signs to Església de Sant Pere – has the best-value rooms in any of three Palafrugell resorts. Unfortunately it only opens from June to September. Good, clean little rooms, some with balconies and all sharing bathrooms, cost €13.20 per person (€11.70 in low season).

Tambucho (☎ 972 61 40 46, Plaça de Sant Pere 1), back a little from the beach, is a relaxed restaurant where you can eat well (they do a reasonable *fondue bourguignon*) by candlelight. Main courses cost from €10.80 to €15. Overlooking the beach is *Les Voltes (☎ 972 61 55 48, Les Voltes 7)*, with a pleasant outside dining area beneath the arches from which it takes its name. On offer are fairly standard Catalan dishes for similar prices to those at Tambucho.

Getting There & Away Buses from the SARFA station in Palafrugell run to La Siesta Camping, Calella, Llafranc and back to La Siesta and Palafrugell, a return trip of 30 minutes (€0.90). They go about every

half-hour from 7.40 am to 8.30 pm in July and August; the service reduces during the rest of the year to three or four buses daily from November to February.

Llafranc
postcode 17211 • pop 172

Barely 2km north-east of Calella de Palafrugell and now merging with it along the roads back from the rocky coast between them, Llafranc has a smaller bay but a longer stretch of sand, is a bit more fashionable and lively, and gets more crowded. The tourist office (☎ 972 30 50 08), a kiosk on Carrer de Roger de Llúria just back from the western end of the beach, opens June to September, the same hours as Calella de Palafrugell's office.

Things to See & Do From the **Far de Sant Sebastià** (Sant Sebastià Lighthouse) and **Ermita de Sant Sebastià** (Sant Sebastià Hermitage) up on Cap de Sant Sebastià, the cape to the east of the town, there are tremendous views in both directions. It's a 30- or 40-minute walk up: head up the steps from the harbour, then follow the road to the right. You can walk on to Tamariu, too, but check with the tourist office about the most scenic of the several routes available.

Places to Stay & Eat In a pine wood, *Camping Kim's (☎ 972 30 11 56)* is on Camí de la Font d'en Xeco, about 750m back from the beach. It opens April to September and charges €17.45 for two people, a site and car parking space.

Residencia Montaña (☎ 972 30 04 04, Carrer de Cesàrea 2), off Plaça del Promontori, is not a bad deal. Doubles cost up to €37.85 plus IVA. *Pensió Celimar (☎ 972 30 13 74, Carrer de Carudo 12)*, also off Plaça del Promontori, is more modern, opens year round and has doubles with bathroom costing €39 plus IVA.

La Pasta (☎ 972 61 22 97, Carrer de Cipsela 1) is popular for its pizzas and salads costing around €5. The waterfront is lined with restaurants, but none are overly inspiring. You are paying for the sea views. Tucked away a block from the waterfront is a more genuine eating experience, *La Sal* (☎ 972 30 01 92, *Carrer de Perre Pascuet 2)*. Seafood is the name of the game and you can eat well for around €21. It closes on Monday.

Getting There & Away See the Getting There & Away section under Calella de Palafrugell, earlier in the chapter, for information on bus services. The Llafranc stop is on Carrer de la Sirena, up the hill on the Calella side of town.

Tamariu
postcode 17212 • pop 89
Three or four kilometres north up the coast from Llafranc as the crow flies, and nearly twice as far by road, Tamariu is smaller and attracts a quieter, more select Catalan crowd. Its beach has some of the cleanest waters on Spain's Mediterranean coast. The tourist office (☎ 972 62 01 93), in the middle of the village on Carrer de la Riera, opens 10 am to 1 pm and 5 to 8 pm Monday to Saturday, and 10 am to 1 pm Sunday and holidays (June to September).

Places to Stay & Eat About 1km back from the beach on Carrer de la Riera, *Camping Tamariu* (☎ 972 62 04 22) opens May to September and charges €15.90 plus IVA for two people, a tent and a car.

Hotel Sol d'Or (☎ 972 62 01 72, *Carrer de la Riera 18)*, 500m nearer to the beach, opens June to September. Doubles with bathroom cost €39.40 plus IVA. *Hotel Es Furió* (☎ 972 62 00 36, *Carrer del Foraió 5–7)* is just back from the beach and has spacious, cheerfully decorated doubles costing up to €68.50 (as little as €42 in slow periods). It opens mid-March to mid-November.

The beachfront is lined with seafood eateries. *Restaurant Royal* (☎ 972 62 00 41) is one of the best and does a reasonable fideuá for about €12.

Getting There & Away SARFA buses from Palafrugell run to Tamariu three or four times daily, from mid-June to mid-September only (€0.90, 15 minutes).

A rough road will take you on to Aiguablava (see under Beaches near Begur later).

Begur
postcode 17255 • pop 2700
The **castle**, dating from the 10th century, on a rock above the village is still pretty much in the state in which it was left by Spanish troops who wrecked it in 1810 to impede the advance of Napoleon's army. Dotted around the village are half a dozen towers built for defence against 16th- and 17th-century pirates. There's a tourist office (☎ 972 62 45 20) at Avinguda del Onze de Setembre 5.

Places to Stay The pine-shaded *Camping Begur* (☎ 972 62 32 01), open April to September, is about 2km south on the road from Palafrugell. *Hotel Rosa* (☎ 972 62 30 15, *Carrer de Forgas i Puig 6)*, a few steps towards the castle from the church, has nice rooms with bathroom; singles/doubles with buffet breakfast cost up to €42.45/65.60 (€28.85/51.10 in slow periods).

Getting There & Away SARFA (☎ 972 62 24 26), at Plaça de Forgas 6, runs three buses daily to Barcelona's Estació del Nord (2¼ hours) via Palafrugell. One bus daily runs Monday to Friday between Begur and Girona (€4.25, 1½ hours), leaving at around 6 pm from Girona and 7.30 am from Begur. It stops at Pals, Peratallada and Ullastret on the way.

Beaches near Begur
You can reach a series of smallish beaches, on an enticing stretch of coast, by turning east off the Palafrugell road 2km south of the centre of Begur. About 2km down is a turning to the black sand beach of **Platja Fonda** (1km). Half a kilometre farther on is the turning to **Fornells** (1km), a small village on one of the most picturesque bays of the whole Costa Brava, with a marina, beach and incredibly blue waters.

The large but friendly *Hotel Aiguablava* (☎ 972 62 20 58, fax 972 62 21 12) overlooking most of this has doubles for €88.95

plus IVA (closed mid-November to mid-February). *Hotel Bonaigua* (☎ *972 62 20 50, fax 972 62 20 54)*, back up the street a little, charges €64.90 plus IVA (closed October to late April). Back up at the Fornells turning, *Restaurant Ondina* (☎ *972 62 30 52)*, open April to October, has four double rooms at €48.10 plus IVA.

One kilometre on from the Fornells turning is **Aiguablava**, with a slightly bigger and busier beach, and the *Parador Nacional de la Costa Brava* (☎ *972 62 21 62, fax 972 62 21 66)* enjoying lovely views back across the Fornells bay. Doubles start at €117.20 plus IVA.

Another road from Begur leads a couple of kilometres east to **Aiguafreda**, a beach on a lovely cove backed by pine-covered hills, and, a bit farther south, the slightly more built-up **Sa Tuna** beach. If you fancy staying, try *Hostal Sa Rascassa* (☎ *972 62 42 47, fax 972 62 41 91, Cala d'Aiguafreda 3)* in Aiguafreda. They have doubles costing up to €72.10, including breakfast.

Getting There & Away A Bus Platges (beach bus) service runs from Plaça de Forgas in Begur between late June and mid-September.

PALS

Six kilometres inland from Begur is the pretty walled town of Pals. The main monument is the 15m **Torre de les Hores** (clock tower) but what makes the trip worthwhile is simply wandering around the uneven lanes and poking your nose into one medieval corner or another. From the **Mirador del Pedró** you can see north-east across the coastal plains to the sea, with the Illes Medes in the background. Five kilometres east (and a few kilometres north of Begur) is the southernmost point of the Platja de Pals, about 10km of sand stretching all the way to L'Estartit.

Pensió Barris (☎ *972 63 67 02, Carrer del Enginyer Algarra 51)* is simple but clean and open year round. They charge €21/30 for singles/doubles. Pals is on the one-bus-a-weekday route between Begur and Girona.

Liberty Beach

The gigantic transmission installations back from the Platja de Pals were, until mid-2001, used by the American station known as the International Broadcasting Bureau. In the days of the Cold War the IBB had a rather more catchy name: Radio Liberty. Propaganda broadcasts in a babble of languages were beamed into Eastern bloc countries as part of the USA's campaign to undermine the Communist bloc regimes. While people from Pals and beyond relaxed on the beach through long summer days, the airwaves above them were laden with messages of a brave new tomorrow to the people of Eastern Europe.

ASA ANDERSSON

PERATALLADA

Visiting Peratallada is a favourite day trip for Catalans. Although only one of several touchingly cute villages in this green patch of Girona province it has been singled out for special treatment. Its narrow streets and fine 11th-century castle/mansion (now a luxury hotel and restaurant) have been supplemented by other places to stay, enticing restaurants and a sprinkling of low-key boutiques. During the week in the off season most of these shut and you have the hamlet largely to yourself. Weekends are another story and summer worse still.

COSTA BRAVA

Places to Stay & Eat

You could stay at *Ca l'Aliu* (☎ 972 63 40 61, Carrer de la Roca 6), a simple *casa de pagès* (country house with rooms to let) in the village that charges up to €42.10 for a double. If you want sheer medieval luxury you will cede to the temptation of the *Castell de Peratallada* (☎ 972 63 40 21, fax 972 63 40 11, @ casteperat@aplitic.com, Plaça del Castell 1). This will cost up to €150.25 a double. Those wanting a little class but without such an investment can try *Hostal La Riera* (☎ 972 63 41 42, Carrer de la Riera 6). This diminutive hideaway has just six rooms, all very bucolic with ceilings done in ceramic from La Bisbal d'Empordà (see later). Doubles cost up to €66.10.

One of the best restaurants is *Can Bonay* (☎ 972 63 40 34, Plaça de les Voltes 13). Splash out on the *menú de degustación* (a gourmet selection of specialities), in which you are treated to such local delights as partridge and goose, in this fine 17th-century building. You'll spend about €30.

Getting There & Away

Peratallada is on the Begur-Girona bus line (one a day on weekdays).

ULLASTRET

The hamlet of Ullastret, about 4km from Peratallada and 7km from the main local town, La Bisbal d'Empordà, is nice but nothing special. About 1km farther to the north-east, however, is one of the best preserved Iberian settlements in Catalunya, Puig de Sant Andreu d'Ullastret (more commonly known simply by the name of the hamlet). It is a leafy, green location with, on its eastern side, a clear vantage point overlooking the surrounding fields. Parts of the walls, gates, silos, water cisterns and other elements, most dating to the 3rd century BC, have been identified. The hillock was settled in the 6th century BC and abandoned towards the end of the 2nd century BC, some time after the Romans had taken control of the area.

Excavations at the Iberian settlement continue and in 2000 remains of an unusual two-storey palace were uncovered. Some 70% of the site remains to be examined and only two hectares of a total of 11 can be visited. Archaeologists hope this will be increased as their work progresses.

You can enter the grounds from 10 am to 8 pm, Tuesday to Sunday. The timetable is reduced from October to May to 10 am to 2 pm and 4 to 6 pm. Wandering around (please don't clamber over the walls and other ruins) is free. Admission to the modest museum with artefacts found at this and other Iberian sites costs €1.80.

A wonderful overnight option for loose wallets is *Mas Crisarán* (☎ 972 76 90 00, Fonolleres) in Parlavà, 5km north-west of Ullastret. It is part of the Rusticae club of quality small hotels. The building dates from the 15th century and contains six alcoves (nine rooms in all) done up and supposed to be evocative of different worlds – Africa, India and so on. A double with breakfast costs €168.30 plus IVA.

The Begur-Girona bus calls by Ullastret and Parlavà.

LA BISBAL D'EMPORDÀ
postcode 17100 • pop 7400

La Bisbal is a local hub and best known for its ceramic production. If you approach from the west (ie, coming from Girona) you will not fail to notice the parade of ceramics stores lining the main road into town. Some of it can make attractive souvenirs, so those with vehicles might like to stop by and snoop around the shops.

The old centre of the town is worth a little exploration, although few monuments of particular note stand out. One exception is the Castell-Palau Episcopal, a one-time Romanesque castle later converted into a bishop's residence and tarted up with Gothic and Renaissance bits and bobs. The Església de Santa Maria, although in one way or another around since 904, received a major makeover in the mid-18th century, the most visible result of which was its present baroque facade.

Places to Stay

Fonda Pilar (☎ 972 64 00 27, Carrer de Coll i Vehí 28) has cheap, austere rooms for

COSTA BRAVA

about €12 per person. Better is **Pensió Adarnius** (☎ *972 62 21 98, Avinguda de les Voltes 7*). It is on the main drag through town and its rooms are reasonably spacious and comfortable. A double costs €37.90.

Getting There & Away
Fairly frequent buses run between Girona (€2.60, 45 minutes) and Palafrugell and stop here, although as elsewhere on the Costa Brava, services drop drastically at the weekend and in winter.

CASTELL DE PÚBOL
The Castell de Púbol at La Pera, just south of the C-66 and 22km north-west of Palafrugell, forms the southernmost point of north-eastern Catalunya's 'Dalí triangle', whose other elements include the Teatre-Museu Dalí in Figueres and the Cadaqués area, where the artist spent much of his life.

Salvador Dalí bought the Gothic and Renaissance mansion – which includes a 14th-century church – in 1968 and gave it to his wife, Gala, who lived here without him until her death. Local lore has it that the notoriously promiscuous Gala was still sending for young village men almost right up to the time she died in 1982, aged 88. On her death, Dalí himself moved into Púbol, but abandoned it after the fire (which nearly burnt him to a crisp) in 1984 to live out his last years at Figueres.

The castle was done up by Dalí in his inimitable style, with lions' heads staring from the tops of cupboards, statues of elephants with giraffes' legs in the garden and a stuffed giraffe staring at Gala's tomb in the crypt. The strength of the artist's passion for Gala is shown by motifs and reminders of her all over the castle. A visit is in effect a tour of the couple's tortured relationship. The blue bedroom in which Dalí nearly burnt to death now has a bright red fire extinguisher standing ready in the corner. There are many other sumptuous beds in other rooms. In the garage is the blue Cadillac in which Dalí took Gala for a last drive round the estate – after she had died.

Take the time to have a look around the little town as well – it's a gem of sandy-coloured stone houses all huddled together, typical of the area.

The mansion opens mid-March to the end of October only. From mid-June to mid-September the hours are 10.30 am to 7.15 pm daily. For the remaining months it opens 10.30 am to 5.15 pm daily (closed Monday) Admission costs €4.20 (seniors and students €3). SARFA buses between Pala-frugell and Girona run along the C-66.

GIRONA
postcode 17080 • pop 71,858
Northern Catalunya's largest city, Girona (Gerona in Castilian) sits in a valley 36km inland from Palafrugell. Its impressive medieval centre, climbing a hill above the Riu Onyar, makes it well worth a visit.

The Roman town of Gerunda lay on the Via Augusta, the highway from Rome to Cádiz (Carrer de la Força in Girona's old town follows part of the line of the Via Augusta). Taken from the Muslims by the Franks in 797, Girona became capital of one of Catalunya's most important counties, falling under the sway of Barcelona in the late 9th century. Its wealth in medieval times produced many fine Romanesque and Gothic buildings, which have survived repeated attacks and sieges down the centuries.

Orientation
The narrow streets of the old town climb above the eastern bank of the Onyar and are easy to explore on foot. Several roads and footbridges link it to the new town across the river. The train station is 1km to the south-west, on Plaça d'Espanya off Carrer de Barcelona, with the bus station behind it on Carrer de Rafael Masó i Valentí.

Information
The tourist office (☎ 972 22 65 75) is towards the southern end of the old town, at Rambla de la Llibertat 1. It opens 8 am to 8 pm Monday to Friday, 8 am to 2 pm and 4 to 8 pm Saturday, and 9 am to 2 pm on Sunday. Another office operates at the airport, but only when charter flights are due.

There are branches of La Caixa bank, with ATMs, on Carrer dels Abeuradors off

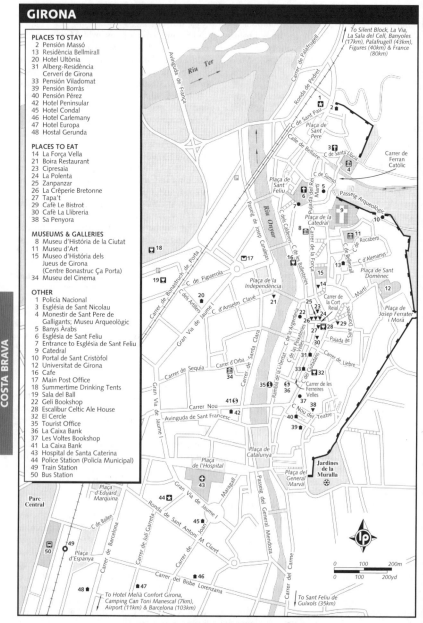

GIRONA

PLACES TO STAY
2 Pensión Massó
13 Residència Bellmirall
20 Hotel Ultònia
31 Alberg-Residència
   Cerverí de Girona
33 Pensión Viladomat
39 Pensión Borràs
40 Pensión Pérez
42 Hotel Peninsular
45 Hotel Condal
46 Hotel Carlemany
47 Hotel Europa
48 Hostal Gerunda

PLACES TO EAT
14 La Força Vella
21 Boira Restaurant
23 Cipresaia
24 La Polenta
25 Zanpanzar
26 La Crêperie Bretonne
27 Tapa't
29 Cafè Le Bistrot
30 Cafè La Llibreria
38 Sa Penyora

MUSEUMS & GALLERIES
8 Museu d'Història de la Ciutat
11 Museu d'Art
15 Museo d'Història dels
   Jueus de Girona
   (Centre Bonastruc Ça Porta)
34 Museu del Cinema

OTHER
1 Policía Nacional
3 Església de Sant Nicolau
4 Monestir de Sant Pere de
   Galligants; Museu Arqueològic
5 Banys Àrabs
6 Església de Sant Feliu
7 Entrance to Església de Sant Feliu
9 Catedral
10 Portal de Sant Cristòfol
12 Universitat de Girona
16 Cafe
17 Main Post Office
18 Summertime Drinking Tents
19 Sala del Ball
22 Geli Bookshop
28 Escalibur Celtic Ale House
32 El Cercle
35 Tourist Office
36 La Caixa Bank
37 Les Voltes Bookshop
41 La Caixa Bank
43 Hospital de Santa Caterina
44 Police Station (Policía Municipal)
49 Train Station
50 Bus Station

Rambla de la Llibertat and on Carrer Nou just across the Riu Onyar. The main post office is at Avinguda de Ramon Folch 2, also across the river.

The Policía Nacional, Carrer de Sant Pau 2, is at the northern end of the old town; the Policía Municipal are at Carrer de Bernat Bacià 4. The Hospital de Santa Caterina (☎ 972 18 26 00) is at Plaça de l'Hospital 5, also west of the river.

Two good bookshops for maps and local guides are Les Voltes on Plaça del Vi and Geli at Carrer de la Argenteria 18.

Catedral

The fine baroque facade of the cathedral stands at the head of a majestic flight of steps rising from Plaça de la Catedral. Most of the building, however, is much older than its facade. Repeatedly rebuilt and altered down the centuries, it has Europe's widest Gothic nave (23m). The cathedral's museum, through the door marked 'Claustre Tresor', contains the masterly Romanesque *Tapís de la Creació* (Tapestry of the Creation) and a Mozarabic illuminated *Beatus* manuscript from 975. The €3 admission fee for the museum also admits you to the beautiful 12th-century Romanesque cloister, whose 112 stone columns have some fine, although rather weathered, carving. From the cloister you can see the 13th-century Torre de Carlemany bell tower, also Romanesque. The cathedral opens 10 am to 2 pm and 4 to 7 pm daily (mornings only on Sunday). It is closed on Monday from October to April.

Museu d'Art

Next door to the cathedral, in the 12th- to 16th-century Palau Episcopal, the bulk of the art museum's collection covers the Romanesque and Gothic periods including woodcarvings, sculpture, paintings and several grand altarpieces. Smaller collections covering the 16th to the 20th centuries are scattered over the upper floors of the building. It opens 10 am to 6 pm (to 7 pm in summer), Tuesday to Saturday, and 10 am to 2 pm on Sunday and holidays. Admission costs €1.80.

Museu d'Història de la Ciutat

Just off Plaça de la Catedral on Carrer de la Força, this museum traces the history of the city from ancient times to the present. Dioramas, explanatory boards, videos, various odds and ends ranging from Neolithic tools to instruments used to accompany the *sardana* (Catalunya's national dance) all help bring the town's story to life. It's a curious museum but interesting if you want to get to know the city and the Catalans more. It opens 10 am to 2 pm and 5 to 7 pm Tuesday to Saturday (mornings only on Sunday). Admission costs €1.20.

Església de Sant Feliu

Girona's second great church stands downhill from the cathedral. The 17th-century main facade, with its landmark single tower, is on Plaça de Sant Feliu, but the entrance is round the side. Put €0.60 in the slot inside the door to light up the interior. The nave has 13th-century Romanesque arches but 14th- to 16th-century Gothic upper levels. In the northernmost of the chapels, at the far (western) end of the church, there's a masterly Catalan Gothic sculpture, Aloi de Montbrai's alabaster *Crist Jacent* (Recumbent Christ).

Banys Àrabs

The 'Arab baths' on Carrer de Ferran Catòlic are, although modelled on earlier Muslim and Roman bathhouses, actually a 12th-century Christian affair in Romanesque style. They are nonetheless reminiscent of the Arab baths in Palma de Mallorca. The Girona version are the only public baths yet discovered from medieval Christian Spain, where, in reaction to the Muslim obsession with water and cleanliness, washing almost came to be regarded as ungodly. The baths contain a changing room, the *apodyterium*, followed by the *frigidarium*, *tepidarium* and *caldarium*, with respectively cold, warm and hot water. It opens 10 am to 7 pm Tuesday to Saturday, and 10 am to 2 pm on Sunday and holidays, in the summer; 10 am to 2 pm daily except Monday, the rest of the year. Admission costs €1.20.

COSTA BRAVA

Passeig Arqueològic

Across the street from the Banys Àrabs, steps lead up into lovely gardens that follow the city walls up to the 18th-century Portal de Sant Cristòfol gate, from which you can walk back down to the cathedral.

Monestir de Sant Pere de Galligants

Down across the little Riu Galligants, this 11th- and 12th-century Romanesque monastery has another lovely cloister with some marvellous animal and monster carvings on the capitals of its pillars. The monastery houses Girona's **Museu Arqueològic** (Archaeology Museum), whose exhibits range from prehistoric to medieval times and include Roman mosaics and medieval Jewish tombstones. It opens 10.30 am to 1.30 pm and 4 to 7 pm (10 am to 2 pm and 4 to 6 pm in winter), Tuesday to Saturday, and 10 am to 2 pm on Sunday and holidays. Admission costs €1.80.

Església de Sant Nicolau

This pretty Lombard-style 12th-century Romanesque church which stands in front of the Monestir de Sant Pere de Galligants is unusual in having an octagonal tower, and also three apses laid out in a trefoil plan.

The Call

Until 1492, Girona was home to Catalunya's second most important medieval Jewish community (after Barcelona), and its Jewish quarter, the Call, centred on Carrer de la Força. For an idea of medieval Jewish life and culture here, visit the **Museu d'Història dels Jueus de Girona**, aka the Centre Bonastruc Ça Porta, entered from Carrer de la Força. It was named after Jewish Girona's most illustrious figure, a 13th-century Cabbalist philosopher and mystic. The centre, which is a warren of rooms and stairways around a courtyard, hosts limited exhibitions and is a focal point for studies of Jewish Spain. It opens 10 am to 8 pm (to 6 pm in winter) and Sunday and holidays from 10 am to 3 pm. Admission costs €1.80.

Passeig de la Muralla

You can walk along a good length of the top of the city walls, the Passeig de la Muralla, from Plaça de Josep Ferrater i Mora, just south of the Universitat de Girona building at the top of the old town, down to Plaça del General Marvà near Plaça de Catalunya. This southern part of the old town dates from the 13th century onwards – a bit younger than the more northerly area centred on the cathedral, where the Roman and early medieval towns stood.

Museu del Cinema

In 1998 Spain's first cinema museum opened its doors in the Casa de les Aigües and has proven one of the town's biggest hits. The extensive Col.lecció Tomàs Mallol begins with shadow puppets and proceeds with displays that recount the evolution of entertainment on screen, from the magic lantern through to the first still cameras, from fairground moving-picture attractions of the late 19th century through to the earliest celluloid hits, a handful of which you can see. Several opportunities arise to see how some of these contraptions worked. Among the many items of equipment on show is a variety of cameras and projectors from as far back as the 1920s and even a couple of examples of 1930s TV sets. The museum opens 10 am to 8 pm Tuesday to Sunday, May to September; 10 am to 6 pm Tuesday to Saturday and 11 am to 3 pm Sunday, the rest of the year. Admission costs €3.

Places to Stay – Budget

The nearest camping ground is *Camping Can Toni Manescal* (☎ 972 47 61 17, *Fornells de la Selva*), 7km south of Girona. It only holds 140 people but opens year round. Two people pay €12.20 per night.

Girona has a good modern youth hostel, the *Alberg-Residència Cerverí de Girona* (☎ 972 21 80 30, *Carrer dels Ciutadans 9*), which is well placed in the old town. It's only available from July to September. High-season rates are charged year round.

There are several pensiones and hostales in the old town. In July and August the better ones fill up quickly. *Pensión Pérez*

(☎ 972 22 40 08, Plaça de Bell.lloc 4) has a gloomy entrance stairway but clean, adequate singles/doubles costing €10.20/ 17.45. The owners have another cheap place with the same phone number, the **Pensión Borràs**, round the corner at Travessera d'Auriga 6.

Pensión Massó *(☎ 972 20 71 75, Plaça de Sant Pere 12)* has rooms with shared facilities for €18 a double; the sign just says '*Habitacions*'.

One of the nicest cheaper places in the old town is **Pensión Viladomat** *(☎ 972 20 31 76, Carrer dels Ciutadans 5)*. Comfortable rooms with shared facilities cost €12/24; there are a few doubles with bathroom for €36.

The fairly modern **Hotel Peninsular** *(☎ 972 20 38 00, Carrer Nou 3)*, just west of the Onyar, has 68 rooms at €18/35.45 with shared facilities, or €33/43.30 with bathroom, all plus IVA. **Hostal Gerunda** *(☎ 972 20 22 85, Carrer de Barcelona 34)*, near the train station, has doubles with bathroom for €22.25.

Places to Stay – Mid-Range & Top End

The attractive little **Residència Bellmirall** *(☎ 972 20 40 09, Carrer de Bellmirall 3)* is in a lovely medieval building with rooms costing €29.90/47.60, or €31.75/51.60 with shower and toilet, including breakfast.

Everything else in this price range is in the new town west of the Onyar. **Hotel Condal** *(☎ 972 20 44 62, Carrer de Joan Maragall 10)* and **Hotel Europa** *(☎ 972 20 27 50, fax 972 20 03 56, Carrer de Julí Garreta 21)* both have doubles costing from €36 to €39. **Hotel Ultònia** *(☎ 972 20 38 50, fax 972 20 33 34, Gran Via de Jaume I 22)* is ugly on the outside but has well equipped doubles costing €66.10 plus IVA (except in August, when prices shoot up to €84.15).

Top of the tree are the modern **Hotel Melià Confort Girona** *(☎ 972 40 05 00, fax 972 24 32 33, Carrer de Barcelona 112)*, where a double costs €87.15 plus IVA, and **Hotel Carlemany** *(☎ 972 21 12 12, fax 972 21 49 94, Plaça de Miquel Santaló)*, with doubles for €93.15 plus IVA.

Places to Eat

The cafes under the arcades on Rambla de la Llibertat and nearby Plaça del Vi are good places to soak up a bit of atmosphere. Several of those on Rambla de la Llibertat offer decent paella for €5.10 or more.

Tapa't *(Carrer de la Cort Reial)* has a great range of tapas from €1.95. There are vegetarian goodies at **La Polenta** *(Carrer de la Cort Reial 6)*, where main courses cost up to €7.20. Another veggie option, although not exclusively so, is **Sa Penyora** *(☎ 972 21 89 48, Carrer Nou del Teatre 3)*.

A great little Basque tavern and restaurant is **Zanpanzar** *(☎ 972 21 28 43, Carrer de la Cort Reial 10–12)*. It's usually packed with locals and offers *pinxos* (Basque tapas) and some fine meat dishes. Round off with *goxua intxaursaltsarekin*, a Basque tart consisting of biscuit, apple and an amazing nut sauce. Expect to fork out about €18 per head.

For tempting savoury and sweet crepes, head for **La Crêperie Bretonne** *(☎ 972 21 81 20, Carrer de la Cort Reial 14)*. This is the local branch of a popular eatery in Perpignan (southern France). They keep cooking until midnight, except on Sunday, when they are closed.

Cafè Le Bistrot *(☎ 972 21 88 03, Pujada de Sant Domènec)*, on one of the most picturesque stairways in the old town, is a treat. Vaguely bohemian, it serves salads, *pizzes de pagès* (good, little bread-based pizzas) and crepes for between €3 and €4.20. They also offer tasty lunch set menus that change daily. Also nice is the calm **Cafè La Llibreria** *(☎ 972 20 48 18, Carrer de les Ferreries Velles)*, doing light meals such as lasagne or *escalivada* (grilled red peppers and aubergines) for €4.20 or green salads for up to €3.60.

La Força Vella *(Carrer de la Força 4)* has a four-course *menú* for €9. Much better lit and easily more inviting is **Cipresaia** *(☎ 972 22 24 49, Carrer de Blas Fournàs 2)*, where you can tuck into paella and fideuá. It closes on Monday night and Tuesday.

Plaça de la Independència in the new town is a popular munching area. The busy **Boira Restaurant** *(☎ 972 20 30 96, Plaça*

COSTA BRAVA

de la Independència 17) is an old stalwart. They do reasonable Catalan dishes and you should be lightened by not much more than €15 for a full meal.

Entertainment

Students make the nightlife here, so in summer things tend to calm down. Thursday is actually the big night, as most people head for the coast at the weekend.

The old town has lots of good bars and cafes for evening *copas* (drinks) along Rambla de la Llibertat and around Carrer de Carreras Peralta. A seemingly nameless *cafe (Carrer de les Ballesteries 23)* stays open longer than some and is a popular spot overlooking the river. If the Irish theme is your thing, try *Escalibur Celtic Ale House (Carrer de la Cort Reial)*. *El Cercle (☎ 972 22 45 29, Carrer dels Ciutadans 8)* is a charming place for a quiet drink carved out of a medieval warren of stone arches and timber.

You can keep going to 3 am or so near the river just north of the old town, where streets such as Carrer de Palafrugell and Ronda de Pedret harbour several lively and varied music bars. On the former, *Silent Block* at No 20 is good, while *La Via* at Ronda de Pedret 66 is also busy.

In summer, a series of drinking tents *(las carpas)* go up in the park west of the railway line – that's where the action is at that time of year. Across the road, the cybertechno *Sala del Ball (☎ 972 21 55 39, Carrer del Riu Güell 2)* is Girona's dance destination on Thursday nights. For dancing you can also try *La Sala del Cel (☎ 972 21 46 64, Ronda de Pedret 118)*.

Getting There & Away

Air Girona's airport (☎ 972 47 43 43), 11km south of the centre just off the A-7 and N-II, is devoted to summer charter flights for Costa Brava tourists. The occasional Buzz flight from London also lands here, along with a weekly service from Madrid.

Bus Barcelona Bus (☎ 972 20 24 32) runs to/from Barcelona's Estació del Nord (€8.70, 1¼ hours) and Figueres (€3.50, 50 minutes) three to seven times daily. SARFA (☎ 972 20 17 96) runs buses to most parts of the Costa Brava. TEISA (☎ 972 20 02 75) runs eight services daily (four on Sunday) to Besalú (€2.30, 50 minutes) and Olot (€4, 1¼ hours).

Train Girona is on the railway between Barcelona, Figueres and Portbou on the French border. There are around 20 trains daily to Figueres (€2 to €2.30 in 2nd class, 30–40 minutes) and Barcelona (€4.75 to €5.50, 1½ hours), and about 15 to Portbou and/or Cerbère (€3.10 to €3.60). A few trains go through to Montpellier in France, or beyond.

Getting Around

There's no airport bus service. You can call a taxi on ☎ 972 20 10 20 or ☎ 972 22 23 33, which from the city to the airport is likely to cost between €9 and €11.

Parking in the old town is fraught, but you can leave your metal steed in several parking areas across the river.

AROUND GIRONA
Banyoles
postcode 17820 • pop 11,570

Although some form of settlement has existed here since Roman times, the main reason for dropping in is not any man-made splendour but rather the natural curio of its figure-of-eight *estany* (lake). Fed by subterranean aquifers feeding off the Riu Fluvià, the level of the lake has the disconcerting habit of ebbing and flowing, on occasion at least, with dramatic haste. It is a favourite spot with locals for pottering about in shallow-bottom boats.

Regular TEISA buses run from Girona and Figueres.

Besalú
postcode 17850 • pop 1991

In the 10th and 11th centuries, pretty Besalú was the capital of an independent county that stretched as far west as Cerdanya, before it came under Barcelona's control in 1111.

Most picturesque of all is the view of the village across the tall, crooked 11th-century pont fortificat (fortified bridge), with its two tower-gates, from the southern side of the Fluvià.

The tourist office (☎ 972 59 12 40) on the arcaded central square, Plaça de la Llibertat, opens 10 am to 2 pm and 4 to 7 pm daily but only from June to mid-October. It hands out a decent map-brochure, sells €0.60 tickets for the Miqvé (a 12th-century Jewish ritual bath by the river) and does worthwhile guided visits to the Miqvé, the bridge and the Romanesque Església de Sant Vicenç, otherwise normally closed. Have a look at the 11th-century Romanesque church of the Monestir de Sant Pere, with an unusual ambulatory (walkway) behind the altar, and the 12th-century Romanesque Casa Cornellà.

Places to Stay & Eat There are three good little places to stay. *Habitacions Venència* (☎ 972 59 12 57, Carrer Major 8) has singles/doubles for €15.65/27. *Fonda Siqués* (☎ 972 59 01 10, fax 972 59 12 43, Avinguda del President Lluís Companys 6) offers doubles with bathroom for up to €39. *Residència Marià* (☎ 972 59 01 06, Plaça de la Llibertat 7) has doubles with bathroom, TV and heating (handy in winter) for €27.

Restaurant Can Quei (☎ 972 59 00 85), facing Església de Sant Vicenç, has a three-course *menú* for €8.40 including wine. It closes on Wednesday. An old favourite is *Restaurant Pont Vell*, by the bridge, where good Catalan main courses can cost up to €11.10. The classiest operation is *Els Fogons de Can Llaudes* (☎ 972 59 08 58, Prat de Sant Pere 6), opposite the Monestir de Sant Pere. It's set in an elegant stone former chapel and offers imaginative twists on old themes. Main courses cost from €7.50 to €17.15. You'd pay the latter for the *solomillo*, a tender loin slab of beef bathed in a raisin-based sauce.

Getting There & Away The N-260 road from Figueres to Olot meets the C-66 from Girona at Besalú. See the Girona and Figueres sections for information on TEISA bus services to Besalú and onto Olot. The stop in Besalú is on the main road just west of Fonda Siqués.

TORROELLA DE MONTGRÍ
postcode 17257 • pop 8020

On the Riu Ter about 30km north-east of Girona and 15km north of Palafrugell, the agreeable old town of Torroella de Montgrí is the funnel through which travellers to the coastal resort of L'Estartit must pass.

The tourist office (☎ 972 75 19 10) is on Carretera de l'Estartit.

Things to See & Do
About 100m south of the porticoed central square, Plaça de la Vila, in an old mansion at Carrer Major 28, the Museu del Montgrí will tell you about local history and archaeology, and a bit about the Illes Medes off L'Estartit. It opens 10 am to 2 pm and 6 to 9 pm (5 to 7 pm from October to March) Monday to Saturday, and 11 am to 2 pm on Sunday and holidays (closed Tuesday and holidays from October to March). Admission is free. Three blocks north of Plaça de la Vila is the Església de Sant Genis, which is mainly 15th-century Gothic (with fine ceiling tracery) but has an 18th-century baroque main facade at the western end.

Overlooking the town from the top of the 300m limestone Montgrí hills to the north, the impressive but empty Castell de Montgrí was built between 1294 and 1301 for King Jaume II in his efforts to bring to heel the disobedient counts of Empúries, to the north. There's no road and by foot it's a 40-minute climb from Torroella. Head north from Plaça del Lledoner along Carrer de Fàtima, at the end of which is a sign pointing you to the castle.

Places to Stay & Eat
Open year round apart from December and a block north of Plaça de la Vila, *Pensió Mitjà* (☎ 972 75 80 03, Carrer de l'Església 14) has bare but decent singles/doubles with bathroom and TV for €15.65/31.25. They do food too.

The *cafes* on Plaça de la Vila are the best place for snacks and people-watching.

Getting There & Away
AMPSA (☎ 972 75 82 33) at Plaça d'Espanya 19 (three blocks west, then two south,

COSTA BRAVA

from Plaça de la Vila) runs hourly buses to L'Estartit from June to September and about half that during the rest of the year. The same company runs two to four buses daily to Girona (one hour). SARFA (☎ 972 75 90 04) at Passeig de Catalunya 61 (three blocks east, then one north, from Plaça de la Vila) has three or four buses daily to Barcelona's Estació del Nord (1¾ hours), Palafrugell (25 minutes) and Figueres (1¼ hours).

VERGES
postcode 17142 • pop 1127
About 15km east of Girona, this town has little to offer, but if you happen to be in the area on Holy Thursday (Easter) make an effort to see the rather macabre evening procession, the Dansa de la Mort. People dressed up as skeletons dance the Dance of Death through the streets in a festivity that seems to have little to do with the Last Supper! The fun usually starts at about 10 pm. Girona-Torroella buses pass through here.

L'ESTARTIT & ILLES MEDES
postcode 17258 • pop 915
L'Estartit, 6km east of Torroella de Montgrí, is at the top end of the long, wide Platja de Pals but otherwise has nothing over any other Costa Brava package resort – except for the Illes Medes (Islas Medes). The group of rocky islets barely 1km offshore are home to some of the most abundant marine life on Spain's Mediterranean coast.

The main road in from Torroella de Montgrí is called Avinguda de Grècia as it approaches the beach; the beachfront road is Passeig Marítim, at the northern end of which is the tourist office (☎ 972 75 19 10).

Illes Medes
The shores and waters around these seven islets, an offshore continuation of the limestone Montgrí hills, have been protected since 1985 as a Reserva Natural Submarina (Underwater Natural Reserve), which has brought a proliferation in their marine life and made them Spain's most popular goal for snorkellers and divers. Some 1345 plant and animal species have been identified here. There's a big bird population too; one

of the Mediterranean's biggest colonies of yellow-legged gulls (8000 pairs) breeds here between March and May.

A series of kiosks by the harbour at the northern end of the beach offer snorkelling and glass-bottomed boat trips to the islands. Other boat trips go to a series of caves along the coast to the north, or combine these with the Illes Medes. A two-hour snorkelling trip to the Illes Medes costs anything up to €15. Trips go frequently every day from June to September and, depending on demand, in April, May and October. Snorkelling, diving and other activities all tend to cost more in the peak months of July and August.

Diving
The range of depths (down to 50m), and the number of underwater cavities and tunnels around the Illes Medes contribute much to their attraction. On and around rocks near the surface are colourful algae and sponges as well as octopuses, crabs and some large and small fish. Below 10 or 15m, cavities and caves harbour lobsters, scorpion fish, large conger eels and groupers. If you get down to the sea floor you may see angler fish, thornback rays and marbled electric rays.

At least half a dozen outfits in L'Estartit can take you out scuba diving, at the Medes or off the mainland coast – the tourist office has a list of them. It's worth shopping around before taking the plunge. If you're already a qualified diver, a single two-hour trip usually costs up to €25.25 per person. If you need to rent all the gear, the extra cost will be somewhere between €12 and €21. Night dives are possible too (usually about €27). If you're a novice, you can can do a one-day introductory course for around €42 or a full, five-day PADI Open Water Diver course for €240 to €360.

Places to Stay
Apart from the eight camping grounds in and around the town, budget accommodation doesn't really exist unless you're on a package. Two of the camping grounds, *La Sirena* (☎ 972 75 15 42, fax 972 75 09 44 *Avinguda de la Pletera s/n*) and *Les Medes*

(☎ 972 75 18 05, fax 972 75 04 13, Paratge Camp de l'Arbre), open year round.

Some of the better options are opposite the harbour at the northern end of the beach. **Hotel Les Illes** *(☎ 972 75 12 39, fax 972 75 00 86, Carrer de les Illes 55)* has singles/doubles with bathroom for €32.60/45.60 with breakfast. A cheap if very plain deal is **Pensió Santa Clara** *(☎ 972 75 17 67, fax 972 75 06 41, Passeig Marítim 18)*, where rooms cost €21.65/39.70.

Places to Eat

The northern end of Passeig Marítim, by the roundabout, is swarming with eateries, as is its immediate vicinity. These places are all pretty similar, presenting a mix of Spanish fare and straightforward chicken-and-chips-style meals.

For something with a little more class, try **Restaurant Robert** *(☎ 972 75 01 87, Passeig Marítim 59)*. The old house, set in luxuriant gardens, looks like it should perhaps be in the Swiss Alps. It ain't cheap though and the budget conscious might want to stick to the set lunch menu for €10.50.

Getting There & Away

AMPSA buses to Torroella de Montgrí (about one hourly) and Girona (three or four daily) go from Passeig Marítim, 150m south of the tourist office. SARFA runs buses to Barcelona three or four-times daily.

L'ESCALA & EMPÚRIES
postcode 17130 • pop 5942

L'Escala, on the coast 11km north of Torroella de Montgrí, is a pleasant medium-sized resort on the southern shore of the Golf de Roses. It's close to the ancient town of Empúries (Ampurias in Castilian) and, a few kilometres farther north, the wetlands of the Parc Natural dels Aiguamolls de l'Empordà.

Orientation & Information

If you arrive by SARFA bus, you'll alight on L'Escala's Plaça de les Escoles, where you'll find the tourist office (☎ 972 77 06 03) at No 1. The tourist office's summer hours are 9 am to 8 pm Monday to Saturday

and 10 am to 1 pm on Sunday. Empúries is 1km round the coast to the north-west of the town centre.

Empúries

Empúries was probably the first, and certainly one of most important, Greek colonies on the Iberian Peninsula. Early Greek traders, pushing on from a trading post at Masilia (modern Marseilles in France), set up a new post around 600 BC at what's now the village of Sant Martí d'Empúries, then an island. Soon afterwards they founded a mainland colony nearby, which forms part of the site you visit today. The colony came to be called Emporion (literally 'market') and remained an important trading centre, and conduit of Greek culture to the Iberians, for centuries.

Empúries was also the place where, in 218 BC, Roman legions landed in Spain to cut off Hannibal's supply lines in the Second Punic War. About 195 BC they set up a military camp and by 100 BC had added a town. A century later it had merged with the Greek one. Emporiae, as the place was then known, was abandoned in the late 3rd century AD after raids by Germanic tribes. Later, an early Christian basilica and cemetery stood on the site of the Greek town, before the whole place, after over a millennium of use, disappeared altogether, to be rediscovered by archaeologists at the turn of the 20th century.

Many of the ancient stones now laid bare don't rise more than knee-high. You need a little imagination – and perhaps the aid of a taped commentary (€1.80 from the ticket office) – to make the most of it.

The Site In spring and summer the site opens 10 am to 8 pm, with a pedestrian entrance from the seafront promenade in front of the ruins; just follow the coast from L'Escala to reach it. At other times the opening hours are 10 am to 6 pm and the only way in is the vehicle approach from the Figueres road, about 2km from central L'Escala. Admission costs €2.40.

The Greek town lies in the lower part of the site, closer to the shore. Main points of

COSTA BRAVA

interest include the thick southern defensive walls; the site of the Asklepion, a shrine to the god of medicine, with a copy of his statue found here; and the *agora* (town square), with remnants of the early Christian basilica and the Greek *stoa* (market complex), beside it.

A small museum separates the Greek town from the larger Roman town on the upper part of the site (the Museu d'Arqueologia in Barcelona has a better Empúries collection). Highlights of the Roman town include mosaic floors of a 1st-century-BC house, the Forum, and the strong 1st-century-BC walls, said to have been built by Julius Caesar. Outside the walls are the remains of an oval amphitheatre.

A string of brown-sand beaches stretches along in front of the site. On one stands a Greek stone jetty.

Places to Stay
Camping The nearest camp site to the centre of L'Escala is the small *Camping La Escala* (☎ *972 77 00 84, Camí d'Ample 21)*, about 700m south of La Platja. It opens mid-April to late September. There are four other sites 2km to 4km east of the centre in the Riells and Montgó areas of town and a further half-dozen or so along or near the beach within a few kilometres north of Empúries.

Hostels The *Alberg d'Empúries* (☎ *972 77 12 00, Les Coves 41)* is just south of the Empúries ruins. It has room for 68 people, in dorms of six or more. High-season rates are charged from April to September.

Hostales, Pensiones & Hotels A good bet, although often booked up in high season, is *Hostal Mediterrà* (☎ *972 77 00 28, fax 972 77 45 93, Carrer de Riera 22–4)*, a block west of Carrer del Pintor Joan Massanet. Singles/doubles with shower cost €15.40/30.80 in summer. Equally good is *Pensió Torrent* (☎ *972 77 02 78, Carrer de Riera 28)* with rooms costing €12/26.15. Singles are hard to come by in summer.

A step up in quality is *Hostal El Roser* (☎ *972 77 02 19, fax 972 77 45 29, Carrer*

de l'Església 7), on the first street on the right as you go down Carrer de Santa Màxima from Plaça de les Escoles. Good-sized modern rooms with TV and bathroom are €22.55/35.45 plus IVA. In high season half-board (which is obligatory) costs €31.25 per person.

On Passeig de Lluís Albert, 10 minutes' walk east along the seafront from La Platja, *Hotel Voramar* (☎ *972 77 01 08)* at No 2 has rooms for €31.25/59.20 plus IVA; *Hotel Bonaire* (☎ *972 77 32 33)* at No 4 charges €31.95/63.85 plus IVA for B&B.

Places to Eat
L'Escala is famous for its *anchoas* (anchovies) and good fresh local fish, both of which are likely to crop up on *menús*.

The seafront restaurants are mostly expensive but, if your wallet is fat enough, try *Els Pescadors* (☎ *972 77 07 28, Port d'En Perris 5)*, in the next bay west from La Platja (five minutes' walk), which does superb baked and grilled seafood, *suquet* (seafood stew) and rice dishes. You will pay from €18 to €24 a head unless you opt for the *menú* at €13.20. *L'Olla* and *Volantí*, also on Port d'En Perris, both do pizzas for around €4.20 to €5.70.

A really cute place for a simple *torrada* (open toasted sandwich) with various toppings and other light meals is the attractively decorated *Café dell'Arte* (☎ *972 77 44 96, Carrer de Calvari 1)*, a few minutes' walk in from the seafront.

Getting There & Away
SARFA has one bus from Barcelona (via Palafrugell) on weekdays (1½ hours), rising to three on Sunday. Five run daily to Figueres (50 minutes) and two to Girona (one hour).

PARC NATURAL DELS AIGUAMOLLS DE L'EMPORDÀ
This natural park preserves the remnants of marshes that once covered the whole coastal plain of the Golf de Roses, an important site for migrating birds. Birdwatchers have spotted over 100 species a day in the March to May and August to

October migration periods, which bring big increases in the numbers of wading birds and even the occasional flamingo, glossy ibis, spoonbill or rare black stork. There are usually enough birds around to make a visit worthwhile at any time of year.

The best place to head for is El Cortalet information centre (☎ 972 45 42 22), 1km east off the Sant Pere Pescador–Castelló d'Empúries road. Marked paths lead to a 2km stretch of beach and a number of hides *(aguaits)* where you can view saltwater marshes and their bird life. From the top of the Observatori Senillosa, a former silo, you can see out across the whole park. The paths are always open, but morning and evening are the best times for watching birds (and mosquitoes!). The information centre opens 9.30 am to 2 pm and 4.30 to 7 pm mid-June to mid-September (3.30 to 6 pm the rest of the year).

The nearest places to El Cortalet that you can reach by bus are Sant Pere Pescador, 6km south (served by four or five SARFA buses daily from L'Escala and Figueres), and Castelló d'Empúries, 4km north.

CASTELLÓ D'EMPÚRIES
postcode 17487 • pop 3640
This was the capital of Empúries, a medieval Catalan county that maintained a large degree of independence up to the 14th century. At the heart of the narrow streets in the old part of town you'll find Plaça dels Homes, with a tourist office (☎ 972 15 62 33) in a 14th-century building.

The finest monument is the **Església de Santa Maria** on Plaça de Jacint Verdaguer, a large 13th- and 14th-century Gothic church with a fine Romanesque bell tower remaining from an earlier church on the site.

Places to Stay & Eat
Of the eight options here, *Hotel Canet* *(☎ 972 25 03 40, fax 972 25 06 07, Plaça del Joc de la Pilota 2)*, a modernised 17th-century mansion in the centre, has elegant singles/doubles with bathroom and breakfast for €27/45.10 (plus IVA) and a swimming pool in an interior courtyard. Its restaurant is reasonably priced.

In the newer part of town just to the south there are several options. *Hostal Ca L'Anton (☎ 972 25 05 09, Carrer de Santa Clara 23)* has rooms for €21/30.90; *Pensió/Fonda Serratosa (☎ 972 25 05 08, Carrer de Santa Clara 14)* charges €14.40 per person plus IVA.

For your grumbling tummy, head for *El Portal de la Gallarda*, on the street of the same name about 50m away from the left flank of the church. It's partly set behind a Romanesque gate and you can snack on *torrades* (€3) in the garden.

Getting There & Away
SARFA runs up to 15 buses daily to Figueres (15 minutes), as few as three to Cadaqués (50 minutes), three daily to/from Girona (45 minutes) and up to four to Barcelona's Estació del Nord (1½ hours).

EMPURIABRAVA
Turn up here on anything but a brilliant summer's day and melancholy is bound to set in. Awkward-looking holiday-makers from various northern climes potter about the wide streets and press their noses up against the windows of plasticised holiday costa restaurants and souvenir shops. Unless of course they are at the local German bakery or in a *Kneipe* (tavern) sipping on a fine German pils.

Only a few kilometres from Castelló d'Empúries, Empuriabrava is in effect the 'new town' extension of that infinitely more charming village. And it is a curious animal. With grid pattern precision a system of canals flanked by luxurious housing (mostly of the holiday variety) has been carved out just inland from the beach. Here wealthy locals and foreigners park their speed boats outside the front door, or timeshare interlopers look on in bemused envy. Curious but disconcertingly devoid of soul. Still, the beach area shakes in summer, with a small but concentrated troop of bars at the Riu La Muga end of Avinguda de Fages de Climent. Four discos keep things moving into the wee hours.

The bulk of the accommodation is made up of holiday apartments. For information on their agents and the nine hotels and six camping grounds around here, go to the tourist office (☎ 972 45 08 02, e turisme@ empuriabrava.com) at Carrer de Puigmal 1. It opens 9 am to at least 8 pm daily. Regular SARFA buses between Figueres and Roses call in here.

ROSES

postcode 17480 • pop 11,590

From Roses, a sizable town on the northern flank of the gulf of the same name, you can clearly make out one of the Costa Brava's biggest eyesores – a mountainous beehive-like concrete apartment block that blights the coast at the southern end of Empuriabrava.

As if in response, Roses (which some believe may be the site of the ancient Greek settlement of Rodes) boasts the impressive seaward wall of its 16th-century citadel. Inside little is left, apart from the ruins of a Romanesque church. Other than that there is not an awful lot more to the place. At least it is a real town and in that respect marginally more attractive than Empuriabrava. The main town beaches are OK but nothing spectacular – see Around Roses for more possibilities. As you head east around the coast (you can walk or drive), a couple of nicer options include **Platja de Canyelles Petites** and **Platja de l'Almadrava** (aka Canyelles Grosses).

The tourist office (☎ 902 10 36 36), at Avinguda de Rhode 101, is a useful stop for searching out accommodation options in and around Roses – almost 50 pensiones and hotels litter the place. The tourist office can also help you with lists of agents dealing in short-term apartment lets.

In summer Roses offers a busy nightlife. The heaviest concentration of bars is in the old centre, just in off Plaça de Sant Pere. *Intermezzo (Carrer de Joan Badosa 47)* is one of the best of them.

Le Rachdingue (☎ 972 53 00 23), on the Roses-Vilajuïga road between Vilajuïga and Pau, about 8km north-west of Roses, is one of the Costa Brava's meccas for lovers of a broad range of club music. Big name DJs from around Europe are wheeled in to this *masia* (country house) to spin their sets of house, jungle and the like. Clubbers from all over Europe make a special effort to get here. It is especially active in summer (the pool comes in handy!). Admission (including one drink) ranges from €9 to €15.

AROUND ROSES

If you have a vehicle, you can get well beyond the crowds of Roses into the southern end of the Parc Natural del Cap de Creus (see also that section later in this chapter). About 6km east of Roses, an asphalt road runs up into the hills behind the town and along the rugged and largely empty coast to **Cala Montjoi**. The beach is on the pebbly side but the inlet is a fine getaway.

Chef Ferran Adrià chose a magnificent spot, with views across the bay and out to sea, to site his gastronomic heaven – *El Bulli (972 15 04 57, e bulli@grn.es)* – one of Spain's top restaurants. Each season sees Adrià indulging himself with new experiments in international and Mediterranean cooking. The setting alone is worth the effort of getting here. A full meal (go with the flow and be guided by the chef's suggestions) can cost around €100 a head including wine. It closes Monday and Tuesday and from mid-October to mid-March.

Another 5km of mostly dirt track (driveable) lead around to a still wilder location, **Cala Jóncols**. Again the beach is grey and pebbly but the location, deep inside a protected bay, is splendid. There is even a place to stay and eat. *Hotel Cala Jóncols (☎ 972 25 39 70)* offers modest rooms and full board for €57.10 per person (€42.10 in slow periods and mid-week) plus IVA. You can eat on the terrace or inside in inclement weather. It makes a wonderful base for coastal walks. The hotel also caters for (mostly German) divers and will even serve up food to those on visiting boats. You can arrange to be taken to and from here by sea taxi from Empuriabrava and nearby Santa Margarita. Call well ahead to book in summer.

From Roses walkers have several options. Perhaps the most exhilarating is the **Camí de Ronda**, a coastal walking path that continues around to Cadaqués.

CADAQUÉS & AROUND
postcode 17488 • pop 1878

If you have time for only one stop on the Costa Brava, you can hardly do better than Cadaqués. Little more than a whitewashed village round a rocky bay, it and the surrounding area have a special magic – a fusion of wind, sea, light and rock – that isn't dissipated even by the throngs of mildly fashionable summer visitors.

Some of that magic is due to Salvador Dalí, who spent family holidays here in his youth and lived much of his later life at nearby Port Lligat. The empty moonscapes, odd-shaped rocks and barren shorelines that litter Dalí's paintings weren't just a product of his fertile imagination. They're strewn all round the Cadaqués area in what Dalí termed a 'grandiose geological delirium'.

The country here is drier than farther south. The sparseness continues to dramatic Cap de Creus, 8km north-east of Cadaqués, lending itself to some coastscapes of almost (if you'll permit us, Senyor Dalí) surreal beauty.

Thanks to Dalí and other artists, Cadaqués has pulled in an artistic, offbeat and celebrity crowd for decades. One visit by the poet Paul Éluard and his Russian wife Gala in 1929 caused an earthquake in Dalí's life: he broke with his family, ran off to Paris with Gala (who was to become his lifelong obsession and, later, his wife) and joined the surrealist movement. In the 1950s, after Dalí's success in the USA, the crowd he attracted was more jet-setting – Walt Disney, the Duke of Windsor and Greek ship-owner Stavros Niarchos. In the 1970s Mick Jagger and Gabriel García Márquez turned up. Today the crowd is neither so creative nor so famous – and a lot bigger – but Cadaqués' atmosphere remains.

Information

The tourist office (☎ 972 25 83 15) is at Carrer del Cotxe 2. It opens 10 am to 2 pm and

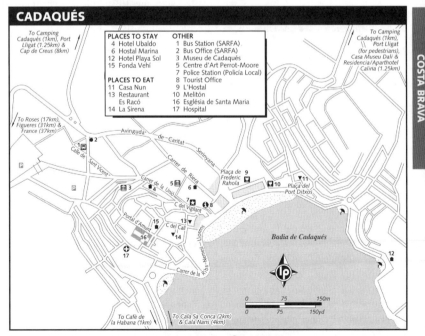

CADAQUÉS

To Camping
Cadaqués (1km), Port
Lligat (1.25km) &
Cap de Creus (8km)

To Camping
Cadaqués (1km),
Port Lligat
(for pedestrians),
Casa Museu Dalí &
Residencia/Aparthotel
Calina (1.25km)

PLACES TO STAY
4 Hotel Ubaldo
6 Hostal Marina
12 Hotel Playa Sol
15 Fonda Vehí

PLACES TO EAT
11 Casa Nun
13 Restaurant
Es Racó
14 La Sirena

OTHER
1 Bus Station (SARFA)
2 Bus Office (SARFA)
3 Museu de Cadaqués
5 Centre d'Art Perrot-Moore
7 Police Station (Policía Local)
8 Tourist Office
9 L'Hostal
10 Melitón
16 Església de Santa Maria
17 Hospital

To Roses (17km),
Figueres (31km) &
France (37km)

Avinguda de Caritat

Calle de Sant Vicent

Carrer de Riera

Carrer de la Unió

C. del Vigilant

Portal d'Amunt

C. del Call

Carrer Nemesi Llorens

Carrer de la Ribera

Plaça de Frederic Rahola

Plaça del Port Ditxos

Badia de Cadaqués

Carrer de la Ribera

To Café de la Habana (1km)

To Cala Sa Conca (2km) & Cala Nans (4km)

0   75   150m
0   75   150yd

COSTA BRAVA

4 to 7 pm (closed Wednesday afternoon and Sunday). The Policía Local (☎ 972 15 93 43) are a few steps behind the tourist office, on Carrer del Vigilant. There's a hospital (☎ 972 25 88 07) on Carrer de Guillem Bruguera, just west of the church.

The Town

Cadaqués is perfect for wandering, either around the town or along the coast. The 16th- and 17th-century **Església de Santa Maria**, with a gilded baroque altarpiece, is the focus of the older part with its narrow hilly streets.

Two art museums worth visiting are the **Centre d'Art Perrot-Moore** off Carrer del Vigilant, founded by Dalí's secretary and focusing on Dalí and Picasso. It was closed at the time of writing and there was no clear indication when it might reopen. The **Museu de Cadaqués**, Carrer de Narcís Monturiol 15, includes Dalí among other local artists. It generally opens 11 am to 1.30 pm and 3 to 8 pm daily; the cost of admission depends on the temporary exhibition being held.

Port Lligat

Port Lligat, a 1.25km walk from Cadaqués, is a tiny settlement around another lovely bay, with fishing boats pulled up on its beach. The **Casa Museu Dalí** here began as a fisherman's hut and was steadily altered and enlarged by Dalí, who lived here (apart from a dozen or so years abroad during and around the Spanish Civil War) from 1930 to 1982. It's the house with a lot of little white chimney pots and two egg-shaped towers, overlooking the western end of the beach.

Visits must be booked (☎ 972 25 80 63, allow three or four days in summer) and you are allowed a grand total of about 30 minutes inside. From mid-June to mid-September the house opens 10.30 am to 9 pm daily. From mid-March to mid-June and from mid-September to early January the hours are 10.30 am to 6 pm (closed Monday). The rest of the year it is shut. Admission costs €7.80 (students and seniors €4.80).

While here you can also join trip's on Dalí's boat, the *Gala*, to Cap de Creus. The jetty is just below the Casa Museu.

Beaches

Cadaqués' main beach, and several others along the nearby coasts, are small, with more pebbles than sand, but their picturesqueness and beautifully blue waters make up for that. Overlooking Platja Llaner on the southern side of the bay is Dalí's parents' holiday home; out the front is a statue by Josep Subirachs dedicated to Federico García Lorca, in memory of his stay in the 1920s.

About 2km south of Cadaqués, **Cala Sa Conca** is a pretty little beach easily reached on foot from the town. A little farther on you reach **Cala Nans**, also enticing. You can follow the Camí de Ronda and hike around to Roses across the southern limits of the Parc Natural del Cap de Creus. A similar track takes you beyond Port Lligat to the north as far as the cape itself.

Red Alert

Back in the 1890s, a Greek diver by the name of Georges Kontos arrived in Cadaqués, contracted to dive for coral. Red coral. For centuries this prized animal, found on the Catalan and Roussillon (France) coast, had been a major export business. In the 18th century Begur was the coral capital of the coast, but Cadaqués and other towns were never far behind. Red coral is the most prized by jewellers, and Catalan divers searched far and wide (elsewhere in the Mediterranean, Morocco, Portugal and even the Cape Verde islands) for the precious material.

Kontos' descendants continued the diving tradition but 'over-fishing' has left relatively little red coral intact off the Catalan coast. Only a handful of divers are still licensed and when they retire no more licences will be issued. The problem is that illegal divers will always be attracted to the increasingly rare red gold which has, in the past, been exported to Italian jewellers for as much as €2400 per kilo.

COSTA BRAVA

Places to Stay

Let's get one thing straight – Cadaqués, especially in high season, is anything but cheap. **Camping Cadaqués** (☎ *972 25 81 26)*, about 1km from central Cadaqués on the road to Port Lligat, has room for about 500 people and can get crowded. Two people with a tent and car pay €17.30 plus IVA. It opens from Setmana Santa to September.

Fonda Vehí (☎ *972 25 84 70, Carrer de l'Església 5)*, near the church, has single/double rooms with shared facilities costing €13.20/24. It tends to be booked up for July and August.

Hostal Marina (☎ *972 25 81 99, Carrer de Frederic Rahola 2)* is probably a better option, and has doubles costing up to €33 with washbasin only or €48.10 with bathroom.

Hotel Ubaldo (☎ *972 25 81 25, Carrer de la Unió 13)*, towards the back of the old part of town, has good rooms with bathroom, some with balcony, for €53.70/70.60 plus IVA.

Hotel Playa Sol (☎ *972 25 81 00, fax 972 25 80 54, Platja Pianc 5)* on the eastern side of the bay has doubles/triples for up to €132.20/164.70 plus IVA. Loners can take a double for €109.40. Rooms have air-con, satellite TV, and breakfast is included. There's a nice pool area too.

In Port Lligat, **Residencia/Aparthotel Calina** (☎ *972 25 88 51)*, near the small beach, has a range of pleasant modern rooms and one-room apartments costing up to €75.15.

Places to Eat

The eastern part of the central beachfront is lined with spots proffering uninspired *menús* for up to €9, or pizzas for about €4.80.

Restaurant Es Racó, (☎ *972 15 94 80, Carrer del Dr Callis 3)* does a fine *parrillada de pescado* (mixed seafood grill) for €13.20 per person. Its balcony overlooking the western half of the beach catches some breeze. **Fonda Vehí's** 2nd-floor restaurant does three-course *menús* for €7.50 to €9 plus IVA.

La Sirena (☎ *972 25 89 74)*, in a quiet little patio off Carrer del Call, is a romantic little eating hideaway. The blue-on-white decor is fine and transports you to the classic dreamed of Mediterranean setting. It is closed on Thursday out of high season.

Casa Nun (☎ *972 25 88 56, Plaça del Port Ditxos 6)* is another stylish bijou restaurant set back on a dainty square. From the tables outside you can look out over the Mediterranean. Prices are mid-range for local standards – around €12 for a main course. They close from Tuesday evening to Thursday lunchtime.

Entertainment

L'Hostal, facing the beachfront *passeig* has live music on many nights. Press clippings posted outside proclaim that one night in the 1970s Dalí called it the '*lugar más bonito del mundo*' ('the most beautiful place on earth'). The beachfront **Melitón** bar has a fine *terraza* (terrace) but with prices to match. If that doesn't bother you it's equally enchanting for breakfast. **Café de la Habana**, a Cadaqués classic about 1km from the centre heading south along the coastal esplanade, can get lively too.

Getting There & Away

SARFA (☎ *972 25 87 13)* has buses to Castelló d'Empúries and Figueres (one hour) up to eight times daily (three in winter), to Girona (1½ hours) three times daily (one in winter) and to Barcelona (2¼ hours) two to five times daily.

CADAQUÉS TO THE FRENCH BORDER

The proud and craggy countenance of Spain's easternmost point is an inevitable stop for anyone with the wheels or legs to carry them around here. Beyond the peninsula, the Costa Brava continues its march northwards to the French border. A string of low-key coastal towns, particularly El Port de la Selva and Llançà, are not bad stops and particularly favoured by the French who pour across the frontier for a slight *frisson* of contact with Spain. Locals almost speak better French than Spanish!

COSTA BRAVA

Cap de Creus

Eight kilometres north-east of Cadaqués by road, Cap de Creus is the most easterly point of the Spanish mainland and a place of sublime, rugged beauty. With a steep, rocky coastline indented by dozens of lovely, turquoise-watered coves, it's an especially wonderful place to be at dawn or sunset. Atop the cape stand a lighthouse and a quirky little English-run restaurant. The **Bar Restaurant Cap de Creus** (☎ *972 19 90 05*) opens year round. You can eat anything from carrot cake to UK-Indian cuisine. They also have four double rooms upstairs, for which they charge €48.10 to €72.10.

More tempting walking, with some spectacular little beaches as reward en route, suggests itself west of the eyesore that is the Club Méditerranée. Follow the GR11 for the 13km inland walk west to El Port de la Selva across this northern end of the Parc Natural del Cap de Creus. Side tracks (not well indicated) lead down to some great little inlets, such as **Cala Portaló** and, about halfway along the route, **Cala Tavallera**. You need to take food and fresh water with you. On summer weekends you may well find yourself sharing the pebbly beach with yachties. For other beaches closer to El Port de la Selva, see the following section.

El Port de la Selva

The first town as you head west out of the Parc Natural del Cap de Creus, El Port de la Selva is a low-key fishing and yachties' haven, laid out north-to-south along a lick of land closing off the eastern side of the eponymous bay. There is not a great deal to the place and the town beach is no great shakes. The views across the bay, however, are pleasant and it makes a nice base for some walks east into the park. Coastal walking tracks lead you out along the jagged edges of the coast (which takes on an especially temperamental appearance when the tramuntana blows) in the direction of Cap de Creus. About 3km traipsing (and just a little scrambling) brings you to a lovely little inlet, **Cala Fornells**. It's on the pebbly side, but a magnificent little spot with not a drink stand in sight (so bring

plenty of water and food). On a calm day the water is like a mirror.

Places to Stay & Eat Should you want to stay in El Port de la Selva you have several options. Prices are high however. **Pensión Sol y Sombra** (☎ *972 38 70 60, Carrer Nou 8*) has clean if small rooms that are about as good as you will find in this price range here. Doubles start at around €40.90 plus IVA.

Ca L'Herminda (☎ *972 38 70 75, Carrer de l'Illa 7*) is the place to head for a little splurge at dinner time. They do a succulent *suquet de peix* (a kind of mixed fish hotpot) for two for €35.45. The various sea critters, accompanied by potatoes, melt in your mouth.

For an after-dinner drink or three head to the only really happening bar in town, **Gus Bar** (*Carrer de Lloia 1*), north along the waterfront.

Monestir de Sant Pere de Rodes

Another possible reason for basing yourself in El Port de la Selva is to make an excursion to this spectacularly located Romanesque monastery, which looms at an altitude of 500m in the hills south-west of the town.

Founded in the 8th century, it later became the most powerful monastery between Figueres and Perpignan (in France). The great triple-naved, barrel-vaulted basilica is flanked by the fine square Torre de Sant Miquel bell tower and a two-level cloister. The buildings are fine but the setting more so. Follow the walking tracks up behind the monastery to the ruined castle higher up and enjoy the splendid views out to sea. The monastery opens 10 am to 8 pm daily except Monday, June to the end of September. The rest of the year it closes at 5.30 pm. Admission costs €1.80 (students €0.90) or it is free on Tuesday.

Getting There & Away The monastery is on a back road over the hills between Vilajuïga, 8km to its west, and El Port de la Selva, 5km north-east. Each town is served by three or four SARFA buses from

Figueres daily, but there are no buses to the monastery. Vilajuïga is also on the railway between Figueres and Portbou.

Llançà to France

From El Port de la Selva, the coast road proceeds around the bay to the growing residential sprawl of Llançà. The town is, if anything, a larger version of El Port de la Selva. Because the railway line between France and Barcelona passes through here, along with the busy N-260 highway, the town has developed much more than El Port de la Selva. The town beach is nothing special, but coastal walking paths lead you to more attractive options not a great deal farther out of the centre.

Beyond Llançà, the towns of **Grifeu**, **Colera** and **Portbou** are the only inhabited stops along the coast north. None are remarkable, if you except the extraordinary sight of the masses of railway sidings as you descend onto Portbou from the high hill roads from the south or north. It is much like its twin, **Cerbère**, just over on the French side of the frontier. Both towns are equipped to adjust the gauge of trains travelling in either direction to/from the standard European gauge in France and the extra-wide version used in Spain.

FIGUERES
postcode 17600 • pop 33,600
Twelve kilometres inland from the Golf de Roses, Figueres (Figueras in Castilian) is a humdrum town (some might say a dive) with a single attraction: Salvador Dalí. In the 1960s and '70s Dalí created here, in the town of his birth, the extraordinary Teatre-Museu Dalí. Whatever your feelings about old Salvador, this is worth every minute you spend on it.

Orientation

From the bus and train stations, on Plaça de l'Estació, it's a 10-minute walk north-west to the central boulevard, the Rambla. The Teatre-Museu Dalí is 200m north of the Rambla, with most of the sleeping and eating options concentrated within a few blocks of it.

Information

The tourist office (☎ 972 50 31 55) on Plaça del Sol opens 9 am to 9 pm Monday to Saturday, and 9 am to 3 pm on Sunday, June to mid-September; 8.30 am to 3 pm and 4.30 to 7.30 pm Monday to Friday, and 9.30 am to 1.30 pm and 3.30 to 7.30 pm Saturday, the rest of the year.

There's no shortage of banks or ATMs in the central area. American Express is at the travel agency Viatges Figueres (☎ 972 50 91 00) on Carrer de Peralada 28.

The post office is on Carrer de Santa Llogàia. You can go on-line at a couple of places along Carrer de Sant Antoni. Bar Arcadia (☎ 972 67 38 91) at No 7 opens 9 am to 10 pm daily except Sunday. Down the road at Pizz@fono (☎ 972 67 71 77), a takeaway pizza joint at No 27, you can navigate until 11 pm (closed Monday).

The police are on Carrer de Pep Ventura. A Creu Roja (Red Cross; ☎ 972 50 17 99) post is at Carrer de Santa Llogàia 67 and there's a hospital on Ronda del Rector Aroles.

Teatre-Museu Dalí

Salvador Dalí was born in Figueres in 1904 and went to school here. Although his career took him for spells to Madrid, Barcelona, Paris and the USA, he remained true to his roots and lived well over half his adult life at Port Lligat, near Cadaqués, on the coast east of Figueres. Between 1961 and 1974 Dalí converted Figueres' former municipal theatre, ruined by a fire at the end of the Civil War, into the Teatre-Museu Dalí. 'Theatre-museum' is an apt label for this multidimensional trip through one of the most fertile (or disturbed) imaginations of the 20th century, full of surprises, tricks and illusions, and containing a substantial portion of his life's work. 'The museum should not be considered as a museum, it is a gigantic surrealist object, everything in it is coherent, there is nothing which escapes my net of understandings,' explained its creator with characteristic modesty.

Even outside, the building aims to surprise, from the collection of bizarre sculptures outside the entrance on Plaça de Gala

COSTA BRAVA

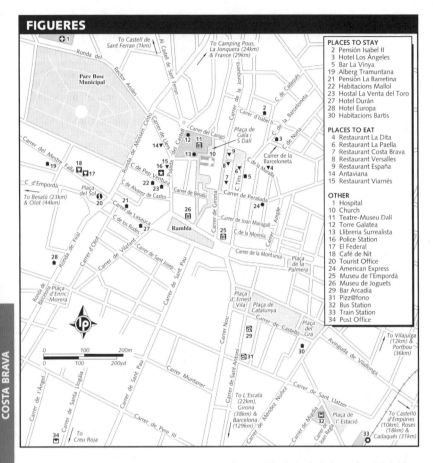

FIGUERES

i Salvador Dalí to the pink wall along Pujada del Castell, topped by a row of Dalí's trademark egg shapes and what appear to be female gymnast sculptures.

Inside, the ground floor (level 1) includes a semicircular garden area on the site of the original theatre stalls. In its centre is a classic piece of weirdness called *Taxi Plujós* (Rainy Taxi), composed of an early Cadillac – said to have belonged to Al Capone – and a pile of tractor tyres, both surmounted by statues, with a fishing boat balanced precariously above the tyres. Put a coin in the slot and water washes all over the inside of

the car. The Sala de Peixateries (Fish Shop Room) off here holds a collection of Dalí oils including the famous *Autoretrat tou amb tall de bacon fregit* (Self-Portrait with Fried Bacon) and *Retrat de Picasso*. Beneath the former stage of the theatre is the crypt, with Dalí's plain tomb.

The stage area (level 2), topped by a glass geodesic dome, was conceived as Dalí's Sistine Chapel. Part of a ballet set, the large egg-head-breasts-rocks-trees backdrop was one of Dalí's many ventures into the performing arts. If proof were needed of Dalí's acute sense of the absurd, *Gala mirando el*

Mar Mediterráneo (Gala looking at the Mediterranean Sea) would be it. The work appears from the other end of the room, with the help of coin-operated viewfinders, to be a portrait of Abraham Lincoln. Off this room is the Sala del Tresor, where paintings such as *La panera del pa* (Breadbasket) show that Dalí was a master draughtsman, too.

One floor up (level 3) you come across the Sala de Mae West, a living room whose components, viewed from the right spot, make up a portrait of Ms West: a sofa for her lips, twin fireplaces for nostrils, impressionist paintings of Paris for eyes. On the top floor (level 5) is a room containing works by other artists from Dalí's own collection, including El Greco's *Sant Pau* (St Paul).

In 2000 the museum acquired the Owen Cheatham collection of 37 magnificent jewels designed by Dalí. It was planned to have them housed in a separate annex of the museum by the end of 2001.

The museum opens 9 am to 7.15 pm daily from July to September and for most of this period there are night sessions from 10 pm to 12.30 am. Queues are long on summer mornings. It opens 10.30 am to 5.15 pm daily, October to June (closed on Monday until the end of May, on 1 January and 25 December). Admission costs €6 and €7.20 for the summer night sessions.

Other Things to See & Do

The **Museu de l'Empordà** at Rambla 2 combines Greek, Roman and medieval archaeological finds with a sizable collection of art, mainly by Catalan artists but there's also some works lent by the Museo del Prado in Madrid. It opens 11 am to 7 pm Tuesday to Saturday and 10 am to 2 pm Sunday and holidays, mid-June to mid-September; 11 am to 1.30 pm and 3 to 7 pm Tuesday to Saturday and 11 am to 1.30 pm Sunday, the rest of the year. Admission costs €1.80.

At Rambla 10, the **Museu de Joguets**, Spain's only toy museum, has more than 3500 Catalunya- and Valencia-made toys from the pre-Barbie 19th and early 20th centuries. It opens 10 am to 1 pm and 4 to 7 pm Wednesday to Monday, and 11 am to

1.30 pm Sunday (also 5 to 7 pm July to September). It closes mid-January to the end of February. Admission costs a rather hefty €4.50.

The large 18th-century **Castell de Sant Ferran** stands on a low hill 1km north-west of the centre. Built in 1750, it saw almost no action in the following centuries. After abandoning Barcelona, Spain's Republican government held its final meeting of the Civil War on 1 February 1939 in the castle's dungeons. It opens 10.30 am to 2 pm daily (until 8 pm from July to mid-September). Admission costs €2.10.

Places to Stay – Budget

Camping Pous (☎ 972 67 54 96), north of the centre on the N-II towards La Jonquera, is small and charges €12 for a tent site, car and two people. It closes in December. Don't sleep in the Parc Bosc Municipal: people have been attacked there at night.

The *Alberg Tramuntana* (☎ 972 50 12 13, Carrer d'Anicet de Pagès 2), a youth hostel two blocks west of the tourist office, has only 56 places (in dorms of four to 24) but opens nearly year round; high-season rates are charged from July to September.

Habitacions Bartis (☎ 972 50 14 73, Carrer de Méndez Núñez 2), on the way into the centre from the bus and train stations, has adequate singles/doubles for €10.20/16.25 plus IVA.

Bar La Vinya (☎ 972 50 00 49, Carrer de Tins 18), three short blocks east of the Teatre-Museu Dalí, has bare rooms up the street on Carrer de la Muralla for €7.20/14.40.

Pensión Isabel II (☎ 972 50 47 35, Carrer d'Isabel II 16) has reasonable rooms with bathroom for €16.85. *Hostal La Venta del Toro* (☎ 972 51 05 10, Carrer de Pep Ventura 5) has bare but adequate doubles costing €22.25, or one with its own shower for €24. *Habitacions Mallol* (☎ 972 50 22 83), along the street at No 9, charges €12/20.75.

A better quality place to sleep is *Pensión La Barretina* (☎ 972 67 64 12, Carrer de Lasauca 13), where comfortable rooms with their own bathrooms cost €21/36.

COSTA BRAVA

Hotel Los Ángeles (☎ *972 51 06 61, Carrer de Barceloneta 10)* is good value with spacious rooms for €25.10/36 plus IVA. *Hotel Europa* (☎ *972 50 07 44, Ronda de Firal 37)* is another respectable mid-range hotel. Rooms with bathroom cost €23.75/35.75 plus IVA.

Places to Stay – Mid-Range

Hotel Durán (☎ *972 50 12 50, fax 972 50 26 09, Carrer de Lasauca 5)*, just off the top end of the Rambla, has a bit more style. Comfortable, homely rooms cost €41.50/59.50 plus IVA.

Places to Eat

Carrer de La Jonquera, just down the steps east of the Teatre-Museu Dalí, is lined with cheaper restaurants, among them *Restaurant España* (No 20), *Restaurant Versalles* (No 18) and *Restaurant Costa Brava* (No 10), offering basic three-course *menús* from €6.90. *Restaurant La Paella*, two short blocks east on Carrer de Tins, does one for €7.50. None is a great culinary experience but they are quick and easy.

A quality leap upwards is *Restaurant La Dita* (Carrer de la Muralla 7)* where you can try a mix of Mediterranean dishes and a few vegetarian options for up to €6.

Restaurant Viarnés (☎ *972 50 07 91, Pujada del Castell 23)* offers traditional cooking, with the emphasis on seafood. Main courses cost from €9 to €15. The nearby *Antaviana* (☎ *972 51 03 77, Carrer de Llers 5)* is another of the Mediterranean cooking crowd. They have a lunch *menú* for €7.20. It is closed on Sunday and Tuesday evening.

The excellent restaurant of the *Hotel Durán* (Carrer de Lasauca 5)* is a big step up, serving Catalan and Spanish specialities like *conill rostit amb cargols* (rabbit roasted with snails). You won't get much change from €21 for a full meal.

Entertainment

Two of the grooviest cafe-bars in town are right next to one another on Carrer del Mestre Falla – *Café de Nit* and *El Federal*. In fact this street hosts pretty much all Figueres' 'nightlife'. Locals tend to get a taxi to Empuriabrava on the coast to strut their stuff.

Getting There & Away

Bus Barcelona Bus (☎ 972 50 50 29) runs to Girona (€3, 50 minutes) seven times daily, and on to Barcelona six times daily (€10.50, 2¼ hours).

SARFA serves Castelló d'Empúries 10 to 20 times daily (€0.90) and Cadaqués (€3, one hour) up to eight times daily. TEISA runs to Besalú (€1.90) and Olot (€3.55) two or three times daily.

Train Figueres is on the railway between Barcelona, Girona and Portbou on the French border, and there are regular connections to Girona (€2 to €2.30 in 2nd class, 30 to 40 minutes), Barcelona (€6.75 to €7.75, 2¼ hours) and to Cerbère and the French border (€1.80).

AROUND FIGUERES

Hard to imagine that just a few kilometres outside Figueres, let's face it, is a bit of a dump, such pleasant country should soothe the eyes. Take the C-252 road northeast out of town for a refreshing little excursion. A couple of daily buses issue forth from Figueres along this stretch of road.

Vilabertran

In this settlement a couple of kilometres outside Figueres is located what started life as an Augustinian convent. The 11th-century Romanesque church, with its three naves and fine Lombard bell tower is outstanding. Also of great charm is the cloister, in which the Catalan newspaper *Avui* has installed a permanent art collection. In one of the church's chapels you can see a beautiful 14th-century, silver-plated crucifix.

The whole complex opens 10 am to 1.30 pm and 3 to 6.30 pm (to 5.30 pm from October to May). It is shut on Monday and on Sunday afternoons. Admission costs €2.40 but is free on Tuesday.

Peralada

Five kilometres up the road through lush countryside, Peralada is known above all for the **Castell-Palau dels Rocabertí**. Built in the 16th century and altered over the succeeding centuries, the castle with its round towers has rather a French air. It is private property and inside it is given over to a casino and restaurant. Unless you are gambling or eating you cannot get in. The gardens are also largely off limits. The only other way in is to turn up for a classical music performance during the July to August concert season.

The rest of the town is also worth a wander, with several medieval churches and convents and pleasantly winding lanes.

Places to Eat For elegant dining it is hard to resist temptation at the *Restaurant Cal Sagristà (☎ 972 53 83 01, Carrer de la Rodona 2)*, in the old town. Charmingly lit and with a cosy, intimate ambience, you may well feel induced to treat your palate to *calamars farcits amb pilotilles de peix* (calamari stuffed with bits of fish) for €10.80. It closes Monday night and Tuesday. Meat-lovers will be in heaven at a summertime option just outside town on the road to Vilabertan. *Can Poncelas (☎ 972 53 82 81)* is located in an old farmhouse with a shady garden out the back. It is the perfect lazy afternoon lunch stop.

PARATGE NATURAL D'INTERÈS NACIONAL DE L'ALBERA

This is a little visited but interesting park divided into two parts. To the west is the Requesens-Baussitges sector and to the east the park around **Sant Quirze de Colera**, a wonderful dark stone Romanesque church.

From Peralada you could follow the road east to Garriguella (just to the north of which is a centre for the reintroduction of tortoises to the area). From there head north to Vilamaniscle and on to Sant Quirze de Colera. Several small walking trails provide fun for the day.

A more challenging day hike in the western sector is worth considering. With your own vehicle, head for Cantallops, a few kilometres east of the A-7 motorway. A 6km dirt trail leads from there on to Requesens. From here you can follow trails to make a circular trip to the highest peak in the range, **Puig Neulós** (1256m), right on the border with France. You have several options, but one would see you heading off north-west for Sant Martí d'Albera (on the French side of the frontier), and then veering north-east for the peak via Coll de l'Ullat and Roc dels Tres Termes. From Puig Neulós, which offers startling views south across the Alt Empordà *comarca* (district) and north across the plains of Roussillon, you wind south towards Requesens (don't forget to take a look at the nearby castle). The whole thing should take about six to seven hours. You will need the Mapa Comarcal (1:50,000) of the Alt Empordà.

Places to Stay

Can Pau (☎ 972 55 48 81, Carretera Comarcal s/n) is the only accommodation option in Cantallops. They charge €30 for modest doubles. Otherwise the nearest options are a camp site in Garriguella, *Camping Vell Empordà (☎ 972 53 02 00)* and a huddle of pensiones at Sant Climent Sescebes.

Getting There & Away

Getting in and around the area by public transport is difficult as only a few towns beyond the park are served by intermittent bus runs (often no more than one a day) from Figueres.

NORTH-WEST OF FIGUERES

Another area attracting little attention from foreigners is the hilly zone north-west of Figueres. One route worth considering (especially with lunch in mind) would be to exit Figueres north along the N-II and take the turn-off west for Pont de Molins on the Riu La Muga. A few kilometres west of this village, those with wheels and rumbling tummies are strongly urged to call in at *Restaurant El Molí (☎ 972 52 92 71)*. This grand old stone-walled mill, with its dark timber exposed beams, tasteful dining area in Isabelline style and river views, is the perfect location for a long lunch. It is a favourite with Catalans from as far off as Barcelona. If you really like it you can even

COSTA BRAVA

stay in one of a couple of rooms. Doubles cost €62.50. The place shuts down from November to early April.

Another 6km brings you to **Boadella**, where you can drive up to the grand dam of the same name. In spite of the signs forbidding such activities, some locals like to camp in the area and swim in the dam waters. You can keep motoring north to **Darnius** (a couple of restaurants and one *pensión*) and on through winding hill country to **Maçanet de Cabrenys**, a fusty old mountain village used by Catalans as a base for walking in the surrounding hills. There is a handful of small hotels. Pop into *Bar La Pau* (*Plaça de la Vila*) for a glimpse of village life. The men play cards, the families noisily carry on their business at other marble top tables and in a deep corner a largely unheeded TV babbles on to itself. Another

15km west brings you to Coustouges, in French territory.

One or two buses run daily from Figueres to Maçanet de Cabrenys via Boadella and Darnius.

La Jonquera

The last town on your way north out of Catalunya into France (or the first on your way in, depending on how you look at it), this place has lived long on the passing road trade but since passport and customs checks were dropped between Schengen countries in 1995 (see the Facts for the Visitor chapter for more details) it has suffered from neglect as tourists elect to belt on down the highway. Understandable really, because there ain't much to stop for. A few hotels and restaurants cater for those who can't bear the thought of another kilometre.

Costa Daurada & the South-West

From Vilanova i la Geltrú (see the Around Barcelona chapter) to the Valencian border stretches the Costa Daurada (Golden Coast), a series of not very exciting resorts along a mainly flat coast varied by occasional promontories and above all by the Delta de l'Ebre (Ebro in Spanish), which protrudes 20km out into the Mediterranean Sea. Along the way, however, are the fine old Roman capital of Tarragona and the modern extravaganza of Port Aventura – Spain's answer to EuroDisney. Excursions inland take you to some of the (surprisingly) least-travelled parts of Catalunya. From the ruins of the Carthusian Monestir de Escaladei to the picturesque villages of Siurana and Horta de Sant Joan (where Picasso spent some time); from the flats of the Delta de l'Ebre (and flamingo-watching) to the heights of Mont Caro (with views seemingly clear across all Spain and far out to sea), the visitor anxious to put distance between himself and the holiday *costas* (coasts) doesn't need to go far to penetrate deep into the real Catalunya of the south-west.

TARRAGONA

postcode 43080 • pop 112,795

Tarragona was first occupied by the Romans, who called it Tarraco, in the 2nd century BC. In 27 BC Augustus made it the capital of his new Tarraconensis province (which covered an area from Catalunya to Cantabria in the north and as far as Almería in the south-east) and stayed here until 25 BC while directing campaigns in Cantabria and Asturias. Tarragona was abandoned when the Muslims arrived in AD 714, but was reborn as the seat of a Christian archbishopric in 1089. Today it's a mainly modern city, but its rich Roman remains and fine medieval cathedral make it an absorbing place.

Highlights

- Exploring Tarragona's Roman past
- Reaching the pretty village of Siurana
- Taking in the magnificent views from Mont Caro
- Contemplating the ruins of Escaladei, followed by lunch and local red wines
- Tucking into seafood on a summer evening in Tarragona's Serrallo fishing port
- Watching the *castellers* of Valls build their human towers
- Touring around Els Ports de Beseit and getting to know the village of Horta de Sant Joan
- Flamingo-watching in the Delta de l'Ebre

Tarraco, An Archaeological Guide by Xavier Aquilué and others will help you unravel Tarragona's ancient history and complicated archaeology; one place selling it is the Museu Nacional Arqueològic de Tarragona. The city is a gold mine for archaeologists, who continue to make finds to this day. In February 2001, for example, remains of ancient warehouses were discovered in a former car pound in the port area.

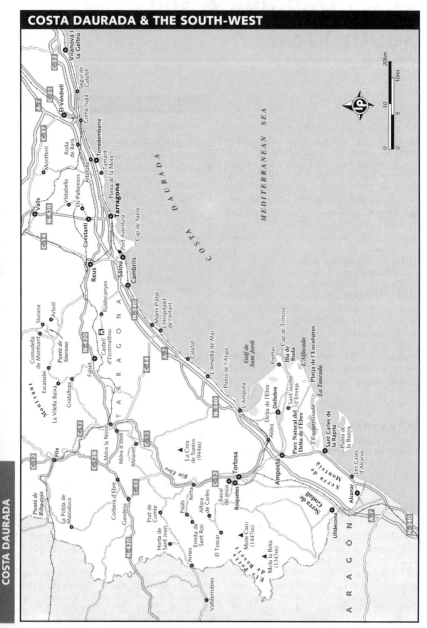

COSTA DAURADA & THE SOUTH-WEST

MEDITERRANEAN SEA

COSTA DAURADA

Orientation

The main street is Rambla Nova, which runs roughly north-west from a cliff top overlooking the Mediterranean. A couple of streets to the east, and parallel, is Rambla Vella, which marks the beginning of the old town and, incidentally, follows the line of the Via Augusta, the Roman road from Rome to Cádiz.

The train station is half a kilometre south-west of Rambla Nova, near the seafront, and the bus station is about 2km inland, just to the west off Plaça Imperial de Tàrraco.

Information

The main tourist office (☎ 977 24 50 64, fax 977 24 55 07), Carrer Major 39, opens 10 am to 2 pm and 4.30 to 7 pm Monday to Friday, and 10 am to 2 pm at the weekend and holidays (and extra hours from July to September). There's also a Catalunya regional tourist office (☎ 977 23 34 15), Carrer de Fortuny 4, which opens 9.15 am to 2 pm and 4 to 7.30 pm Monday to Saturday (closed Saturday afternoon). Several information booths around town open 10 am to 2 pm at the weekend and in summer.

All the city's monuments bar the cathedral are closed on Monday. You will soon come to notice that, aside from the cathedral, the theme is decidedly Roman. Pick up the handy *Ruta Arqueològica Urbana* brochure from the tourist office. It details more than 30 locations throughout the old town where Roman remains can be viewed, some of them in shops and restaurants. If they are not too busy with customers, shop owners are generally happy for individuals (no groups!) to drop in and take a look.

The main post office *(correus/correos)* is on Plaça Corsini. The Guàrdia Urbana (municipal police; ☎ 092 or ☎ 977 24 03 45) has a station at Carrer de Pare Palau 7. There's a hospital (☎ 977 23 27 14) on Passeig de Torroja. Several countries have consulates in Tarragona.

Catedral

Sitting grandly at the top of the old town, Tarragona's cathedral is a treasure house deserving 1½ hours or more if you're to do it justice. Built between 1171 and 1331 on the site of a Roman temple, it combines Romanesque and Gothic features, as typified by the main facade on Pla de la Seu. The entrance is by the cloister on the north-western side of the building.

The cloister has Gothic vaulting and Romanesque carved capitals, one of which shows rats conducting what they think is a cat's funeral, until the cat comes back to life! Rooms off the cloister house the **Museu Diocesà**, with a broad collection extending from Roman hairpins to some lovely 12th- to 14th-century polychrome woodcarvings of a breast-feeding Virgin. Of prime importance is the collection of 45 tapestries.

The interior of the cathedral, which is over 100m long, is Romanesque at the north-eastern end and Gothic at the south-western end. The aisles are lined with 14th- to 19th-century chapels and hung with 16th- and 17th-century tapestries from Brussels. The arm of St Thecla, Tarragona's patron saint, is normally kept in the Capella de Santa Tecla on the south-eastern side. The choir in the centre of the nave has 15th-century carved walnut stalls. The marble main altar was carved in the 13th century with scenes from the life of St Thecla.

The cathedral opens 10 am to 7 pm daily (except Sunday and holidays) July to mid-October; 10 am to 2 pm mid-November to the end of March; and 10 am to 1 pm and 4 to 7 pm, the rest of the year. The €1.85 admission charge includes a detailed booklet.

Museu d'Història de Tarragona

This museum comprises four separate Roman sites around the city and the 14th-century noble mansion which now serves as the **Museu Casa Castellarnau**, Carrer dels Cavallers 14. The mansion, furnished in 19th-century fashion, provides insight into how the other half lived on a street that for centuries was one of *the* addresses in town. While on that street, take a look at the **Conservatori** (No 10), the local music conservatorium, which has a fine pillared courtyard and a remarkable ceramic fountain off to the left beyond the entrance.

COSTA DAURADA

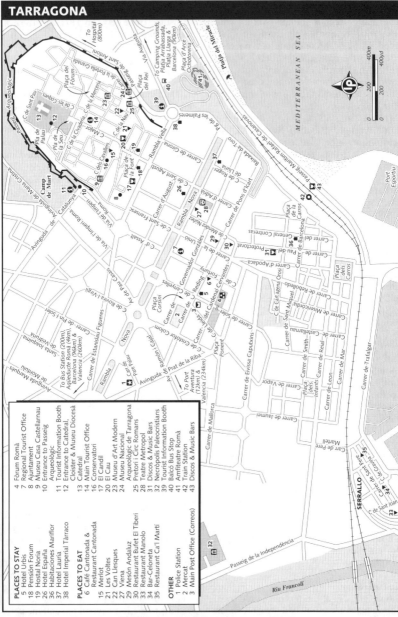

TARRAGONA

PLACES TO STAY
5 Hotel Urbis
18 Pensión Forum
19 Hostal Noria
26 Hotel España
36 Habitaciones Mariflor
37 Hotel Lauria
38 Hotel Imperial Tárraco

PLACES TO EAT
6 Café Cantonada &
  Restaurant Cantonada
15 Merlot
21 Les Voltes
22 Can Llesques
27 Viena
29 Mesón Andaluz
30 Restaurant Bufet El Tiberi
33 Restaurant Manolo
34 Bar-Celoneta
35 Restaurant Ca'l Marti

OTHER
1 Police Station
2 Mercat
3 Main Post Office (Correos)
4 Fòrum Romà
7 Regional Tourist Office
8 Ajuntament
9 Museu Casa Castellarnau
10 Entrance to Passeig
   Arqueologic
11 Tourist Information Booth
12 Entrance to Catedral,
   Cloister & Museu Diocesà
13 Catedral
14 Main Tourist Office
16 Conservatori
17 El Candil
20 El Cau
23 Museu d'Art Modern
24 Museu Nacional
   Arqueologic de Tarragona
25 Pretori i Circ Romans
28 Teatre Metropol
31 Discos & Music Bars
32 Necròpolis Paleocristians
39 Tourist Information Booth
40 Balcó Bus Stop
41 Amfiteatre Romà
42 Train Station
43 Discos & Music Bars

COSTA DAURADA

For the Roman circuit, start with the **Pretori i Circ Romans** on Plaça del Rei, which includes part of the vaults of the Roman circus where chariot races were held. The circus, 300m long, stretched from here to beyond Plaça de la Font. The views from the top of the squat tower, or Pretori (and known to some as the Torre de Pilat after Pontius Pilate), are among the best you will get of the city. These buildings mark off the south-eastern corner of what was the provincial forum, a huge area surrounded by porticoes which was the central gathering place for people from all over the province. You can see a few remnants of it on Plaça del Fòrum. The most curious part of a visit here is to walk along the almost 100m-long subterranean passage below the circus. You can see a little of the seating and climb (mostly restored) stairs to what was the top level of the arena.

Close to the beach is the well preserved **Amfiteatre Romà**, where gladiators battled each other, or wild animals, to the death. In its arena are the remains of 6th- and 12th-century churches built to commemorate the martyrdom of the Christian bishop Fructuosus and two deacons, whom they say were burnt alive here in 259.

By Carrer de Lleida are remains of the **Fòrum Romà**, dominated by several imposing columns. The north-western half of this site was occupied by a judicial basilica (where legal disputes were settled), from which the rest of the forum stretched downhill to the south-east. Linked to the site by a footbridge is another excavated area with a stretch of Roman street. This forum was the hub of public life for the Roman town but was less important, and much smaller, than the provincial forum, the navel of all Tarraconensis province.

The **Passeig Arqueològic** is a peaceful walk around part of the perimeter of the old town between two lines of city walls; the inner ones are mainly Roman while the outer ones were put up by the British during the War of the Spanish Succession.

All these places open 9 or 10 am to 9 pm Tuesday to Saturday and 9 am to 3 pm Sunday, June to September; and tend to open 10 am to 1.30 pm and 4 to 6.30 pm (10 am to 2 pm Sunday and holidays) the rest of the year. Admission to each costs €1.85.

Museu Nacional Arqueològic de Tarragona

This carefully presented museum on Plaça del Rei gives further insight into Roman Tarraco, but most explanatory material is in Catalan or Castilian. Exhibits include part of the Roman city walls, frescoes, sculpture and pottery. A highlight is the large, almost complete *Mosaic de Peixos de la Pineda* showing fish and sea creatures. In the section on everyday arts you can admire ancient fertility aids including an outsize stone penis, symbol of the god Priapus. The museum opens 10 am to 8 pm Tuesday to Saturday and 10 am to 2 pm on Sunday and holidays, in the summer; the weekday times change to 10 am to 1.30 pm and 4 to 7 pm the rest of the year. Admission costs €2.45 and entitles you to enter the museum at the **Necròpolis Paleocristians**. This large Christian cemetery of late Roman and Visigothic times is on Passeig de la Independència on the western edge of the town centre and boasts some surprisingly elaborate tombs. Unfortunately only the tiny museum was open at the time of writing, as restoration work on the necropolis had brought to an indefinite halt.

Museu d'Art Modern

This modest art gallery at Carrer de Santa Anna 8 is at its most interesting when temporary exhibitions take place. It opens 10 am to 8 pm Tuesday to Saturday (with a 3 to 5 pm lunch break on Saturday) and 11 am to 2 pm on Sunday. Admission is free.

Beaches

The town beach, **Platja del Miracle**, is reasonably clean but can get terribly crowded. **Platja Arrabassada**, 1km north-east across the headland, is longer, and **Platja Llarga**, beginning 2km farther out, stretches for about 3km. Bus Nos 1 and 9 from the Balcó stop on Via Augusta go to both (€0.75). You can get the same buses along Rambla Vella and Rambla Nova.

COSTA DAURADA

A Little Modernista Excursion

Tarragona's master of Modernisme was Josep Maria Jujol (1879–1949), a student of and collaborator with the grand Gaudí on various projects but virtually unknown outside Catalunya.

He worked on a handful of projects in Barcelona, the epicentre of this architectural movement, but also received commissions in the province around his native town. Those mad about Modernisme might like to undertake a small tour of his more outstanding accomplishments, though in Tarragona itself about the only way you'll get to admire his work is by looking inside the Teatre Metropol at Rambla Nova 46 (where, as was often the case, Jujol had to work with a limited budget). Jujol was a devout Catholic and decided to create an allegory of the Church as a boat sailing the high seas of life. To contemplate the undulating ceiling is to have the impression of being submerged and looking up to see the bottom of ships' hulls ploughing through the sea.

A short way north of town (take the TP-2031 road or one of up to 10 buses a day) in **Els Pallaresos** you can take a look at the Casa Bofarull. The most interesting element of this *masia* (country house) is the arcade with its slender columns resembling part of a cloister. A few kilometres on in **Vistabella** is Jujol's Església del Sagrat Cor, damaged during the Civil War. Farther north in **Montferri** (on the T-204, about midway along and south off the C-37 road that links Valls and El Vendrell) is his curious Ermita de Nostra Senyora de Montserrat. The sharp triangles and parabolic arches will no doubt remind you of Gaudí.

Getting in to any of these three buildings outside Tarragona is hit and miss. They are not yet on any tourist trail to speak of.

Places to Stay

There are eight camping grounds on or close to the beaches within 11km north-east of the city along the N-340. The nearest is *Camping Tàrraco* (☎ 977 23 99 89) behind Platja Arrabassada, but others, such as *Camping Las Palmeras* (☎ 977 20 80 81) at the far end of Platja Llarga, are better. Most grounds open from April to September. The only one that opens year round is *Camping Tamarit Park* (☎ 977 65 01 28), 4km farther beyond La Palmeras. You are looking at between €4.50 and €5.20 per person at these camping grounds, plus around the same per tent and per car.

The *Alberg Sant Jordi* youth hostel (☎ 977 24 01 95, *Avinguda del President Lluís Companys 5*), about 300m north-west of the bus station, has 192 beds but during the academic year most are taken up by students. The hostel's high season is from April to August.

Habitaciones Mariflor (☎ 977 23 82 31, *Carrer del General Contreras 29*), housed in a drab block near the train station, has clean rooms with shared bathrooms for €12.65/24.10.

Plaça de la Font in the old town has three adequate *pensiones* (guesthouses), though one was closed at the time of writing. *Pensión Forum* (☎ 977 23 17 18) at No 37 charges €15.10/30.15 for small, clean en-suite rooms. *Hostal Noria* (☎ 977 23 87 17) at No 53 is a bit better value at €16.30/27.75 but is often full.

Hotel España (☎ 977 23 27 12, *Rambla Nova 49*) is a well positioned but unexciting one-star hotel where en-suite rooms cost €19.90/36.15 plus IVA. The three-star *Hotel Lauria* (☎ 977 23 67 12) at No 20 is a worthwhile splurge at €33.15/51.20 plus IVA, with a good location and a pool. A comfortable option though less inspired in terms of placement is *Hotel Urbis* (☎ 977 24 01 16, *fax 977 24 36 54, Carrer de Reding 20*). Rooms cost up to €57.25/72.30 plus IVA.

Hotel Imperial Tàrraco (☎ 977 23 30 40, *Passeig de les Palmeres s/n*) is the best in town, with a great position overlooking the Mediterranean and rooms for €75.30/96.70 plus IVA. Several of the better hotels offer big discounts on Friday, Saturday and Sunday night.

A 'gigantic surrealist object' – the Teatre-Museu Dalí in Figueres

¡Coliflor!, Palafrugell market

Spanning the Fluvià, the *pont fortificat* (fortified bridge) affords wonderful views of medieval Besalú.

Packed in tight at Llafranc's harbour on the Costa Brava

Serene Siurana hanging on a cliff edge in the morning fog

Walks wind out from Siurana and the area acts as a magnet for rock-climbers.

Places to Eat

There are a couple of cafes and eateries on Rambla Nova, including *Viena* at No 50, which has croissants and a vast range of *entrepans* (sandwiches) from €1.80.

For an all-you-can-eat Catalan buffet (€9 per person), head for the stylish *Restaurant Bufet El Tiberi (Carrer de Martí d'Ardenya 5)*. It closes Sunday night and Monday. Nearby *Mesón Andaluz (Carrer de Pons d'Icart 3)*, a local favourite (upstairs), has a good three-course *menú del día* (fixed-price meal) for €9. *Café Cantonada (Carrer de Fortuny 23)* has reasonable tapas, while next door, *Restaurant Cantonada* has pizzas and pasta from around €5.

If cheese is your thing, try a cheese platter *(taula de formatges)* at *Can Llesques* (☎ 977 22 29 06, *Carrer de Natzaret 6)*, a pleasant little spot looking onto Plaça del Rei. They do more than a hundred other dishes too, mostly combinations of anything imaginable on two slices *(llesques)* of bread and costing less than €6.

If you'd like to eat under the vaults of the former Roman circus try *Les Voltes* (☎ 977 23 06 51, *Carrer de Trinquet Vell 12)*. The food itself is a little overpriced for what you are served, but the *menú del día* is not bad at €9.

One of Tarragona's seriously classy addresses is the understated *Merlot* (☎ 977 22 06 52, *Carrer dels Cavallers 6)*, where you'll find all sorts of inventive dishes based upon Catalan classics. This refreshing place has heavy, exposed stone walls that are lightened by paintings and other decoration. You'll probably part company with about €24. It closes on Sunday and Monday lunch time.

The quintessential Tarragona seafood experience can only be had in the Serrallo, the town's fishing port. About a dozen bars and restaurants here sell the day's catch and during summer weekends in particular the place is packed. Most of the restaurants close their kitchens fairly early – by 10.30 pm. *Bar-Celoneta* (☎ 977 24 00 16, *Plaça de Narcís Monturiol s/n)* is a rowdy, spit-and-sawdust place if you want to go cheap and cheerful with the locals. They have a

lunch *menú* for €5.90. *Restaurant Ca'l Martí* (☎ 977 21 23 84, *Carrer de Sant Pere 12)* is a little more classy and has a broad range of sea fare as well as that backstreet feel in a convivially noisy environment. The set meal costs €9.65, and a-la-carte fish main courses start at €10.25. It closes on Sunday evening and Monday. *Restaurant Manolo* (☎ 977 22 34 84, *Carrer de Gravina 61–63)* is doubtless one of the better establishments in the Serrallo. The setting is elegant and attracts a better-healed but still predominantly local clientele. Try the *parrillada de pescado*, a mixed fish grill, for €22.60. It closes on Sunday evening.

Entertainment

El Candil (Plaça de la Font 13) is a popular, relaxed bar-cafe with a student clientele. *El Cau (Carrer de Trinquet Vell)*, in one of the vaults of the Roman circus, is similar, but with music. *Café Cantonada* (see Places to Eat), with its pool table, is nice for a drink or two.

The main concentration of nightlife is along the waterfront behind the train station, and in some of the streets in front of it, such as along Carrer de la Pau del Protectorat. The big night is Thursday, as most of the punters are young students from the small towns outside Tarragona, who tend to go home for the weekend.

Getting There & Away

Lying on main routes south from Barcelona, Tarragona is well connected. The easiest way to get to Barcelona is by train.

Air Charter flights for passengers on package holidays in the area land at the small airport at Reus, north-west of Tarragona. There is no public bus service but transport is organised to meet the flights.

Bus Services run to Barcelona (€7.40, 1½ hours, nine buses Monday to Friday and one or two at the weekend), Valencia (€13.90, 3½ hours, nine daily), Lleida (two hours, up to six daily), Zaragoza (€11.95, 2¾ hours, up to six daily) and La Seu d'Urgell (3¼ hours, one daily). Other buses run daily to Madrid (€22.90) and other Spanish cities. For information try calling ☎ 977 22 91 26 (they may even answer).

Train Up to 40 regional and long-distance trains a day run to/from Barcelona, taking one to 1½ hours. Most stop at Estació Sants and Passeig de Gràcia stations, and the cheapest fare is €4 in 2nd class. Only three stop at Sitges (€2.50, one hour). Up to 12 trains run daily to Valencia (€12.65 in (slow) 2nd class, two to 3½ hours) and as many as nine a day to Lleida (€4.60, one to two hours) and Zaragoza (€13.60, three to 3¾ hours). Three trains daily run to Madrid; the cheapest costs €29.55.

AROUND TARRAGONA
Altafulla
postcode 43893 • pop 1675

Once a Roman holiday resort for affluent citizens of Tarragona, this little town was converted into a fortified settlement in the wake of the Muslim invasion. The original medieval core of Altafulla is small but charming, all white and cream whitewashed walls with rose-coloured stone portals and windows. It is topped by a 13th-century castle (much tampered with in the 17th century). Altafulla, about 10km east of Tarragona, is definitely, as they say, 'worth a detour'.

The *Alberg Casa Gran (☎ 977 65 07 79, Plaçeta 12)*, in the old part of town, is one of the region's more enchantingly placed youth hostels, with room for 65 people. There's a scattering of restaurants in the old and newer parts of town. While only six buses run to Altafulla from Tarragona at the weekend, up to 30 operate during the week. They take 20 to 30 minutes.

Around Altafulla

One of the few unspoiled stretches of coastline along the Costa Daurada is the protected parkland at **Punta de la Mora**. Conservationists have fought to keep this area free of building. A nice walk is to head for the woods of l'Arboçar from Tarragona's Platja Llarga, and then head down to the cove. Another walk leads from **Platja de la Mora** to a medieval watchtower, from

where you can walk to the small beach of **Calabeig**. Platja de la Mora itself is a change from the general run of broad, flat beaches between Tarragona and Sitges, having tree-covered promontories that poke out into the sea at either end. Development is also comparatively inconspicuous. Tarragona's bus No 9 terminates at Platja de la Mora.

About 1km east along the coast is the **Castell de Tamarit**. There has been a fort here since Roman times, and Tamarit was a major base during the reconquest of this part of Catalunya from the Muslims. The partly rebuilt castle is in decent shape but private property. To get here, follow the signs to Camping Tamarit from the N-340 highway (a short way farther east is Altafulla's beach). Among the streets of holiday homes that surround the castle is the site of their predecessor: the archaeological remains of a Roman seaside villa. The **Vil.la Romana dels Munts** on Passeig del Fortí opens 10 am to 1.30 pm and 4 to 7.30 pm (3 to 5.30 pm October to April) Monday to Saturday, and 10 am to 2 pm on Sunday and holidays. Admission costs €1.85.

As you head north-east along the N-340 you soon reach the **Arc de Barà**, a 2nd-century Roman arch smack in the middle of the main road. Off to the right on the seaside is the curious **Roc de Sant Gaietà** residential district. Huddled on a rocky point over the sea, this collection of houses built in various mock traditional styles from around the Spanish peninsula is a curious animal indeed. You can wander around and eat at a seaside terrace bar/restaurant. Roc de Sant Gaietà is on the bus route between Tarragona and El Vendrell (the bus drops you at the highway turn-off, from where it's about a half-hour walk).

Salou
postcode 43840 • pop 7265

Get off the train, close your eyes for a second and imagine a hamlet of modest houses and a handful of villas (a couple of them with Modernista touches). Now open your eyes. Well, the villas are still there and the leafy Carrer de Barcelona is actually quite nice. The waterfront and beach are pleasant, though no better than other beaches up and down the Costa Daurada. And then there is the Salou of today. A rabbit warren of apartment and hotel blocks, whose ground floors are taken up with karaoke bars, authentic English pubs, Dutch *eetcafés* (pubs that serve meals) and so on. Masses of tourists pile in from all over Europe – and it has to be said there seems to be a fair Catalan and Spanish contingent too. Beats me. If you want information on all this and more, call in at the Patronat Municipal de Turisme (☎ 977 35 01 02) at Passeig de Jaume I 4. It opens 9.30 am to 1.30 pm and 4 to 8 pm daily.

Should you end up here and want a room in a hotel, you could do worse than trying something along Carrer de Barcelona, in the oldest part of the town (which is not saying a lot). The modest ***Hotel Niza*** *(☎ 977 38 13 91, Carrer de Barcelona 23)*, with singles/doubles at €24.10/36.15, is handy for the train station and doesn't quite have the hyper-touristy feel of the big block-booked hotels. One of the good things to come out of Salou (apart from the train) is *coca de Salou*, the local version of this Catalan pastry. Almond-based and sprinkled with candied fruit, you can get some in ***Pastisseria Ramon*** *(Carrer de Barcelona 4)*.

European charter flights use the small airport at Reus to funnel tourists into Salou and the surrounding area.

Up to nine trains a day leave for Tarragona (€1.05, 15 minutes) and Barcelona (€5.05, one hour 20 minutes). Local buses from several stops along the waterfront Passeig de Jaume I will take you to Tarragona, Port Aventura and farther down the coast to Cambrils.

Port Aventura

Port Aventura (☎ 902 20 22 20), 7km west of Tarragona, is Spain's biggest and best funfair-adventure park. If you have €27.75 to spare (€20.50 for children aged five to 12), it can make an amusing day out, especially if you have ankle-biters in tow. In 1998 Universal Picture Studios bought up the park and have begun filling it with Americanisms that may or may not appeal. Woody Woodpecker is the new mascot of a park that is billed as a 'world of fun for all ages'. Rocky & Bullwinkle, that famous Catalan pair, have also been catapulted to star status in the park. Sarcasm aside, the park has plenty of spine-tingling rides and other attractions. The latest big addition was a virtual submarine created by Universal at a staggering cost of just over €27,000.

The funfair opens 10 am to 8 pm (until 10 pm at the weekend; until midnight from around mid-June to mid-September) daily from Setmana Santa (Holy Week, the week leading up to Easter Sunday) to the end of October. Night tickets, valid from 7 pm, cost €20.50.

Trains run to Port Aventura's own station, about a 1km walk from the site, several times a day from Tarragona (€2.30 return) and Barcelona (€7.90 return). By road, take exit 35 from the A-7, or the N-340 from Tarragona. Parking costs €3.65.

Inland

Roman Aqueduct The Aqüeducte Romà, 4km inland on the N-240 Lleida road, is a fine stretch of two-tiered aqueduct (also known as the Pont del Diable, or Devil's Bridge) 217m long and 27m high. Bus No 5 to Sant Salvador from Tarragona's Plaça Imperial de Tàrraco, every 10 to 20 minutes, will take you there.

Centelles About 6km north of Tarragona in Constantí is another reminder of the Roman presence around the empire's one-time Spanish capital. The Centelles villa is especially important for its palaeo-Christian mosaics. It opens 10 am to 1.30 pm and 3 to 5.30 pm (4 to 7.30 pm from June to September) daily except Monday. Admission costs €1.85. From Tarragona regular buses run to Constantí (€1.05, 20 minutes).

EL VENDRELL & AROUND

Now a busy farming town and traffic junction, El Vendrell started life as a Phoenician trading settlement. The old centre is not unpleasant to wander around although there is not a great deal to see other than the

Castles in the Air

It's difficult to know how to classify making human castles, but to many a Catalan, the *castellers* are as serious in their sport as any footballer.

The 'building' of *castells* is particularly popular in central and southern Catalunya and the number of fans is growing. Teams *(colles)* from various parts of Catalunya compete in the summer and you are most likely to see castellers in town festivals *(festes majors)*.

Erecting human towers is not a new pastime. Its golden age was in the 1880s, when the most daring castellers raised nine and on occasion even 10 human storeys. Now, 62 colles have been registered by the Coordinadora de Colles Castelleres. Of these, two teams (the Vella dels Xiquets de Valls and the Joves Xiquets de Valls), can trace their roots back a century. 'Castle-fever' is spreading – teams have sprung up, as it were, in Mallorca and France, and as far away as Mexico and Argentina.

It's very much an amateur sport. The club will pay team members' travel costs and supply a team jersey, but that's as far as the remuneration goes. It was once an exclusively male preserve but women now form up to a quarter of some colles.

The 'Castles'

The idea is to 'build' human layers of a 'castle' and then to successfully undo it without everyone tumbling in a heap – easier said than done. The first level of the *tronco* (trunk) is a wide and solid scrum of people, together known as the *pinya*. The most popular teams 'playing' at home can get a thousand people chiming in to be part of the pinya!

Above this you build your castle. About the best any team has recorded is a *quatre de nou* or *tres de nou*: a four-by-nine or three-by-nine castle. That means nine storeys of people, three or four in the core levels tapering to two then one person at the top. Often the base pinya does not provide enough buttressing, so you get more of the same on the second level. That is called the *folre*. Hence, the result might be a *quatre de nou amb folre* (a four-by-nine with folre). Sometimes a team will add some support to the third level *(manilles)*. When one is built without any extra support at the lower levels *net* (clean).

If all goes well, the whole structure is topped off by a kid *(anxaneta)* who serves as a pinnacle, or *agulla*. When the anxaneta waves his or her arm the castell is complete. If it can be dismantled without collapsing in a heap, the castell is *descarregat*. There are more permutations of this activity than crenellations on your average stone castle.

---

baroque **Església del Salvador Transfigurat** and a couple of museums. One museum is dedicated to the playwright Àngel Guimerà, whose family came from El Vendrell (although he was born in the Canary Islands).

El Vendrell is on the *rodalies* (local) train line 4 from Barcelona (€3.10). It is also connected to Tarragona by bus (about 40 minutes, up to 14 buses daily).

Down on the coast, El Vendrell's local beach, **Coma-ruga**, is a long broad strip of sand with a residential backdrop. Heading east along the coast towards Vilanova i la Geltrú, there are several more fine beaches along the same lines, such as **Platja de** **Calafell**, **Segur de Calafell** and **Cunit**. They are all on rodalies line 2 from Barcelona.

Just outside **Calafell** town (about 1km inland from the Calafell train station on the coast) you can visit a spruced-up Iberian citadel. It's difficult to know what to think of this kind of thing. Archaeologists have done their work in excavating the place and now it makes a modest buck as a kind of 'Iber-Town'. So the reconstructed mud houses have been injected with a suitable ragbag of ceramic objects and other odds and ends...

It opens 11 am to 2 pm and 6 to 9 pm in August; admission costs €3.05. On summer evenings *nits ibèriques* (Iberian nights) are

Castles in the Air

Teams sometimes concentrate on a level, say seven, ranging from a *nou de set* (nine people by seven storeys) through to the really tricky two- and one-person levels. Those involving two castellers per storey are *torres* (towers) and those with one per level are *pilars* (pillars). It is rare to get above either six or seven storeys. To keep team members humming, someone usually belts out some strident tunes on a *gralla*, something like a kazoo.

It is tempting to think the sky's the limit on what castellers can achieve, but perhaps it is more prosaically a question of human strength and persistence. The virtually unthinkable, *castells de deu* (10 levels) had until 1998 not been achieved since the 19th century. Another challenge is a *quatre de nou sense folre* (a four-by-nine without folre), also unheard of in more than 100 years. Equally tricky and rarely pulled off is the *cinc de vuit* (eight storeys of five people) that is sometimes referred to as a *catedral* (cathedral).

JANE SMITH

When & Where

The two teams from Valls have a long and venerable history in this odd branch of the construction industry. Until recently they had been overshadowed by Els Castellers de Vilafranca del Penedès but this all changed at the biennial championship day held in Tarragona's bullring in October 2000. The Vella romped home ahead of their nearest rivals, the Joves Xiquets, with Els Castellers de Vilafranca limping home in third place. The next championship get-together will be in October 2002.

Otherwise, these and many other teams turn up at festes all over Catalunya. The standard afternoon program involves three competing colles, each with four castles to make – around three hours of sweaty work. The action takes place in town squares – just turn up and join the crowd. The season lasts roughly from February to December.

staged from 10.30 pm, with scenes of Iberian life including the occasional clash with Romans (who always get booed). For €6.05 you can be a part of this. For more information call ☎ 977 69 46 83.

From Calafell the coast road leads to Vilanova i la Geltrú; see the Around Barcelona chapter.

VALLS
postcode 43800 • pop 20,090

Not much remains of old Valls, but the place warrants a mention if only as a cradle of that strange and now greatly repopularised activity, the building of human castles. The

Catalan police force, the Mossos d'Esquadra (see the boxed text 'La Policía – Who's Who' in the Facts for the Visitor chapter), has its origins in the Esquadres de Valls, established by a local noble in the early 18th century to combat anti-Madrid bandits. The town is also the epicentre of the *calçotada* – the spring onion event featuring *romesco* sauce (see the Out to Eat in Catalunya special section).

If you do drop in, the small old core of town has a few streets and buildings of interest, including the Gothic **Església de Sant Joan**, rebuilt after the Civil War. From Valls the N-240 highway from Tarragona

COSTA DAURADA

continues north to Montblanc (see the Central Catalunya chapter).

REUS & AROUND

Reus retains even today the air of a self-satisfied, successful middle-class commercial town. For much of the second half of the 19th century it was the second most important city in Catalunya and a major centre for the export of textiles and brandy. Birthplace of Gaudí, it boasts a series of Modernista mansions, many of which, however, are less than inspiring. Their presence testifies to the one-time prosperity of Reus' family businesses. For information about the town and surrounding districts, the tourist office (☎ 977 34 59 43), Plaça de la Llibertat s/n, opens 9.30 am to 1.30 pm and 4 to 7 pm (5 to 7 pm on Saturday) Monday to Saturday.

Plaça del Mercadal, the central square, is graced on one side by Domènech i Montaner's striking Modernista **Casa Navàs** (at No 5). The tourist office has a route map for those interested in inspecting the remaining 30-odd Modernista mansions around the town centre. Nearby on Plaça de Sant Pere is the Gothic **Església Arxipestal de Sant Pere**, finished in 1569.

In the unlikely event you want to stay in Reus, you have a choice of several pensiones and hotels. **Hostal Simonet** (☎ 977 34 59 74, Raval de Santa Anna 18) is central and has pleasant air-con rooms as well as a relaxing courtyard and a good restaurant. A double can cost up to €60.25. The restaurant offers such locally prized dishes as *cargols a la llauna* (snails) for €9.05 or highly un-Catalan options like *filet de canguro amb fruites de bosc* (kangaroo fillet in wild fruit sauce). You'll pay up to €24.10 per head.

Regular trains connect Reus with Barcelona and Tarragona, as do buses. The trip from Tarragona takes 15 to 20 minutes.

Siurana

The castle of Siurana was one of the last two Muslim bastions to fall to the reconquering Christians in Catalunya (the other was Miravet – see North of Tortosa later in the chapter). Today it lies in ruins above the

pretty huddle of a village inhabited by just one family, occasionally accompanied by small groups of holiday-makers and trekkers.

About 3km of winding road slice up through a red rock gorge, bringing you to a rise and the village which, bunched up on a high spur, affords long views down to the Pantà de Siurana (Siurana Dam) and west to the forbidding rock walls of the **Serra de Montsant**. Walking trails wind out from the village, and rock climbers flock to the area.

Siurana boasts a hotel, a camp site, a refuge and a pleasant little *casa de pagès* (country house with rooms to let), ***Can Roig*** (☎ 977 82 14 50, Carrer Major 6). This charming, refurbished stone house in the middle of the village has double rooms for €30.15. A handful of bars and restaurants situated in rustic houses keep hunger and thirst at bay. Those without cars could consider hitching, as public transport (in the form of one or two evening buses from Tarragona and Reus) only goes as far as **Cornudella de Montsant**, leaving you 9km short of your objective. Call the tourist office in Cornudella de Montsant (☎ 977 82 18 00) to confirm bus times.

Those with their own transport could choose to head north-east for Prades and on to Poblet (see the Central Catalunya chapter) or deeper west into the hilly El Priorat *comarca* (district).

Cartoixa d'Escaladei & Around

From Cornudella de Montsant, a wonderfully narrow and picturesque road (the TV-7021) hugs the rugged southern face of the Montsant westwards to Escaladei, which is located in a valley below the mountain range. In 1162 Alfons II convinced the Charterhouse monks of Grenoble, in France, to establish a monastery in recently reconquered territory. It was the order's first *priorat* (priory) in Catalunya and soon extended its authority (and name – El Priorat) over the whole comarca. Abandoned in 1835 and subsequently largely destroyed, what remains now is an atmospheric ruin, presided over by the neo-classical facade of the monastery's church. It opens 10 am to 1.30 pm and 3 to 5.30 pm (4 to 7.30 pm

June to September) Tuesday to Saturday, and morning only on Sunday. Admission costs €2.45.

The ruins are about a 1km walk from the village of Escaladei, the life of which revolves around the Cellers de Scala Dei. The wine-making tradition that the monks brought to the area centuries ago lives on today, and Escaladei reds (which are heavy and potent) are considered among the best from El Priorat. If you wish to stay here overnight, your one choice is *Hostal Els Troncs* (☎ 977 83 00 78, *Rambla Cartoixa 9*), with simple but comfortable doubles for €30.15. A couple of restaurants, including *El Rebost de la Cartoixa* (☎ 977 82 71 49, *Rambla Cartoixa 15*) put on some fine hearty spreads, best accompanied by the local tipple.

There are no buses here so you'll be glad of your own wheels. A web of narrow roads spreads out across the comarca of El Priorat, and simply touring around and popping into villages along the way is a pleasure. The road south-west of Escaladei passes such endearing little spots as **La Vilella Alta** and **La Vilella Baixa**. In the latter, houses are built one over the other in a curious fashion, obligated by the dramatically uneven terrain. **Gratallops** is in itself not as interesting, but does boast some good restaurants for local cooking. Try for a window seat at *La Font* (☎ 977 83 91 72, *Carrer de Valls 41*), where a huge whack of *ternasco* (a cut of beef) will fill you up – expect to pay about €15 per head.

Sant Miquel d'Escornalbou

A pretty, tree-lined road leads up to the Castell-Monestir de Sant Miquel d'Escornalbou, 4km west of the village of **Riudecanyes** (itself quite a fetching little town). Dating from 1153, much of the castle-monastery complex is in ruins; parts have been rebuilt but hardly to exacting historical criteria. The most interesting elements are the church (from the 12th and 13th centuries), cloister and chapterhouse.

It opens 10 am to 1.30 pm and 3 to 5.30 pm (4 to 6.30 pm June to September) Tuesday to Saturday, and morning only on

Sunday. Admission costs €2.45. Regular buses make the half-hour trip to Riudecanyes from Reus. Then you're on your own.

SOUTH TO THE DELTA DE L'EBRE

The coast that stretches south-west from touristy Salou is somewhat similar. The apartments, hotels and standard seafood restaurants continue, albeit with diminishing density, from Salou into **Cambrils**, 6km on. Quite a way in from the coast, Cambrils still retains an intact old town, although not a great deal of specific interest is to be found. And so it goes on down to **Miami Platja** and **L'Hospitalet de l'Infant**. The cove of **Calafat** is pleasant enough but hardly a secret.

A few kilometres on, **L'Ametlla de Mar** distinguishes itself by being a true, working fishing village. It has a small town beach, just beyond which the trawling vessels tie up for the night in the port. It's a quiet little place that seems to have remained largely indifferent to the seaside tourism, though you can get rooms in one of a couple of hotels, and holiday apartments are often up for rent.

From here the highways take you into the Delta de l'Ebre.

DELTA DE L'EBRE

The Delta de l'Ebre (Ebro in Spanish), formed by silt brought down by the Riu Ebre, sticks 20km out into the Mediterranean near Catalunya's southern border. Dotted with reedy lagoons and fringed by dune-backed beaches, this flat and exposed wetland is northern Spain's most important water bird habitat. The October–November migration season sees the bird population peak, with an average of 53,000 ducks and 15,000 coots, but the birds are also numerous in winter and spring. Ten per cent of all water birds wintering on the Iberian Peninsula do so here.

Nearly half the delta's 320 sq km are given over to rice-growing. Some 77 sq km, mostly along the coasts and around the lagoons, form the Parc Natural del Delta de l'Ebre.

Orientation

The delta is a seawards-pointing arrowhead of land with the Ebre flowing eastwards across its middle. The town of Deltebre straggles about 5km along the northern bank of the river at the centre of the delta. Deltebre's western half is called Jesús i Maria and the eastern half La Cava. Facing Deltebre on the southern bank is Sant Jaume d'Enveja. Roads crisscross the delta to Deltebre and beyond from the towns of L'Ampolla, Amposta and Sant Carles de la Ràpita (an ugly place but the seafood is fresh), all on the N-340. Three river-crossing car ferries *(transbordadors)*, running from early morning till nightfall, link Deltebre to Sant Jaume d'Enveja. They charge €0.30 per pedestrian and €1.85 for a car with two people.

Information

The tourist office, or Centre d'Informació (☎ 977 48 96 79), Carrer de Martí Buera 22, in Deltebre is next to an **Ecomuseu**, which has some examples of delta environments and an aquarium-terrarium of delta species. Both open 10 am to 2 pm (until 1 pm at the weekend) and 3 to 6 pm, and close on Sunday afternoon. Admission to the museum costs €1.20.

There's another information office, with a **bird museum**, at La Casa de Fusta, by L'Encanyissada lagoon about 10km southwest of Deltebre. It opens 10 am to 2 pm and 3 to 6 pm daily except Monday. Other offices are in Sant Carles de la Ràpita, Amposta and L'Ampolla.

Things to See & Do

A good way to explore the delta is by bicycle and you can rent one for about €8 per day from several places in Deltebre. Early morning and evening are the best times for **bird-watching**, and good areas include L'Encanyissada and La Tancada lagoons and Punta de la Banya, all in the southern part of the delta. L'Encanyissada has two observation towers and La Tancada one (others are marked on a map you can pick up at the Centre d'Informació). Punta de la Banya is joined to the delta by

a 5km sand spit with the wide, long and sandy Platja de l'Eucaliptus (beach) at its northern end. La Tancada and Punta de la Banya are generally the best places to see greater flamingoes, the delta's most spectacular birds. Almost 2000 of the birds nest here, and since 1992 the delta has been one of only five places in Europe where they reproduce.

Olmos (☎ 977 48 05 48) is one of a couple of companies that run daily **boat trips** for tourists from Deltebre to the mouth of the Riu Ebre and to the Illa de Buda at the delta's tip. Trips last 1½ hours and cost around €5 per person. Boats go daily but the frequency depends on the season: in summer both companies do several trips daily.

Amposta celebrates its *festa major* (main festival) in the third week of August and the locals indulge in much merriment, the running of bulls and other taurine torment – part of a long tradition that will not appeal to all observers.

Places to Stay & Eat

Camping Mediterrani Blau (☎ *977 47 90 46, Platja de l'Eucaliptus)* opens from April to September with room for 240 people in a small eucalyptus grove, charging €3.05 plus IVA per each person, car and tent. It also has a restaurant. There are two more camping grounds, open year round, at Riumar, 10km east of Deltebre.

Restaurant Can Salat (☎ *977 48 02 28, Carrer de Adrià VI 1)* in the centre of La Cava has a few adequate rooms and charges €12.05 per person. The *Delta Hotel* (☎ *977 48 00 46, fax 977 48 06 63, Avinguda del Canal, Camí de la Illeta s/n)*, on the northern edge of Deltebre by the road to Riumar, has nice modern singles/doubles costing up to €35.85/59.35 (including breakfast) plus IVA.

The most pleasant places to eat are out by Riumar and the mouth of the river. *Restaurante Galach* (☎ *977 26 75 03)*, by the Llacuna Garxal (the end of the road as it were), serves Ebre specialities including *anguilas* (eels), *angules* (baby eels), and also shellfish.

Getting There & Away

The delta is easiest to get to and around with your own wheels but it is possible to reach it by bus or a train and bus combination. Autocars Hife (☎ 902 11 98 14) runs buses to Jesús i Maria and La Cava from Tortosa (one hour) up to four times daily (twice a day on Saturday, Sunday and holidays), and from Amposta (30 minutes) once or twice daily.

SOUTH TO VALENCIA

All roads and the railway south of the delta lead to the neighbouring region of Valencia, a fascinating area that warrants a book of its own. For some tempting hints, get hold of Lonely Planet's *Spain*.

The Serra de Montsià forms an uncompromising, rocky barrier between you and the hinterland as you head south. There's not too much to hold you up on your way although, if you don't fancy halting at the next main city of Castelló (in Valencia), the small seaside town of **Les Cases d'Alcanar** has some pleasant, shallow beaches and a handful of places to stay. The small port is fronted by a bevy of seafood restaurants. The town's festa major on 15 August features a strange local version of the *correbous*, or running of the bulls, in which some are tossed into the water!

If you have your own transport, an inland detour would take you about 10km via Alcanar to **Ulldecona**, a town founded by the Muslims. About 1km west are the remnants of a hill-top castle erected by the Muslims and later taken over by the Knights Templar. You can wander in at any time.

TORTOSA

postcode 43500 • pop 29,600

Home 2000 years ago to Iberian tribes, Tortosa has seen them all come and go: Greeks, Romans, Visigoths and Muslims. The town was on the northern front line between Christian and Muslim Spain for four centuries.

A tourist booth (☎ 977 44 25 67, fax 977 58 58 52) on Avinguda de la Generalitat opens 10 am to 1.30 pm and 4 to 8 pm Tuesday to Saturday (morning only on Sunday). Another booth on Carrer de Ferran Arasa opens similar hours.

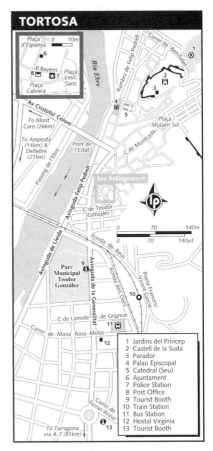

TORTOSA

1 Jardins del Príncep
2 Castell de la Suda
3 Parador
4 Palau Episcopal
5 Catedral (Seu)
6 Ajuntament
7 Police Station
8 Post Office
9 Tourist Booth
10 Train Station
11 Bus Station
12 Hostal Virginia
13 Tourist Booth

The old town, concentrated in the eastern end of the city north of the Ebre, is watched over by the imposing **Castell de la Suda**, an Islamic fortress *(suda)* where a small, medieval Arab cemetery has been unearthed and in whose grounds now stands a *parador* (a high-class, state-run hotel). The Gothic **Catedral** (or *Seu*) dates from 1347 and contains a pleasant cloister and some baroque additions. It opens 9 am to 1 pm and 4 to 8 pm daily. Other attractions include the **Palau Episcopal** and the lovely **Jardins del Príncep**, perfect for a stroll.

About the cheapest place to stay is

Hostal Virginia (☎ 977 44 41 86, Avinguda de la Generalitat 133), where singles/doubles with bathroom cost up to €19.90/27.15. If you have some spare dosh, then splurge on the fine ***Parador (☎ 977 44 44 50)***. Elegant rooms cost €65.10/81.35.

The train and bus stations are opposite each other on Ronda dels Docs. There are regular trains as well as two buses daily (€4.75, one to 1½ hours) to Tarragona. Trains also run to Vinaròs (in Valencia). Up to six buses run daily to Barcelona (around €6, two hours), and two to four into the Delta de l'Ebre area. Lleida is about two hours away by bus (up to four buses run daily).

ELS PORTS DE BESEIT

About 10km west of Tortosa rises the mountainous chain known as Els Ports de Beseit (Gates of Beseit), beyond which stretch the magnificently wild and woolly Maestrazgo uplands in the regions of Valencia and Aragón. If you have your own transport, it would be well used here.

For breathtaking views of the whole area, head 27km west from Tortosa through Roquetes to **Mont Caro** (1447m). After crossing the river plain, the road starts a series of switchbacks that seems to lift you as if on an escalator above the mountain spurs and Ebro plain. The drive up is a pleasure and when you arrive (try to ignore the TV transmission stations) you will be rewarded with views out across the Delta de l'Ebre, as well as up and down the Catalan coast and deep into the hinterland. You may well be accompanied by mountain goats.

Another drive through Roquetes takes you past a turn-off for the sleepy village of **Alfara de Carles** and up into the densely wooded hillside of **El Toscar**, site of a gushing spring and a bar with views back down the valley. At the time of writing plans were afoot to create Catalunya's second biggest natural park here, the Parc Natural del Ports de Tortosa-Beseit.

NORTH OF TORTOSA

The C-12 road north out of Tortosa roughly follows the Riu Ebre, and is lined with citrus orchards reminiscent more of Valencia

than Catalunya. After 13km you pass through **Xerta**. Stop to buy one of the mountainous bags of sweet oranges, on whose proceeds the village lives. A side road west of Xerta leads 10km to the hill-top village of **Päuls**, a few kilometres beyond which a driveable track trundles up to the **Ermita de Sant Roc**, where locals fill up on spring water and engage in shady weekend picnics (barbecue facilities are available).

Three kilometres beyond Xerta the road forks. You can follow the right fork (C-12) 20km north-east to the turn-off for **Miravet** (on the road to Móra d'Ebre). Miravet is a tall, compact medieval town that seems to cascade directly into a bend of the Ebre, just where a local river barge still ferries cars and people to the other side. Up on a hill behind the village stand the empty walls of the **Castell de Miravet**, one of Muslim Catalunya's last strongholds. It was later expanded and played a role in many of the wars that rolled across the Catalan countryside. It is closed for restoration. Turivet (☎ 977 40 76 26), Carrer Verge de Gràcia 5, is a local private tourist office. It provides guides and loads of information on all of south-western Catalunya.

Getting here using public transport is not easy. Trains on a branch of the Madrid-Barcelona line call in at Móra d'Ebre. From there you can get a taxi (☎ 609 22 68 21 or ☎ 977 40 75 13).

Horta de Sant Joan & Around

The left fork after Xerta (on the C-12) takes you along a pretty back-country route, still in the shadow of Els Ports de Beseit. After 8km, take the T-333 road west (you pass the village of Prat de Comte after 5km) and follow the signs for Alcañiz (in the region of Aragón). After 10km you reach a turn-off to the right (north) for Horta de Sant Joan.

Surrounded by strange rock formations and almond stands, with Els Ports de Beseit in the distance, this pretty medieval village not only makes a nice initial base for treks into the Ports and beyond, but is worth looking at in its own right. The porticoes and narrow lanes of the village centre were just as fascinating to Picasso, who spent two long periods here, from 1898 to 99 and in 1909. In the **Centre Picasso** (☎ 977 43 53 30) you can see copies of some of the many sketches and paintings he did in, or that were inspired by, Horta. He later claimed he had learned everything he knew about painting here. The centre opens 11 am to 1.30 pm Tuesday to Sunday; admission costs €1.85. Take time to walk out to the 13th-century **Convent de Sant Salvador**, 2km across the fields and clearly visible from the village in the shadow of a conical hill.

A couple of *cases de pagès* offer accommodation in Horta, as does the ***Hotel Miralles*** *(☎ 977 43 51 14, Avinguda de la Generalitat 21)*. Rooms are spotless and comfortable, though not particularly inspiring. Singles/doubles cost €21.10/30.15. A couple of restaurants and bars will keep starvation at bay. Transport options are limited to a couple of buses a day from Tortosa, leaving at 1.30 pm and 5.30 pm; call Autocars Hife (☎ 902 119814) to be sure. The trip takes about 1½ hours.

If you have a car, it is tempting to make a little side trip west (via Arnes) into the region of Aragón. Eleven kilometres in you reach the picturesque village of **Valderrobres**, topped by an impressive (if partly ruined) Gothic church and castle complex.

From here there are several options. To keep within Catalan bounds, one would be to return eastwards and then, after about 5km, turn north to Calaceite, where you hit the N-420 highway, which you take east for **Gandesa**, 23km away back in Catalunya. This is a big town and a minor transport hub in the area. It lay at the heart of the last great clash of the Spanish Civil War, the Battle of the Ebre, which lasted from July to September 1938. It was the single most violent encounter of the war, leaving about 21,000 dead. The village of **Corbera d'Ebre**, about 6km east of Gandesa, was so badly destroyed under Nationalist bombardment that after the war it was abandoned and a new town built nearby. The bombed-out ghost town can still be visited today. From here the N-420 highway leads east to Reus and Tarragona. Buses with La Hispano Igualadina (☎ 977 77 06 98) run from Tarragona to Alcañiz (in Aragón) via Reus, Falset, Móra d'Ebre, Corbera d'Ebre and Gandesa. Up to four a day of these reach Gandesa (of which two proceed to Alcañiz).

COSTA DAURADA

Central Catalunya

The interior of central Catalunya figures, along with the south-western *comarcas* (districts) covered in the Costa Daurada chapter, among the least-travelled areas of the region. There are several reasons for this. With so much to offer along the coast and in the Pyrenees, the bulk of tourists and travellers, whether foreign or Spanish, tend not to bother much with the interior. It is also true that much of the area between Barcelona and Lleida is fairly flat and uninspiring stuff.

That said, there are plenty of little unexpected jewels for those prepared to dig around a little. It doesn't require a great effort either. From the splendours of the Cistercian monasteries west of the Penedès wine region to some Romanesque surprises and the appealing foothill country of the pre-Pyrenees, you won't be disappointed.

Lleida itself is a worthwhile stop and travelling in this area has the added attraction of plunging you into 'deep Catalunya'. You want to hear nothing but Catalan? You've come to the right place.

This chapter is divided into three rough routes that presuppose you are travelling from Barcelona to Lleida (or the other way around).

ACROSS THE CONCA DE BARBERÀ

This hilly, green, back-country district comes as a refreshing surprise in the otherwise drab flatlands that surround you along the A-2 toll road towards Lleida.

Vineyards and woods succeed one another across rolling green hills, studded with occasional medieval villages and monasteries.

Reial Monestir de Santes Creus

If you follow the A-2 out of Barcelona, the first turn-off (exit 11) of interest that you strike after passing through the Penedès wine region is for this medieval monastery.

Cistercian monks moved in here in 1168

Highlights

- Touring the great Cistercian monasteries, especially at Poblet
- Inspecting the high fortress of Cardona – and staying the night there
- Witnessing the 'donkey' antics of Carnaval in Solsona
- Exploring Àger and the Montsec area

and from then on the monastery developed as an important centre of learning and as a launch pad for the repopulation of the surrounding territory. The monks were turfed out in 1835, and the site was subsequently badly damaged as it was used in turn as a barracks and a prison.

You first enter the complex through a baroque portal that leads into a long square up to the facade of the church, which is part Romanesque and part Gothic. Turn right to get to the ticket office, from where you enter the glorious 14th-century cloister. The warm sandstone lends it a particular glow in the late-afternoon light. Off the cloister is the chapterhouse, an exquisite construction of interlaced vaults and columns, above which is the grand dormitory. A passage connects the cloister with its older, but less captivating, counterpart. Of most interest off to the right in this second cloister are the

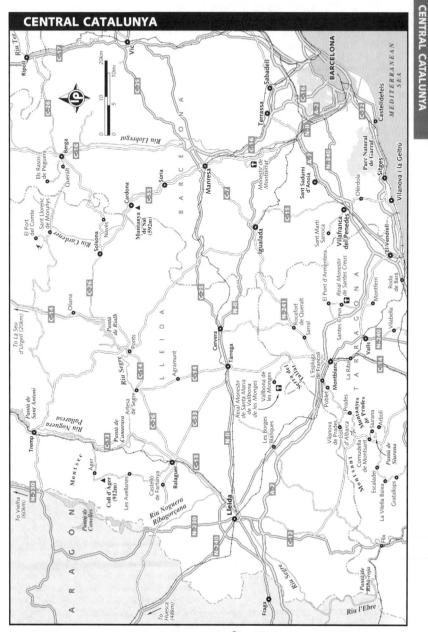

CENTRAL CATALUNYA

royal apartments where the count-kings (*comtes-reis*; rulers of the joint state of Catalunya and Aragón) often stayed during Holy Week. The church, begun in the 12th century, is a lofty Gothic structure in the French tradition. It houses the tombs of count-kings Pere el Gran and Jaume II.

The monastery opens 10 am to 1.30 pm and 3 to 5.30 pm (until 7 pm mid-March to mid-September) daily except Monday. Admission costs €3.65 except on Tuesday, when it's free. Or you can purchase a €6.05 ticket valid for this monastery and those of Poblet and Vallbona de les Monges (see Reial Monestir de Santa Maria de Poblet and Vallbona de les Monges later in the chapter). There's a handful of places to eat in the shadow of the monastery walls.

Getting there without a car is painful, as the only way is a bus from Valls at noon or 6.15 pm. Only one bus goes the other way at around 8.30 am.

Montblanc
postcode 43400 • pop 5750
An important town in medieval times, Montblanc has remained surprisingly intact. In particular, the 15th-century walls are an impressive testimony to the city's past. More than 2km long, they once sported 28 towers, of which 17 remain. Once inside the gates, make for the **Església de Santa Maria la Major**, a fine Gothic church with a Plateresque (a highly ornamented, early Renaissance Spanish style of architecture) entrance. Also worth a peek is the simple Romanesque **Església de Sant Miquel**. The three-arched bridge spanning the Riu Francolí is also Romanesque. Just strolling around town turns up all sorts of little gems.

On the feast day of Sant Jordi (St George), 23 April, Montblanc celebrates its *setmana medieval* (medieval week). Local tradition has it that St George slew the dragon here. For a week the townsfolk get down to the serious business of medieval banquets and dancing, dodging *dracs* and *dimonis* (dragons and demons) and, of course, fire-running *(correfoc)*.

Regular trains from Barcelona to Tarragona via Reus (Ca4 Regional line) stop at

Montblanc. Buses with La Hispano Igualadina (☎ 977 77 06 98) stop at Montblanc on their way between Tarragona, Reus and Tàrrega. Vilana buses (☎ 902 10 13 63) covering the Tarragona-Lleida route call in as often as six times a day.

L'Espluga de Francolí
postcode 43440 • pop 3670
You are more than likely to pass through this shady and appealing little village en route to the Monestir de Poblet. It makes an agreeable lunch stop, and while hanging about you might want to inspect the 13th-century **Església Vella de Sant Miquel**, which displays some Byzantine elements.

The *Hostal Senglar* (☎ 977 87 01 21, Plaça Montserrat Canals 1) is about the best bet if you decide to stay. Rooms with balconies and pleasant views cost €28.65/43.05 plus IVA. The restaurant is also good but there are other options. Good local fare at reasonable prices can be had at the tiny *Casa Nostra* (☎ 977 87 04 77), directly in front of the Sant Miquel church. Their *menú del día* (fixed-price meal) costs €9.05.

The Barcelona-Reus-Tarragona train to Montblanc also calls in here, as do the buses (see Montblanc earlier).

Reial Monestir de Santa Maria de Poblet
The jewel in the crown of the Conca de Barberà is this imposing, fortified monastery, devoted to Santa Maria. It was founded by Cistercian monks from southern France in 1151 and lies about a 40-minute walk outside L'Espluga de Francolí. It became the most important monastery in Catalunya and the burial place of many of its rulers. After it was expropriated in 1835 it was sacked and left to go to rack and ruin. That you can enjoy it in its present state is in no small measure due to the community of Cistercian monks, now numbering 32, who moved back in after the Civil War and set about restoring the place. However, no amount of restoration can replace the copious works of art and the invaluable library that were destroyed or stolen in the years of neglect.

As well as being a defensive measure, the abbey's triple line of walls also symbolised the monks' isolation from the vanities of the outside world. Even before entering the complex the majesty of the place cannot fail to impress you. A portal gives access to a long uneven square, the Plaça Major, which is flanked by several dependencies including the small Romanesque **Capella de Santa Caterina**. The nearby **Porta Daurada** (Golden Gate) is so called because its bronze panels were overlaid with gold to suitably impress the visiting emperor Felipe II in 1564.

Once inside the **Porta Reial** (Royal Gate), flanked by hefty octagonal towers, you will be led through a worn Romanesque entrance to the grand cloister, of Romanesque origins but largely Gothic in style. With its peaceful fountain and pavilion, the two-level cloister is a marvellous haven. You will be led from the cloister to the head of the church, itself a typically tall and austere Cistercian Gothic creation, to witness the sculptural glory in alabaster that is the altarpiece and the Panteón de los Reyes (Kings' Pantheon). The raised alabaster coffins, restored by Frederic Marès (see Museu Frederic Marès in the Barcelona chapter), contain such greats as Jaume I (the conqueror of Mallorca and Valencia) and Pere III. Also along the tour you will be taken upstairs to the monks' dormitory and for a walk around the exposed upper gallery of the cloister. Later on come the library and, downstairs, the cellars where the monks used to make wine. They still cultivate wine grapes, mostly for the Raïmat winery (in the Costers del Segre area in Lleida province) and for Codorníu (see Penedès Wine Country in the Around Barcelona chapter).

The monastery opens 10 am to 12.30 pm and 3 to 6 pm (until 5.30 pm in winter); admission costs €3.05, (students €1.85). One-hour guided tours (in Catalan and/or Spanish) start every 15 to 30 minutes. You'll find a tourist information office (☎ 977 87 12 47) in the compound.

On the way between the monastery and L'Espluga de Francolí are the Torres vineyards of the **Castell de Milmanda** (☎ 619 83

13 14), at whose centre stands the 11th-century fortified estate (or 'castle') that lends its name to the Chardonnay produced here. (For more about the Torres enterprise see Penedès Wine Country in the Around Barcelona chapter.) It opens for visits and tastings from 10 am to 2 pm and 4 to 8 pm (mornings only on Sunday and holidays).

Over Easter and the summer months you can stay across the road from the monastery at the cheerful *Hostal Fonoll (☎ 977 87 03 33)*. Singles/doubles start at around €14/18 without bathroom, €25/32 with.

On weekdays, up to three of the six daily Vilana buses operating between Tarragona and Lleida call at Poblet.

Around Poblet

The rolling and densely wooded countryside that spreads south towards Prades, west to Vilanova de Prades and east as far as La Riba has been declared an area of natural interest. Although not a park as such, it is a soothing area and offers some pleasant walks in hilly surroundings (the highest point, the Tossal de Baltassana, is 1200m). The GR7 long-distance walking route passes through here, linking Montblanc to Prades. Those with transport could wend their way south into the striking Serra de Montsant (see the Costa Daurada & the South-West chapter).

Reial Monestir de Santa Maria de Vallbona de les Monges

Swinging away to the north from Montblanc (take the C-14 and then branch west along the LP-2335), country roads guide you up through tough countryside into the low hills of the Serra del Tallat and towards yet another Cistercian complex. This one is the Reial Monestir de Santa Maria de Vallbona de les Monges, the most important surviving Cistercian convent in Catalunya. Around 20 nuns still live and pray here.

To visit, you must join a guided tour in Catalan, and enter the cloister from the ticket office. Two sides of the cloister are under restoration and it is clear that over the years the entire complex has weathered some fierce storms, the most telling of which was its sack during the Civil War. The cloister is largely Romanesque, though the corner leading into the chapterhouse is Gothic. The tall, narrow church is transitional from Romanesque to Gothic. That it is bereft of virtually all decoration and the choir stalls that once occupied the back of the church is due to the flames of war.

The monastery opens 10.30 am (from noon on Sunday and holidays) to 1.30 pm and 4.30 to 6.45 pm daily except Monday. Admission costs €1.85 unless you have picked up the €6.05 pass (see Reial Monestir de Santes Creus). There is a tourist information office (☎ 973 33 05 67) at Passeig Montesquiu s/n.

Getting to this place without a car is a challenge as only one bus a day rumbles in from Lleida (departing at noon). Another returns to Lleida the following day at 8 am – which is not very helpful really.

IGUALADA TO LLEIDA
Igualada
postcode 08700 • pop 31,855
A centre of industry in central Catalunya, few people take the time to so much as pass through here. Understandable really, although Igualada is not totally devoid of interest. A few remnants of its old town remain and the **Museu de la Pell** (Leather Museum) is a curious place. There was a time when every shoe in Spain was equipped with soles made in Igualada and in this museum you can find out how the leather business worked until well into the 20th century. The museum is at Carrer del Doctor Joan Mercader s/n and opens 11 am to 1 pm and 4 to 6.30 pm Tuesday to Friday; and 11 am to 2 pm at the weekend and on holidays. If this doesn't grab you, keep moving.

Cervera
postcode 25200 • pop 6950
During the War of the Spanish Succession this ancient town sided with the Bourbon king Felipe V – a prudent choice. Perhaps it is no coincidence that almost three centuries earlier Isabel of Castilla and Ferdinand of Aragón agreed (in what is now the auditorium on the long and winding Carrer Major) to marry and thus unite the two great Spanish crowns. Felipe V's reward to the town was to create a new **university** here, after suppressing the remaining Catalan institutions. It is a lavish baroque building and well worth visiting, as is the **Paeria**, or town hall, on the other end of Carrer Major in the heart of what remains of the old town. Note especially the grotesque figures leering from its balconies. Virtually next door is the **Església de Santa Maria**, a mixed Romanesque and Gothic job. Take a wander through the medieval streets in the heart of town; part of the medieval town walls also remain.

Cervera is on the rather slow Regional train line that runs between Barcelona and Lleida via Terrassa and Sabadell. Three trains run from Barcelona and six from Lleida (one hour 10 minutes) daily. People with their own wheels who are heading roughly south and have time to spare could do worse than follow the road for Rocafort de Queralt (31km away). It twists, turns, rises and drops in some pretty countryside well away from the tourist trails. At Rocafort you can pick up the C-241 for Montblanc and Poblet.

Tàrrega
postcode 25300 • pop 10,255
Next stop on the train line from Cervera to Lleida, Tàrrega was founded by the Romans and in the Middle Ages was an important local hub. Though not the most fascinating of towns, the old centre is worth a brief wander along arcaded streets and past some fine medieval houses intermingled with the occasional Modernista fantasy. The 14th-century Gothic **Creu del Pati** in the central Plaça Major is an exquisite piece of sculpture. You are unlikely to want to hang around too long and you can pick up one of the six daily trains running between Cervera and Lleida.

Agramunt
postcode 25310 • pop 4803
A detour north of Tàrrega is worth your while if you are into Romanesque art. The

Roman aqueduct, Tarragona

Bringing life to the walls of Tarragona

Tarragona's 12th-century cathedral combines Romanesque and Gothic styles.

Mist shrouds the little-visited valleys of central Catalunya.

Gothic detail on Lleida's towering La Seu Vella

Autumn fields in the central plains

remarkable **Església de la Mare de Déu dels Socors** is adorned with a beautiful main entrance portal, flanked by 15 columns that in turn support the same number of arches. The church dates from the 13th century, although the entrance was completed in the mid-14th century. A couple of daily buses connect Agramunt with Balaguer (see Balaguer later in the chapter).

Bellpuig

Another stop on the Cervera-Lleida line, you could drop in here to inspect the lavish **Mausoleu de Ramon III Folc de Cardona**, executed in Carrara marble by Italian Renaissance artists and now housed in the 16th-century Església de Sant Nicolau in the town centre. Ramon was viceroy in Sicily and Naples before his immortalisation in stone. If it's closed you might be able to get the keys from the *ajuntament* (town hall), virtually across the road.

About half a kilometre south of town on the road to Belianes stands the **Convent de Sant Bartomeu**, founded by the same Ramon in 1505 and sacked in the 19th century. The cloisters are worth a look. It opens 10 am to 1.30 pm and 3 to 5.30 pm (until 6.30 pm from June to September) Tuesday to Saturday, and morning only on Sunday.

MANRESA TO THE RIU SEGRE

Starting in one of central Catalunya's most important towns, on the C-16 toll road out of Barcelona, this route then describes a northward arc (on the C-55) as far as the medieval town of Solsona. From there you can head west to pick up the C-14 road and follow the Riu Segre south-west (via the C-26 and C-13 roads) into Lleida.

Igniting Ignatius' Faith

JANE SMITH

From March 1522, the Basque Ignatius Loyola (1491–1556), founder of the Society of Jesus (Jesuits), stayed in Manresa for a year, lived the life of a humble beggar and composed the basis of *The Spiritual Exercises*.

Religion, however, was a relatively new experience for Ignatius. The portrait he later painted of himself as a young man was that of a vainglorious knight – a career that came juddering to a halt when a cannon ball landed on his legs in 1521. For a while it looked as though he wouldn't survive the blow. During his long and painful convalescence he read a great deal about Christ and the saints.

Ignatius saw the light, and when able to travel again, went to Montserrat to confess his sins (it took him three days). Thereupon he hung up his sword for good and proceeded to Manresa.

His *Exercises* would become a salient spiritual guide for the devout throughout Christendom. Loyola's path, however, was not so clear. In 1523 he made a pilgrimage to the Holy Lands and then returned to Europe, where he embarked upon years of theological study. Ordained in 1535, he had long acquired many followers and in 1540 he created the order of the Society of Jesus. A military man still, he became its General. Under his direction the order dedicated itself above all to education and taking the Word to any part of the world – frequently bringing its members into great danger. He was made a saint in 1622.

CENTRAL CATALUNYA

Manresa
postcode 08240 • pop 66,320

A big commercial centre in the Catalan heartland, Manresa was the scene of the first assembly of the nationalist Unió Catalanista in 1897, which published the *Bases de Manresa* (see History in the Facts about Catalunya chapter).

Not a great deal of the old town remains but you can't miss the great bulk of the **Basílica de Santa Maria**, atop the Puig Cardener hill in the centre of town. Its huge Gothic nave is second in size only to that of the cathedral in Girona. The unique Romanesque **Pont Vell**, whose eight arcs span the rather less impressive Riu Cardener, was rebuilt after destruction in the Civil War.

Manresa celebrates its *festa major* (main festival) in the second half of August. It opens on a Saturday with the *correaigua*, in which thousands of citizens collect in the central streets of town to be bombarded with flour, confetti, water and other liquids for about an hour. A week later they're back for the more traditional correfoc!

Getting to Manresa is easy. Rodalies trains from Barcelona via Terrassa run here regularly. They take about 1¼ hours and a ticket costs €3.30. From Manresa buses stream out to various parts of the region. Regular buses continue along our route to Súria, Cardona and Solsona, from where you can connect on to Lleida.

Súria
postcode 08260 • pop 6282

Known above all for its important potassium salt deposits, Súria lies along the Riu Cardener and boasts a small old town centre with a couple of Romanesque churches and the remains of a castle tower. Súria is on the Barcelona-Manresa-Solsona bus route run by Alsina Graells. ATSA buses provide up to eight more services from Manresa.

Cardona
postcode 08261 • pop 6445 • elevation 506m

Long before you arrive, you espy in the distance the outline of the impregnable 18th-century fortress high above the town of Cardona, which itself lies next to the Muntanya de Sal (Salt Mountain). Until 1990 the salt mines were an important source of income to the people of Cardona, who now more than ever rely on local agriculture and a trickle of tourism. The little tourist office (☎ 93 869 27 98), Avinguda del Rastrillo s/n, is just outside the town walls and opens 10 am to 1 pm weekdays, 10 am to 2 pm and 4 to 6 pm on Saturday and 10 am to 2 pm on Sunday.

The **castle** (follow signs uphill from the town to the Parador) was built over a predecessor on the same site and its multiple lines of walls and ramparts were tested during the War of the Spanish Succession and again by Napoleon's troops, to no avail. The single most remarkable element of the castle buildings is the lofty and spare Romanesque **Església de Sant Vicenç**. To get in, stop at the warden's office on the right as you enter the castle (and now hotel) courtyard. The bare stone walls were once covered in bright frescoes, some of which can be contemplated in the Museu Nacional d'Art de Catalunya in Barcelona. The church opens 10 am to 1 pm and 3 to 5 pm (until 6 pm June to September) and admission costs €2.45.

A quick wander around the town itself is worth the effort. The views back to the castle from Plaça de la Fira and the adjacent Balcó de Cardona are impressive. It is possible to visit the Muntanya de Sal, about 2km out of town. It has become an offbeat tourist attraction since the mines closed.

A couple of modest *pensiones* (guesthouses) are relatively cheap for an overnight stay. **Pensió Borrasca** (☎ 93 869 27 30, *Carrer del Escorxador 12*) has some rooms with countryside views; singles/doubles cost €21.10/30.15. If you can afford it the magnificent **Parador** (☎ 93 869 12 75, *fax 93 869 16 36, e cardona@parador.es*) is *the* place to be. The sprawling castle grounds make a magical setting. Try for one of the doubles with baldachins (for that extra medieval touch). Singles/doubles cost €84.35/105.45. There are also some suites for €132.55.

Restaurant Perico (*Plaça del Vall*) is a reasonable food stop. You can settle for the lunch *menú* at €7.25 or try something like

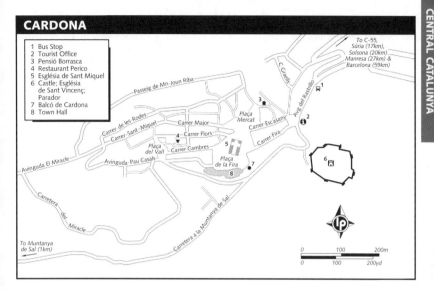

CARDONA

1 Bus Stop
2 Tourist Office
3 Pensió Borrasca
4 Restaurant Perico
5 Església de Sant Miquel
6 Castle; Església
  de Sant Vincenç;
  Parador
7 Balcó de Cardona
8 Town Hall

filet d'estruç amb cor de carxofa farcit (fillet of ostrich with stuffed artichoke hearts) for €10.55.

Cardona is served by the Alsina Graells Barcelona-Manresa-Solsona bus route. Up to seven buses run daily from Manresa (40 minutes). ATSA buses provide up to seven more services from Manresa. Both companies have a few onward services to Solsona.

Solsona
postcode 25280 • pop 6658

They call the people of Solsona *matarucs*, or donkey-killers, which seems a very odd tag until you hear what the townsfolk's favourite festive activity used to be.

Every February the high point of Solsona's carnival fun was the hoisting of a donkey by the neck up the town bell tower (Torre de les Hores). The donkey, literally scared to death, not unreasonably would shit and piss on its way up, much to the delight of the drink-addled crowd below – to be hit by a glob of either substance was, they say, a sign of good fortune for the coming year. Animal rights people have put an end to this particularly bizarre form of torture and the donkey nowadays is a water-spraying fake.

Apart from that, Solsona is a fairly normal and not unpleasant stop. A Roman settlement, it later fell to the Muslims and was finally recovered by Guifré el Pelós early in the 9th century. Today it is a busy agricultural centre.

Information The tourist office (☎ 973 48 23 10), Carretera de Bassella 1, is just outside the old town centre and a few minutes' walk from the bus station. It opens 9 am to 1 pm and 4 to 7 pm (10 am to 2 pm on Sunday and holidays).

Things to See The grandiose 12-arched **bridge** that leads into the town has been said to be 'too much bridge for so little river'. Of most interest is the **Catedral de Santa Maria**, with Romanesque apses, Gothic nave and baroque touches (such as the facade). The pretty little cloister was a dust bowl of renovation works at the time of writing. Behind the cathedral in Plaça del Palau is the 18th-century neo-classical **Palau Episcopal**, which houses a considerable collection of medieval art gathered from churches in the surrounding district. It opens 10 am to 1 pm and 4 to 6 pm (4.30 to

CENTRAL CATALUNYA

7 pm May to September) Tuesday to Saturday, and 10 am to 2 pm on Sunday. Admission costs €1.85. It's also worth wandering the narrow streets of the old town.

Places to Stay & Eat Should you want or need to hang about the cheapest option is the straightforward *Pensió Pilar (☎ 973 48 01 56, Carrer dels Dominics 2)*, where rooms cost €7.85 per person. More enticing is the Modernista *Hostal Sant Roc (☎ 973 48 08 27, Plaça de Sant Roc 2)*. It looks distinctly like Puig i Cadafalch's Casa Amatller in Barcelona. Singles/doubles with bathroom cost €15.10/27.15.

A few places to eat are scattered about the old town, but you should take the trouble to make for *La Cabaña d'En Geli (☎ 973 48 29 57, Carretera de Sant Llorenç 35)*. Here you can expect good, hearty local cooking and better Catalan wines. The only snag is that you can also expect about €25 to take leave of your wallet.

Getting There & Away Two to four Alsina Graells buses run daily from Barcelona via Manresa and Cardona to Solsona. The trip takes two hours and costs €9.25. Two of these buses go on to La Seu d'Urgell (€5.95, 1¼ hours) and Andorra (€7.35, two hours). One Alsina Graells bus daily heads to Lleida (two hours 20 minutes) via Artesa de Segre and Balaguer, departing at 6.40 am. From Lleida it leaves at 1.30 pm. Other buses run to Berga, one via Cardona and the other via Navès.

Balaguer
postcode 25600 • pop 13,040
An important agricultural centre astride the Riu Segre, Balaguer is one of those places worth popping into if you happen to be passing by and are in no particular hurry. The old town climbs steeply away from the river on the west bank, ultimately reaching the Gothic Església de Santa Maria. A few vestiges of the city walls and the one-time Muslim fortress can also be seen, and to round off you could sip a coffee on the grand colonnaded Plaça del Mercadal. Balaguer is 25 minutes from Lleida by Alsina

Graells bus. Other buses run up to three times a day between Balaguer and Tàrrega and two times a day to/from Agramunt. Balaguer is also on the slow, but in places rather picturesque, Lleida–La Pobla de Segur railway line.

Around Balaguer
If you have transport, a curious 8km detour will take you west to **Castelló de Farfanya**. Originally a Muslim defensive position against Christian counties to the mountainous north, the latter dislodged the invaders in 1116, converting the castle to their own purposes and installing a church, parts of which remain. Various towers poke out about the place, overlooking a quiet farming hamlet rarely bothered by sightseers.

Montsec
Before leaving Balaguer for Lleida (a boring trip across the flatlands), you might be tempted by an interesting excursion northwards. It could be done as a little circuit on its own or viewed as the first leg of a trip into the Pyrenees. Your own wheels are virtually a must, though the odd bus will get you part of the way.

The main objective is **Àger**, a village lying in the valley of the same name. If coming from Balaguer, you will see it to the north-east as you reach the top of Coll d'Àger (912m). Away to the north stretches the natural wall of Montsec, a popular area for walks, caving, hang-gliding and climbing. The village is draped over a hill like a mantle, protruding from the top of which is the intriguing ruin of the Església de Sant Pere.

You can stay at one of a handful of *cases de pagès* (country houses with rooms to let) or a *hostal* (budget hotel). If you don't want to hang about or are headed for Lleida or elsewhere to the south, east or west, you can continue east along a serpentine road until you hit the main Tremp-Balaguer road, then turn right (south). The first half of this drive, winding above the Riu Noguera Pallaresa and through steep rock gorges past the Pantà de Camarasa dam, is a pleasure. Once back at the Balaguer crossroads you can proceed south-east for the N-II national highway (or head south-west to the provincial capital, Lleida, and join it there) for either Barcelona or west towards Zaragoza.

LLEIDA
postcode 25080 • pop 112,207

So you've arrived. Lleida (or Lérida in Spanish, which is what you will have seen on road signs coming in from Aragón to the west) is a likeable place with a long, varied history. If you have followed any of the three routes in this chapter, you may feel this is the end of the road, but that is a mat-

ter of choice. Lleida makes a decent starting point for heading north into Catalunya's western Pyrenees. Or indeed you could move west beyond the scope of this book into Aragón and, eventually, to Madrid.

Orientation

The centre spreads around the southern side of a hill dominated by the old cathedral, La Seu Vella, with Carrer del Carme, Carrer de Sant Joan, Plaça de Sant Joan and Carrer Major forming a mainly pedestrianised axis from north-east to south-west. The train station is at the north-eastern end of Rambla

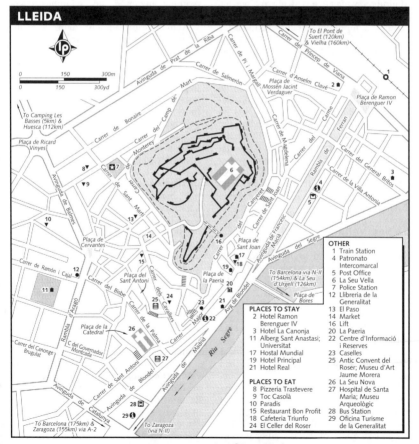

OTHER
1 Train Station
4 Patronato Intercomarcal
5 Post Office
6 La Seu Vella
7 Police Station
12 Llibreria de la Generalitat
13 El Paso
14 Market
16 Lift
20 La Paeria
22 Centre d'Informació i Reserves
23 Caselles
25 Antic Convent del Roser; Museu d'Art Jaume Morera
26 La Seu Nova
27 Hospital de Santa Maria; Museu Arqueològic
28 Bus Station
29 Oficina Turisme de la Generalitat

PLACES TO STAY
2 Hotel Ramon Berenguer IV
3 Hotel La Canonja
11 Alberg Sant Anastasi; Universitat
17 Hostal Mundial
19 Hotel Principal
21 Hotel Real

PLACES TO EAT
8 Pizzeria Trastevere
9 Toc Casolà
10 Paradís
15 Restaurant Bon Profit
18 Cafeteria Triunfo
24 El Celler del Roser

de Ferran, with the bus station 1.25km away on Carrer de Saracíbar, off Avinguda de Madrid.

Information

Turisme de Lleida's Centre d'Informació i Reserves (☎ 902 25 00 50), Carrer Major 31 bis, is the municipal tourist office. It opens 11 am to 8 pm (until 1.30 pm on Sunday) and is the best place for city information. For information on the rest of Lleida province (including much of the Pyrenees) you can try the Oficina de Turisme de la Generalitat (☎ 973 27 09 97), Avinguda de Madrid 36, which opens 10 am to 2 pm and 3.30 to 6 pm Monday to Friday. Another good place for provincial information is the Patronato Intercomarcal (☎ 973 24 54 08), Rambla de Ferran 18. It opens 8 am to 3 pm weekdays.

The main post office (correus/correos) is on Rambla de Ferran. It opens 8.30 am to 8 pm weekdays and 10 am to 2 pm on Saturday. The Policía Nacional (☎ 973 24 40 50) has a station at Carrer de Sant Martí s/n.

If you're heading for the Pyrenees, Caselles, at Carrer Major 46, has some material on the mountains. For material on just about any subject concerning Catalunya that you care to name, try the Llibreria de la Generalitat (☎ 973 28 19 30), Rambla d'Aragó 43.

La Seu Vella

Lleida's 'old cathedral' towers above all else in position and grandeur. It stands within a recinte (compound) of defensive walls erected between the 12th and 19th centuries.

The main entrance to the recinte (open 8 am to 9 pm daily; admission free) is from Carrer de Monterey on its western side, but during the cathedral's opening hours you can use the extraordinarily ugly ascensor (lift) from above Plaça de Sant Joan (€0.36).

The cathedral was built in sandy-coloured stone in the 13th to 15th centuries on the site of a former mosque (Lleida was under Muslim control from 719 to 1149). It's a masterpiece of the Transitional style,

though it only recently recovered from 241 years' use as a barracks, which began as Felipe V's punishment for the city's opposition in the War of the Spanish Succession.

A 70m octagonal bell tower rises at the south-western end from the cloister, whose windows have exceptionally fine Gothic tracery. The spacious but rather austere interior, used as stables and dormitories during the military occupation, has a forest of slender columns with carved capitals.

The cathedral opens 10 am to 1.30 pm and 3 to 5.30 pm (4 to 7.30 pm from June to September) Tuesday to Saturday, and morning only on Sunday and holidays. Admission costs €2.45.

Above the cathedral are remains of the Islamic fortress (suda) and residence of the Muslim governors, known as the Castell del Rei or La Suda.

An alternative way to reach the complex from the centre of town is by the local L15 bus, which you can catch from the bus or train station. It operates from 10 am to 1.30 pm and 4 to 8 pm (3 to 5.30 pm from October to May) Monday to Saturday, and 10 am to 2.30 pm on Sunday and holidays. Buses depart every 30 minutes.

Carrer Major & Around

A 13th-century Gothic mansion, **La Paeria** has housed the city government almost since its inception. The 18th-century neoclassical **La Seu Nova** on Plaça de la Catedral was built when La Seu Vella was turned into barracks.

Opposite is the **Hospital de Santa Maria**, with a Gothic courtyard. It now houses the **Museu Arqueològic**, which includes Iberian and Roman finds from the Lleida area. It opens noon to 2 pm and 5.30 to 8.30 pm Tuesday to Saturday from October to May. In June it opens a little longer and the remaining months only 11 am to 2 pm.

Carrer dels Cavallers and Carrer de la Palma climb from Carrer Major up through the old part of town. The **Antic Convent del Roser** at Carrer dels Cavallers 15, with an unusual three-storey cloister, houses the **Museu d'Art Jaume Morera** and its collection of work by Lleida-associated artists.

Places to Stay

Camping Les Basses (☎ *973 23 59 54*) at Km 5 on the N-240 to Huesca charges €3.80 per person, per tent and per car. Lleida's youth hostel, *Alberg Sant Anastasi* (☎ *973 26 60 99, Rambla d'Aragó 11)*, has room for 120 and no high season, but it's used as a student residence from mid-September to June, during which time you may have trouble getting in.

The friendly *Hostal Mundial* (☎ *973 24 27 00, fax 973 24 26 02, Plaça de Sant Joan 4)*, with an entrance on Carrer Major, is hard to beat, with its range of worthy rooms costing from €7.25 for a small but clean single with washbasin to around €19 for a double with bathroom. It also offers cheap meals and the place is often full with students.

Convenient for the train station are *Hotel La Canonja* (☎ *973 23 80 14, fax 973 22 25 81, Carrer del General Britos 21)* and *Hotel Ramon Berenguer IV* (☎ *973 23 73 45, fax 973 23 95 41, Plaça de Ramon Berenguer IV 2)*. At the former you are looking at singles/doubles for €14.50/27.15 plus IVA for fairly uncaptivating but clean and quiet digs, while the latter charges €27.95/35.40. In both cases rooms come with own bathroom.

If you're looking for marginally more style, one good central option is the *Hotel Principal* (☎ *973 23 08 00, fax 973 23 08 03, Plaça de la Paeria 8)*, with its main entrance on Carrer Major and rooms with TV, phone and the usual features for €33.15/41 (about €6 off at weekends). Another is the modern *Hotel Real* (☎ *973 23 94 05, Avinguda de Blondel 22)*, which charges up to €49.40 plus IVA.

Places to Eat

Despite the many pleasant cafes around Plaça de Sant Joan and elsewhere, the options for an actual meal in the town centre are limited, especially in the evening. *Cafeteria Triunfo* on Carrer Major, just off Plaça de Sant Joan, has a *menú* for €5.75.

The cheapest food deal in town is *Restaurant Bon Profit (Carrer dels Cavallers 37)*. The area is home to many black and North African migrants, and the eatery serves up all sorts of mains, including cous-cous, starting at €3.

Lleida is Catalunya's snail-eating capital. So many *cargols* are swallowed during the annual Aplec del Cargol snail feast, held on a Sunday in early May, that some of them have to be imported. *El Celler del Roser* (☎ *973 23 90 70, Carrer del Cavallers 24)* serves the slithering things *a la llauna* (baked on tin over hot coals), as well as other Catalan fare. They close on Sunday evening and Monday.

A less central hunting ground is the area around Plaça de Ricard Vinyes, north-west of La Seu Vella, where you'll find good places like *Pizzeria Trastevere* (☎ *973 24 80 42, Carrer del Camp de Mart 27)* with pasta and pizzas from around €5.70, and *Toc Casolà*, down the street at No 12, which serves a decent lunch *menú* for €7.85. It also serves snails.

Vegetarians should take a look at *Paradis* (☎ *973 27 27 95, Carrer de Joan Baget 20)*, where you shouldn't need to spend more than €12 a head.

Entertainment

Lleida is unlikely to be remembered in years to come as one of Spain's hot nightlife capitals, but for an overnighter there's a fairly satisfying concentration of bars along the western half of Carrer de Bonaire and some of the side streets. They don't really get hopping until Thursday. One bar that *is* busy most nights of the week is *El Paso*, *(Carrer de Sant Martí 25)*. Take care in this part of town because it's a trifle dodgy.

Getting There & Away

Bus For general bus timetable information you can call ☎ 973 26 85 00. Daily services by Alsina Graells (☎ 973 27 14 70) include up to 13 buses (three on Sunday) to Barcelona (€12.35, 2¼ to 2¾ hours); two to El Pont de Suert and Vielha (€9.10, 2¾ hours); one (except Sunday) to La Pobla de Segur, Sort, Llavorsí and Esterri d'Àneu (€12.25, three hours) and two to La Seu d'Urgell (2½ hours). Other buses go to Tarragona (six daily), and westwards to Zaragoza (four or five daily Monday to

Saturday; one on Sunday) and Barbastro and Huesca (in Aragón; four to six daily).

Train Lleida is on the main Barcelona-Zaragoza-Madrid line. Around 20 trains daily run to Barcelona, most taking about two hours, although some dawdle for four. Second-class fares start at €7.60. There are up to 10 trains daily to Zaragoza (€8.50, around 1¾ hours) and up to five to Madrid. Other direct services run to Tarragona (from €4, 1¼ hours, 10 daily), La Pobla de Segur

(€4, two hours, three daily), Valencia, San Sebastián and as far afield as Galicia, Andalucía and Cerbère (in France).

Car & Motorcycle The quickest routes to Barcelona, Tarragona and Zaragoza are by the A-2. You can avoid tolls by taking the N-II to Barcelona or Zaragoza, or the N-240 to Tarragona. The main roads north are the C-13 to La Seu d'Urgell (via the C-26 and C-14 roads), the N-230 to Vielha and the N-240 to Barbastro and Huesca (in Aragón).

The Pyrenees

Although not as high as those in neighbouring Aragón, and lacking Aragón's glaciers, the Catalan Pyrenees constitute a formidable mountain range. Far below peaks of stark magnificence wind beautiful valleys, and the lower ranges and plains offer up all manner of natural wonders. The range's variety is remarkable. While the northwestern corner, especially the Val d'Aran, is astonishingly green and could easily be mistaken for Alpine scenes in Austria or northern Italy, the vistas become distinctly barren and forbidding farther west. Water seems to burble forth across the range as if from nowhere. Even after a rainless summer, mountain streams and brooks maintain their animated passage. Waterfalls crash in torrents in the most unlikely places and glacial lakes rest undisturbed like mirrors to the heavens.

If you have time to sample only one area of the Catalan Pyrenees, make for the Parc Nacional d'Aigüestortes i Estany de Sant Maurici and its environs, a jewel-like area of lakes and dramatic peaks.

Aside from the natural beauty of the mountains and valleys and the obvious attractions of walking, skiing and other activities, the Catalan Pyrenees and their foothills have a rich cultural heritage, notably many lovely Romanesque churches and monasteries, often tucked away in remote valleys. These are mainly the product of a time of prosperity and optimism in the 11th and 12th centuries, after Catalunya had broken ties with France in AD 988 and as the Muslim threat from the south receded. The distant past also remains alive in the distinctly medieval atmosphere of some of the mountain towns and villages.

Places to Stay

The best deals on accommodation in the north-western part of the Pyrenees are frequently the *cases de pagès* (country houses with rooms to let). In the bigger towns you can find cheapish hotels but in the smaller

Highlights

- Walking to the top of the Pica d'Estats mountain on the French border
- Long walks about the peaks, lakes and forests of the Parc Nacional d'Aigüestortes i Estany de Sant Maurici
- White-water rafting on the Noguera Pallaresa rapids
- Skiing in Baqueira-Beret
- Chowing down on a steaming bowl of *olla aranesa*, a thick mountain stew
- Searching out splendid Romanesque churches, from Ripoll to the Vall de Boí
- Catching the *cremallera* railway up the Vall de Núria and walking to the peaks along the French border
- Exploring the lush green Val d'Aran and its little villages
- Being mesmerised by the Estany de Certascan, the Pyrenees' largest natural lake

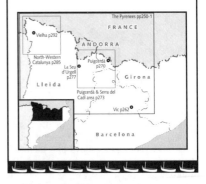

villages near walking areas choices are more limited. Suggestions are made in the course of the chapter but you are advised to pick up a copy of the handy annual guide, *Residències – Casa de Pagès – Guia*, for €3.65. It has a near-complete list of these private houses offering rooms.

THE PYRENEES

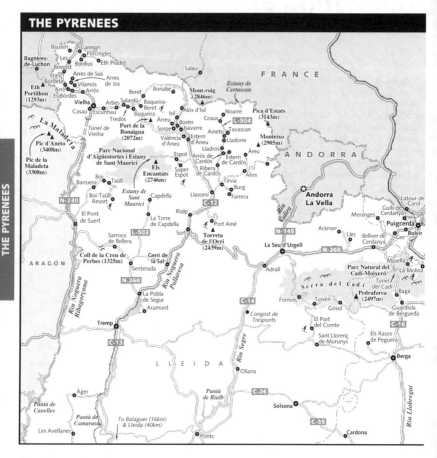

THE PYRENEES

Getting Around

Public transport, especially in the north-west, is extremely limited. Those wanting to explore mountain valleys and their set-tlements, or reach some base points for walking, will need their own wheels or the time and patience to combine hitching (if you so choose) with walking. The only alternative in some cases is a taxi.

OLOT

postcode 17800 • pop 27,644

The hills around Olot, little more than pimples, are the volcanoes of the Parc Natural de la Zona Volcànica de la Garrotxa. Admittedly they're extinct or dormant volcanoes, although one erupted as recently as 11,500 years ago! Olot, if not the world's prettiest place, is an obvious base for the park.

Information

The Patronat Municipal de Turisme (☎ 972 26 01 41) at Carrer del Bisbe Lorenzana 15, opposite the bus station, has the best town maps. It opens 9 am to 3 pm and 5 to 8 pm weekdays, 10 am to 2 pm and 5 to 8 pm Saturday and 10 am to 2 pm Sunday; with reduced hours late September to late June.

The Casal dels Volcans (☎ 972 26 62 02) concentrates on information about the Parc Natural de la Zona Volcànica de la Garrotxa. It's in the Jardí Botànic on Avinguda de Santa Coloma de Farners, 1km south-west of Plaça de Clarà. It opens 9 am (10 am on Saturday) to 2 pm and 4 to 6 pm (5 to 7 pm July to September) Monday to Saturday, and 10 am to 2 pm Sunday.

Things to See
The **Museu Comarcal de la Garrotxa**, Carrer de l'Hospici 8, covers Olot's growth as an early textile centre and includes a

collection of local 19th-century art. It opens 11 am to 2 pm and 4 to 7 pm daily except Tuesday, Sunday and holiday afternoons.

The **Jardí Botànic**, a botanical garden of Olot-area flora, contains the interesting **Museu dels Volcans**, covering local flora and fauna as well as volcanoes and earthquakes. It opens 10 am to 2 pm and 4 to 6 pm (5 to 7 pm July to August) daily except Tuesday, Sunday and holiday afternoons.

Four **volcanoes** stand sentry on the fringes of Olot. Head for Volcà Montsacopa, 500m north of the centre, or Volcà La Garrinada, 1km north-east of the centre. Paths lead to their craters.

Places to Stay & Eat
Camping Les Tries (☎ 972 26 24 05, *Avinguda de Pere Badosa s/n*), on the eastern edge of town, opens from Setmana Santa to October. The ***Torre Malagrida*** youth hostel (☎ 972 26 42 00, *Passeig de Barcelona 15)* is an unusual early-20th-century modernist building. The high season, pricewise, is March to September.

The central ***Hostal Residència Garrotxa*** (☎ 972 26 16 12, *Plaça de la Móra 3*) offers bare but big singles/doubles with private shower for €11.30/22.60 plus IVA. ***Pensión Narmar*** (☎ 972 26 98 07, *Carrer de Sant Roc 1)*, near the central Plaça Major, has good, modern rooms starting at €17.50 for singles with shared bathroom and €30.15 for doubles with own bathroom. Prices include breakfast.

Aparthotel Perla D'Olot (☎ 972 26 23 26, *fax 972 27 04 74, Avinguda de Santa Coloma de Farners 97)* has 30 rooms with own kitchen, bathroom and TV at €19.60/ 42 for a single/double plus IVA.

Pensión Narmar runs a restaurant with main dishes (including trout and chicken) from €4.60 and a *menú* (fixed-price meal) for €6.70. If you have transport and want to head where the locals go for good Catalan cooking, try ***Els Ossos*** (☎ 972 26 61 34), 2.5km out of town on the road to Santa Pau. The *ànec amb peres* (duck cooked in pears) is delicious. You'll shed close to €24, unless you turn up on Thursday, when the place is closed.

Getting There & Away

Bus TEISA (☎ 972 26 01 96) runs buses to: Barcelona (at Carrer de Pau Claris 117; €11.20, two to 2½ hours, two to four times daily); Girona via Besalú (€4, 1¼ hours, eight times daily, three buses on Sunday); Figueres via Besalú (€3.65, one hour, three times daily); Ripoll (most via Sant Joan de les Abadesses; €3, one hour, three or four times daily); and Camprodon (€2.45, 45 minutes, once or twice daily).

Car & Motorcycle The easiest approach from Barcelona is by the A-7 and C-63. The N-260 runs west to Ripoll and east to Besalú and Figueres, passing Olot on a northerly ring road.

PARC NATURAL DE LA ZONA VOLCÀNICA DE LA GARROTXA

This park surrounds Olot on all sides but the most interesting area is between Olot and the village of Santa Pau, 10km south-east.

Volcanic eruptions began here about 350,000 years ago and the most recent one, at Volcà del Croscat, happened 11,500 years ago. There are about 30 volcanic cones in the park which stretch up to 160m high and 1.5km wide. Together with the lush vegetation, a result of fertile soils and a damp climate, these create a landscape of unusual beauty. Between the woods are crop fields, a few hamlets and scattered stone farmhouses.

Information

The main information office for the park is the Casal dels Volcans in Olot. Another is the Centre d'Informació Can Serra (☎ 972 19 50 74), beside the GI-524 Olot-Banyoles road, 4.5km from the centre of Olot.

Walking

The heart of the park encompasses the Fageda d'en Jordà beech wood and two of the biggest volcanoes, Volcà de Santa Margarida and Volcà del Croscat; all of which are included in the marked walking route

No 1, an 11km, four-hour circuit from the Centre d'Informació Can Serra. Moving east from the beech wood to the Volcà de Santa Margarida, you pass the little 11th-century Romanesque Església de Sant Miquel de Sacot. You then ascend 100m to the 330m-wide crater of Santa Margarida, containing a small Romanesque hermitage. From Santa Margarida you head north across the GI-524 and around the Volcà del Croscat, part of which has been quarried, enabling you to see its lava strata. At least three other well marked routes allow you to roam the park with ease.

Santa Pau

postcode 17811 • pop 1390
The old part of the village, perched picturesquely on a rocky outcrop, contains a porticoed plaza, the Romanesque Església de Santa Maria and a locked-up baronial castle.

Castellfollit de la Roca

postcode 17856 • pop 1006
This village on the N-260, 8km north-east of Olot, stands atop a crag composed of several layers of petrified lava – most easily viewed from the road north of the village. It is at its most impressive from a distance.

Places to Stay & Eat

Just off the GI-524 and close to the most interesting parts of the natural park are two pleasant, small, country camping grounds, which open year round: *Camping La Fageda* (☎ 972 27 12 39) and *Camping Lava* (☎ 972 68 03 58), 4km and 7km from the centre of Olot, respectively. *Restaurant Can Xel*, about halfway between the two on the GI-524, can provide meals. Wild camping is banned throughout the Garrotxa district, which stretches from east of Besalú to west of Olot, and from the French border to south of Sant Feliu de Pallerols.

In Santa Pau, there are 10 quaint old rooms with bathrooms at *Bar-Restaurant Cal Sastre* (☎ 972 68 00 49, Cases Noves 1) on Placeta dels Balls in the old part of the village. Doubles start at around €42.20.

[continued on page 261]

MOVING MOUNTAINS

The Pyrenees are becoming increasingly known to mountain sports enthusiasts. Long overshadowed by the glamour of the Alps, this rugged mountain range is now attracting more and more skiers, trekkers, mountain climbers, white-water rafting enthusiasts and other adventure sports addicts from around the country and abroad. Facilities are being improved all the time although in many respects they still lag behind those of the Alps.

Skiing

Baqueira-Beret in the Val d'Aran is one of Spain's biggest and best ski resorts, and by far the most sophisticated of Catalunya's 11 downhill ski areas. La Molina near Puigcerdà is also good, and there are several others, ranging from the reasonable if slightly rough-around-the-edges Boí-Taüll Resort near the regional frontier with Aragón to the tiny beginners' weekender spots at Els Rasos de Peguera and Vall de Núria.

Travel agencies in Catalunya offer affordable packages for one day or longer on the slopes. If you want to set it up yourself on the spot, a day's ski pass *(forfait)* costs up to €30 per day (depending on resort and season) or up to €120 for five days; equipment rental costs €10.25 to €15 per day. It is cheapest to rent directly at the resorts. Ski school costs up to €25 per hour for individual tuition or around €97 for five days of group lessons.

You can find a range of accommodation, from mid-priced *hostales* (budget hotels) upwards, either in or near most resorts.

The high season – when the slopes are most crowded and prices for ski passes, ski school and accommodation are at their peak – is the Christmas to New Year holiday period, February, Setmana Santa (Holy Week, the week leading up to Easter Sunday) and weekends almost all season long.

Pistes are all graded green *(verde)* for beginners, blue *(azul)* for easy, red *(rojo)* for intermediate and black *(negro)* for difficult, although there's some variation in criteria between resorts.

Here follows a brief summary of Catalunya's downhill ski centres, from east to west:

resort	pistes	lifts	ski pass (€)	information (☎)
Vallter 2000	14	9	20.50	972 13 60 75
Vall de Núria	10	4	19.50	972 73 20 44
La Molina	31	13	25.35	972 89 21 64
Masella	37	13	25.35	972 89 00 53
Els Rasos de Peguera	9	5	20.50	93 821 05 84
El Port del Comte	34	15	18.10	973 48 09 50
Port Ainé	30	9	22.90	973 62 03 25
Tavascan	5	2	15.10	973 62 30 89
Super Espot	31	10	21.70	973 62 40 58
Baqueira-Beret	53	27	29.55	973 63 90 10
Boí-Taüll Resort	41	15	24.70	902 30 44 30

Cross-Country (Nordic) Skiing More than half a dozen cross-country skiing areas are also dotted across the Catalan Pyrenees. These places boast trails ranging from 17km in total at the smallest centres, such as Tavascan, to 50km at Sant Joan de l'Erm and Virós-Vall Ferrera. It costs from €3.65 to €6 per day to gain access to these trails.

Walking

The Catalan Pyrenees present some stunning walking and trekking opportunities. You can do anything from pleasant half-day wanders to full-day treks. You could also undertake much longer walks, staying overnight in mountain refuges *(refugis)* that offer basic dormitory accommodation. Small hostales and other accommodation are also available in many Pyrenean villages.

If you're relying on a refuge you should try to reserve places or at least establish that it's not going to be full. Contact numbers are given for most of those mentioned in this chapter and tourist offices can often tell you whether a booking is needed. Nearly all the refuges mentioned in this chapter are run by two Catalan alpine clubs based in Barcelona, the Federació d'Entitats Excursionistes de Catalunya (FEEC; ☎ 93 412 07 77, Ⓦ www.feec.es), at La Rambla 61, 1r, 08002 Barcelona, and the Centre Excursionista de Catalunya (CEC; ☎ 93 315 23 11), at Carrer del Paradis 10. A night in a refuge costs up to around €8. Normally FEEC refuges allow you to cook there, but CEC ones don't. Moderately priced meals are often available.

The terrain ranges from dense forest to windswept mountain crests and peaks, and from glacial lakes to broad open fields. The scope is broad and the going can get long and tough at times but the rewards are often spectacular.

When to Walk In general, the best time to walk is between about mid-June and mid-September. Late July and August can get busy in some areas, making it more problematic to find accommodation. The weather is unpredictable at any time of the year but outside the summer months snow and ice at high altitudes become an impediment to those not equipped to deal with them.

What to Bring For your average short walks that don't involve any great change in altitude, you will need only a minimum of items. Firstly, a good pair of comfortable trainers (runners) should be sufficient, although of course there is nothing to stop you

JANE SMITH

taking along your walking boots. A change of socks is handy for the end of the day. A small day-pack containing an extra layer of clothing should temperatures drop and some kind of wet weather gear (like a poncho) are often helpful. Depending on the season, sun block, sun-glasses and hat are recommended. You need as detailed a map as possible of the area you are walking in (ideally scaled at 1:25,000) and a compass should be a standard item in any walker's pack.

If you are not sure how long you will be out and about, a water flask and some food are essential. Mixed nuts and dried fruit are good, although you may want to prepare a packed lunch for day-long walks, especially if you cannot be sure of chancing on an eatery at the right moment.

In the mountains things are tougher and you need to kit yourself out properly for walking. This means first and foremost sturdy, and prefer-ably waterproof, walking boots. Invest some money in decent, thick socks too. You can find yourself in loose scree and other tough terrain where trainers will be of no use at all. Extendable walking poles can be very handy on steep stretches, whether you are heading up or down, as they redistribute some of the effort away from the legs to the arms, helping you move faster as you go up and acting as brakes on the way down. When you start using these things you'll wish *Homo erectus* had never stood up and probably become insanely jealous of all quadrupeds. There are times, however, when the poles become a nui-sance, so you'll appreciate being able to collapse them and stick them into your pack.

The aforementioned cold and wet weather gear becomes essential in the mountains – you never know when a change will turn your beautiful sunny day into wet, howling misery. If you have room, carry a pair of soft shoes to change into at the end of the day's march.

You may laugh, but if you encounter difficulties while off the beat-en track a mobile phone can come in handy. Some sort of medical kit is also essential. It should at least include plasters (if only for blistered feet) and some kind of disinfectant cream for cuts and abrasions.

Free camping is possible in some parts of the mountains, so you have the option of carrying a tent, sleeping bag and cooking utensils. Most campers will set up in a valley below the peaks they aim to climb but of course if you are doing serious hikes of several days you will have to carry all this stuff with you – which is no fun on mountain ascents!

Maps & Books Nothing like the UK's Ordnance Survey maps really exists in Spain. Several publishers produce maps of varying quality that cover certain parts of Catalunya. For a brief survey of regional and walking maps see the Facts for the Visitor chapter.

The main map publisher for the Pyrenees is Editorial Alpina. Maps come scaled at 1:25,000, 1:40,000 or 1:50,000. The latter two are sufficient for walking but only just. Always go for 1:25,000 where available. Unfortunately some areas of the Pyrenees simply have not been covered at that scale. The Alpina maps traditionally came with small red- or orange-covered booklets which contained useful listings information (on such things as refuges and transport) and suggested itineraries. These are being overhauled and repackaged as glossier green-covered booklets. They are titled *Mapa y Guía Excursionista* and come in Catalan or Spanish (generally they cost €4.70). One hopes the map quality is improving as sometimes they can be unreliable.

Editorial Alpina also produces a series of maps in cooperation with the French Rando Editions, scaled at 1:40,000 and 1:50,000. They come in a predominantly yellow colour. Though again, it's best to get something scaled at 1:25,000 if you can. The map covering the Pica d'Estats in this series, for instance, is OK and covers a wide

MARTIN HARRIS

area but if your main concern is climbing the mountain itself and sticking to neighbouring areas, you are better off with Alpina's 1:25,000 map.

Finally, the Institut Cartogràfic de Catalunya puts out several maps, also scaled at 1:25,000. Some hikers say they are better than Editorial Alpina's maps but the trails are not always accurately marked. No 1, covering the Parc Nacional d'Aigüestortes i Estany de Sant Maurici, is probably one of the most useful.

Walking guides to Catalunya are hard to come by in languages other than Catalan and Spanish. The Catalan Pyrenees are, to some extent, covered in several more general walking guides to the entire Pyrenees chain. Lonely Planet's *Walking in Spain* covers a few routes, as does Kev Reynolds' *Walks & Climbs in the Pyrenees*.

On the Trail When walking you may often be left scratching your head as to where certain trails lead, even if you have a map and compass. You need to keep your eyes peeled for some helpful signs – on some trails you will actually come across signposts at key junctions. This is especially the case in the Parc Nacional d'Aigüestortes i Estany de Sant Maurici, the Val d'Aran and Vall de Núria.

The long-distance GR trails *(senders de Gran Recorregut/senderos de Gran Recorrido)* are generally intermittently marked out with red and white painted markers. On occasion they may be so painted (perhaps bending to one side) as to indicate which path (of several) to follow or which paths (with a cross) *not* to follow. Yellow and white markings refer to shorter PR trails *(senders de Petit Recorregut/senderos de Petit Recorrido)*. Local forest wardens and volunteers sometimes apply paint splodges of no particular colour to indicate local trails. For instance, the last stages of the ascent of the Pica d'Estats from the French side are marked by intermittent yellow dots.

Where no paint is used, keep a lookout for deliberately placed piles of stones. They often appear where there is virtually no discernible trail at all – ideally each one will bring you within sight of the following mound.

All these aids are indispensable for keeping to the right track but placement and clarity vary greatly. You are bound to have moments of hesitation and it is remarkably easy to lose your way.

Where to Walk Various suggestions for specific walks are scattered throughout the text of the Pyrenees chapter. What follows is a brief summary of some areas you might like to concentrate your efforts on.

Long-Distance Trails The coast-to-coast GR11 long-distance footpath traverses the entire Pyrenees from Cap de Creus on the Costa Brava to Hondarribia on the Bay of Biscay. Its route across Catalunya goes by way of La Jonquera, Albanyà, Beget, Setcases in the upper Ter valley, the Vall de Núria, Planoles, Puigcerdà, Andorra, south of the Pica d'Estats (3143m; Catalunya's highest peak), over to the Parc Nacional d'Aigüestortes i Estany de Sant Maurici, then on to the southern flank of the Val d'Aran and into Aragón. Several variants splinter off the main route along the way. The whole route would take the experienced walker about 1½ months to walk! If you intend to follow a good stretch of this route, consider investing in *Through the Spanish Pyrenees, GR11: A Long Distance Footpath* by Paul Lucia.

Another major long-distance path is the GR7, which starts in Andorra, heads south across Catalunya via La Seu d'Urgell, Tuixén and Solsona. One of the nicest stretches of this path is where it enters the Serra de Montsant and the Prades area. The terrain is a mix of high woodland and vineyards, and you can visit places like the Carthusian Monestir de Escaladei along the way. The trail crosses the Riu Ebre (Ebro in Spanish) and heads on into Aragón.

An intriguing path is the GR107, which links Queralt and Montsegur in France. This is part of the so-called Camí dels Bonshomes (Good Men's Way; the path the Cathars took as they fled persecution). It winds through Gósol, Bagà and across the Serra del Cadí to Bellver de Cerdanya before crossing the Pyrenees into France.

The GR92 follows the coast to Portbou from the Riu Llobregat, while a couple of routes lead to Montserrat, one from Barcelona (the GR6) and another from Puigcerdà (the GR4).

Several other GR routes meander across the region, along with a plethora of shorter PR paths. Many are still being signposted, such as the GR65-5, which begins in Tarragona and heads along the route of the old Roman road to Zaragoza. It was one of the many trails that later joined the Camino de Santiago, Spain's most important pilgrimage route across the north of the country to Santiago de Compostela. Only the relatively small stretch in Catalunya has had its signposting completed.

Parc Natural de la Zona Volcànica de la Garrotxa Although not overly taxing, you can undertake many pleasant walks among the long-extinct volcanoes of this park. The vegetation is particularly healthy owing to the rich volcanic soil from which it springs. You can choose between strolls of a few hours and longer walks.

Vall de Núria The spectacular valley and gorge is a wonderful one-off experience in itself, whether you walk it or take the handy *cremallera* (an electric narrow-gauge, cog-wheel railway). When you reach the top you find yourself in mountain pasture land, dominated by the somewhat monolithic religious sanctuary. From here you have plenty of choices of day walks up to the frontier with France and levels close to 3000m. You can follow paths into France, walk the mountain crest line or simply turn back to Núria. Most of the walks are fine for those of average fitness and require no particular mountain skill.

Serra del Cadí & Cerdanya The stark rock walls of the north face of this pre-Pyrenean range are a rock-climber's delight, as is the famed Pedraforca (2497m). But the range is laced with trails good for hikers in no way inclined to scale sheer stone walls!

To the north, the stretch of the Pyrenees running across the Cerdanya area may not be the highest on offer in Catalunya but it still contains some mighty fine surprises. There are plenty of opportunities for bagging some modest peaks and spotting lakes. A series of refuges makes it possible to walk for days on end in the area, and the GR11 runs right through here.

Parc Nacional d'Aigüestortes i Estany de Sant Maurici & Around Catalunya's only national park is a wonderland of natural beauty. Walks will take you through dense forest to bare, snow-covered mountain ridges, past glacial lakes and up to some fine peaks of almost 3000m. Other walks offer rushing streams, dramatic waterfalls and grassy plains. The combination of hotels, *cases de pagès* (country houses with rooms to let), camping grounds and refuges allows you to opt either for long day trips after which you return to base or for more ambitious treks with overnight stops in refuges.

Vall de Cardós & Vall Ferrera These two picturesque valleys, not much visited by foreigners, are full of surprises. Walking options range from soothing country strolls through valley villages with Romanesque churches and bridges, past babbling brooks and through open country-side, to far more exhilarating possibilities, such as the ascent of the Pica d'Estats (3143m) – a wonderful hike past streams, waterfalls, picture-postcard lakes and the bare lunar rockscapes of the high Pyrenees. Plenty of peaks and glacial lakes are waiting to be discovered around here.

Val d'Aran This, the greenest corner of the region, offers a host of beautiful walks. They range from fairly easy strolls through rolling hills and woods (the Val de Toran is a good example) through to more challenging and longer treks reaching into the Pyrenees. Some walkers choose to approach the Parc Nacional d'Aigüestortes i Estany de Sant Maurici from this valley. Challenging routes reach across into Aragón and the Pic d'Aneto (3408m) and its glaciers from the peaceful highland plains of the Plan dera Artiga de Lin. Other routes takes you west to the challenging Maladeta massif.

Mountain Climbing

Pedraforca in the Serra del Cadí offers some of the most exciting ascents. If you are serious about the sport and want to identify more locations in the Pyrenees suitable for scaling, contact the FEEC (see under Walking earlier for details).

White-Water Rafting

The Riu Noguera Pallaresa around Llavorsí and Sort has some of Spain's most exciting white water and is a centre for **rafting**, **canoeing** and **hydrospeeding** (water-tobogganing). A stage of the White-Water World Cup championships was held here in July 2001, the first time Spain hosted the event.

The turbulent Noguera Pallaresa has a string of grade 3 and 4 drops (on a scale of 1 to 6). Descents on the river are best undertaken in May and June. Numerous local companies offer outings along with other adventure sports possibilities.

JANE SMITH

Cycling

Cycling is a fairly popular pastime in Catalunya and mountain biking attracts a growing number of disciples all the time.

To make the task of finding enjoyable mountain routes a little easier, bike centres are being set up in various locations across northern Catalunya. These Centres BTT (*bicicleta tot terreny*; mountain bike) offer maps and information and provide about 100km of marked circuits, as well as bike hire and repair. Approved by the Catalan and French cycling federations, the central office (☎ 972 58 06 39, fax 972 58 25 35, [e] info@banyoles-agenda.com) is at Passeig de la Generalitat 21 in Banyoles, near Girona.

Other Activities

You can go horse riding almost anywhere in the Pyrenees region – there are *hípicas* (riding stables) all over the place. Another sport that's taking off here is parapenting, a cross between hang-gliding and parachuting. Other operators organise activities such as bungee-jumping *(puenting)*, kayaking, caving and cave-diving *(barranquismo)*, in which participants don wet suits and follow watercourses and gorges using a combination of climbing and swimming skills. Tourist offices are generally the first port of call for information on local outfits offering these and other activities.

[continued from page 252]

RIPOLL
postcode 17500 • pop 10,953
• elevation 691m

Ripoll, 30km from Olot in the next valley west, is a shabby industrial town. It can claim, however, with some justice, to be the birthplace of Catalunya. At its heart, in the Monestir de Santa Maria, is one of the finest pieces of Romanesque art in Spain.

Back in the 9th century Ripoll was the power base from which the local strongman, Guifré el Pelós (Wilfred the Hairy), succeeded in uniting several counties of the Frankish March along the southern side of the Pyrenees. Guifré went on to become the first count of Barcelona. In AD 879, to encourage repopulation of the Pyrenees valleys, he founded the Monestir de Santa Maria, the most powerful monastery of medieval Catalunya.

Orientation & Information

The tourist office (☎ 972 70 23 51), Plaça del Abat Oliba, opens 9.30 am to 1.30 pm and 4 to 7 pm. The Monestir de Santa Maria is virtually next door.

Monestir de Santa Maria

Following its foundation in AD 879, the monastery grew rapidly richer, bigger and more influential. From the mid-10th to mid-11th centuries, under famous abbots such as Arnulf and Oliba, it was Catalunya's spiritual and cultural heart. A great five-naved basilica was built, and adorned in about 1100 with a stone portal that ranks among the high points of Romanesque art. The decline began in the 12th century, when Poblet replaced Ripoll as the burial place of Catalan royalty. The monks were evicted during 19th-century anticlerical reforms and two fires left the basilica in ruins by 1885. It was later restored in a rather gloomy imitation of its former glory. The most interesting feature inside now is the restored tomb of Guifré el Pelós.

You can visit the basilica and its great portal, now protected by a wall of glass, 8 am to 1 pm and 3 to 8 pm daily (free). A chart (in Catalan) near the portal helps to interpret the feast of sculpture: a medieval vision of the universe, from God the Creator, in the centre at the top, to the month-by-month scenes of daily rural life on the innermost pillars.

Down a few steps to the right of the doorway is the monastery's beautiful *claustre* (cloister) open 10 am to 1 pm and 3 to 7 pm daily. It costs €0.65 to visit. It's a two-storey affair, created in the 12th to 15th centuries.

Museu Etnogràfic de Ripoll

Next door to the Monestir de Santa Maria, this museum, in part of the medieval Església de Sant Pere, covers local crafts, industries and religious art. It opens 9.30 am to 1.30 pm and 3 to 7 pm (to 6 pm from late September to late March). Admission costs €1.85.

Places to Stay & Eat

The friendly *Hostal Paula (☎ 972 70 00 11, Carrer de Berenguer 8)* is barely a stone's throw from the Monestir de Santa Maria. Its 11 rooms, modernised with sparkling bathrooms, cost €20/32.10 for a single/double. *Hostal del Ripollès (☎ 972 70 02 15, Plaça Nova 11)* has quite decent rooms, some looking over the square, for €27.15/39.20.

There are a few nondescript eating places in the centre of Ripoll. A couple that locals prefer include *Can Villaura (☎ 972 70 08 00, Carretera de Barcelona s/n)* and *Hostal de Rama (☎ 972 70 38 02, Carretera de Sant Joan)*. They are both just outside the town centre. The former is best for solid workers' lunches, while the other is a favourite for big family events. They both have fairly broad menus and serve local fare. Can Villaura is the cheaper of the two.

For more modern cuisine, try *Reccapolis (☎ 972 70 21 06, Carretera de Sant Joan 68)*. They often organise their menu around a culinary theme (say, mushrooms).

Getting There & Away

The bus and train stations are almost side by side on Carrer del Progrés, 600m south-east of the centre. Connections with Barcelona,

Ribes de Freser and Puigcerdà are all much better by train than bus. Trains run to Barcelona (two hours, about 12 daily), Ribes de Freser (20 minutes, up to nine daily) and Puigcerdà (1¼ hours, five daily). There is also a bus that runs to Guardiola de Berguedà in the Serra del Cadí area.

RIU TER TO VIC
The road south from Ripoll leads along the Riu Ter into the flatlands of La Plana de Vic and the city of the same name. Lovers of peaceful walks in the woods might make for the **Serra de Sobremunt**, in pre-Pyrenean hill country to the west of the river. At Sant Hipòlit de Voltregà take the BV-4608 road towards Sant Boi de Lluçanès. This brings you into a stretch of nearly alpine country with dense pine woods. Wandering around in here in search of *rovellons* (a variety of wild mushroom) is a popular autumn activity but even in summer it makes a nice, cool escape from the heat.

VIC
postcode 08500 • pop 30,155
Situated in the plains, Vic is not often considered a highlight of the region, but it may surprise you! It has an attractive historic centre and some good restaurants. Being on the *rodalies* (local) train line makes it a straightforward day trip from Barcelona too. A farming city that has been inhabited since it was known as Ausa to the Celt-Iberians, Vic was traditionally one of Catalunya's leading religious centres. The power of the bishops of Vic stretched far and wide, and may explain the surprising number of (mostly baroque and more modern) churches crammed into the old town today.

Orientation & Information
The tourist office (☎ 93 886 20 91), Carrer de la Ciutat 4, is just off Plaça Major and opens 9 am to 8 pm Monday to Friday, 10 am to 2 pm and 4 to 7 pm Saturday, and

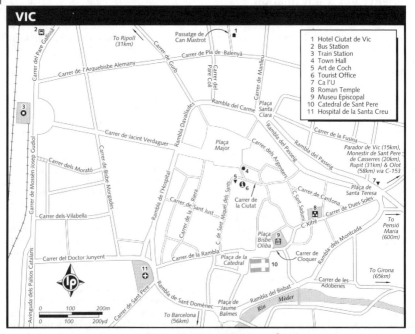

VIC

To Ripoll (31km)

Passatge de Can Mastrot

Carrer del Pare Galissà
Carrer de l'Arquebisbe Alemany
Carrer de Gurb
Carrer de Pla de Balenyà
Carrer del Pare Coll
Carrer de Manlleu
Rambla del Carme
Plaça Santa Clara
Carrer de Jacint Verdaguer
Rambla Davallades
Plaça Major
Carrer dels Argenters
Rambla del Passeig
Carrer de la Fusina
Carrer de Mossèn Josep Gudiol
Carrer dels Morató
Carrer de Bisbe Morgades
Rambla de l'Hospital
Carrer de Sant Just
Carrer de Sant Miquel dels Sants
Carrer de la Ciutat
Carrer de Sant Sadurní
Carrer de Cardona
Plaça de Santa Teresa
Carrer dels Vilabella
Carrer de Sant Pere
Carrer de Sant Domènec
Plaça Bisbe Oliba
Carrer de Dues Soles
Carrer dels Montcada
Carrer del Doctor Junyent
Avinguda dels Països Catalans
C-Xifré
Plaça de la Catedral
Carrer de la Rambla
Carrer de Cloquer
Rambla del Bisbat
To Pensió Maria (600m)
To Girona (65km)
Carrer de les Adoberies
Plaça de Jaume Balmes
Riu Mèder
To Barcelona (56km)

Parador de Vic (15km), Monestir de Sant Pere de Casserres (20km), Rupit (31km) & Olot (58km) via C-153

1 Hotel Ciutat de Vic
2 Bus Station
3 Train Station
4 Town Hall
5 Art de Coch
6 Tourist Office
7 Ca l'U
8 Roman Temple
9 Museu Episcopal
10 Catedral de Sant Pere
11 Hospital de la Santa Creu

0   100   200m
0   100   200yd

10 am to 1 pm on Sunday. Plaça Major, the largest of Catalunya's central squares, is lined with medieval, baroque and Modernista mansions. It is still the scene of regular markets, hence its other name, Plaça del Mercadal.

Things to See & Do

Just wandering around the city is pleasant enough but the highlights are the **Catedral de Sant Pere** and the **Museu Episcopal**. The former is a neo-classical Goliath of rather gloomy taste flanked by a stout Romanesque bell tower. Inside, the dark, square-based pillars are lightened somewhat by murals by Josep Maria Sert (he had to do them twice because the first set was destroyed by fire in 1936). It is worth the €1.85 to enter the Romanesque crypt, see the treasury rooms and above all wander into the stone lace-work splendour of the Gothic cloister. Across Carrer de Cloquer, the Museu Episcopal holds a fine collection of medieval art and other pieces. A new building is being raised on the site, so a selection of the museum's most prized possessions is temporarily on display at the **Hospital de la Santa Creu**, Rambla de l'Hospital 52. On Carrer Xifré stands the largely reconstructed remains of a **Roman temple**.

In September the city hosts the Mercat de Música, a somewhat chaotic event over several days in which Catalan, national and foreign acts of various schools of Latin rock and pop get together to jam. Around 100,000 spectators turn up for the fun.

Places to Stay

Hotel options are a little thin. ***Pensió Maria*** *(☎ 93 889 31 02, Carrer del Canigó 29 & 54)* is a little way out of the centre and has basic doubles for €18.10. ***Hotel Ciutat de Vic*** *(☎ 93 889 25 51, fax 93 889 14 47, Passatge de Can Mastrot s/n)* is a great deal more comfortable but you pay for the luxury – at around €84.35 per double. ***Parador de Vic*** *(☎ 93 812 23 23, fax 93 812 23 68, Bac de Sau)* is, for just a little more money (up to €90.40 per double), a much more enticing option if you have the transport. This

remake of a grand country mansion is about 15km west of the city and located right on the Pantà de Sau dam. Take the C-153 road for Olot and, after 4km, the Tavernoles turnoff. Follow it to the end.

Places to Eat

Several good restaurants beckon for attention. ***Ca l'U*** *(☎ 93 886 35 04, Plaça de Santa Teresa 4)* is a big old *hostal* (budget hotel) dining hall where you can tuck into good Catalan home cooking. A full meal will cost about €18.10, although the weekday lunchtime set menu costs €9.65. It opens Tuesday to Sunday lunchtime. *Art de Coch* *(☎ 93 886 40 33, Carrer de Sant Miquel dels Sants 1)* is in the heart of the old town and offers a mix of traditional Catalan and also more creative dishes. Try the *suquet de cloïsses fines amb bacallà i carxofes*, a clam stew with cod and artichokes. A set menu can cost €14.50, while a la carte you are likely to go closer to €30. It closes on Sunday.

Getting There & Away

Regular rodalies trains (line C3) run here from Barcelona (€3.30, up to 1½ hours). Buses run to towns in the *comarca* (district). Plaça Major is a five minute walk south-east.

AROUND VIC
Rupit

An enchanting excursion north-east of Vic takes you 31km along the C-153 road towards Olot to the town of Rupit, a splendid old village set amid rugged grazing country – the flat-top mountains around here come as quite a surprise. It is no secret with locals and on weekends the car park just outside fills with tour buses (mostly from Barcelona). Still, there's a good reason for all this. You cross a suspension footbridge made in the 1940s to reach the village, full of quaint old 17th-century houses, a baroque church vaguely reminiscent of those found in Portugal and tucked-away squares. Carrer del Fossar, which climbs the hill along the spine of which part of the village is spread-eagled, is especially enticing. Rupit is on the GR2 long-distance walking trail and is also a good base for less ambitious rambles in the area. A quick stroll out of town takes you over a busy brook and up the other side to a small chapel from where there are splendid views.

Places to Stay & Eat A pleasant place to stay, *Hostal Estrella (☎/fax 93 852 21 71, Plaça de Bisbe Font 1)* has prim rooms overlooking the square and the countryside. Rooms start at around €42 per person for half-board *(media pensión)*, which seems reasonable as the food is very good. Try the *ànec amb peres* (duck prepared with pears in a rich sauce). If you opt to eat but not stay, you are looking at around €21 for a meal with wine.

Getting There & Away Getting here without your own car is a trifle problematic. An Empresa Pous de Manlleu bus (☎ 93 850 60 63) leaves Carrer de Casp 30 in Barcelona at 6 pm Monday to Friday and at 11 am on Saturday, and returns at 8 am (with an extra service at 5 pm at weekends and holidays). The bus calls in at Vic on the way. The trip takes about two hours from Barcelona (€12 return).

Around Rupit

If you have your own wheels you might also pop into **Tavertet**, 15km back towards Vic on the C-153 and then 13km south along a narrow, winding road. The views across a broad gorge and south-west over the Pantà de Sau dam towards La Plana de Vic are breathtaking, and you'll find a bijou Romanesque chapel and a couple of restaurants catering to day-trippers.

Monestir de Sant Pere de Casserres

This isolated Benedictine monastery, a Romanesque jewel set in a sharp bend of the Riu Ter, is accessible from Vic if you've got your own transport. If you're really keen you can pick up a route map in the Vic tourist office and make the five-or-so-hour walk here (but then you have to get back!). The less ambitious could drive to the Parador de Vic, situated on the dam, and walk the almost 4km from there.

VALL ALTO DEL TER

From Ripoll, this upper part of the Riu Ter valley reaches north-east to the small pleasant towns of Sant Joan de les Abadesses and Camprodon (950m), then north-west to the modest Vallter 2000 ski centre (2150m), just below the French border. The area is a more agreeable overnight stop than Ripoll and from the upper reaches there are some excellent walks west to the Vall de Núria.

The C-38 road leaves the Riu Ter valley at Camprodon to head over the 1513m Coll d'Area pass into France.

Information

Sant Joan de les Abadesses has one tourist office (☎ 972 72 05 99) and Camprodon has two (☎ 972 74 09 36, ☎ 972 74 00 10). Salvat bookshop at Carrer del Beat Miró 8 in Sant Joan stocks Editorial Alpina mapguides and other guidebooks.

Skiing

Lying at 2150m in an impressive mountain bowl, about a kilometre from the French border, **Vallter 2000** (☎ 972 13 60 75) is the easternmost Pyrenean ski resort and snow can be unreliable. It has 14 pistes of all grades, nine lifts and a ski school. A day's lift pass costs €20.50. You can rent gear at the resort, Setcases or Camprodon.

In summer, the Telecadira Jordi Pujol chair lift opens 11 am to 4 pm late July to early September. It rises to the Cafeteria Les Marmotes at 2535m, from where, on a good day, there are magnificent views.

Walking

The fit and well equipped can undertake excellent full-day walks west from the uppermost part of the Riu Ter valley to the Vall de Núria, 10km to 12km away as the crow flies. Follow the Editorial Alpina *Puigmal* map-guide.

One route takes you through Tregurà de Dalt (1400m), north-west over the Coll dels Tres Pics pass (2400m), and down to the Federació d'Entitats Excursionistes de

Catalunya's (FEEC; see under Walking in the Moving Mountains special section for details) small Coma de Vaca refuge (closed) at the top of the steep Gorges del Freser valley, then north-west up to the Coll de Torreneules (2585m), and down to the Vall de Núria (1970m). Shorter walks down in the valley or higher up are also possible.

Sant Joan de les Abadesses

In Sant Joan de les Abadesses the restored 12th-century **bridge** over the Ter is worth a look, though the **Museu del Monestir** on Plaça de l'Abadessa is perhaps of greater interest. This monastery, another Guifré el Pelós foundation, began life as a nunnery but the nuns were expelled in 1017 for alleged licentious conduct. Its elegant 12th-century church contains the marvellous *Santíssim Misteri*, a 13th-century polychrome woodcarving of the descent from the cross, composed of seven life-size figures. Also remarkable is the Gothic altarpiece of Santa Maria La Blanca, carved in alabaster. The elegant 15th-century late-Gothic cloister is charming. The monastery complex opens from at least 10 am to 2 pm and 4 to 6 pm (to 7 pm May, June and September) daily (at the weekend only from November to mid-March); and 10 am to 7 pm daily in July and August. Admission costs €1.25.

Camprodon

A favoured summer retreat and walkers' and skiers' base, Camprodon is a pretty little

THE PYRENEES

The Legend of Comte Arnau

Sant Joan de les Abadesses is one of many places in the country north of Ripoll associated with perhaps the strangest of Pyrenean legends: that of Comte Arnau, the wicked medieval count of Mataplana, who cheated his workers of their due payments of wheat and had more than his quota of lust for local womanhood. It seems the insatiable count came by tunnel to Sant Joan from Campdevànol, 10km west, for covert trysts with the abbess and other nuns. When the abbess, his favourite, died, her pious replacement barred him from the convent but (thanks to help from the devil) he still got in – and carried on.

Eventually, Arnau fell in love with a local lass, whose only refuge was the nunnery at Sant Joan. Arnau forced his way into the convent to find his beloved dead – from fear and misery, it's surmised. However, her corpse revived just long enough to give the count a good ticking-off for his misdeeds. Overcome by remorse, Arnau retired to the Serra de Mogrony where, condemned to eternal misery for his sins, his tortured soul still wanders, returning on thundery nights (and, some say, under a full moon) to the convent: a horrific vision on horseback with a pack of balefully howling dogs.

If you visit Sant Joan or other villages in the region in summer, you might be lucky enough to catch one of the occasional re-enactments of bits of the Arnau legend. Or you can look at his supposed residence, the Castell de Mataplana, at Gombrèn, about 11km north-west of Ripoll on the GI-401.

ASA ANDERSSON

place boasting a lovely Romanesque bridge and the equally beguiling 12th-century Monestir de Sant Pere. Isaac Albéniz, one of Spain's few notable composers, was born here.

Setcases
Another 11km to the north-west, this hamlet is said to have been founded by a blind shepherd and his seven sons. They could not have imagined that it would one day be a popular spot for walkers and skiers (making for Vallter 2000) to spend their nights. In spite of recent development, it is not an unattractive spot.

Molló
Only 3km along the main road to France from Camprodon, it is worth a stop here to admire the fine Romanesque Església de Santa Cecilia.

Beget
Capping the end of a long and winding mountain lane that trails off here into a heavily wooded valley, this hamlet is a joy to behold. The 12th-century Romanesque church is accompanied by an implausible array of roughly hewn (but immaculately maintained) houses, all scattered about stone-paved lanes. Through it gushes a busy mountain stream. Beget is on the GR11 long-distance walking route. The place has a permanent population of 12 and the rest of the well kept houses belong to well lined pockets from well out of town!

Places to Stay
There are many accommodation options, including camping grounds near Sant Joan and Camprodon and the good *Camping Conca de Ter* (☎ 972 74 06 29) at Vilallonga de Ter, 5km north-west of Camprodon; it opens year round, charging €17 plus IVA for two people with a car and tent.

Hostal Janpere (☎ 972 72 00 77, Carrer del Mestre Andreu 3), in Sant Joan de les Abadesses, has good rooms with bathroom costing €18.10 per person.

In Camprodon *Can Ganansi* (☎ 972 74 01 34, Carrer de Josep Morera 9), 100m south

of the central Plaça d'Espanya, has doubles with bathroom and TV for up to €36.15.

North-west up the valley from Camprodon, the villages of Vilallonga de Ter, Tregurà de Dalt (5km up a steep side road, 12km from Camprodon) and Setcases (11km off) have at least one *pensión* (guesthouse) or hostal each. Setcases has half a dozen.

You can stay in two places in Beget. *El Forn* (☎ 972 74 12 30, Carrer de Josep Duñach 'En Feliça' 9) is a cosy house kept in good order. Doubles cost €58. Full board costs €45.20 per person. A little more basic but fine is *Can Joanic* (☎ 972 74 12 41, Carrer de Bell Aire 14), with doubles at €30.15.

Places to Eat
You'll find a few cheap and (sometimes) cheerful little restaurants in central Camprodon and other towns – often the *menú* (set-price meal) won't exceed about €7.25. Some local favourites are a little less obvious to find for the uninitiated and require your own wheels (or a taxi). *Restaurant El Serrat* (☎ 972 13 60 19) is a delightful, rustic sort of place in the village of Tregurà de Dalt. It is good for country cooking.

For a limited menu of venison and other hunters' favourites, but above all for the lush green setting, try to get a place at the table of *Can Po* (☎ 972 74 10 45) in the village of Rocabruna, which is about 10km north-east of Camprodon on the road to Beget. Regional president Jordi Pujol occasionally drops by for a feed here. Closing times are particularly fickle (and in winter they open only at the weekend) so if possible call ahead. Both of the little hotels in Beget have inviting restaurants.

Getting There & Away
Güell i Güell runs around seven buses daily from Ripoll to Sant Joan de les Abadesses (15 minutes) and Camprodon (40 minutes). The only daily bus north-west from Camprodon, as far as Setcases (30 minutes), leaves in the early afternoon and returns soon after. TEISA runs a couple of buses daily from Olot to Sant Joan de les Abadesses and Camprodon. There are no buses to Rocabruna or Beget.

VALL DE NÚRIA & RIBES DE FRESER

Around AD 700, so the story goes, Sant Gil (St Giles) came from Nîmes in France to live in a cave in an isolated mountain valley 26km north of Ripoll, preaching the Gospel to shepherds. Four years later, apparently fleeing Visigothic persecution, Sant Gil hurriedly hid a wooden image of the Virgin and Child he had carved, a cross, his cooking pot and the bell he had used to summon the shepherds. They stayed hidden until 1079, when an ox miraculously led some shepherds to the spot. The statuette, the Mare de Déu de Núria, became the patron of Pyrenean shepherds and Núria's future was assured. The first historical mention of a shrine here was made in 1162.

Sant Gil would recoil in shock if he came back today. The large, grey Santuari de Núria (a sanctuary complex) squatting at the heart of the valley is an eyesore and the crowds would make anyone with hermitic leanings run a mile. Núria, however, remains almost pristine, a mountain-ringed wide, green bowl that is the starting point for numerous fine walks. It's also fun getting there, via the Gorges de Núria – the green, rocky valley of the thundering Riu Núria – either on foot or by the little *cremallera* (an electric narrow-gauge, cogwheel railway) from Ribes de Freser, which rises over 1000m on its 12km journey.

Bring warm clothes as the high altitude can bring quite a temperature drop. In winter Núria is a small-scale ski resort with 10 short runs.

Orientation

Unless you're walking to Núria across the mountains, you must approach from the small town of Ribes de Freser, on the N-152 14km north of Ripoll. The cremallera starts at Ribes-Enllaç station, just off the N-152 at the southern end of Ribes de Freser, and makes two stops on the way to Núria: at Ribes-Vila station, near the northern end of Ribes de Freser after 1 km, and at the village of Queralbs (1200m) after 6km. There's a road from Ribes de Freser to Queralbs, from where it's the cremallera or your feet.

Information

Núria's tourist office (☎ 972 73 20 20) is in the Santuari de Núria complex. It opens 8.30 am to 6.30 pm (to 8 pm July to September) daily.

Ribes de Freser's main tourist office (☎ 972 72 77 28) is at Plaça de l'Ajuntament 3.

Santuari de Núria

The large 19th- and 20th-century building dominating the valley contains a hotel, restaurants and exhibition halls as well as the *santuari* (sanctuary) itself, which holds the sacred *símbols de Núria*. The sanctuary has the same opening hours as the information office. The Mare de Déu de Núria sits behind a glass screen above the altar and is in the Romanesque style of the 12th century, so either Sant Gil was centuries ahead of his time or this isn't his work! Steps lead up to the bell, cross and cooking pot (all dating back to at least the 15th century). To have a prayer answered, you should put your head in the pot and ring the bell while you say it.

Walking

If you plan on doing some walking you'd be advised to get Editorial Alpina's *Puigmal* map-guide before arriving at Núria. If you want to walk up to Núria, you can avoid the first unexciting 6km from Ribes de Freser by taking the cremallera (or road) to Queralbs, saving your energies for the steepest and most spectacular part of the approach – about three hours up the track climbing the Gorges de Núria. Or take the cremallera up and walk down! The track is OK by hikers' standards, but this is not a Sunday afternoon stroll for the seriously unfit.

From the Vall de Núria (where you're advised to fill in a route sheet at the information office before heading off), you can cap several 2700m to 2900m peaks on the main Pyrenees ridge in about 2½ to four hours' walking for each peak (one way). For instance, the walk up and down the Pic de Noucreus (2799m), north-east of the valley, can be done in about five hours all in. From that peak you are poised on the

French frontier and you happen to be on the GR11 long-distance route. This you can follow east or west. Another trail descends into France and an enticing series of mountain lakes.

A Puigmal Circuit Bagging the area's highest peak (2913m) is within the grasp of most moderately fit walkers. Head to the back of the sanctuary and towards the short ski lift that heads north-west from there: shortly after it you cross a bridge over a stream, from where you need to bear right and upwards (you'll see a sign for Puigmal). After a brief stroll through woods and across a stream you come to a sign pointing off left to Puigmal and right to Finestrelles. Take the former and follow the blue paint splodges that guide you high above the dry riverbed to join a walking path that follows the riverbed, which you eventually cross a couple of times as you reach high, green but treeless pasture. The path remains clear. The last stretch is a fairly steep walk to the top and the whole hike should take you about 2½ hours. Early in the summer (as late as June) you may find some snow and ice up here.

The views from the top are sensational, and paths lead away into neighbouring French Cerdagne (west) and to the south. To the north, you can follow a gentle crest to the Pic del Segre (2844m). First you pass along the west flank of a low rise, then dip down and next find yourself scrambling up a path through red stones to the top. From here you can see the sanctuary below in the Vall de Núria – to reach it continue walking north from the Pic del Segre to a signposted pass, the Coll de Finestrelles. If you started your day early enough, you could spend about an hour proceeding up the Pic de Finestrelles (2829m) before returning to the path and beginning the gentle, if longish, march down to Núria. Your path takes you through lush green grazing land and roughly follows the course of the Finestrelles stream to your starting point. The countryside is pleasing to the eye and you may get lucky and see chamois and other four-legged creatures (horses abound).

Places to Stay & Eat

Wild camping is banned in the whole Ribes de Freser–Núria area.

Núria There's a cheap and basic *zona d'acampada* (camping area with limited facilities) behind the sanctuary. Space is limited (bookings ☎ 972 73 20 20).

The *Alberg Pic de l'Àliga* youth hostel (☎ 972 73 20 48) is up at the top of the cable car *(telecabina)* on the eastern side of the valley. It has 138 places in dorms of four to 14. High-season prices (plus a €0.60 surcharge) apply all year except April, June, October and November. The cable car runs from 9 am to 6.35 pm (8.15 pm July to September) daily, and also from 9.30 to 10 pm on Friday and Saturday.

The *Hotel Vall de Núria* (☎ 972 73 20 00) in the sanctuary building has 65 comfortable singles/doubles with bathroom and TV. Prices range from €39.50/52.90 (for Monday to Friday nights most of the year) to €70.40/91.45 in August. It closes in May and December but has some apartments that open year round. The hotel restaurant has a *menú* for €13.30. Also in the sanctuary building are the *Autoservei* self-service cafeteria and the *Bar Finestrelles*, both of which have starters costing about €3.65 and main courses for around €6. The bar and hotel restaurant close in slow periods, but the cafeteria generally opens daily. There's also a shop in the sanctuary building selling food.

Ribes de Freser You'll find that *Fonda Vilalta* (☎ 972 72 70 95, Carrer de Cerdanya 6) has a variety of basic but clean doubles that cost €19.30, €25.35 (with views and shower) or €31.35 (with views and fully equipped bathroom). Another reasonable option is the *Hotel Els Caçadors* (☎ 972 72 77 22, fax 972 72 80 01, Carrer de Balandrau 24–26). Rooms are comfortable and cost up to €17.20 plus IVA per person. You are warmly counselled to cough up the extra €4.25 per person for the amazing buffet breakfast – loads of cold meats, cheeses, juice, cereal and sweet pastries. The same people also opened a three-star place across the road in 1999, where prices start at €23.20 per person plus IVA.

There are three lower mid-range hotels, with doubles at up to €43.70, on Carrer de Sant Quintí.

Queralbs This delightful hamlet of stone houses with slate roofs makes a very pretty base. The only place to stay is *Pensió L'Avet* (☎ *972 727 377, Carrer Major 7)*, a pleasant old house (often open only at weekends) with six doubles at €30.15. Make sure you don't leave your passport with the guy who runs it, as he isn't always around and you may have trouble tracking him down when you want to leave!

The town is short on eating options so it's best to bring your own in slow periods or have a car to get to another town, such as Fornells de la Muntanya, 2km south off the Ribes de Freser–Puigcerdà road. There you'll find *Ca Casa Nova*, a simple country restaurant serving great meat dishes. It's popular with hunters and other mountain types, except when it closes on Monday evening and Tuesday.

Getting There & Away
Transports Mir runs between Ripoll and Ribes de Freser, with two or three buses a day from Monday to Friday and one on Saturday.

About six RENFE trains run daily to Ribes-Enllaç from Ripoll (20 minutes), and Barcelona (2¼ hours).

The cremallera (☎ 972 73 20 20), operating since 1931, runs from Ribes-Enllaç to Núria and back six to 12 times daily depending on the season (€8.30/13.30 one way/return; about 45 minutes one way). All trains stop at Ribes-Vila and Queralbs, and some connect with RENFE trains at Ribes-Enllaç. It's a spectacular trip, particularly after Queralbs as the train winds up the Gorges de Núria.

CERDANYA
Cerdanya, along with French Cerdagne across the border, occupies a low-lying basin between higher reaches of the Pyrenees to the east and west. Cerdanya and Cerdagne, once a single Catalan county,

were divided by the Treaty of the Pyrenees in 1659 but still have a lot in common. It's in areas like this that you have the strongest sense of being neither in Spain nor in France but in Catalunya. Local tourist offices make a big thing of being in Cerdanya and stock brochures and information on both the Spanish and French sides of the district.

Walkers should get a hold of Editorial Alpina's *Cerdanya* map and guide booklet (scaled at 1:50,000).

Puigcerdà
postcode 17520 • pop 6580
• elevation 1202m

Just a couple of kilometres from the French border, the capital of Catalan Cerdanya, Puigcerdà (puh-cher-**da**), is not much more than a way station, but it's a jolly little one, particularly in summer and during the ski season. A dozen Spanish, Andorran and French ski resorts lie within 45km.

Orientation & Information Puigcerdà stands on a small hill, with the train station at the foot of its south-western side. Just off Plaça de l'Ajuntament (reached by a few minutes' climb up some flights of steps) is the tourist office (☎ 972 88 05 42) at Carrer de Querol 1. It opens 9 am to 1 pm and 4 to 7 pm (morning only on Monday) weekdays, and 10 am to 1.30 pm and 4.30 to 7.30 pm Saturday. If you ask the right questions you can get buckets of information here, including lots on possible walking options all over Cerdanya, skiing, local transport and more.

Another office (☎ 972 14 06 05), by the Park Hotel near the southern entrance to town, opens Sundays; opening hours tend to vary.

You'll find plenty of banks on the main squares. The post office *(correus/correos)* is at Avinguda del Coronel Molera 11. The Guàrdia Urbana (municipal police; ☎ 908 83 11 60) are based in the town hall *(ajuntament)* on Plaça de l'Ajuntament. The Hospital de Puigcerdà (☎ 972 88 01 50) is central at Plaça de Santa Maria 1.

Things to See Despite having been seriously damaged in the Civil War, the town

THE PYRENEES

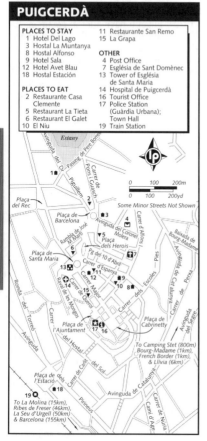

PUIGCERDÀ

PLACES TO STAY
1 Hotel Del Lago
3 Hostal La Muntanya
8 Hostal Alfonso
9 Hotel Sala
12 Hotel Avet Blau
18 Hostal Estación

PLACES TO EAT
2 Restaurante Casa Clemente
5 Restaurant La Tieta
6 Restaurant El Galet
10 El Niu
11 Restaurante San Remo
15 La Grapa

OTHER
4 Post Office
7 Església de Sant Domènec
13 Tower of Església de Santa Maria
14 Hospital de Puigcerdà
16 Tourist Office
17 Police Station (Guàrdia Urbana); Town Hall
19 Train Station

centre retains a relaxed and old-fashioned air. Only the **tower** of the 17th-century **Església de Santa Maria** remains, on Plaça de Santa Maria. The rest of the church fell victim to the war. The 13th-century Gothic **Església de Sant Domènec** on Passeig del 10 d'Abril was also wrecked but was later rebuilt. Some 14th-century Gothic murals inside somehow survived the civil-war destruction. The **estany** (lake) in the north of town, created for irrigation, is surrounded by turn-of-the-20th-century summer houses built by wealthy Barcelona families.

Places to Stay On the Llívia road, *Camping Stel (☎ 972 88 23 61)* opens year round and charges €21.15 plus IVA for two people with a car and tent.

Right outside the train station, *Hostal Estación (☎ 972 88 03 50, Plaça de l'Estació 2)* has plain but adequate singles/doubles with bathroom for €18.10/30.15 plus IVA. Downstairs there's a handy cafe.

Up in town, the friendly *Hostal Alfonso (☎ 972 88 02 46, Carrer d'Espanya 5)* is a bit better at around €36.15 for large doubles with bathroom. *Hostal La Muntanya (☎ 972 88 02 02, Avinguda del Coronel Molera 1)* is clean, if somewhat like a little hospital ward, and charges €30.15 per double. Singles are hard to come by in either place.

Hotel Sala (☎ 972 88 01 04, Carrer d'Alfons I 17) has straightforward rooms for €15.10/30.15 (with shared bathroom), or €21.10/39.20 (with private bathroom).

Hotel Del Lago (☎ 972 88 10 00, fax 972 14 15 11, Avinguda del Dr Piguillem s/n), near the lake, has an old-fashioned style and a nice garden. Singles/doubles cost €42.20/57.25 plus IVA. Top of the tree is *Hotel Avet Blau (☎ 972 88 25 52, fax 972 88 12 12, Plaça de Santa Maria 14)*, a fine old mansion overlooking the centre of the village. Comfortable doubles cost up to €84.35 plus IVA.

Places to Eat For cheap, no-nonsense food you could do worse than *El Niu (Carrer d'Alfons I 15)*, where the €7.25 *menú* appears to offer just two courses but is actually three (one of which is usually trout) with wine thrown in too. Another straightforward option is *Restaurante San Remo (☎ 972 88 00 05, Carrer de Ramón Cosp 9)*, with a *menú* for €6.65.

Restaurante Casa Clemente (☎ 972 88 11 66, Avinguda del Dr Piguillem 6) has a more interesting *menú* for €9.95 and a range of other dishes. *Restaurant La Tieta (☎ 972 88 01 56, Carrer dels Ferrers 20)* is an intimate, cavernous place where you can choose from an interesting menu. The *carpaccio de salmó* (thin strips of garnished uncooked salmon) is good at €8.45.

Restaurant El Galet (☎ 972 88 22 66, *Plaça de Santa Maria 8)* is a welcoming little dining option with a timber ceiling and a menu of Catalan dishes at moderate prices. They close on Monday evening and Tuesday.

La Grapa (☎ 972 14 00 85, *Carrer de Querol 4)* is a cocktail and *cava* (Catalan 'champagne') bar that also offers an appetising range of munchies, from salads and crepes through to *torrades* (open toasted sandwiches) and cheese platters.

Getting There & Away Puigcerdà is something of a local transport hub.

Bus Alsina Graells (☎ 973 35 00 20) runs two buses daily (one at weekends) to Barcelona (three hours) via the 5km Túnel del Cadí; two or three daily to La Seu d'Urgell (one hour); and one to Lleida (3½ hours). The buses stop at the train station. The tourist office has timetables.

To get to Andorra you can take the train to Latour-de-Carol and then catch a bus (a journey of 2¼ to 2¾ hours). You can also reach Andorra la Vella by changing buses in La Seu d'Urgell.

Train About six trains run daily to Ribes de Freser, Ripoll and Barcelona (€6.80, 3¼ hours). Five in each direction make the seven-minute hop across the border to Latour-de-Carol in France, where they connect with trains from Toulouse or Paris, and with the narrow-gauge Train Jaune (or Tren Groc in Catalan) down the Têt valley to Perpignan. Puigcerdà station has details on the French trains.

Car & Motorcycle From Barcelona, the C-58 toll road feeds into the C-16C/C-16, which approaches Puigcerdà through the Túnel del Cadí (which is a toll road). Bicycles are not allowed in the tunnel.

The N-152 from Ribes de Freser climbs west along the northern flank of the Rigard valley – with the pine-covered Serra de Mogrony rising to the south – to the 1800m Collado de Toses pass, and then winds down to Puigcerdà.

The main crossing into France is at Bourg-Madame, immediately east of Puigcerdà, from where roads head to Perpignan and Toulouse.

Around Puigcerdà

Llívia Six kilometres north-east of Puigcerdà across flat farmland, the little town of Llívia (population 975) is a piece of Spain in France. Under the 1659 Treaty of the Pyrenees Spain ceded 33 villages to France, but Llívia was a 'town' and so, together with the 13 sq km of its municipality, remained a Spanish possession.

The interest of Llívia's tiny medieval nucleus, near the top of the town, centres on the **Museu Municipal** at Carrer dels Forns 4 and the 15th-century Gothic **Església de Nostra Senyora dels Àngels**, just above the museum. The museum is in what's claimed to be Europe's oldest pharmacy, the Farmacia Esteva, which was founded in 1415. The church contains an 18th-century baroque altarpiece and a processional cross given to Llívia by Carlos I. There's a tourist office (☎ 972 89 63 13) in the museum and both open 10 am to 1 pm and 3 to 6 pm (to 7 pm April to September) Tuesday to Saturday (and Monday in July and August), and 10 am to 2 pm on Sunday in summer. Admission costs €0.95 From the church you can walk up to the ruined **Castell de Llívia**, where, during the short-lived period of Islamic dominion in the Pyrenees, the Muslim governor Manussa enjoyed a secret dalliance (or so legend has it) with Lampègia, daughter of the Duke of Aquitaine.

You can stay in Llívia in one of several hotels and dine on the balconies of the *Restaurant Can Ventura* (☎ 972 89 61 78, *Plaça Major 1)*, a ramshackle building dating from 1791. The food is traditional Catalan and delightful, with main courses costing around €12. They close on Monday and Tuesday.

At the time of writing, one or two Alsina Graells buses and one TEISA bus daily connected Puigcerdà train station with Llívia. Otherwise, it's not a long walk, and the road is flat and quiet. You only cross about 2km of France before entering the Llívia enclave and, apart from an abandoned border post just past Camping Stel and a couple of French road signs, you'd hardly know you'd left Spain.

La Molina & Masella These two ski resorts lie either side of the 2537m Tosa d'Alp, about 15km south of Puigcerdà. La Molina is one of Catalunya's biggest ski centres. Altogether it has 31 pistes of all grades, totalling 27km, at altitudes of 1600m to 2537m. The resort straggles about 4km up the hill from La Molina proper (where the train station is) to 'Super Molina', where some lifts start and you'll find the information and bookings office (☎ 972 89 20 31).

Masella (☎ 972 14 40 00) has some long forest runs among its 37 pistes totalling 49km; the majority are blue (easy) or red (intermediate). The lift system is more limited than La Molina's. A one-day pass at each resort costs €25.35, and both resorts offer equipment rental and ski schools (La Molina has three).

Places to Stay The *Alberg Mare de Déu de les Neus (☎ 972 89 20 12)* youth hostel is in the bottom part of La Molina near the train station. It has 148 places in rooms ranging from doubles to a 38-person dorm. Mid-season prices are charged from December to April and during July and August. High-season rates are applied on most winter weekends.

Other accommodation is mostly on the expensive side and many skiers stay in Puigcerdà or even farther afield. *Hostal 4 Vents (☎ 972 89 20 97, Pista Standard s/n)*, about halfway up the hill to 'Super Molina', has doubles for about €60 but opens only in winter (like most places here). *Hotel Adserà (☎ 972 89 20 01)* is another option at about the same price.

Getting There & Away La Molina is on the Barcelona–Ribes de Freser–Puigcerdà railway, with about six trains daily each way. In the ski season there's a bus service from Puigcerdà. Most people come by car; the easiest route from Barcelona is by the

C-58 toll road and the C-16C/C-16 through the Túnel del Cadí. Roads also wind down to La Molina and Masella from the N-152 west of the Collado de Toses.

Northern Cerdanya

The N-260 highway rolls out south-west from Puigcerdà along the Riu Segre valley towards La Seu d'Urgell. It cuts its path between the main Pyrenees chain to the north and the range made up mainly of the Serra del Cadí and Serra de Moixeró to the south. For details of the latter ranges, see later in the chapter.

You can get along this valley by catching one of the daily buses (up to three) that run between Puigcerdà and La Seu d'Urgell.

Bolvir Only about 6km from Puigcerdà, Bolvir has a little Romanesque church and, more importantly, a luxurious and characterful place to stay. *Torre del Remei (☎ 972 14 01 82, fax 972 14 04 49, Camí Reial s/n)* is a tastefully decorated Modernista mansion. The rooms are superb and the dining is equally tempting. It also has a pool. The eleven rooms don't come cheaply (a double costs anything from €157 to €254) and neither does the food – expect to lighten your wallet by about €36 per head.

Meranges & Around Another kilometre on from Bolvir, take the Ger turn-off for an excursion into the mountains. Ger itself is of little interest, although you'll find several places to stay. A minor asphalted road winds its way west and then north through the broad, arid Valltova valley to Meranges, a dishevelled little stone farming village that makes few concessions to the passing tourist trade.

If you need to refuel you can pick up huge filled bread rolls at the local bar, *Cal Joan*, for around €3. Alternatively you can opt to shell out a bit more (up to €73 for a double room) for a stay in the charming *Can Borrell (☎ 972 88 00 33, Carrer de Retorn 3)*, a rustic hideaway that has been tastefully redecorated for a modestly discerning clientele. The restaurant is fine if a little expensive – mains cost €12 or more.

The much-photographed peaks of Els Encantats in the Catalan Pyrenees

Last one home buys the drinks...

Lakes abound in the rare splendour of the Parc Nacional d'Aigüestortes i Estany de Sant Maurici.

The jewel-like Estany de Sant Maurici, the largest lake in Catalunya's only national park

Vic's large and attractive Plaça Major

Detail of La Seu d'Urgell's cathedral

It's always nice to travel with a friend.

PUIGCERDÀ & SERRA DEL CADÍ AREA

That's about all there is to recommend Meranges, which for most people is a pit stop on the way higher up into the Pyrenees.

Those with their own vehicles can proceed along a sliver of road that worsens as it approaches the **Refugi de Malniu**, at 2130m. Here you can park your car for €1.80, and stay overnight for €3.65. The *refugi* (refuge) also provides snacks and full meals (the latter for €9.95). It's possible to walk from Meranges to the refuge, but it is quite a climb.

Right behind the refuge is the charming little reed-covered **Estany Sec** (the misnamed

'dry lake'). The refuge is also right on the path of the long-distance GR11 walk, which approaches from Guils de Cerdanya (also reachable by car along a combination of road and piste) in the east and continues west to Andorra.

From the refuge you can wander off and take in a trio of lakes in about an hour's walking. Head away north-east from the refuge and you will hit the path that takes you first to the large **Estany Malniu** (follow the sign to the 'Llac de Malniu' and the yellow and white paint splodges indicating the path). You emerge at the south-eastern corner of the lake. To reach the next one, **Estany Mal** (which is virtually dry), head north and bear slightly away from the Estany Malniu. At first you'll be guided by fence posts, then by telltale cairns. You will reach a boggy clearing that you must cross, and then bear slightly to the left. From Estany Mal a visible path leads you east for about 10 minutes to the **Estany Guils** – a shimmering pool at the foot of the mountain wall that shuts you in from France. The return trip has one potentially tricky element. Make sure that the path you take through the clearing to come back is the same as that on which you came. It is easy to lose your bearings here and you could wind up cursing and swearing as you clamber about in a trackless tangle of dense scrub and boulders.

Another possibility, which will take about seven hours all in, is to follow the GR11 for about 20 minutes west of the refuge and then head off north along a trail to **Puigpedrós** (2914m), the third highest peak in Cerdanya. From there you follow the crest west to the **Tosseta de l'Esquella**, at which point you drop south again to reach the GR11 and head east back to the point of departure. You will want to have Alpina's *Cerdanya* map with you.

Bellver de Cerdanya If you're tooting along the N-260 and in no particular rush, duck into the old quarter of this town. Although somewhat dilapidated and scarred by various reconstruction projects, the small porticoed square and nearby much-modified Gothic church are worth a quick look. The town is used by many as a launch pad for walks into the northern reaches of the Parc Natural del Cadí-Moixeró. The GR107 route leads from Queralt across the park to Bellver de Cerdanya, and then proceeds north across the Pyrenees and into France. A couple of hotels and camping grounds line the highway around here.

Other excursions (you'll need your own vehicle) north from the N-260 would take you to the villages of **Lles** and **Aränser**, both good bases for walking and (in winter) cross-country skiing.

SERRA DEL CADÍ

The Serra del Cadí and its eastern extension, the Serra de Moixeró, together form one of the finest pre-Pyrenean ranges, rising steeply along the southern side of the N-260.

The northern face of the Cadí – rocky and fissured by ravines known as *canales* – looks daunting enough but the range's most spectacular peak is Pedraforca (2497m), a southern offshoot with probably the best rock climbing in Catalunya.

Pedraforca and the main Cadí range also offer some excellent mountain walking for those suitably equipped and experienced. This together with the dramatic scenery, attractive villages and some unpaved hill roads that non-4WD vehicles could manage in dry conditions make the area well worth some time. The options are numerous from the northern and southern sides but here we focus on Pedraforca and the south.

Orientation

The area around Pedraforca is most easily reached from the C-16, along the B-400, which heads west 1.5km south of Guardiola de Berguedà. Pedraforca looms mightily into view about halfway to the village of Saldes, which sits 1215m high at its foot, 15km from the C-16. The main Cadí range runs east to west about 5km north of Saldes. The Refugi Lluís Estasen (see Places to Stay & Eat) is under the northern face of Pedraforca, 2.5km north-west of Saldes. You can reach it by footpath from Saldes or by a partly paved road that turns north off the B-400 about 1km west of Saldes. Park at the Mirador de Gresolet, from where it's a 10-minute walk up to the refuge.

Information

The Parc Natural del Cadí-Moixeró's main information office, the Centre d'Informació (☎ 93 824 41 51), is in the pleasant little village of **Bagà** (walk down to the stone bridge across the stream) on the C-16 4km north of Guardiola de Berguedà. The office is a mite inconveniently placed at Carrer de la Vinya 1, on the Gisclareny road on the western edge of Bagà. It opens 9 am to 1.30 pm and 3.30 to 6.30 pm weekdays; 10 am to 2 pm and 4 to 6.30 pm Saturday; and 10 am to 2 pm on Sunday and holidays.

Some information on the park is available from the tourist offices (these are *not* park offices, however) at the service area at the northern end of the Túnel del Cadí (☎ 973 51 02 07), in Bellver de Cerdanya (☎ 973 51 00 29), in Tuixén (☎ 973 37 00 30) and in La Seu d'Urgell (☎ 973 35 15 11).

In Saldes, the Centre d'Informació Massís del Pedraforca (☎ 93 825 80 05) opens 11 am to 2 pm and 5 to 7 pm daily from June to September, but at weekends only the rest of the year. It has information only on the Saldes and Pedraforca area.

Editorial Alpina's *Serra del Cadí – Pedraforca* map-guide covers the Saldes-Tuixén route, Pedraforca, the main Cadí range and its northern slopes. For areas east of Saldes you will need the *Moixeró – Tossa d'Alp* map-guide.

Walking

Pedraforca The name means 'Stone Fork' and the approach from the east makes it clear why. The two separate rocky peaks, the northern Pollegó Superior (2497m) and southern Pollegó Inferior (2400m), are divided by a saddle called L'Enforcadura. The northern face, rising near-vertically for 600m, has some classic rock climbs; the southern has a wall that sends alpinists into raptures.

It is also quite possible to walk up Pedraforca, but certainly exhilarating. From Refugi Lluís Estasen (see under Places to Stay & Eat) you can reach the Pollegó Superior summit in about three strenuous hours – either southwards from the refuge, then up the middle of the fork from the south-eastern side (a path from Saldes joins this route); or westwards up to the Collada del Verdet, then south and east to the summit. The latter route has some hairy precipices and requires a good head for heights, but is classed as a walk rather than a climb. It's not suitable for coming down: you must use the first route.

Other Walks Walkers can ascend Comabona (2530m), towards the eastern end of the main Cadí ridge, in about four or five hours from the Refugi Lluís Estasen. Puig de la Canal del Cristall (2563m) and Puig de la Canal Baridana (2647m; the highest in the range) are longer walks that may require a night in the hills.

There are various routes of one to two days right across the Cadí, from Saldes, the Refugi Lluís Estasen or Gósol, to the Riu Segre valley. If you want to stay overnight in the mountains, the FEEC's small **Refugi Prat d'Aguiló** (☎ 973 25 01 35), at 2037m on the northern slopes, has room for up to 38 and a kitchen.

Gósol

The B-400 continues paved from Saldes to the pretty stone village of Gósol (about 6km). Pedraforca looks slightly less daunting from here. The Vila Vella, the original Gósol, which dates back at least to the 9th century, is now abandoned. It sits on the hill south of the present village and is worth a look. Picasso spent some of 1906 painting in the village and there's a museum just off Plaça Major with a section devoted to him.

Tuixén & Beyond

An unpaved road west from Gósol climbs the 1625m Coll de Josa pass then descends past the picturesque hamlet of Josa del Cadí to Tuixén (1206m), another attractive village on a small hill. From Tuixén, scenic paved roads lead north to La Seu d'Urgell (36km away) and south to Sant Llorenç de Morunys (28km away), which is on a beautiful cross-country road from Berga to Organyà.

Places to Stay & Eat

There are *pensiones* (guesthouses) and/or *hostales* (budget hotels) in Bagà, Guardiola de Berguedà and Sant Llorenç de Morunys as well as at several spots along the Riu Segre valley (such as Bellver de Cerdanya – see earlier).

Saldes & Around There are at least four camping grounds along the B-400 between the C-16 and Saldes, some open year round. In Saldes, *Can Manuel* (☎ 93 825 80 41), on the plaza, offers accommodation with

THE PYRENEES

half-board only, which costs €21.70 per person. Saldes has a couple of food stores.

The FEEC's *Refugi Lluís Estasen (☎ 93 822 00 79)* near the Mirador de Gresolet (see Orientation) opens year round with 100 places, meals and a warden in summer, and about 30 places in winter. When the refuge is full you can sleep outside but tents are not allowed.

Gósol By the road at the eastern end of the village, *Hostal Cal Francisco (☎ 973 37 00 75)* has singles/doubles for €16.30/30.15. The smaller *Hostal Can Triuet (☎ 973 37 00 72, Plaça Major 4)*, in the centre, requires you to take at least half-board which costs €27 per person.

Tuixén The friendly *Can Farragetes (☎ 973 37 00 34, Carrer del Coll 7)* has doubles with bathroom for €19.30 and serves food in the bar. There are a couple of other places nearby. The small *Camping Molí de Fórnols (☎ 973 37 00 21)*, open year round, is about 4km north of Tuixén, down by the Riu de la Vansa off the La Seu d'Urgell road. It charges €13.90 for two people including car and tent space.

Getting There & Around
Berga, Guardiola de Berguedà and Bagà are all on the Alsina Graells bus routes from Barcelona to Puigcerdà and La Seu d'Urgell via the Túnel del Cadí. There's a bus between Guardiola de Berguedà and Ripoll once or twice daily Monday to Saturday.

Getting to Saldes, Gósol or Tuixén basically requires your own transport. You might consider hitching – this is feasible along the B-400 as far as Saldes or Gósol in July or August, or at weekends during the other summer months, but there won't be much traffic at other times.

LA SEU D'URGELL
postcode 25700 • pop 10,661
• elevation 691m
The valley town of La Seu d'Urgell (la se-u dur-**zhey**) is Spain's gateway to Andorra, 10km north. It has a fine medieval cathedral and is a pleasant place to spend a night.

When the Franks evicted the Muslims from this part of the Pyrenees in the early 9th century, they made La Seu the seat of a bishopric and capital of the counts of Urgell. It has been an important market and cathedral town since the 11th century and also played a key role in the history of Andorra.

Information
The tourist office (☎ 973 35 15 11) is at the northern entrance to town, at Avinguda de les Valls d'Andorra 33. It opens 9 am to 9 pm daily, July to mid-September; and 10 am to 2 pm and 4 to 7 pm Monday to Saturday, the rest of the year. The staff can give you pamphlets describing walking and horse-riding itineraries in the area. You can also get information at the *consell comarcal* (administrative centre for the comarca; ☎ 973 36 01 55), at Passeig de Joan Brudieu 15. It opens weekday mornings only.

The Policía Municipal (☎ 973 35 04 26) are based in the town hall *(casa de la ciutat)* at Plaça dels Oms 1. There's a hospital (☎ 973 35 00 50) at the southern end of Passeig de Joan Brudieu.

Llibreria Ribera de Antich on Carrer de Sant Ot is a good source of maps and local guides.

Catedral de Santa Maria & Museu Diocesà
Looming on the southern side of Plaça dels Oms, the 12th-century *seu* (cathedral) is one of Catalunya's most outstanding Romanesque buildings despite various remodellings over the centuries. It is one of more than a hundred Romanesque churches lining what has come to be known as the Ruta Romànica from Perpignan (in France) to the Urgell district.

The western facade, through which you enter, is decorated in typical Lombard style. The inside is dark and plain but still impressive, with five apses, some murals in the southern transept and a 13th-century Virgin-and-Child sculpture in the central apse.

From inside the cathedral you can enter the good Museu Diocesà. This encompasses the fine cloister and the 12th-century

Romanesque Església de Sant Miquel, as well as some good medieval Pyrenean church murals, sculptures and altarpieces and a rare 10th-century Mozarabic *Beatus* (illustrated manuscript of the Apocalypse).

The cathedral and museum open 10 am to 1 pm and 4 to 6 pm (morning only on Sunday) daily. The cloister opens Sunday mornings only. Admission to the church is free; admission to the cloister and Església de Sant Miquel costs €0.90, or €2.15 if you want to see the museum too (which is well worthwhile).

Places to Stay

Camping En Valira (☎ 973 35 10 35, *Avinguda del Valira*) has room for 1200 people charging €13.90 for two people with a car and tent. It opens year round.

The modern *Alberg La Valira* youth hostel (☎ 973 35 38 97, *Carrer de Joaquim Viola Lafuerza 57*) has spacious public areas and 100 places in eight-bunk dorms. The

mid-season is March to mid-September. There's little other cheap accommodation.

By contrast there are lots of good lower mid-range hotels. *Hotel Avenida* (☎ 973 35 01 04, *Avinguda de Pau Claris 18*) is a decent bet, with bright singles/doubles for either up to €21.70/31.95 or €23.95/40.70 plus IVA: the more expensive ones are bigger and recently renovated. On a fairly quiet street, *Residència Duc d'Urgell* (☎ 973 35 21 95, *Carrer de Josep de Zulueta 43*) has nice modern rooms with TV and bathroom for €28.35/40.40. *Hotel Andria* (☎ 973 35 03 00, *Passeig de Joan Brudieu 24*) has sizable rooms with a certain antiquated charm but generally offers half-board only at up to €47.60 per person. The bigger 56-room *Hotel Nice* (☎ 973 35 21 00, *Avinguda de Pau Claris 4–6*) is a better deal, with smart rooms for €34.20/46.25.

La Seu's *Parador* (☎ 973 35 20 00, fax 973 35 23 09, *Carrer de Sant Domènec s/n*), built around the restored cloister of the

THE PYRENEES

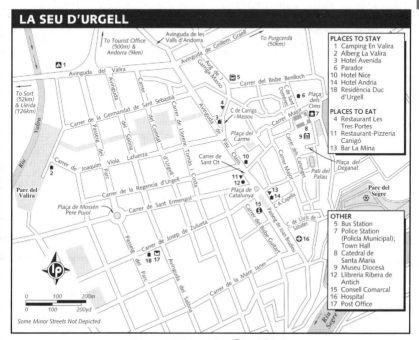

LA SEU D'URGELL

PLACES TO STAY
1 Camping En Valira
2 Alberg La Valira
3 Hotel Avenida
6 Parador
10 Hotel Nice
14 Hotel Andria
18 Residència Duc
   d'Urgell

PLACES TO EAT
4 Restaurant Les
  Tres Portes
11 Restaurant-Pizzeria
   Canigó
13 Bar La Mina

OTHER
5 Bus Station
7 Police Station
  (Policía Municipal);
  Town Hall
8 Catedral de
  Santa Maria
9 Museu Diocesà
12 Llibreria Ribera de
   Antich
15 Consell Comarcal
16 Hospital
17 Post Office

Some Minor Streets Not Depicted

14th-century Sant Domènec convent, is suitably luxurious with doubles at €90.40 plus IVA.

Places to Eat
Bar La Mina (☎ 973 35 10 51, *Passeig de Joan Brudieu 24*) does good pizzas for €4.70 and a range of main courses from €5.45. Watch the world go by at its outside tables. *Restaurant-Pizzeria Canigó* (☎ 973 35 10 43, *Carrer de Sant Ot 3)* has a wide range of options; the *parrillada de carne* (mixed meat grill) is good value at €7.25.

A homely little place is *Restaurant Les Tres Portes* (☎ 973 35 29 07, *Carrer de Garriga i Massou 7)*; main courses cost €7.25 to €10.85 and you can eat in the garden.

The *Hotel Avenida*, *Hotel Nice* and *Hotel Andria* offer Catalan and Spanish food, with *menús* at around €10.

Getting There & Away
Bus The bus station is on the northern edge of the old town. Alsina Graells (☎ 973 35 00 20) runs four or five buses daily to Barcelona, two of which go via Solsona and Ponts, and one of which (which does not run on Sunday) goes via the Túnel del Cadí (€14.95, 3½ hours); three buses daily to Puigcerdà (€4.05, one hour); and two daily to Lleida (€6.95, 2½ hours). La Hispano Andorrana runs up to seven buses daily to Andorra la Vella (€2.05, 30 minutes). Hispano Igualadina runs one bus daily to Tarragona (3¼ hours). Two buses daily crawl along in all-stops mode to Sort from 1 July to mid-September; otherwise they run on Monday and Friday only. The trip costs €3.05 and you must book a day in advance (☎ 973 62 07 33 or ☎ 973 62 08 02).

Car & Motorcycle The N-260 heads 6km south-west to Adrall, then turns off west over the hills to Sort. The C-14 carries on south to Lleida, threading through the towering Tresponts gorge about 13km beyond Adrall.

PALLARS SOBIRÀ & PALLARS JUSSÀ
The trans-Pyrenean highway, the N-260, drops 6km south of La Seu d'Urgell before turning west at Adrall to head across a range of high hills and down into the next valley, that of the Riu Noguera Pallaresa. The rapids of this mountain river slice through the middle of the north-western comarca of Pallars Sobirà (Upper Pallars).

The comarca includes some of the most dramatic scenery in the Catalan Pyrenees, ideal for rugged walks ranging from hours to days. The area is also replete with enchanting little villages and hamlets, some strung along verdant valleys and others hidden from the average passer-by's view high up in the hills. Action sports from cross-country skiing to white-water rafting are added attractions.

A good portion of the Parc Nacional d'Aigüestortes i Estany de Sant Maurici (see later in the chapter) falls within its boundaries, while Catalunya's best skiing lies just beyond in the neighbouring Val d'Aran. The Riu Noguera Pallaresa cuts a dramatic swathe from north to south and is Spain's best white-water torrent.

The river continues south into the neighbouring comarca of Pallars Jussà (Lower Pallars), characterised by a much drier and less mountainous terrain, although its northern tip reaches into the national park. Together they form a fascinating travel target in which you could easily spend many days exploring.

Sort
postcode 25560 • pop 1571
The only significant roads leading into this part of Catalunya are the N-260 (from La Seu d'Urgell in the east and La Pobla de Segur in the south), and the C-28 that winds its way in from the Val d'Aran in the north-west. All converge on the *comarcal* capital, Sort, a useful point of reference.

The tourist office (☎ 973 62 10 02), at Avinguda dels Comtes del Pallars 21, has information on the whole area. It opens 8 am to 3 pm Monday to Friday; 10 am to 1 pm and 5 to 8 pm Saturday; and 10 am to 1 pm Sunday. Several rafting outfits and other adventure sport crowds have offices here, so you can check out what's available before taking the next sensible step –

leaving. What little of the medieval *Saort* that remains is in lamentable shape and the town has little to recommend it other than the suggested cursory information stop. Should you get stuck here, however, there are several hotel and restaurant options.

South of Sort

Gerri de la Sal A straggly town on the Riu Noguera Pallaresa about 14km south of Sort, Gerri de la Sal is named after its extant riverside salt pans. As early as the 9th century an important Benedictine monastery complex existed on the other side of the river. Its most recent heir is the 12th-century **Col.legiata de Santa Maria**. This charming mix of Romanesque and later interventions is set amid vegetable and flower gardens on the banks of the Noguera Pallaresa, where there is also a shady restaurant. Locals like to take a dip here in the warmer months.

Gerri is about a 15-minute bus ride from either Sort or La Pobla de Segur, but there are only two services daily at the most. There are rooms in town if you need them.

La Pobla de Segur Only a few kilometres farther south of Gerri de la Sal the highway plunges into a tunnel only to emerge among the strangely bulbous rock walls of the **Congost de Collegats**. Emerging from this bizarre landscape, you find yourself in altogether different surrounds. Clearly the Pyrenees are receding and giving way to more sunburnt territory. La Pobla de Segur lies strung along a ridge; or rather, a strange rank of suburban apartment blocks tails out incongruously from the tiny nucleus of the old town. Until the 20th century, it was as much a backwater as many other villages in the area, but boomed with the hydroelectricity business generated by the building of the nearby Talarn dam. Although it's an important junction on the southern side of the Pyrenees, you may well merely pass through here.

Beyond La Pobla de Segur The N-260 highway veers north-west to El Pont de Suert (for details see Val d'Aran later in the chapter). The road is a pretty one, which soon sets to gaining altitude in a series of switchbacks after an initial flat run. After you pass the **Coll de la Creu de Perbes** (1325m), the scenery reverts to the greener, lusher land more akin to the landscape farther north.

South of La Pobla de Segur, the C-13 road follows the course of the Riu Noguera Pallaresa southwards to **Tremp**, a busy agricultural centre in the low hills rolling away from the Pyrenees (a couple of buses crisscrossing this part of Catalunya call in here, as well as Lleida–La Pobla de Segur trains). The river and road continue southwards, the former joining the Riu Segre, which along with the highway proceeds to Balaguer (see the Central Catalunya chapter).

North of Sort

Things get a great deal more interesting north of Sort. Between here and Llavorsí is the most popular stretch of the river for white-water rafting. A growing number of firms offer complete novices the chance to barrel down the rapids, as well as providing other waterborne options such as hydrospeeding (water-tobogganing), canoeing and kayaking. When you feel like getting out of the river there is canyoning, walking, climbing, mountain biking, horse riding or *ponting* (jumping from bridges, to which you are attached by ropes).

Llavorsí This is the principal base and starting point for white-water fun on the river, although companies are scattered about other towns (including Sort and Rialp) too.

White-Water Rafting The Noguera Pallaresa has no drops of more than grade 4 (on a scale of 1 to 6), but it's exciting enough to attract a constant stream of white-water fans from April to August. It's at its best in May and June.

The best stretch (and the standard beginners' dash) is the 14km that starts in Llavorsí and ends downriver at Rialp – from where you are then driven back up (if you wish) to Llavorsí. The standard raft outing on this stretch costs between €27 and €31 per person. A faster surge on a hydrospeed costs €42.20. Other longer rides down to Sort and beyond will cost more.

At least one company, Yeti Emotions (☎ 973 62 22 01), at Carrer de Borda Era d'Alfons s/n in Llavorsí, organises a high-grade trip for experienced rafters, beginning higher upstream.

You can do adventure weekend packages combining rafting with other activities (such as mountain-bike excursions) for around €72 to €157 (the cost depends in part on the type of accommodation and time of year).

For all trips you need to bring your own swimming costume, towel and change of clothes. Generally all the other gear is provided.

Places to Stay Llavorsí is the most pleasant base in the area, being much more of a mountain village than Rialp or Sort. *Camping Riberies* (☎ 973 62 21 51) has a good riverside site and charges €3.50 per person, per tent and per car, but opens from mid-June to mid-September only. *Camping Aigües Braves* (☎ 973 62 21 53), about 1km north beside the river, charges the same.

Hostal del Rey (☎ 973 62 20 11), *Hostal La Noguera* (☎ 973 62 20 12) and *Hotel Lamoga* (☎ 973 62 20 06) all overlook the river. They charge €28.95, €31.35 and €46.60, respectively, for a double room with bathroom.

Vall de Cardòs

Heading north into the hills along the L-504 road from Llavorsí, this is a remarkably pretty valley and little appreciated by tourists from beyond Catalunya. It leads to some challenging mountain walking possibilities and in winter there are some modest winter sports options too. Editorial Alpina's *Pica d'Estats* map-guide is useful here. There is no public transport up the valley.

Lladrós & Lladorre The first few villages you pass through heading north are humdrum but Lladrós and Lladorre, the latter graced with a charming Romanesque church,

are pretty stone hamlets oozing bucolic charm. You can stay at *Casa Serra* (☎ 973 62 31 17), a casa de pagès on the main road in Lladorre. Double rooms cost €24.10.

A turn-off just before you reach Lladrós takes you east to **Esterri de Cardós**, another fine mountain village at the centre of which you can admire the single nave, 11th-century Església de Sant Pere i de Sant Pau. There are four cases de pagès here.

Tavascan The greenery thins out as you push on another 5km to the delightful little village of Tavascan. It's a huddle of well kept houses, among which nest some hotels and cases de pagès. For many centuries a charming Romanesque bridge connected them with the village church – the bridge remains but the modern road provides the main route of access. One gentle walking option is a circuit that follows in part the GR11 route and takes in Lladorre and other villages. It's fairly clearly marked and takes five to six hours.

Casa Feliu (☎ 973 62 31 63), on the main thoroughfare, is a modest place to stay, with clean doubles costing up to €27.75. Otherwise you have four other hotels to choose from, several of which have restaurants. Five kilometres north-west of Tavasan along a dirt road is the *Bordes de Graus* camping ground (☎ 973 62 32 46), a pleasant site where you are charged €3.80 per person, per tent and per car.

Around Tavascan Tavascan is pretty but it's above all a launch pad for numerous excursions into some of the stunning surrounding territory. What follows is a taster – there is plenty more. The local tourist information booth (☎ 973 62 30 79) in Tavascan – on the main road at the northern end of the village – can provide information on hiring 4WD 'taxis' to access some of the main natural sights in the area. Day and half-day 4WD excursions to some of the lakes cost around €15 per person.

Estany de Certascan & Pla de Boavi A rough dirt trail leads 13km north-east out of Tavascan towards the Estany de Certascan, the largest natural lake in the entire Pyrenees. The road is pretty bad, although more robust normal cars can make it. You're better off with a 4WD, especially on the last 6km or so, which wind upwards from a turn-off that's high in the mountains above the Riu Lladorre valley. The drive is quite splendid in itself. You arrive at a parking area just below a small dam; at this point your feet take over. About an hour's climb follows the hilly contour in a broad rising arc to a small lake and then on to the *Refugi de Certascan* (☎ 945 13 71 82), which has room for 30 people and offers meals. It opens from early June to mid-September.

The strange, wavy rock formations just in front of the refuge hide one of the Pyrenees' most majestic sights – the glacial lake of Estany de Certascan, which is 1km across, has a circumference of about 4km and is about 90m deep. This great mass of water is cupped as though in a large breakfast bowl, and if you have about three hours you can walk around its western shore and climb the Pic Senó, the highest point on the lip of the bowl and smack on the French border. Other walking trails wind their way to the east (where more pretty lakes await you) and west of the lake. Make sure you have Alpina's *Pica d'Estats* map for planning excursions hereabouts.

Back at the Riu Lladorre valley turn-off, you could proceed east about 6km to the **Pla de Boavi**, a beautiful wooded plain where you can camp. From here a trail zigzags uphill to a fork where two streams split. Following Riu de Broate eastwards would eventually bring you to the Pica d'Estats mountain (see later under Vall Ferrera). If you're feeling fit you could do the round trip from the camping ground in a long day's walking (reckon on 13 hours there and back).

Further Excursions The dirt road that leaves Tavascan for Graus (and its camping ground) continues on along the Riu de Tavascan and up to the *Alberg-Refugi la Pleta del Prat* (☎ 973 62 30 79), which is run by the local municipal council and opens all year (call ahead to be sure). The refuge makes a great base for round-trip walking

excursions, of anything up to five or so hours, to some pretty glacial lakes, such as Estany Mariola, Estany del Diable, Estany Blau and Estany Flamisella. A fairly tough assignment is the ascent of Mont-roig (2864m). The refuge has 60 bunk beds and a restaurant/cafeteria service. In winter it is used as a base for some modest downhill and cross-country skiing. It rents out ski gear.

Vall Ferrera

Greener than the Vall de Cardòs, this valley is another pleasant surprise, hiding several pretty villages and bringing still more good walking country within reach – the ascent of the Pica d'Estats, the region's highest peak, is generally undertaken from here. Get hold of Alpina's *Pica d'Estats* map and be aware that there is no public transport.

Alins & Around The valley's capital and a curious little town, Alins was in medieval times a centre of iron production. The whole valley was rich in the stuff, which explains its name (from *ferro*, meaning 'iron').

A dirt road leads east out of Alins and follows the Riu Tor (take the first right fork) about 10km to the highest settlement in the Pyrenees (and, it is claimed, the third highest in all Spain), **Tor** (1649m). It has long been abandoned, though for a while a handful of hippies moved in. The track continues for another serpentine 7km south-east to Port de Cabús, a mountain pass on the border with Andorra (at which point the track becomes asphalted road). An alternative walking trail follows a gorge east to the Port Negre dels Pallars pass into Andorra. These passes were traditionally long-favoured crossings for contraband smugglers between Andorra and Spain.

Àreu Five kilometres north of Alins, Àreu is a much prettier little hamlet and a favourite base for hikers planning an ascent of the Pica d'Estats, to the north-west. It is actually divided into two separate hamlets, each with a Romanesque church, Sant Climent in the lower part and Sant Feliu de la Força up the road.

Numerous walking possibilities open up here. You could try the ascent of **Monteixo** (2905m), the highest point in the range of the same name east of the village. A signposted trail heads east across the river about 1km along the dirt road north of Àreu. The GR11 long-distance route also passes just north of here on its east-west Pyrenees traverse. The big one, however, is the Pica d'Estats, for which see later.

Places to Stay & Eat As is often the case in this part of the north-west of Catalunya, the best deals for accommodation are at cases de pagès, or country homestays. There are several in Àreu, all of which seem reasonable. It is hard to beat *Casa Gallardó (☎ 973 62 43 44, Carrer La Força s/n)*, in the upper part of the village, where rooms are spotless if in some cases a little small, and the family is friendly. Who can argue at up to only €18 for a double room?

Eating options are limited. The *Pica d'Estats* camping ground *(☎ 973 62 43 47)*, east of the main road as you head north through the village, has an uninspiring restaurant where you can eat dinner for about €9. If you feel like splashing out, head for the *Hotel Vall Ferrera (☎ 973 62 43 43)*, where the main road enters town. The restaurant is too brightly lit but some of the dishes are mouthwatering. Try, for instance, the *carn de corder amb bolets* (lamb with mushrooms) – the lamb is of average quality but the abundance of mushrooms in the sauce is heavenly. Expect to pay €24.10 for a full meal.

Pica d'Estats At 3143m, this is the highest peak in Catalunya. From the top you have simmering 360° views across Catalunya, Andorra and France. Wild camping is tolerated, and some choose to pitch tents around the lakes (see later in the section) and tackle the peak from there.

The mountain can be approached from several directions in Catalunya and France. The classic approach is from the Vall Ferrera. About 10km of driveable piste takes you north from Àreu and then east to a point short of the *Refugi de Vall Ferrera (☎ 973*

62 07 54). You can sleep and eat here (there's space for up to 35 people), although if you have your own vehicle and intend to return from the Pica d'Estats (or other walks) in the same day, it isn't really necessary. Hundreds of cars line up here on the day before the Diada Nacional de Catalunya (Catalunya's national day; 11 September). They disgorge hordes of Catalans who hike up to the lakes to camp, with a view to tackling the mountain the next day.

Although fitter and faster walkers can generally do this hike in a 10-hour round trip, you would be wise to calculate 12 hours (including your lunch stop at the top). This means that from Àreu you need to start driving by 6 am so that you begin walking with the first light of dawn.

From the parking spot you follow the piste a couple of hundred metres to a signpost that points you across the river and on to the refuge (about 15 minutes). From the refuge a confusion of tracks leads away up the hill. Follow the stream through the trees a little way and weave up along the principal trails – you need to be headed up and north. At a signposted fork follow the Pica d'Estats sign (not the Areste one). You will find yourself on a high trail moving west above the upper Vall Ferrera and then bending around north up the Barranc de Sotllo (Sotllo gorge). The countryside is splendid, with waterfalls deep in the gorge giving way to lush green pasture.

After wandering along this plain, a series of little, rising plateaux brings you to the first of two admirable glacial lakes, the **Estany de Sotllo**. Thus far takes about 2½ hours. You skirt around the western bank of the lake and continue onwards and upwards, gaining another 100m in altitude to reach the second lake, the **Estany d'Estats**. Here again you make for the western side and follow a trail that climbs up and beyond the lake to a plain behind it.

Here before you rises the stone and scree wall you must clamber up to reach the **Port de Sotllo pass** (2894m). This is a steep and fairly strenuous path, the way marked by the usual little piles of stones. Once at the pass (about one to 1½ hours), you find yourself looking across to the other side and into France. The experienced can tackle the peak by following the rugged crest to the right but the majority take the 'easy' way. You descend into France and follow a trail that drops just below the pass, bears right over a ridge and then proceeds east in the shadow of the mountain's northern wall. To your left lie several little lakes sparkling in among the natural slag heaps of brown and scorched red stone.

The trail takes you to a point east of the peak, from where you gradually veer right and head upwards among the rocks and scree to approach the summit from the opposite side to the Port de Sotllo. All but the fit will be feeling the effects of the previous hours' walking and this last stretch, in which you gain plenty of altitude, seems excruciatingly endless (that's how it felt to the author, anyway!). If you don't faint from joy when you reach the cross marking the summit, then sit down for lunch and enjoy the limitless views. To the north the plains of southern France stretch away interminably beyond the mountains, while to the south the two lakes you admired on the way up seem like tiny puddles.

Several trails head north farther into France, including one to the **Refuge de l'Estaing du Pinet**, which you could reach before nightfall. You need to get hold of the *Pica d'Estats-Aneto* map published by Rando Editions and the Generalitat. It's scaled at 1:50,000, however.

From Port de Sotllo you have the option of heading down to the first of the little lakes on the French side and then heading west back across the border. From the pass you can head north-west to the FEEC's **Refugi Broate**, with space for 18 people and cooking facilities. You will probably want to sleep there, although the fast and determined could push on several hours to the camp site in the Pla de Boavi (see earlier).

Valls d'Àneu

To proceed to the next valleys west, you return to Llavorsí and the C-12 highway, along which you proceed north. After 12km you pass the turn-off on the left for Espot –

this is the most popular way into the Parc Nacional d'Aigüestortes i Estany de Sant Maurici (for which see later). Six kilometres farther on, after passing an artificial lake on the right where you can hire rowing boats and canoes to potter about in, you arrive at Esterri d'Àneu.

Esterri d'Àneu The nerve centre of the valley of the same name, this lively little town is a popular low-level base for the ski fields of Baqueira-Beret in the Val d'Aran to the north-west (see under Val d'Aran later in the chapter). At one time or another Basque tribes must have held some clout here, as the name Esterri, meaning 'people behind the walls', is Basque.

No outstanding monuments of the old centre remain but the place is pleasant enough and in summer and winter it springs to life with travellers enjoying mountain sports in the area. This is also where the daily bus up the Riu Noguera Pallaresa valley terminates, except in summer when it goes on to the Val d'Aran.

Places to Stay & Eat About the cheapest place to stay in town is the ***Fonda Agustí*** (☎ 973 62 60 34, Plaça de l'Església 6). Doubles cost up to €26 and the square is a shady little retreat. For around the same money you can also seek out one of the four cases de pagès. Otherwise you can choose from about a half-dozen other hotels. The main road is lined with cheerful eateries, although nothing much stands out for culinary greatness.

To Port de la Bonaigua The C-12 forks at Esterri d'Àneu. The main road, which from here on is the C-28, starts to climb and almost immediately takes you through València d'Àneu, a place more clearly devoted to accommodating skiers with its, at times, astonishingly ugly hotels. The road climbs quickly above the tree line to the Port de la Bonaigua mountain pass, where ski lifts and a couple of roadside cafes operate at the height of the winter season. From the pass, the road drops into the Val d'Aran (see later in the chapter).

THE PYRENEES

Vall d'Isil Among the various valleys making up the Valls d'Àneu, this is surely the most intriguing. Follow the C-12 directly north through Esterri d'Àneu and you are led over a bridge across the Riu Noguera Pallaresa, which you now follow up into a mountain valley. After passing Isavarre on your right you shortly wind up in **Borén**, a pleasant little hideaway banked along a stream. Cross the bridge on the stream and do the 1½-hour stroll to **Àrreu** and the Romanesque Església de Mare de Deu.

From here the road bears north a few kilometres to **Isil**. Situated on the right bank, this place remains a gem with its unspoiled rural stone houses slung low beneath moss-covered slate roofs and nobler buildings rising higgledy-piggledy to several storeys. The largely Romanesque Església de Sant Joan Baptista presides over affairs and the town loses its collective head in a fiery display of occasion with bonfires for *La Nit de Sant Joan* on the evening of 23 June. The left side of the river is showing signs of probably inevitable tourist development, as Catalan and a few savvy Spanish tourists pile in. You can stay at *Alberg-Refugi Casa Sastres* (☎ 973 62 65 22, *Carrer de les Escoles s/n)*. There's room for 45 and you can get simple home-cooked meals too. Bed and breakfast costs €11.15, or €19.90 for half-board.

Another 3km of asphalt take you to the half-abandoned **Alós d'Isil**. Keep your eyes peeled for the endearing Romanesque **Monestir de Sant Joan d'Isil** on the right of the road, which it is thought belonged to the Knights Templar. The place is strangely engaging in its tumbledown way. This rare air of being almost untouched by time, something shared to some extent by the rest of the valley (at least outside peak summer and winter tourist seasons), could one day become a thing of the past if plans to blast a road tunnel through to Salau, in France, ever come to fruition.

From Alós, the asphalt gives way to dirt. Four kilometres along you reach the rather cute *Refugi del Fornet* (☎ 973 62 65 20), with room for 40 people. Bunk and breakfast costs €12.05. It has showers and the

wardens provide meals. In summer you can use it as a base for walks, mountain bike rides and so on. In winter cross-country skiers take over, using this as a base for the Bonabé cross-country skiing station another 5km or 6km along the dirt road. The same road pushes on to **Montgarri** in the Val d'Aran and then drops south to the Pla de Beret and to the Baquiera-Beret ski area (see under Val d'Aran later in the chapter). The road is not always passable, especially in winter, so check beforehand.

Getting There & Around
Here more than ever you will be glad to have your own wheels. Alsina Graells runs one bus daily (at 7.30 am) from Barcelona to La Pobla de Segur (11.35 pm), Sort (12.20 pm), Rialp, Llavorsí (12.34 pm) and Esterri d'Aneu (12.50 pm). From June to October it continues to the Val d'Aran. The return bus leaves Esterri d'Àneu at 1.40 pm and arrives in Barcelona at 7 pm. The fare from Barcelona to Esterri d'Àneu is €20.80.

Alsina Graells also has a daily bus (except on Sunday) from Lleida to Esterri d'Àneu (€12.25) via Tremp, La Pobla de Segur, Sort, Rialp and Llavorsí. It leaves Lleida at 4.30 pm and arrives in Esterri d'Àneu at 7.35 pm. It returns the following morning at 5.30 am. Irritatingly, it pulls into La Pobla de Segur at 6.32 am, just two minutes after the only other Barcelona-bound service heading out of this area leaves!

A couple of slow buses run between La Seu d'Urgell and Sort in summer; see Getting There & Away under La Seu d'Urgell for more details.

In addition to the buses, a minor branch railway line connects Lleida to La Pobla de Segur – up to three trains a day service this line and the trip takes about 2½ hours.

PARC NACIONAL D'AIGÜESTORTES I ESTANY DE SANT MAURICI & AROUND
Catalunya's only national park extends 20km east to west and only 9km from north to south, but packs in more beauty than most areas 100 times its size. The product of glacial action over two million years, it's

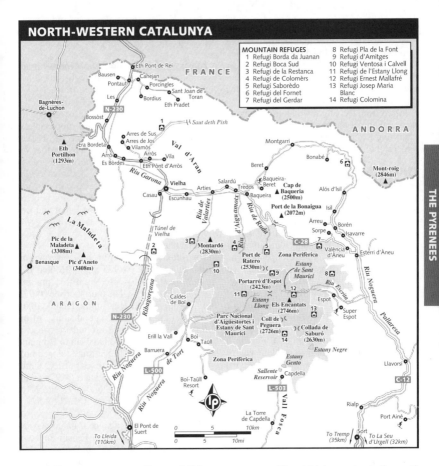

NORTH-WESTERN CATALUNYA

MOUNTAIN REFUGES
1 Refugi Borda da Juanan
2 Refugi Boca Sud
3 Refugi de la Restanca
4 Refugi de Colomèrs
5 Refugi Saborèdo
6 Refugi del Fornet
7 Refugi del Gerdar
8 Refugi Pla de la Font
9 Refugi d'Amitges
10 Refugi Ventosa i Calvell
11 Refugi de l'Estany Llong
12 Refugi Ernest Mallafré
13 Refugi Josep Maria Blanc
14 Refugi Colomina

essentially two east–west valleys at 1600m to 2000m altitudes lined by jagged 2600m to 2900m peaks of granite and slate. Against this backdrop, pine and fir forests and open bush and grassland – bedecked with wild flowers in spring and early summer – combine with some 200 *estanys* (small lakes or tarns) and countless streams and waterfalls to create a wilderness of rare splendour.

The national park (whose boundaries were extended in 1996 to cover 141.2 sq km) lies at the core of a wider area of wilderness; this outer area is known as the *zona perifèrica* (perimeter belt) and includes some magnificent high country to the north and south. The total area covered is 408.5 sq km and is monitored by park rangers, who ensure that activities permitted between the two boundaries do not adversely affect the area (see Park Rules under Information later for details).

Although the park's main valleys are easily accessible and there are numerous marked walking routes, once off the main trails it's not hard to lose your way, and the peaks themselves are mainly for mountaineers only. The whole park is normally under snow from December to April.

Chamois are relatively abundant. In summer they prefer to stick to high altitudes but you may spot some lower down when they feed in the early morning and evening. Deer are more common at lower altitudes. Spectacular birds that you may spot include the capercaillie and golden eagle.

Apart from its natural wonders, the region also contains a cluster of Catalunya's most charming Romanesque churches, in the Boí and Taüll areas south-west of the park.

Orientation

Approaches One main approach to the park is from the village of Espot (1320m), 4km east of its eastern boundary. An 8km paved road leads up to Espot from the C-147 highway 12km north of Llavorsí.

The other main approach – and in summer the easier one if you're dependent on buses (see Getting There & Away later) – is from the L-500, which heads north-east off the N-230 Lleida-Vielha road 2km north of El Pont de Suert. From this turning it's 15km to the turning for Boí (another 1km east), then a farther 1.5km to the turning for the park, which begins 4km east.

Walkers can also enter the park by passes from the Vall Fosca to the south and the Val d'Aran to the north.

The Park The two main valleys are those of the Riu Escrita in the east and the Riu de Sant Nicolau in the west. The Escrita flows out of the park's largest lake, the 1km-long **Estany de Sant Maurici**. The Sant Nicolau's main source is Estany Llong, 4km west of Estany de Sant Maurici across the 2423m Portarró d'Espot pass. Downstream from Estany Llong (3km), the Sant Nicolau runs through a particularly beautiful stretch known as **Aigüestortes** (Twisted Waters).

Apart from the valley openings at the eastern and western ends, virtually the whole perimeter of the park is formed by mountain crests, with numerous spurs of almost equal height reaching in towards the centre. One of these spurs, reaching in from the south, ends in the twin peaks Els Encantats (2746m and 2733m), which tower over Estany de Sant Maurici and form a scene so photographed that it has almost become the park's emblem.

Maps & Guides Editorial Alpina's map-guides are adequate, although they don't show every single trail. *Sant Maurici – Els Encantats* covers the eastern half of the park and its approaches; *Vall de Boí* covers the western half and its approaches; *Montsent de Pallars* covers the Vall Fosca; and *Val d'Aran*, naturally, covers the Val d'Aran. A better map of the whole area is the Institut Cartogràfic de Catalunya's *Parc Nacional d'Aigüestortes i Estany de Sant Maurici*, scaled at 1:25,000. The help of guides can be enlisted at the Espot and Boí information offices.

Information

Tourist Offices National park information offices in Espot (☎ 973 62 40 36) and Boí (☎ 973 69 61 89) open 9 am to 1 pm and 3.30 to 7 pm daily. The tourist office (☎ 973 69 40 00) in Barruera, on the L-500, 10km up from the N-230, is a good source of information on the area around the western side of the park. It opens 10 am to 2 pm and 4 to 7 pm Monday to Saturday (closed holidays). There are other tourist offices south of the park in El Pont de Suert (☎ 973 69 06 40), La Torre de Capdella (☎ 973 25 22 31) and La Pobla de Segur (☎ 973 68 02 57).

Money Boí has a Caixa de Catalunya ATM just up the road from the Pensió Pey (see under Places to Stay later). In Espot and Barruera there are branches of La Caixa bank.

Park Rules Private vehicles cannot enter the park. From Espot, they can go as far as the park entrance; on the western side they must stop about 2.5km short of the park on the approach from the L-500. Jeep-taxis, however, offer easy transport into the park from Espot and Boí (see Getting Around).

Wild camping is not allowed in the park, nor are swimming or other 'aquatic activities' in the lakes and rivers. Hunting, fishing, mushroom-picking and just about every other kind of potentially harmful activity are banned. Most such activities are allowed in the zona perifèrica but are subject to control (to avoid such problems as overfishing). Indeed, the weird shape of the park's western end is due to the protests of locals who wanted several important lakes kept open to them for fishing.

Romanesque Churches

The Vall de Boí south-west of the park is dotted with some of Catalunya's loveliest little Romanesque churches. Two of the finest are at Taüll, 3km east of Boí. **Sant Climent de Taüll** at the entrance to the village, with its slender six-storey bell tower, is a gem, not only for its elegant, simple lines but also for the art that once graced its interior until the works were transferred to museums in the 20th century. The central apse contains a copy of a famous 1123 mural that now resides in Barcelona's Museu Nacional d'Art de Catalunya. At its centre is a Pantocrator (Christ figure) whose rich Mozarabic-influenced (a civilisation of Moorish Spain) colours, and expressive but superhuman features, have become a virtual emblem of Catalan Romanesque art. Other art from this church has found its way to museums as far away as Boston, USA! The church supposedly opens 10.30 am to 2 pm and 4 to 8 pm daily – but don't count on it.

Santa Maria de Taüll, up in the old village centre and possessing a five-storey tower, is also well represented in the Barcelona museum but lacks the *in situ* copies that add to the interest of Sant Climent. However, it's another elegant building and the only other one of this group of churches that opens (so they say) daily.

Other Romanesque churches in the area are at Boí, Barruera, Durro, Erill la Vall, Cardet and Coll. Erill la Vall's has a slender six-storey tower to rival Sant Climent's. All of these, however, can only be entered on (free) guided tours at fixed hours two or three times a week; the tourist office in Barruera has the timetable.

Walking

The park is crisscrossed by plenty of paths – ranging from well marked to unmarked – enabling you to pick routes and circuits to suit yourself. You can find details of all the mountain refuges mentioned under Places to Stay later in the chapter.

East–West Traverse You can walk right across the park in one day. The full Espot to Boí (or vice-versa) walk is about 25km long and takes nine hours but you can shorten this by using jeep-taxis to/from Estany de Sant Maurici and/or Aigüestortes (3km downstream from Estany Llong). From Espot (1300m) to Estany de Sant Maurici (1900m) is 8km (two hours). A path then climbs up to the Portarró d'Espot pass (2423m), where there are fine views over both of the park's main valleys. From the pass you descend to Estany Llong and Aigüestortes (1820m; about 3½ hours from Estany de Sant Maurici). Then you have around 3.5km to go to the park entrance, 4km to the L-500 and 2.5km south to Boí (1260m) – a total of about three hours.

Shorter Walks Numerous good walks of three to five hours return will take you up into spectacular side valleys from Estany de Sant Maurici or Aigüestortes.

From the eastern end of Estany de Sant Maurici, one path heads south 2.5km up the beautiful Monestero valley to Estany Monestero (2171m), passing Els Encantats on the left. This walk takes you south from the Refugi Ernest Mallafré through wooded country that follows the course of a chirpy stream (the path is on the western side and for a while is quite a way above stream). Within the first hour you will have meandered across a charming meadow threaded by the stream and a higher pasture called the Prat del Monestero. Shortly afterwards you reach the lake.

Ahead of you is the rock wall of mountain peaks dominated by the Pic de Peguera. About two hours out from the Estany de Sant Maurici you reach the foot of this wall and a sign pointing to Peguera. From here it's steep uphill going – the last bit across what seems like a sea of boulders and rocks – to the final plateau before reaching the Coll de Peguera pass (2726m). All in, the average walker will need three to four good

THE PYRENEES

hours to reach the pass, from where you have great views south. At this point you could turn back. Alternatively, you could turn this into a more challenging expedition by following the Pic de Peguera over a challenging crest line (for which you will need an hour or so). You could then turn back or proceed to the Coll de Monestero and head east for the Estany Negre before then heading down to Espot – a very long day.

Heading north-west from Estany de Sant Maurici, another beautiful walk leads 3km up by Estany de Ratero to Estany Gran d'Amitges (2380m). You could instead continue from Estany de Ratero to Port de Ratero, a fine mountain pass with great views. Or, from Planell Gran (1850m), 1km up the Sant Nicolau valley from Aigüestortes, a path climbs 2.5km south-east to Estany Gran de Dellui (2370m). You can descend to Estany Llong (3km) – about four hours from Aigüestortes to Estany Llong.

A good walk of three to four hours one way from Espot goes south-west up the Peguera valley to the Refugi Josep Maria Blanc (2350m) by Estany Tort. A marked turning to the right just out of Espot, on the road up to the small ski resort of Super Espot, points the way. Push on a little farther from Estany Tort to reach the enchanting Estany Negre, or Black Lake. This walk is the first half of the route to the Refugi Colomina (see Other Traverses).

Other Traverses Serious walkers have many options for extended trips in and out of the park. Details can be found in Lonely Planet's *Walking in Spain*.

One of the most attractive areas to head to is the lake-rich basin south of the middle part of the park. The Refugi Colomina here is about four hours from the Refugi Josep Maria Blanc via the 2630m Collada de Saburó pass, or about seven hours from Estany de Sant Maurici by the more difficult Coll de Peguera. You can reach the Refugi Colomina from the south by a half-day walk up from the village of Capdella at the head of the Vall Fosca, 20km north off the N-260 La Pobla de Segur–El Pont de Suert road. (Capdella, sometimes spelt Cabdella, is not

to be confused with La Torre de Capdella, which is 8km farther south.) From July to September you can shorten the walk by taking a cable car from the Sallente reservoir to Estany Gento.

The most obvious route between the park and the Val d'Aran to the north is via Estany de Ratero and the Port de Ratero pass (2530m) over to the Refugi de Colomèrs (2125m), in a fine lake-strung valley – it's not too long a day from Estany de Sant Maurici. From the Refugi de Colomèrs it's about 10.5km down the Vall de l'Aiguamotx, mostly by a partly paved road, to Tredòs. A slightly longer alternative, diverging at Port de Ratero, is via the Refugi Saborèdo (2310m) and the Ruda valley (east of the Riu d'Aiguamotx). There are also good, more westerly routes using the Refugi Ventosa i Calvell at the head of Vall de Boí and the Refugi de la Restanca on the Aran side. For walks to the latter see the Val d'Aran section later.

Skiing

The Boí-Taüll Resort (☎ 973 69 60 44) is one of Catalunya's more promising areas, with 51 pistes (most fairly easy) covering 39km. A day pass costs €23.95. You can also ski around Espot at the optimistically denominated Super Espot slopes (☎ 973 62 40 58). These consist of 32 pistes over 38km and a day pass costs €21.70.

Places to Stay

Camping At Espot the small *Camping Solau* (☎ 973 62 40 68) is at the top of the village and opens year round, and *Camping Vorapark* (☎ 973 62 41 08), 1km up towards the park entrance, opens from mid-April to the end of September. Two bigger camping grounds below the village have summer-only seasons. At Taüll, *Camping Taüll* (☎ 973 69 61 74) opens year round. There are three camping grounds on the L-500 between El Pont de Suert and Boí.

Mountain Refuges Five refuges in the park and seven more inside the zona perifèrica provide accommodation for walkers. In general they tend to be staffed from early or mid-June to September, and for some weeks in the first half of the year for skiers. At other times several of them leave a section open where you can stay overnight; if you are unsure call ahead or ask at the park information offices.

In the Park You don't usually need to book for these except during August. The Espot park office can contact the Refugi Ernest Mallafré, Refugi d'Amitges and Refugi Josep Maria Blanc for you to check on availability.

Refugi Ernest Mallafré (☎ 973 25 01 18), sometimes called ***Refugi Sant Maurici***, near the eastern end of Estany de Sant Maurici (1885m), is run by the FEEC and has 24 places, with meals available. ***Refugi d'Amitges (☎ 973 25 00 07)*** at Estany Gran d'Amitges (2380m) in the north of the park is run by the Centre Excursionista de Catalunya (CEC; see under Walking in the Moving Mountains special section for details) and has 66 places. Meals are available.

Refugi de l'Estany Llong (☎ 629 37 46 52 for reservations) near Estany Llong (2000m) is run by the national park, with 40 places and a kitchen. ***Refugi Josep Maria Blanc (☎ 93 423 23 45 for reservations)*** near Estany Tort (2350m) is run by the CEC, with 40 places and meals available when staffed.

In the north-west of the park, the CEC's ***Refugi Ventosa i Calvell (☎ 973 29 70 90)*** has 80 places.

Zona Perifèrica South of the park by Estany de Colomina (2395m), ***Refugi Colomina (☎ 973 68 10 42 for reservations)*** is run by the FEEC and has 40 places and meals available, when staffed.

Refugi de Colomèrs (☎ 973 64 05 92), north of the park in the lovely Circ de Colomèrs (2130m), is run by the FEEC, with 40 places and meals available when staffed. ***Refugi Saborèdo (☎ 973 25 30 15)***, north of the park in the lake-strewn Circ de Saborèdo (2310m), is run by the FEEC and has 21 places.

The FEEC's ***Refugi de la Restanca (☎ 608 03 65 59)*** has 80 places.

Hostales & Hotels The villages of Espot, Boí and Taüll have a range of accommodation options. There are hostales and/or cases de pagès in Barruera, El Pont de Suert, Capdella and La Torre de Capdella.

Espot The following places are all near the centre of this small village. The friendly, family-run ***Residència Felip (☎ 973 62 40 93)*** has clean singles/doubles, with shared bathrooms, for €12.05/24.10 (€18.10/30.15 in July and August) including breakfast. ***Casa La Palmira (☎ 973 62 40 72, Carrer de Marineta s/n)*** has rooms with bathroom for €14.50/28.95. ***Hotel Roya (☎ 973 62 40 40, Carrer de Sant Maurici s/n)*** has rooms with shower or bath for €30.15/48.20. The big ***Hotel Saurat (☎ 973 62 41 62, Carrer de Sant Martí s/n)*** has doubles for up to €57.25 plus IVA.

Boí On the small village square, ***Pensió Pey (☎ 973 69 60 36)*** has doubles for €39.20 plus IVA. In the peak summer season they charge €30.15 per person for half-board. ***Hostal Fondevila (☎ 973 69 60 11)***, on the right as you enter the village, has similar prices.

Cases de pagès have cheaper rooms with shared bathrooms. To find ***Casa Cosan (☎ 973 69 60 18)*** and its nice garden, head down into the village from the square, bear right and ask. The seven rooms are just €9.65 per person. ***Casa Guasch (☎ 973 69 60 42)*** charges €14.20 per person; take the lane along the right side of the Pensió Pey, then fork to the right down the hill.

Taüll Although 3km uphill from Boí, Taüll is more picturesque and a nicer place to stay. ***Restaurant Sant Climent (☎ 973 69 60 52)***, on the road into the village from Sant Climent church, is a new stone building with rooms for €9.05/18.10, or €12.05/24.10 with bathroom.

Casa Chep or ***Xep (☎ 973 69 60 54, Plaça de Santa Maria)***, up in the village, has rooms for €10.85/21.70, and a kitchen is available. ***Casa Llovet (☎ 973 69 60 32, Plaça de Franc)***, an atmospheric old four-storey stone house, charges €9.65 per person. Follow

Carrer de l'Església up from the Santa Maria church to find it.

Places to Eat

In Espot, *Casa La Palmira's* (see under Places to Stay) restaurant is popular but some of the best food can be had at *Restaurant Juquim* (☎ 973 62 40 09), on the main square. Its *menú* is varied and costs €10.55. Try the soups. Otherwise, *Hotel Saurat* (see Espot under Places to Stay) has a slightly pricier but pleasant dining room.

About 100m up the road heading out of Espot towards the park is the slightly elusive *Restaurant La Clossa* (☎ 973 62 41 34). The dining area is newish but feels warm and woody and the food is fine and moderately priced, but the opening days seem chosen to fit only periods of maximum passing trade.

In Boí, *Pensió Pey* (see under Places to Stay) does set *menús* for €10.85 or *bocadillos* (filled rolls) and other snacks. Right opposite the Sant Climent church in Taüll, *Restaurant Mallador* is set in a tumbledown house with a leafy garden – a perfect place for lunch.

Espot has a couple of supermarkets and Boí has one small one.

Getting There & Away

See Getting There & Around under Pallars Sobirà & Pallars Jussà earlier in the chapter for an overall picture of transport in this area. Additional information, mainly pertaining to the southern approaches to the park, follows.

Bus The Alsina Graells buses from Barcelona, Lleida and La Pobla de Segur to Esterri d'Àneu will stop, if requested, at the Espot turning on the C-12, from where you have an 8km uphill walk (or hitch, if you so choose).

In addition, from July to mid-September, a daily Alsina Graells bus runs from El Pont de Suert to Caldes de Boí at 11.15 am. The trip takes 30 minutes and on the way the bus stops at Barruera and the Boí turn-off *(el Cruce de Boí)* on the L-500. Going the other way the bus leaves at 2 pm.

During the same period (and on Friday only the rest of the year) an Alsina Graells bus connects La Pobla de Segur with El Pont de Suert. The trip takes an hour and the bus stops at Senterada en route. From here the L-503 road heads north to Capdella – that part of the trip is up to you. During school terms (which counts most of the summer, Easter and so on) you can get the Monday to Friday school bus from La Pobla de Segur, which leaves at 5.15 pm and reaches Capdella an hour later.

Taxi For a taxi in Boí call ☎ 973 69 60 15 or ☎ 973 69 60 36. In Espot call ☎ 973 62 41 05.

Getting Around

Once you're close to the park, the easy way to get inside it is by jeep-taxi from Espot or Boí. Fleets of these rattly white knights, whose drivers congregate loudly in local bars during their off-duty moments, run a more or less continuous shuttle service between Espot and Estany de Sant Maurici, and between Boí and Aigüestortes, saving you, respectively, 8km and 10km of walking. The one-way fare for either trip is €3.65 per person and the services run from outside the park information offices in Espot and Boí, from 8 am to 8 pm July to September, and 9 am to 6 pm the rest of the year; in July or August you may have to queue. You can also do several excursions with these taxis, for instance to the Estany Negre or the Estanys d'Amitges from Espot. Prices hover at around €10.25 per person for this kind of trip.

VAL D'ARAN

With its grave, grey stone houses, lush green valleys, alpine countryside, and chic ski resorts, the Val d'Aran seems to have as much or more in common with its northern neighbour, France, than with the rest of Catalunya – let alone Spain.

What an extraordinary thought that for some the first taste of Spain might be to cross the frontier here at Eth Pont de Rei (The King's Bridge). As you wind down the tight valley, thickly wooded mountains (some of

2000m or more) rising both steeply and gently to either side, it is hard to guess what lies beyond. There is none of the bare brown rock of other parts of the Pyrenees, the sunscorched plains farther south in Catalunya or the deplorable tourist *costas* (coasts). It is like funnelling oneself into what then opens out as a boundless panorama.

Apart from those coming to ski, many visitors who enter the country here do in fact barrel their way southwards. This is a great shame, because the greenest corner of Catalunya has much to offer.

The comarca's only natural opening is northwards to France, to which it gives its river, the Riu Garona (Garonne), flowing down to Bordeaux. Thanks to this geography, Aran's native language is not Catalan but Aranese *(aranés)*, a dialect of Occitan or the *langue d'oc* – the old Romance language of southern France (still spoken in some areas there). Most Aranese, however, can switch equally happily between Catalan, Spanish and French.

While munching your way through the area, you'll generally find the trout is good. You should try to get a taste of *olla aranesa*, the local version of the mountain stew you find in the Catalan Pyrenees – full of meat, sausage, beans, carrots, cauliflower, leeks, celery and rice. The French have had some influence on local cooking too, so you should have little trouble finding crepes!

History

Despite the valley's northwards orientation, Aran has been tied politically to Catalunya since 1175, when Alfons II took it under his protection to forestall the designs of rival counts on both sides of the Pyrenees. In 1312, following one of many French takeover bids, the Aranese voted by popular referendum to stay with Catalunya – perhaps because in practice this meant a large degree of independence. The major hiccup came with a Napoleonic occupation from 1810 to 1815.

For all its intriguing past, the Val d'Aran is in danger of being overrun by tourism, which since the opening of the Baqueira-Beret ski resort in 1964 has replaced farming and herding as the economic mainstay. A valley that, until the 1960s was probably still a pocket of scattered stone villages centred on quaint, pointy-towered Romanesque churches, is being swamped by ski-apartment development. That said, most of the villages retain an old-fashioned core and from Aran's pretty side valleys walkers can continue over the mountains in any direction, notably southwards to the Parc Nacional d'Aigüestortes i Estany de Sant Maurici and westwards into the Pyrenees of Aragón, Catalunya's neighbouring region.

Orientation

The Val d'Aran (population about 7000) is some 35km long and is considered to have three parts: Naut Aran (Upper Aran), which is the eastern part, aligned east-west; Mijaran (Middle Aran) around Vielha; and Baish Aran (Lower Aran), where the Riu Garona flows north-east to France. Six bears live in the valley too (often crossing over from the French side of the Pyrenees) – they are closely monitored by satellite but otherwise unlikely to be seen.

Editorial Alpina's *Val d'Aran* (1:40,000) is a useful aid.

Vielha

**postcode 25530 • pop 3896
• elevation 975m**

Vielha is the Val d'Aran's junction town and this, the Aranese spelling of its name, is more common than the Catalan and Castilian version, Viella.

Orientation The bus stops are on Avenguda deth Alcalde Calbetó Barra, essentially a short walk north of the main roundabout. The road is part of the N-230 to France. The town centre is south-east of the roundabout along the C-28, which is at first called Avenguda de Castièro, then, from the central square Plaça dera Glèisa onwards, Avenguda deth Pas d'Arró.

Information The Val d'Aran's main tourist office (☎ 973 64 01 10), at Carrèr de Sarriulèra 5, opens from at least 10 am to 1 pm and 4.30 to 7.30 pm daily. There are banks

THE PYRENEES

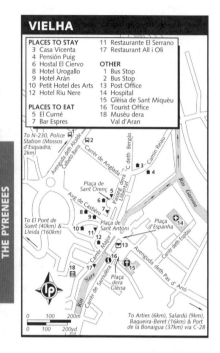

VIELHA

PLACES TO STAY
3 Casa Vicenta
4 Pensión Puig
6 Hostal El Ciervo
8 Hotel Urogallo
9 Hotel Arán
10 Petit Hotel des Arts
12 Hotel Riu Nere

PLACES TO EAT
5 El Curné
7 Bar Espres

11 Restaurante El Serrano
17 Restaurant All i Oli

OTHER
1 Bus Stop
2 Bus Stop
13 Post Office
14 Hospital
15 Glèisa de Sant Miquèu
16 Tourist Office
18 Musèu dera
    Val d'Aran

along Avenguda de Castièro and Avenguda deth Pas d'Arró. The post office is at Carrèr de Sarriulèra 4. The Mossos d'Esquadra (Catalunya's regional police; ☎ 973 64 20 44) are based 2km from the centre along the N-230 highway to France. There's a hospital (☎ 973 64 00 66) on Carrèr deth Espitau off Avenguda deth Pas d'Arró.

Things to See The small old quarter is around Plaça dera Glèisa and across the little Riu Nere just west of the square. The **Glèisa de Sant Miquèu**, a church on Plaça dera Glèisa has a mix of 12th- to 18th-century styles and a 13th-century main portal. It contains some notable medieval artwork, especially the 12th-century *Crist de Mijaran*, an almost life-sized wooden bust thought to have been part of a Descent from the Cross group. The **Musèu dera Val d'Aran**, Carrèr Major 11, recounts Aran's history up to the present. It opens 5 to 8 pm Tuesday to Friday; 10 am to 1 pm and 5 to

8 pm Saturday; and 10 am to 1 pm Sunday. Admission costs €1.25. In high summer the opening times are generally longer.

Places to Stay For some of the cheaper places, head down Passeg dera Llibertat, north off Avenguda de Castièro just west of Plaça dera Glèisa. *Hostal El Ciervo* (☎ *973 64 01 65, Plaça de Sant Orenç 3)*, just off Passeg dera Llibertat, has ageing but adequate singles/doubles for €15.10/24.10, or €21.10/30.15 with bathroom. On Camin Reiau, a north-east extension of Passeg dera Llibertat, *Pensión Puig* (☎ *973 64 00 31)* at No 6, with no sign except for a 'P', has doubles for €16.90; *Casa Vicenta* (☎ *973 64 08 19)* at No 7 is much better at €33.15 for doubles with bathroom and breakfast.

For a bit more comfort, *Hotel Urogallo* (☎ *973 64 00 00, Avenguda de Castièro 7)*, *Hotel Arán* (☎ *973 64 00 50, Avenguda de Castièro 5)* and *Hotel Riu Nere* (☎ *973 64 01 50, Carrèr de Sant Nicolau 2)* have doubles with bathroom ranging from €30 to €40 in the low season and €54 to €73 in the high season.

Petit Hotel des Arts (☎ *973 64 18 48, Carrèr dera Palha 15)* is a rather bijou, spick-and-span sort of place with attractive doubles for €48.80.

Places to Eat A cosy little bar and restaurant in a charming old house, *El Curné* (☎ *973 64 16 23, Plaça de Sant Orenç)* serves main courses which start at about €6.

An unassuming little place is *Bar Espres* (*Passeg dera Llibertat 3)*, where staff will sell you Aranese products or whip you up a quick tapa or two. *Restaurant El Serrano* (☎ *973 64 01 50, Carrèr de Sant Nicolau 2)* does some reasonable Aranese dishes. A bowl of the traditional local broth, olla aranesa, costs €4.55.

Restaurant All i Oli (☎ *973 64 17 57, Carrèr Major 9)* is one of the costlier places in town with a *menú* for €15.10. Anyone for snails?

East of Vielha

The main attraction as you head east is skiing, the best in Catalunya.

Salardú Nine kilometres east of Vielha, Salardú's little nucleus of old houses and narrow streets has largely resisted the temptation to sprawl. Unfortunately, however, if you come in May, June, October or November, you'll find only a few hotels open. The tourist office (☎ 973 64 57 26) is by the car park near the middle of the village and opens in summer only. Otherwise call the town hall *(ayuntamiento)* on ☎ 973 64 40 30. In the apse of the village's 12th- and 13th-century **church** you can admire the 13th-century crucifixion carving, *Crist de Salardú*.

Places to Stay & Eat Just above the main road towards the eastern end of the village, ***Xalet-Refugi Juli Soler Santaló*** *(☎ 973 64 50 16)* has dormitory places for €9.05 and bunk rooms for €14.50 per person, plus a kitchen and cafeteria. You may find yourself being obliged to pay €26.55 per person for half-board.

The large ***Alberg Era Garona*** youth hostel *(☎ 973 64 52 71)* nearby has room for 180 people; the high season is December to April and July and August. In the centre, ***Refugi Rosta*** *(☎ 973 64 53 08, fax 973 64 58 14, Plaça Major 1)* is an 18th-century place full of character with dormitory bunks for €11.60 per person and double rooms for €27.75 in July and August or €33.75 in the ski season (prices include breakfast). It closes at most other times. There's a great wood-panelled bar, where you can eat sausage, pâté or crepes for €3 to €4.55, as well as a good dining room.

Pensión Montaña *(☎ 973 64 41 08, Carrèr Major s/n)* has doubles for €24.70. ***Residència Aiguamòg*** *(☎ 973 64 54 96, Carrèr de Sant Andreu 12–14)*, near the centre, has quaint singles/doubles with bathroom for up to €18.10/36.15. ***Hotel Deth Pais*** *(☎ 973 64 58 36, fax 973 64 45 00, Carrèr de Santa Paula s/n)* has nice pine-panelled rooms with bathroom for €37.35 plus IVA, single or double. There are also five more expensive places to stay.

Baqueira-Beret Baqueira (Vaquèira in Aranese), 3km east of Salardú, and Beret, 8km north of Baqueira, form Catalunya's premier ski resort, favoured by the Spanish royal family, no less! Its good lift system gives access to 47 varied pistes totalling 77km (larger than any other Spanish resort), amid fine scenery at between 1500m and 2510m, and there's a big ski school. A one-day lift pass costs €27.75.

In summer the Bosque and Mirador chair lifts open from some time in July to some time in September to carry you from Baqueira almost to the top of Cap de Baqueira (2500m) for around €10.85.

There's nowhere cheap to stay in Baqueira, and nowhere at all at Beret. Many skiers stay down the valley in Salardú, Arties or Vielha. Information on packages is available from Baqueira-Beret's Central de Reservas (☎ 973 64 44 55, fax 973 64 44 88), Apartado 60, 25530 Vielha. The cheapest five-day packages including room, breakfast and lifts start at around €150 per person. The price tag depends on where and when you go, and you could easily find yourself paying €1200 per person for a good apartment at New Year (the most expensive time).

Walking If you have a vehicle to get to Beret (some 8km north up a hairpin road from Baqueira), a nice shortish walk is the 5km from Beret along the headwaters of the Riu Noguera Pallaresa to the abandoned village of **Montgarri**, where there is a 16th-century shrine.

More spectacular routes head south up into the mountains on the northern fringes of the Parc Nacional d'Aigüestortes i Estany de Sant Maurici. The following three can all be done partway by vehicle and end at mountain refuges for those who want to linger or head on over into the national park. You can find details of the mountain refuges mentioned under Places to Stay under Parc Nacional d'Aigüestortes i Estany de Sant Maurici.

From the village of **Tredòs**, slightly east of and below Salardú, a road ascends the valley of the Riu d'Aiguamotx. You can get a car about 8km up, to a level of about 1850m. From there it's a 2.5km walk up to the Refugi de Colomèrs at 2125m, set in a beautiful lake-strewn bowl. From the refuge there are easy marked circuit walks of two and four hours.

Another walk from Tredòs would be to head south-east up the valley of the Riu de Ruda to the Refugi Saborèdo, some 12km up at 2310m, in another fine lake-dotted cirque. You can drive about two-thirds of the way.

From the town of **Arties**, 3km west of Salardú, you could head 8km up the Riu de Valarties valley to the Refugi de la Restanca. It's drivable for about the first 4.5km; from there you must walk the steeper part, about 3.5km, up to the refuge at 2000m. From the refuge you can walk for about one hour south-west up to the Estany de Mar, amid extremely rugged scenery at 2250m, or spend a day climbing and descending 2830m Montardó (to the east), with magnificent views.

If you happen to stop at Arties, call in at the **Hotel Valarties** (☎ 973 64 43 64, fax 973 64 21 74, Carrer Major 3). Set in a house that is a heterodox mix of local building tradition and tarty avant-garde, it houses a restaurant known to skiers and walkers for miles around. You can stay too if you want, although it's a touch expensive with doubles costing up to €56.65 in the high season.

The Refugi de Colomèrs and Refugi de la Restanca are a short day's walk from each other, on the GR11. From the Refugi de la Restanca, the GR11 heads about five hours west to the **Refugi Boca Sud** (☎ 973 69 70 52), near the southern end of the Túnel de Vielha. From there, if you continue on the GR11, it's two days (with a night's camping or in a refuge) past the Maladeta massif over to Benasque in Aragón.

North of Vielha

Most people heading north just race up the highway to France which is a pity because the hills hide some exquisite countryside with fine walking trails and an assortment of curious villages and hamlets.

Arròs, Vila & Other Villages You can approach this string of villages in several ways. Turn right off the highway at **Eth Pònt d'Arròs** and climb the few kilometres

into **Arròs** itself. Suddenly you seem to have left the cheapness of ski-tourism behind and this sleepy village makes a much better choice of place to stay than the valley towns. You have a choice of five tiny cases de pagès. The biggest is **Casa Mariun** (☎ 973 64 03 41, Carrèr del Centre 13). A double costs €21.10 and there is space for 10 people.

El Raconet (☎ 973 64 17 30, Carrèr de Crestalhera 3) is a cosy little stone-walled house converted into a charming country restaurant. The setting alone makes it worthwhile. Solid country cooking is on offer and you should not have to pay out more than about €18.10 per head.

A couple of kilometres east and uphill is the even sleepier hamlet of **Vila**. The main reason for calling in here is for food. **Casa Maite** (☎ 973 64 26 39, Carrèr de Sant Miquel 28) is a rustic mountain hideaway where you'll feel you'd like to stay well beyond the last course. A meal can cost around €18.10.

Without a 4WD you can't make much more progress on wheels, although several hikes are signposted around here.

Back in Arròs, those with wheels could turn off northwards for the Saut deth Pish waterfall. It's a worthwhile exercise. The road takes you up along a narrow heavily wooded valley. After 7km you pass the **Refugi Borda da Juanun**, where you can pick up something to eat. Another kilometre on and you reach **Els Artiguetes**, a small, signposted plain. Stop at this point and you can look west to the glaciers of the Pic d'Aneto in Aragón. From here 4km of rough but driveable dirt trail takes you to a plain and the thundering **Saut deth Pish** waterfall ('pish', or piss, is the rather colourful Aranese word for waterfall). The refuge here is being rebuilt.

After heading back down to Arròs you could (with wheels) continue driving about villages farther west – head for **Vilamòs** (6km of rising hairpin bends) and **Arres**. The former is bigger but a little less intriguing than the latter, which is divided into upper and lower parts (Arres de Sus and Arres de Jos, respectively). Vilamòs lies towards the southern end of a pretty mountain walk north to Canejan in the Val de Toran (see under Val de Toran later), the signposted PR114.

Plan dera Artiga de Lin Branch west off the main highway at **Es Bòrdes**, a typically cute Aranese village, and keep following the road as it twists its way up into heavily wooded country. The drive alone is a delight, following the course of the Joèu stream as you gain altitude to reach the high mountain pastures of the Plan dera Artiga de Lin plain (Heidi would feel very much at home here). Hikers will start feeling the call of the wild, as a couple of trails lead off into the tall forbidding mountains of the Aragonese Pyrenees, capped by the Pic d'Aneto.

A couple of kilometres short of the plain is a delightfully simple local *eatery* (look for the 'brasseria' signs). Open from about Easter to November for lunch only, you have a limited choice of grilled meats to tuck into. Accompanied by some salad and washed down with a bottle of red wine, you will feel pleasantly heavy at a cost of about €15.10 per head.

You can also reach the Plan dera Artiga de Lin on foot, following the short-distance PR115 route from the village of **Casau**, just outside Vielha. A pleasant hour's circuit walk would take you through the woods to the **Uelhs deth Joèu**, a cascade that gives rise to the Arriu Joèu. The Vielha tourist office has a brochure describing this stroll.

Bossòst Arriving in Bossòst you will be struck by the pleasant tree-lined, riverside boulevard that the N-230 becomes as it enters this town. You might also be astounded by the uninterrupted line-up of tourist-tack shops selling everything from porcelain statue lampstands to flamenco dancer dolls (*trés* interesting).

Before racing towards France, make a brief stop to head a few steps west of the main thoroughfare into the backstreets. In between the typical Aranese houses with snowproof roofs and balconies bedecked with flowers you'll run into the 12th-century **Església de l'Assumpció de Maria.**

Apart from the awful concrete reconstruction of part of the apse (who allowed *that*?), it is a fine example of the small-scale rural Romanesque architecture typical of this part of the country. The northern entrance is capped by a black marble tympanum featuring a Pantocrator (a Christ figure) and symbols of the Evangelists.

About eight hotels volunteer their services if you need to stay overnight. Doubles start at €30.15. There are several places to eat at in town, although they are nothing special.

An alternative route into France from here involves taking a side road west from the southern end of Bossòst to **Eth Portilhon**. It climbs steeply for about 8km to this mountain pass (1292m) before dropping over the other side and leading you 7km to Bagnères-de-Luchon. As so often happens when crossing from Spain into France, this orderly, well kept little town comes as a bit of a shock after those in Catalunya. However well kept the latter towns are, they still retain a touch of the dishevelled that seems a trademark of all Spain.

Les Sitting astride the pounding Riu Garona, this is another pleasant little Aranese town to wander about or spend a night in if it's getting late in the day. If you decide to stay you could do worse than *Hotel Europa* (☎ 973 64 80 16, Carrèr d'Aran 8), in the middle of the town and on the river. A sizable double costs €34.95 plus IVA. Its restaurant isn't too bad either.

Val de Toran From Les you are about 7km from the French border. About 1½ km short of the border you should, if you have wheels and time, take the turn-off to the right for **Canejan**. This narrow country lane leads you into lush green country that seems so far removed from Spain as to be barely possible. It is a charming drive, and there is an alternative signposted walking trail that starts shortly after crossing the bridge over the Riu Garona (look for the sign to the left – it's the long-distance GR211 path). It takes you on a climb directly up to Canejan, whereas by road you come in around the back. The town is a trifle run-down but charming all the same and, best of all, placed such that it gives you broad views south down the Val d'Aran.

Follow the GR211 through the countryside to the tiny settlements of **Porcingles**, **Sant Joan de Toran** and **Eth Pradet**. At Sant Joan there is a popular lunchtime restaurant, *Bar Comidas Juan*, in among the dozen or so too-cute-to-be-true stone houses. You can also get to Sant Joan by car, following the road lower down in the valley from Canejan. Branch trails lead off to the other two hamlets too (for Eth Pradet it's a brief but steep climb along a dirt track). The GR211 continues enticingly eastwards across the top of the comarca, hugging the lower contours of the mountain range that marks the frontier with France.

Getting There & Around

Bus Two Alsina Graells buses run daily between Barcelona and Vielha (€21.45) via Lleida and El Pont de Suert. Lleida to Vielha (€9.10), where there is usually a half-hour wait for the connection, takes three hours. From June to October a daily Alsina Graells bus connects Barcelona and Vielha via La Pobla de Segur, Llavorsí, the Espot turning on the C-12, Port de la Bonaigua and Salardú (the total journey time is about seven hours). At the time of writing the southbound departure from Vielha was at 11.44 am.

A local bus service runs from four (at weekends) to nine times daily along the valley from Baqueira to Les or Pontaut (for Eth Pont de Rei) via Vielha and the intervening villages. Several others run from Vielha either to Baquiera or to Les/Pontaut. The trip from one end of the valley to the other takes up to an hour. A single ticket for any destination is €0.75 (or €6.05 for a book of 10 tickets). To get into the side valleys and hills you have to go under your own steam.

Car & Motorcycle The N-230 from Lleida and El Pont de Suert reaches Aran through the 5.25km Túnel de Vielha (built in the 1940s and showing its age), then heads north from Vielha to the French border at Eth Pont de Rei. Continuing as the French N-125, it reaches the Toulouse-Pau road at Montréjeau, 46km from the border.

From the Vall de la Noguera Pallaresa, the C-28 crosses the Port de la Bonaigua pass (2072m) – sometimes closed in winter – into Naut Aran, meeting the N-230 at Vielha.

Language

Catalunya is, officially at least, a bilingual region. Since gaining its autonomous status at the end of the 1970s, the regional government has embarked on a vigorous campaign to revive Catalan *(català)*, a language that since 1714 had frequently been subject to bans and censorship.

The effects have been quite remarkable. Few would argue that Catalan is a viable, living language. Ongoing programmes of 'linguistic normalisation' suggest it will continue to gain ground as the area's first language. However, Spanish, or more correctly Castilian *(castellano)*, remains for many the language of choice.

Both Latin languages, the differences go back in part to the way the various modern Latin tongues spun off from the mother tongue of Rome. While the indigenous people of the Roman province of Tarraconensis (which included Catalunya) tended to pick up Latin from settlers and soldiers, those of the remoter provinces apparently learned from more educated classes. In addition, a sound shift that occurred to a greater or lesser extent in the Latin spoken from Italy across France and into Catalunya barely touched the rest of Spain. To this day many Spanish words derive from an older, more classical version of Latin than their equivalents in Catalan, French or Italian.

Traditionally, big cities and the coast have always been more open to varied influences than the rural hinterland. And so it is that in the coastal resorts and Barcelona you are much more likely to encounter Castilian as a first language. Your chances of striking English speakers and (on the Costa Brava especially) French speakers are also not so bad. Inland, Catalan rules. This is not to say locals don't speak Castilian but that they don't do so as a matter of course and sometimes even feel uncomfortable about it.

Foreigners will encounter no ill-feeling for muddling through in Castilian – that in itself is appreciated. If you go the whole hog and try your hand at Catalan, you should earn extra brownie points. It's worth the effort to try at least one language.

Castilian Spanish

Pronunciation
Vowels
Unlike English, each of the vowels in Spanish has a uniform pronunciation which doesn't vary. For example, the Spanish 'a' has one pronunciation rather than the numerous pronunciations we find in English, such as 'cake', 'care', 'cat', 'cart' and 'call'. Many words have a written accent. This acute accent (as in *días*) indicates a stressed syllable and doesn't change the sound of the vowel. Vowels are pronounced clearly even if they are in unstressed positions or at the end of a word.

a	somewhere between the 'a' in 'cat' and the 'a' in 'cart'
e	as in 'met'
i	somewhere between the 'i' in 'marine' and the 'i' in 'flip'
o	similar to the 'o' in 'hot'
u	as in 'put'

Consonants
Some consonants are the same as their English counterparts. The pronunciation of other consonants varies according to which vowel follows. The Spanish alphabet also contains the letter ñ, which is not found in the English alphabet. Until recently, the clusters **ch** and **ll** were also officially separate consonants, and you're likely to encounter many situations – for example, in lists and dictionaries – in which they are still treated that way.

b	soft, as the 'v' in 'van'; also (less commonly) as in 'book' when word-initial or when preceded by a nasal such as 'm' or 'n'
c	as the 'th' in 'thin'

ch as in 'choose'
d   sometimes not pronounced at all
g   as in 'go' when initial or before 'a', 'o' or 'u'; elsewhere much softer. Before 'e' or 'i' it's a harsh, breathy sound, a bit like 'ch' in Scottish *loch*.
h   always silent
j   a harsh, guttural sound similar to the 'ch' in Scottish *loch*
ll similar to the 'y' in 'yellow'
ñ   a nasal sound like the 'ni' in 'onion' or the 'ny' in 'canyon'
q   always followed by a silent 'u' and either 'e' (as in *que*) or 'i' (as in *aquí*); the combined sound of 'qu' is like the 'k' in 'kick'
r   a rolled 'r' sound; longer and stronger when initial or doubled
s   often not pronounced, especially at the end of a word; thus *pescados* (fish) is pronounced 'peh-cow' in Andalucía
v   same as 'b'
x   as the 'x' in 'taxi' when between two vowels; as the 's' in 'say' before a consonant
z   as the 'th' in 'thin'

Greetings & Civilities

Hello.	*¡Hola!*
Goodbye.	*¡Adiós!*
Yes.	*Sí.*
No.	*No.*
Please.	*Por favor.*
Thank you (very much).	*(Muchas) gracias.*
You're welcome.	*De nada.*
Excuse me.	*Perdón/Perdone.*
Sorry/Excuse me.	*Lo siento/Discúlpeme.*

Useful Phrases

Do you speak English?	*¿Habla inglés?*
Does anyone speak English?	*¿Hay alguien que hable inglés?*
I (don't) understand.	*(No) entiendo.*
Just a minute.	*Un momento.*
Could you write it down, please?	*¿Puede escribirlo, por favor?*
How much is it?	*¿Cuánto cuesta/vale?*

Getting Around

What time does the ... leave/arrive?	*¿A qué hora sale/ llega el ...?*
boat	*barco*
bus (city)	*autobús/bus*
bus (intercity)	*autocar*
metro/ underground	*metro*
plane	*avión*
train	*tren*

next	*próximo*
first	*primer*
last	*último*
1st class	*primera clase*
2nd class	*segunda clase*

I'd like a ... ticket.	*Quisiera un billete ...*
one-way	*de solo ida*
return	*de ida y vuelta*

Where is the bus stop?	*¿Dónde está la parada de autobús?*
I want to go to ...	*Quiero ir a ...*
Can you show me (on the map)?	*¿Me puede indicar (en el mapa)?*
Go straight ahead.	*Siga/Vaya todo derecho.*
Turn left.	*Gire a la izquierda.*
Turn right.	*Gire a la derecha.*
near	*cerca*
far	*lejos*

Around Town

I'm looking for ...	*Estoy buscando ...*
a bank	*un banco*
the city centre	*el centro de la ciudad*
the embassy	*la embajada*
my hotel	*mi hotel*
the market	*el mercado*
the police	*la policía*
the post office	*los correos*
public toilets	*los aseos públicos*
a telephone	*un teléfono*
the tourist office	*la oficina de turismo*

the beach	*la playa*
the bridge	*el puente*
the castle	*el castillo*
the cathedral	*la catedral*

Signs – Spanish

Entrada	Entrance
Salida	Exit
Abierto	Open
Cerrado	Closed
Información	Information
Prohibido	Prohibited
Habitaciones Libres	Rooms Available
Ocupado/Completo	No Vacancies
Comisaría	Police Station
Servicios/Aseos	Toilets
Hombres	Men
Mujeres	Women

the church	*la iglesia*
the hospital	*el hospital*
the lake	*el lago*
the main square	*la plaza mayor*
the mosque	*la mezquita*
the old city	*la ciudad antigua*
the palace	*el palacio*
the ruins	*las ruinas*
the sea	*el mar*
the square	*la plaza*
the tower	*el torre*

Accommodation

Where is a cheap hotel?	*¿Dónde hay un hotel barato?*
What's the address?	*¿Cuál es la dirección?*
Do you have any rooms available?	*¿Tiene habitaciones libres?*

I'd like ...	*Quisiera ...*
a bed	*una cama*
a single room	*una habitación individual*
a double room	*una habitación doble*
a room with a bathroom	*una habitación con baño*
to share a dorm	*compartir un dormitorio*

How much is it per night/person?	*¿Cuánto cuesta por noche/persona?*
May I see it?	*¿Puedo verla?*
Where is the bathroom?	*¿Dónde está el baño?*

Food

breakfast	*desayuno*
lunch	*almuerzo/comida*
dinner	*cena*

I'd like the set lunch.	*Quisiera el menú del día.*
Is service included?	*¿El servicio está incluido?*
I'm a vegetarian.	*Soy vegetariano/ vegetariana.* (m/f)

Time & Dates

What time is it?	*¿Qué hora es?*
It's one o'clock.	*Es la una.*
It's two o'clock.	*Son las dos.*
It's five past six.	*Son las seis y cinco.*
It's half past eight.	*Son las ocho y media.*
today	*hoy*
tomorrow	*mañana*
yesterday	*ayer*
in the morning	*de la mañana*
in the afternoon	*de la tarde*
in the evening	*de la noche*

Monday	*lunes*
Tuesday	*martes*
Wednesday	*miércoles*
Thursday	*jueves*
Friday	*viernes*
Saturday	*sábado*
Sunday	*domingo*

January	*enero*
February	*febrero*
March	*marzo*
April	*abril*
May	*mayo*
June	*junio*
July	*julio*
August	*agosto*
September	*setiembre/ septiembre*
October	*octubre*
November	*noviembre*
December	*diciembre*

Health

I'm ...	*Soy...*
diabetic	*diabético/a*
epileptic	*epiléptico/a*
asthmatic	*asmático/a*

Emergencies – Spanish

Help!	¡Socorro!/¡Auxilio!
Call a doctor!	¡Llame a un doctor!
Call the police!	¡Llame a la policía!
Where are the toilets?	¿Dónde están los servicios?
Go away!	¡Váyase!
I'm lost.	Estoy perdido/a.

I'm allergic to ...	Soy alérgico/a a ...
antibiotics	los antibióticos
penicillin	la penicilina

antiseptic	antiséptico
aspirin	aspirina
condoms	preservativos/condones
contraceptive	anticonceptivo
diarrhoea	diarrea
medicine	medicamento
nausea	náusea
sunblock cream	crema protectora contra el sol
tampons	tampones

Numbers

0	cero
1	uno, una
2	dos
3	tres
4	cuatro
5	cinco
6	seis
7	siete
8	ocho
9	nueve
10	diez
11	once
12	doce
13	trece
14	catorce
15	quince
16	dieciséis
17	diecisiete
18	dieciocho
19	diecinueve
20	veinte
21	veintiuno
22	veintidós
23	veintitrés
30	treinta
31	treinta y uno
40	cuarenta
50	cincuenta
60	sesenta
70	setenta
80	ochenta
90	noventa
100	cien/ciento
1000	mil

one million   un millón

Catalan

Pronunciation

Catalan sounds are not hard for an English-speaker to pronounce. You should note, however, that vowels will vary according to whether they occur in stressed or unstressed syllables. Unstressed vowels are never accented. Stressed vowels may or may not carry an acute (**é**) or a grave (**è**) accent. Vowels with a grave accent are pronounced with the mouth slightly more open than unaccented vowels, while vowels with an acute accent are more closed.

Vowels
- **a** when stressed, as the 'a' in 'father'; when unstressed, as in 'about'
- **e** when stressed, as in 'pet'; when unstressed, as the 'e' in 'open'
- **i** as the 'i' in 'machine'
- **o** when stressed, as in 'pot'; when unstressed, as the 'oo' in 'zoo'
- **u** as the 'u' in 'humid'

Consonants
- **b** pronounced 'p' at the end of a word
- **c** hard before 'a', 'o', and 'u'; soft before 'e' and 'i'
- **ç** pronounced 'ss'
- **d** pronounced 't' at the end of a word
- **g** hard before 'a', 'o' and 'u'; before 'e' and 'i', as the 's' in 'measure'
- **h** always silent
- **j** as the 's' in 'pleasure'

r   as in English in the middle of a word;
    silent at the end
rr a rolled 'r' sound at the beginning of a
    word; stressed more in the middle of
    a word
s   as in 'so' at the beginning of a word; as
    'z' in the middle of a word
v   pronounced as 'b' in Barcelona; pro-
    nounced a 'v' in some other areas
x   mostly as in English; sometimes 'sh'

Other letters are pronounced approximately
as in English. There are a couple of odd
combinations:

l.l repeat the 'l'
tx   like 'ch'
qu   like 'k'

Greetings & Civilities

Hello.	*Hola.*
Goodbye.	*Adéu.*
Yes.	*Sí.*
No.	*No.*
Please.	*Sisplau/Si us plau.*
Thank you (very much).	*(Moltes) gràcies.*
You're welcome.	*De res.*
Excuse me.	*Perdoni.*
May I?/Do you mind?	*Puc?/Em permet?*
Sorry/Forgive me.	*Ho sento/Perdoni.*
What's your name?	*Com et dius?* (inf) *Com es diu?* (pol)
My name's ...	*Em dic ...*
Where are you from?	*D'on ets?*

Language Difficulties

Do you speak English?	*Parla anglès?*
Could you speak in Castilian please?	*Pot parlar castellà sisplau?*
I (don't) understand.	*(No) ho entenc.*
Could you repeat that?	*Pot repetir-ho?*
Could you write it down, please?	*Pot escriure-ho, sisplau?*
How do you say ... in Catalan?	*Com es diu ... en català?*

Signs – Catalan

Entrada	Entrance
Sortida	Exit
Obert	Open
Tancat	Closed
Informació	Information
Comissaria	Police Station
Lavabos	Toilets

Getting Around

What time does the ... leave?	*A quina hora surt ...?*
boat	*le vaixall*
bus	*l'autobús*
flight	*le vol*
train	*le tren*
I'd like a ... ticket.	*Voldria un bitllet ...*
one-way	*d'anada*
return	*d'anar i tornar*
Where is the ...?	*On és ...?*
bus station	*l'estació d'autobusos*
train station	*l'estació de tren*
metro station	*la parada de metro*
How do I get to ...?	*Com puc arribar a ...?*
I want to go to ...	*Vull anar a ...*
Please tell me when we get to ...?	*Pot avisar-me quan arribem a ...?*
baggage claim	*recollida d'equipatges*
departures	*sortides*
exchange	*canvi*
platform	*andana*

Around Town

I'm looking for ...	*Estic buscant ...*
a bank	*un banc*
the city centre	*el centre de la ciutat*
the hotel	*el hotel*
the market	*el mercat*
the police	*la policia*
the post office	*correus*
a public toilet	*els lavabos públics*
a restaurant	*un restaurant*
the telephone centre	*la central telefònica*
the tourist office	*l'oficina de turisme*

the beach	la platja
the bridge	el pont
the castle	el castell
the cathedral	la catedral
the church	l'església
the hospital	el hospital
the lake	el llac/el estany
the mosque	la mesquita
the old city	el casc antic
the palace	el palau
the ruins	les ruïnes
the sea	el mar
the square	la plaça
the tower	la torre

What time does it open/close?	A quina hora obren/tanquen?

I want to change ...	Voldria canviar ...
some money	diners
travellers cheques	txecs de viatge

Accommodation

Is there a campsite/ hotel near here?	Hi ha algun càmping/ hotel a prop d'aquí?
Do you have any rooms available?	Hi ha habitacions lliures?

I'd like ...	Voldria ...
a single room	una habitació individual
a double room	una habitació doble
to share a dorm	compartir un dormitori

I want a room with a ...	Vull una habitació amb ...
bathroom	cambra de bany
double bed	llit de matrimoni
shower	dutxa

How much is it per night/person?	Quant val per nit/persona?
Does it include breakfast?	Inclou l'esmorzar?
Are there any cheaper rooms?	Hi ha habitacions més barates?
I'm going to stay for (one week).	Em quedaré (una setmana).
I'm leaving now.	Me'n vaig.

Shopping

Where can I buy ...?	On puc comprar ...?
How much does this cost?	Quant val això?

Where is the nearest ...?	On és ... més propera/proper?
bookshop	la llibreria
camera shop	la botiga de fotos
department store	el gran magatzem
greengrocer	la fruiteria
laundrette	la bugaderia
market	el mercat
newsagent's shop	el quiosc
pharmacy	la farmàcia
supermarket	el supermercat
travel agency	la agència de viatges

condoms	preservatius/condons
deodorant	desodorant
razor blades	fulles d'afaitar
sanitary towels	compreses
shampoo	xampú
shaving cream	crema d'afaitar
soap	sabó
sunblock cream	crema solar
tampons	tampons
tissues	mocadors de paper
toilet paper	paper higiènic
toothbrush	raspall de dents
toothpaste	pasta de dents

envelope	sobre
magazines	revistes
map	mapa
newspapers	diaris
pen (ballpoint)	bolígraf
postcards	postals
stamp	segell

Time & Dates

One thing to remember when asking about times in Catalan: minutes past the hour (eg, quarter past, twenty-five past) are referred to as being before the next hour. Thus 'half past two' becomes *dos quarts de tres* (two quarters to three) and 'twenty past nine' becomes *un quart i cinc de deu* (one quarter and five minutes to ten). Thus, 'twenty to ten' becomes *tres quarts menys cinc de deu* (three quarters minus five minutes to ten) and 'ten to five' becomes *tres quarts i cinc de cinc* (three quarters and five minutes to five).

What time is it?	*Quina hora és?*
It's one o'clock.	*És la una.*
It's two o'clock.	*Són les dues.*
It's quarter past six.	*És un quart de set.*
It's half past eight.	*Són dos quarts de nou.*
today	*avui*
tomorrow	*demà*
yesterday	*ahir*
in the morning	*del matí*
in the afternoon	*de tarda*
in the evening	*de nit*

Monday	*dilluns*
Tuesday	*dimarts*
Wednesday	*dimecres*
Thursday	*dijous*
Friday	*divendres*
Saturday	*dissabte*
Sunday	*diumenge*

January	*gener*
February	*febrer*
March	*març*
April	*abril*
May	*maig*
June	*juny*
July	*juliol*
August	*agost*
September	*setembre*
October	*octubre*
November	*novembre*
December	*desembre*

Numbers

0	*zero*
1	*un, una*
2	*dos, dues*
3	*tres*
4	*quatre*
5	*cinc*
6	*sis*
7	*set*
8	*vuit*
9	*nou*
10	*deu*

11	*onze*
12	*dotze*
13	*tretze*
14	*catorze*
15	*quinze*
16	*setze*
17	*disset*
18	*divuit*
19	*dinou*
20	*vint*
21	*vint-i-un*
22	*vint-i-dos*
23	*vint-i-tres*
30	*trenta*
31	*trenta-un*
40	*quaranta*
50	*cinquanta*
60	*seixanta*
70	*setanta*
80	*vuitanta*
90	*noranta*
100	*cent*
1000	*mil*

one million	*un milió*

FOOD

breakfast	*esmorzar*
lunch	*dinar*
dinner	*sopar*
dessert	*postres*
a drink	*una beguda*

Can I see the menu please?	*Puc veure el menú, sisplau?*
I'd like the set lunch, please.	*Voldria el menú del dia, sisplau.*
The bill, please.	*El compte, sisplau.*
Bon appetit/Cheers!	*Bon profit/Salut!*

Popular Catalan Dishes

allioli
  garlic sauce
calçots
  shallots, usually served braised with an almond dipping sauce; a seasonal Catalan delicacy
coca
  dense, flat pastry, especially popular during St Joan (John) celebrations, when it's decorated with candied peel or pine nuts

crema catalana
　creme caramel with a burnt toffee sauce
ensaimada mallorquina
　sweet Mallorcan pastry
escalivada
　roasted red peppers, onion and aubergine
　in olive oil
escudella i carn d'olla
　winter dish of soup and meatballs
fuet
　thin, dried pork sausuage, native to Cat-
　alunya
mel i mató
　dessert of curd cheese with honey
mongetes seques i botifarra
　haricot beans with thick pork sausage
pa amb tomàquet (i pernil)
　crusty bread rubbed with ripe tomatoes,
　garlic and olive oil, often topped with
　cured ham
paella
　rice, seafood and meat dish (Valencian in
　origin)
sobrassada
　spreadable red sausage; a speciality in
　Mallorca

Drinks

fruit juice	*suc*
mineral water	*aigua mineral*
(still)	*(sense gas)*

tap water	*aigua de l'aixeta*
tiger nut drink	*orxata*
soft drinks	*refrescos*

black coffee	*cafè sol*
long black	*doble*
iced coffee	*cafè gelat*
decaffeinated coffee	*cafè descafeinat*
tea	*te*

coffee ...	*cafè ...*
with liqueur	*carajillo* (*cigaló* in northern Catalunya)
with a little milk	*tallat*
with milk	*amb llet*

Catalunya is famous for its *cava*, the region's 'champagne'.

beer	*cervesa*
rum	*rom*
whisky	*whisky*
muscatel	*moscatell*
ratafia (liqueur)	*ratafia*

a glass of ... wine	*un vi ...*
red	*negre*
rosé	*rosat*
sparkling	*d'agulla*
white	*blanc*

Glossary

Items listed below are in Catalan/Castilian Spanish where they start with the same letter. Where the two terms start with different letters, they have their own entry – identified as Catalan (C) or Spanish (S). Identified in the same way are words given in only one or the other language, either because that term is predominantly used by all or because the word is the same in both languages. In a few other cases, the Spanish alone is given as the only difference is the addition of accents for the Catalan.

abierto (S) – open
ajuntament/ayuntamiento – city or town council or hall
alberg de joventut/albergue juvenil – youth hostel; not to be confused with *hostal*
alcalde – (C & S) mayor
altar major/mayor – high altar
apartat de correus/apartado de correos – post office box
arribada – (C) arrival
ascensor – (C & S) lift (elevator)
autonomía – (S) autonomous community or region: Spain's 50 *provincias* are grouped into 17 of these, one of which is Catalunya
autopista – (C & S) tolled dual-lane highway
autovía – (S) toll-free dual-lane highway

bakalao – (S) ear-splitting Spanish techno music; not to be confused with *bacalao* (salted cod)
Barcelonin – (C) inhabitant/native of Barcelona
barri/barrio – district, quarter of Barcelona
biblioteca – (C & S) library
bodega – (S) literally, a cellar (especially a wine cellar); also means a winery, or a traditional wine bar likely to serve wine from the barrel
bombero – (S) fireman; *cuerpo de bomberos* means fire brigade
botiga – (C) shop

caixer automàtic/cajero automático – automatic teller machine (ATM)
call – (C) Jewish quarter in medieval Barcelona (and other Catalan towns)
canvi/cambio – in general, small change; also currency exchange
canya/caña – a small glass of beer
cap/cabo – cape (headland or promontory)
cap de setmana – (C) weekend
capella/capilla – chapel
capella major/capilla mayor – chapel containing the high altar of a church
capgròs – (C) huge-headed figure seen at traditional Catalan festivals
Carnestoltes/Carnaval – carnival; a period of fancy-dress parades and merrymaking ending on the Tuesday 47 days before Easter Sunday
carrer/calle – street
carretera – (C & S) highway
carta – (C & S) menu
casa de pagès/casa rural – a village or country house or farmstead with rooms to let
castell/castillo – castle
castellers – (C) human-castle builders
catedral – (C & S) cathedral
celler – (C) see *bodega*
cercanías – (S) local trains serving Barcelona's airport, suburbs and some outlying towns
cerrado – (S) closed
cerveseria/cervecería – beer bar
chiringuito – (S) small shop or stall; often a makeshift food stall at the seaside
claustre/claustro – cloister
comarca – (C & S) district, a grouping of *municipios*
comedor – (S) dining room
comissaria/comisaría – National Police station
compte/cuenta – bill (check)
consigna – (C & S) left-luggage office or lockers
copes/copas – drinks (literally, glasses); *anar de copes/ir de copas* is to go out for a few drinks

cor/coro – choir (part of a church, usually in the middle)
corcho – (S) cork
correfoc – (C) fire-running, a part of many a Catalan *festa* where people run about the streets chased by fire-breathing dragons and the like
Correus i Telègrafs/Correos y Telégrafos – post office
costa – (C & S) coast
cremallera – (S) an electric narrow-gauge, cog-wheel railway line

duro – (C & S) hard; also a common name for a five ptas coin

entrada – (C & S) entrance
església – (C) church
estació d'autobusos/estación de autobuses – bus station
estanco – (S) tobacconist's shop
estany – (C) lake

far/faro – lighthouse
farmacia – (S) chemist's shop (pharmacy)
ferrocarril – (C & S) railway
festa/fiesta – festival, public holiday or party
festa major/fiesta mayor – a town or village's main annual festival
FGC – (C) Ferrocarrils de la Generalitat de Catalunya, local trains operating alongside the metro in Barcelona
fin de semana – (S) weekend
fira/feria – (trade) fair
flamenc/flamenco – means flamingo and Flemish as well as flamenco music and dance

gallec/gallego – Galician; a native of Galicia
garum – (Latin) a spicy, vitamin-rich sauce made from fish entrails found throughout the former Roman Empire, including Barcelona
gegant – (C) a huge figure, usually representing kings, queens and other historical figures, often seen parading around at *festes*
Generalitat de Catalunya – autonomous regional government of Catalunya

gitano – (C & S) the Romany people, formerly called Gypsies

hostal – (C & S) commercial establishment providing accommodation in the one to three star category; not to be confused with *alberg de joventut*

iglesia – (S) church
IVA – *impuesto sobre el valor añadido/impost sobre el valor afegit*, or value-added tax (VAT)

lavandería – (S) laundry
llac/lago – lake
llegada – (S) arrival
llibreria or **llibreteria/librería** – bookshop
llista de correus/lista de correos – poste restante
llitera/litera – couchette or sleeping carriage

madrileño – (S) a person from Madrid
marisquería – (S) seafood eatery
marxa/marcha – action, life, 'the scene'
masia – (C) country house or farmhouse
menjador – (C) dining room
menú del día – (S) fixed-price meal available at lunchtime, sometimes in the evening too
mercat/mercado – market
Modernisme – (C) modernism; the architectural and artistic style, influenced by Art Nouveau and sometimes known as Catalan modernism, whose leading practitioner was Antoni Gaudí
Modernista – (C & S) an exponent of Modernisme
moll/muelle – wharf or pier
monestir/monasterio – monastery
Morisc/Morisco – a Muslim converted (often only superficially) to Christianity in medieval Spain
moro – (C & S) 'Moor' or Muslim (usually in a medieval context); also pejorative term for North Africans
mudéjar – (S) a Muslim living under Christian rule in medieval Spain; also refers to their decorative style of architecture
municipio (C & S) – town council or hall

muntanya/montaña – mountain
museu/museo – museum

obert – (C) open
oficina de turisme/turismo – tourist office

palau/palacio – park
pantà/presa – dam
Pantocrator – (from Greek) Christ the All-Ruler or Christ in Majesty, a central emblem of Romanesque art
parador – one of a chain of state-run, high-class hotels, often set in magnificent castles or mansions
parc/parque – park
pensión – (C) guesthouse
penya/peña – a club, usually of flamenco or football fans
pica pica – (C) snacks/snacking
pinxos/pinchos – Basque for *tapes/tapas*
piscina – (C & S) swimming pool
plaça/plaza – public square
plaça de braus/plaza de toros – bullring
plat combinat/plato combinado – literally, combined plate; a large serving of meat/seafood/omelette with trimmings
Plateresque – a highly ornamented, early Renaissance Spanish style of architecture
platja/playa – beach
poble/pueblo – village
pont/puente – bridge; also means the extra day or two off that many people take when a holiday falls close to a weekend
porta/puerta – gate or door
porto/puerto – port
provincia – (C & S) province; Spain is divided into 50 of them
puenting – (S) bungee jumping (from a bridge)

REAJ – (S) Red Española de Albergues Juveniles, the Spanish HI youth hostel network
Reconquista – the Christian reconquest of the Iberian Peninsula from the Muslims (8th to 15th centuries)

refugi/refugio – shelter or refuge, especially a mountain refuge with basic accommodation for hikers
reial/real – royal
RENFE – (S) Red Nacional de los Ferrocarriles Españoles, the national rail network
retaula/retablo – altarpiece
riu/río – river
rodalies – (C) see *cercanías*

sacristía – sacristy, the part of a church in which vestments, sacred objects and other valuables are kept
sardana – (C) traditional Catalan folk dance
serra/sierra – mountain range
Setmana Santa/Semana Santa – Holy Week, the week leading up to Easter Sunday
sida – (C & S) AIDS
sortida/salida – exit or departure
suro – (C) cork

tancat – (C) closed
tapes/tapas – bar snacks traditionally served on a saucer or lid *(tapa)*
taquilla – (C & S) ticket window
targeta de crèdit/tarjeta de crédito – credit card
tarjeta telefónica – (S) phonecard
terrassa/terraza – terrace; often means a cafe or bar's outdoor tables
tienda – (S) shop
torre – (C & S) tower
tramuntana/tramontana – north wind
transbordador – (S) river-crossing car ferry
turisme/turismo – means both tourism and saloon car; *el turismo* can also mean the tourist office

urbanització/urbanización – suburban housing development

vall/valle – valley
VIH – HIV
v.o. – *versión original*, a foreign-language film subtitled in Spanish

Lonely Planet Guides by Region

Lonely Planet is known worldwide for publishing practical, reliable and no-nonsense travel information in our guides and on our Web site. The Lonely Planet list covers just about every accessible part of the world. Currently there are 16 series: Travel guides, Shoestring guides, Condensed guides, Phrasebooks, Read This First, Healthy Travel, Walking guides, Cycling guides, Watching Wildlife guides, Pisces Diving & Snorkeling guides, City Maps, Road Atlases, Out to Eat, World Food, Journeys travel literature and Pictorials.

AFRICA Africa on a shoestring • Botswana • Cairo • Cairo City Map • Cape Town • Cape Town City Map • East Africa • Egypt • Egyptian Arabic phrasebook • Ethiopia, Eritrea & Djibouti • Ethiopian Amharic phrasebook • The Gambia & Senegal • Healthy Travel Africa • Kenya • Malawi • Morocco • Moroccan Arabic phrasebook • Mozambique • Namibia • Read This First: Africa • South Africa, Lesotho & Swaziland • Southern Africa • Southern Africa Road Atlas • Swahili phrasebook • Tanzania, Zanzibar & Pemba • Trekking in East Africa • Tunisia • Watching Wildlife East Africa • Watching Wildlife Southern Africa • West Africa • World Food Morocco • Zambia • Zimbabwe, Botswana & Namibia
Travel Literature: Mali Blues: Traveling to an African Beat • The Rainbird: A Central African Journey • Songs to an African Sunset: A Zimbabwean Story

AUSTRALIA & THE PACIFIC Aboriginal Australia & the Torres Strait Islands •Auckland • Australia • Australian phrasebook • Australia Road Atlas • Cycling Australia • Cycling New Zealand • Fiji • Fijian phrasebook • Healthy Travel Australia, NZ & the Pacific • Islands of Australia's Great Barrier Reef • Melbourne • Melbourne City Map • Micronesia • New Caledonia • New South Wales • New Zealand • Northern Territory • Outback Australia • Out to Eat – Melbourne • Out to Eat – Sydney • Papua New Guinea • Pidgin phrasebook • Queensland • Rarotonga & the Cook Islands • Samoa • Solomon Islands • South Australia • South Pacific • South Pacific phrasebook • Sydney • Sydney City Map • Sydney Condensed • Tahiti & French Polynesia • Tasmania • Tonga • Tramping in New Zealand • Vanuatu • Victoria • Walking in Australia • Watching Wildlife Australia • Western Australia
Travel Literature: Islands in the Clouds: Travels in the Highlands of New Guinea • Kiwi Tracks: A New Zealand Journey • Sean & David's Long Drive

CENTRAL AMERICA & THE CARIBBEAN Bahamas, Turks & Caicos • Baja California • Belize, Guatemala & Yucatán • Bermuda • Central America on a shoestring • Costa Rica • Costa Rica Spanish phrasebook • Cuba • Cycling Cuba • Dominican Republic & Haiti • Eastern Caribbean • Guatemala • Havana • Healthy Travel Central & South America • Jamaica • Mexico • Mexico City • Panama • Puerto Rico • Read This First: Central & South America • Virgin Islands • World Food Caribbean • World Food Mexico • Yucatán
Travel Literature: Green Dreams: Travels in Central America

EUROPE Amsterdam • Amsterdam City Map • Amsterdam Condensed • Andalucía • Athens • Austria • Baltic States phrasebook • Barcelona • Barcelona City Map • Belgium & Luxembourg • Berlin • Berlin City Map • Britain • British phrasebook • Brussels, Bruges & Antwerp • Brussels City Map • Budapest • Budapest City Map • Canary Islands • Catalunya & the Costa Brava • Central Europe • Central Europe phrasebook • Copenhagen • Corfu & the Ionians • Corsica • Crete • Crete Condensed • Croatia • Cycling Britain • Cycling France • Cyprus • Czech & Slovak Republics • Czech phrasebook • Denmark • Dublin • Dublin City Map • Dublin Condensed • Eastern Europe • Eastern Europe phrasebook • Edinburgh • Edinburgh City Map • England • Estonia, Latvia & Lithuania • Europe on a shoestring • Europe phrasebook • Finland • Florence • Florence City Map • France • Frankfurt City Map • Frankfurt Condensed • French phrasebook • Georgia, Armenia & Azerbaijan • Germany • German phrasebook • Greece • Greek Islands • Greek phrasebook • Hungary • Iceland, Greenland & the Faroe Islands • Ireland • Italian phrasebook • Italy • Kraków • Lisbon • The Loire • London • London City Map • London Condensed • Madrid • Madrid City Map • Malta • Mediterranean Europe • Milan, Turin & Genoa • Moscow • Munich • Netherlands • Normandy • Norway • Out to Eat – London • Out to Eat – Paris • Paris • Paris City Map • Paris Condensed • Poland • Polish phrasebook • Portugal • Portuguese phrasebook • Prague • Prague City Map • Provence & the Côte d'Azur • Read This First: Europe • Rhodes & the Dodecanese • Romania & Moldova • Rome • Rome City Map • Rome Condensed • Russia, Ukraine & Belarus • Russian phrasebook • Scandinavian & Baltic Europe • Scandinavian phrasebook • Scotland • Sicily • Slovenia • South-West France • Spain • Spanish phrasebook • Stockholm • St Petersburg • St Petersburg City Map • Sweden • Switzerland • Tuscany • Ukrainian phrasebook • Venice • Vienna • Wales • Walking in Britain • Walking in France • Walking in Ireland • Walking in Italy • Walking in Scotland • Walking in Spain • Walking in Switzerland • Western Europe • World Food France • World Food Greece • World Food Ireland • World Food Italy • World Food Spain **Travel Literature:** After Yugoslavia • Love and War in the Apennines • The Olive Grove: Travels in Greece • On the Shores of the Mediterranean • Round Ireland in Low Gear • A Small Place in Italy

Lonely Planet Mail Order

onely Planet products are distributed worldwide. They are also available by mail order from Lonely Planet, so if you have difficulty finding a title please write to us. North and South American residents should write to 150 Linden St, Oakland, CA 94607, USA; European and African residents should write to 10a Spring Place, London NW5 3BH, UK; and residents of other countries to Locked Bag 1, Footscray, Victoria 3011, Australia.

INDIAN SUBCONTINENT & THE INDIAN OCEAN Bangladesh • Bengali phrasebook • Bhutan • Delhi • Goa • Healthy Travel Asia & India • Hindi & Urdu phrasebook • India • India & Bangladesh City Map • Indian Himalaya • Karakoram Highway • Kathmandu City Map • Kerala • Madagascar • Maldives • Mauritius, Réunion & Seychelles • Mumbai (Bombay) • Nepal • Nepali phrasebook • North India • Pakistan • Rajasthan • Read This First: Asia & India • South India • Sri Lanka • Sri Lanka phrasebook • Tibet • Tibetan phrasebook • Trekking in the Indian Himalaya • Trekking in the Karakoram & Hindukush • Trekking in the Nepal Himalaya • World Food India **Travel Literature:** The Age of Kali: Indian Travels and Encounters • Hello Goodnight: A Life of Goa • In Rajasthan • Maverick in Madagascar • A Season in Heaven: True Tales from the Road to Kathmandu • Shopping for Buddhas • A Short Walk in the Hindu Kush • Slowly Down the Ganges

MIDDLE EAST & CENTRAL ASIA Bahrain, Kuwait & Qatar • Central Asia • Central Asia phrasebook • Dubai • Farsi (Persian) phrasebook • Hebrew phrasebook • Iran • Israel & the Palestinian Territories • Istanbul • Istanbul City Map • Istanbul to Cairo • Istanbul to Kathmandu • Jerusalem • Jerusalem City Map • Jordan • Lebanon • Middle East • Oman & the United Arab Emirates • Syria • Turkey • Turkish phrasebook • World Food Turkey • Yemen **Travel Literature:** Black on Black: Iran Revisited • Breaking Ranks: Turbulent Travels in the Promised Land • The Gates of Damascus • Kingdom of the Film Stars: Journey into Jordan

NORTH AMERICA Alaska • Boston • Boston City Map • Boston Condensed • British Columbia • California & Nevada • California Condensed • Canada • Chicago • Chicago City Map • Chicago Condensed • Florida • Georgia & the Carolinas • Great Lakes • Hawaii • Hiking in Alaska • Hiking in the USA • Honolulu & Oahu City Map • Las Vegas • Los Angeles • Los Angeles City Map • Louisiana & the Deep South • Miami • Miami City Map • Montreal • New England • New Orleans • New Orleans City Map • New York City • New York City City Map • New York City Condensed • New York, New Jersey & Pennsylvania • Oahu • Out to Eat – San Francisco • Pacific Northwest • Rocky Mountains • San Diego & Tijuana • San Francisco • San Francisco City Map • Seattle • Seattle City Map • Southwest • Texas • Toronto • USA • USA phrasebook • Vancouver • Vancouver City Map • Virginia & the Capital Region • Washington, DC • Washington, DC City Map • World Food New Orleans **Travel Literature**: Caught Inside: A Surfer's Year on the California Coast • Drive Thru America

NORTH-EAST ASIA Beijing • Beijing City Map • Cantonese phrasebook • China • Hiking in Japan • Hong Kong & Macau • Hong Kong City Map • Hong Kong Condensed • Japan • Japanese phrasebook • Korea • Korean phrasebook • Kyoto • Mandarin phrasebook • Mongolia • Mongolian phrasebook • Seoul • Shanghai • South-West China • Taiwan • Tokyo • Tokyo Condensed • World Food Hong Kong • World Food Japan **Travel Literature:** In Xanadu: A Quest • Lost Japan

SOUTH AMERICA Argentina, Uruguay & Paraguay • Bolivia • Brazil • Brazilian phrasebook • Buenos Aires • Buenos Aires City Map • Chile & Easter Island • Colombia • Ecuador & the Galapagos Islands • Healthy Travel Central & South America • Latin American Spanish phrasebook • Peru • Quechua phrasebook • Read This First: Central & South America • Rio de Janeiro • Rio de Janeiro City Map • Santiago de Chile • South America on a shoestring • Trekking in the Patagonian Andes • Venezuela **Travel Literature**: Full Circle: A South American Journey

SOUTH-EAST ASIA Bali & Lombok • Bangkok • Bangkok City Map • Burmese phrasebook • Cambodia • Cycling Vietnam, Laos & Cambodia • East Timor phrasebook • Hanoi • Healthy Travel Asia & India • Hill Tribes phrasebook • Ho Chi Minh City (Saigon) • Indonesia • Indonesian phrasebook • Indonesia's Eastern Islands • Java • Lao phrasebook • Laos • Malay phrasebook • Malaysia, Singapore & Brunei • Myanmar (Burma) • Philippines • Pilipino (Tagalog) phrasebook • Read This First: Asia & India • Singapore • Singapore City Map • South-East Asia on a shoestring • South-East Asia phrasebook • Thailand • Thailand's Islands & Beaches • Thailand, Vietnam, Laos & Cambodia Road Atlas • Thai phrasebook • Vietnam • Vietnamese phrasebook • World Food Indonesia • World Food Thailand • World Food Vietnam

ALSO AVAILABLE: Antarctica • The Arctic • The Blue Man: Tales of Travel, Love and Coffee • Brief Encounters: Stories of Love, Sex & Travel • Buddhist Stupas in Asia: The Shape of Perfection • Chasing Rickshaws • The Last Grain Race • Lonely Planet … On the Edge: Adventurous Escapades from Around the World • Lonely Planet Unpacked • Lonely Planet Unpacked Again • Not the Only Planet: Science Fiction Travel Stories • Ports of Call: A Journey by Sea • Sacred India • Travel Photography: A Guide to Taking Better Pictures • Travel with Children • Tuvalu: Portrait of an Island Nation

LONELY PLANET

ON THE ROAD

Travel Guides explore cities, regions and countries, and supply information on transport, restaurants and accommodation, covering all budgets. They come with reliable, easy-to-use maps, practical advice, cultural and historical facts and a rundown on attractions both on and off the beaten track. There are over 200 titles in this classic series, covering nearly every country in the world.

 Lonely Planet Upgrades extend the shelf life of existing travel guides by detailing any changes that may affect travel in a region since a book has been published. Upgrades can be downloaded for free from **www.lonelyplanet.com/upgrades**

For travellers with more time than money, **Shoestring** guides offer dependable, first-hand information with hundreds of detailed maps, plus insider tips for stretching money as far as possible. Covering entire continents in most cases, the six-volume shoestring guides are known around the world as 'backpackers bibles'.

For the discerning short-term visitor, **Condensed** guides highlight the best a destination has to offer in a full-colour, pocket-sized format designed for quick access. They include everything from top sights and walking tours to opinionated reviews of where to eat, stay, shop and have fun.

CitySync lets travellers use their Palm™ or Visor™ hand-held computers to guide them through a city with handy tips on transport, history, cultural life, major sights, and shopping and entertainment options. It can also quickly search and sort hundreds of reviews of hotels, restaurants and attractions, and pinpoint their location on scrollable street maps. CitySync can be downloaded from **www.citysync.com**

MAPS & ATLASES

Lonely Planet's **City Maps** feature downtown and metropolitan maps, as well as transit routes and walking tours. The maps come complete with an index of streets, a listing of sights and a plastic coat for extra durability.

Road Atlases are an essential navigation tool for serious travellers. Cross-referenced with the guidebooks, they also feature distance and climate charts and a complete site index.

LONELY PLANET

ESSENTIALS

Read This First books help new travellers to hit the road with confidence. These invaluable predeparture guides give step-by-step advice on preparing for a trip, budgeting, arranging a visa, planning an itinerary and staying safe while still getting off the beaten track.

Healthy Travel pocket guides offer a regional rundown on disease hot spots and practical advice on predeparture health measures, staying well on the road and what to do in emergencies. The guides come with a user-friendly design and helpful diagrams and tables.

Lonely Planet's **Phrasebooks** cover the essential words and phrases travellers need when they're strangers in a strange land. They come in a pocket-sized format with colour tabs for quick reference, extensive vocabulary lists, easy-to-follow pronunciation keys and two-way dictionaries.

Miffed by blurry photos of the Taj Mahal? Tired of the classic 'top of the head cut off' shot? **Travel Photography: A Guide to Taking Better Pictures** will help you turn ordinary holiday snaps into striking images and give you the know-how to capture every scene, from frenetic festivals to peaceful beach sunrises.

Lonely Planet's **Travel Journal** is a lightweight but sturdy travel diary for jotting down all those on-the-road observations and significant travel moments. It comes with a handy time-zone wheel, a world map and useful travel information.

Lonely Planet's eKno is an all-in-one communication service developed especially for travellers. It offers low-cost international calls and free email and voicemail so that you can keep in touch while on the road. Check it out on **www.ekno.lonelyplanet.com**

FOOD & RESTAURANT GUIDES

Lonely Planet's **Out to Eat** guides recommend the brightest and best places to eat and drink in top international cities. These gourmet companions are arranged by neighbourhood, packed with dependable maps, garnished with scene-setting photos and served with quirky features.

For people who live to eat, drink and travel, **World Food** guides explore the culinary culture of each country. Entertaining and adventurous, each guide is packed with detail on staples and specialities, regional cuisine and local markets, as well as sumptuous recipes, comprehensive culinary dictionaries and lavish photos good enough to eat.

OUTDOOR GUIDES

For those who believe the best way to see the world is on foot, Lonely Planet's **Walking Guides** detail everything from family strolls to difficult treks, with 'when to go and how to do it' advice supplemented by reliable maps and essential travel information.

Cycling Guides map a destination's best bike tours, long and short, in day-by-day detail. They contain all the information a cyclist needs, including advice on bike maintenance, places to eat and stay, innovative maps with detailed cues to the rides, and elevation charts.

The **Watching Wildlife** series is perfect for travellers who want authoritative information but don't want to tote a heavy field guide. Packed with advice on where, when and how to view a region's wildlife, each title features photos of over 300 species and contains engaging comments on the local flora and fauna.

With underwater colour photos throughout, **Pisces Books** explore the world's best diving and snorkelling areas. Each book contains listings of diving services and dive resorts, detailed information on depth, visibility and difficulty of dives, and a roundup of the marine life you're likely to see through your mask.

LONELY PLANET

OFF THE ROAD

Journeys, the travel literature series written by renowned travel authors, capture the spirit of a place or illuminate a culture with a journalist's attention to detail and a novelist's flair for words. These are tales to soak up while you're actually on the road or dip into as an at-home armchair indulgence.

The range of lavishly illustrated **Pictorial** books is just the ticket for both travellers and dreamers. Off-beat tales and vivid photographs bring the adventure of travel to your doorstep long before the journey begins and long after it is over.

Lonely Planet **Videos** encourage the same independent, tough-minded approach as the guidebooks. Currently airing throughout the world, this award-winning series features innovative footage and an original soundtrack.

Yes, we know, work is tough, so do a little bit of deskside dreaming with the spiral-bound Lonely Planet **Diary** or a Lonely Planet **Wall Calendar**, filled with great photos from around the world.

TRAVELLERS NETWORK

Lonely Planet Online. Lonely Planet's award-winning Web site has insider information on hundreds of destinations, from Amsterdam to Zimbabwe, complete with interactive maps and relevant links. The site also offers the latest travel news, recent reports from travellers on the road, guidebook upgrades, a travel links site, an online book-buying option and a lively traveller's bulletin board. It can be viewed at **www.lonelyplanet.com** or AOL keyword: lp.

Planet Talk is a quarterly print newsletter, full of gossip, advice, anecdotes and author articles. It provides an antidote to the being-at-home blues and lets you plan and dream for the next trip. Contact the nearest Lonely Planet office for your free copy.

Comet, the free Lonely Planet newsletter, comes via email once a month. It's loaded with travel news, advice, dispatches from authors, travel competitions and letters from readers. To subscribe, click on the Comet subscription link on the front page of the Web site.

LONELY PLANET

You already know that Lonely Planet produces more than this one guidebook, but you might not be aware of the other products we have on this region. Here is a selection of titles that you may want to check out as well:

Andalucía
ISBN 1 86450 191 X
US$17.99 • UK£10.99

Barcelona
ISBN 1 86450 143 X
US$14.99 • UK£8.99

Barcelona city map
ISBN 1 86450 174 X
US$5.99 • UK£3.99

Europe on a shoestring
ISBN 1 86450 150 2
US$24.99 • UK£14.99

Madrid
ISBN 1 86450 123 5
US$14.99 • UK£8.99

Mediterranean Europe
ISBN 1 86450 154 5
US$27.99 • UK£15.99

Read This First: Europe
ISBN 1 86450 136 7
US$14.99 • UK£8.99

Spain
ISBN 1 86450 192 8
US$24.99 • UK£14.99

Spanish phrasebook
ISBN 0 86442 475 2
US$5.95 • UK£3.99

Walking in Spain
ISBN 0 86442 543 0
US$17.95 • UK£11.99

Western Europe
ISBN 1 86450 163 4
US$27.99 • UK£15.99

World Food Spain
ISBN 1 86450 025 5
US$12.95 • UK£7.99

Available wherever books are sold

Index

Text

Boxed Text

MAP LEGEND

BOUNDARIES

━━ ━ ━ ━ ━ ━	International
━ ━ ━ ━ ━ ━	Regional
─ ─ ─ ─ ─ ─	Provincial

HYDROGRAPHY

	Coastline, Lake
	River, Creek
⊙	Spring, Rapids
	Waterfalls

ROUTES & TRANSPORT

	Motorway
	Major Road
	Minor Road
	Other Road
═ ═ ═ ═ ═ ═	Unsealed Road
	Motorway (City)
	Through Route (City)
	Major Road (City)
	Street, Lane (City)

	Pedestrian Mall
	Steps on Road
⊃ ═ ═ ═	Tunnel
	Path Through a Park
━━━▣━━	Tram Line, Stop
├─┼─●─┼─	Railway, Station
─●─	Metro, Station
┼─┼─┼▣┼─	Cable Car, Terminus
─ ─ ─▣─ ─	Ferry Route, Terminal

AREA FEATURES

⊛	Park, Gardens
✕	Cemetery

	Building, Hotel
	Market

	Beach, Desert
	Urban Area

MAP SYMBOLS

◉ **BARCELONA**	Major City
● Tarragona	City
● Igualada	Town
● Aramunt	Village
•	Point of Interest
♦	Place to Stay
🅰	Camping Ground
▼	Place to Eat
⬚	Pub or Bar
✈	Airport
	Ancient or City Wall

⊖	Bank
⊼	Beach
▣ ▣	Bus Station, Stop
⊡	Castle or Fort
⌂	Cave
⊡ ✝	Church or Cathedral
⊞	Cinema
	Cliff or Escarpment
⊡	Embassy or Consulate
⊕	Hospital
⊡	Internet Cafe
⚓	Lighthouse
☀	Lookout
⚑	Monument
▲	Mountain or Hill

⌒	Mountain Range
⊞	Museum
→	One-Way Street
⊡	Parking
)(	Pass
⊡	Police Station
⊡	Post Office
⊠	Shopping Centre
⚐	Ski Area
⊞	Stately Home
⊡	Swimming Pool
⊡	Theatre
⊙	Tourist Information
⊡	Transport
⊡	Zoo

Note: not all symbols displayed above appear in this book

LONELY PLANET OFFICES

Australia
Locked Bag 1, Footscray, Victoria 3011
☎ 03 8379 8000 fax 03 8379 8111
email: talk2us@lonelyplanet.com.au

USA
150 Linden St, Oakland, CA 94607
☎ 510 893 8555 TOLL FREE: 800 275 8555
fax 510 893 8572
email: info@lonelyplanet.com

UK
10a Spring Place, London NW5 3BH
☎ 020 7428 4800 fax 020 7428 4828
email: go@lonelyplanet.co.uk

France
1 rue du Dahomey, 75011 Paris
☎ 01 55 25 33 00 fax 01 55 25 33 01
email: bip@lonelyplanet.fr
www.lonelyplanet.fr

World Wide Web: www.lonelyplanet.com *or* **AOL keyword: lp**
Lonely Planet Images: lpi@lonelyplanet.com.au